S0-AWY-858

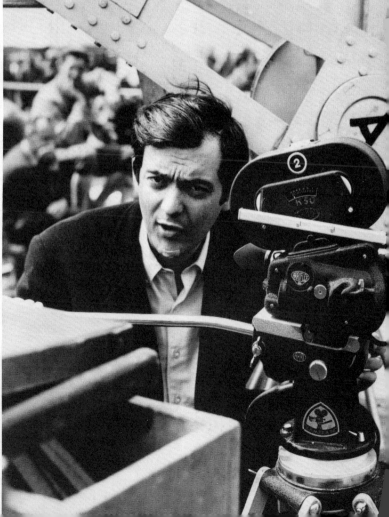

Dictionary of Literary Biography • Volume Twenty-six

American Screenwriters

Dictionary of Literary Biography

1: *The American Renaissance in New England*, edited by Joel Myerson (1978)

2: *American Novelists Since World War II*, edited by Jeffrey Helterman and Richard Layman (1978)

3: *Antebellum Writers in New York and the South*, edited by Joel Myerson (1979)

4: *American Writers in Paris, 1920-1939*, edited by Karen Lane Rood (1980)

5: *American Poets Since World War II*, 2 volumes, edited by Donald J. Greiner (1980)

6: *American Novelists Since World War II*, Second Series, edited by James E. Kibler, Jr. (1980)

7: *Twentieth-Century American Dramatists*, 2 volumes, edited by John MacNicholas (1981)

8: *Twentieth-Century American Science-Fiction Writers*, 2 volumes, edited by David Cowart and Thomas L. Wymer (1981)

9: *American Novelists, 1910-1945*, 3 volumes, edited by James J. Martine (1981)

10: *Modern British Dramatists, 1900-1945*, 2 volumes, edited by Stanley Weintraub (1982)

11: *American Humorists, 1800-1950*, 2 volumes, edited by Stanley Trachtenberg (1982)

12: *American Realists and Naturalists*, edited by Donald Pizer and Earl N. Harbert (1982)

13: *British Dramatists Since World War II*, 2 volumes, edited by Stanley Weintraub (1982)

14: *British Novelists Since 1960*, 2 volumes, edited by Jay L. Halio (1983)

15: *British Novelists, 1930-1959*, 2 volumes, edited by Bernard Oldsey (1983)

16: *The Beats: Literary Bohemians in Postwar America*, 2 volumes, edited by Ann Charters (1983)

17: *Twentieth-Century American Historians*, edited by Clyde N. Wilson (1983)

18: *Victorian Novelists After 1885*, edited by Ira B. Nadel and William E. Fredeman (1983)

19: *British Poets, 1880-1914*, edited by Donald E. Stanford (1983)

20: *British Poets, 1914-1945*, edited by Donald E. Stanford (1983)

21: *Victorian Novelists Before 1885*, edited by Ira B. Nadel and William E. Fredeman (1983)

22: *American Writers for Children, 1900-1960*, edited by John Cech (1983)

23: *American Newspaper Journalists, 1873-1900*, edited by Perry J. Ashley (1983)

24: *American Colonial Writers, 1606-1734*, edited by Emory Elliott (1984)

25: *American Newspaper Journalists, 1901-1925*, edited by Perry J. Ashley (1984)

26: *American Screenwriters*, edited by Robert E. Morsberger, Stephen O. Lesser, and Randall Clark (1984)

Yearbook: 1980, edited by Karen L. Rood, Jean W. Ross, and Richard Ziegfeld (1981)

Yearbook: 1981, edited by Karen L. Rood, Jean W. Ross, and Richard Ziegfeld (1982)

Yearbook: 1982, edited by Richard Ziegfeld; associate editors: Jean W. Ross and Lynne C. Zeigler (1983)

Documentary Series, volume 1, edited by Margaret A. Van Antwerp (1982)

Documentary Series, volume 2, edited by Margaret A. Van Antwerp (1982)

Documentary Series, volume 3, edited by Mary Bruccoli (1983)

Documentary Series, volume 4: *Tennessee Williams*, edited by Margaret A. Van Antwerp and Sally Johns (1984)

Dictionary of Literary Biography • Volume Twenty-six

American Screenwriters

Edited by
Robert E. Morsberger
Stephen O. Lesser
and
Randall Clark

A Bruccoli Clark Book
Gale Research Company • Book Tower • Detroit, Michigan 48226

Ref
PN
1998
A2
A585
1984

Advisory Board for
DICTIONARY OF LITERARY BIOGRAPHY

Louis S. Auchincloss
John Baker
D. Philip Baker
A. Walton Litz, Jr.
Peter S. Prescott
Lola L. Szladits
William Targ

Matthew J. Bruccoli and Richard Layman, *Editorial Directors*
C. E. Frazer Clark, Jr., *Managing Editor*

Manufactured by Edwards Brothers, Inc.
Ann Arbor, Michigan
Printed in the United States of America

Copyright © 1984
GALE RESEARCH COMPANY

Library of Congress Cataloging in Publication Data
Main entry under title:

American screenwriters.

  (Dictionary of literary biography; v. 26)
  "A Bruccoli Clark book."
  Includes index.
  1. Screen writers—United States—Biography. I. Mors-
berger, Robert Eustis, 1929- . II. Lesser, Stephen O.
III. Clark, Randall. IV. Series.
PN1998.A2A585 1984 791.43'7'0922 [B] 83-25414
ISBN 0-8103-0917-3

Contents

138347

Plan of the Series

. . . Almost the most prodigious asset of a country, and perhaps its most precious possession, is its native literary product—when that product is fine and noble and enduring.

Mark Twain*

The advisory board, the editors, and the publisher of the *Dictionary of Literary Biography* are joined in endorsing Mark Twain's declaration. The literature of a nation provides an inexhaustible resource of permanent worth. It is our expectation that this endeavor will make literature and its creators better understood and more accessible to students and the literate public, while satisfying the standards of teachers and scholars.

To meet these requirements, *literary biography* has been construed in terms of the author's achievement. The most important thing about a writer is his writing. Accordingly, the entries in *DLB* are career biographies, tracing the development of the author's canon and the evolution of his reputation.

The publication plan for *DLB* resulted from two years of preparation. The project was proposed to Bruccoli Clark by Frederick G. Ruffner, president of the Gale Research Company, in November 1975. After specimen entries were prepared and typeset, an advisory board was formed to refine the entry format and develop the series rationale. In meetings held during 1976, the publisher, series editors, and advisory board approved the scheme for a comprehensive biographical dictionary of persons who contributed to North American literature. Editorial work on the first volume began in January 1977, and it was published in 1978.

In order to make *DLB* more than a reference tool and to compile volumes that individually have claim to status as literary history, it was decided to organize volumes by topic or period or genre. Each of these freestanding volumes provides a biographical-bibliographical guide and overview for a particular area of literature. We are convinced that this organization—as opposed to a single alphabet method—constitutes a valuable innovation in the presentation of reference material. The volume plan necessarily requires many decisions for the

*From an unpublished section of Mark Twain's autobiography, copyright © by the Mark Twain Company.

placement and treatment of authors who might properly be included in two or three volumes. In some instances a major figure will be included in separate volumes, but with different entries emphasizing the aspect of his career appropriate to each volume. Ernest Hemingway, for example, is represented in *American Writers in Paris, 1920-1939* by an entry focusing on his expatriate apprenticeship; he is also in *American Novelists, 1910-1945* with an entry surveying his entire career. Each volume includes a cumulative index of subject authors. The final *DLB* volume will be a comprehensive index to the entire series.

With volume ten in 1982 it was decided to enlarge the scope of *DLB* beyond the literature of the United States. By the end of 1983 twelve volumes treating British literature had been published, and volumes for Commonwealth and Modern European literature were in progress. The series has been further augmented by the *DLB Yearbooks* (since 1981) which update published entries and add new entries to keep the *DLB* current with contemporary activity. There have also been occasional *DLB Documentary Series* volumes which provide biographical and critical background source materials for figures whose work is judged to have particular interest for students. One of these companion volumes is entirely devoted to Tennessee Williams.

The purpose of *DLB* is not only to provide reliable information in a convenient format but also to place the figures in the larger perspective of literary history and to offer appraisals of their accomplishments by qualified scholars.

We define literature as the *intellectual commerce of a nation*: not merely as belles lettres, but as that ample and complex process by which ideas are generated, shaped, and transmitted. *DLB* entries are not limited to "creative writers" but extend to other figures who in this time and in this way influenced the mind of a people. Thus there will be volumes for historians, journalists, publishers, and screenwriters. By this means readers of *DLB* may be aided to perceive literature not as cult scripture in the keeping of cultural high priests, but as at the center of a nation's life.

DLB includes the major writers appropriate to each volume and those standing in the ranks immediately behind them. Scholarly and critical counsel has been sought in deciding which minor figures to include and how full their entries should be.

Wherever possible, useful references will be made to figures who do not warrant separate entries.

Each *DLB* volume has a volume editor responsible for planning the volume, selecting the figures for inclusion, and assigning the entries. Volume editors are also responsible for preparing, where appropriate, appendices surveying the major periodicals and literary and intellectual movements for their volumes, as well as lists of further readings. Work on the series as a whole is coordinated at the Bruccoli Clark editorial center in Columbia, South Carolina, where the editorial staff is responsible for the accuracy of the published volumes.

One feature that distinguishes *DLB* is the illustration policy—its concern with the iconography of literature. Just as an author is influenced by his surroundings, so is the reader's understanding of the author enhanced by a knowledge of his environment. Therefore *DLB* volumes include not only drawings, paintings, and photographs of authors, often depicting them at various stages in their careers, but also illustrations of their families and places where they lived. Title pages are regularly reproduced in facsimile along with dust jackets for modern authors. The dust jackets are a special feature of *DLB* because they often document better than anything else the way in which an author's work was launched in its own time. Specimens of the writers' manuscripts are included when feasible.

A supplement to *DLB*—tentatively titled *A Guide, Chronology, and Glossary for American Literature*—will outline the history of literature in North America and trace the influences that shaped it. This volume will provide a framework for the study of American literature by means of chronological tables, literary affiliation charts, glossarial entries, and concise surveys of the major movements. It has been planned to stand on its own as a vade mecum, providing a ready-reference guide to the study of American literature as well as a companion to the *DLB* volumes for American literature.

Samuel Johnson rightly decreed that "The chief glory of every people arises from its authors." The purpose of the *Dictionary of Literary Biography* is to compile literary history in the surest way available to us—by accurate and comprehensive treatment of the lives and work of those who contributed to it.

The *DLB* Advisory Board

Foreword

The American screenwriter has received very little serious study. Even among film scholars, emphasis has most often been placed on the director rather than the writer, and literary scholars have denied the screenwriter the attention given to his closest relative, the playwright. But the screenwriter is no less a writer simply because he writes for a visual medium. Like any other writer, the screenwriter is interested in telling a story, and like any other literary figure, the best screenwriter's works will be marked by recurring concerns, themes, motifs, and images.

What does make the screenwriter different from other writers are the requirements of the film medium. He must be prepared to tell his story with a minimum of dialogue and in a limited amount of time. The story must be conceived entirely in visual terms; it must be properly paced and have mass appeal. Although it is a written work, the screenplay is not composed to be read. It is not meant to exist apart from the motion picture.

As the American motion picture has developed over the past decades, the status of the screenwriter has changed, and the screenplay has emerged as a new form of literature. The earliest movies were one-reel "quickies" that were entirely improvised and required no script. As silent films became longer, writers were needed to provide continuity and dialogue in the form of title cards, which at first contained short phrases but soon became more sophisticated. In particular, Anita Loos's titles for the highly successful 1916 film *Intolerance* proved that audiences were willing to read titles while they viewed a motion picture.

The screenwriter achieved true prominence with the advent of sound in 1927. Title cards were replaced by spoken dialogue, and Hollywood recruited playwrights to provide the dialogue for its films. Throughout the 1930s virtually everyone writing motion pictures had a stage background, and screenplays reflected the literary qualities of theater work. By the end of the decade, screenwriters had begun to recognize that the motion picture had a different set of requirements from the stage play and began writing their scripts accordingly. Hollywood began to rely less on screenplays by playwrights and more on scripts by a new kind of writer, the professional screenwriter who worked within his medium and understood its demands.

The screenwriter is, of necessity, a collaborator. In pre-1970s Hollywood, almost all screenplays were written by two or more people, with writers encouraged to develop a specialty: dialogue, gags, polishing a script. Collaboration on scripts in the 1930s was so common that the screenplay was likened to an assembly-line product. Because of regulations established by the Writers Guild, it is possible for a writer to make significant contributions to a film but receive no credit and for a credited writer to have little to do with the finished screenplay. The screenplay may be further altered by producers, directors, actors, editors, and cinematographers so that the completed film bears only a remote resemblance to the screenplay. Still, it is by the film that most screenwriters must be judged, and the work of a talented screenwriter is often recognizable no matter how many other hands were involved.

American Screenwriters contains studies of the careers of sixty-five significant motion-picture writers. Obviously, not every important figure is in the volume; instead, what is offered is a representative sample of the hundreds of screenwriters who have worked in Hollywood, ranging from the artistically important to the commercially successful to the relatively obscure. (A second volume of *American Screenwriters* is in progress.) Because this is a study of screenwriters, only writers who wrote primarily for the screen—or those who wrote in other media but had noteworthy film achievements—are included. Novelists who wrote for motion pictures part-time to supplement their income—William Faulkner, Raymond Chandler, F. Scott Fitzgerald—are not included. Playwrights whose film careers consisted mostly of adapting their own works, such as Neil Simon and Tennessee Williams, have been omitted, as have performers who wrote their own material, such as Mae West, Charlie Chaplin, and W. C. Fields. The filmographies in this volume include only movies for which writers received official screen credit; uncredited contributions are discussed in text.

–Randall Clark

Acknowledgments

This book was produced by BC Research. Karen L. Rood is senior editor for the *Dictionary of Literary Biography* series. Margaret A. Van Antwerp was the in-house editor.

The production manager is Lynne C. Zeigler. Art supervisor is Alice A. Parsons. The production staff included Mary Betts, Patricia Coate, Claudia Ericson, Lynn Felder, Kathleen M. Flanagan, Joyce Fowler, Laura Ingram, Nancy H. Lindsay, Walter W. Ross, Patricia C. Sharpe, Joycelyn R. Smith, and Meredith Walker. Jean W. Ross is permissions editor. Joseph Caldwell, photography editor, did the photographic copy work for the volume. Some entries were solicited by Tracey Thompson.

No record of screenwriters' careers is complete without visual evidence of their most memorable films. Muriel Hamilton of Hampton Books, Newberry, South Carolina, and Fred Zentner of Cinema Bookshop, London, generously gave of their time and energy to help assemble movie stills and other illustrative materials for this volume. To them the editors would like to express their deepest gratitude.

Valuable assistance was also given by the staff at the Thomas Cooper Library of the University of South Carolina: Lynn Barron, Sue Collins, Michael Freeman, Gary Geer, Alexander M. Gilchrist, Jens Holley, David Lincove, Marcia Martin, Roger Mortimer, Harriet B. Oglesbee, Jean Rhyne, Karen Rissling, Paula Swope, and Ellen Tillett.

Dictionary of Literary Biography • Volume Twenty-six

American Screenwriters

Dictionary of Literary Biography

James Agee
(27 November 1909-16 May 1955)

Andrea Rosenwein

See also the Agee entry in *DLB 2, American Novelists Since World War II*.

MOTION PICTURES: *The Quiet One* (Museum of Modern Art, 1949), narration;
The African Queen (United Artists, 1951), screenplay by Agee and John Huston;
Genghis Khan (Italian Film Exports, 1952), narration;
The Bride Comes to Yellow Sky (half of *Face to Face*) (RKO, 1953), screenplay;
White Mane (Rembrandt Films and Contemporary Films, 1953), script;
The Night of the Hunter (United Artists, 1955), screenplay;
Green Magic (Italian Film Exports, 1955), script.

TELEVISION: *The Blue Hotel, Omnibus* (NBC, late 1940s), script;
Abraham Lincoln, Omnibus (NBC, 1953), scripts.

BOOKS: *Permit Me Voyage* (New Haven: Yale University Press, 1934);
Let Us Now Praise Famous Men, photographs by Walker Evans (Boston: Houghton Mifflin, 1941; London: Owen, 1965);
The Morning Watch (Boston: Houghton Mifflin, 1951; London: Secker & Warburg, 1952);
A Death in the Family (New York: McDowell, Obolensky, 1957; London: Gollancz, 1958);
Agee on Film: Reviews and Comments (New York: McDowell, Obolensky, 1958; London: Owen, 1963);
Agee on Film, Volume II: Five Film Scripts (New York: McDowell, Obolensky, 1960; London: Owen, 1965)—includes *The Blue Hotel, The African*

James Agee (photo by Florence Homolka)

Queen, The Bride Comes to Yellow Sky, Noa Noa, The Night of the Hunter;
The Collected Poems of James Agee, edited by Robert Fitzgerald (Boston: Houghton Mifflin, 1968; London: Calder & Boyars, 1972);
The Collected Short Prose of James Agee, edited by Fitzgerald (Boston: Houghton Mifflin, 1968;

London: Calder & Boyars, 1972).

OTHER: *Notes for a Moving Picture: The House*, in *New Letters in America*, edited by Horace Gregory (New York: Norton, 1937), pp. 37-55.

PERIODICAL PUBLICATIONS: *Any Seventh Son*, *Phillips Exeter Monthly*, 31 (June 1927): 107-109;
Man's Fate—A Film Treatment of the Malraux Novel, *Films*, 1 (1939): 51-60;
Dedication Day, *Politics*, 3 (April 1946): 121-125.

James Agee was an eclectic writer, shifting easily among fiction, documentary prose, movie criticism, and screenwriting. His talents ultimately won him a Pulitzer prize in 1958 for *A Death in the Family* and an Academy award nomination in 1951 for *The African Queen*. But he died in relative obscurity, not living long enough to enjoy the fruits of his efforts. His screenplay with John Huston for the movie classic *The African Queen* was filmed on location in Africa without him, for he suffered the first of a series of heart attacks in 1951 and was too weak to make the trip. He died at the age of forty-five before his adaptation of *The Night of the Hunter*, a movie acclaimed by critics such as Kenneth Seib as "perhaps one of the two or three finest 'horror' movies produced in the last two decades," was released in 1955. Two years after Agee's death, the publication of *A Death in the Family* finally brought his work recognition which it never received during his life. Agee became a symbol of the artist struggling in a commercial society, pouring his talents into movie and book reviews instead of writing fiction. Agee himself felt guilty about this, holding stringent standards for himself as an artist, yet succumbing to his desires for money and alcohol.

James Rufus Agee was born in Knoxville, Tennessee, and attended St. Andrew's School, outside Sewanee, where he received Episcopal schooling. He attended Knoxville High School from 1924 to 1925 and graduated from Phillips Exeter Academy in Exeter, New Hampshire, in 1928. From there Agee went to Harvard, where he was editor of the *Advocate*; he graduated in 1932. From 1939 to 1948 he was the movie reviewer for *Time* magazine, and from 1942 to 1948 he wrote the film column for the *Nation*. Agee was married three times, to Olivia Saunders; to Alma Mailman, by whom he had a son, Joel; and to Mia Fritsch, by whom he had a daughter, Julia Teresa.

John Huston, Agee's good friend and movie collaborator, described the writer in the introduc-

tion to *Agee on Film, Volume II* as being about "six-two and heavy but neither muscular nor fat—a mountaineer's body. He was always gentle towards his fellow humans with that kind of gentleness usually reserved for plants and animals." Houston claimed that Agee's physical self-destruction was implicit in his psychological makeup, and indeed, on 16 May 1955, a final heart attack ended his life. It is ironic that Agee's prolific output yielded only three major works and a few short stories in print and a small scattering of feature-length films and documentaries on the screen.

Agee's earliest scripts, never filmed, were highly experimental in nature. The first, *Notes for a Moving Picture: The House* (1937), anticipated the modern film in its call for the use of color and black and white in the same frame and its Dada-like directions for neon signs that "spell out semi-intelligible names for suspense." Agee's second script, *Man's Fate—A Film Treatment of the Malraux Novel* (1939), was a described picture rather than a formal shooting script, similar to *The House*. Written in a similar manner was a later satire, *Dedication Day* (1946).

In the late 1940s, Agee wrote the commentary for Helen Levitt's documentary about a Negro boy in Harlem, *The Quiet One*, and then began work on commercial scripts. Under contract to Huntington Hartford, Agee wrote a script based on Stephen Crane's "The Blue Hotel" in 1948-1949 that was never filmed but was adapted by NBC television for *Omnibus*. In 1951, he collaborated with John Huston on the script for *The African Queen*, adapted from the novel by C. S. Forester.

In the early 1950s Agee adapted another Stephen Crane short story for Huntington Hartford. Entitled *The Bride Comes to Yellow Sky*, the film was released by RKO as half of *Face to Face*, a pair of filmed short stories; the other story included was Joseph Conrad's "The Secret Sharer," adapted for the screen by Aeneas MacKenzie. During this time, Agee also wrote narration for a Filipino movie, *Genghis Khan*, released by Italian Film Exports in 1952. A commission by the Ford Foundation for *Omnibus* produced Agee's scripts on the life of Lincoln for television in 1953.

That same year, Agee wrote an original treatment of the life of Paul Gauguin, *Noa Noa*, which has not been produced. Agee wrote commentary and narration for an Italian travel film, *Green Magic* (1955), and also adapted for the screen Davis Grubb's novel *The Night of the Hunter*, which was released by United Artists in 1955. During this time, he worked with *New York Times* music critic Howard

Taubman on the shooting script for "Tanglewood," about the Berkshire music festival. Just before his death, Agee sketched out an allegorical fantasy about elephants.

In all of his scripts, Agee paid close attention to photographic technique. He saw the camera's function as capturing surface detail without sentimentalization. No matter how carefully he outlined the process of filming, he wanted the result to simulate reality. He called for the use of orthochromatic film, for example, to achieve the look of the grainy newsreel in *Man's Fate*. "If you can invent something worth watching, the camera should hold still and clear, so that you can watch it," Agee once wrote.

Agee was equally emphatic in his views on film cutting, saying that the power and honesty of screen images lie "in juxtaposition and careful series, in rhythm, and in a rhythmic and spatial whole." In *Noa Noa*, his detailed instructions for the king's funeral scene include as many as eight shots for each beat of Chopin's "Funeral March."

Detailed directions in Agee's screenplays are not limited to technical instructions, and in many instances he provides so many acting and scenery suggestions that the director could conceivably have nothing of his own to do if he were to follow all of Agee's written indications. Agee's scripts read like well-crafted fiction. The use of the first-person plural in directions is reminiscent of a novelist elucidating his viewpoint. The richness of imagery in his directions is sometimes difficult to render on the screen but contains an almost Shakespearean appeal on paper.

A unity of theme threads many of Agee's screenplays together. According to Victor Kramer, Agee frequently adapted literary works in which the "regenerate or unregenerate Adamic motif is basic. He was fascinated with the idea of the confrontation of innocence with evil—a situation which is immediately obvious in both of the Stephen Crane stories for which he did scripts, 'The Blue Hotel' and 'The Bride Comes to Yellow Sky.'" *The Blue Hotel* shows a Swede unbalancing a peaceful prairie town; the other script describes the drunken gunman Scratchy as "turned loose with both hands" on quiet little Yellow Sky.

The Night of the Hunter is Agee's most searching treatment of the innocence versus evil theme. Faithfully adapted from Grubb's novel of terror, the movie concerns two children who are mercilessly hounded by a psychopathic preacher because they know where their father hid some stolen money. The sumptuous settings in the country are juxtaposed against the corruption of the townspeople

in the film. The audience sees through the eyes of the children, sharing experiences from their naive point of view. Their river trip, a journey into nature, brings forth images of helpless rabbits and sinister spiders, and the end of their journey is shown with the images of a canary in a lighted window. Stylized cinematic effects help the audience relate to the children's plight.

Directed by Charles Laughton and produced by Paul Gregory, *The Night of the Hunter* diverges from Agee's original script in many ways. The film, starring Robert Mitchum, Lillian Gish, and Shelley Winters, employs numerous comic effects to relieve tension for the audience. Laughton altered some of the cinematic devices called for in Agee's script; yet his respect for Agee's intentions is apparent in the camera movements, grouping and compositions, and helicopter shots. The novel, cluttered with ponderous verbiage, has been streamlined by Agee, and what remains is effectively translated to the screen by Laughton.

Another mediocre novel that Agee tightened and successfully adapted for the screen was *The African Queen*, C. S. Forester's story about a prudish old maid and a simple, crass cockney, who find themselves forced together on a dilapidated riverboat in Africa during World War I. The missionary's sister and the engineer fall in love when her courage and his pragmatism combine toward a common goal—to destroy a German gunboat. The theme of courage and moral conviction, which surfaces in the character of the little boy in *The Night of the Hunter*, appears again in *The African Queen*. Rose refuses to accept defeat, even when the boat propeller shaft is twisted and a blade breaks off. Her tenacity overwhelms Charlie, who ultimately gives in to her whims at every juncture.

Forester's novel, though filled with action, explains the characters' motivations in too great detail. "Resolve was hardening in Rose's heart." "There was within her a lust for adventure." Sentences such as these are not only trite but redundant. Agee gets rid of deadwood descriptions and fashions two dynamic individuals whose moral values collide. Humphrey Bogart was given the Academy Award for Best Actor for his portrayal of Charlie Allnut, and Katharine Hepburn played a convincing Rose Sayer.

Though the script is commercial by nature, Agee's attention to meaningful detail gives it spunk entirely lacking in the original story. Agee's concern with sound and image supporting each other is apparent in numerous scenes of *The African Queen*, notably Rose's serving tea at the mission. The scene,

Katharine Hepburn and Humphrey Bogart in The African Queen. *Agee collaborated with John Huston on this adaptation of C. S. Forester's novel.*

which does not take place in the book, juxtaposes Charlie's growling stomach with the decorum of the formal situation. Typically, Agee wrote more than a full page of directions about sound and gestures for this short, comic scene.

The rich imagery of Agee's directions is also evident in the script for *The African Queen*. Rose's struggle with her inhibited virginal world is brought out in the very first scene as Rose plays the organ in a missionary church. The directions call for her to "pump the pedals vigorously" of the "reedy organ," "spreading with her knees the wings of wood." Later, when the orgasmic excitement of shooting the rapids in Charlie's boat subsides, Rose sits back: "Despite an empty feeling in her stomach and a pounding heart, she wears a smile of satisfaction."

Because Agee's work was interrupted by illness, it is difficult to attribute an exact portion of the detail of this script to him. Besides his precise descriptions of action, however, it seems clear that he influenced the making of the movie with his anticipation of its need for a distinguishing rhythm. He greatly admired the director John Huston, but he

felt that the overall rhythm of Huston's work might be improved. Agee wrote the falls sequences of the movie to have the effect of a mounting series of suspenseful scenes. Only when Rose and Charlie have run the current does the audience get relief. Huston's direction, as well as John Collier's and Peter Viertel's collaboration, cannot be underrated in assessing the merit of the film.

Some critics say that *The Blue Hotel* and *The Bride Comes to Yellow Sky* are Agee's finest scripts. "There is a precision, a tightness, and a unified effect to each of these that Agee failed to achieve in the other, more original scenarios," according to Kenneth Seib.

The Blue Hotel centers around the figure of a Swede, an alien staying overnight in a small whistle-stop town, whose fate rests in the hands of several men, or, by implication, humanity. Generally, Agee is faithful to Crane's short story, fleshing out characters presented in the original and adding the farmer and Scully's daughter to act as foils in the drama. Agee is able to extend the symbolism introduced by Crane, showing in visual terms what Crane began in verbal description.

The train that brings the Swede and the other passengers to Fort Romper symbolically connects the town with the outside world. The train begins and ends the screenplay; it is a reminder that the town is a microcosm and that the incident could have occurred anywhere that the transcontinental express ran. Other graphic symbols can be found in the script: the steel engraving of the "Stag at Bay," the record player, and the allusions to the Swede as a Christ figure ("a tired Pilgrim on the homestretch to Paradise"). When the Gambler kills the Swede, the audience does not see the Gambler's face; anyone at the table could have killed the Swede, but fate would have it that the Gambler was approached by the intruder.

Agee's one major deviation from Crane's text concerns the timing of the Easterner's confession. In the original, the Easterner does not reveal that the innkeeper's son was cheating at cards until sometime after the Swede's death. In Agee's script, Johnnie is accused immediately after the card game, after the Swede has left the hotel but before his death. The audience, therefore, is aware that if something happens to the Swede, the guests of the inn are responsible. By this device, the death of the Swede takes on an even more tragic character than in the original story. The screenplay ends with a closeup of the Easterner's face taking on an expression of sorrow, tenderness, and hopelessness of expiation. Crane's message that "every sin is a collab-

Agee (center) as Frank Gudger in The Bride Comes to Yellow Sky. *This movie, for which Agee wrote the screenplay, was one of two filmed short stories released under the title* Face to Face.

oration" is then brought home with a camera long shot showing the three figures going inside, and then only the starlit sky, slowly turning.

Like his other adaptations, *The Bride Comes to Yellow Sky* is faithful both to the theme and the tone of the original story. This time, however, Agee takes considerable liberties with Crane's tale, focusing on the town and its inhabitants. The bartender in the story becomes a woman in the script; the salesman becomes a major character. Agee introduces Frank Gudger, a benign jailbird whose presence emphasizes the passing of frontier life. Besides working as scriptwriter and technical consultant, Agee acted the part of Gudger, whose name is first seen in his book *Let Us Now Praise Famous Men* (1941). Agee doubtless saw this part as a caricature of himself; he played the role of another drunk in the Lincoln series.

Like *The Blue Hotel*, the screenplay for *The Bride Comes to Yellow Sky* uses visual symbolism to convey Crane's theme. When Potter crosses the threshold of his home with his wife, Gudger throws torn-up pictures from early West murder stories

into the wind. Scratchy Wilson, the last of the old-guard bad guys, drags a "real shock of a necktie" "snakily" from its hook; Potter's conservative tie is contrasted. In the end, when he wants to have a showdown with Potter and discovers that his only rival in town has given up the old ways and gotten married, Scratchy "turns both revolvers in his hands, looking at them, then puts them with finality into their holsters." The Old West is dead.

Like many of the female characters portrayed in Agee's screenplays, Crane's bride is "not pretty, nor was she very young." Rose of *The African Queen* is "early thirties, tight-featured and tight-haired." Agee's women have grit in a time when the country still saw them as passive and peroxided. In *Noa Noa* Gauguin's wife Mette is described as a "woman of courage," and Rose and Rachel of *The Night of the Hunter* are both strong in their moral convictions.

Agee's own concept of moral strength, which was carefully honed during his religious upbringing, revealed itself in his attitudes about artists' responsibilities. "The real effort has always been, simply, to be true to my own soul," he says through his

7

character Gauguin in *Noa Noa*. In *Noa Noa* Agee's most ambitious script, Gauguin fights against society and the government in an attempt to realize his quest for beauty and innocence. He flees from a monetarily successful life in Paris and takes up residence in Tahiti to pursue a life of artistic integrity.

Agee's view that the artistic impulse derives from individual suffering is seen in his portrayal of Gauguin as a Christ figure, and the scenario is strewn with crucifixes and religious allusions. Agee's cinematic directions are extremely detailed, and at one point he calls for the camera to be moved and cut to make a cross over Gauguin's body.

Although the screenplay was never produced and was blasted by critics Genevieve Moreau and Kenneth Seib for its "obvious and facile symbolism" and its "unbelievably bad dialogue," its themes are a dramatic representation of the views Agee espoused in his other writings. "The desire of any critic, like that of any artist, who has a right even to try to defend or practice an art—as perhaps of any human being who has a right even to try to defend or practice living—cannot be satisfied short of perfect liberty, discipline, and achievement, though the attempt may be wholly loved and honored," he said in a review for the *Nation* in 1946.

As a critic, Agee praised most the films which blended reality with imagination and sought to uncover the depths of the human condition. He also held every film responsible to its potential, no matter what its genre. Of Hitchcock's *Spellbound*, he stated that the film had "only suggestions of the hair-raising movie this had every right and obligation to be." In contrast to his views of the pretentious films ground out by the Hollywood "factory" of the 1940s, he applauded the silent era in his most sustained—and most famous—piece of criticism, *Comedy's Greatest Era*. He felt that these films, which relied so heavily on the visual image, possessed a naturalness which deteriorated with the introduction of sound.

Agee's incisive comments on film were well regarded by both the public and other critics. Only two years after Agee had begun writing for the *Nation* in 1941, W. H. Auden wrote in a letter to the editors of the magazine that Agee's articles "belong in that very select class—the music critiques of Berlioz and Shaw are the only other members I know—of newspaper work which has permanent literary value." When Agee's criticism was collected

in *Agee on Film: Reviews and Comments* (1958) after his death, critic Arthur Knight called him "the best movie critic this country has ever had."

A final analysis of Agee's contributions to film must take into account his philosophical intentions as well as his actual cinematic achievements. An intense dedication to cinema and the new medium of television put him in the vanguard of these art forms. Agee approached movies with scholarly deliberation before it was common practice to do so, and he tried to give television artistic legitimacy through his literate experimental dramas. His screenplays are adapted from works of literature and deal with the lives of great men in history. James Agee cannot be faulted if the industry so rarely reached his high ideals of artistic integrity, for, with his sense of self-doubt, ultimately even he had difficulty reaching them.

Letters:
Letters of James Agee to Father Flye (New York: Braziller, 1962).

References:
Alfred T. Barson, *A Way of Seeing: A Critical Study of James Agee* (Amherst: University of Massachusetts Press, 1972);

Genevieve Fabre, "A Bibliography of the Works of James Agee," *Bulletin of Bibliography*, 24 (May-August 1965): 145-148, 163-166;

Victor A. Kramer, *James Agee* (Boston: Twayne, 1975);

Kramer, "James Agee Papers at the University of Texas," *Library Chronicle of the University of Texas*, 8, no. 2 (1966): 33-36;

Erling Larsen, *James Agee* (Minneapolis: University of Minnesota Press, 1971);

David Madden, ed., *Remembering James Agee* (Baton Rouge: Louisiana State University Press, 1974);

Genevieve Moreau, *The Restless Journey of James Agee* (New York: Morrow, 1977);

Peter H. Ohlin, *Agee* (New York: Obolensky, 1966);

Kenneth Seib, *James Agee: Promise and Fulfillment* (Pittsburgh: University of Pittsburgh Press, 1968).

Papers:
The University of Texas has a large collection of Agee's literary manuscripts and correspondence.

Zoë Akins

(30 October 1886-29 October 1958)

Anthony Slide

MOTION PICTURES: *Sarah and Son* (Paramount, 1930), screenplay;
Anybody's Woman (Paramount, 1930), screenplay by Akins and Doris Anderson;
The Right to Love (Paramount, 1930), screenplay by Akins;
Women Love Once (Paramount, 1931), screenplay;
Once a Lady (Paramount, 1931), screenplay by Akins and Samuel Hoffenstein;
Working Girls (Paramount, 1931), screenplay;
Christopher Strong (RKO, 1933), screenplay;
Outcast Lady (M-G-M, 1934), screenplay;
Camille (M-G-M, 1936), screenplay by Akins, Frances Marion, and James Hilton;
Accused (Criterion/United Artists, 1936), screenplay by George Barraud; dialogue;
Lady of Secrets (Columbia, 1936), screenplay by Akins and Joseph Anthony;
The Toy Wife (M-G-M, 1938), screenplay;
Zaza (Paramount, 1938), screenplay;
Desire Me (M-G-M, 1947), screenplay by Akins and Marguerite Roberts.

SELECTED PLAYS: *The Magical City* (New York, Bandbox Theatre, 1915-1916 season);
Papa (New York, Little Theatre, 10 April 1919);
Footloose (New York, Greenwich Village Theatre, 10 May 1919);
Déclassée (New York, Empire Theatre, 6 October 1919);
Daddy's Gone A-Hunting (New York, Plymouth Theatre, 31 August 1921);
The Varying Shore (New York, Hudson Theatre, 5 December 1921);
The Texas Nightingale (New York, Empire Theatre, 20 November 1922);
A Royal Fandango (New York, Plymouth Theatre, 12 November 1923);
The Moon-Flower (New York, Astor Theatre, 25 February 1924);
First Love (New York, Booth Theatre, 8 November 1926);
The Crown Prince (New York, Forrest Theatre, 23 March 1927);
The Furies (New York, Shubert Theatre, 7 March 1928);

Zoë Akins

The Love Duel (New York, Ethel Barrymore Theatre, 15 April 1929);
The Greeks Had a Word For It (New York, Sam H. Harris Theatre, 25 September 1930);
The Old Maid (New York, Empire Theatre, 7 January 1935);
O Evening Star! (New York, Empire Theatre, 8 January 1936).

BOOKS: *Interpretations: A Book of First Poems* (New York: M. Kennerley, 1912; London: G. Richards, 1912);
Papa (New York: M. Kennerley, 1913);
Cake Upon the Waters (New York: Century, 1919);
Déclassée, Daddy's Gone A-Hunting, and *Greatness* (New York: Boni & Liveright, 1923);

Such a Charming Young Man (New York: French, 1924);

The Old Maid (New York & London: Appleton-Century, 1935);

The Little Miracle (New York & London: Harper, 1936);

The Hills Grow Smaller (New York & London: Harper, 1937);

Forever Young (New York: Scribners, 1941);

Mrs. January and Mr. Ex (New York: French, 1948).

Zoë Akins was born in Humansville, Missouri. Raised in a well-to-do and strongly political Republican family, she fell in love with the stage after seeing productions of touring companies at various St. Louis theaters. She wrote her first play at the age of twelve, and her early poetry was published in William Marion Reedy's *St. Louis Mirror*, a journal that had earlier recognized the talents of Fannie Hurst, Sara Teasdale, and Edgar Lee Masters. Her first professional work for the stage was a three-act comedy titled *Papa*. It was performed with moderate success in many cities throughout the United States, but ran for only twelve performances when finally produced at the Little Theatre in New York, on 10 April 1919. *The Magical City*, written after *Papa*, was her first play to be produced in New York. A one-act melodrama in verse, it was performed by the Washington Square Players at the Bandbox Theatre during their 1915-1916 season.

It was *Déclassée* that gained Akins the critical and public acclaim she desired. The play opened at the Empire Theatre in New York on 6 October 1919 and starred Ethel Barrymore as Lady Helen Haden, the self-styled "last of the mad Varricks." Lady Haden "has lived a little recklessly in an effort to make life a trifle more endurable" and becomes involved with a man who has committed the unpardonable sin of cheating at cards. This English society drama, written by a woman from Missouri, has its origins not in the trashy magazine romances of the period, but in the writing of Elinor Glyn and in the short works of Saki. Its melodramatic, overblown style typifies Akins's later writings for both the stage and the screen.

Akins followed *Déclassée* with a number of plays, some of which were critical and popular successes and others which were disastrous failures, including *Daddy's Gone A-Hunting* (1921), starring Marjorie Rambeau; *The Varying Shore* (1921), starring Elsie Ferguson; *The Moon-Flower* (1924), from the Hungarian play by Lajos Biro and starring Elsie Ferguson; *The Furies* (1928), starring Laurette Taylor; and *The Greeks Had a Word For It* (1930),

starring Verree Teasdale. Akins probably reached the pinnacle of her stage career with the production of *The Old Maid*, an adaptation of a novella by Edith Wharton, for which she received the 1935 Pulitzer Prize for drama. *The Old Maid* opened at the Empire Theatre in New York on 7 January 1935 and starred Judith Anderson.

The playwright described her stage plays as written "from the heart for the great collective heart," a remark that caused one wit to say of her writing, "It's the curse of an Akins heart." In her plays, Akins concerned herself only with beauty; anything sordid or ugly had no place in her philosophy. In a 1941 interview, she commented, "No, I've never seen Saroyan, Irwin Shaw, or Blitzstein. . . . I'm sorry, but I don't know Steinbeck's *Grapes of Wrath*. . . . As for his *Mice and Men*, I just couldn't bear to see that morbid thing; my nerves, my whole being would go to pieces."

As early as 1924 various film producers had begun purchasing the screen rights to Akins's plays. In 1925 *Daddy's Gone A-Hunting* was filmed by M-G-M and *Déclassée* by Corinne Griffith Productions; *The Moon-Flower* was filmed as *Eve's Secret* in the same year by Paramount; and in 1929 First National also filmed her play *Déclassée* as *Her Private Life*, following it in 1930 with *The Furies*. The $8,000 Paramount paid for the motion picture rights to *The Moon-Flower*, a large sum in 1925, indicated the film industry's interest in the commercial possibilities of Akins's plays.

In 1928 Akins moved to California for her health. Less than two years later she was under contract to Paramount, writing six films during 1930 and 1931, and contributing original stories or plays for three others. Four of her first five screenplays—*Sarah and Son* (1930), *Anybody's Woman* (1930), *The Right To Love* (1930), and *Once a Lady* (1931)—were written for Ruth Chatterton, one of the new breed of film stars whom the talkies had lured away from the stage. Critics considered her a worthy successor to Jeanne Eagels in the field of emotional drama. The haughtily elegant Chatterton could provide the necessary self-sacrificing melodramatics for *Sarah and Son*, in which a mother separated from a no-good husband sells her baby to a wealthy oil man; or for *Once a Lady*, which demanded that she adopt a heavy accent to portray a Russian eccentric married to an English politician whose political plans force her to give up both him and her child. In *Anybody's Woman*, Chatterton is cast in the unlikely role of a chorus girl who is too good for her wealthy lawyer husband. In *The Right To Love*, Chatterton plays a double role: that of a mother who prevents her daughter's marriage to a young country boy, and the daughter herself as she grows up and encourages her child to experience the romance she has missed.

The non-Chatterton films fared poorly with the critics. "Heaves too much in the clinches," commented *Variety* in June 1931 about *Women Love Once* (1931), in which a wealthy socialite (Eleanor Boardman) steals a happily married artist (Paul Lukas) away from his wife and daughter. Lukas was also featured in *Working Girls* (1931), a saga of two beautiful blondes from the country who learn of city life from a couple of slickers.

Of the films based on Akins's material but scripted by others, the best is undoubtedly *Girls About Town* (1931), directed by George Cukor and featuring Kay Francis, Joel McCrea, and Lilyan Tashman. The comedy in this yarn about two gold diggers is fresh and vibrant, and the dialogue is pleasantly risqué. In 1932 Akins prepared a script for Paramount based on A. J. Cronin's 1931 novel *Hatter's Castle*. An adaptation of this novel was eventually filmed by Paramount British in 1948, but Akins's script does not appear to have been used.

Like the elite who peopled her films, Akins lived in a grand and aloof manner. Screenwriter Anita Loos recalled, "She considered the film colony vulgar and could only breathe the rarefied air of Pasadena, that elegant suburb built in the eighties by retired tycoons and still so snobbish that it looked down on movie stars. Zoë purchased an Edwardian mansion, furnished it with opulence, and engaged a staff of British servants." Her search for gentility reached its zenith in 1932 when she married Hugo Rumbold, the son of Sir Horace Rumbold, a former British ambassador to Austria-Hungary. Her husband died within months of their wedding.

Paramount was not the only studio to adapt Akins's material for the screen. In 1932 her play *The Greeks Had a Word For It* was filmed by Samuel Goldwyn as *The Greeks Had a Word for Them* and the following year RKO-Radio filmed Akins's play *Morning Glory* (produced earlier at the Pasadena Playhouse) as a vehicle for Katharine Hepburn. It was a classic Akins plot, involving an egotistical young actress from Kansas who is determined to rise to the pinnacle of her profession and prove she is more than just a "morning glory." Originally considered for Constance Bennett, this role gave Hepburn her first Academy Award for Best Actress.

In late 1933 Akins adapted Gilbert Frankau's best-selling novel, *Christopher Strong*, for RKO. It was originally to have starred Ann Harding, but when she became unavailable, Hepburn was sub-stituted. The story of an aviatrix who falls in love with a married man and eventually renounces her love by the theatrical expedient of crashing her plane and killing herself, *Christopher Strong* garnered mixed reviews. *Variety* found the characters to be merely glamorous stage puppets, while Mordaunt Hall in the *New York Times* praised Akins and the film's director, Dorothy Arzner, for their "marked intelligence." In recent years, the film has taken on considerable significance with women's groups because of its supposedly feminist viewpoint and famous woman director. Whatever success the film had on its initial release, however, was due entirely to the popularity of Hepburn and the novels of Frankau. In addition to their collaboration on *Christopher Strong*, Arzner and Akins had previously worked together on three other feature films: *Sarah and Son, Anybody's Woman*, and *Working Girls*.

A sojourn followed at M-G-M, where Akins must surely have felt in her element; there she was in the realm of the film industry's leading producer, Irving Thalberg—the aristocrat of filmmakers. Her first M-G-M script, *Outcast Lady* (1934), was based on Michael Arlen's 1924 novel *The Green Hat*, which had already been produced as a silent film with Greta Garbo titled *A Woman of Affairs* (1928). Transformed into a vehicle for Constance Bennett, the story required considerable changes because of the censorship restrictions placed on the industry by the Hays Office. As *Variety* noted in November 1934, *Outcast Lady* was "the chassis of *The Green Hat* with the motor taken out . . . dull, jumbled, and pointless."

The happiest pairing at M-G-M came in 1936 when Akins collaborated with director George Cukor on *Camille*. The story of the world's most romantic heroine, Marguerite Gauthier, and her handsome young lover, Armand Duval, was a natural for Akins's talents. Cukor was a great admirer of Akins the playwright and described her as one of America's most gifted artists. He recalls that the script, as he shot it, was entirely hers, despite her sharing credit with two other fine writers, James Hilton and Frances Marion. *Camille* was a box-office and artistic triumph, largely due to the popularity of its two stars, Greta Garbo and Robert Taylor. The film also received widespread praise from critics, who found the dialogue natural and unaffected and lauded the screenwﬁers' close adherence to Alexandre Dumas fils's original story.

The Toy Wife (1938) was an original Akins script for Luise Rainer, a follow-up to the actress's two Academy Award-winning performances in *The Great Ziegfeld* (1936) and *The Good Earth* (1937).

Robert Taylor and Greta Garbo in a scene from Camille

Rainer plays a flighty "toy wife" in the New Orleans of the 1880s, whose frivolous ways bring unhappiness and disaster to her husband and to herself. Some critics complained that Akins did not seem to realize she was writing for the screen and not the stage, where actors were accustomed to declaiming their lines; others felt she paid too much attention to the manner and speech of the New Orleans aristocracy and not enough to character development.

Her next project, with George Cukor at Paramount, was *Zaza* (1938), the third film version of the play that Mrs. Leslie Carter had first made famous as leading lady in 1899. Claudette Colbert starred as the French vaudeville actress who falls in love with a married man (Herbert Marshall); because of his marital status, she knows they must part. At her opening in Paris, Zaza, knowing Marshall is in the audience, sings a song of parting. She later goes on to become a great success, but her happiness is tinged with loss. Interference from the Hays Office again hurt the script, but most critics agreed with *Life* magazine that the film was "moderately interesting." While Akins's play *The Old Maid*

was being brought to the screen by Warner Bros. in 1939 as a vehicle for Bette Davis, she continued to collaborate with George Cukor on M-G-M's production of *Pride and Prejudice*. Cukor was later replaced as director by Robert Z. Leonard, and the Akins script was apparently completely rewritten by Aldous Huxley and Jane Murfin. Akins did not receive screen credit when the film was released in 1940.

It was six years before Akins wrote again for the screen. Again the director was George Cukor, and the film went through six title changes before its release in 1947 as *Desire Me*, a vehicle for Greer Garson. Sonya Levien and Marguerite Roberts collaborated with Akins on the adaptation of Leonhard Frank's novel about a man who pretends his best friend is dead in order to acquire his wife and property. Mervyn LeRoy replaced Cukor as director halfway through the production. The film was apparently an unhappy experience for all concerned, with Cukor's, LeRoy's and Levien's names being removed from the credits. The critics called the plot hackneyed and sentimental.

H. B. Warner, Luise Rainer, and Melvyn Douglas in The Toy Wife

Although she continued to write plays and continued to see her early works adapted by others for the screen, Akins never again wrote a screenplay. At her death in Los Angeles on 29 October 1958, one of her friends and colleagues, Sonya Levien, recalled, "She was brilliantly young and vital to the very last."

Papers:
Zoë Akins's papers are at the Huntington Library, San Marino, California. In addition, there is a collection of literary manuscripts, including plays, screenplays, and stories, at the Department of Special Collections, University Research Library, University of California, Los Angeles.

Jay Presson Allen

(3 March 1922-)

Nick Roddick

California State University, Long Beach

MOTION PICTURES: *Marnie* (Universal, 1964), screenplay;

The Prime of Miss Jean Brodie (20th Century-Fox, 1969), screenplay;

Cabaret (Allied Artists, 1972), screenplay;

Travels with My Aunt (M-G-M, 1972), screenplay by Allen and Hugh Wheeler;

Funny Lady (Columbia, 1975), screenplay by Allen and Arnold Schulman;

Just Tell Me What You Want (Warner Bros., 1980), screenplay;

Prince of the City (Orion/Warner Bros., 1981), screenplay by Allen and Sidney Lumet;

Deathtrap (Warner Bros., 1982), screenplay.

TELEVISION: *The Borrowers* (NBC, 1973), script;

Family [series] (ABC, 1976-1980), creator and story consultant.

SELECTED PLAYS: *The Prime of Miss Jean Brodie* (Torquay, U.K., Princess Theatre, 5 April 1966; New York, Helen Hayes Theatre, 16 January 1968);

Forty Carats (New York, Morosco Theatre, 26 December 1968);

Sand Albert (London, Piccadilly Theatre, 6 November 1972).

BOOKS: *Spring Riot* (New York: Rinehart, 1948);

Forty Carats (New York: Random House, 1969);

The Prime of Miss Jean Brodie (New York: French, 1969);

Just Tell Me What You Want (New York: Dutton, 1975).

Although Jay Presson Allen has written novels, plays, and television scripts and although she has written only eight screenplays in nearly twenty years, she is best known for her work in motion pictures, for which she has achieved consid-

Mike Nichols and Jay Presson Allen, mid-1970s

erable critical acclaim and financial success. By the beginning of the 1980s, she had also established herself as an important Hollywood producer.

Allen was born Jacqueline Presson in San Angelo, Texas, daughter of Albert Jeffrey and Wilhilmina Miller Presson. "Somewhat" educated in Texas, she moved to New York in the late 1940s with ambitions to become an actress. Instead, she married and settled in Connecticut, where she wrote two unproduced plays and a novel, *Spring Riot* (1948).

Allen's first marriage ended in divorce, and on 17 March 1955 she was married to Lewis Maitland Allen, a theater and movie producer. Never particularly fond of her given name, she decided to use her first initial when writing (the more elaborate form, Jay, is the work of a Social Security clerk, she says). With her first screenwriting credit—*Marnie* in 1964—she adopted her married name as her professional name.

One of Allen's two early plays, "The First Wife," was scheduled for Broadway production in the early 1960s. The production fell through, but the play was optioned by Hal Wallis; it was filmed as *Wives and Lovers* from a screenplay by Edward Anhalt in 1963, giving Allen her first contact with

Maggie Smith in the title role of Allen's second film, The Prime of Miss Jean Brodie. *Smith won the Academy Award as best actress for her performance in this 1969 movie.*

Hollywood. Partly autobiographical, the play deals with the problems of getting one's first play on the Broadway stage and with the social rituals of suburban Connecticut.

Shortly after *Wives and Lovers* was released, Allen received an offer from Alfred Hitchcock to work on his film *Marnie*. Enthusiastic about the experience of working with Hitchcock, Allen describes him as "absolutely extraordinary, a natural teacher," but she is a good deal more reserved about the film, to which she was a comparative latecomer, replacing two earlier screenwriters. *Marnie* is the story of a young woman (Tippi Hedren) with a compulsive urge to steal and many sexual problems, all of which are traced back to a traumatic childhood incident involving her prostitute mother and a sailor client. The movie was Hitchcock's worst-received film in years, and because the earlier writers did not receive screen credit, much of the blame for the movie's failure came to rest on Allen. Yet she should receive at least some credit for the intensive, nightmare quality of the movie, whose reputation has grown over the years. The screenplay, an efficiently structured adaptation of Winston Graham's novel, provides hints of derangement in the heroine's apparently banal comments, but it is Hitchcock's handling of her moments of complete derangement that makes the movie succeed.

Marnie was the first of Allen's six films that center on female characters. With her second film, *The Prime of Miss Jean Brodie* (1969), she began a series of screenplays dealing with women whose control of their lives and their worlds is not as total as they would have others believe. She had first adapted Muriel Spark's novel as a play, which premiered in London in 1966 before moving to Broadway in 1968. These adaptations, which achieved critical and commercial success, represent Allen's finest work.

In the film Miss Brodie (Maggie Smith, who won an Oscar), a teacher in a private girls' academy, is more concerned with the aesthetic welfare of her charges than with the breadth of their education. Her influence is both positive—an alternative to the unimaginative approach of much British education—and pernicious. For example, cultivating in her charges an admiration for Mussolini, she urges them to fight for Franco in the Spanish Civil War. In Allen's adaptations Miss Brodie is a more dramatic figure than she was in the novel. Because Allen makes her a larger-than-life figure who is more sympathetic and comic than twisted and complex, Miss Brodie commands the audience's interest and sympathy without incurring contempt. Such a change, which produced a highly effective but less probing film, is in many ways symptomatic of Allen's screenwriting technique: taking a literary original, she streamlines and simplifies, adding such dramatic focal points as the movie's final confrontation between Miss Brodie and the girl she has underestimated. As a result, the novel and the issues on which it touches—repression, sexual awakening, education, and fascism—become accessible to a wider and more diverse public, even if those issues become slightly blurred in the process.

Allen's next project, *Cabaret* (1972), has many similarities to *The Prime of Miss Jean Brodie* in its period, its central character, and its theme. Based on Christopher Isherwood's *Goodbye to Berlin*; its stage version, *I Am a Camera*, by John van Druten; and on the stage musical *Cabaret*, by Fred Ebb and John Kander, the film is the story of a young Englishman (Michael York) in Berlin on the eve of the Nazi takeover and of his experiences with chanteuse Sally Bowles (Liza Minnelli, who won an Oscar) and German aristocrat Maximillian von Heune (Helmut Griem). The movie is best remembered for its musical numbers in the Kit-Kat Club, a seedy focus for the upheaval in Germany as the Nazis took power. Working on *Cabaret* was not a happy experience for Allen; she was replaced as screenwriter by Hugh Wheeler while the film was still being shot, but she received sole screenplay credit on the grounds—established by the Writers Guild—that the basic construction of the screenplay was complete before Wheeler began work.

Allen shared screenplay credit with Wheeler on her next film, *Travels with My Aunt* (1972), though in this case their positions were reversed. Wheeler had adapted Graham Greene's novel as a vehicle for Katharine Hepburn, but when Hepburn was unhappy with his screenplay, the studio decided to start over with a new screenwriter and a new star. Allen rewrote the script, and Maggie Smith played Aunt Augusta, an extravagant woman who, in an apparent effort to ransom a former lover, travels around Europe with her conventional former-bank-manager nephew (Alec McCowen), her devoted manservant (Lou Gossett), and briefly, a hippy named Tooley (Cindy Williams). *Travels with My Aunt* is a highly entertaining film, but it bears unmistakable signs of haste and last-minute change.

For *Funny Lady* (1975), written to provide Barbra Streisand a sequel to the successful *Funny Girl* (1968), Allen shared screenwriting credit with Arnold Schulman, who also wrote the original story. The film picks up the Fanny Brice story after her divorce from gambler Nick Arstein (Omar Sharif) and charts her increasing professional success and decreasing personal happiness during her marriage to songwriter and impresario Billy Rose (James Caan). *Funny Lady* was a failure critically and at the box office, but Allen was one of the few people to emerge from it with some credit. Her touch is clearly discernible in the dialogue: in Fanny's early exchanges with Billy and in the final break with Nicky, Allen's wry humor provides perfect material for Streisand's mixture of aggression and vulnerability.

Following *Funny Lady*, Allen virtually retired from Hollywood for four years. She wrote a novel, *Just Tell Me What You Want* (1975), and created and served as story consultant for the television series *Family*, about an upper-middle-class Pasadena family who faces problems with everyday common sense. Allen was not directly responsible for all the episodes, but the series's middlebrow treatment of sensitive issues clearly bears her trademark.

In September 1979, Allen signed a six-picture deal with Warner Bros. to produce rather than write. Yet despite her statement that "I didn't want to write any more. I was tired of it," she has written the screenplays for four of the six films she produced. The first was an adaptation of her novel *Just Tell Me What You Want* (1980), about financier Max Herschel (Alan King) and his mistress and protégée, Bones Burton (Ali MacGraw), who leaves him for another man but is drawn back to him by his energy and power. The film's reception was mixed, possibly because its director, Sidney Lumet, had little experience directing comedy.

Allen continued working with Lumet, however. After she produced *It's My Turn* (1980), a comedy-drama about a woman with career and romantic problems, she produced and wrote with Lumet *Prince of the City* (1981), based on Robert Daley's book about a New York City police officer. Played by Treat Williams in the film, this officer is asked to investigate corruption in the police department but finds himself ostracized by his friends and eventually charged with perjury. The production of this film was an enormous undertaking. In order to capture all the details of the story, Allen and Lumet fashioned a film that ran for nearly three hours and had hundreds of speaking parts. Although not a financial success, the film has received much critical acclaim and was considered by many critics to be one of the best films of 1981.

Lumet and Allen followed *Prince of the City*

Michael York and Liza Minnelli in a scene from Cabaret. *Minnelli won an Oscar for her portrayal of singer Sally Bowles.*

with the film version of Ira Levin's long-running mystery play, *Deathtrap* (1982). In the film a prominent playwright (Michael Caine), who has not had a hit in several years, pretends to murder a former student (Christopher Reeve), who has written a sure success, although the two have actually conspired to murder the playwright's wealthy wife (Dyan Cannon). The film, which suffered from staginess and excessive length, received mixed reviews and was a mild financial success.

Jay Presson Allen's best work is marked by her inclination toward sophisticated comedy. Her de-partures from a style that features wry, rapid-fire dialogue, often centering on the notion of marital and sexual conflict, have been *Cabaret*, *Marnie*, and *Prince of the City*—films with which she has seemed least happy. As with so many Hollywood professionals of the postwar years, hers is a talent which does not always seem to suit the times.

Reference:

Marjorie Rosen, Interview with Allen, *Los Angeles Times*, 11 May 1975.

Edward Anhalt
(28 March 1914-   )

Nick Roddick
California State University, Long Beach

SELECTED MOTION PICTURES: *Problem Child* [documentary] (Independent, 1935), script;

Thunder of the Sea [documentary] (Lutheran Radio Pictures, 1936), script;

Strange Voyage (Monogram, 1946), screen story and screenplay by Anhalt and Edna Anhalt, as Andrew Holt;

Avalanche (Producers Releasing Corporation, 1946), screen story and screenplay by Anhalt and Edna Anhalt, as Andrew Holt;

Bulldog Drummond Strikes Back (Columbia, 1947), screenplay by Anhalt and Edna Anhalt;

The Gentleman from Nowhere (Columbia, 1948), screen story and screenplay;

The Crime Doctor's Diary (Columbia, 1949), screen story by Anhalt and David Dressler; screenplay;

Panic in the Streets (20th Century-Fox, 1950), screen story by Anhalt and Edna Anhalt;

The Sniper (Columbia, 1952), screen story by Anhalt and Edna Anhalt;

The Member of the Wedding (Columbia, 1952), screenplay by Anhalt and Edna Anhalt;

Not as a Stranger (United Artists, 1955), screenplay by Anhalt and Edna Anhalt;

The Pride and the Passion (United Artists, 1957), screenplay by Anhalt and Edna Anhalt;

The Young Lions (20th Century-Fox, 1958), screenplay;

In Love and War (20th Century-Fox, 1958), screenplay;

The Restless Years (Universal-International, 1959), screenplay;

The Sins of Rachel Cade (Warner Bros., 1961), screenplay;

The Young Savages (United Artists, 1961), screenplay by Anhalt and J. P. Miller;

Girls! Girls! Girls! (Paramount, 1962), screenplay by Anhalt and Allan Weiss;

A Girl Named Tamiko (Paramount, 1962), screenplay;

Wives and Lovers (Paramount, 1963), screenplay;

Becket (Paramount, 1964), screenplay;

The Satan Bug (United Artists, 1965), screenplay by Anhalt and James Clavell;

Boeing, Boeing (Paramount, 1965), screenplay;

Edward Anhalt

Hour of the Gun (United Artists, 1967), screen story and screenplay;

The Boston Strangler (20th Century-Fox, 1968), screenplay;

In Enemy Country (Universal, 1969), screenplay by Anhalt and Alfred Hayes;

The Madwoman of Chaillot (Warner Bros., 1969), screenplay;

Jeremiah Johnson (Warner Bros., 1972), screenplay by Anhalt and John Milius;

Luther (American Express Films [New York] / Ely Landau Organisation [London] / Cinevision [Montreal], 1974), screenplay;

The Man in the Glass Booth (American Film Theater, 1975), screenplay;

Escape to Athena (I.T.C., 1979), screenplay by Anhalt and Richard S. Lochte;

Green Ice (I.T.C., 1981), screenplay by Anhalt, Ray

18

Hassett, Anthony Simmons, Robert De Laurentiis.

TELEVISION: "A Time for Killing," *The Bob Hope Chrysler Theater* (NBC, 1965), script;
QB VII (ABC, 1974), script;
Contract on Cherry Street (NBC, 1977), script;
Nowhere to Hide (1977), script;
The Day Christ Died (CBS, 1980), script by Anhalt and James Lee Barrett;
Madame X (NBC, 1981), script.

PERIODICAL PUBLICATION: "The Camera-man's Part in Television Production," *American Cinematographer*, 24 (January 1943): 8-9, 30-35; 24 (February 1943): 46-47, 78.

Edward Anhalt was born in New York City. Educated at George Washington High School, he was part of an experiment funded by the Carnegie Foundation which took fifty children with exceptional IQs and placed them into an accelerated educational program. From there he went on to study journalism at Columbia, but he left in his sophomore year. Anhalt won a Rockefeller Foundation grant to Princeton in 1935 and in 1937 received a fellowship to study documentary film technique under Willard Van Dyke. For two years he worked as cameraman and film editor in the field of socially conscious documentary, collaborating with Van Dyke, Pare Lorentz, and Ralph Steiner. Joining CBS in 1938, he became chief television cameraman, wrote the first study of television camera work to appear in *American Cinematographer*, directed Eugene Loring and the American Ballet Theatre in a television version of Aaron Copland's *Billy the Kid*, and was involved in the first color television transmission.

Anhalt and his wife Edna had contributed several short stories to pulp magazines, and it was these stories that took them to Hollywood. Their first joint screen credit, as Andrew Holt (the pseudonym they had used for their pulp stories), was *Strange Voyage* (1946), an adventure melodrama about death and betrayal during a search for buried treasure in the desert of Baja California. Andrew Holt's next effort went to the other end of the climatic scale; whereas the characters in *Strange Voyage* die of thirst in the desert, those in *Avalanche* (1946) are trapped by snow in the mountains.

Dropping the Holt pseudonym after *Avalanche*, the Anhalts moved on to the Columbia "B" unit. While their first two pictures used a fairly basic plot structure—murderous tensions between people cut off from the world—Anhalt's three Columbia movies (the first coscripted with Edna) have plot lines of nearly impenetrable complexity. The first, *Bulldog Drummond Strikes Back* (1947), has H. C. McNeile's aristocratic hero solving a case of mistaken identity among heiresses in postwar London. For his next two films, both starring Warner Baxter, Anhalt said that "the film story could be anything I chose to invent, providing the star wore a dinner jacket and was not obliged to run up or down stairs." *The Gentleman from Nowhere* (1948) tells the story of a New York night watchman who is persuaded by an insurance investigator to go to California and impersonate a chemical company executive who has mysteriously disappeared. After uncovering an accounting swindle, the night watchman reveals that he is, in fact, the missing executive and thereby gets his old job back. *The Crime Doctor's Diary* (1949) is the ninth and last film in a series based on the Crime Doctor radio program. In the movie the Crime Doctor helps an ex-con clear himself of a frame-up involving an arson attempt; the real culprit is the ex-con's jilted girl friend.

The Anhalts were given their first chance to work on an "A" film when they were hired by 20th Century-Fox to collaborate on *Panic in the Streets* (1950). Daniel Fuchs, who was responsible for most of the ideas retained in the final version of the film, received credit for adapting the Anhalts' screen story; Richard Murphy received credit for the screenplay. The film depicts the attempts of a public health official to track down two petty criminals who have contracted a deadly virus from a man they killed during a robbery. The criminals avoid the authorities and the health inspector, who, hampered in his efforts by a local police captain, cannot announce why they are being sought for fear of creating mass panic. *Panic in the Streets* won the Anhalts an Academy Award for Best Motion Picture Story.

After *Panic in the Streets*, the Anhalts worked on a Western, *Red Mountain*, for Hal Wallis, receiving credit in the Screen Achievement Record as "contributors to screenplay construction." Long before its release in April 1952, however, they had signed a contract with independent producer Stanley Kramer, whose films were being distributed through Columbia. Their job, in addition to writing, was to function as a producing team, replacing Val Lewton, who had died in 1951. The Anhalts' first credit for Kramer was as associate producers of *My Six Convicts* (1952). Their second was *The Sniper* (1952) for which, in addition to producing, they supplied the original screen story. *The Sniper*, which was directed by Edward Dmytryk, bears a close resemblance to *Panic in the Streets*, both in its semidocumentary approach and in its portrayal of a liberal reformer blocked by a corrupt establishment. The film was based on actual case studies of snipers, researched extensively in conjunction with the Los Angeles Police Department and supported by legislators eager to see changes in the laws regarding sex offenders; Columbia touted it as "Hollywood's first major motion picture to deal frankly with the nationally increasing problem of sex-murderers." *The Sniper* deals with a young psychopath whose only method of sexual expression is to shoot women with a high-powered rifle; he makes indirect attempts to get help before the murders are committed, but when he is unable to find help, he kills. The plot highlights the callousness of civic authorities unwilling to respond to the need that prompted these murders; the city is only interested in eradicating the symptom, not in treating the cause. The Anhalts received their second Academy Award nomination for the screen story.

After *The Sniper*, the Anhalts worked as associate producers of one more Kramer film, *Eight Iron Men* (1952), before writing their first full screenplay for him, *The Member of the Wedding*, (1952), which was one of the Kramer company's more successful early efforts. Adapted from the highly successful Broadway play by Carson McCullers (itself a dramatization of her own 1946 novel), the screenplay is more representative of her work than of the Anhalts' since it adheres very closely to the play. Well over three-quarters of the film takes place in the Addams kitchen, ruled over by the black cook Bernice, and in the yard outside, where twelve-year-old Frankie Addams hovers between childhood and adolescence; the only expanded scenes—Frankie's nighttime odyssey through the town and her encounter with a young soldier in a bar—are taken from the novel. The film's climax, though, seems to bear the Anhalt stamp of an action which eloquently summarizes the theme of a story: Frankie, having convinced herself that she is going to leave home forever in her newly won role as a "member of the wedding," packs her bag and hides in her brother's honeymoon car. Despite gentle attempts to persuade her, she will not get out and finally has to be dragged kicking and screaming in her grown-up dress into the dust of the road as bride and groom speed away.

Beginning with *The Member of the Wedding*, Anhalt worked almost entirely as an adapter; his next project for Kramer, *Not as a Stranger* (1955),

allowed him to develop his rather unusual way of working on an adaptation. He read Morton Thompson's novel several times and then ripped it apart, pinning up the pages that excited him and throwing away the rest. "Then I would thread my continuity between that excitement, frequently changing the general moral tone of the book, or its purpose, to fit that excitement." *Not as a Stranger* was a lengthy study of the problems of an idealistic young doctor, one of the first of Stanley Kramer's big projects of the 1950s. It also marked Kramer's debut as a director.

The Anhalts' next script for Kramer was also their last for him and their last as a team. *The Pride and the Passion* (1957), adapted from a short novel by C. S. Forester, was Kramer's entry into the epic-movie league. In the movie, a group of guerrillas advised by a British army officer move a huge gun across Spain so that it can be used against Napoleon's invading army (Frank Sinatra played the guerrilla chief, Cary Grant the adviser). Forester visited the location and pronounced himself pleased with the adaptation: "The Anhalts did a good job compressing characters and expanding incidents." According to Anhalt, *The Pride and the Passion* "lost most of the money previous pictures had earned and was a catalyst for my divorce from Edna"—he has since remarried twice—"and our joint divorce from Stanley." At the time of the break with Kramer, in November 1956, Edward Anhalt's salary was $1,500 a week. The dual break did nothing to affect his screenwriting career; his first solo picture, *The Young Lions* (1958), is one of his most successful.

The Young Lions is adapted from the novel by Irwin Shaw; eight authors had produced thirteen unusable scripts before Anhalt was given the assignment. The film charts two parallel military experiences that run from the late 1930s to the end of World War II, that of a young Nazi officer, Christian Diestl, and that of a young Jewish GI, Noah Ackerman. Although the novel's portrayal of Ackerman's persecution by anti-Semitic NCOs and his general disillusionment with the army were toned down in the movie as a result of military pressure, it is the character of Diestl that underwent the greatest change. In Shaw's novel, he is an unreconstructed Nazi to the end; in Anhalt's screenplay he suffers pangs of disillusionment with the war and disgust with Hitler (when he learns about the concentration camps) and commits suicide by walking into the line of fire of the first American soldier he sees (who is, of course, Ackerman). Anhalt's screenplay for *The Young Lions* shows him at his

Scene from the 1957 movie The Pride and the Passion, *the last of eight films that Anhalt wrote with his wife Edna*
(photo by Ken Danvers)

strongest, stringing together action sequences so that the audience is guided smoothly through the complexities of history and narrative.

Anhalt followed *The Young Lions* with four films, all for different studios. Three of these efforts were undistinguished. *In Love and War* (1958) tells the interlocking stories of three young marines during the war in the Pacific and on leave back home in California. *The Restless Years* (1959), based on an unproduced play by Patricia Joudry, is a late 1950s youth drama in which the kids overcome the prejudices of adults in a small-town community. *The Sins of Rachel Cade* was completed in November 1959 but not released until April 1961. His next project, *The Young Savages* (1961), was slightly better. A story of gang youths that avoided portraying the delinquents as either degenerate monsters or angelic victims of social deprivation, the film struck the balance that Anhalt achieved later more memorably with *The Boston Strangler* (1968).

After *The Young Savages*, Anhalt began work-

ing for Hal Wallis, for whom he made five films. The first three are largely forgettable, and Anhalt has suggested that they were chores Wallis made him complete before he would let him have a crack at *Becket*. *Girls! Girls! Girls!* (1962) is an Elvis Presley vehicle; *A Girl Named Tamiko* (1962) is about a Russian-Chinese photographer who uses a receptionist at the U.S. embassy in Tokyo to gain entrance to the United States; *Wives and Lovers* (1963) is a slightly risqué comedy about the seductions, material and physical, held out to a young playwright on the road to success. During this period, Anhalt also worked briefly on *Cleopatra* (1962).

Becket (1964), Anhalt's fourth film for Wallis, won him a second Oscar, this one for best screenplay based on material from another medium. In adapting Jean Anouilh's play, Anhalt felt "the main problem was to stop it from being a play, to stop it from being theatrical, and to make it real. I had to make the two men into people who were really living in the time that they lived and

Richard Burton and Peter O'Toole in Becket, *for which Anhalt won his second Oscar*

talking in conversational rather than theatrical terms." He removed Anouilh's characteristic rhetoric, altered the characters into more historically realistic personages, and deemphasized the playwright's concern with theatrical devices. *Becket* was an enormous success, and it showed Anhalt at his best, the adapter with a strong cinematic sense who has no qualms about altering aspects of the original that he finds unsatisfactory and who is extremely skillful at "opening up" a play or a novel in such a way that the new scenes blend into the fabric of the original. The film's success made Anhalt one of the highest-paid screenwriters in the business; in 1965 he was receiving a minimum of $5,000 a week.

In the interim between *Becket* and his last Wallis film, Anhalt wrote his first television script, "A Time for Killing," for *The Bob Hope Chrysler Theater*. He also wrote the first of two genre films directed by John Sturges, *The Satan Bug* (1965), a science-fiction film about a serum capable of starting a fatal,

worldwide chain reaction. The second Sturges film was *Hour of the Gun* (1967), a western depicting Wyatt Earp and Doc Holliday after the gunfight at the OK Corral. In 1965 Anhalt did one more film with Hal Wallis, the movie adaptation of Marc Camoletti's play *Boeing, Boeing*, about two Paris-based journalists who come into comic conflicts over their involvements with several airline stewardesses. Anhalt was distinctly unimpressed by the play: "I thought it was absolutely appalling. I mean, I really thought it was bad"—and even improved by the screenplay, the result was still mediocre.

In 1968 Anhalt wrote *The Boston Strangler*, based on the case study of schizophrenic Albert de Salvo, who murdered thirteen women between June 1962 and January 1964. The screenplay treats the subject in a straightforward manner, neither voyeuristically nor sensationally. The story is split in two parts; the first half covers the police hunt for the murderer, the second the interrogation of de

Salvo, who gradually realizes what he has done. At one level, *The Boston Strangler* is a superior thriller; at another, it is a disturbing portrayal of a psychopath and of police reaction to him.

In the 1970s Anhalt scripted four movies. *Jeremiah Johnson* (1972), written with John Milius, is the balladlike story of an ex-soldier who, in the 1830s, sets out to become a trapper in the Rocky Mountains. The film charts his initiation first into survival, then into the ways of the Indian. Finally, the murder of Johnson's Indian wife and adopted child sends him on an orgy of revenge. The film consists of a careful structuring of the story's development around moments of significant action. Structuring stories—and bringing out the values inherent in a situation, a character, or a location—is what has consistently characterized Anhalt's best work as a screenwriter. When speaking of his work with *Jeremiah Johnson*'s director Sidney Pollack, Anhalt has stressed the extent of his own contribution to the visual conceptualization of the film (as well as of Pollack's to the dialogue): "I feel that I do as much directing as he does, even though I never direct anything, because a lot of that is in the script."

Anhalt next scripted two productions for Ely Landau's American Film Theater, movie versions of John Osborne's *Luther* (1974) and Robert Shaw's

The Man in the Glass Booth (1975). The two projects are oddities, neither faithful to the major stage productions nor films in their own right. *Luther*, to which Anhalt seems to have been drawn very little, is the less successful of the two, chopping up Osborne's play and toning down the anger and torment of his hero. *The Man in the Glass Booth* is based on the 1968 Broadway play by Robert Shaw, who insisted that his name be removed from the film credits because Anhalt's screenplay removed a crucial ambiguity—whether or not the central character is a Nazi war criminal.

In 1974 Anhalt was responsible for the script of the first of the big television movies, *QB VII*, from the Leon Uris novel and with a theme similar to *The Man in the Glass Booth*, the unmasking of a Nazi war criminal, this time a former concentration camp doctor. The process of adapting novels for television, said Anhalt, requires two things: first, the removal of the kind of inconsistency a novelist can camouflage ("The television audience is far more sophisticated than those who read novels and some of the things in books just won't wash on television"); and second, the establishment of a strong continuity: "The audience must understand everything, all the time."

After *QB VII*, there were plans for Anhalt to

Tony Curtis and Henry Fonda in a scene from The Boston Strangler, *based on the case study of convicted murderer Albert de Salvo*

do further television work, including a special on Thomas Jefferson and scripting for the *Eleanor and Franklin* series. He did neither but wrote two television films in 1977. *Contract on Cherry Street* was a crime drama which marked Frank Sinatra's first dramatic appearance in a made-for-televison movie; *Nowhere to Hide*, produced by Anhalt, who also played a small role in the film, was about a federal agent protecting a criminal turned informant.

Anhalt returned to motion pictures with *Escape to Athena* (1979), a war movie about a group of World War II prisoners on a Greek island run by a German commandant and inhabited by a resistance leader. The film was unsuccessful, and after its release Anhalt returned to television writing. In 1980 he cowrote *The Day Christ Died* from a book by Jim Bishop that examines the political background of the Crucifixion. The film received good reviews but complaints from Bishop, since Anhalt claimed he

had to update certain aspects of the book because of recent archaeological and theological discoveries. In 1981 he wrote the script for *Madame X* (the seventh version of that story) and again acted in the television film in a small role. That same year he worked on the theatrical film *Green Ice* (1981), about an elaborate emerald robbery in South America. The film was released in Europe in 1981 but was not distributed in the United States, where it was sold directly to cable television.

Although his output has diminished since the beginning of the 1970s, Edward Anhalt has established himself as a versatile screenwriter. After a career of over thirty-five years, he is recognized as a master craftsman in his field.

References:
"Life of a Wordsmith," *Time* (16 April 1965): 6;
J. D. Marshall, *Blueprint on Babylon* (Los Angeles: Phoenix House, 1978), pp. 73-91.

John Balderston
(22 October 1889- 8 March 1954)

James Moore
Mount San Antonio College

MOTION PICTURES: *The Mummy* (Universal, 1932), screenplay;
Berkeley Square (20th Century-Fox, 1933), screenplay by Balderston and Sonya Levien;
The Bride of Frankenstein (Universal, 1935), adaptation by Balderston and William Hurlbut;
Mad Love (M-G-M, 1935), screenplay by Balderston, Guy Endore, and P. T. Walfson;
The Lives of a Bengal Lancer (Paramount, 1935), screenplay by Balderston, Waldemar Young, and Achmed Abdullah;
The Mystery of Edwin Drood (Universal, 1935), screenplay by Balderston and Gladys Unger;
The Man Who Lived Again (Universal, 1936), screenplay by Balderston, L. duGarde Peach, and Sidney Gilliat;
The Last of the Mohicans (United Artists, 1936), adaptation by Balderston, Paul Perez, and Daniel Moore;
Beloved Enemy (United Artists, 1936), screen story; screenplay by Balderston, Rose Franken, and William Brown Melony;

Romance and Riches (Grand National, 1937), screenplay;
The Prisoner of Zenda (United Artists, 1937), screenplay by Balderston, Donald Ogden Stewart, and Wells Root; filmed again (M-G-M, 1952), screenplay by Balderston and Noel Langley;
Victory (Paramount, 1940), screenplay;
Little Old New York (20th Century-Fox, 1940), screen story;
Smilin' Through (M-G-M, 1941), screenplay by Balderston and Stewart;
Scotland Yard (20th Century-Fox, 1941), screenplay by Balderston and Samuel G. Engel;
Tennessee Johnson (M-G-M, 1942), screenplay by Balderston and Root;
Stand By For Action (M-G-M, 1943), screenplay by Balderston, George Bruce, and Herman J. Mankiewicz;
Gaslight (M-G-M, 1944), screenplay by Balderston, Walter Reisch, and John Van Druten;
Red Planet Mars (United Artists, 1952), screen story

John Balderston

and screenplay by Balderston and Anthony Veiller.

PLAYS: *Dracula* (New York, Fulton Theatre, 5 October 1927), adapted from Bram Stoker's novel by Balderston and Hamilton Deane;

Berkeley Square (London, St. Martin's Theatre, 6 October 1928); revised version (London, Lyric Theatre, 6 March 1929), by Balderston and J. C. Squire;

Red Planet (New York, Cort Theatre, 17 December 1932), by Balderston and J. E. Hoare;

Farewell Performance (London, 1936).

BOOKS: *Genius of the Marne: A Play in Three Scenes*
(New York: N. L. Brown, 1919);

A Morality Play for the Leisure Class (New York & London: Appleton, 1924).

John Balderston was a journalist and playwright before turning to the screen in 1931. In his later years he lamented that so few of his screenplays were his alone. But he was nearly always more successful in collaboration than on his own, and film was a suitable medium for his kind of romantic writing. Working mainly for Universal from 1931 to 1936, Balderston was a principal figure in the Golden Age of Horror. *Dracula* (1931), *Frankenstein* (1931), *The Mummy* (1932), and *The Bride of Frankenstein* (1935), all of which he contributed to, are now classics. In most of his other successful work, Balderston speculated about identity switches, time travel, or interplanetary communication. He was at home with the fantastic, and his best work is either poignantly or whimsically scary or genuinely frightening.

John Balderston was born in Philadelphia to Anglo-American parents, Lloyd and Mary Balderston, who divided their time during his early life between America and England. Graduated from Columbia, he was a reporter and copyreader on Philadelphia newspapers from 1907 to 1910, then the New York correspondent for the *Philadelphia Record* from 1911 to 1914. Most of the time between 1914 and 1931 he spent in London, first as a war correspondent for McClure's Newspaper Syndicate; next as a Director of Information for the Great Britain-United States Committee on Public Information (1917-1918); then as editor of the literary-political magazine *The Outlook* (1920-1924); longest as the chief London correspondent for the *New York World* (1924-1931). Balderston married Marion A. Rubicam on 7 March 1921.

Always close to the London theatrical scene, he wrote the play *Genius of the Marne* in 1919; in 1924 he adapted his book *A Morality Play for the Leisure Class* for the stage and completed the play "Tongo." All of these plays were unproduced. In 1926 with J. C. Squire, editor of *London Mercury*, Balderston wrote *Berkeley Square*, a romantic fantasy based on Henry James's *The Sense of the Past*. *Berkeley Square* was a hit on the London stage; revived, it was again successful in 1929.

In 1927 Balderston reworked actor Hamilton Deane's London stage version of Bram Stoker's *Dracula*. Starring Bela Lugosi, the Deane-Balderston version was a hit in New York; it toured America for several years and was the basis for the 1931 Universal film directed by Tod Browning.

138347

Lugosi, who also starred in the 1931 movie, established the definitive Dracula persona with his performance, taking guidance for his pallidly sensual performance from the Deane and Balderston script.

After Balderston went to Hollywood in 1931, he attempted playwriting only twice more, then wrote only for the screen. In 1932, he collaborated with J. E. Hoare on *Red Planet*. The play closed quickly in New York, but Balderston later resurrected it in one of his final screenplays, *Red Planet Mars*. In 1936 his stage adaptation of the maudlin novel by the Hungarian Lajos Zilahy, *Farewell Performance*, pleased London audiences but not the critics.

Though there is some controversy about his credit, it is generally accepted that Balderston's first work for the screen was *Frankenstein*, directed by James Whale. Balderston apparently adapted Peggy Webling's stage version for the Universal film, but Garrett Fort and Francis Faragoh got the screenplay credit; on the typescript for the screenplay, Balderston is credited with "composition," but this credit was not noted on the film itself. Balderston insisted for the rest of his life that *Frankenstein* had been constructed upon his framework and that he deserved more credit.

Balderston's first solo screenplay was *The Mummy* (1932), based on a story by Nina Putnam and Richard Schayer. As Im-Ho-Tep, Boris Karloff plays a 3,000-year-old Egyptian buried alive for the blasphemous act of trying to bring back his beloved princess from the dead. The Egyptian revives when a young archaeologist reads aloud from the same scroll Im-Ho-Tep had been using three millennia earlier. Im-Ho-Tep tracks down an Englishwoman who is the reincarnation of his princess; the goddess Isis, however, intervenes, and he is consigned again to the dead.

In 1933 Balderston collaborated with Sonya

Elsa Lanchester and Boris Karloff in The Bride of Frankenstein

Levien on the screenplay for his own *Berkeley Square*. Young American Peter Standish (Leslie Howard) is able to strike a deal with the ghost of his ancestor, another Peter Standish. They will trade places, and the young American astonishes eighteenth-century London with his twentieth-century knowledge. Problems arise when he falls in love with Helen Pettigrew, knowing he is fated to marry her sister Kate. Balderston's play had been criticized for never probing the weightier notions of James's novel on which it had been based, but the screenplay was praised for its charm and sophistication.

Balderston followed *Berkeley Square* with what is probably his finest film, *The Bride of Frankenstein* (1935). Almost the entire *Frankenstein* troupe was reunited to produce the sequel, for which Balderston and William Hurlbut shared screenplay credit. *The Bride of Frankenstein* was possibly the crowning achievement of horror's golden era. One reason for the nearly unanimous approval of the film is the rather deliberate attempt—sometimes credited to Whale, sometimes to Balderston—to be closer in spirit to Mary Shelley's novel than the first Frankenstein film.

In the opinion of critic R. H. W. Dillard, a passage near the end of Shelley's *Frankenstein* provides the key to understanding the monster; it is this vision of the monster's humanity that Balderston and Hurlbut emphasized in their film. In Shelley's book, as they flee across the ice floes of the frozen North, the monster accuses his maker: "I ought to be thy Adam, but I am rather thy fallen angel, whom thou drives from joy for no misdeed. . . . Make me happy, and I shall again be virtuous."

As the film begins, the monster (Karloff), having survived the fire at the end of the original film, roams the countryside, horrified by his own face mirrored in a stream, persistently being misunderstood by villagers and peasants alike. He kills, but he also makes alliances with true innocents—children, a blind hermit. Under the hermit's guidance, he learns to speak and says his key line: "Alone BAD, friends GOOD."

For *The Bride of Frankenstein*, Balderston created Dr. Pretorius, a fascinating villainous influence on the monster-maker Dr. Frankenstein (Colin Clive). In Dillard's view, Pretorius, one of Dr. Frankenstein's former teachers, externalizes his pupil's weakness and evil. Pretorius has already experimented with creating tiny beings—two and one-half to five inches high—kept in jars, and his is an unredeeming, careless, semiscientific curiosity. He convinces Dr. Frankenstein that they must work together: "We will create his mate. That should be lots of fun."

Pretorius and the monster inevitably meet, in a burial vault where the monster has taken refuge. Pretorius is there to select a skeleton upon which to construct the mate. Drinking and smoking with the monster, Pretorius wins him over, and the monster confesses, "I love the dead. I hate the living." Yet the solution, in the monster's own words, is "Woman—friend—wife."

In the end, however, when the mate (Elsa Lanchester) is brought to life in the laboratory, she is attracted to Dr. Frankenstein and screams in horror at the monster's ugliness. As he destroys self, bride, and Pretorius, the monster says, "She is like the rest." What would have made the monster happy was love, and it is the monster's gradual humanization throughout this film that makes *The Bride of Frankenstein* the most poignant of all horror films.

Balderston next collaborated with P. T. Walfson and Guy Endore on *Mad Love* (1935), Peter Lorre's first American film. *Mad Love* came from the novel *The Hands of Orlac* by Maurice Renard; in it, Lorre plays a scientist who grafts the hands of an executed knife-murderer onto the arms of an injured pianist. In love with the pianist's wife, the scientist falls prey to his own handiwork—the pianist becomes a fine knife-thrower.

The Lives of a Bengal Lancer (1935), a swashbuckling adventure, was cowritten by Balderston with Waldemar Young and Achmed Abdullah. It tells the story of three British officers at India's northwest frontier who are battling the

Monte Blue in The Lives of a Bengal Lancer. *This 1935 film received six Academy Award nominations, including one for screenwriters Balderston, Waldemar Young, and Achmed Abdullah.*

treacherous Mohammed Khan, a supposed ally of the British. The film was nominated for six Academy awards, including those for best picture and best screenplay. It also inspired a series of at least eleven films between 1935 and 1939 dealing with the nineteenth-century British Empire in India and the Sudan and with the French Foreign Legion.

Within the year following the release of *The Lives of a Bengal Lancer*, Balderston completed five films: *The Mystery of Edwin Drood* (1935), *The Man Who Lived Again* (1936), *The Last of the Mohicans* (1936), *Beloved Enemy* (1936), and *Romance and Riches* (1937). This productive period climaxed with the 1937 version of *The Prisoner of Zenda*, based on the 1894 novel by Anthony Hope. By 1937, in one critic's words, Hope's novel was already "a clanky old museum piece," but in the film version of this tale of honor and true monarchy, Balderston achieved a seemingly effortless fusion of plot, character, tone, and mood. His dialogue holds the

smile and the steel in graceful tension.

The film tells the story of Rudolf Rassendyll (Ronald Colman), an Englishman on holiday in Ruretania, where it is discovered that he bears an uncanny resemblance to the king. Pressed into "kingship" by loyalists when the monarch is abducted, the elegantly roguish impostor Rassendyll falls in love with Flavia (Madeleine Carroll), the king's betrothed. Developments in their relationship provide some of the film's most delightful and amusing moments—such as Rudolph's response to Flavia's remark that he seems different from the boyish swain she has not seen in years: "I certainly feel different."

Perhaps the film's best feature is Balderston's parody of the "Die, Saxon Dog!" school of dueling patois, evident in the climactic confrontation between Rassendyll and the villainous Rupert of Hentzau:

Rupert: Where did you learn to fight?

Charles Boyer and Ingrid Bergman in a scene from Gaslight. *Balderston, Walter Reisch, and John Van Druten received an Academy Award nomination for their screenplay, and Bergman won her first Oscar for her performance in this film.*

Rudolf: On the playing field of Eton.

Rupert: You English are a stubborn lot.

Rudolf: Well, England expects every man to do his duty.

Rupert: Where did you learn such roller-skating tactics?

Rudolf : Coldstream Guards, my boy. Come on, when does the fencing lesson begin?

According to Donald Ogden Stewart, who wrote additional dialogue for *The Prisoner of Zenda* (and consequently shared screenplay credit), the script for the film was "nearly perfect." M-G-M used it almost verbatim when the film was remade in 1952 starring Stewart Granger.

After *The Prisoner of Zenda*, Balderston's credits thinned, and he was assigned to films which were markedly different from his more successful work. For example, he was one of the corps of writers who worked without credit on *Gone with the Wind*. In 1940 he was reunited with *The Prisoner of Zenda* director John Cromwell on *Victory* for Paramount, but this adaptation of Joseph Conrad's novel was a failure. The same year for 20th Century-Fox he wrote the screen story for *Little Old New York*, a romantic adventure of no consequence.

In 1943 Balderston was one of the collaborators responsible for *Stand By For Action*, in which an American destroyer crew picks up a group of refugee women and their babies and goes on to sink a battleship. The previous year he had co-written with Wells Root *Tennessee Johnson*, the film biography of Andrew Johnson.

Balderston, Walter Reisch, and John Van Druten adapted Patrick Hamilton's Broadway hit *Angel Street* into *Gaslight* (1944). There had been an earlier film version of the play, but this one has proven more memorable. Director George Cukor said the film had "a good scenario because it moved out of the confines of the stage . . . it seems to move up and down and around." A marvelously moody piece of Victoriana, it tells the story of a suave criminal (Charles Boyer) who marries the heiress of a famous opera singer in order to find the jewels she has inherited. To distract his wife (Ingrid Bergman) from his nightly searches in the attic of the gaslit house, he tries to drive her insane. Despite the melodramatic plot, *Gaslight* is a subtle study in both suspense and psychology. It was nominated for best screenplay and won Ingrid Bergman her first Oscar.

Two of Balderston's films were remade in the early 1950s. *The Prisoner of Zenda*, with Noel Langley listed as collaborator, succeeded again in 1952, but *I'll Never Forget You* (1951), an updating of *Berkeley Square*, with screenplay by Ranald MacDougall, did not. Neither was Balderston's own reworking of his 1932 play *Red Planet* successful. *Red Planet Mars* (1952) presents scientists who are able to communicate with Mars. The Martians warn the Earthlings that they must do several things right away—return to faith, cause a counterrevolution in Russia, and stabilize "our way of life." The film was dismissed as a piece of anti-Communist propaganda.

John Balderston died in Beverly Hills in 1954. Charged by both his theatrical and cinematic critics with failing to probe deeply enough into his speculations, he was nevertheless a lively and inventive thinker. His position in the ranks of major fantasy writers is secure.

References:

Carlos Clarens, *An Illustrated History of the Horror Film* (New York: Capricorn, 1967);

R. H. W. Dillard, "Even a Man Who is Pure at Heart: Poetry and Danger in the Horror Film," in *Man And The Movies*, edited by W. R. Robinson (Baton Rouge: Louisiana State University Press, 1967);

"Dracula: It All Started in a Theatre," *Performing Arts*, 12 (September 1978);

Roy Huss and T. J. Ross, eds., *Focus on the Horror Film* (Englewood Cliffs, N.J.: Prentice-Hall, 1972).

Papers:

Screenplays by John Balderston are on file at the American Film Institute, Los Angeles, California.

Alvah Bessie
(4 June 1904-   )

Gabriel Miller
Rutgers University

MOTION PICTURES: *Northern Pursuit* (Warner Bros., 1943), screenplay by Bessie and Frank Gruber;

The Very Thought of You (Warner Bros., 1944), screenplay by Bessie and Delmer Daves;

Hotel Berlin (Warner Bros., 1945), screenplay by Bessie and Jo Pagano;

Objective, Burma! (Warner Bros., 1945), screen story;

Smart Woman (Allied Artists, 1948), screenplay by Bessie, Louis Morheim, and Herbert Margolis;

Passage West (Paramount, 1951), story as Nedrick Young;

España otra vez (Pandora, S. A., 1968), screenplay by Bessie, Jaime Camino, and Norman Green.

SELECTED TELEVISION: *The Sex Symbol* (ABC, 7 September 1974), script adapted by Bessie from his novel *The Symbol*.

BOOKS: *Dwell in the Wilderness* (New York: Covici Friede, 1935; London: Constable, 1936);

Men in Battle: A Story of Americans in Spain (New York: Scribners, 1939);

Bread and a Stone (New York: Modern Age, 1941; London: Gerald G. Swan, 1948);

The Un-Americans (New York: Cameron, 1957; London: Calder, 1957);

Inquisition in Eden (New York: Macmillan, 1965);

The Symbol (New York: Random House, 1967; London: Bodley Head, 1967);

Spain Again (San Francisco: Chandler & Sharp, 1975);

One for My Baby (New York: Holt, Rinehart & Winston, 1980);

Alvah Bessie's Short Fictions (San Francisco: Chandler & Sharp, 1982).

OTHER: *The Heart of Spain*, edited by Bessie (New York: Veterans of the Abraham Lincoln Brigade, 1952).

Alvah Bessie, novelist, screenwriter, union worker, and critic, was born in New York City. His father, Daniel N. Bessie, was a successful inventor, manufacturer, and stockbroker, though not a par-

Alvah Bessie

ticularly good father or husband, and Bessie has, in both his fiction and nonfiction, expressed his contempt for everything his father stood for. Bessie attended Dewitt Clinton High School, then went on to Columbia College, where he began writing poetry. After graduation in 1924, he worked as an actor with the Provincetown Players and the Theatre Guild, but convinced he would never make a very good actor, Bessie sold his library of one thousand books for a dollar each and went to Paris. There he secured a job on the *Paris Times*, an English-language newspaper which came out in the afternoon with translations from the French morning papers.

That job and the stay in France were short-lived (though he absorbed enough French to translate several books), and he returned to New York in 1929, where he held a variety of jobs, none of them lasting very long, before the onset of the Depression. In 1931, now married, without work and without a hope of finding any in New York, Bessie and his wife went to Vermont to work as a houseman and maid at a wealthy couple's summer home. They stayed on in Vermont, where Bessie earned money writing book reviews and occasionally selling short stories (some of his short stories were included in volumes of best short stories from 1931 to 1934) and digging potatoes for local farmers. It was also during this time that he began to read material on Marxism; his subsequent dedication to the Marxist philosophy of equality and his hatred of fascism were to become shaping forces in his life, prompting personal and political commitments that would have profound effect on his career and on his artistic vision.

In 1935 Bessie received a Guggenheim Fellowship and completed his first novel, *Dwell in the Wilderness*, the chronicle of an American family from 1876 to 1925. Later that year he returned to New York City to work as assistant editor of the Sunday magazine section of the *Brooklyn Daily Eagle*. Early in 1937, aroused by his support of the Spanish Republic in its war against Franco, Bessie quit the *Eagle* to work for the Spanish Information Bureau, a New York-based organization that assisted the Spanish Republican government. Then in 1938 he left the United States to fight for the Republic as part of the international volunteer unit known as the Abraham Lincoln Brigade. His experiences during that war are described in his book *Men in Battle* (1939).

When he returned from Spain, Bessie wrote for the *New Masses* and served as its drama critic while writing his second novel, *Bread and a Stone* (1941), a fact-based case history of the effects of environment on an individual.

In January of 1943, offered a contract by Warner Bros., Bessie resigned his position at *New Masses* and left for California. His career as a screenwriter was to be brief, as he would be blacklisted by the late 1940s. In the short time he worked for Warner Bros., he received three screenplay credits: *Northern Pursuit* (1943), *The Very Thought of You* (1944), and *Hotel Berlin* (1945).

Based upon the story "Five Thousand Trojan Horses" by Leslie T. White, *Northern Pursuit* was designed as a wartime vehicle for Errol Flynn. The screenplay is credited to Frank Gruber and Bessie, although several other writers, including William

Bessie in Spain, 1939, as a member of the Abraham Lincoln Brigade. Bessie's experiences during the Spanish Civil War are described in his book Men in Battle *(1939).*

Faulkner, had a hand in it. Raoul Walsh directed this film about Nazi saboteurs in Canada who plan to bomb the St. Lawrence seaway. All the Nazis but one (Helmut Dantine) are killed by an avalanche; he is found by two Mounties, one of whom (Flynn) pretends to be a Nazi sympathizer in order to be led to the German's base.

The Very Thought of You, cowritten with director Delmer Daves, is a slight comedy about two soldiers who pick up two girls and fall in love with them. The story centers around Dave (Dennis Morgan) and Janet (Eleanor Parker) and Janet's family, which disapproves of wartime romances. After some ado, the family sees the light and love triumphs. Bessie placed the story in New York, where the dialogue could be spiced with banter about New York and

New Yorkers, but in revisions the setting was changed to Pasadena, and whatever humor there had been in the script disappeared.

Bessie's third Warner Bros. film, *Hotel Berlin*, is merely an updating of the 1932 classic *Grand Hotel* set during the decline of Nazi Germany. The film has fine melodramatic moments arising from the usual concoction of stories about lives intertwined. Bessie collaborated with Jo Pagano.

After *Hotel Berlin* Bessie worked on one more film for Warner Bros., providing the screen story for *Objective, Burma!* (1945), which earned him an Academy Award nomination. Another war film starring Errol Flynn and directed by Raoul Walsh, *Objective, Burma!*, is a far better film than *Northern Pursuit*, depicting realistically the attempts of a band of American paratroopers to find and destroy a Japanese post in Burma.

After leaving Warner Bros., Bessie scripted *Smart Woman* (1948) with Louis Morheim and Herbert Margolis from a story by Adela Rogers St. John. In this film Constance Bennett plays an attorney who specializes in getting gangsters freed; she is opposed by a crusading district attorney (Brian Aherne) whose job it is to clean up the city. They fall in love, with predictable complications. Bessie was not pleased with this film: "The story was a lulu," he remarked, "and I hope no one ever saw the film." Just as he was finishing work on this script, Allied Artists, probably hearing Bessie was being investi-

gated by the House Un-American Activities Committee, fired him.

In 1947 Bessie and nine others were summoned before HUAC and asked whether they were members of the Communist party. They refused to cooperate. Bessie was sentenced to a one-year prison term in Texarkana; he began serving in 1950. During this year Bessie sold, under the name of Nedrick Young, an original story called "Cross of Gold"; it was produced in 1951 as *Passage West* and starred John Payne. Based on an idea suggested by Abraham Polonsky and on material Bessie picked up in the WPA California Guide, it takes place in the nineteenth century and concerns a group of convicts who escape from a Nevada prison and make their way to California. En route, they take over a wagon train of immigrants going to California to found a religious community, and during the journey they are reformed by the immigrants' example.

Released from prison in 1951, Bessie found work hard to come by. He was finally offered a job as an assistant editor and assistant public relations man for the International Longshoreman and Warehouseman's Union paper, the *Dispatcher*. Later he went to work as a light man, stage manager, and announcer for the hungry i nightclub in San Francisco. During this time, he wrote a novel and one work of nonfiction. His experiences with HUAC, the blacklist, and his prison sentence were documented in *Inquisition in Eden* (1965). He also

The Hollywood Ten, with two of their attorneys, before arraignment on contempt of Congress charges, Washington, D.C., 9 January 1950. Front row (left to right): Herbert Biberman, attorneys Martin Popper and Robert W. Kenny, Albert Maltz, Lester Cole. Second row: Dalton Trumbo, John Howard Lawson, Alvah Bessie, Samuel Ornitz. Third row: Ring Lardner, Jr., Edward Dmytryk, and Adrian Scott.

dealt with this material in *The Un-Americans* (1957), a largely autobiographical novel about a man who fights in Spain and is later jailed for refusing to cooperate with a congressional committee.

Bessie's best work of this period is his Hollywood novel, *The Symbol* (1967). Although dismissed by many critics as a rehash of the life of Marilyn Monroe, the novel is substantially more than this. Here Bessie returns to his earlier fictional themes of loneliness and frustration, developing them within an interesting narrative structure. The central characters are effectively drawn, especially the protagonist Wanda Oliver; few Hollywood novels have so intelligently explored the psychology of the actress. Bessie adapted the novel for the 1974 television film *The Sex Symbol*. Unfortunately, the project was threatened by the possibility of libel suits and was severely edited before being aired.

Since the blacklist, Bessie has had little contact with Hollywood. He contributed some uncredited rewrite work to the film *Executive Action* (1973), a melodrama that blames right-wing corporate and military powers for the assassination of John F. Kennedy, for which Dalton Trumbo, another member of the Hollywood Ten, received main credit.

Bessie's major film project in recent years was a Spanish film, *España otra vez (Spain Again)*, released in 1968. Bessie not only collaborated on the script but also appeared in this film, which concerns the experiences and emotional reactions of a doctor (Mark Stevens) who fought on the Republican side during the Spanish Civil War and returns to Spain thirty years later. The film won a prize from the Spanish government-controlled National Syndicate of Entertainment and was entered as Spain's official entry for the Academy Award for Best Foreign Film. It has never been released in the United States. Bessie's book *Spain Again* (1975) contains portions of the screenplay as well as his own reactions to Spain after his return following a thirty-year absence.

Bessie's novel *One for My Baby* was published in 1980. He still writes essays, reviews, and political pieces. A collection of Bessie's best short stories and a previously unpublished novella, *The Serpent Was More Subtil*, was published under the title *Alvah Bessie's Short Fictions* in 1982. Bessie resides in San Rafael, California, where he is working on his autobiography and the film version of his novel *Bread and A Stone*.

Reference:

Gabriel Miller, Introduction to *Alvah Bessie's Short Fictions* (San Francisco: Chandler & Sharp, 1982).

Papers:

Bessie's papers are housed at the State Historical Society of Wisconsin, Madison.

Charles Brackett
(26 November 1892-9 March 1969)

Sam Frank

MOTION PICTURES: *Enter Madam!* (Paramount, 1935), screenplay by Brackett and Gladys Lehman;

College Scandal (Paramount, 1935), screenplay by Brackett, Frank Partos, and Marguerite Roberts;

The Lost Outpost, adaptation by Brackett and Partos (Paramount, 1935);

Without Regret (Paramount, 1935), screenplay by Brackett and Doris Anderson;

Woman Trap (Paramount, 1936), screen story;

Rose of the Rancho (Paramount, 1936), screenplay by Brackett, Partos, Arthur Sheekman, and Nat Perrin;

Piccadilly Jim (M-G-M, 1936), screenplay by Brackett and Edwin Knopf;

Live, Love and Learn (M-G-M, 1937), screenplay by Brackett, Cyril Hume, and Richard Maibaum;

Wild Money (Paramount, 1937), additional dialogue by Brackett and Partos;

Bluebeard's Eighth Wife (Paramount, 1938), screenplay by Brackett and Billy Wilder;

Midnight (Paramount, 1939), screenplay by Brackett and Wilder;

Charles Brackett

What a Life (Paramount, 1939), screenplay by Brackett and Wilder;

Ninotchka (M-G-M, 1939), screenplay by Brackett, Wilder, and Walter Reisch;

Arise, My Love (Paramount, 1940), screenplay by Brackett and Wilder;

Hold Back the Dawn (Paramount, 1941), screenplay by Brackett and Wilder;

Ball of Fire (RKO, 1941), screenplay by Brackett and Wilder;

The Major and the Minor (Paramount, 1942), screenplay by Brackett and Wilder;

Five Graves to Cairo (Paramount, 1943), screenplay by Brackett and Wilder;

The Lost Weekend (Paramount, 1945), screenplay by Brackett and Wilder;

To Each His Own (Paramount, 1946), screenplay by Brackett and Jacques Thery;

The Emperor Waltz (Paramount, 1948), screenplay by Brackett and Wilder;

Miss Tatlock's Millions (Paramount, 1948), screenplay by Brackett and Richard L. Breen;

A Foreign Affair (Paramount, 1948), screenplay by Brackett, Wilder, and Breen;

Sunset Boulevard (Paramount, 1950), screenplay by Brackett, Wilder, and D. M. Marshman, Jr.;

The Mating Season (Paramount, 1951), screenplay by

Brackett, Reisch, and Breen;

The Model and the Marriage Broker (20th Century-Fox, 1951), screenplay by Brackett, Reisch, and Breen;

Niagara (20th Century-Fox, 1953), screenplay by Brackett, Reisch, and Breen;

Titanic (20th Century-Fox, 1953), screenplay by Brackett, Reisch, and Breen;

The Girl in the Red Velvet Swing (20th Century-Fox, 1955), screen story and screenplay by Brackett and Reisch;

Teenage Rebel (20th Century-Fox, 1956), screenplay by Brackett and Reisch;

Journey to the Center of the Earth (20th Century-Fox, 1959), screenplay by Brackett and Reisch.

BOOKS: *The Counsel of the Ungodly* (New York & London: Appleton, 1920);

Week-End (New York: McBride, 1925); London: Melrose, 1928);

That Last Infirmity (New York: Day, 1926);

American Colony (New York: Liveright, 1929);

Entirely Surrounded (New York: Knopf, 1934).

OTHER: *The Lost Weekend*, by Brackett and Billy Wilder, in *Best Film Plays, 1945*, edited by John Gassner and Dudley Nichols (New York: Crown, 1946).

Though Charles Brackett is best remembered for his collaboration with Billy Wilder, he was a man of many facets. He wrote and/or produced forty films; wrote five published novels; was decorated by the French army; owned several businesses; was president of a law firm, the Screen Writers Guild, and the Academy of Motion Picture Arts and Sciences; was vice-president of a bank; and won five Academy awards.

Charles Brackett was born on 26 November 1892 in Saratoga Springs, New York. His parents were Edgar Truman Brackett, a distinguished lawyer and state senator, and Mary Emma Corliss Brackett. Little is known about Brackett's childhood except that he was raised in a well-to-do, conservative household. Years later he commented that "it was the theory of my parents that a child should vegetate, and I did."

His scholastic achievements included a baccalaureate from Williams College in 1915 and a law degree from Harvard in 1920. During his stay at Williams, he found he enjoyed editing the school paper and acting with the drama society more than studying.

Brackett's stay at Harvard was interrupted by World War I. He enlisted in the American Expeditionary Force, becoming vice-consul at St. Nazaire, France. He was commissioned as a second lieutenant and assigned as assistant liaison officer on the staff of General Contanceau, commander of the eleventh region. Brackett's war duty culminated with his being awarded the Médaille d'Honneur en Argent for services rendered the French army.

During the war, Brackett found time to write a short story entitled "War." While finishing his law degree at Harvard, he sent the story to an agent who discouraged him, saying it was subject to censorship. At his mother's urging, Brackett sent the story to the *Saturday Evening Post*. The *Post* accepted it, requesting more stories. Brackett's next submission was a novel entitled *The Counsel of the Ungodly*, which was serialized in the *Post* (1919) in three parts. It was published in book form in 1920.

Brackett graduated from Harvard with honors in 1920. Prior to graduating, he married Elizabeth Barrows Fletcher, a well-bred Easterner like himself. They were married for twenty-eight years and had two children, Alexandra Corliss and Elizabeth Fletcher.

From 1920 to 1925 Brackett practiced law but continued to write, contributing short stories to the *Saturday Evening Post*, *Collier's*, and other magazines. He also wrote two more novels, one of which—*Week-End* (1925)—caught the eye of Harold Ross, editor of a new magazine called the *New Yorker*. Ross invited Brackett to be the magazine's drama critic. He held the post for three years, earning fame for his wit and style and becoming a member of the informal club of writers who met at the Algonquin Hotel as well.

Brackett left the *New Yorker* in 1929. He wrote another novel, *American Colony* (1929), and held a brief, unproductive screenwriting job at RKO. Discouraged, he returned to New York, where he joined his father's law firm and sat on the Board of Directors of the Adirondacks Trust Company. Though he later became successful as a screenwriter and producer, Brackett remained active with the law firm as a senior member and with the trust company as vice-president.

While Brackett's stint at RKO did not result in any produced screenplays, he had sold three of his short stories to Hollywood in the 1920s, and those sales, coupled with his background as a drama critic, led to Brackett's being offered a six-week contract in 1932 to join the Paramount stable of writers. He accepted and stayed on at Paramount until 1950, only occasionally working on "loan-out" to other

studios. Brackett received no screen credit at Paramount until 1935, and he was confined mostly to the committee writing of second features until 1938. He was on the verge of returning to the world of law and finance in 1937 when Paramount production executive Manny Wolfe introduced him to a fiery Viennese screenwriter named Billy Wilder and pronounced them a team. They were a dissimilar pair. Wilder was feisty, volatile, enthusiastic, and full of ideas. Brackett was low-keyed and reserved and not given to displays of emotion. Wilder dressed in sport clothes and was politically liberal. Brackett dressed in tailored three-piece suits and held arch-conservative views. Nevertheless, they got along famously, as much because of their differences as despite them.

During their first four years as a team, Brackett and Wilder wrote three scripts for Mitchell Leisen, two for Ernst Lubitsch, and one each for Howard Hawks and Jay Theodore Reed. Their first assignment was *Bluebeard's Eighth Wife* (1938) for Lubitsch, a comedy with Gary Cooper as an often-married Casanova and Claudette Colbert as the woman who sets him straight. This was followed by *Midnight* (1939), a screwball comedy directed by Leisen, an adept director of sophisticated material. Claudette Colbert is a penniless chorine trying to crash Paris society with the aid of a cab driver played by Don Ameche. *What a Life* (directed by Jay Theodore Reed) and *Arise, My Love* (for Leisen) were two other minor Brackett-Wilder efforts in 1939 and 1940. The first was based on a play by Clifford Goldsmith and the subsequent radio series *Henry Aldrich*. Jackie Cooper played Henry. The second featured Ray Milland and Claudette Colbert in a romantic drama set against the Spanish Civil War, one of the few instances in which Hollywood acknowledged that conflict onscreen.

Their final film for 1939, *Ninotchka* (cowritten with Walter Reisch, who later became Brackett's collaborator at 20th Century-Fox), was both their first major artistic and commercial success and their first of three consecutive films about opposites attracting. The others are *Hold Back the Dawn* and *Ball of Fire*, both released in 1941.

The title character of *Ninotchka* (Greta Garbo) is a Communist official sent to Paris to sell some jewels which the Politburo contends are the property of "the people." Ninotchka is a woman for whom affairs of state take precedence over affairs of the heart, until she meets her match in a suave gigolo (Melvyn Douglas) who makes her realize the importance of love. *Ninotchka*'s depiction of romance within the context of political satire was

Greta Garbo and Melvyn Douglas in Ninotchka

daring for its time. Brackett and Wilder were nominated for an Academy award for their screenplay.

Hold Back the Dawn also concerns a gigolo (Charles Boyer), but a far less romantic one than *Ninotchka*'s. Boyer's goal is to seduce a mousy grammar-school teacher (Olivia de Havilland) into marriage so that he can legally enter the United States from Mexico. The film suggests that even the least worthy of men—like Boyer's gigolo—have a core of genuine feeling that can be tapped and nurtured. Had the script been written by Wilder or Brackett alone, the ending—in which Boyer and de Havilland run to each other at the Mexican border for a heartrending fade out—might have been either a denunciation of emotional corruption or a saccharinely sentimental affirmation of romantic love. Wilder's sharp-tongued cynicism was tempered by Brackett's soft-edged romanticism and vice versa.

Ball of Fire is the story of a sedate, scholarly bachelor (Gary Cooper) who, while researching an essay on American slang for a new encyclopedia,

meets a brassy nightclub performer played by Barbara Stanwyck. In this film, the softening of hearts is mutual. The singer brings a much-needed woman's touch to the scholar and his asexual colleagues, while they pierce her defenses with gentle temperaments. Thematically, *Ball of Fire* and *Hold Back the Dawn* are linked by their concern for emotional redemption. Two clear points emerge: 1) that cultural opposites can indeed be compatible, and 2) that without love one is never really whole.

The cumulative success of *Ninotchka*, *Hold Back the Dawn*, and *Ball of Fire* allowed Brackett and Wilder to expand their base of power at Paramount. Beginning with *The Major and the Minor* (1942), Wilder became a director, and with *Five Graves to Cairo* (1943), Brackett became a producer. (Brackett produced all his own screenplays after this point and also produced, but did not write, thirteen other films, including *The Uninvited* [1944], *Garden of Evil* [1954], *Woman's World* [1955], *The Virgin Queen* [1955], *D-Day, the Sixth of June* [1956], *The King and I* [1956], *The Gift of Love* [1958], *Ten North Frederick*

[1958], *The Remarkable Mr. Pennypacker* [1959], *Blue Denim* [1959], *High Time* [1960], and *State Fair* [1962].)

The Major and the Minor presents Ginger Rogers as a woman returning to the Midwest from New York. Lacking adult train fare, she disguises herself as a twelve-year-old to get by at half-price. The scheme backfires when she gets mixed up with a gentlemanly major (Ray Milland) who insists on escorting her back home. The film's thematic implications are as sly as they are numerous: 1) that adults and teenagers are equals when it comes to sexual deceit; 2) that adults are afraid to admit they can be sexually attracted to adolescents; and 3) that people can waste a lot of precious time and energy playing games when they could accomplish so much more by being direct and honest, with themselves and with each other.

Their next film, *Five Graves to Cairo*, is a relatively sophisticated war drama taken from the headlines of the time. A British agent (Franchot Tone) endeavors to learn the secret of Rommel's desert campaign. The five graves of the title are German supply depots located at strategic points in the Egyptian desert. *Five Graves to Cairo* differs from similar war films in that action is subordinate to characterization. It was a welcome change from the melodramatic, stereotypical war movies of the period. It was also a huge financial success, confirming Brackett and Wilder as Hollywood's best-known and most powerful filmmaking team.

In December of 1944, Lincoln Barnett wrote an article on them for *Life*. Entitled "The Happiest Couple in Hollywood," it discussed in detail their backgrounds, views, and methods of collaboration. He described their office as an informal suite with a coffeehouse ambience and bedrooms where the writers took after-lunch naps. Wilder formulated plots, with Brackett acting as sounding board. "Every syllable of every line of dialogue is exhaustively discussed. No word or bit of business, no fade-in, camera angle or dissolve is recorded until both partners agree fully on its dramatic value. . . . Wilder is galvanic, facile, prolific with ideas, endowed with visual imagination. Brackett is critical, contemplative, gifted with a graceful literary style and taste. When Wilder sparks off a salvo of suggestions, Brackett sorts good from bad and imparts to the best of them adroit turns of action and phrase. . . . Wilder is an instructive dramatist who envisages story ideas through the camera's mobile eye. Brackett is primarily a novelist, attuned to the niceties of continuity and construction." The pic-

ture Barnett paints of the Brackett-Wilder working relationship is idyllic, though perhaps not an accurate one. According to Maurice Zolotow in his book *Billy Wilder in Hollywood*, the two writers were often at each other's throats.

Regardless of how well Brackett and Wilder did or did not get along, the fact remains that during the 1940s they were easily the most successful writers in Hollywood. By 1945, each was receiving $2,500 a week for writing, plus fees for producing and directing. By 1948 their weekly salaries were $5,000 apiece, and their first five hits had grossed nineteen million dollars, according to *Daily Variety*. After *Five Graves to Cairo*, they went their separate ways for a year; after that, Brackett teamed with Wilder only on every second picture he made.

Their next project was *The Lost Weekend* (1945), a film about alcoholism and a more personal effort than usual for Brackett, whose wife was an alcoholic. *The Lost Weekend*, adapted from the novel by Charles R. Jackson, is an account of five days in the life of Don Birnam (Ray Milland), a writer by profession who cannot stop drinking long enough to write the novel he has talked about for years. His brother has lost patience with him, but his girlfriend (Jane Wyman) still clings to the hope of a cure. The closest Birnam gets to a cure is the drunk ward of a hospital, where delirium tremens are a way of life. Despite this horrifying glimpse of the future, he runs away from the hospital, only to have the D.T.'s in his home. But he still keeps drinking, unable to get a grip on his sickness. *The Lost Weekend* was a compromise between realism and polished entertainment, and it received public and critical acclaim. It won Academy awards for best picture, best screenplay, and best adaptation; Ray Milland won the Oscar for best actor.

To Each His Own (1946) was Brackett's first collaboration apart from Wilder since *Bluebeard's Eighth Wife*. The original idea was his, and the co-writer was Jacques Thery. In this film Olivia de Havilland plays a woman who bears the illegitimate child of a pilot who was killed in World War I. The film was very popular, and de Havilland won an Oscar for best actress.

Back with Wilder, Brackett wrote *The Emperor Waltz* (1948), a romance with Bing Crosby as a victrola salesman peddling his wares to Emperor Franz Josef at the turn of the century. It was the team's only flop; the film was released briefly after being shelved by Paramount for two years.

While Paramount was deciding what to do with *The Emperor Waltz*, Brackett cowrote with

Ray Milland (far right) as alcoholic writer Don Birnam in The Lost Weekend, *Brackett's tenth collaboration with Billy Wilder, who also directed the film*

Richard L. Breen a crazy comedy called *Miss Tatlock's Millions* (1948), in which a stunt man schemes with a con man to impersonate an heir to a fortune. Brackett worked next with Wilder and Breen on *A Foreign Affair*, a postwar comedy-drama. A congresswoman (Jean Arthur) visits Berlin to check on American troop morale, but she encounters more than she bargained for, including the black market, an urbane officer, and a cabaret singer (Marlene Dietrich) who was friendly with the Nazis.

Just before *A Foreign Affair* was released, Brackett's wife Elizabeth died on 7 June 1948. Five and a half years later, he married his former sister-in-law, Lillian Fletcher. They remained married until his death.

Sunset Boulevard (1950) was Brackett's last collaboration with Wilder. It is arguably their finest script (cowritten with D. M. Marshman, Jr.) as well as one of the most scathing movies ever made about Hollywood. A hack screenwriter, Joe Gillis (William Holden), becomes the gigolo of washed-up movie queen Norma Desmond (Gloria Swanson). When she discovers that Joe is spending his nights co-

writing a screenplay with another woman, she shoots him in a jealous rage. Ironically, this murder puts her back in the public eye. For one last time, she appears before the cameras, totally insane, beckoning the audience to adore her.

In a public relations paper for the Directors Guild, Brackett explained that "*Sunset Boulevard* came about because Wilder, Marshman and I were acutely conscious of the fact that we lived in a town which had been swept by social change as profound as that brought about in the old South by the Civil War. Overnight, the coming of sound brushed aside gods and goddesses into obscurity. We had an idea of a young man happening into a great house where one of these ex-goddesses survived. At first we saw her as a kind of horror woman—an embodiment of vanity and selfishness; . . . as we went along, our sympathies became deeply involved with the woman who had been given the brush by thirty million fans. At the end, we had to give her the only happiness we could see for her—the twilight happiness of the mad."

The screenplay for *Sunset Boulevard* won

Brackett, Wilder, and Marshman the Academy Award. However, soon after making this critical and commercial triumph, Brackett and Wilder split as a team. The separation was not unexpected; reportedly, Wilder had long wanted to work with other writers. Though he did not express it at the time, Brackett was deeply bitter about the breakup. Years later, on his deathbed, he expressed his feelings to Garson Kanin: "Don't you think it was odd? What he did? There was no reason. . . . We had our disagreements, of course, but they were always professional, never personal. And I don't think we ever had a serious quarrel."

After the split with Wilder, Brackett's collaborators were Walter Reisch, Richard L. Breen, or both. His final film for Paramount, *The Mating Season*, was cowritten with Reisch and Breen in 1951. He broke with Paramount as the result of a long-standing feud with production head Sam Briskin, the final blow of which was Briskin's objection to Brackett's trips to New York, where he spoke on behalf of the Academy of Motion Picture Arts and Sciences to the Motion Picture Advertising Association. Briskin claimed these trips delayed film production; Brackett insisted he did not have to answer to anyone about his comings and goings.

Right after he left Paramount, Brackett signed with 20th Century-Fox, where he remained for the rest of his career. During this period, Brackett cowrote and/or produced fifteen films, including *Titanic* (1953), for which he won his third Oscar. In 1957 he received the Writers Guild Laurel Award for his contributions to motion pictures.

Brackett's career at Fox ceased on 18 September 1962. On that date, Darryl F. Zanuck fired most of his top executives in a move aimed at restructuring the company. He also ceased payment of salaries under unexpired contracts, including Brackett's. Brackett filed a breach-of-contract suit against Fox and Zanuck in October 1962; the suit was settled out of court six weeks later. Brackett could easily have gone to work for another studio,

Gloria Swanson starred as faded movie queen Norma Desmond in Sunset Boulevard, *Brackett's last collaboration with writer-director Billy Wilder.*

but he chose retirement instead. He lived in retirement at his home in Beverly Hills for the next seven years until his death.

The movies that Charles Brackett made with Billy Wilder are clearly his best, and Wilder's finest also. Their hallmarks are polished production values, solid storylines and characters, biting wit, and an impeccably stylish approach to sophisticated subject matter. Furthermore, the films that Wilder cowrote with Brackett generally have more dramatic substance than the ones he later cowrote with I. A. L. Diamond. Brackett and Wilder were masters of the fine art of telling a story on film that entertains as it comments and tempers cynicism with sentiment.

Contemporary screenwriters may be more "realistic" in baring social truths, but Brackett and Wilder were adept at baring emotional truths in order to get at the social ones. Therein lay their genius as a team and, more important, Brackett's genius as a collaborative screenwriter.

References:

James Agee, *Agee on Film* (New York: McDowell, Obolensky, 1958);

Lincoln Barnett, "The Happiest Couple in Hollywood," *Life* (11 December 1944): 98-112;

Garson Kanin, *Hollywood* (New York: Viking, 1974), pp. 176-181;

Steve Seidman, *The Film Career of Billy Wilder* (Boston: G. K. Hall, 1977), pp. 16-17.

Joseph Wechsberg, "Idea-a-Minute-Men," *Liberty* (4 May 1946): 18-19, 59;

Maurice Zolotow, *Billy Wilder in Hollywood* (New York: Putnam's, 1977);

Zolotow, "Ninotchka: The Movie That Never Should Have Been Made," *Los Angeles* (December 1976): 88-99.

Papers:

The Academy of Motion Picture Arts and Sciences in Beverly Hills, California, has a large folder of materials on Charles Brackett and copies of the scripts for *Ninotchka* and *The Lost Weekend* and a copy of a draft for *Sunset Boulevard*.

Leigh Brackett

(7 December 1915-18 March 1978)

Alain Silver and Elizabeth Ward

See also the Brackett entry in *DLB 8, Twentieth-Century American Science Fiction Writers.*

MOTION PICTURES: *The Vampire's Ghost* (Republic, 1945), screen story; screenplay by Brackett and John K. Butler;

The Big Sleep (Warner Bros., 1946), screenplay by Brackett, William Faulkner, and Jules Furthman;

Crime Doctor's Manhunt (Columbia, 1946), screenplay;

Rio Bravo (Warner Bros., 1959), screenplay by Brackett and Furthman;

Gold of the Seven Saints (Warner Bros., 1961), screenplay by Brackett and Leonard Freeman;

Hatari! (Paramount, 1962), screenplay;

El Dorado (Paramount, 1967), screenplay;

Rio Lobo (National General, 1970), screenplay by Brackett and Burton Wohl;

The Long Goodbye (United Artists, 1973), screenplay;

The Empire Strikes Back (20th Century-Fox, 1980), screenplay by Brackett and Lawrence Kasdan.

TELEVISION: "Death of a Cop," *Alfred Hitchcock Presents* (NBC, 1960), script;

"Terror at Northfield," *Alfred Hitchcock Presents* (NBC, 1960), script;

"The Face in the Window," *Checkmate* (CBS, 1961), script by Brackett and Harold Clements;

"The Body Beautiful," *Archer* (NBC, 1975), story and script;

"Four-Pound Brick," *The Rockford Files* (NBC, 1975), story; script by Brackett and Juanita Bartlett.

BOOKS: *No Good from a Corpse* (New York: Coward-McCann, 1944);

Shadow over Mars (Manchester, U.K.: Pemberton, 1951); republished as *The Nemesis from Terra*

Leigh Brackett (photo by Jay Kay Klein)

(New York: Ace, 1961);

The Starmen (New York: Gnome Press, 1952; London: Museum Press, 1954); republished as *The Galactic Breed* (New York: Ace, 1952); republished again as *The Starmen of Llyrdis* (New York: Ballantine, 1976);

The Sword of Rhiannon (New York: Ace, 1953; London: Boardman, 1955);

The Big Jump (New York: Ace, 1955);

The Long Tomorrow (Garden City: Doubleday, 1955; London: Mayflower, 1962);

An Eye for an Eye (Garden City: Doubleday, 1957; London: Boardman, 1958);

The Tiger Among Us (Garden City: Doubleday, 1957; London: Boardman, 1958); republished as *Fear No Evil* (London: Transworld, 1960);

Rio Bravo (New York: Bantam, 1959);

13 West Street (New York: Bantam, 1962; London: Transworld, 1962);

Follow the Free Wind (Garden City: Doubleday, 1963);

Alpha Centauri—or Die! (New York: Ace, 1963);

The People of the Talisman / The Secret of Sinharat (New York: Ace, 1964);

The Coming of the Terrans (New York: Ace, 1967);

Silent Partner (New York: Putnam's, 1969);

The Halfling and Other Stories (New York: Ace, 1973);

The Ginger Star (New York: Ballantine, 1974; London: Sphere, 1977);

The Hounds of Skaith (New York: Ballantine, 1974; London: Sphere, 1976);

The Reavers of Skaith (New York: Ballantine, 1976);

The Best of Leigh Brackett, edited by Edmond Hamilton (Garden City: Doubleday, 1977).

OTHER: *The Best of Planet Stories No. 1: Strange Adventures on Other Worlds*, edited by Brackett (New York: Ballantine, 1975);

The Best of Edmond Hamilton, edited by Brackett (Garden City: Doubleday, 1977).

Leigh Brackett was born in Los Angeles. Her father, William Franklin Brackett, was a certified public accountant and aspiring writer who died in 1919. Brackett's childhood was spent in Los Angeles, New Orleans, and Boston, where she attended public elementary schools and a convent secondary school, and on the California coast, where she spent extended periods with her grandfather. Her earliest literary experience, under her grandfather's tutelage, centered on Arthur Conan Doyle, Edgar Rice Burroughs, and Rudyard Kipling (she committed long portions of Kipling's *Jungle Book* to memory). She began her own writing at age nine by jotting down sequels to current films, particularly those starring Douglas Fairbanks. What Brackett called her "serious" writing began at age thirteen. After the completion of her formal schooling, Brackett's grandfather offered to subsidize her attempts at commercial authorship. She produced two socially conscious novels, numerous short stories, and several poems, none of which was published, all of which she later destroyed. She had been acquainted with another aspiring author, Ray Bradbury, since her school days in Los Angeles and received encouragement from him and local magazine editors Forrest J. Ackerman and Henry Kuttner, who advised her to concentrate on short fantasy and science-fiction stories for the pulp market. Following this advice, Brackett made her first sale, "Martian Quest," in late 1939, at age twenty-four, to *Astounding Science-Fiction*.

Brackett continued to sell short stories to science-fiction magazines through the early 1940s. She wrote her first screenplay, *The Vampire's Ghost*, in 1944, but it was extensively rewritten by John K. Butler after it was sold to Republic Pictures. Brackett called the completed film "a Republic ten-day wonder and very horrible it was."

Her first novel was published in 1944. *No Good from a Corpse*, a crime melodrama written in the hard-boiled style, brought Brackett to the attention of producer/director Howard Hawks. Assuming that the novelist was male, Hawks contacted Brackett's agent and requested that "he" come in for an

Lauren Bacall and Humphrey Bogart in The Big Sleep

interview. After his initial surprise when a diminutive, twenty-nine-year-old female appeared for "his" interview, Hawks hired Brackett to help William Faulkner complete an adaptation of Raymond Chandler's 1939 novel *The Big Sleep*. The self-discipline and organized procedures that had helped Brackett survive in the pulp and genre markets helped her now to produce quickly a new draft of *The Big Sleep*. As Brackett later described it, Faulkner greeted her on her first day of work, opened a copy of Chandler's novel, and assigned her alternate chapters to adapt. That was their first and last conference. Working in separate offices, she and Faulkner blocked out the novel in sections and handed the material to Hawks as it was written. Hawks in turn extended many scenes and patched together what the writers had produced. It was only after shooting had begun that Hawks, who now had too much material, hired Jules Furthman to shorten the script and revise the ending.

Because of the length of time over which the script for *The Big Sleep* evolved, it is difficult to separate Brackett's work from that of her collaborators, but it is clear that her most significant contribution to the film was in the area of "tough" dialogue. In fact, when Humphrey Bogart joined the project, he went to Brackett to discuss lines he found too genteel and assumed she had written. When he learned that those lines were Faulkner's and that her lines were what he considered the "toughest" in the script, he nicknamed her "Butch" and began to consult her whenever he wanted a passage hardened or tightened up. To master this idiom before writing her first novel, Brackett had studied Steinbeck, Hemingway, Kipling, Chandler, and Dashiell Hammett because "they got so much into so little."

Judging from Brackett's subsequent work for

Howard Hawks, it would seem that she quickly assimilated Hawks's thematic preoccupation with male/female relationships. Such relationships in Hawks's films begin antagonistically but, through a series of challenges which man and woman meet together, evolve into sexual liaisons. As Brackett later observed, "Mr. Hawks does not like conventional heroines. He does not like 'nice' girls: he finds them exceedingly dull. . . . My taste in heroines is somewhat similar to theirs [Hawks's and Furthman's] so I was able to work well within that framework."

Brackett's next assignment after *The Big Sleep* was *Crime Doctor's Manhunt* (1946) for Columbia Pictures. This return to the "B" film after her experience with *The Big Sleep* may have disheartened Brackett. She took an original story by another writer and in craftsmanlike fashion produced a script which became a forgettable entry in Columbia's short-lived series of *Crime Doctor* melodramas. This work reinforced for Brackett the dichotomy between high- and low-budget productions. As she later discovered, both Republic and Columbia encouraged her to produce scripts with shot notations and elaborate descriptions of action. This request was to diminish the amount of invention which would later be required of the director working on a short schedule and a tight budget. Hawks, in contrast, insisted on being given only "master" scenes with a minimum of stage action indicated. Brackett much preferred this method. "Basically you put in as little description as you can possibly get away with. I've always worked that way, except when I was forced to do the other, which I hate doing. No director worth his salt wants some writer telling him where to put his camera."

In 1946 Brackett married Edmond Hamilton, a science-fiction and comic-book author. She returned to writing fiction (except for an occasional radio play), and in 1949 she and Hamilton moved to a hundred-year-old farmstead in Kinsman, Ohio. Through the 1950s, Brackett concentrated on fantasy and science-fiction writing, both in short-story and novel forms.

Brackett's science-fiction work typically follows an estranged male through a hostile environment or culture. Challenges to his personal skill and honor are overcome; as a sidelight, a personal goal is often achieved. The alien protagonist is an exceptional man who prefers to work alone but rarely gets the opportunity. Like the characters played by John Wayne in *Rio Bravo* (1959), *El Dorado* (1967), and *Rio Lobo* (1970), which she would later write, Brackett's typical protagonist complains when someone

Poster for the second film Brackett wrote for John Wayne—the only one of three for which she received sole screenplay credit

comes unsolicited to his aid.

Another important element, which is common to Brackett's film scripts and genre fiction, is the presence of an antagonistic female character. Typically, this is a woman of power and independence who initially frustrates or complicates the actions of the hero. In the novels and stories the woman's presence is often a catalyst of danger and conflict, but in the films it is more often simply a device for comic relief. The narrative concepts of both Brackett's prose fiction and her film scripts are firmly rooted in genre traditions. The "epic" quality and heroic constructions of her science fiction may emerge in radically different milieus from those of Chandler and his dark, urban streets, but the conflicts are similar. Brackett's mysteries and her later westerns are less monumental in scale than her fantasy romances, but the moral victories, whether over mobsters, cattle barons, or intergalactic warlords, are affirmations of the same values.

Brackett had two crime novels published in 1957: *The Tiger Among Us* and *An Eye for an Eye*. The latter was used as the basis for a CBS television pilot entitled "Markham" in 1964, and the former was filmed in 1962 as *13 West Street*. Brackett did not participate in either of these projects. Her first active film work in over a dozen years was again for Howard Hawks, on *Rio Bravo*. Again the cowriter was Furthman, but on this screenplay he and Brackett worked simultaneously and in collaboration. Because Furthman preferred to discuss scenes and concepts and disliked the physical act of writing, Brackett was the recorder of their story conferences with Hawks. As she described it: "I would put on paper the scenes that Mr. Hawks and Mr. Furthman had talked out, shape them, reshape them if necessary, and put them together, adding a few things of my own in the process." Over several months, as Hawks repeatedly changed his mind about which story elements he wanted, Brackett used this process to produce four successive drafts of *Rio Bravo*. After shooting began, Hawks continued to use spare moments on the set to make notes on additional changes, and Brackett would turn these into formal revisions.

The film which resulted from this collaboration has acquired the critical reputation of one of the most extraordinary and well-constructed post-World War II westerns, despite the fact that *Rio Bravo* shares little common ground with the "classic" Westerns from *Iron Horse* (1924) to *High Noon* (1952). For whereas the traditional thematic preoccupations of the Western are with American

John Wayne in Rio Bravo

expansionism and frontier conflicts with lawless elements, *Rio Bravo* uses its "Westernness" to assume this framework but concentrates on the moral dilemmas of the characters who exist within it. The lawman, John T. Chance (John Wayne), like the figures in Brackett's fantasy novels, is a moral prototype. His sense of duty and his desire to fulfill that duty are part of an epic posture which is held tenaciously in the face of numerous antagonists and which motivates the film's other, more tarnished characters.

Hawks would not wait another twelve years before soliciting Brackett's participation in a project. Brackett did produce another "B" script, adapted from Steve Frazee's western novel *Desert Guns*, which had been bought by Warner Bros. as an off-season project for its television contract players. The result, *Gold of the Seven Saints*, was released in 1961. By that time, Brackett was again at work for Hawks on *Hatari!* (1962). The procedure for scripting this film was somewhat unusual, even for Hawks. He had already spent half a year in Africa filming thousands of feet of action with wild animals and big game trappers. From this material Brackett was assigned to interpolate connecting scenes and to devise a plot. None of Brackett's first four drafts was acceptable, since none incorporated enough of the African material which Hawks envisioned as the core of the film. Because Hawks wanted individual scenes more than a narrative, he and Brackett eventually charted all the existing action scenes and developed lines between two or three of them or, as she put it, "devise[d] the people scenes." When a draft had been produced using this process and shooting began, Brackett stood by on the set. If Hawks altered or added characters to fit the actors he wanted to use, Brackett worked into the night to provide still more revisions for the next day. The resultant film was, as might be expected, uneven.

While in Hollywood working primarily for Hawks from 1958 to 1962, Brackett produced her first teleplays: two Alfred Hitchcock shows, "Death of a Cop," and "Terror at Northfield," both in 1960; and one of the *Checkmate* series episodes, "The Face in the Window," in 1961. After completion of *Hatari!*, Brackett returned to Kinsman, Ohio, and fiction writing. In 1963 *Follow the Free Wind*, a fictional biography of a mountain man, was published. This was her last hardcover novel. It received favorable reviews, the most attention in literary circles since her *The Long Tomorrow* in 1955, and eventually a Silver Spur Award from the Western Writers' Association in 1964, but Brackett returned to the pulp market and science-fiction paperbacks. In the late 1960s she accepted two more script assignments from Howard Hawks.

Both *El Dorado* and *Rio Lobo* were conscious reworkings of earlier Hawks/Brackett collaborations, particularly *Rio Bravo*. Both films starred John Wayne, older, portlier, and slower than he was as John T. Chance. While the situation and supporting characters were similar in many respects, the Wayne characterization clearly evolved in the course of four films (including *Hatari!*). Perhaps this was because Brackett always knew the actor for whom she was writing, and "if you know who you're writing for, it helps . . . you learn to utilize what the actor has that is peculiarly his own." In adapting Harry Brown's novel for *El Dorado* and reworking an earlier script for *Rio Lobo*, Brackett realigned the narrative focus to accommodate the strengths of the Wayne character and to underscore his resilience. The earlier righteousness and even antagonism of Chance were mitigated, and the result bore some resemblance to the world-weary but stubbornly idealistic Philip Marlowe in *The Big Sleep*.

Having come almost full circle in her work for Hawks, Brackett would appropriately complete her film-writing career by returning to Chandler and the Marlowe character. In 1971 she was hired by her former agent Elliott Kastner to adapt Chandler's novel *The Long Goodbye*. Brackett's first draft emerged from several story conferences in London with Kastner and director Brian G. Hutton, who left the project after a disagreement. He was replaced by Robert Altman, who gave Brackett the line he wished to follow. As she had with Faulkner, Brackett blocked out the chapters, streamlined the narrative, and produced a complete script in a week's time. From that point until shooting began, Brackett made only minor changes. Some of the film's sequences were improvised by Altman, but essentially things were as Brackett had rendered them. The film's ending, in which Marlowe kills his friend, was frequently attributed to Altman, but Brackett explained to *Films in Review* that this was not so: "Actually, the ending, where Marlowe commits the murder, was in the script before Altman came onto it. The ending of the book was totally inconclusive. You had built up a villain, you feel that Marlowe has been wounded in his most sensitive heart as it were—he's trusted this man as his friend, the friend has betrayed him, what do you do? We said let's just face up to it. He kills him. . . . I don't know whether we were right to do it but I don't regret having done it. It felt right at the time."

Leigh Brackett died of cancer in Lancaster, California on 18 March 1978. She had completed a draft of *The Empire Strikes Back*, the sequel to *Star Wars*, produced by George Lucas, who has been an admirer of her science fiction. Brackett's science fiction had contained numerous prototypes of Luke Skywalker, Han Solo, and Leia Organa, the figures in Lucas's film. Brackett had explained in an article written in the 1950s that "I've been fascinated with the old Celtic mythology and folklore, and the names carry such magic, at least to me, that I tend to use them in exotic interplanetary settings." Her fascination and use of unfuturistic Celtic names for her space heroes seemed to anticipate the cultish, mystic homilies of Lucas's Obi Wan Kenobi, created more than a score of years later. However much she might have influenced Lucas's conceptions, Brackett died during the early stages of the project. Lawrence Kasdan's revisions and new drafts of *The Empire Strikes Back* made after Brackett's death have somewhat diluted her contributions. Nonetheless, Brackett's themes are apparent throughout the finished picture, most notably in the tough-talking relationship that develops between Han Solo and Princess Leia. Of all the genres in which she wrote, science fiction was Brackett's avowed favorite, and it seems appropriate that her final screen credit be in that genre.

References:

Robert E. Briney, *Destiny + 10* (Summer 1954): 54-56;
Donald Chase, *Filmmaking: the Collaborative Art* (Boston: Little, Brown, 1975);
"A Conversation with Leigh Brackett," *Films in Review* (August-September 1976): 76, 413-421;
Hedda Hopper, "They Call Her for Salty Dialogue," *Los Angeles Times*, 28 December 1965, IV: 10;
R. Shatzlin, "The Big Sleep," *Take One*, 2 (January 1979): 29.

Mel Brooks
(28 June 1926-)

Tom Stempel
Los Angeles City College

MOTION PICTURES: *New Faces* (National Pictures/20th Century-Fox, 1954), sketches by Brooks, Ronny Graham, Paul Lynde, Luther Davis, and John Cleveland;
The Critic (Pintoff-Crossbow Productions, 1963), narration;
The Producers (Sidney Glazier Productions/Embassy Pictures, 1968), screenplay;
The Twelve Chairs (Twelve Chairs Co./UMC Pictures, 1970), screenplay;
Blazing Saddles (Warner Bros., 1974), screenplay by Brooks, Norman Steinberg, Andrew Bergman, Richard Pryor, and Alan Uger;
Young Frankenstein (20th Century-Fox, 1974), screenplay by Brooks and Gene Wilder;
Silent Movie (20th Century-Fox, 1976), screenplay by Brooks, Ron Clark, Rudy DeLuca, and Barry Levinson;
High Anxiety (20th Century-Fox, 1977), screenplay by Brooks, Clark, DeLuca, and Levinson;
History of the World–Part I (20th Century-Fox, 1981), screenplay.

PLAYS: *New Faces of 1952*, sketches by Brooks and Ronny Graham (New York, Royale Theatre, 16 May 1952);
Shinbone Alley, book by Brooks and Joe Darion (New York, Broadway Theatre, 13 April 1957);
All-American, book by Brooks (New York, Winter Garden Theatre, 19 March 1962).

SELECTED RECORDINGS: *2,000 Years*, by Brooks and Carl Reiner (Capitol, 1960);
2,000 and One Years, by Brooks and Reiner (Capitol, 1961);
At the Cannes Film Festival, by Brooks and Reiner (Capitol, 1961);
2,000 and Thirteen, by Brooks and Reiner (Warner Bros., 1973).

Mel Brooks was born Melvin Kaminsky in Brooklyn, New York, to Max and Kate Brookman Kaminsky. His comedy career began at an early age with humorous routines he performed for his classmates at school, routines that he later incorporated into his films. As a young man, Brooks worked at various jobs at resorts in the Catskills before changing his name to avoid identification with a well-known musician of the time, Max Kaminsky. He attended Virginia Military Institute in 1944, and from 1944 to 1946 he served with the U.S. Army in a combat engineering group in Europe.

In 1947 he began to write gags for a young comic he had met before the war, Sid Caesar. When in 1949 Caesar began appearing on a television variety show, *The Admiral Broadway Revue*, he hired Brooks as a writer. Renamed *Your Show of Shows* in 1950, the program employed many young comedy writers, including Woody Allen, Neil Simon, Carl Reiner, and Larry Gelbart. The group worked together in a chaotic manner: ideas were thrown back and forth, developed, thrown out, put back, and completely rewritten. In such a situation it would be impossible to define precisely what each writer contributed, but there is some agreement that Brooks specialized in the various interview routines

Mel Brooks (photo by Maureen Lambray)

used in the show. (He and Carl Reiner later developed the comic interview form for a series of records in which Brooks played a 2000-year-old man.) Brooks also undoubtedly contributed to the brilliant movie parodies on the program, and, like other writers on the show who turned to screenwriting, he has written a number of movie parodies for the screen. Indeed, the parody has become the dominant form for Brooks's films to date.

While writing for television, Brooks developed some sketches with Ronny Graham for the Broadway revue *New Faces of 1952*. The same year he married Florence Baum, a dancer. The marriage ended in divorce in 1959, and in August 1964 Brooks married Anna Maria Italiano (actress Anne Bancroft). *New Faces of 1952* was so successful that it was filmed as *New Faces* in 1954, and, although Brooks was not directly involved with the film, he was given his first screen credit as a writer. His next Broadway efforts were less successful. He and Joe Darion wrote the book for *Shinbone Alley* (1957), a musical based on Don Marquis's Archy and Mehitabel stories, and he also wrote the book for the musical *All-American* (1962). Neither did well as theatrical productions.

Brooks worked on Caesar's second show, *Caesar's Hour*, until it went off the air in 1957. He had some success with the 2000-year-old man records, and he worked on the screenplay for *The Ladies' Man* (1961), a Jerry Lewis film. Little of his work was retained for that film, and he received no screen credit.

In 1962 Brooks went to see an abstract animated film by Norman McLaren and was distracted by an old man sitting behind him complaining that the film made no sense. Brooks was inspired to ask his friend Ernest Pintoff to make a similar animated film for which he ad-libbed a narration inspired by the old man's complaints. *The Critic* (1963) won an Academy Award for best animated short film and has been playing in art theaters ever since. In 1965 Brooks and Buck Henry created the television series *Get Smart*, which spoofed the then-popular spy shows. The series ran for five seasons, but Brooks was only minimally involved with the program once it was on the air.

Since the early 1960s, Brooks had been working on an idea titled "Springtime for Hitler," first in novel form, then as a play. Brought together with Academy-Award-winning producer Sidney Glazier by their agent, he convinced Glazier that "Springtime for Hitler" should be made into a film, with Glazier as producer and Brooks as director. Glazier and Joseph E. Levine financed the film, whose title was changed to *The Producers* to avoid offending Jewish theater owners.

In *The Producers* (1968), a timid accountant (Gene Wilder) tells a shady Broadway producer (Zero Mostel) that he could make a fortune by over-financing a sure-fire flop. They select the script "Springtime for Hitler," hire an inept director and actors, and then sell shares in the show in excess of one thousand percent. The play is so awful it is a hit, and the producers wind up in jail. Although the film won Brooks his second Academy Award, for Best Original Screenplay, and became a cult favorite, it was years before it made back its costs.

Brooks's next film, *The Twelve Chairs* (1970), was also financially unsuccessful. Based on the 1928 novel *Twelve Chairs* by Russian writers Ilya Ilf and Yevgenyi Petrov, the film shows a man's search for the family diamonds, which his mother had sewn into one of the dining-room chairs during the Russian revolution. Brooks wrote the film as a tribute to the Russian literary tradition, which fascinates him. His next attempt at writing a screenplay alone was another literary adaptation, of Oliver Goldsmith's eighteenth-century comedy *She Stoops to Conquer.* Brooks was unable to get financing for this project, and the script was never produced.

With his first two films unsuccessful financially, Brooks had difficulties finding a new project that could secure studio financing. Finally a story editor at Warner Bros. sent him a treatment for a comedy Western, "Tex X," written by Andrew Bergman. Brooks agreed to rewrite the material, but insisted that he be joined by Bergman and several other writers, including Richard Pryor. Brooks said later, "I decided that this would be a surrealist epic. For nine months we worked together like maniacs. We went all the way—especially Richard Pryor, who was very brave and far-out and catalytic. I figured my career was finished anyway, so I wrote berserk, heartfelt stuff about white corruption and racism and Bible-thumping bigotry. We used dirty language on the screen for the first time, and to me the whole thing was like a big psychoanalytical session."

The film, retitled *Blazing Saddles* (1974), was an enormous hit with the public. Its budget was $2.6 million, and by early 1979 it had returned $37.2 million in film rentals. Some critics complained that most of the humor in the film comes from tasteless language and actions, but much of the comedic impact is derived from the unexpected juxtaposition of crassness with the purity of the Western. This film made Brooks's reputation as a comic filmmaker and gave him the freedom to make the films he wanted.

Gene Wilder, who had appeared in both *The Producers* and *Blazing Saddles*, suggested the idea for *Young Frankenstein* (1974), a spoof of the old Frankenstein films. Wilder developed the first draft of the script, and Brooks later joined him in rewriting it. In *Young Frankenstein*, Victor Frankenstein's grandson Freddie (Gene Wilder) returns to Transylvania to continue his grandfather's experiments. He succeeds in bringing the monster (Peter Boyle) back to life, only to lose control of it. In *Young Frankenstein*, Brooks is able to spoof the conventions of the horror film, particularly the first two sequels to *Frankenstein* (1931), *Bride of Frankenstein* (1935) and *Son of Frankenstein* (1939), while still working with a well-developed plot, something *Blazing Saddles* lacked. Many critics feel *Young Frankenstein* is Brooks's most successful work.

Following the success of *Blazing Saddles* and *Young Frankenstein*, Brooks briefly returned to television with a series that lasted less than a season. *When Things Were Rotten* was an attempt to parody the Robin Hood legend in the way *Blazing Saddles* parodied the Western. Unfortunately, television denied Brooks the vulgarity that had made *Blazing Saddles* so successful, and Brooks and the other writers were unable to develop the sustained characterizations and humor that had made *Get Smart* a hit ten years before.

Silent Movie (1976) is perhaps the most imaginatively conceived of Brooks's films, but the conception is not completely realized. The screenplay, written with Ron Clark and two writers from *The Carol Burnett Show*, Barry Levinson and Rudy DeLuca, is uneven; sequences range from clever to conventional to terrible. The film is a silent movie about an alcoholic director (Brooks) who convinces the head of Sunshine Studios that the only way to avoid takeover from the conglomerate Engulf and Devour is to let him make a silent film. The Studio Chief (Sid Caesar) will not agree to finance the film unless the director can entice some big-name stars to appear; Burt Reynolds, James Caan, Paul Newman, Liza Minnelli, and Anne Bancroft are signed for the movie. (The film's final title card informs the audience that "This is a true story,"

Scenes from three Brooks movies. Top: Zero Mostel, Kenneth Mars, and Gene Wilder in The Producers *(1968); Wilder and Peter Boyle in* Young Frankenstein *(1974). Bottom: Dom De Luise, Brooks, Bernadette Peters, and Marty Feldman in* Silent Movie *(1976).*

indicating perhaps Brooks's problems in getting the film made.) *Silent Movie* earned $21 million on a $4.4 million budget.

Working with the team that wrote *Silent Movie*, Brooks next wrote, directed, and starred in *High Anxiety* (1977), a comic homage to Alfred Hitchcock. Although there are amusing sequences in the film, it is structured primarily to give Brooks a chance to parody Hitchcock's style. The film is weak because it merely provides the audience a detached if amused appreciation of the parodies. At the box office, *High Anxiety* was the least successful of Brooks's films since before *Blazing Saddles*.

Two perceptive analysts of Brooks's career, Kenneth Tynan in the *New Yorker* (1978) and Lawrence Weschler in the *Village Voice* (1977), raised basically the same question about Brooks's film career: can he and should he continue to make films that are parodies of other films and film styles? Brooks himself seems to have considered this problem, for after having toyed with making films such as "A World War II picture to end all World War II pictures," a remake of Ernst Lubitsch's *To Be or Not to Be*, and a Busby Berkeley-style musical, he announced in November 1978 that his next project would be *History of the World—Part I*. The film was finally released in 1981, with Brooks as writer, producer, director, and star. The film depicted five separate periods during the earth's history: the Stone Age, ancient Egypt during the time of Moses, the end of the Roman Empire, the Inquisition, and the French Revolution. There are also "previews"

for the nonexistent "History of the World—Part II." The film was an enormous failure for Brooks, ranking with *High Anxiety* as among his least successful films financially. Reviews were uniformly unfavorable. Brooks then went to work on a previously announced project, the remake of *To Be or Not to Be*.

Perhaps because of these two failures, Brooks has begun to turn his attention away from screenwriting and toward producing. His company Brooksfilms has had three successes since 1980. *The Elephant Man* (1980), was nominated for Academy Awards for Best Picture, Best Director (David Lynch), Best Actor (John Hurt), and Best Screenplay (Lynch, Christopher Devore, Eric Bergen). *My Favorite Year* (1982) earned an Oscar nomination for star Peter O'Toole, as did *Frances* (1982) for Jessica Lange and Kim Stanley.

Biographies:

Bill Alder and Jeffrey Fineman, *Mel Brooks: The Irreverent Funnyman* (Chicago: Playboy Press, 1976);

William Holtzman, *Seesaw: A Dual Biography of Anne Bancroft and Mel Brooks* (Garden City: Doubleday, 1979).

References:

Joshua Logan, *Movie Stars, Real People, and Me* (New York: Delacorte, 1978);

Ralph Rosenblum and Robert Karen, *When the Shooting Stops* (New York: Viking, 1979).

Harry Brown

(30 April 1917-   )

Joseph R. Millichap
University of Tulsa

MOTION PICTURES: *The True Glory* [documentary] (Columbia, 1945), screen story and screenplay by Brown and others;

The Other Love (United Artists, 1947), screenplay by Brown and Ladislas Fodor;

Arch of Triumph (United Artists, 1948), screenplay by Brown and Lewis Milestone;

Wake of the Red Witch (Republic, 1949), screenplay by Brown and Kenneth Gamet;

Sands of Iwo Jima (Republic, 1949), screen story;

screenplay by Brown and James Edward Grant;

The Man on the Eiffel Tower (RKO, 1950), screenplay;

Kiss Tomorrow Goodbye (Warner Bros., 1950), screenplay;

Only the Valiant (Warner Bros., 1951), screenplay by Brown and Edmund H. North;

A Place in the Sun (Paramount, 1951), screenplay by Brown and Michael Wilson;

Bugles in the Afternoon (Warner Bros., 1952),

screenplay by Brown and Geoffrey Homes;

The Sniper (Columbia, 1952), screenplay;

Eight Iron Men (Columbia, 1952), screenplay adapted by Brown from his play *A Sound of Hunting*;

All the Brothers Were Valiant (M-G-M, 1953), screenplay;

Many Rivers to Cross (M-G-M, 1955), screenplay by Brown and Guy Trosper;

The Virgin Queen (20th Century-Fox, 1955), screenplay by Brown and Mindret Lord;

D-Day, the Sixth of June (20th Century-Fox, 1956), screenplay by Brown and Ivan Moffat;

Between Heaven and Hell (20th Century-Fox, 1956), screenplay;

The Deep Six (Warner Bros., 1958), screenplay by Brown, John Twist, and Martin Rackin;

The Fiend Who Walked the West (20th Century-Fox, 1958), screenplay by Brown and Philip Yordan;

Ocean's Eleven (Warner Bros., 1960), screenplay by Brown and Charles Lederer.

PLAY: *A Sound of Hunting* (New York: Lyceum Theatre, 20 November 1945).

SELECTED BOOKS: *The End of a Decade* (Norfolk, Conn.: New Directions, 1940);

The Poem of Bunker Hill (New York: Scribners, 1941);

The Violent: New Poems (Norfolk, Conn.: New Directions, 1943);

A Walk in the Sun (New York: Knopf, 1944; London: Secker & Warburg, 1944);

Artie Greengroin, P.F.C. (New York: Knopf, 1945; London: Secker & Warburg, 1945);

Poems: 1941-1944 (London: Secker & Warburg, 1945);

A Sound of Hunting (New York: Knopf, 1946);

The Beast in His Hunger (New York: Knopf, 1949);

The Stars in Their Courses (New York: Knopf, 1960; London: Cape, 1961);

A Quiet Place to Work (New York: Knopf, 1968);

The Wild Hunt (New York: Harcourt Brace Jovanovich, 1973).

Harry Brown is an author of poetry, fiction, and drama, but he is probably best known for his twenty screenplays. Most of Brown's screenplays are adaptations, and he tended to work close to his literary sources. No dominant subject, style, or theme marks Brown's body of work because his choice of materials, approaches, and ideas was eclectic. Brown seems to be a literary figure capti-

vated by Hollywood; he came to movies from literature, and after making a reasonable living he went back to fiction writing. He occasionally succumbed to the pressure of the Hollywood system, involving himself with weak properties. As a result, his screenwriting is uneven in terms of artistic quality and commercial success. Nonetheless, Harry Brown has produced several fine works for the screen.

Harry Peter McNab Brown was born in Portland, Maine, the son of Harry McNab and Bessie Hiles Brown. He attended Harvard University from 1936 to 1938 but left without taking his degree. At Harvard he began his writing career as a poet, winning several awards for his verses, and in 1940 his first collection of poems, *The End of a Decade*, was published by New Directions. Later poetry collections included *The Poem of Bunker Hill* (1941), *The Violent: New Poems* (1943), *Poems: 1941-1944* (1945), and *The Beast in His Hunger* (1949). During the prewar years Brown worked as a copyboy for *Time* and as a subeditor for the *New Yorker*.

In 1941 Brown enlisted in the U.S. Army, and from 1942-1945 he served with *Yank*, the army magazine, in England. His major contribution to *Yank* was a series of humorous sketches about army life written under the pseudonym Artie Greengroin, which were later collected under the title *Artie Greengroin, P.F.C.* (1945). A more important publication during this period was Brown's *A Walk in the Sun* (1944), a novel depicting an Italian beachhead operation. In 1946 *A Walk in the Sun* was adapted for the screen by Robert Rossen and directed by Lewis Milestone; the result was a film regarded as Milestone's best since *All Quiet on the Western Front* (1930).

Brown left the service in 1945 and wrote a realistic drama about the Italian campaign entitled *A Sound of Hunting*; it was produced on Broadway in late 1945. He also wrote a poem that was used in the World War II documentary *The True Glory* (1945), for which he received his first screen credit. Through his connection with Milestone, Brown readily found work in Hollywood, writing the screenplay for *The Other Love* in 1947. He and Ladislas Fodor adapted Erich Maria Remarque's *Flotsam* (1941) for this film about a woman dying from tuberculosis and her doctor-husband who attempts to save her. Unfortunately, the screenplay wrings too much sentiment from Remarque's realistic story.

Brown's next effort, *Arch of Triumph* (1948), suffered from a similar soap-opera quality. Brown and Milestone collaborated on the screenplay for this film, basing it on Remarque's 1947 novel of the same title. Both the film and the novel center on the

John Wayne in Sands of Iwo Jima, *for which Brown received his first Academy Award nomination*

relationship between Ravic (Charles Boyer), a Czech surgeon forced to flee Nazi Germany, and Joan Madou (Ingrid Bergman), a neurotic cabaret singer. Ravic meets Madou as he sinks into the demimonde and is forced, as an unlicensed physician, to perform abortions for prostitutes. His loss of values is symbolized by his brutal murder of the German agent who had tortured Ravic's wife to death years before. Joan Madou's disintegration is represented by her abandonment of Ravic for a rich actor who can advance her career. The story ends when Madou is shot by the jealous actor and dies in Ravic's arms. He leaves her body for the police to find and walks out in the foggy dawn of 1 Sep-

tember 1939—the day on which World War II began. Remarque handled this potentially sensational subject matter with realism and restraint; the Brown-Milestone version surrenders realism to the productions code and restraint to popular melodrama. The film was an artistic failure and a financial disaster; it cost $4 million and only earned $1.5 million.

With *Wake of the Red Witch* (1949), Brown turned from international melodrama to action and adventure on the high seas. The film, directed by Edward Ludwig, was adapted from Garland Roark's book of the same title; Kenneth Gamet collaborated with Brown on the screenplay. John

Wayne starred in this tale set in the South Seas. *Wake of the Red Witch* defies easy summary as adventures and plots abound in a contest of wills between a South Seas tyrant and a tough sea captain. The plot includes sunken treasure, castaways, man-eating sharks, tribal orgies, and a final battle between the captain and a giant squid. Clearly the picture was in the tradition of Republic Studios, which nurtured John Wayne as an action hero.

A better effort was *Sands of Iwo Jima* (1949), for which Brown adapted his own story and collaborated with James Edward Grant on the screenplay. Brown received his first Academy Award nomination for this generally realistic re-creation of the Pacific campaign. Documentary footage of island landings balanced some of the excesses of emotion in the film's stories about the members of a marine rifle squad. The story recalls *A Walk in the Sun* as it follows the squad, bloodied at Tarawa landing, to the triumphant ascent of Mount Suribachi and the famous raising of the American flag. Unlike Brown's earlier war story, *Sands of Iwo Jima* is marred by the standardized, sentimentalized brawls and love affairs of the marines when they are back at

the staging areas in New Zealand. This compilation of service-film clichés keeps *Sands of Iwo Jima* from becoming a really fine war film.

Brown next wrote the screenplay for *The Man on the Eiffel Tower* (1950), an adaptation of George Simenon's Inspector Maigret novel *A Battle of Nerves* (1931). This mystery stays close to its source and succeeds best in evoking a Parisian atmosphere. Brown's next two films were produced by William Cagney, James Cagney's brother, and directed by Gordon Douglas, Brown's favorite director of any he worked with during his film career. As a starring vehicle for James Cagney, Brown adapted *Kiss Tomorrow Goodbye* (1950) from Horace McCoy's novel of the same title. The movie, intended to be in the same vein as Cagney's earlier *White Heat* (1949), did not succeed, for the most part because of a confusing script. *Only the Valiant* (1951), adapted from Charles Marquis Warren's novel, was Brown's first attempt at the Western genre. Under Douglas's direction it proved an interesting yarn of cavalry and Indians with as many conflicts among the horse soldiers as between them and the Apaches.

It was *A Place in the Sun* (1951) that established

Lobby poster and scene featuring stars Clift and Taylor in the film which many critics consider Brown's finest screen work

Harry Brown as a critically and professionally respected screenwriter. Adapting Theodore Dreiser's 1925 novel, *An American Tragedy*, Brown and collaborator Michael Wilson changed the original setting to a contemporary one, excised some of Dreiser's themes about social injustice, and generally distilled the essence of the tragedy promised by the novel's title. (Brown despised collaborating on films and described this project as "the one time I even discussed a script with the 'other' writer.") In all, it was a solid job of screenwriting which in turn was ably translated to film by director George Stevens and the cast, which included Elizabeth Taylor, Montgomery Clift, and Shelley Winters. Brown and Wilson won an Academy Award and a Writers Guild Award for their screenplay; Stevens won an Oscar for Best Director; and the film was nominated for Best Picture.

After this artistic triumph Brown went back to writing mediocre films with *Bugles in the Afternoon* (1952), a routine cavalry Western adapted with Geoffrey Homes from an Ernest Haycock novel. More intriguing is Brown's screenplay for *The Sniper* (1952), written from a fact-based screen story by Edward and Edna Anhalt. The film was extensively researched and promoted by its studio as the first motion picture to deal frankly with the problem of sex murderers. Brown said of it, "*The Sniper*, a very underrated film, struck me, and still strikes me, as doing exactly what it set out to do. And what it set out to do, believe me, was a lot." Edward Dmytryk, who directed *The Sniper*, also directed Brown's next film, *Eight Iron Men* (1952), the screen version of Brown's play *A Sound of Hunting*. Unfortunately, the change in title reflects the change in dramatic emphasis, as Brown's realistic play set during the Italian campaign becomes a standard war movie, complete with combat action and dramatized reveries about women back home. Brown said that Dmytryk managed to "mess up [the film] irreparably with his direction."

In 1953 Brown returned to the setting of the South Seas with *All the Brothers Were Valiant*, an adaptation of material from a story by Ben Ames Williams about two feuding brothers who are whaling captains. *Many Rivers to Cross* (1955), co-scripted with Guy Trosper from a story by Steve Frazee, is a silly Western spoof about a frontiersman and the woman who pursues him.

In the mid-1950s Brown worked on a script that he feels is his best, "The Enchanted Cup," co-written with Charles Brackett. Brown described the screenplay, based on a novel updating the legend of Tristan and Isolde, as a "fairy tale for adults." Dar-

Bette Davis as Elizabeth I in The Virgin Queen

ryl Zanuck found it too downbeat to be filmed, and it has never been produced.

Brown rates *The Virgin Queen* (1955) with *The True Glory* as his most satisfying screenplay that has been produced. Bette Davis, who had portrayed Elizabeth I in *The Private Lives of Elizabeth and Essex* (1939), also starred in this film, which seems to draw on the earlier movie for its basic characterization of Elizabeth as a strong, passionate, and lonely woman.

Brown's next movie, *D-Day, the Sixth of June* (1956), provides more romance than war story, as most of the plot concerns an attenuated affair between two lovers (Robert Taylor and Dana Wynter) in a London apartment. Ivan Moffat assisted Brown with this adaptation of Lionel Shapiro's novel. The war in the Pacific is the subject of *Between Heaven and Hell* (1956), a predictable story of a young man who finds his identity in combat. Similar subject matter is treated in *The Deep Six* (1958), about a naval gunnery officer torn between his combat duties and his pacifist convictions. He finally abandons his pacifism when his friend is killed in battle. In the same year, Brown also worked with Philip Yordan on *The Fiend Who Walked the West* (1958), a remake of Ben Hecht and Charles Lederer's 1947 film *Kiss of Death*.

In 1960 Lewis Milestone hired Brown to develop a script for *Ocean's Eleven* as a vehicle for the Sinatra "Rat Pack"—including Dean Martin, Sammy Davis, Jr., Peter Lawford, and Joey Bishop. Coauthored with Charles Lederer from a story by George Clayton Johnson and Jack Golden Russell, the screenplay concerns the heist of money from Las Vegas gambling casinos by a group of eleven ex-commandos led by Danny Ocean (Frank Sinatra). This was Brown's last film script.

Brown married June Jollie Clark de Brown in 1959; they have a son, Jarred Jollie Clark Brown. He retired to Mexico in 1959 and returned to fiction

writing. In 1960 his novel *The Stars in Their Courses* was published; it was later filmed as *El Dorado* (1967). Brown's other books include the novels *A Quiet Place to Work* (1968) and *The Wild Hunt* (1973).

Harry Brown produced a group of diverse, uneven screenplays ranging from the genre formulas of Westerns to the artistic quality of *A Place in the Sun*. When he was challenged by a novel such as Dreiser's *An American Tragedy*, he could produce fine work indeed. During his Hollywood career he was in every sense a professional screenwriter—a literate, intelligent, creative craftsman.

Clyde Bruckman
(1894-4 January 1955)

Joseph Adamson III

SELECTED MOTION PICTURES: *Rouged Lips* (Metro, 1923), titles;
The Three Ages (Joseph M. Schenk Productions, 1923), story and titles by Bruckman, Jean Havez, and Joseph Mitchell;
Our Hospitality (Joseph M. Schenk Productions, 1923), story, titles, and scenario by Bruckman, Havez, and Mitchell;
Sherlock, Jr. (Metro, 1924), story by Bruckman, Havez, and Mitchell;
The Navigator (Metro-Goldwyn, 1924), story and titles by Bruckman, Havez, and Mitchell;
Seven Chances (Metro-Goldwyn, 1925), scenario by Bruckman, Havez, and Mitchell;
Keep Smiling (Monty Banks Pictures, 1925), story by Bruckman, Monty Banks, and Herman Raymaker;
For Heaven's Sake (Paramount, 1926), story by Bruckman, Ted Wilde, and John Grey;
The General (United Artists, 1927), story by Bruckman and Buster Keaton;
The Cameraman (M-G-M, 1928), story by Bruckman and Lew Lipton;
Welcome Danger (Paramount Famous Lasky, 1929), story by Bruckman, Lex Neal, and Felix Adler;
Feet First (Paramount-Publix, 1930), story by Bruckman, Grey, and Alfred A. Cohn;
Professor Beware (Paramount, 1938), adaptation by

Bruckman and Jack Cunningham;
Blondie Goes to College (Columbia, 1942), screen story by Bruckman and Warren Wilson;
So's Your Uncle (Universal, 1943), screenplay by Bruckman and Maurice Leo;
Honeymoon Lodge (Universal, 1943), screenplay;
Swingtime Johnny (Universal, 1944), screenplay;
Weekend Pass (Universal, 1944), screenplay;
Moon Over Las Vegas (Universal, 1944), screenplay by Bruckman and George Jeske;
South of Dixie (Universal, 1944), screenplay;
Twilight on the Prairie (Universal, 1944), screenplay;
Under Western Skies (Universal, 1945), screenplay by Bruckman and Stanley Roberts;
She Gets Her Man (Universal, 1945), screen story and screenplay by Bruckman and Wilson.

Clyde Adolph Bruckman was a gagman, writer, and director of some of the greatest films of the Golden Age of comedy. While better known than many screenwriters working in the early comedy films, he is not nearly so famous as the many classic comedies to which he lent his talents, including one of the most famous and revered of all silent films, *The General* (1927). He worked with Mack Sennett, Hal Roach, Buster Keaton, Laurel and Hardy, W. C. Fields, Harry Langdon, and Harold Lloyd, as well as with such lesser lights as Monty Banks, Abbott and Costello, the Three Stooges, and

Robert Woolsey. He has one of the most impressive records in the annals of a very productive period.

Bruckman was born in San Bernardino, California. He completed high school, which gave him the academic edge over most of his colleagues, and after a few years as a newspaper reporter (a common apprenticeship for film writers), he became involved with comedy filmmaking in 1919 or 1920 when Monty Banks and Al St. John were working for Warner Bros. in its formative years. Through the efforts of Harry Brand, Keaton's publicity man and later director of publicity for 20th Century-Fox, Bruckman joined the Buster Keaton unit in 1921. Bruckman worked happily and profitably for Keaton for five years, first on short subjects and later on feature-length films.

Keaton's features were produced for an average of $200,000 apiece and grossed between $500,000 and $750,000. Critical reception to the films was strongest when Keaton first hit the film scene on his own (after years as Fatty Arbuckle's sidekick), although some of the pictures received surprisingly lukewarm reviews on their initial release. Many of the films, feature and short, are now considered classics. The credits for Keaton's early short comedies read "Written and Directed by 'Buster' Keaton and Eddie Cline." But the importance of Bruckman, Jean Havez, and Joseph Mitchell, fully acknowledged by Keaton, was finally made public in 1923 with the move to features and more detailed title cards. Though Bruckman credited Keaton with the bulk of the creativity and often considered himself overpaid and overcredited, Keaton more than once singled out Bruckman and Havez as his favorite gag writers, a distinction he did not lavish indiscriminately. In return, Bruckman valued working with Keaton and learning from Keaton's vast store of comic experience.

The short comedies tended to revolve around the Keaton character's tribulations in securing the love of the girl he has set his sights on or the approval of her family, usually by performing some fairly meaningless task or donning a uniform. This theme continued as the basis for the first Keaton-Bruckman-Havez-Mitchell feature, *The Three Ages* (1923), constructed as a parody of D. W. Griffith's 1916 film *Intolerance* and intercutting three episodes about the struggles of a lover with a formidable competitor in the Stone Age, the Roman Empire, and the modern day. With *Our Hospitality* (1923), set in the early nineteenth century and based on early American family feuds, the historical accuracy and romantic imagery characteristic of the best Keaton features are first exhibited. The film is

intricately constructed, each sequence providing balance, parallel, or counterpoint for other sequences. It also marks the beginning of the "falling, sleeping, waking, and winning" pattern that critic Daniel Moews has perceived in the Keaton features, wherein an early sequence showing Keaton bungling a required task is balanced, after the interval of a night's sleep or a short nap, by a sequence of Keaton succeeding at the same task, usually by drawing on an adaptive ingenuity and employing common devices for uses other than that for which they were intended.

This theme appeared in its most pronounced form in the next feature, *Sherlock, Jr.* (1924), in which the bulk of the footage is devoted to a film-within-a-film: the Keaton character, unsuccessful at solving a simple crime in real life, dreams of himself as a great, invincible detective who foils schemes mirroring those that had tripped him up in reality. *Sherlock, Jr.* is a marvel of clockwork precision—a series of gags setting each other off like weights on a scale.

The Navigator (1924) delves deeper into the conflict of man versus machine than any of the previous Keaton features and, like *The Boat* (1921), uses the sea as a metaphor for life's journey—beginning by careful plan and deliberate navigation, foundering on choppy waters, ending marooned, stranded, totally at sea.

Seven Chances, made in 1925 more or less against Keaton's will, was based on a 1916 play bought by Keaton's producer Joseph Schenck, who coerced his star to adapt it for the screen. The resulting film is a less-than-perfect transformation of theatrical dialogue into brilliant pantomime, but it continues the passion for symmetrical design interwoven with social satire developed in the earlier films—comedy of manners fashioned into visual comedy of patterns.

Except for some title-writing on a Metro feature, *Rouged Lips* (1923), Bruckman worked exclusively for Keaton from 1921 to 1925. After *Seven Chances*, however, he was increasingly in demand at other comedy units and began to free-lance profitably, returning first to his former associate Monty Banks for his feature *Keep Smiling* (1925) and then joining the Harold Lloyd unit on *For Heaven's Sake* (1926). Both of these films are pleasant examples of 1920s comedy, revolving around some of the same themes as the Keaton pictures—efforts to please the girl and her father, the gulf between wealth and poverty, complications arising from mistaken identities—without the corresponding fatalism and tight narrative structure found in Keaton's work.

Both films received enthusiastic reviews.

In 1927 Bruckman returned to Keaton with a story idea of his own. In the years since he had worked with Keaton, two major changes had occurred in the making of comedy features. First, comedy had been revolutionized by Chaplin's adroit mixture of laughs, tears, and spectacle in *The Gold Rush* (1925). With this film, the short, fast-paced, moderately budgeted feature comedies of the early 1920s gave way to long, lavish productions with strong narrative lines. Second, American feature filmmaking, formerly preeminent in the world market, had begun to be influenced by the sophisticated visuals of German directors and the dynamic montages of Soviet filmmakers. American directors became conscious of camera movement and image juxtaposition, with improved film stock and optical technology abetting this new visual awareness. Bruckman was impressed with the increasing seriousness of Keaton's work; the dynamic finale of *Battling Butler* (1926) convinced him that his old boss could capitalize on the new trends in comedy filmmaking to realize an affecting film based on a true incident from the Civil War as documented in William Pittenger's popular novel *The Great Locomotive Chase* (originally published in 1863 as *Daring and Suffering*). The book is a firsthand account of an extremely hazardous Union raid into Confederate territory in 1862, written by one of a band of eight men who commandeered a Confederate locomotive in Big Shanty, Georgia, and proceeded north, destroying track and tearing down telegraph lines along the way. The Union band was pursued by three Southerners who chased them first on foot, then on a "truck-car" which was hurled from the track when it hit a stretch of rail removed by the Union raiders.

Many of these incidents were retained in *The General*, which Keaton cowrote and codirected with Bruckman with the admonition "It's got to be so authentic it hurts." The Civil War period was plausibly recreated, with efforts made to locate actual narrow-gauge railroad track in Oregon and to restore vintage locomotives. The basic change in the story was to tell the tale from the Confederate point of view, consolidating the three Southern pursuers into one man, Johnny Gray (Keaton), and integrating a romance into the adventure. In the film, the Union raid is a success (in reality, most of the men were caught and hanged), forcing Gray to enter the camp to retrieve his locomotive, the *General*, and undergo pursuit by Union soldiers.

The General has been seen as a mockery of the insanity of war, a shattering of romantic illusions and heroic conventions, and an essay on man versus machine. It is now considered a classic silent film; in the British Film Institute's 1972 worldwide poll of the greatest films of all time, it was the only American silent film ranking in the top ten. Critical reaction was less enthusiastic when the film was released in 1927; it was greeted as just another Buster Keaton film and criticized for its lack of "variety" (most of the action takes place on the train).

After *The General*, Bruckman began to work as a director, although he probably continued to make major contributions to the story and gag content of the films on which he worked. Some of these include Monty Banks's *Horse Shoes* (1927) and *A Perfect Gentleman* (1928), as well as some of the early Laurel and Hardy two-reelers, including the very first, *Putting Pants on Philip* (1927). On the Laurel and Hardy films, Bruckman had the advantage of working with two excellent comedy minds, Leo McCarey and Stan Laurel. McCarey was concerned with structure and supervised the construction and execution of each two-reeler; Laurel was concerned with comedy pacing and discussed it with Bruckman at great length.

In 1928 Bruckman worked with Keaton again at M-G-M on *The Cameraman*, the story of an aspiring news photographer. This feature, though delightful and consistently funny, reflects Keaton's decreasing control over his films. It has less of the pure Keaton vision than its predecessors, and its gags create the impression of a mechanical, big-studio production.

More autonomous was the Harold Lloyd comedy unit, on which Bruckman worked after *The Cameraman*. He was given story and direction credit on Lloyd's first sound film, *Welcome Danger* (1929)—which combined elements of *The Cameraman*, *For Heaven's Sake*, *Horse Shoes*, and Lloyd's earlier *A Sailor-Made Man* (1921)—depicting a young botanist who becomes involved in a dope ring in San Francisco's Chinatown. The film was completed as a silent by Mal St. Clair, and Bruckman directed the new dialogue sequences and supervised the dubbing on the silent shots; it became Lloyd's highest-grossing film, possibly because of the novelty of hearing one of the silent idols speak. After *Welcome Danger*, Bruckman directed two more films for Lloyd: *Feet First* (1930)—much of the story work was later attributed to him—and *Movie Crazy* (1932).

One of Bruckman's skills was his ability to adapt to the comic persona with whom he was working. The skill is evident in the two comedies that he directed for W. C. Fields (from scripts writ-

Above and opposite page: Buster Keaton in three of the films he made with Bruckman, The Navigator *(top),* Sherlock, Jr. *(bottom), and* The General *(at right)*

(Museum of Modern Art Film Stills Archive)

ten by Fields), *The Fatal Glass of Beer* (1933) and *Man on the Flying Trapeze* (1935). Bruckman suggested more two-reel story ideas, but disagreements between producer Mack Sennett and Fields forced an end to a successful collaboration.

Failing to secure more directing assignments, Bruckman went back to writing and in 1938 worked on Lloyd's *Professor Beware*, a pastiche of routines from previous Lloyd films and from Keaton's *College* (1927) that climaxed in a chase borrowed from *For Heaven's Sake*. *Professor Beware* starred Lloyd as a meek Egyptologist who must cope with a variety of problems while traveling across the country to secure a trip to Egypt. The film received disappointing reviews and box-office returns, and Lloyd virtually retired from filmmaking.

With most of the old-style comedy units closed or closing, Bruckman had difficulty finding work. He finally joined Jules White's short-subject unit at Columbia Pictures, where comedy was being performed but in the most slapdash way. The Columbia shorts were shot in three days and given to theaters as a bonus for renting the Columbia features. The talents employed were chiefly, like Bruckman, veterans of earlier days, now pitting their ingenuity and know-how against severe time and budget restrictions. Here the famous vaudeville

act Ted Healy and his Stooges became, without Ted Healy, the Three Stooges; Mack Sennett clown Andy Clyde adopted a grizzled hayseed characterization; Harry Langdon reworked routines from his great features; and Buster Keaton himself showed up in search of employment. At Columbia, Bruckman and Keaton recycled gags from *The General* in *Mooching Through Georgia* (1939), *Horse Shoes* in *Pardon My Berth Marks* (1940), *Man on the Flying Trapeze* and *Spite Marriage* in *Nothing But Pleasure* (1939), *Movie Crazy* and *The Haunted House* in *The Spook Speaks* (1940), and Keaton's 1930s feature *An Old Spanish Custom* in *Pest from the West* (1939). In the Three Stooges films, elements of Chaplin's *The Great Dictator* (1940) turn up in *You Nazty Spy* (1940) and *I'll Never Heil Again* (1941), with Moe masquerading as Hitler. This kind of "borrowing" was not unusual in the comedy business, as many comedy writers and directors took funny bits and gags from each other.

The trend of borrowing continued when Bruckman did some feature-film writing during the 1940s, using ideas from Keaton's *College* for *Blondie Goes to College* (1942) at Columbia and mining *Movie Crazy* and other past triumphs for a string of short B-pictures made at Universal and featuring Vera Vague, Joan Davis, Leon Errol, and the Andrews

Sisters. These films are chiefly marital mix-up stories, involving mistaken identities, convoluted complications, and jokes about the preposterous shenanigans some people will go through to part rich fools from their money. Most of the films are barely more than an hour in length and never opened in New York except as second offerings of double bills.

Bruckman's best work during the 1940s was done without credit on an Abbott and Costello feature called *In Society* (1944). The film was generally considered one of the team's best and was well received when first released, except by critics who were keeping a running count of what now seemed like ancient routines. Most of Abbott and Costello's successful bits of patter (such as "Who's On First") were refashioned versions of old burlesque classics, and the visual comedy provided by Bruckman and others provided a welcome sense of variety. For *In Society*, Bruckman employed a plot twist used in the Monty Banks film *Keep Smiling* and a gag about riding a bull backwards from *Welcome Danger*. The end result is quite funny, and the film brought in an enormous return on its B-picture budget.

But the borrowing was easy to overdo. Harold Lloyd filed suit against Universal Pictures and Clyde Bruckman for $400,000 in damages for copyright infringement when *So's Your Uncle* came on the screen with the "magician's coat" sequence from *Movie Crazy* intact. In 1947, Lloyd was finally awarded $40,000, and the Ninth United States Circuit Court of Appeals stated that "evidence is conclusive that the lifting was deliberately intended." Bruckman never worked in features again.

With the 1950s came a new medium—television. Bruckman was reunited with Keaton for *The Buster Keaton Show*, reworking old silent comedy bits, and he later worked with Abbott and Costello on their television show, adding his own favorite theme of the hopeful suitor trying to win the girl's father's approval.

But none of this work provided enough of a steady income for Bruckman to live on. The work at Columbia continued, but White's unit was winding down—making fewer pictures a year and spending less per picture. Modern, assembly-line production techniques, inimical to the informal spirit that had made the silent classics possible, made Bruckman angry. "I often wish," he told Rudi Blesh in the early 1950s, "that I were back there, with Buster and the gang, in *that* Hollywood. But I don't have the lamp to rub."

Bruckman was eventually forced to auction his prize possessions to pay rent on his Santa Monica apartment. He began to drink heavily, which led to marital difficulties with his wife Gladys and further trouble finding work. This desperate situation reached a climax in December 1954. Telling Keaton he was going on a hunting trip, Bruckman borrowed his friend's .45 automatic, and on 4 January 1955 he parked his car in a lot adjacent to a restaurant at Twentieth Street and Wilshire Boulevard in Santa Monica, walked into the men's room, and pulled the trigger.

References:

Rudi Blesh, *Keaton* (New York: Macmillan, 1966), pp. 148-156, 191-260, 268-277, 297-307, 365;

Tom Dardis, *Keaton: The Man Who Wouldn't Lie Down* (New York: Scribners, 1979);

Leonard Maltin, *The Great Movie Shorts* (New York: Crown, 1972), pp. 6-8, 156-157;

Daniel Moews, *Keaton: The Silent Features Close Up* (Berkeley: University of California Press, 1977);

Adam Reilly, *Harold Lloyd: The King of Daredevil Comedy* (London: Deutsch, 1977), pp. 86-92, 108-126, 223.

Sidney Buchman

(27 March 1902-23 August 1975)

Jay Boyer
Arizona State University

MOTION PICTURES: *Daughter of the Dragon* (Paramount, 1931), dialogue;

No One Man (Paramount, 1932), screenplay by Buchman and Agnes Brand Leahy;

Thunder Below (Paramount, 1932), screenplay by Buchman and Josephine Lovett;

The Sign of the Cross (Paramount, 1932), screenplay and dialogue by Buchman and Waldemar Young;

If I Had A Million (Paramount, 1932), screenplay by Buchman, Claude Binyon, and others;

From Hell to Heaven (Paramount, 1933), screenplay by Buchman and Percy Heath;

The Right to Romance (RKO, 1933), screenplay by Buchman and Henry McCarty;

All of Me (Paramount, 1934), screenplay by Buchman and Thomas Mitchell;

Whom the Gods Destroy (Columbia, 1934), screenplay;

His Greatest Gamble (RKO, 1934), screenplay by Buchman and Harry Hervey;

I'll Love You Always (Columbia, 1935), screenplay by Buchman and Vera Caspary;

Love Me Forever (Columbia, 1935), screenplay by Buchman and Jo Swerling;

She Married Her Boss (Columbia, 1935), screenplay;

The King Steps Out (Columbia, 1936), screenplay;

Theodora Goes Wild (Columbia, 1936), screenplay;

Adventure in Manhattan (Columbia, 1936), screenplay by Buchman, Harry Sauber, and Jack Kirkland;

The Music Goes 'Round (Columbia, 1936), screen story;

Holiday (Columbia, 1938), screenplay by Buchman and Donald Ogden Stewart;

Mr. Smith Goes to Washington (Columbia, 1939), screenplay;

The Howards of Virginia (Columbia, 1940), screenplay;

Here Comes Mr. Jordan (Columbia, 1941), screenplay by Buchman and Seton I. Miller;

The Talk of the Town (Columbia, 1942), screenplay by Buchman and Irwin Shaw;

A Song to Remember (Columbia, 1945), screenplay;

Over 21 (Columbia, 1945), screenplay;

Sidney Buchman

Jolson Sings Again (Columbia, 1949), screen story and screenplay;

Saturday's Hero (Columbia, 1951), screenplay by Buchman and Millard Lampell;

The Mark (Continental, 1961), screenplay by Buchman and Stanley Mann;

Cleopatra (20th Century-Fox, 1962), screenplay by Buchman, Joseph L. Mankiewicz, and Ranald MacDougall;

The Group (United Artists, 1966), screenplay;

La Maison sous les arbres (The House under the Trees), released in the United States as *The Deadly Trap* (National General, 1972), screenplay by Buchman and Eleanor Perry.

PLAYS: *This One Man* (New York, Morosco

61

Theatre, 21 October 1930);
Storm Song (Philadelphia, 1931).

OTHER: *Mr. Smith Goes to Washington* and *Here Comes Mr. Jordan*, by Buchman and Seton I. Miller, in *Twenty Best Film Plays*, edited by John Gassner and Dudley Nichols (New York: Crown, 1943);
Over 21, in *Best Film Plays, 1945*, edited by Gassner and Nichols (New York: Crown, 1946).

Sidney Buchman was born in Duluth, Minnesota. Following education at the University of Minnesota, Columbia, and Oxford, he traveled for a year in Europe, working for a short time as an assistant stage director at the Old Vic in London. Two of his plays were produced when he returned to New York. *This One Man* was produced on Broadway in 1930, and *Storm Song* opened in Philadelphia in 1931. Neither was well received, and he decided to try his hand at screenwriting. He left for Hollywood and joined the staff at Paramount. His first film work was writing dialogue for a Fu Manchu serial, *Daughter of the Dragon* (1931); he rose to prominence as a screenwriter by 1932 with his adaptation of Wilson Barrett's play *The Sign of the Cross* for Cecil B. De Mille.

In 1934 Buchman went to work for Harry Cohn at Columbia. It was at this studio that Buchman did much of his best screenwriting; the comedies to which he contributed between 1935 and 1942 are the films for which he is best remembered. He worked on several undistinguished films before having his first major success with *Theodora Goes Wild* (1936), taken from a Mary McCarthy story and starring Irene Dunne as a proper young New England girl who writes a racy, best-selling novel.

Theodora Goes Wild was Irene Dunne's first notable comedy; it was such a success that Harry Cohn wanted to try her in another, and he decided to film Arthur Richman's play *The Awful Truth*. Buchman worked on this film starring Dunne and Cary Grant, but his contributions were not substantial enough to earn him screen credit.

Cary Grant starred in two more of Buchman's memorable comedies from this period, *Holiday* (1938) and *The Talk of the Town* (1942). *Holiday* was adapted by Buchman and Donald Ogden Stewart from Philip Barry's play and directed by George Cukor. Grant plays a free-spirited young man engaged to a young woman whose family does not approve of him. Jilted by the woman, he winds up marrying her sister (Katharine Hepburn) instead. In *The Talk of the Town*, written by Buchman and

Cary Grant and Katharine Hepburn in a publicity shot for Holiday

Irwin Shaw, an anarchist (Grant) fleeing the police hides out in a house rented by a law professor (Ronald Colman) and tries to convince the professor that the law is not always right. Matters are complicated when both men fall in love with the woman (Jean Arthur) who owns the house.

As different as these comedies are in tone, character, and plot, they share a fundamental situation. In each, human goodness is defined in the context of a corrupt world, one filled with infidelities, hypocrisy, and injustice. Goodness always wins out in the final moments. For much of the time, though, its powers are called into question. This is perhaps most obviously the case in *Mr. Smith Goes to Washington* (1939) and *Here Comes Mr. Jordan* (1941).

The Frank Capra-Robert Riskin team had come up with a string of hits for Harry Cohn in the 1930s, and when Riskin left Columbia in 1938, Buchman was chosen to be the scenarist for the next Capra project, *Mr. Smith Goes to Washington*. Buchman had collaborated with Capra twice before without receiving credit, once on *Broadway Bill* (1934) and again on *Lost Horizon* (1937), both times successfully. Now, working from a Lewis Foster short story, "The Gentleman from Montana," Buchman locked himself into a suite at the Desert Inn in Palm Springs and turned out at breakneck pace the script which was to be made into one of Capra's finest films.

Like *Mr. Deeds Goes to Town* (for which Riskin wrote the screenplay in 1936), *Mr. Smith Goes to Washington* pits rural virtue against big-city evils. When an incumbent state senator dies, Jefferson Smith (James Stewart) is chosen to serve the last two months of his term by the corrupt politicians who want someone who will not interfere with the land fraud they have under way. Smith is energetic and more intent on doing good than anyone had foreseen; when he learns of the fraud, he refuses to cooperate. Smith is accused of buying up the land himself, and to forestall his removal from the Senate, he undertakes a filibuster, hoping to find a

public forum for his defense. Smith convinces the public, as well as a cynical government employee (Jean Arthur) of his innocence. Buchman was nominated for an Oscar for his screenplay.

Here Comes Mr. Jordan tells the story of Joe Pendleton, a prizefighter who is killed in an airplane accident. His death was a mistake—Pendleton was fated to survive the accident, but an overly zealous celestial messenger removed his soul prematurely. Pendleton's body was cremated; he needs a new one and selects that of Bruce Farnsworth, a malicious millionaire financier. Joe reverses Farnsworth's way of living, setting free a man who had been framed and imprisoned for a stock swindle and returning to small investors the money out of which they have been cheated. *Here Comes Mr. Jordan* was an enormous financial success and won Academy awards for best screenplay and best story, with nominations for best picture, best director (Alexander Hall), and best cinematography. In 1978 Warren Beatty and Buck Henry

James Stewart as Jefferson Smith in Mr. Smith Goes to Washington, *Buchman's third collaboration with director Frank Capra*

directed a remake of *Here Comes Mr. Jordan* under the title *Heaven Can Wait*.

It would be a mistake to see *Mr. Smith Goes to Washington* and *Here Comes Mr. Jordan* as prototypical of Buchman's work, and a mistake as well to find in them too many similarities. But they do share certain characteristics which seem to have contributed to their popular and critical appeal. Both films are about old-fashioned heroes, uncomplicated men who refuse to complicate the simple principles by which they live. In the best and worst senses, both men are innocents. The worlds that Smith and Pendleton enter are rotting from within, with self-interest the motivating force, and innocence in a corrupt and dangerous world is ignorance as well. Smith and Pendleton are virtuous men, but they are also slightly laughable. Smith and Pendleton are

heroic figures not because they are more virtuous than anyone else who might come fresh to corruption but rather because they refuse to succumb to it. If virtue is to triumph over evil in the worlds depicted by Buchman, then a learning process must be undergone. In both films, a woman plays a pivotal role in the education of the protagonist.

Buchman would never again create characters as memorable as Smith and Pendleton, nor would his talents ever be as impressive as they are in the comedies from 1935 to 1942. His subsequent films are often entertaining, though, and just as often skillfully written. Perhaps the best of these are his musical biographies of the 1940s—*A Song to Remember* (1945) and *Jolson Sings Again* (1949)—and one of his last films, *The Mark* (1961).

A Song to Remember, which Buchman wrote and

Robert Montgomery and Edward Everett Horton in Here Comes Mr. Jordan, *winner of Academy Awards for best original story and screenplay in 1941*

produced, is a highly fictionalized account of the life of Frédéric Chopin. Buchman traces the composer's life from childhood and his relationship with Professor Joseph Elsner, his mentor, through Chopin's flight from Poland and his arrival in Paris, where he falls in love with Madame Dudevant, better known as George Sand. Although Buchman took liberties with the truth, he succeeded in his study of the man; the film received generally positive reviews, and star Cornel Wilde was nominated for an Oscar as best actor.

Buchman had worked without credit on the 1947 film *The Jolson Story*, which follows Al Jolson's career from his Washington, D.C., boyhood through his rise in burlesque and vaudeville and finally to the pinnacle of his career and the failure of his marriage. The sequel, *Jolson Sings Again*, while not as successful as the original, is still an impressive film. Buchman produced and wrote the screenplay alone, working with essentially the same cast (Larry Parks, William Demarest, Ludwig Donath, Bill Goodwin, and Tamara Shane). He examines Jolson's despondency over his broken marriage, career collapse, and embittered retirement and portrays the entertainer's amazing comeback. Buchman was nominated for an Academy award for his screenplay.

In September 1951, Buchman was brought before the House Un-American Activities Committee and questioned about membership in the Communist party. Buchman admitted he had been a party member from 1938 to 1945. He refused "on deep principle of conscience" to name others in his party cell because he felt it "repugnant to an American to inform on his fellow citizens." When he failed to answer two additional subpoenas in January 1952, Buchman was indicted for contempt of Congress, and in 1953 he was found guilty. He was given a relatively light sentence—one year's probation and a $150 fine—but was blacklisted and unable to work.

Buchman went to Europe after his conviction, but he maintained ties with the film industry and in 1961 was hired by 20th Century-Fox as a writer and a producer. His first produced screenplay after the blacklist was *The Mark* (1961), about a child molester just released from prison and trying to lead a normal life. Other scripts followed, including *Cleopatra* (1962), *The Group* (1966), and his last, an English-language French film entitled *La Maison sous les arbres (The House under the Trees)* and released in the United States as *The Deadly Trap* (1972). In 1965 he was given the Writers Guild's highest honor, the Laurel Award, for excellence throughout his years as a writer. Sidney Buchman died of cancer in Cannes, where he had lived for a decade, on 23 August 1975.

A close inspection of Buchman's best films reveals how little they depend on plot machinations. All of these films are fantasies in their way, all at least once removed from the workaday world, as if Buchman had to distance viewers from reality in order to allow a perspective from which to study his people. This is important, for Buchman's best films are first and foremost about people. They are character studies in the most honorable and far-reaching sense of the phrase, studies of human beings and the dilemmas in which they find themselves. And while that in itself is not a formula for great scriptwriting, it may well be what all great film scripts have in common.

References:
Richard Corliss, *Talking Pictures* (Woodstock, N.Y.: Overlook Press, 1974), pp. 275-283;
Ted Sennett, *Lunatics and Lovers* (New Rochelle: Arlington House, 1973);
Bob Thomas, *King Cohn* (New York: Putnam's, 1967).

Robert Buckner
(28 May 1906-   )

John P. Driscoll
University of Washington

MOTION PICTURES: *Gold Is Where You Find It* (Warner Bros., 1937), screenplay by Buckner and Warren Duff;

Love Honor and Behave (Warner Bros., 1938), screenplay by Buckner, Clements Ripley, Michel Jacoby, and Lawrence Kimble;

Comet over Broadway (Warner Bros., 1938), screenplay by Buckner and Mark Hellinger;

The Oklahoma Kid (Warner Bros., 1938), screenplay by Buckner, Duff, and Edward E. Paramore;

Dodge City (Warner Bros., 1939), screenplay;

You Can't Get Away with Murder (Warner Bros., 1939), screenplay by Buckner, Don Ryan, and Kenneth Gamet;

Angels Wash Their Faces (Warner Bros., 1939), screenplay by Buckner, Michael Fessier, and Niven Busch;

Espionage Agent (Warner Bros., 1939), screen story;

Virginia City (Warner Bros., 1940), story and screenplay;

Knute Rockne–All American (Warner Bros., 1940), screen story and screenplay;

Sante Fe Trail (Warner Bros., 1940), screen story and screenplay;

My Love Came Back (Warner Bros., 1940), screenplay by Buckner, Ivan Goff, and Earl Baldwin;

Dive Bomber (Warner Bros., 1941), screenplay by Buckner and Frank Wead;

Yankee Doodle Dandy (Warner Bros., 1942), screen story; screenplay by Buckner and Edmund Joseph;

The Desert Song (Warner Bros., 1944), screenplay;

Confidential Agent (Warner Bros., 1945), screenplay;

Rogue's Regiment (Universal, 1948), screenplay; screen story by Buckner and Robert Florey;

Sword in the Desert (Universal, 1949), screen story and screenplay;

Deported (Universal, 1950), screenplay;

Free For All (Universal, 1950), screenplay;

Bright Victory (Universal, 1951), screenplay;

When in Rome (M-G-M, 1952), story;

The Man Behind the Gun (Warner Bros., 1953), screen story;

A Prize of Gold (Columbia, 1955), screenplay by Buckner and John Paxton;

Robert Buckner

To Paris with Love (Continental, 1955), screenplay;

Safari (Columbia, 1956), screen story;

Love Me Tender (Fox, 1957), screenplay;

Triple Deception (Rank, 1957), screenplay by Buckner and Bryan Forbes;

From Hell to Texas (Fox, 1958), screenplay by Buckner and Wendell Mayes;

Moon Pilot (Buena Vista, 1962), screenplay.

TELEVISION: *Hong Kong* (ABC, 1960-1961), creator;

Return of the Gunfighter (NBC, 1967), script adapted by Buckner from his story with Burt Kennedy.

SELECTED BOOKS: *Sigrid and the Sergeant* (New York: Appleton-Century-Crofts, 1957; London: Heinemann, 1958);

Tiger by the Tail (London: Heinemann, 1960);
Moon Pilot (New York: Pocket Books, 1961).

Robert Henry Buckner might be called both a "writer's writer" and what is referred to in film circles as an "old pro." Although his novels achieved only limited success, his short stories and screenplays were much praised. His stories were published by prestigious magazines and were often reprinted. Although the ability to turn a phrase does not guarantee the capacity to write visually, this talent, among others, enabled Buckner to write from his earliest days for top-budget pictures in one of the most successful and productive studios, Warner Bros., where he became a writer/producer. Buckner was good at feeling the public pulse; even in his best scripts he tended to write for the vast viewing public.

Buckner was born to a landowning family at Crewe, Virginia. While at the University of Virginia, where he took premed courses, he was editor of the college newspaper. After graduating in 1927, he continued his studies in medicine and science at Edinburgh University in Scotland, where he received an M.A. degree in 1928, and at the Ecole Polytechnique in Paris. While on the Continent, he contributed fiction and travel sketches to several British magazines, including *Punch*, *Pearson's*, and *Bystander*, and worked as a tour guide, English teacher, and courier for a British exporting firm.

Having given up his plans to become a doctor, Buckner went to England and wrote for the *London Daily Mail* and the *New York World*. Upon returning to the United States in 1933, he worked for several publishing firms and later entered into a business partnership with an advertising agency which specialized in financial accounts. When the Depression brought an end to this venture, Buckner returned to publicity and journalism, writing in Europe for British publications and in America for such magazines as *Harper's Bazaar*, *Cosmopolitan*, *Atlantic Monthly*, and *Redbook*. He also spent time in Abyssinia as a free-lance war correspondent. In 1937 he married Mary Duckett Doyle; they had two children, Robert, Jr., and Sharon Courtoux.

During his years on the Continent, Buckner met Cecil Brandon. This brief acquaintance and some long weeks of research in the Belgium War Office and at the Admiralty Archives in London resulted in Buckner's short story "The Man Who Won the War," based on an event from Brandon's life. Buckner submitted his story to twenty top magazines before it was finally accepted by *Atlantic Monthly*. The interest it aroused was astounding;

Atlantic Monthly had never received so much correspondence about any article or story published. *Reader's Digest* picked up the story for its April 1936 issue, and it was included in *The Best Short Stories of 1936*.

When the story was purchased by Columbia Pictures in 1936, Buckner was put under long-term contract and assigned to work on its script. Although the story never reached the screen, Buckner profited from the experience by learning about screenwriting. In 1937 he worked for Warner Bros., where his first screenplay, *Gold Is Where You Find It*, resulted in a successful film. The plot revolves around the struggles between farmers and miners in nineteenth-century California; the hero, a mine superintendent, meets the rancher's daughter and eventually comes to understand the environmental and human costs of mining.

Buckner remained at Warner Bros. until 1945, writing films for contract performers such as Errol Flynn and James Cagney. Because of the success of *Gold Is Where You Find It*, he was frequently called upon to produce fast-paced Western scripts. *The Oklahoma Kid* (1938) stars James Cagney and Humphrey Bogart, who plays the outlaw who challenges him in the old West; this was followed by *Dodge City* (1939), in which Errol Flynn portrays a man trying to bring law and order to a lawless town. Also in 1939, Buckner wrote two crime dramas, both about young men who get involved with criminals—*You Can't Get Away with Murder* and *Angels Wash Their Faces*. The fourth Western Buckner worked on, *Virginia City* (1940), was another box-office success, although critics were not impressed. The plot concerns intrigue over a gold shipment from Nevada to the Confederacy during the latter months of the Civil War and the struggle between a Union captain (Errol Flynn) and a Confederate officer (Randolph Scott).

Working from the papers provided by Knute Rockne's widow, Buckner fashioned one of his best screenplays, *Knute Rockne–All American* (1940). Buckner's screenplay closely matches real events from the coach's life with one exception—a scene depicting the inspiration for Rockne's famous backfield shift takes place in a theater. Even when faithfully following events from Rockne's life, Buckner skillfully molds scenes to flesh out the emotional power inherent in them.

Santa Fe Trail (1940), a story with Civil War overtones, is about an extended fight between Southerner Jeb Stuart and John Brown, the abolitionist. The film was criticized for its lack of perspective and its historical inaccuracies.

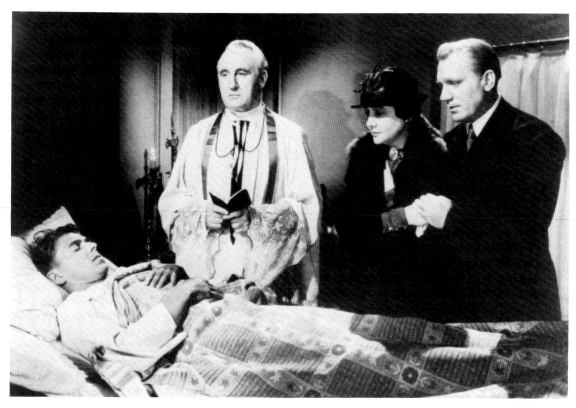

Ronald Reagan with Donald Crisp, Ruth Robinson, and Pat O'Brien in Knute Rockne—All American

Dive Bomber (1941) was beautifully timed to coincide with current events, and it was popular with both critics and the public. The title is misleading; the film is not about dive-bombing but is concerned almost entirely with the new field of aviation medicine. The story revolves around a young navy doctor's fight to prevent pilots' blackouts at the end of a power dive. Buckner and coauthor Frank Wead fashioned a screenplay around experimentation in pressure chambers, doctors forming hypotheses, and flight testing in the air.

Following the success of *Dive Bomber*, Buckner had his first opportunity to write and produce a film. *Yankee Doodle Dandy* (1942), directed by Michael Curtiz, is a musical biography based on the life and times of George M. Cohan. Cohan's colorful stage and personal life is told in flashback from a visit of the elderly Cohan to President Roosevelt's White House study and ends with Cohan's receiving a congressional medal for his patriotic song "Over There." Buckner received his only Academy Award nomination for this screenplay; the film was nominated for best picture, and James Cagney won the award as best actor for his portrayal of Cohan.

After *Yankee Doodle Dandy*, Buckner began

working more as a producer and, consequently, writing fewer screenplays. Between 1943 and 1950 he produced all his own scripts. As a producer for Warner Bros., he produced but did not write *Gentleman Jim* (1942), *Mission to Moscow* (1943), *Uncertain Glory* (1944), *God Is My Co-Pilot* (1945), *San Antonio* (1945), *Devotion* (1946), *Cheyenne* (1947), and *Life with Father* (1947).

Buckner's screenplay for *The Desert Song* (1944) was based on Sigmund Romberg's operetta; it was the third time the operetta had been filmed. Buckner's last screenplay for Warner Bros. was *Confidential Agent* (1945), based on Graham Greene's novel. In the film, an agent of Loyalist Spain goes to London in 1937 to interfere with a Fascist business deal which would have supplied needed material for the Fascist cause. The film was praised for adhering to Greene's novel.

In 1948 Buckner joined Universal Studios, where he worked under conditions different from those at Warner Bros. He produced films only from his own scripts, and those scripts reflected a new freedom from the heavy studio hand of earlier years. His first film at Universal, *Rogue's Regiment* (1948), is about the attempts of a foreign legionnaire to track down a Nazi officer. *Sword in the Desert*

(1949) depicts the flight of European refugees in World War II. *Deported* (1950) presents an American gangster involved with the Italian black market. *Free For All* (1950) is a comedy about a man who invented a synthetic gasoline.

For his last picture at Universal, Buckner won the Writers Guild Award. *Bright Victory* (1951) is a serious story about a blind veteran (Arthur Kennedy) who adjusts to life after the war. Much of the story takes place at Valley Forge Hospital, where the ex-soldier struggles past despair through a woman's love and courage. Although some critics found Buckner's script flawed because of its tilt toward conventional romance, it was generally well received.

Buckner left Universal in 1951 and in 1952 wrote the story for a light comedy, *When in Rome*, for M-G-M; he then worked on another Western for Warner Bros., *The Man Behind the Gun* (1953). In 1955, he wrote two films for the British studio Warwick, *A Prize of Gold*, about a plan to steal a shipment

of gold from a plane in Berlin, and *To Paris with Love*, a comedy about a worldly man who decides to take his son on a trip to Paris. While in England, Buckner also wrote the jungle drama *Safari* (1956) for Columbia.

Buckner returned to Westerns with *Love Me Tender* (1957), a Civil War drama that was Elvis Presley's first film. *From Hell to Texas* (1958), co-written with Wendell Mayes, was based on Charles O. Locke's highly regarded novel *The Hell-Bent Kid*, about a young man who accidentally kills a man and then must elude the posse that pursues him.

From Hell to Texas was Buckner's last produced screenplay. After his many years working in the film medium, he wanted to return to fiction writing. He worked six months on a novel, *Sigrid and the Sergeant* (1957), trying to forget the habits he had learned while writing motion pictures. Buckner did his first work for television in 1960, creating the television series *Hong Kong*. He wrote his last screenplay, *Moon Pilot*, in 1961; it was filmed by Walt Disney Produc-

James Cagney with his sister Jeanne Cagney, Joan Leslie, Walter Huston, and Rosemary DeCamp in Yankee Doodle Dandy

tions in 1962. In 1967, Buckner wrote the Western television film *Return of the Gunfighter*, which some critics praised as a return to the Hollywood Westerns of years past.

Robert Henry Buckner was a Hollywood contract writer in every sense of the term. He worked on whatever film was assigned to him without ever receiving the critical acclaim of other, better known screenwriters, but he had steady, lucrative employment and contributed to successful and popular motion pictures for over thirty years.

Borden Chase
(11 January 1900-8 March 1971)

Blake Lucas

MOTION PICTURES: *Under Pressure* (Fox, 1935), screenplay by Chase, Noel Pierce, and Lester Cole;

Blue, White and Perfect (20th Century-Fox, 1942), story;

Harrigan's Kid (M-G-M, 1943), story;

Destroyer (Columbia, 1944), screenplay by Chase, Frank Wead, and Lewis Meltzer;

The Fighting Seabees (Republic, 1944), screen story; screenplay by Chase and Aeneas MacKenzie;

This Man's Navy (M-G-M, 1945), screen story and screenplay;

Flame of the Barbary Coast (Republic, 1945), screenplay;

I've Always Loved You (Republic, 1946), story and screenplay;

Tycoon (RKO, 1947), screenplay by Chase and John Twist;

Red River (United Artists, 1948), story; screenplay by Chase and Charles Schnee;

The Man from Colorado (Columbia, 1948), screen story;

The Great Jewel Robbery (Warner Bros., 1950), screen story and screenplay;

Montana (Warner Bros., 1950), screenplay by Chase, James R. Webb, and Charles O'Neal;

Winchester '73 (Universal-International, 1950), screen story and screenplay by Chase and Robert L. Richards;

Iron Man (Universal-International, 1951), screenplay by Chase and George Zuckerman;

Lone Star (M-G-M, 1952), story and screenplay;

Bend of the River (Universal-International, 1952), screenplay;

The World in His Arms (Universal-International, 1952), screenplay;

Borden Chase

Sea Devils (RKO, 1953), screen story and screenplay;

His Majesty O'Keefe (Warner Bros., 1954), screenplay by Chase and James Hill;

Vera Cruz (United Artists, 1955), screen story;

The Far Country (Universal-International, 1955), screen story and screenplay;

Man Without a Star (Universal-International, 1955), screenplay by Chase and D. D. Beauchamp;

Backlash (Universal-International, 1956), screenplay;

Night Passage (Universal-International, 1957), screenplay;

Ride a Crooked Trail (Universal-International, 1958), screenplay;

Gunfighters of Casa Grande (M-G-M, 1965), screen story by Chase and Patricia Chase; screenplay by Chase, Patricia Chase, and Clarke Reynolds.

SELECTED BOOKS: *East River* (New York: Crowell, 1935);

Sandhog (Philadelphia: Penn Publishing, 1938);

Blazing Guns on the Chisholm Trail (New York: Random House, 1948);

Diamonds of Death (Toronto & London: Popular Publications, 1949);

Red River (London: Sampson Low, 1949).

Borden Chase played a key role in the development of the postwar Western. His efforts in that genre and his scripts for related adventure films were instrumental in establishing the ambivalent action heroes who dominated the period. He wrote important screenplays for several major directors, including King Vidor, Howard Hawks, and especially Anthony Mann. His narratives have a keen edge of moral complexity and often provide exceptional dramatic conflict between protagonist and antagonist. Although his writing has faults, notably a tendency for dialogue to state the author's moral and social position too explicitly, these faults are compensated for by his gift for narrative structure.

Chase was born Frank Fowler in Brooklyn, New York. He left school at fourteen and joined the U.S. Navy at seventeen. After leaving the navy, he worked at several jobs, including prizefighter, taxi driver, high diver in a carnival, driver of a milk wagon, construction worker, commercial diver, and shipyard worker. He even worked in the bootlegging and protection rackets before taking a job as a sandhog for the Holland Tunnel. He married his first wife, concert pianist Lee Keith, while he was working on the Eighth Avenue subway tunnels; they have a daughter, Barrie Chase (born 1934), who became an actress-dancer and made several film appearances in the 1960s. Chase has since remarried twice.

Chase's earliest writings were inspired by his experiences as a sandhog. *East River* (1935), his first novel, is about men tunneling under New York's East River; this was followed by the similar *Sandhog*

(1938), about the death of a young tunnel worker. Several years before *Sandhog* was published, Chase sold it to Fox and came to Hollywood to work on the script of the film version, *Under Pressure* (1935), changing his name to Borden Chase because he felt his own name was too colorless for a writer. *Under Pressure* is the film which most clearly expresses his personal experiences. The central conflicts which animate Chase's later work are present in embryonic form in the relationship between the film's protagonists, friends who battle one another throughout the film only to have the friendship reconfirmed by the film's end.

After working on *Under Pressure*, Chase returned to the East and became a writer of fiction which was published in such magazines as *Argosy* and the *Saturday Evening Post*. Between 1935 and 1944, six of his works were filmed, although Chase did not have anything to do with the screenplays. *Dr. Broadway*, one of the films based on a short story by Chase, was the first film directed by Anthony Mann. Chase made a brief trip to Hollywood to work on a project called "Black Gold" that was never completed, then returned for good to work on *Destroyer* (1944). Subsequent screenplays written or cowritten by Chase include *The Fighting Seabees* (1944) and *This Man's Navy* (1945).

Some Chase screenplays of the period find the writer venturing in different directions. *I've Always Loved You* (1946), a romantic melodrama with a musical background, is entirely atypical of him, although he is the sole author of both story and screenplay. *Tycoon* (1947) is a rather labored and tedious action drama centered on a mining entrepreneur. *Flame of the Barbary Coast* (1945) is more interesting, a Chase original which eloquently foreshadows the writer's major works. John Wayne plays a cattleman who becomes involved with a singer and a gambler on the Barbary Coast shortly after the turn of the century. The singer (Ann Dvorak), long the mistress of an unsavory gambler (Joseph Schildkraut), finally switches her affection to the cattleman. Both the historical aspects and interpersonal relationships of the story prefigure *Bend of the River* (1952), although *Flame of the Barbary Coast* is not in the same class.

Chase came into his own with his first Western, *Red River*, released in 1948 after long postproduction delays. Chase had written the story, published serially in the *Saturday Evening Post* as "The Blazing Guns of the Chisholm Trail," before being engaged to write the screenplay. Based on a historical incident, the opening of the Chisholm Trail, the story sets the pattern for much of the

John Wayne as Tom Dunson and Walter Brennan as Groot in Chase's first Western, Red River

writer's subsequent work, describing a journey and centering on conflict between two principal characters who have a familial relationship. When the story begins, Tom Dunson (John Wayne) is traveling with a wagon train, but he decides to strike out on his own with his faithful friend Groot (Walter Brennan). He leaves behind his fiancée Fen (Coleen Gray), and when the wagon train is attacked by Indians and she is killed, Dunson is hardened by feelings of guilt. Subsequently, he takes over a vast amount of land in Texas by fighting the Mexicans who claim title and adopts the orphan Matthew Garth (Montgomery Clift).

Most of the story takes place ten years after the adoption, when Dunson must find a way to take his cattle to market. Matthew, who has become as good with a gun as his adopted father, and gunman Cherry (John Ireland) join the drive to Missouri. The journey proves arduous, and some of the men are unwilling to keep their pledge and see it

through to the end. The obsessed Dunson is a hard taskmaster and kills several of those who attempt to desert. When Dunson refuses to accept the alternative of driving the herd to Abilene and becomes deranged in his treatment of the men, Matt stands against him. The wounded Dunson is left behind, vowing to kill Matt. For the climax of the film, Chase had planned for Dunson to die, mortally wounded by Cherry but reconciled with Matt, who refused to draw against him. However, director Howard Hawks engaged a second screenwriter, Charles Schnee, and altered this ending so that Dunson lives and eventually makes Matt an equal partner. Although problematic as a result of the differing artistic personalities of Chase and Hawks, *Red River* is one of the films most widely regarded as a classic of its genre. Chase received his only Academy Award nomination for this film, and he concentrated on the Western form in most of his subsequent screenplays.

Chase contributed the screen story for *The Man from Colorado* (1948) but did not write the screenplay. Nevertheless, this second credit on a Western is an important one, as it shows Chase intensifying the conflict between protagonist and antagonist. In this case two friends come into conflict after the Civil War, the first becoming a corrupt judge (Glenn Ford) and the second (William Holden) having to take a stand against him. Chase worked on the screenplay of *Montana* (1950), an Errol Flynn vehicle, but on this Western his presence is less compelling because other writers were involved; one of them, Western novelist Ernest Haycox, was the author of the story. Chase's only original screenplay between *Red River* and *Winchester '73* (1950) is a crime narrative, *The Great Jewel Robbery* (1950). With *Winchester '73*, Chase capitalized on the success of *Red River* with a second outstanding film in which his personality is unmistakable.

The conflict in *Winchester '73* is between two brothers, one of whom, Lin McAdam (James Stewart), must avenge the death of their father at the hands of the other. The weapon of the title is brand-new and coveted by all of the major male characters. Lin has won the rifle in a shooting contest, but his brother steals it, and it passes from hand to hand, permitting introduction into the story of incidents and characters only tangentially related to the principal conflict. Before film's end there has been a valiant stand by a small cavalry troop against warring Indians, a bank holdup, and conflict involving a frontier gambler and a psychotic outlaw. The final shoot-out between the brothers takes place high in rocky terrain, the physical environment commenting expressively on the elemental nature of the violence.

Despite the fact that *Winchester '73* was adapted from a novel by Stuart Lake and that Chase was the second of two writers to work on the screenplay, it is not difficult to discern the extent to which the narrative reflects his major concerns. The characteristic Chase film relates the story of a journey, during the course of which the paths of some characters cross and recross. Lin's pursuit of his brother easily permits Chase to accentuate the journey aspect of the narrative, and characters cross paths at several points in the story in the unexpected manner Chase favors. Fortunately, Chase found in director Anthony Mann a collaborator who pro-

Rock Hudson and John McIntire in Winchester '73

vided the harmony which was missing in *Red River*.

Winchester '73 initiated an important relationship for Chase in addition to the one with Mann. Aaron Rosenberg, the film's producer who was responsible for the involvement of both Chase and Mann, made intelligent use of both of them on many of his later A-budget Universal-International productions. Of nine films written or cowritten by Chase for that studio, only the last, *Ride a Crooked Trail* (1958), was not produced by Rosenberg. Chase's second film for Rosenberg, *Iron Man* (1951), was a prizefighting drama that does not appear to have had much significance for Chase, although personal experience had provided him with some insight into the fighter's milieu. In more familiar territory, Chase wrote an original screenplay called *Lone Star* (1952) for M-G-M. The story of statehood for Texas, it has a strong narrative focus, centering on a protagonist (Clark Gable) and a sympathetic antagonist (Broderick Crawford) in love with the same woman (Ava Gardner). Chase was not pleased with the film, saying of its director, "Vincent Sherman was the only one who destroyed a picture of mine completely."

Chase followed this experience with one of his greatest successes and finest works, *Bend of the River* (1952), for which Rosenberg reunited him with Mann and James Stewart. The story relates the opening up of Oregon territory and the resultant conflict between gold miners and farmers. Glyn McLintock (Stewart), a former raider of the Kansas-Missouri border, is leading a group of farmers to their new settlement, hoping to prove by his actions that he has reformed. He saves the life of Emerson Cole (Arthur Kennedy), another former raider, who in turn saves McLintock's life in an encounter with an Indian raiding party. For two-thirds of the film the two men remain friends, but they are ultimately separated by differences of character. Cole steals the settlers' supplies and abandons McLintock in the wilderness; in their final battle Cole and McLintock fight it out in the raging river, and the body of the defeated Cole is washed away. The settlers forgive McLintock's past, and he is fully integrated into the group.

Few Westerns possess as much physical action and intriguing character development as *Bend of the River*. The arduous journey to the settlement is only the first phase of the story. McLintock must return to Portland and fight for supplies that his group has already bought. The second journey to the settlement is marked by violent encounters, culminating in those with Cole. Cole and McLintock are alike in many ways: they have similar backgrounds, possess

similar skills, and are both attracted to the same woman. Initially, Cole is the more likable of the two men. Unlike McLintock, he is relaxed and has a sense of humor. The story turns on the crucial moral difference between the two men: Cole lets the promise of riches persuade him to abandon the settlers, while McLintock does not. The effect of Cole's becoming the villain in the last third of the film is exceptionally powerful. Obsessed with proving his moral worth, McLintock often lapses into a violent stance as chilling as that of Cole—his outlaw double—and Cole is arguably the most memorable villain in Chase's work, shaped by the writer's appreciation of the character's attractiveness and mystery.

Rosenberg next assigned Chase to adapt Rex Beach's novel for the 1952 film *The World in His Arms*. The best of three maritime adventures Chase wrote from 1952 to 1954, the film relates the story of a sea captain and sealer (Gregory Peck) who comes to San Francisco to buy Alaska and falls in love with a Russian countess (Ann Blyth). Ultimately he must sail to Sitka to rescue her from an unwanted marriage to the villain (Carl Esmond). The film reunited Chase with Raoul Walsh, who had directed *Under Pressure*. *Sea Devils* (1953), also directed by Walsh, is similarly vivid and colorful but lacks the passion and drive that characterize *The World in His Arms*. This Chase original describes the romance of a beautiful British spy (Yvonne De Carlo) and a smuggler (Rock Hudson) during the Napoleonic era. *His Majesty O'Keefe* (1954) relates the adventures of another captain (Burt Lancaster), who is thrown overboard by his mutinous crew and becomes king of the island of Yap in the Fijis after opening up the copra trade.

Lancaster's production company was responsible for Chase's next major work, *Vera Cruz* (1955). Although Chase is credited only with the screen story for this film telling of two adventurers in Mexico during the period of conflict between Maximilian and the Juaristas, its narrative structure and central characteristics call attention to the significance of his involvement. Two men, Trane (Gary Cooper) and Erin (Lancaster), transport gold for Maximilian but align themselves with the Juaristas, to whom the gold rightfully belongs. Trane is unable to betray the Juaristas and kills Erin. The similarity of the Trane-Erin relationship to that between McLintock and Cole in *Bend of the River* is striking. Again, the taciturn hero is a less colorful figure than the villain, and again the two men enter into an ambivalent friendship before coming into conflict late in the story. There are subtle differences between *Bend of the River* and *Vera Cruz*, attributable in large part to the differences between directors Anthony Mann and Robert Aldrich. *Vera Cruz* honors the traditional moral opposition of hero and villain but undercuts it at the same time. Another major commercial success and a film of continuing reputation, *Vera Cruz* confirms Chase's position as a central figure of the 1940s and 1950s whose narrative structures are adaptable to the intentions of different works which have in common the modernization of the Western form.

Chase's ability is again evident in *Man Without a Star* (1955), produced by Rosenberg and directed by King Vidor. Although less intense than *Vera Cruz* or the Mann films and more modest than *Red River*, this range-war Western is a well-constructed and highly rewarding film. The protagonist, Dempsey Rae (Kirk Douglas), is a wandering protagonist with a phobia for barbed wire. Shifting sides as the story progresses, Dempsey ends up defending the wire he hates, then rides on, the wire foregrounded in the last image to imply that he is fated to encounter it no matter where he goes. Unlike most Chase protagonists, Dempsey is not assimilated into any community. Dempsey is an eternal romantic, and he therefore occupies a special place in Chase's world. A nostalgia for open spaces combined with a consciousness of the tragic implications of this nostalgia is not unexpected in a Chase work.

In comparison *Backlash* (1956) seems less creative, overly familiar. Jim Slater (Richard Widmark) is searching for the man he believes murdered his father. It appears that his father is one of a group of five men buried in unmarked graves and that a sixth man, still alive somewhere, is responsible for the deaths of the others. Ultimately, after confrontations with several incidental antagonists, Jim discovers that the murderer he is searching for is his father. The narrative structure of the film is a reprise of that used for *Winchester '73*, with characters crossing paths until the final confrontation between hero and villain. Although Jim's response to his father's villainy is interesting, the conflict between the two men never achieves the intensity of that between the two brothers in the earlier film.

The Far Country (1955) is the quintessential Borden Chase Western. The final Rosenberg production to unite Mann, Chase, and Stewart, it crystallizes all the writer's major themes, narrative devices, and moral concerns into one elaborate, beautifully moderated adventure. The exciting story is about a journey to Alaska made by several characters, principally Jeff Webster (Stewart), a man callous in his dealings with others; his com-

panion, Ben Tatem (Walter Brennan), a garrulous old man; the villain, Gannon (John McIntire), a corrupt judge; a woman of the world, Ronda Castle (Ruth Roman), whose allegiances to both hero and villain are ambivalent; and a young Frenchwoman, Renee Vallon (Corinne Calvet), who adores Jeff and brings out his finer instincts. The story begins in Seattle, where Jeff, Ben, and Ronda board a steamboat which will take them to Skagway, the first stop on the way to the goldfields in Dawson. Jeff is taking a cattle herd north to sell and has already made enemies. On their first journey he is unjustly accused of murder. In Skagway, Gannon holds a humorous trial which results in a skeptical understanding between Jeff and himself; he frees Jeff but impounds his cattle. Jeff meets Renee, whose tomboyish ways fail to soften him. He rustles his own cattle in the night and travels north with Ronda, who is going to start a business in Dawson. Jeff sells the cattle to her instead of to the Dawson women who have been sustaining the miners with great effort. Renee has also come north with the group, and her anger over Jeff's selfishness is matched only by her frustrated affection for him. Jeff and Ben stake their claim and make a strike, but Gannon has arrived in Dawson and has been systematically stealing claims by using hired gunmen. Jeff is indifferent until he and Ben are ambushed and Ben is killed. He then assumes the social responsibility that has been thrust on him and fights it out with Gannon. Ronda also makes a choice; having aligned herself with Gannon, she steps out in front of a bullet meant for Jeff during the final gunfight. Jeff prevails, killing Gannon and his henchmen.

Chase is very insistent about the moral and social issues of this story. To some critics, the good people are too good and Jeff only becomes an admirable human being when he joins them. In contrast to Ronda, Renee is not permitted to be sexually expressive, as if this would undermine her role in the story as a young innocent. As for Jeff, his honesty and self-reliance are essentially positive qualities. From the moment he knocks an antagonist off the steamboat with a vicious swing of his saddle, he is an appealing hero. The climax, in which his actions affirm the virtues of friendship and justice, is satisfying, but it would be much less so if Jeff were an uncomplicated and selfless figure throughout the story.

Mann was also originally set to direct Stewart in *Night Passage* (1957) but withdrew and was replaced by James Neilson. Once again Chase settled for a variation on familial conflict. Grant McLaine (Stewart), troubleshooter for a railroad, must recover a payroll and shoot it out with the thieves, including his brother, the Utica Kid (Audie Murphy). Chase permits the Utica Kid to redeem himself in this story, shifting sides in the final fight and dying to save his brother.

Night Passage was Chase's last major work, followed by only two more films. Encouraged by Audie Murphy's capable performance as the Utica Kid, Chase wrote another good characterization for that actor in *Ride a Crooked Trail* (1958). Murphy plays Joe Maybe, an outlaw posing as a sheriff who develops positive relationships and lives down his past. Although the story is predictable in every way, it is competently told.

Although Chase never retired and continued to work on screenplays to the time of his death, only one of the films he wrote was produced after 1958, and that was not until 1965. When asked if his conservative political views were the reason for his inactivity during the 1960s, Chase replied, "Well, I don't think that I've forgotten how to write, but nobody seems to be interested in my writing, which is quite all right. I can dish it out, and I can take it too. I hope when I get to Spain [he was contemplating a move to Europe with his third wife] there'll be some work for me, and I think I'll like it there."

Chase's last film, *Gunfighters of Casa Grande* (1965), revived the familiar archetypes of two men who ride together until moral conflicts force them apart. Joe Daylight plans to sell Mexican cattle in the United States, and when his partner discovers that Daylight does not plan to pay the needy Mexicans from whom the cattle were obtained, he rebels. After *Gunfighters of Casa Grande*, Chase wrote another screenplay for Anthony Mann, "Sierra Trail." It was completed in 1966, but when Mann died, the project was abandoned. In 1970 Chase completed his final screenplay, "The Way It Was," an attempt to portray the old West realistically, drawn from the reminiscences of old-timers. It was never filmed, and Chase died shortly after completion of the script.

Borden Chase stamped his own vision on his screenplays. The changes of the Western landscape in films of the postwar period are unimaginable without his contributions. Working from a thorough knowledge of genre conventions, he knew how to revitalize those conventions and significantly alter them without betraying the tradition which had brought them into being.

References:
Richard Corliss, *Talking Pictures* (Woodstock, N.Y.: Overlook Press, 1974), pp. 123-129;
Jim Kitses, *Horizons West* (Bloomington & London: Indiana University Press, 1969), pp. 49-53;
Kitses, "The Rise and Fall of the American West," *Film Comment*, 6 (Winter 1970-1971): 14-21; includes interview with Chase and Chase filmography.

Delmer Daves
(24 July 1904-17 August 1977)

Jay Boyer
Arizona State University

MOTION PICTURES: *So This Is College* (M-G-M, 1929), story and screenplay by Daves and Al Boasberg;
Shipmates (M-G-M, 1931), adaptation by Daves and Lou Edelman; dialogue by Daves and Malcolm S. Boylan;
Divorce in the Family (M-G-M, 1932), story by Daves and Maurice Rapf; screenplay;
Clear All Wires (M-G-M, 1933), continuity;
No More Women (Paramount, 1934), story by Daves and Grant Leenhouts; screenplay by Daves and Lou Breslow;

Dames (Warner Bros., 1934), screenplay by Daves and Robert Lord;
Flirtation Walk (Warner Bros./First National, 1934), story by Daves and Edelman; screenplay;
Stranded (Warner Bros., 1935), adaptation and screenplay;
Page Miss Glory (Cosmopolitan/Warner Bros., 1935), screenplay by Daves and Lord;
Shipmates Forever (Warner Bros., 1935), story and screenplay;
The Petrified Forest (Warner Bros., 1936), screenplay by Daves and Charles Kenyon;

Delmer Daves

The Go-Getter (Warner Bros., 1937), screenplay;

The Singing Marine (Warner Bros., 1937), screen story and screenplay;

She Married An Artist (Columbia, 1937), screenplay by Daves and Gladys Lehman;

Professor Beware (Paramount, 1938), screenplay;

Love Affair (RKO, 1939), screenplay by Daves and Donald Ogden Stewart; filmed again as *An Affair to Remember* (20th Century-Fox, 1957), screenplay by Daves and Leo McCarey;

$1,000 a Touchdown (Paramount, 1939), screen story and screenplay;

The Farmer's Daughter (Paramount, 1940), story;

Safari (Paramount, 1940), screenplay;

Unexpected Uncle (RKO, 1941), screenplay by Daves and Noel Langley;

The Night of January 16th (Paramount, 1941), screenplay by Daves, Robert Pirosh, and Eve Greene;

You Were Never Lovelier (Columbia, 1942), screenplay by Daves, Michael Fessier, and Ernest Pagano;

Destination Tokyo (Warner Bros., 1943), screenplay by Daves and Albert Maltz;

Stage Door Canteen (United Artists, 1943), screen story and screenplay;

The Very Thought of You (Warner Bros., 1944), screenplay by Daves and Alvah Bessie;

Hollywood Canteen (Warner Bros., 1944), screen story and screenplay;

The Red House (United Artists, 1947), screenplay;

Dark Passage (Warner Bros., 1947), screenplay;

Task Force (Warner Bros., 1949), screen story and screenplay;

Bird of Paradise (20th Century-Fox, 1951), screen story and screenplay;

Treasure of the Golden Condor (20th Century-Fox, 1953), screenplay;

Drum Beat (Warner Bros., 1954), screen story and screenplay;

White Feather (20th Century-Fox, 1955), screenplay by Daves and Leo Townsend;

Jubal (Columbia, 1956), screenplay by Daves and Russell S. Hughes;

The Last Wagon (20th Century-Fox, 1956), screenplay by Daves, James Edward Grant, and Gwen Bagni Gielgud;

A Summer Place (Warner Bros., 1959), screenplay;

Parrish (Warner Bros., 1961), screenplay;

Susan Slade (Warner Bros., 1961), screenplay;

Rome Adventure (Warner Bros., 1962), screenplay;

Spencer's Mountain (Warner Bros., 1963), screenplay;

Youngblood Hawke (Warner Bros., 1964), screenplay;

The Battle of the Villa Fiorita (Warner Bros., 1965), screenplay.

Delmer Daves was born in San Francisco, California. Raised in Los Angeles, he graduated from Polytechnic High School, studied engineering at Stanford University, and took a law degree at Stanford in 1927. Daves first drew attention to his writing at age eleven, marking up hymnals in a Los Angeles church by reproducing the Gothic print he found there. He put his fascination with calligraphy and his talent for reproduction to more positive use while a university student. He paid his tuition and expenses—some ten thousand dollars in all—by teaching lettering and drawing, working as a draftsman for the city of Palo Alto, and designing bookplates and children's greeting cards. In addition to supporting himself and pursuing his studies, Daves found time to participate in dramatic shows on campus. He was not unfamiliar with theatrical productions, having made his movie debut as an extra at age ten. He worked occasionally in films for the next dozen years, but it was not until he was twenty-three that Daves actively sought a career in the film industry. After receiving his law degree, he returned to Los Angeles. Carrying a letter of introduction from a Stanford friend, he approached director/producer James Cruze, who was working on the film *The Covered Wagon*. Cruze hired Daves as an assistant property man. Daves went to M-G-M a year later. While working there in the property department, he was offered a job as an actor and technical adviser on a collegiate film, *The Duke Steps Out* (1929).

Director Sam Wood hired Daves as a technical adviser on a similar project, *So This Is College* (1929). This was to be the inadvertent beginning of Daves's screenwriting career. In order to get the job, Daves had to submit twenty pages of ideas. In addition to the suggestions he submitted, he wrote a part for himself, thereby increasing his salary and so impressing Wood with his authorial ability that he was made a member of the studio's writing staff. After working for five years without a vacation, Daves put his Hollywood career aside temporarily in 1933, boarded a freighter for Europe, and toured the Continent by bicycle for a year. After returning to this country in 1934, he went to work as a screenwriter for Warner Bros.

Working first with Cruze's gradually failing production company, then for M-G-M and Warner Bros., Daves learned that movies were a commercial product necessarily crafted within the limitations of technical facilities, time, and budget. A good film was one that showed a profit; a good script, one that gave the public the story they wanted. His early scripts, those written between 1929 and 1935, reflect this awareness. They risk little and remain faithful to tried-and-true conventions, primarily those of the romance genre, even when the romances are thinly disguised by the addition of music, comedy, or popular settings and situations.

The most entertaining of Daves's scripts from this period are the Dick Powell-Ruby Keeler vehicles, *Dames* (1934), *Flirtation Walk* (1934), and *Shipmates Forever* (1935). Their general dramatic pattern takes the protagonist from adolescence to adulthood. The protagonist undergoes a series of trials and thereby proves himself an adult, earning maturity through learning or by deed. There are clear delineations of hero and villain in these films. Similarly, there is no confusion about the outcome of the dilemmas they face—the good triumphs over the evil, but only after overcoming the obligatory plot complications.

The scripts on which Daves worked from 1936 to 1954, more than twenty in all, are more diverse in tone, plot, and character than those of his apprenticeship. They risk more, and despite the faults one may find with them, they are generally better written. These films include mysteries and gangster films, *The Night of January 16th* (1941), *The Red House* (1947), *Dark Passage* (1947); adventure films, *The Go-Getter* (1937), *Safari* (1940), *Treasure of the Golden Condor* (1953); theatricals and musicals, *The Singing Marine* (1937), *The Farmer's Daughter* (1940), *You Were Never Lovelier* (1942), *Stage Door Canteen* (1943), *Hollywood Canteen* (1944); romances, *She Married An Artist* (1937), *Love Affair* (1939), *The Very Thought of You* (1944), *Bird of Paradise* (1951); comedies, *Professor Beware* (1938), *$1,000 a Touchdown* (1939), *Unexpected Uncle* (1941); and war movies, *Destination Tokyo* (1943), *Task Force* (1949). These films vary in quality, and sometimes their plots are even more unlikely that those of Daves's apprenticeship movies. But these scripts are generally better written than his earlier work insofar as they look more closely and intelligently at their characters.

This attention to character is particularly evident in such films as *The Petrified Forest* (1936), *Love Affair*, and *Dark Passage*, which represent Daves's best work of this period. The protagonists of these films have several things in common. They are men approaching middle age who undergo change after meeting a woman of kindred spirit. For much of their lives, these protagonists have not been masters of their own fate. Like the women with whom they fall in love, they have been pulled along by forces—familial, judicial, circumstantial—beyond their control. Suddenly they find themselves in situations in which they must take charge of their own destinies, and in doing so they redefine who they are and what they want.

The Petrified Forest, directed by Archie Mayo and adapted from Robert E. Sherwood's Broadway hit by Daves and Charles Kenyon, is fundamentally a study of two people. Alan Squier (Leslie Howard), an ineffectual and failed writer in search of a purpose to his life, wanders into the Black Mesa Bar-B-Q, a seedy restaurant on the edge of the Arizona desert. There he meets Gaby Maple (Bette Davis), a waitress who reads Villon and dreams of going to France to paint. Fleeing from the law, Duke Mantee (Humphrey Bogart) and his gang hide out in the restaurant on their way to Mexico. Having fallen in love with Gaby, Squier makes her the beneficiary of his life insurance policy and asks Mantee to promise to kill him so that Gaby may have the money to go to Paris. Before being shot by the sheriff's posse, Mantee kills Squier.

In the comic, bittersweet *Love Affair*, co-scripted by Daves and Donald Ogden Stewart and directed by Leo McCarey, Daves once again depicts

Humphrey Bogart (far right) accosts a group of travelers in The Petrified Forest. *His henchman (far left) is played by Joe Sawyer; his victims (left to right) are Leslie Howard, Genevieve Tobin, Henry Kolker, and John Alexander.*

two strangers who fall in love and subsequently must take charge of their lives. Michael Marnay (Charles Boyer) and Terry McKay (Irene Dunne) meet on a ship sailing from Europe to New York. Both intend to marry for money and are traveling to meet their wealthy fiancés, but they fall in love with each other. To ensure that they will not throw away the fortunes that await them for a momentary infatuation, they agree to postpone their respective marriage plans and stay apart for six months; if they are still in love at that time, they will reunite. On the night they are to meet, Terry is crippled by an auto accident; rather than chain Michael to an invalid, she lets him think she has changed her mind about marrying him. Michael finally finds Terry, and at the film's end they declare their love for each other.

Both *The Petrified Forest* and *Love Affair* sacrifice plot in favor of investigating the characters and the changes they undergo. Perhaps Daves's most improbable plotting—and most intense character study—of this period is to be found in *Dark Passage*, directed and scripted by Daves from a novel by David Goodis. *Dark Passage* is the story of

Vincent Parry (Humphrey Bogart), an innocent man sent to prison for the murder of his wife. When he escapes to try to find her killer, he is befriended, hidden, then aided in his search by Irene Jansen (Lauren Bacall), a young woman whose father was also imprisoned for a crime he did not commit. To ensure that he can go about his search freely, Parry undergoes plastic surgery. He discovers his wife's murderer, and goes off to live in South America with Irene, having proved his innocence to her if not to the authorities.

In 1943 Daves began working as a director as well as a screenwriter. Beginning with *Destination Tokyo* he directed his own scripts with the exception of *Stage Door Canteen, White Feather* (1955), and *An Affair to Remember* (1957). He directed but did not write *Pride of the Marines* (1945), *To the Victor* (1948), *A Kiss in the Dark* (1948), *Broken Arrow* (1950), *Return of the Texan* (1952), *3:10 to Yuma* (1957), *Cowboy* (1958), *Kings Go Forth* (1958), *The Badlanders* (1958), and *The Hanging Tree* (1959). He also produced all his films beginning with *A Summer Place* (1959).

The best of Daves's scripts are his Westerns of

Charles Boyer and Irene Dunne in Love Affair

the mid-1950s—*Drum Beat* (1954), *White Feather*, *Jubal* (1956), and *The Last Wagon* (1956)—in which plot, character, and theme complement one another gracefully. These films are generally set in the last quarter of the nineteenth century, when a rugged frontier was gradually giving way to modern America. The action tends to take place both in an outpost community and on the open range. The protagonists are frequently men caught between nineteenth- and twentieth-century values and, consequently, between a private code of honor and a code premised on the good of the community. Right and wrong are not easily distinguished in these films, and most of the stereotypes of the Western are blurred in favor of moral and personal ambiguities. Daves may well have felt direct ties with Americans of this era: his grandmother was born in California two months after her family had come West by covered wagon, and his grandfather served

in the Union army and became one of the first Pony Express riders.

Daves drew much of the background material for his screenplay *Drum Beat* from nineteenth-century accounts of the Modoc War. The film is plotted around the conflict between two men of equal strength and purpose—Indian fighter Johnny Mackay (Alan Ladd) and Modoc leader Captain Jack (Charles Bronson). Mackay has been ordered to stop Indian raids on white settlers and the cavalry, but Captain Jack realizes the white men intend to take over the Modoc land, and he continues to fight, preferring annihilation to subjugation. The film focuses on the relationship that develops between these two men, both brave warriors who adhere to a code of honor.

In *White Feather*, the Indian is again portrayed with dignity, and his conquerors find their victory to be both sad and distasteful. *White Feather* recounts

---

the months of the Cheyenne's struggle against the U.S. Cavalry in Wyoming territory. The drama is realized through the sensibility of a man with ties to both the white and Indian worlds, Josh Tanner, a white surveyor who has married an Indian and feels caught between the end of one era and the beginning of the other.

Daves transplanted the plot line of Shakespeare's *Othello* to the mountain ranges of the Wyoming-Montana border in *Jubal*, the story of Shep Horgan (Ernest Borgnine), the owner of a cattle ranch; Mae Horgan (Valerie French), his bored wife who has attracted the attentions of a ranch hand, Pinky (Rod Steiger); and Jubal Troop (Glenn Ford), the new ranch foreman. When Mae shows an interest in Jubal, who refuses her advances, Pinky convinces Shep that Jubal is sleeping with his wife. Shep tries to take revenge, and Jubal kills him in self-defense. When Pinky organizes a lynch mob to kill Jubal, Mae comes to his defense, and Pinky is destroyed. Daves is less concerned here with what his characters do than he is with why they do it, and consequently the film is more complex than a synopsis would indicate; it is a tight study of good and evil and their effects on human relationships.

Evil is of concern to Daves once again in *The Last Wagon*. Collaborating on the script with James Edward Grant and Gwen Bagni Gielgud, Daves uses a familiar revenge plot to develop a context in which an evil deed is to be understood and judged. Comanche Todd (Richard Widmark), a white man raised by Indians, sets out to track down the Harper brothers, the murderers of his Indian wife and children. He kills them all but one, the sheriff Bull Harper, who captures him. Todd and Harper join a wagon train that is attacked by Indians; the survivors of the attack are able to make it back to civilization thanks largely to Todd's skills. At his trial Todd argues successfully that the territory is only sparsely settled and that frontier justice has not yet been superceded fully by the civilian law; furthermore, the lives he has saved must be weighed against those he has taken. There are two standards that must be understood, one in the light of the other.

Daves went on to direct a few more memorable Westerns from 1956 to 1959 (*3:10 to Yuma, The Hanging Tree, Cowboy*), but his only script, *An Affair to Remember*, a remake of *Love Affair*, suggests that Daves's authorial talents had begun to wane. The script, on which he collaborated with Leo McCarey (who directed both versions), is little more than a

fair update of the original.

From 1959 to 1965 Daves worked primarily on melodramatic romances such as *A Summer Place* (1959), *Parrish* (1961), and *Rome Adventure* (1962). Several writers had tried to come up with a workable screenplay from Sloan Wilson's novel *A Summer Place*. Not even Wilson himself was able to produce a version which pleased Jack Warner, so Warner offered Daves the job, allowing him to direct and produce the film as well. While not a critical success, the film showed sufficient profit so that Daves was offered Mildred Savage's novel *Parrish* (Joshua Logan had been working on this project for more than a year). *Parrish* proved profitable, enough so that Daves received offers to write other similar scripts. The best of his last films, *Spencer's Mountain* (1963), is quite different from the romances. Based on Earl Hamner, Jr.'s autobiographical novel — which was also the basis for the television series *The Waltons* — the film explores the changes in the lives of a poor mountain family when the oldest child decides to go to college.

In the United States, Daves has been noted only in passing by film scholars, but in Europe, particularly France and Germany, he has been counted among the most important of Hollywood auteurs. He was given an "hommage" in Paris by *Cinémathèque Française*, and his films were honored in a retrospective at the Oberhausen Film Festival in Germany in 1972. In America, his Western films earned him a special trustee's award from the Western Heritage Association, and he was elected to the National Cowboy Hall of Fame. Daves served as the Regents' Lecturer at the University of California at San Diego, and in 1976 he was made an honorary member of Delta Kappa Alpha, the University of Southern California's film fraternity.

Delmer Daves died from a heart condition in 1977 in La Jolla, California. He was survived by his wife, the former actress Mary Lawrence, whom he had married in 1938, and their three children.

To appreciate a Delmer Daves film is to take his strengths and weaknesses in stride. If his scripts seem old-fashioned or overwritten, it is because they are first of all narratives that often depend on their own peculiar internal definitions. They seek an emotional response before an intellectual one. And if these faults contribute sometimes to the film's failures as cinematic art, these absurdities of plot or character are also responsible for taking us out of our own lives and problems for a time. Delmer Daves is, in short, responsible for giving viewers films in the best and worst Hollywood traditions.

References:

Richard Corliss, ed., *The Hollywood Screenwriters* (New York: Avon, 1972), pp. 251-253;

Corliss, *Talking Pictures* (Woodstock, N.Y.: Overlook Press, 1974), pp. 307-313;

Charles Higham, *Warner Brothers* (New York: Scribners, 1975), pp. 105, 133, 150-151;

William R. Meyer, *Warner Brothers Directors* (New Rochelle, N.Y.: Arlington, 1978), pp. 109-116;

Andrew Sarris, *The American Cinema* (New York: Dutton, 1968), pp. 176-177;

Richard Whitehall, "On the 3:10 to Yuma — Delmer Daves," *Films and Filming*, 8 (May 1963): 48-51;

Whitehall, "A Summer Place," *Films and Filming*, 7 (April 1963): 50-54.

I. A. L. Diamond

(27 June 1920-   )

Sam Frank

MOTION PICTURES: *Murder in the Blue Room* (Universal, 1944), screenplay by Diamond and Stanley Davis;

Never Say Goodbye (Warner Bros., 1946), screenplay by Diamond and James V. Kern;

Two Guys from Milwaukee (Warner Bros., 1946), screenplay by Diamond and Charles Hoffman;

Love and Learn (Warner Bros., 1946), screenplay by Diamond, Eugene Conrad, and Francis Swann;

Romance on the High Seas (Warner Bros., 1948), additional dialogue;

Always Together (Warner Bros., 1948), screenplay by Diamond, Phoebe Ephron, and Henry Ephron;

Two Guys from Texas (Warner Bros., 1948), screenplay by Diamond and Allen Boretz;

It's a Great Feeling (Warner Bros., 1949), screen story;

The Girl From Jones Beach (Warner Bros., 1949), screenplay;

Love Nest (20th Century-Fox, 1951), screenplay;

Let's Make It Legal (20th Century-Fox, 1951), screenplay by Diamond and F. Hugh Herbert;

Monkey Business (20th Century-Fox, 1952), screenplay by Diamond, Ben Hecht, and Charles Lederer;

Something for the Birds (20th Century-Fox, 1952), screenplay by Diamond and Boris Ingster;

That Certain Feeling (Paramount, 1956), screenplay by Diamond, Norman Panama, Melvin Frank, and William Altman;

Love in the Afternoon (Allied Artists, 1957), screenplay by Diamond and Billy Wilder;

Merry Andrew (M-G-M, 1958), screenplay by Diamond and Isobel Lennart;

Some Like It Hot (United Artists, 1959), screenplay by Diamond and Wilder;

The Apartment (United Artists, 1960), screenplay by Diamond and Wilder;

One, Two, Three (United Artists, 1961), screenplay by Diamond and Wilder;

Irma La Douce (United Artists, 1963), screenplay by Diamond and Wilder;

Kiss Me, Stupid (United Artists, 1964), screenplay by Diamond and Wilder;

The Fortune Cookie (United Artists, 1966), screen story and screenplay by Diamond and Wilder;

Cactus Flower (Columbia, 1969), screenplay;

The Private Life of Sherlock Holmes (United Artists, 1970), screenplay by Diamond and Wilder;

Avanti! (United Artists, 1972), screenplay by Diamond and Wilder;

The Front Page (Universal, 1974), screenplay by Diamond and Wilder;

Fedora (United Artists, 1978), screenplay by Diamond and Wilder;

Buddy Buddy (M-G-M / United Artists, 1981), screenplay by Diamond and Wilder.

BOOKS: *Some Like It Hot*, by Diamond and Billy Wilder (New York: New American Library, 1959);

Irma La Douce, by Diamond and Wilder (New York: Midwood-Tower, 1963);

The Apartment and The Fortune Cookie, by Diamond and Wilder (New York: Praeger, 1971).

I. A. L. Diamond (right) with Billy Wilder on the set of their 1970 film The Private Life of Sherlock Holmes

Unlike some screenwriters who feel they do not receive adequate recognition for their work, I. A. L. Diamond prefers to remain in the shadow of his cowriter, director Billy Wilder. Diamond is a talented man who deserves recognition, having helped to create such films as *Love in the Afternoon* (1957), *Some Like It Hot* (1959), and *The Apartment* (1960).

Diamond was born Itek Domnici in Ungheni, Rumania. The family name became Diamond when the Domnicis immigrated to New York in 1929, settling in the Crown Heights section of Brooklyn. Diamond's first name was changed early on to Isadore by a grammar-school teacher who did not like

saying Itek. When asked his name today, he replies "Iz" or "Isadore." His teens were spent at Boys' High School in Brooklyn, where he became a mathematics wizard. He parlayed this talent into championships in New York, New Jersey, and Connecticut in 1936 and 1937. By the time he entered Columbia University in 1938, he had won seventeen gold medals and a gold cup for scholarship.

Though his majors at Columbia were math and physics, Diamond spent a great deal of time writing, especially in a comic vein. His favorite modes of writing at Columbia were sketches and lyrics for musical revues, prepared in tandem with budding composer Lee Wainer. They also turned out weekly revues during summers in the Catskills and the Berkshires. Eventually Diamond changed majors, planning to become a journalist, and began writing for the Columbia *Spectator*. The *Spectator*'s editors liked his manuscripts but not his first name. Though they themselves were Jewish, they wanted by-lines that did not sound Jewish, so they changed Isadore to Ian. Diamond rebelled at this, doing away with the name problem altogether with a private form of irony—he adopted the initials of the Interscholastic Algebra League, for which he had been a teenage champion.

He was planning to attend the Columbia School of Journalism when a story about him and Wainer appeared in the *New York Times* shortly before his graduation from college in 1941. The article pointed out that he and Wainer were the only people in Columbia's history to have written four varsity musicals. This news brought Diamond a ten-week contract offer from Paramount to become a junior writer. He quickly accepted, believing that he would be a failure in Hollywood and that by summer's end he would be attending courses at the School of Journalism. He ended up staying at Paramount for eighteen months, at a steadily increasing salary. Ironically, none of the scripts he wrote in the 1940s for that studio were produced.

In 1943 Diamond left Paramount to free-lance. His first produced script was for a minor Universal horror-musical, *Murder in the Blue Room* (1944), cowritten with Stanley Davis. After the war, he signed with Warner Bros., where he worked on eight forgettable musicals and comedies, always in conjunction with other writers. Among them were *Never Say Goodbye* (1946) with Errol Flynn, and several Jack Carson-Dennis Morgan vehicles, including *Two Guys from Milwaukee* (1946) and *Two Guys from Texas* (1948). Diamond would rather forget these films and all the others he wrote prior to teaming with Wilder because he had no control over the scripts. They were always the end result of committee writing and were spoiled further, he felt, by producers and other executives.

Before moving to Warner Bros., Diamond met and married novelist and screenwriter Barbara Bentley in 1945. She describes her husband as "withdrawn, and anything but gregarious. His friends are almost all old friends and all in his field or allied fields. He is constitutionally not able to stay away from work. When we are on vacation, he may rest the first two days. Then he begins writing poetry, then a sketch. I was married to him for ten years before I noticed that, when I was talking, no one was answering."

In 1951 Diamond signed with 20th Century-Fox, where he cowrote four screenplays, only one of which is notable: *Monkey Business* (1952), which starred Cary Grant and Ginger Rogers and was directed by Howard Hawks. Diamond collaborated with Ben Hecht and Charles Lederer on this film about a scientist who discovers a youth serum and tries it out on himself and others, with hilarious results. The reviews were favorable, audiences liked the film, and it made money. Of Diamond's other collaborative scripts for Fox, one, a political comedy called *Something for the Birds* (1952), had an intriguing idea that was ultimately pasteurized. Victor Mature plays a lobbyist who locks horns with civic-minded Patricia Neal over the issue of federally funded bird sanctuaries. Unfortunately, what could have been a sharp satire degenerates into a clichéd romantic muddle. After completing his obligations to Fox, Diamond free-lanced again, writing a Bob Hope comedy, *That Certain Feeling* (1956), with Melvin Frank, Norman Panama, and William Altman for Paramount.

In 1955 Diamond met Billy Wilder at a Writers Guild dinner. Wilder was impressed with Diamond's skits for the affair and approached him about cowriting a movie. Wilder had worked with several screenwriters after he broke up his partnership with Charles Brackett in 1950 but had not been able to find someone compatible enough to collaborate with on a regular basis. Though their temperaments were dissimilar—Diamond was an introvert while Wilder was an extrovert—they found they shared a common immigrant background and the same sense of humor.

Their first film was *Love in the Afternoon* (1957), a charming throwback to the romantic comedies of Ernst Lubitsch, of whom Wilder had been a protégé. It concerns the virgin daughter (Audrey Hepburn) of a Parisian private detective (Maurice Chevalier) and her fantasies about the men—mainly adulterers—her father investigates, particularly a middle-aged playboy businessman (Gary Cooper). *Love in the Afternoon* has many fine elements, among which are a smoothly witty and sentimental screenplay and a pace that is leisurely without making the film seem overlong. But it was not a financial success when first released because audiences could not accept the fifty-six-year-old Cooper making love to a teenager. Despite its commercial failure, *Love in the Afternoon* is a satisfying, richly textured film that won the Writers Guild Award for 1957.

In its sentimental way *Love in the Afternoon* helped set the tone for future Diamond-Wilder collaborations. All of their scripts deal, in one way or another, with sex, money, or power and how they are employed, particularly by Americans, both for constructive and destructive purposes. Whereas the Brackett-Wilder screenplays are ultimately senti- mental, the sexual tone of the Diamond-Wilder scripts is increasingly tough and cynical, reflecting the changing values of a later era. The Diamond- Wilder formula began with *Some Like It Hot* and culminated with *The Fortune Cookie* (1966). This formula is usually applied to ambitious middle-class American men (often played by Jack Lemmon) who compromise their integrity for material and sexual gains. With each new movie, Wilder and Diamond would go a few steps further in showing the extent to which the American middle-class privately con- dones, and even applauds, corrupt behavior.

Some Like It Hot is perhaps their best script in this vein. Set in Chicago and Miami during the Roaring Twenties, it concerns Jerry and Joe (Jack Lemmon and Tony Curtis), two unemployed jazz

Tony Curtis and Jack Lemmon in Some Like It Hot, *for which Diamond and Wilder won their second Writers Guild Award*

musicians who accidentally witness the St. Valen- tine's Day Massacre and go on the lam to escape being rubbed out. They end up dressing in women's clothes in order to hide out in an all-female jazz band. En route to Miami, they fall in love with a singer named Sugar Kane (Marilyn Monroe). In Miami, Jerry is pursued by a lecherous but rich widower, Osgood Fielding (Joe E. Brown), while Joe, in the guise of a wealthy bachelor, pursues Sugar. In the end, the gangsters are caught and the musicians reveal themselves to their sweethearts. The topper comes when Jerry tells the rich widower he is a man and Fielding coolly replies, "Well, no- body's perfect." (The credit for this famous last line goes to Diamond.) *Some Like It Hot* was a great finan- cial success and firmly established Diamond and Wilder as one of Hollywood's hottest writing teams. It was nominated for an Academy Award for Best Screenplay, and it won Diamond and Wilder a sec- ond Writers Guild award.

With the exception of *Cactus Flower* (1969), all of Diamond's scripts beginning with *Some Like It Hot* have been written in collaboration with Wilder. The nature of that collaboration was described in a 1963 *New York Times* article by Murray Schumach:

> In their office . . . they spend most of their time talking about a script. Diamond estimates that for every week of talk about each script, they get one hour of typing. Each of the writers has the capacity for retaining lines and scenes in his head until it is time to type.
>
> Then, with Diamond at the typewriter and Wilder prowling about the office or apartment, sometimes swinging a light cane, the script begins to take shape. . . . Anyone familiar with the Wilder-Diamond pattern can tell what stage of the script they are on by their hours. When they begin, their office hours are from 10 a.m. to about 5 p.m. Then, as the script progresses, the hours are stretched from 9 to 6. . . . No script is ever finished before the shooting begins. What is not generally realized in Hollywood is that, during the writing sessions, Diamond as well as Wilder plans a good deal of the direction.

As for who contributes what to each screenplay, the evidence at hand suggests that Wilder conjures up the premise and structure and that both toss in their share of witty lines. Though this is the same method of collaboration Wilder had used with Brackett, Diamond had a more pronounced influence on the films because, according to film historian Steve

Jack Lemmon and Shirley MacLaine in The Apartment, *winner of Academy Awards for best screenplay, best director (Wilder), and best picture*

Seidman, "he had more in common personally with Wilder than did Brackett. He was an immigrant from Europe, though he arrived in this country as a boy and knew more English by the time he got to Hollywood than did Wilder. He also shares Wilder's enthusiasm for bridge, old movies, and liberal politics, as well as his chain-smoking habit."

Wilder and Diamond followed *Some Like It Hot* with *The Apartment* (1960), an incisive look at sexual mores in the world of American business. A young accountant (Jack Lemmon) lends his apartment to his superiors for sex with their mistresses; they reward him with a series of promotions. When he falls in love with his boss's mistress (Shirley MacLaine), who has tried to commit suicide in the apartment, he has pangs of conscience and finally resigns after telling off his boss. With *The Apartment*, Diamond and Wilder again had a critical and financial success. They won the Academy Award, the New York Film Critics Award, and the Writers Guild Award for their screenplay; the film won the Academy Award for Best Picture and Wilder won for best director.

Their next film, *One, Two, Three* (1961) was a bawdy farce in the manner of *Some Like It Hot*, though more frenetically paced and certainly more topical. The jokes are taken from headlines of the time; the Berlin Wall, Russian-American relations, the internationality of Coca-Cola, and Communist duplicity are all satirized in this story of a Coca-Cola executive (James Cagney) in West Berlin during the Cold War. Cagney also spoofed his own screen image, at one point threatening a Communist with a grapefruit. *One, Two, Three* is a sharply witty, brightly farcical film; however, upon its release the film was attacked by critics as being un-American and avoided by audiences.

To regain public favor, Wilder and Diamond adapted the stage musical *Irma La Douce* (1963), sans music. They also changed the focus from the title character, a prostitute (Shirley MacLaine), to her pimp (Jack Lemmon). As in the previous films, ethics tangle with sex and money. Lemmon is a Paris cop who has the misfortune to fall in love with Irma, so much so that he ends up moonlighting as a laborer in a butchery so he can impersonate a wealthy

British gentleman and claim her services full-time. There are two ironies here: he is her pimp by day, having been fired from the police force following an unjust accusation of graft, and he does not realize that Irma loves him enough to give up her street life, if only he would ask.

Diamond and Wilder followed *Irma La Douce* with *Kiss Me, Stupid* (1964), in which extramarital sex is used for the purpose of social advancement. Orville J. Spooner is a novice songwriter (Ray Walston) in the town of Climax, Nevada. Trying to impress a famous singer (Dean Martin) and get a tune on the charts, Spooner hires a waitress (Kim Novak) to pose as his wife and sleep with the singer. The plan works until Spooner becomes jealous of the waitress and sleeps with her himself. Ironically, Spooner's real wife makes love to the singer that same night, extracting a promise that he will use one of her husband's songs. *Kiss Me, Stupid* was condemned as smutty, vulgar, cheap, and distasteful. United Artists refused to distribute it, passing the film on to a subsidiary releasing company. The controversy surrounding the film caused Billy Wilder's popularity to go into an enormous decline.

Diamond and Wilder returned in 1966 with *The Fortune Cookie*, their ultimate statement about crooked ethics and material corruption. When tele-vision cameraman Harry Hinkle (Jack Lemmon) is knocked down during a Cleveland Browns football game, his shyster brother-in-law (Walter Matthau) persuades him to sue CBS, the Browns, and the Cleveland stadium for $250,000. Hinkle becomes friends with the player who "injured" him and begins to have doubts about the con; meanwhile, an insurance investigator tries to prove that both Hinkle and his brother-in-law are phonies. Despite critical acclaim, Academy Award and Writers Guild nominations for the screenplay, and an Oscar for Matthau, the film did only moderately well at the box office. Consequently, it would be four years before Wilder made another movie. In the interim, Diamond busied himself with an adaptation of Abe Burrows's play *Cactus Flower*, about an amorous dentist (Walter Matthau) who lusts after a vivacious dumb blonde (Goldie Hawn, who won an Oscar), not realizing his nurse (Ingrid Bergman) is in love with him.

Diamond's next film, *The Private Life of Sherlock Holmes* (1970), was plagued with problems during production. Billy Wilder, who had long wanted to make a film about the detective, had planned an elaborate project to star Peter Sellers and Peter O'Toole. When they both withdrew, Wilder was left with no stars, script, or financing for his film. Since

Jack Lemmon and Walter Matthau in The Fortune Cookie. *Matthau won an Oscar for his portrayal of an ambulance chaser in this 1966 film.*

Diamond was working on *Cactus Flower* when Wilder began the script for *The Private Life of Sherlock Holmes*, he was unavailable at the time, and Wilder used other collaborators on drafts that proved unsatisfactory before calling on Diamond in desperation. By then, Diamond was free of other commitments and rejoined Wilder as a collaborator. They contrived a story in which Holmes aids a Belgian woman whose missing husband is an engineer for a top-secret government project. The film was about to be released as a three-hour road-show movie when it became clear that the public was staying away in droves from these expensive flops, so United Artists panicked and cut the film to 125 minutes, purportedly deleting some of the best scenes. Critical and public reactions were mixed, and the film quickly disappeared from theaters; it has since developed a cult following, particularly among Holmes buffs.

Avanti! (1972) fared better, though it too suffered the critics' disdain and poor distribution. It concerns an American businessman (Jack Lemmon) who goes to claim the body of his father, killed while on vacation in Italy. He meets the daughter of his father's mistress (Juliet Mills), and they too fall in love, finally agreeing to meet once a year, just as their parents had done.

Because their last three films had done poorly, Wilder and Diamond undertook their next script with caution. Universal offered them the opportunity to remake Ben Hecht's and Charles MacArthur's stage hit, *The Front Page*. What emerged in 1974 was a parody of the original, with gratuitous enlargements. Jack Lemmon and Walter Matthau starred. The film was inferior to the first two screen versions of the Hecht-MacArthur play due to its poor dialogue and stereotyped characters. *The Front Page* did make a profit, and Wilder and Diamond were signed to a long-term contract at Universal. Nothing came of it, though, except the film rights to a story in Thomas Tryon's book *Crowned Heads*. The movie that resulted was entitled *Fedora* (1978); financed by a German syndicate as a tax-shelter, it was released by United Artists rather than Universal. It marked a return to the theme of Wilder's earlier *Sunset Boulevard*, telling the story of the legendary, Garbo-like actress who is supposedly in her sixties but looks forty years younger. Critical reaction to *Fedora* was mixed; the film did poorly at the box office and did not receive national release.

Diamond and Wilder's next project was *Buddy Buddy* (1981), which they adapted from the French film *A Pain in the A--* (1974). In their third teaming for Diamond and Wilder, Walter Matthau and Jack Lemmon star, the former as a hit man after a federal witness, the latter as a suicidal neurotic who interferes with the hit man's plans. *Buddy Buddy* was a major release of 1981; it was a financial disaster and received mostly negative reviews; a few critics found it to be a return to their earlier work.

Comparing the films that Wilder had done with Diamond with those he wrote in partnership with Brackett, one finds several similarities: topicality, biting wit, cynical outlook, and, in most instances, consummate storytelling craftsmanship. The major difference between the two collaborations is that for all the caustic wit Wilder displayed in his work with Brackett, those screenplays were tempered by a warmth that is not always evident in Wilder's work with Diamond. The key to the artistic success of the best Wilder-Diamond movies is that they entertain even as they sting. They have much to say about the relationship of sex, money, and scruples in American society, but they also have the good sense and the skill to say it in a way that enlightens without alienating. Wilder and Diamond tell some hard-edged truths about human nature, making us laugh at our follies as we learn about them.

Papers:
The American Academy of Motion Picture Arts and Sciences in Beverly Hills, California, holds several Diamond-Wilder scripts, including those for *Some Like It Hot, The Apartment*, and *The Fortune Cookie*.

Philip Dunne

(11 February 1908-   )

Tom Stempel
Los Angeles City College

SELECTED MOTION PICTURES: *Student Tour* (M-G-M, 1934), screenplay by Dunne and Ralph Spence;

The Count of Monte Cristo (United Artists, 1934), screenplay and dialogue by Dunne, Dan Totheroh, and Rowland V. Lee;

The Melody Lingers On (Reliance, 1935), screenplay by Dunne and Ralph Block;

The Last of the Mohicans (United Artists, 1936), screenplay;

Breezing Home (Universal, 1937), screen story by Dunne and Finley Peter Dunne, Jr.;

Lancer Spy (20th Century-Fox, 1937), screenplay;

Suez (20th Century-Fox, 1938), screenplay by Dunne and Julien Josephson;

Stanley and Livingstone (20th Century-Fox, 1939), screenplay by Dunne and Josephson;

The Rains Came (20th Century-Fox, 1939), screenplay by Dunne and Josephson;

Swanee River (20th Century-Fox, 1939), screenplay by Dunne and John Taintor Foote;

Johnny Apollo (20th Century-Fox, 1940), screenplay by Dunne and Rowland Brown;

How Green Was My Valley (20th Century-Fox, 1941), screenplay;

Son of Fury (20th Century-Fox, 1942), screenplay;

The Late George Apley (20th Century-Fox, 1947), screenplay;

Forever Amber (20th Century-Fox, 1947), screenplay by Dunne and Ring Lardner, Jr.;

The Ghost and Mrs. Muir (20th Century-Fox, 1947), screenplay;

Escape (20th Century-Fox, 1948), screenplay;

The Luck of the Irish (20th Century-Fox, 1948), screenplay;

Pinky (20th Century-Fox, 1949), screenplay by Dunne and Dudley Nichols;

David and Bathsheba (20th Century-Fox, 1951), screen story and screenplay;

Anne of the Indies (20th Century-Fox, 1951), screenplay by Dunne and Arthur Caesar;

Lydia Bailey (20th Century-Fox, 1952), screenplay by Dunne and Michael Blankfort;

Way of a Gaucho (20th Century-Fox, 1952), screenplay;

The Robe (20th Century-Fox, 1953), screenplay;

Demetrius and the Gladiators (20th Century-Fox, 1954), screen story and screenplay;

The Egyptian (20th Century-Fox, 1954), screenplay by Dunne and Casey Robinson;

The View from Pompey's Head (20th Century-Fox, 1955), screenplay;

Hilda Crane (20th Century-Fox, 1956), screenplay;

Three Brave Men (20th Century-Fox, 1957), screenplay;

Ten North Frederick (20th Century-Fox, 1958), screenplay;

Blue Denim (20th Century-Fox, 1959), screenplay by Dunne and Edith Somers;

The Agony and the Ecstasy (20th Century-Fox, 1965), screenplay;

Blindfold (Universal, 1966), screenplay by Dunne and William H. Menger.

BOOK: *Take Two: A Life in Movies and Politics* (New York: McGraw-Hill, 1980).

OTHER: *How Green Was My Valley*, in *Twenty Best Film Plays*, edited by John Gassner and Dudley Nichols (New York: Crown, 1943);

Finley Peter Dunne, *Mr. Dooley Remembers*, edited by Dunne (Boston: Little, Brown, 1963).

Philip Dunne is particularly noted for his screen adaptations of the works of such authors as John O'Hara, John Galsworthy, Lloyd C. Douglas, John P. Marquand, and Kathleen Winsor. Although he has written few original screenplays, he is adept at transforming other writers' works into successful films. Dunne once compared himself and other screenwriters to Italian sculptor Benvenuto Cellini: "Cellini was a craftsman, not an artist. But he was definitely artistic. We're Cellinis, but we're not Leonardos."

Dunne was born in New York City, the son of the former Margaret Ives Abbott and the noted American humorist Finley Peter Dunne. After attending Harvard from 1925 to 1929 (but failing to graduate due to illness), Dunne went to work for the Guaranty Trust Company in New York in 1929, but, as he observed, "people started dropping out of

Philip Dunne, producer Frank Ross, and director Henry Koster on the set of the 1952 film The Robe

buildings, splashing on the sidewalk, and I decided some form of literature would pay better than the stock market."

With a letter of introduction from Quinn Martin, the movie critic for the *New York World* (where Dunne's brother was employed as the assistant drama editor), Dunne obtained a job as a story reader at the Fox studios in Los Angeles in 1930. He soon was asked to leave when he began rewriting the stories he was assigned to summarize. He had a few short stories published, then worked on the screenplay of *Student Tour* (1934) at M-G-M. Dunne collaborated on the screenplay for Edward Small's production of *The Count of Monte Cristo* (1934), but he wrote the screenplay not from the novel, which he had not read, but from a lengthy treatment prepared by Rowland V. Lee, the director, and Dan

Totheroh, who also received screenplay credit.

After working for M-G-M again and at United Artists, Dunne signed a contract with 20th Century-Fox in 1937. The head of production at the recently formed company was Darryl F. Zanuck, who took great pains to perfect scripts before production. For this reason, Zanuck valued writers who could consistently come up with solid scripts ready to shoot. As screenwriters who knew what Zanuck wanted, Dunne, Lamar Trotti, and Nunnally Johnson became the pillars of the Fox screenwriting staff. Dunne remained under contract to the studio for twenty-five years.

Zanuck liked historical films, and Dunne, as a writer of literate prose and dialogue and a self-described "historian manqué," became the studio specialist in historical drama. He was often appalled at the license taken with historical fact in order to enhance the story lines of the films and made an effort to get accurate historical information into his scripts. Along with a sense of history, Dunne also brought to many of his scripts a nostalgia for the past.

Dunne's first large-scale historical films for Fox were *Suez* (1938), an account of the building of the Suez Canal; *Stanley and Livingstone* (1939); and *Swanee River* (1939), the story of Stephen Foster's life and career. Also in 1939, Dunne wrote *The Rains Came*, a contemporary story from the 1937 novel by Louis Bromfield. In this film, the problems of the major characters—an Indian doctor (Tyrone Power) and an English socialite (Myrna Loy)—are overshadowed by an earthquake and flood. Critics complained of Dunne's lack of fidelity to the novel, but Bromfield was so pleased with the film and displeased with the critical reaction to it that he wrote an advertisement for the film stating his approval. On 15 July 1939 Dunne married Amanda Duff; they are the parents of three daughters.

In 1940 Zanuck sent Dunne a screenplay by Liam O'Flaherty, author of *The Informer*. The screenplay was an adaptation of Richard Llewellyn's 1939 novel *How Green Was My Valley*, the story of the disintegration of a Welsh mining family. Dunne disliked the script, describing it as "just a bitter labor diatribe," and suggested that Zanuck drop the project entirely. Zanuck disagreed and assigned Dunne to rewrite the screenplay.

The original screenplay had called for the boy Huw Morgan to grow up into an adult, but when Dunne and Zanuck saw young Roddy McDowall's screen test, they decided to rewrite the script so that Huw remained a boy throughout the film. The story of the Morgan family was seen through his eyes. Huw's father (Donald Crisp) and brothers, and later Huw himself, work in the coal mines in their valley in Wales. The disintegration of the family parallels the destruction of the natural beauty of the valley by the mining operations as Huw's brothers leave home, some because of a dispute with their father, some to start families of their own. Dunne used much narration from the novel, which is written as if the adult Huw were looking back at his past. This use of the adult Huw's viewpoint provides a stylization to the language that Dunne carried over into the parts used in the film's narration. The literary tone and the romantic view of the past evident in the movie are both typical of Dunne's best work. *How Green Was My Valley* was nominated

Sidney Blackmer (second from left), Elissa Landi, and Robert Donat in Dunne's second film, The Count of Monte Cristo

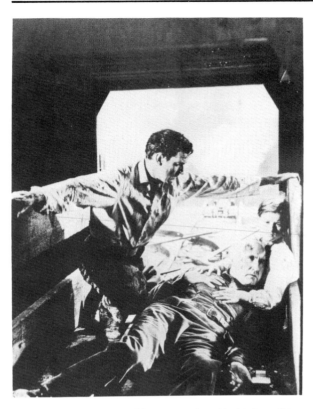

Walter Pidgeon, Donald Crisp, and Roddy McDowall in
How Green Was My Valley, *winner of the Oscar
for Best Picture in 1941*

for an Academy Award for Best Screenplay and won Oscars for Best Picture, Best Director (John Ford), Best Supporting Actor (Donald Crisp), and Best Cinematography.

After writing the historical swashbuckler, *Son of Fury* (1942), Dunne spent World War II as chief of production for the Motion Picture Bureau of the Office of War Information. Working for another screenwriter, Robert Riskin, Dunne was in charge of producing documentaries for distribution overseas.

As a result of his experiences in the OWI, after the war Dunne wanted to work on smaller scale, more realistic feature films rather than the historical epics he had been previously assigned. Instead, the first film Zanuck asked him to write was *Forever Amber* (1947), an adaptation of the long, lurid 1944 novel by Kathleen Winsor about the rise of a lady of questionable morals in the London of Charles II. The novel's racy passages made it a best-seller and had brought it to the attention of the film industry. For this same reason the Production Code office kept a watchful eye on the film. Dunne and his cowriter, Ring Lardner, Jr., had to reduce Amber's

husbands from four to one, her children from three to one, and her many lovers to merely four.

After *Forever Amber*, Dunne wrote three scripts for films directed by Joseph L. Mankiewicz. The first of these three, *The Late George Apley* (1947), was released before *Forever Amber* because of that film's Production Code problems. *The Late George Apley* was based on a novel by John P. Marquand and a play by Marquand and George S. Kaufman. It is the story of a proper Bostonian so concerned with social niceties that he becomes a snobbish clown. Dunne's next film, *The Ghost and Mrs. Muir* (1947), is a charming fantasy about a woman writer who falls in love with a ghost occupying her house. The third film, *Escape* (1948), adapted from the 1926 play by John Galsworthy, is about a man who tries to escape from prison because he believes he is being punished for a just act.

After World War II, Zanuck returned to making films about social issues. In *Pinky* (1949), adapted from the novel by Cyd Ricketts Summer, the subject was race relations. The first writer on the project, Dudley Nichols, wrote a script close to the original story about a Southern black woman who has passed for white while training as a nurse in the North. When she returns to the South, her experiences with the poverty of the black people and the bigotry of the whites force her to decide whether to remain a nurse or become a political symbol for her people. After Dunne was brought in on the project, he suggested reconstructing the story so the question was not whether to be a militant or a nurse, but whether to live as black or white. This shift made the film more dramatic and more comprehensible to the mass audience. The critical reaction to *Pinky* was mixed, but of all the major films released in 1949 dealing with race relations—*Home of the Brave*, *Intruder in the Dust*, *Lost Boundaries*—*Pinky* was the most successful, the second highest grossing film that year.

David and Bathsheba (1951) was originally conceived as one film with three distinct parts, the other two parts to deal with David and Goliath and David and Absalom. After some consideration, Dunne decided he was most interested in the story of David and Bathsheba, commenting that, "You could tell a story which you could not normally tell because of censorship, but it would be sacrosanct because it was out of the Old Testament." Dunne wrote his screenplay in blank verse, and his original dialogue was so convincing that people wrote the studio asking where in the Bible David's final prayer could be found. Made on a budget of $2.1 million, the film grossed $8 million and also brought Dunne his sec-

Jean Simmons, Jay Robinson, and Richard Burton in the first Cinemascope release, The Robe

ond Academy Award nomination.

He then wrote three historical swashbucklers: *Anne of the Indies* (1951), *Lydia Bailey* (1952), and *Way of a Gaucho* (1952). Dunne had to write *Anne of the Indies* in a week since production was scheduled to start and Zanuck was dissatisfied with the work of another writer. Dunne wrote the script based on the stars already hired—Jean Peters, Louis Jourdan—and keeping in mind the decision already made to use stock footage and process plates from a previous Fox pirate picture, *The Black Swan* (1942). Jacques Tourneur directed *Anne of the Indies* and *Way of a Gaucho*, a film made in Argentina to use up company receipts frozen in that country. Zanuck signed Dunne to produce *Way of a Gaucho*, saying, "You like to play politics. You have a big chance now with Peron." When Dunne arrived in Argentina, he discovered that the novel on which the film was to be based, *Gaucho* by Herbert Childs, was completely inaccurate in its depiction of Argentine life and decided to rewrite the script.

Zanuck next approached Dunne to rewrite the screenplay for *The Robe* (1953). Dunne took over the job, noting that the people who had worked on the

script had already made the necessary structural change: in the novel by Lloyd C. Douglas, the Roman Tribune Marcellus who wins the robe of Christ by casting lots for it at the Crucifixion converts to Christianity early in the story; in the script Dunne worked from, the conversion comes only after Marcellus has tried to find and destroy the robe. Dunne's contributions to the script included improved dialogue and increased historical accuracy. The original script portrayed the emperor Tiberius as a madman, which was not only inaccurate but also provided no contrast when Caligula became emperor. Dunne developed Tiberius as "an embittered old warrior who . . . understood what was going to happen to Rome."

The Robe was the first film released in the wide-screen process Cinemascope, and its lucrative box-office returns bolstered Fox's sagging finances. Producer Frank Ross suggested a sequel even before the film was released. As Dunne recalls, "Here we had some of the cast that hadn't been killed off, and all these expensive costumes and sets all ready to go. . . . We didn't have a clue how to go on." Dunne decided that since *The Robe* had been the story of a conversion to Christianity, the sequel should be the story of the temptation of a Christian. He developed the sequel *Demetrius and the Gladiators* (1954), an account of how Marcellus's slave Demetrius (Victor Mature) is tempted by sex—the empress Messalina (Susan Hayward)—and violence —the gladiator ring.

The first draft of the screenplay for *The Egyptian* (1954) was by Casey Robinson, a veteran of many years at Warner Bros. Robinson's script was typical of much of his work, filled with events, plot turns, and many characters. Dunne's contribution as a cowriter was not only to emphasize the historical details but also to provide the sense of a life passing as the elderly Sinuhe recalls his youthful rise as the pharaoh's physician and his descent into degradation with the courtesan Nefer. The final script is more complex and moving than the film, which suffered from poor casting (Marlon Brando and Marlene Dietrich were replaced by Edmund Purdom and Bela Darvi) and, despite Dunne's efforts, historical inaccuracies.

In 1955 Dunne began directing films, demonstrating in his projects intelligence, a respect for the actors and for the scripts. Beginning with *The View from Pompey's Head* (1955), about prejudice in a small Southern town, he directed his own scripts— with the exception of *The Agony and the Ecstasy* (1965)—and directed but did not write *Prince of Players* (1954), *In Love and War* (1958), *Wild in the Country* (1961), and *Lisa* (1962). The films he directed, however, were often too elevated in their subject matter for popular taste, and Dunne's treatment of the script often lent a stolidity to his films. When directing films by other writers, Dunne often had to cut their scripts, as with Moss Hart's script for *Prince of Players* and Clifford Odets's script for *Wild in the Country*. Dunne also reworked Nelson Gidding's script for *Lisa*, emphasizing the nobler qualities of the characters which he felt Gidding had slighted.

In 1957 Dunne wrote *Three Brave Men*, a potentially daring attack on the U.S. government security program that dealt with the unwarranted suspension of a man accused of being a security risk. The film was inspired by a series of Pulitzer Prize-winning newspaper articles by Anthony Lewis, but the film was softened because of studio reluctance to offend government officials. Dunne's adaptation of *Ten North Frederick* (1958) was the first and best adaptation of a novel by John O'Hara and perhaps the best film Dunne directed; it is Dunne's own favorite of his films. The story is a study of a Pennsylvania man's (Gary Cooper) successes and failures at love and politics. Dunne followed *Ten North Frederick* with *Blue Denim* (1959), a well-received film about the problems of a teenage couple (Carol Lynley and Brandon De Wilde) faced with the girl's pregnancy.

In 1962 Dunne was abruptly released from his contract at 20th Century-Fox. The studio had invested so much money in *Cleopatra* that it had to terminate many contracts. A year later, after Zanuck returned to Fox, he brought Dunne back to work at the studio. While still under contract, Dunne had written a treatment of Irving Stone's 1961 novel about Michelangelo, *The Agony and the Ecstasy*. Dunne suggested that an interesting film could be developed from the conflict between Michelangelo and Pope Julius II whom he imagined as "a sort of Quirk and Flagg in the Sistine Chapel." Zanuck saw the treatment and hired Dunne to write the script. The 1965 film directed by Carol Reed toned down some of the comedy. Charlton Heston played Michelangelo and Rex Harrison the Pope.

Dunne's last film was *Blindfold* (1966), which uses the spy-thriller genre to comment on the absurdity of government secrecy. A psychoanalyst (Rock Hudson) is hired to treat a scientist working on a top-secret project, but when the scientist disappears, the analyst is unable to get the government to divulge any information about him. *Blindfold* is one of the few interesting spy spoofs of the 1960s.

Dunne wrote three unproduced scripts for Universal in the late 1960s and early 1970s. He then wrote his reminiscences, which were published as *Take Two: A Life in Movies and Politics* in 1980.

As a screenwriter, Philip Dunne brought a high level of both literacy and craft to his work. He was able to write skillfully for the screen in a variety of styles, as indicated by the wide range of authors whose works he adapted. The emphasis on historical accuracy and the finer qualities of both language and character raised the level of his films beyond that of the average Hollywood script. Dunne will be remembered for the literacy and intelligence he brought to American film.

References:

Peter Bogdanovich, *John Ford* (Berkeley: University of California Press, 1968);

Kenneth L. Geist, *Pictures Will Talk* (New York: Scribners, 1978);

Daniel J. Leab, *From Sambo to Superspade* (Boston:

Houghton Mifflin, 1976);

J. D. Marshall, Interview with Philip Dunne, in *Blueprint on Babylon* (Los Angeles: Phoenix House, 1978).

Papers:
There is a collection of Philip Dunne's papers and scripts in the Department of Special Collections at the University of Southern California Library, Los Angeles.

Julius Epstein
(22 August 1909-   )

Philip Epstein
(22 August 1909-7 February 1952)

Don Kilbourne

SELECTED MOTION PICTURES: *Living on Velvet* (Warner Bros., 1935), screenplay by Julius Epstein;

In Caliente (Warner Bros., 1935), screenplay by Julius Epstein;

Little Big Shot (Warner Bros., 1935), screenplay by Julius Epstein;

I Live for Love (Warner Bros., 1935), screenplay by Julius Epstein;

Stars Over Broadway (Warner Bros., 1935), screenplay by Julius Epstein;

Sons o' Gun (Warner Bros., 1936), screenplay by Julius Epstein and Jerry Wald;

Love on a Bet (RKO, 1936), screenplay by Philip Epstein and P. J. Wolfson;

The Bride Walks Out (Paramount, 1936), screenplay by Philip Epstein and Wolfson;

Grand Jury (RKO, 1936), screenplay by Philip Epstein and Joseph A. Fields;

New Faces of 1937 (RKO, 1937), screenplay by Philip Epstein, Nat Perrin, and Irving S. Brecher;

Confession (Warner Bros., 1937), adaptation by Julius Epstein;

Four Daughters (Warner Bros., 1938), screenplay by Julius Epstein and Lenore Coffee; filmed again as *Young at Heart* (Warner Bros., 1954);

Secrets of an Actress (Warner Bros., 1938), screen story and screenplay by Julius Epstein, Milton Krims, and Rowland Leigh;

The Mad Miss Manton (RKO, 1938), screenplay by Philip Epstein;

There's That Woman Again (Columbia, 1938), screenplay by Philip Epstein, James Edward Grant, and Ken Englund;

Daughters Courageous (Warner Bros., 1939), screenplay;

Four Wives (Warner Bros., 1939), screenplay by the Epsteins and Maurice Hanline;

Saturday's Children (Warner Bros., 1940), screenplay;

No Time for Comedy (Warner Bros., 1940), screenplay;

Strawberry Blonde (Warner Bros., 1941), screenplay;

The Bride Came C.O.D. (Warner Bros., 1941), screenplay;

Honeymoon for Three (Warner Bros., 1941), screenplay by the Epsteins and Earl Baldwin;

The Man Who Came to Dinner (Warner Bros., 1941), screenplay;

The Male Animal (Warner Bros., 1942), screenplay by the Epsteins and Avery Stephen Morehouse;

Casablanca (Warner Bros., 1943), screenplay by the Epsteins and Howard Koch;

Mr. Skeffington (Warner Bros., 1944), screenplay;

Arsenic and Old Lace (Warner Bros., 1944), screenplay;

One More Tomorrow (Warner Bros., 1946), additional dialogue;

Romance on the High Seas (Warner Bros., 1948), screenplay;

My Foolish Heart (RKO, 1949), screenplay;

Take Care of My Little Girl (20th Century-Fox, 1951), screenplay;

Forever Female (Paramount, 1954), screen story and screenplay;

Philip and Julius Epstein (Culver Pictures)

The Last Time I Saw Paris (M-G-M, 1954), screenplay by the Epsteins and Richard L. Brooks;

The Tender Trap (M-G-M, 1955), screenplay by Julius Epstein;

Kiss Them For Me (20th Century-Fox, 1957), screenplay by Julius Epstein;

The Brothers Karamazov (M-G-M, 1958), adaptation;

Tall Story (Warner Bros., 1959), screenplay by Julius Epstein;

Take a Giant Step (United Artists, 1959), screenplay by Julius Epstein and Louis S. Peterson;

Fanny (Warner Bros., 1961), screenplay by Julius Epstein;

Light in the Piazza (M-G-M, 1962), screenplay by Julius Epstein;

Send Me No Flowers (Universal, 1964), screenplay by Julius Epstein;

Return from the Ashes (United Artists, 1965), screenplay by Julius Epstein;

Any Wednesday (Warner Bros., 1966), screenplay by Julius Epstein;

Pete 'n' Tillie (Universal, 1972), screenplay by Julius Epstein;

Once Is Not Enough (Paramount, 1975), screenplay by Julius Epstein;

House Calls (Universal, 1978), screenplay by Julius Epstein, Max Shulman, Alan Mandel, and Charles Shyer.

SELECTED PLAYS: *And the Stars Remain* (New York, Guild Theatre, 12 October 1936);

Chicken Every Sunday (New York, Henry Miller's Theatre, 5 April 1944);

That's the Ticket (Philadelphia, Shubert Theatre, 24 September 1948);

But Seriously. . ., by Julius Epstein (New York,

Henry Miller's Theatre, 27 February 1969).

TELEVISION: *The Pirate* (CBS, 1978), adaptation by Julius Epstein.

OTHER: Howard Koch, comp., *Casablanca: Script and Legend* (Woodstock, N.Y.: Overlook Press, 1973)—includes the screenplay by the Epsteins and Koch.

The careers of Julius and Philip Epstein reached their zeniths with *Casablanca* (1943). With a few exceptions, their other films never gained critical esteem, although many of them were popular with audiences.

Julius and Philip Epstein, twin brothers, were born in New York City. Their father, Henry, was proprietor of a livery stable. The brothers grew up in New York, attended local schools, but went to college at Pennsylvania State University. Julius graduated in 1931 and Philip a year later. They held various jobs after college. Philip worked as an actor in New York, and Julius tried many things, from press agentry to professional boxing. In 1933 they came to Hollywood and began their screenwriting careers. Julius worked on several musicals with Jerry Wald, and Philip wrote some lighthearted detective films, working with several different collaborators. These projects were basically "B" pictures. In 1936, Julius Epstein married Frances Sage. The marriage was dissolved in 1945, and he married Ann Lazlo in 1949.

It was Julius who received the first break when he was assigned to work on the screenplay for *Four Daughters* (1938) with Lenore Coffee. Both writers received Academy Award nominations for their work on this film. Based loosely on the Fannie Hurst play *Sister Act*, *Four Daughters* featured the romantic entanglements of four young women in a musical household. The film proved so popular that it inspired three follow-up films. The first, *Daughters Courageous* (1939), while using basically the same cast, is not a sequel as such; although the family is the same, the thrust here is the return of the father after a twenty-year absence. It was with *Daughters Courageous* that Philip Epstein began his long association with his brother. *Four Wives* (1939) is the true sequel to *Four Daughters*, continuing the saga through the birth of the sisters' children. At this point, the Epsteins left the series; the final film, *Four Mothers* (1940), was passed on to another writer.

The Epsteins' next film was *Saturday's Children*

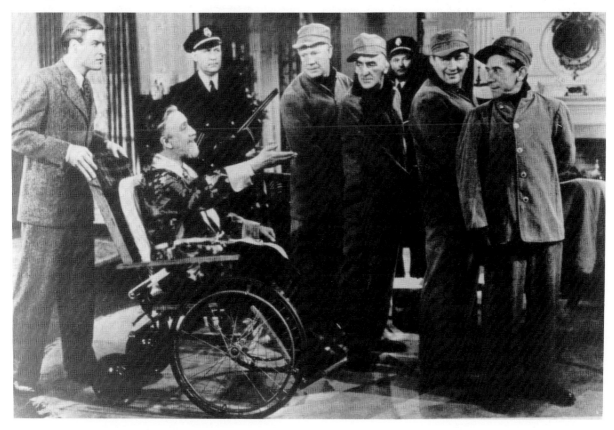

Richard Travis brings Monty Woolley to greet a group of convicts in The Man Who Came to Dinner

(1940), based on Maxwell Anderson's 1927 play about young lovers from the working class. With *No Time for Comedy* (1940), the Epsteins changed direction and began establishing their reputations as versatile writers who showed a good hand at dialogue. It was the first of several adaptations of Broadway comedies for the Epsteins. In the 1939 S. N. Behrman play, the romance between the playwright and his leading lady served as an excuse for bantering about the impossibility of writing comedy during depressing times. The Epsteins decided to develop more interest in the romantic implications and rewrote the roles for James Stewart and Rosalind Russell.

Their other adaptations of Broadway plays were *The Man Who Came to Dinner* (1941) from George S. Kaufman and Moss Hart's 1939 play about an acid-tongued radio celebrity who, confined to a house with a broken leg, wreaks havoc on the lives of the people there, and *Arsenic and Old Lace*, from the 1941 play by Joseph Kesserling about two elderly women who invite lonely old men to

their home and poison them. *Arsenic and Old Lace* was produced in 1941 with Frank Capra as director, but it was held back from release until 1944. As in *No Time for Comedy*, the romantic elements in *The Man Who Came to Dinner* and *Arsenic and Old Lace* were emphasized. The two films were successes both financially and critically.

The Epsteins were proving to be a popular team, especially with their adaptations of successful Broadway plays. They were given two other assignments for adaptation in the early 1940s: *Strawberry Blonde* (1941) and *The Male Animal* (1942). *Strawberry Blonde* was the second film version of James Hagan's *One Sunday Afternoon*, the story of a dentist (James Cagney) who is infatuated with one woman (Rita Hayworth) but marries another (Olivia de Havilland), eventually realizing he has been very lucky in his marriage. Raoul Walsh directed the film. *The Male Animal* was an adaptation of James Thurber and Elliott Nugent's defense of academic freedom and satire of academic life, centering around a college professor (Henry Fonda), his wife

Peter Lorre, Raymond Massey, Josephine Hull, Cary Grant, Priscilla Lane, and Jean Adair in a scene from Arsenic and Old Lace

Left to right: Claude Rains (in dark uniform), Paul Henreid, Humphrey Bogart, and Ingrid Bergman in Casablanca

(Olivia de Havilland), and her ex-football-hero beau (Jack Carson).

Ironically, *Casablanca*, the Epsteins' greatest film success, came from a Broadway flop, *Everybody Comes to Rick's*, a play by Murray Bennett and Joan Allison. Warner Bros. had given the assignment to the Epsteins who had agreed to work with Frank Capra on "Why We Fight," his documentary series for the U.S. Army, and had to come up with the *Casablanca* script quickly. (Their involvement with *Casablanca* forced them to cancel their part in the Capra series.) Howard Koch also worked on the script, and a series of incidents from the play were transformed into a finished screenplay with dramatic continuity. Directed by Michael Curtiz, *Casablanca* tells the story of Rick Blaine, a cynical loner who runs a café in Casablanca, where refugees from World War II come to bargain their way to freedom. Into Rick's life come his former lover and her freedom-fighter husband who cause Rick to drop his cynicism and help them escape from the

Nazis. *Casablanca* won several Academy Awards, including Best Picture and Best Screenplay. The movie's critical reputation has grown over the years, and the film is one of America's favorites.

Casablanca marked the apogee of the Epsteins' careers. They were never to come close to producing another masterpiece. The reason for this lies in part in the fact that, like all movie people at this time, they were at the mercy of the studio system and were assigned projects but were unable to choose their own. Their one joint attempt at controlling their work came when they cowrote and coproduced the Bette Davis vehicle *Mr. Skeffington* (1944). The film is about a woman who marries a man (Claude Rains) to save her brother from prison. When her brother is killed in World War I, she abandons her husband and daughter, returning years later when age and disease have robbed her of her beauty. The critical reaction to *Mr. Skeffington* was very negative.

After *Mr. Skeffington*, the Epsteins took four

years off from films. They turned to the theater and wrote two plays, *Chicken Every Sunday* and *That's the Ticket*. The first opened on Broadway in April 1944; the second never reached New York.

Their next film, *Romance on the High Seas* (1948), marked the end of the Epsteins' long association with Warner Bros. A musical comedy centering on mistaken identity, the movie tells of a suspicious wife (Janis Paige) who hires a struggling singer (Doris Day) to take her place on a cruise. The wife plans to remain at home in order to spy on her husband (Don Defore), who, in turn, has hired a private detective (Jack Carson) to follow his wife on her cruise. It was Doris Day's first film and was generally dismissed by the critics as lighthearted froth, although it was successful with the public.

The Epsteins' next film, *My Foolish Heart* (1949), was a return to sentimental drama. Loosely based on J. D. Salinger's story "Uncle Wiggily in Connecticut," it deals with the emotional breakdown of a pregnant woman (Susan Hayward) after the death of her soldier husband. The dialogue is touching at times, but as a picture of a college girl's growth into womanhood, it is too sentimental. Salinger was so upset by this film that he forbade any of his other works to be adapted for the movies.

Philip Epstein died of cancer in 1952. Shortly before his death the first of the Epsteins' last three films together was released. *Take Care of My Little Girl* (1951) was a critical look at sororities starring Jeanne Crain; unfortunately, the sorority under examination was portrayed as so outrageously snobbish that some of the value of the social protest in the script was lost. *Forever Female* (1954), from J. M. Barrie's 1912 play *Rosalind*, told of a young playwright (William Holden) torn between the love of a budding actress (Pat Crowley) and a fading star (Ginger Rogers). *The Last Time I Saw Paris* (1954), the Epsteins' final collaboration, was a lushly done film starring Elizabeth Taylor and Van Johnson; it was disappointing in that it took F. Scott Fitzgerald's short story "Babylon Revisited" and updated it to a post-World War II maudlin melodrama.

Alone, Julius Epstein wrote *Young at Heart* (1954), a remake of his first success, *Four Daughters*. This time there were three daughters, and although songs were added, the family's musical abilities were relegated to a background role. The result was a nicely done, conventional love story that seemed more old-fashioned than the original.

Epstein then wrote three comedies: *The Tender Trap* (1955), about a swinging bachelor (Frank Sinatra) who gets married; *Kiss Them For Me* (1957), directed by Stanley Donen, chronicling the ro-

mances of naval officers on shore leave; and *Tall Story* (1959), about the relationship between a coed (Jane Fonda) and a basketball star (Anthony Perkins). In 1959 Epstein also produced and wrote *Take a Giant Step*, the story of a young black man growing up in a white middle-class neighborhood. Louis S. Peterson's 1953 play on which the film was based was well regarded, but the film received unfavorable reviews.

Epstein's next film, *Fanny* (1961), was very popular. Based on Marcel Pagnol's trilogy—*Marius* (1931), *Fanny* (1932), and *Césare* (1936)—it is a sentimental story of a young woman (Leslie Caron) in Marseilles and the men in her life. After spending the night with her, the man with whom she is in love (Horst Bucholz) goes off to sea. Finding herself pregnant, Fanny marries an older man (Maurice Chevalier) who loves her. After many years, she and her son are united with her lover.

With *Light in the Piazza* (1962), an adaptation of a novella by Elizabeth Spencer, Epstein moved from France to Italy for the sentimental story of an anxious mother (Olivia de Havilland) whose concern over her retarded daughter (Yvette Mimieux) increases when the girl falls in love with a young Italian (George Hamilton) who does not realize she is retarded. Despite poor reviews, the film was a box-office success.

Since *Light in the Piazza*, Epstein has written *Return from the Ashes* (1965), a drama about a man (Curt Jurgens) romancing his stepdaughter (Samantha Eggar) after his wife's supposed death, and *Once Is Not Enough* (1975), adapted from Jacqueline Susann's novel. Primarily, though, he has written comedies. *Send Me No Flowers* (1964) is a Doris Day-Rock Hudson movie about a man who thinks he has a short time to live and tries to find another husband for his wife. *Any Wednesday* (1966) is the story of a man (Jason Robards) who uses his mistress's (Jane Fonda) apartment for business. *Pete 'n' Tillie* (1972) is about the marital problems of a mismatched couple (Walter Matthau and Carol Burnett); many critics felt it was flawed by its shift from comedy to melodrama after the first half of the film. *House Calls* (1978) deals with the romance between a lecherous doctor (Walter Matthau) and an independent woman (Glenda Jackson) who wins him on her own terms. The film received mixed reviews but was a success with audiences and inspired a television series of the same name.

Julius Epstein has had no screen credits since 1978, but he has done some writing for television. In 1978 he adapted Harold Robbins's novel *The Pirate* into a four-hour television movie depicting

Arab-Israeli tensions in the story of a Jewish-born Arabian sheik whose daughter is a PLO terrorist.

Julius and Philip Epstein were products of the studio system. A review of their film credits reveals few great works. But many of their films, especially those in the 1930s and 1940s, are significant for students of popular culture because they reflect very accurately the tastes and values of their times. At their best, in *Casablanca*, *The Male Animal*, and *The Man Who Came to Dinner*, the Epsteins wrote dialogue that transcends formulaic content. Their scripts are good examples of the extremely compe-tent work done by contract writers during the hey-day of the major studios.

References:

James Agee, *Agee on Film*, volume 1 (New York: Grosset & Dunlap, 1969);

Richard J. Anobile, ed., Michael Curtiz's *Casablanca* (New York: Universe Books, 1974);

Ron Haver, "The True Story of the Filming of *Casablanca*," *Los Angeles* (October 1976): 60-70;

Howard Koch, *As Time Goes By* (New York: Har-court Brace Jovanovich, 1979).

Horton Foote
(14 March 1916-   )

Joseph R. Millichap
University of Tulsa

SELECTED MOTION PICTURES: *Storm Fear* (United Artists, 1956), screenplay;

To Kill a Mockingbird (Universal, 1962), screenplay;

Baby, the Rain Must Fall (Columbia, 1964), screen-play adapted by Foote from his play *The Traveling Lady*;

Hurry Sundown (Paramount, 1967), screenplay by Foote and Thomas Ryan;

Tomorrow (Filmgroup, 1972), screenplay;

Tender Mercies (Universal, 1983), screenplay.

PLAYS: *Texas Town* (New York, Provincetown Playhouse, December 1942);

Only the Heart (New York, Bijou Theatre, 4 April 1944);

Celebration (New York, Maxine Elliot's Theatre, 11 April 1948);

The Chase (New York, Playhouse Theatre, 15 April 1952);

The Trip to Bountiful (New York, Henry Miller's Theatre, 3 November 1953);

The Traveling Lady (New York, Playhouse Theatre, 27 October 1954);

The Dancers (Los Angeles, Fiesta Hall, 28 October 1963);

Gone With the Wind (London, 1971; Los Angeles, Dorothy Chandler Pavilion, 28 August 1973), book by Foote.

TELEVISION: *Only the Heart* (NBC, 1947), script;

Ludie Brooks (CBS, 1951), script;

The Travelers (NBC, 1952), script;

The Old Beginning (NBC, 1952), script;

The Trip to Bountiful (NBC, 1953), script;

Young Lady of Property (NBC, 1953), script;

The Oil Well (NBC, 1953), script;

Rocking Chair (NBC, 1953), script;

Expectant Relations (NBC, 1953), script;

Death of the Old Man (NBC, 1953), script;

Tears of My Sister (NBC, 1953), script;

John Turner Davis (NBC, 1953), script;

The Midnight Caller (NBC, 1953), script;

The Dancers (NBC, 1954), script;

The Shadow of Willie Greer (NBC, 1954), script;

The Roads to Home (ABC, 1955), script;

Flight (NBC, 1956), script;

Drugstore; Sunday Noon (ABC, 1956), script;

Member of the Family (CBS, 1957), script;

Traveling Lady (CBS, 1957), script;

Old Man (CBS, 1959), script;

Tomorrow (CBS, 1960, 1971), script;

The Shape of the River (CBS, 1960), script;

Nights of the Storm (CBS, 1961), script;

Gambling Heart (NBC, 1964), script;

The Displaced Person (PBS, 1977), script;

Barn Burning (PBS, 1980), script.

BOOKS: *Only the Heart* (New York: Dramatists Play Service, 1944);

Roots In a Parched Ground (New York: Dramatists

Play Service, 1952);

The Chase (New York: Dramatists Play Service, 1952);

The Trip to Bountiful (New York: Dramatists Play Service, 1954);

The Traveling Lady (New York: Dramatists Play Service, 1955);

A Young Lady of Property (New York: Dramatists Play Service, 1955);

The Chase [novel] (New York: Rinehart, 1956);

Harrison, Texas (New York: Harcourt, Brace, 1956);

The Midnight Caller (New York: Dramatists Play Service, 1959);

Three Plays (New York: Harcourt, Brace & World, 1962);

Tomorrow (New York: Dramatists Play Service, 1963);

The Screenplay of "To Kill a Mockingbird" [screenplay] (New York: Harcourt, Brace & World, 1964).

Horton Foote is a prolific and successful writer of drama for the theater, the movies, and television.

Six of his plays have received New York productions; at least six of his screenplays have been filmed; another film was made from one of his works; and twenty-seven of his teleplays have been broadcast. All of Foote's original works have been concerned with the mythical small town of Harrison, Texas, whose people and history recall the characters of other modern Southern writers, particularly William Faulkner, Carson McCullers, and Tennessee Williams. Foote's adaptations for television, the stage, and movies include the work of Southern writers Faulkner, Harper Lee, and Margaret Mitchell. Although his contribution to screenwriting has been limited, Foote's screenplays have extended to the film medium his careful assessment of Southern life in the twentieth century.

Horton Foote was born in Wharton, Texas, a small town much like his mythical setting of Harrison. His parents, Albert and Hallie Foote, were middle-class shopkeepers, and Foote spent what he calls a normal childhood in Wharton. After graduation from Wharton High School, he decided on a

Gregory Peck as Alabama lawyer Atticus Finch in To Kill a Mockingbird. *Foote's screenplay won awards from the Academy and the Writers Guild.*

theatrical career, studying at the Pasadena Playhouse from 1933 to 1935 and the Tamara Darkarhovna Theatre School in New York from 1937 to 1939. From 1939 to 1942 he acted in several Broadway plays, including Ernest Hemingway's *The Fifth Column* (1940), and from 1942 to 1945 he managed a production company, Productions Inc., in Washington, D.C., and taught playwriting. Foote married Lillian Valish on 4 June 1945; they have four children.

Foote's first professionally produced play, *Texas Town* (1942), announced the subject matter for all his later work. Foote's important stage works include *Only the Heart* (1944), *The Chase* (1952; a novelization was published in 1956), *The Trip to Bountiful* (1953), and *The Traveling Lady* (1954).

Foote began his television career writing for *Kraft Playhouse* in 1947 and later wrote scripts for *Playhouse 90* and other prestigious series. Eight of his television pieces were published under the title *Harrison, Texas* in 1956. His teleplays include adaptations of his own stage plays and of works by other Southern authors (notably William Faulkner's "Old Man").

Foote's first screenplay was the adaptation of a minor Southern novel, Clinton Seeley's *Storm Fear*, for Cornel Wilde, who produced, directed, and starred in this 1956 film for United Artists. Wilde plays Charlie, a good man gone bad, who robs a bank and retreats to the mountain home of his brother (Dan Duryea) but has his getaway plans spoiled by an unexpected storm. The emphasis of both novel and film is on the revelation of character rather than on plot, and the central figures of Charlie and his girl friend (Lee Grant) resemble other people on the run in Foote's original works. Although Foote created a polished screenplay, the film is slow and stagy. *Storm Fear* was indifferently received by both the critics and the public.

Foote's next screenplay, *To Kill a Mockingbird* (1962), was greeted by an enthusiastic reaction, both critical and popular. The film stays faithful to Harper Lee's Pulitzer Prize-winning novel, concentrating on the lives of a six-year-old girl, Scout (Mary Badham), her ten-year-old brother, Jem (Philip Alford), and their father, Atticus (Gregory Peck), in the small Alabama town of Maycomb during the 1930s. The film traces the children's process of maturing and culminates in an event that is crucial to their maturation, the trial of a black man (Brock Peters) falsely accused of rape. Atticus defends the man but cannot sway the bigoted jury, and although the children realize that hate and bigotry are an integral part of life, they also learn to ap-

George Kennedy (second from left) and John Philip Law (at right) in a scene from Hurry Sundown

preciate the value of courage and integrity. Foote won the Academy Award and the Writers Guild Award for his screenplay; Gregory Peck won an Oscar for Best Actor, and the film was nominated for Best Picture.

These honors undoubtedly stimulated interest in Foote's own works as material for screen adaptation. In 1964 he adapted his play *The Traveling Lady* for the screen; Alan Pakula produced it as *Baby, the Rain Must Fall* with Robert Mulligan directing. In the film Steve McQueen and Lee Remick play an immature ex-convict and his loyal wife who are betrayed by the hostility of a small Texas town which will not give the ex-con a chance to go straight. Foote's screenplay is weakened by puzzling motivation; his hero resembles some of Tennessee Williams's tragic protagonists in his inarticulate rage at a disordered world, but in Foote's screenplay the reason for the tragedy of character seems more obscure than inevitable. Similar problems are evident in *The Chase* (1966), which Lillian Hellman adapted for the screen from Foote's novel and play.

Foote's next screenplay was an adaptation done with Thomas Ryan of K. B. Glidden's novel *Hurry Sundown* (1967), a melodrama about racial problems in the South. The novel is a confused pastiche of Southern melodrama, and while Foote made the best of his material, the film was badly produced and directed by Otto Preminger. The film received scathing reviews and was a financial failure. Foote did not write another screenplay until 1972.

Foote renewed his reputation as a screenwriter with *Tomorrow* (1972), a screen version of his teleplay drawn from William Faulkner's story of the same title. Robert Duvall portrays a taciturn young cotton farmer who raises a child abandoned by a sharecropping family; in taking on this responsibility, the farmer finds capacities for love and growth neither he nor the audience had suspected. The film received only limited distribution, but it is considered by many to be one of the best screen adaptations of a Faulkner work.

Foote has done little screenwriting since 1972, working instead on other projects, notably two successful adaptations of stories by Southern writers for the PBS American Short Story series: Flannery O'Connor's *The Displaced Person*, televised in 1977, and William Faulkner's *Barn Burning*, which aired in 1980. Foote's latest film is *Tender Mercies* (1983), which stars Robert Duval as an aging country singer. Like *Tomorrow*, the film received only limited distribution but excellent reviews; many critics felt it was among the year's best motion pictures.

In his most recent work Foote again offers the intelligent and realistic view of the modern South that has been his greatest strength as both a screenwriter and a dramatist.

Carl Foreman
(23 July 1914-   )

Malvin Wald
University of Southern California

MOTION PICTURES: *Spooks Run Wild* (Monogram, 1941), screen story and screenplay by Foreman and Francis Marion;

Dakota (Republic, 1945), story;

So This Is New York (United Artists, 1948), screenplay by Foreman and Herbert Baker;

Clay Pigeon (RKO, 1949), screen story and screenplay;

Champion (United Artists, 1949), screenplay;

Home of the Brave (United Artists, 1949), screenplay;

Young Man with a Horn (Warner Bros., 1950), screenplay by Foreman and Edmund North;

The Men (United Artists, 1950), screen story and screenplay;

Cyrano de Bergerac (United Artists, 1950), adaptation and screenplay;

High Noon (United Artists, 1952), screenplay;

The Sleeping Tiger (Astor, 1955), screenplay by Foreman and Harold Buchman as Derek Frye;

The Bridge on the River Kwai (Columbia, 1957), screenplay by Foreman and Michael Wilson, credited to Pierre Boulle;

The Key (Columbia, 1958), screenplay;

The Guns of Navarone (Columbia, 1961), screenplay;

The Victors (Columbia, 1963), screenplay;

Mackenna's Gold (Columbia, 1969), screenplay;

Young Winston (Columbia, 1972), screenplay;

Force 10 from Navarone (American International, 1978), screen story;

When Time Ran Out (Warner Bros., 1980), screenplay by Foreman and Stirling Silliphant.

BOOK: *Young Winston: The Screenplay of the Film* (London: Fontana, 1972; New York: Ballantine, 1972).

OTHER: *Three Major Screenplays*, edited by Malvin Wald and Michael Werner (New York: Globe, 1972)—includes Foreman's story treatment and screenplay for *High Noon*.

PERIODICAL PUBLICATIONS: "The Road to the Victors," *Films and Filming* (September 1963): 11-12;

"The Sense of Adventure," *Films and Filming* (November 1969): 14-18;

"Confessions of a Frustrated Screen Writer," *Film Comment*, 6 (Winter 1970-1971): 22-25.

Carl Foreman's career seems broken into two sections—a division created by his break with the

Carl Foreman (right) and Richard Attenborough on the set of the 1972 film Young Winston

film industry during the blacklisting era of the early 1950s. Choosing to leave America for exile abroad, Foreman continued to further his screenwriting career but seemed to concentrate less on human conflict in his writing as his own conflicts grew. His successes did not diminish during the time he went to live and work in London. From the time he arrived in Britain in 1952 to the time he returned to the United States in 1975, his list of accomplishments increased. He was the first American to become head of the British Film Institute and was honored as a Commander of the Order of the British Empire by Queen Elizabeth II for his contributions to the British film industry. Yet after he left the United States, there was a subtle change in theme throughout his screenplays. Without totally abandoning his examination of the human condition, he was more inclined to refrain from controversy and the artistic exploration that marked his earlier films.

Carl Foreman was born on 23 July 1914 in Chicago to Isidore and Fanny Rozin Foreman. Foreman attended the Chicago public schools and studied at the University of Illinois (1932-1933), Northwestern University (1935-1936), and the John Marshall Law School (1936-1937). He dropped out of law school to embark on a career in show business. For several years, between schools and after law school, he tried his hand at a variety of jobs: newspaper reporter, press agent, radio writer, carnival barker, director of little theater, and contributor to fiction magazines. Foreman has been married twice—to Estelle Barr and Evelyn Smith—and has three children.

In 1938 Foreman came to Hollywood, where he worked as a story analyst and a film laboratory technician. Under the auspices of the WPA, he received $85 a month as part of the Federal Writers' Project. He won a scholarship to the League of American Writers' School, where he studied screenwriting under Robert Rossen and Dore Schary. In 1940 he teamed up with another aspiring screenwriter, Charles Marion. They worked on their technique and managed to sell three scripts to Monogram Films, then considered the bottom of the ladder of Hollywood studios.

When World War II broke out, Foreman joined the U.S. Army Signal Corps, in which he served as a writer-producer from 1942 to 1945, and he was fortunate to be associated with Frank Capra in making orientation and training films. Foreman worked on Capra's well-known "Why We Fight" series along with two other soldiers, fledgling producer Stanley Kramer and veteran publicist George Glass.

In 1945, after he left the army, Foreman's career advanced when Republic Studios agreed to purchase his original story *Dakota* (1945), which was made into a film starring John Wayne. The following year, Foreman and his army comrades Kramer and Glass decided to strike out on their own and form an independent film company. Foreman was to serve as writer, vice-president, and treasurer.

Their first venture, *So This Is New York* (1948), an adaptation of Ring Lardner's 1921 novel *The Big Town*, was neither a critical nor a box-office success. In 1949 Foreman sold an original screenplay to RKO for a "B" picture titled *Clay Pigeon*. That same year, Foreman, Kramer, and Glass tried another independent production. This film, *Champion* (1949), proved far more successful than their past attempts. It became a turning point for the star of the film, Kirk Douglas, as well as for the three filmmakers. Foreman received his first nominations for the Academy Award and the Writers Guild Award for this adaptation of the Ring Lardner story about an unscrupulous prizefighter.

The Kramer organization followed *Champion* with another fairly successful film, *Home of the Brave* (1949). Foreman's screenplay was based on Arthur Laurent's Broadway play of the same title about a Jewish soldier who experiences psychosomatic paralysis from guilt feelings over the death of a fellow soldier. Foreman made the hero a black soldier and presented *Home of the Brave* as one of the first films to deal with the anti-Negro feelings in a supposedly democratic army. For his work, Foreman again was nominated for an award by the Writers Guild.

Warner Bros., interested by the progress of Foreman's career, hired him to write the screenplay for *Young Man with a Horn* (1950), a fictionalized version of the life of jazz cornetist Bix Beiderbecke, who died of pneumonia at age twenty-eight. In the film, the hero (Kirk Douglas) works his way up from obscurity to fame as a cornet player; nearly de-

stroyed by marriage to a rich woman (Lauren Bacall), he is saved by the love of a singer (Doris Day). Foreman shared script credit with Edmund North; Michael Curtiz directed.

By this time, the Kramer-Foreman-Glass group was beginning to receive some notice in Hollywood. They responded with another controversial film in 1950, *The Men*, which introduced Marlon Brando to the screen. The film dealt with the problems of hospitalized paraplegic veterans of World War II. Sensitively directed by Fred Zinnemann, the film was highly praised, and Foreman was nominated for both an Academy Award and the Writers Guild Award.

The Kramer group decided upon a change of pace for their next film, and in 1950 Foreman adapted Edmond Rostand's classic romantic play *Cyrano de Bergerac*, about the seventeenth-century French poet and swordsman who thinks he is unlovable because of his extraordinarily large nose and therefore helps the woman he loves to marry a handsome guardsman. Since *Cyrano de Bergerac* depends as much on Rostand's dialogue as it does on plot, Foreman kept the Brian Hooker translation intact and confined himself mainly to expanding a few scenes while also condensing the play to 112 minutes running time. The film was another critical and box-office hit; José Ferrer, who had starred in the 1946 Broadway version of the play, also starred in the film and won the Academy Award for Best Actor.

Foreman decided next to concentrate his energies on a film that was to be the high point of his career: *High Noon* (1952). As Foreman recalled during a lecture at the American Film Institute, the project began when he was asked to do a story about the United Nations and the necessity for free nations to align themselves in a common struggle. The more Foreman pondered, the more he realized that the story could be told in an analogous narrative about the old American West. With a situation involving a frontier town fighting for survival against marauding outlaws, Foreman would deal with the idea of world peace on a smaller-than-global scale. As he began to work on the idea, his enthusiasm mounted. But after submitting a story outline to his agent, Foreman was astonished to find that the agent had read a story along similar lines. Foreman located that short story, "The Tin Star" by John W. Cunningham, purchased the rights, and proceeded to complete the screenplay of *High Noon*.

Foreman's script actually owes little to "The Tin Star." In the story, the marshall's gun hand is crippled by arthritis and he is aided in the shoot-out

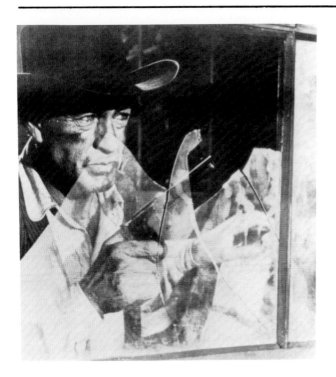

Gary Cooper in his Oscar-winning role as Marshall Will Kane in High Noon

by his deputy, who takes over when the sheriff is killed. *High Noon* opens with the marriage of Marshall Will Kane (Gary Cooper). He is resigning his office and planning to leave town when word comes that an outlaw he sent to prison five years before is returning to kill him. The townspeople, who want no trouble, urge him to leave as planned, but he refuses. No one will help him fight the outlaw and his gang, and his time is running out. (The film runs for eighty-five minutes, which is also the time of the action.) *High Noon* was produced by Kramer and Glass and directed by Fred Zinnemann. Upon its release, the film was recognized as a Western classic. Foreman's screenplay was nominated for an Academy Award and won the Writers Guild Award; Gary Cooper won an Oscar for best actor and the film was nominated as best picture.

Shortly before *High Noon* was released, in September 1951, Foreman was asked to testify before the House Un-American Activities Committee about his membership in the Communist party. Foreman agreed to testify but refused to confirm his membership or to name other party members. He was classified an "unfriendly witness" and as a result found himself shunned by his friends and associates in Hollywood. He had severed his business relationship with Stanley Kramer and announced a production company to be formed with

Gary Cooper, but the company was dissolved when Cooper yielded to political pressure and withdrew. Foreman was unable to find work and made the decision to leave the United States.

In May 1952 Foreman sailed to England. His passport was taken from him, but he was able to stay in England as a working resident while pursuing legal action to have his passport returned. The case went on for three years, and during that time Foreman wrote for British television, worked as an adviser on several British films, and became an assistant to Alexander Korda. For the most part, he refused the offers to ghostwrite scripts, but there were exceptions. In 1955 he and another blacklisted writer, Harold Buchman, wrote *The Sleeping Tiger* as Derek Frye. With Michael Wilson, also a victim of the blacklist, Foreman cowrote *The Bridge on the River Kwai* (1957). The film was set in a Japanese prisoner-of-war camp during the Second World War; a British officer (Alec Guinness) and his men are compelled to build a bridge while an American who has escaped from the camp (William Holden) is on an expedition to destroy it. The film was a great critical and box-office success, winning Academy awards for best picture, best director (David Lean), best actor (Guinness), and best cinematography. It also won the award for best screenplay, but that award was not given to Foreman and Wilson, who had written the screenplay without credit. The award was presented instead to Pierre Boulle, the French author of the novel on which the film is based. Boulle, who could not write in English, received official screenplay credit.

The popularity of *The Bridge on the River Kwai* encouraged Columbia Pictures to defy the blacklist and openly hire Foreman and his company, Open Roads Films, Ltd., to write and/or produce films in England. The first was *The Key* (1958), taken from Jan de Hartog's novel *Stella* about a bereaved woman who permits a series of Navy officers to become her lovers. *The Guns of Navarone* (1961), for which Foreman received another Academy Award nomination, is an adaptation of Alistair MacLean's World War II adventure about a team of saboteurs sent ashore to destroy two huge cannons on a Greek island held by the Nazis. Less successful was another World War II epic, *The Victors* (1963), which Foreman wrote as well as directed. *Mackenna's Gold* (1969), a Western adventure about the search for lost gold, was released in a severely edited form and was a critical and financial disaster. Foreman ended his association with Columbia with *Young Winston* (1972), about the early years of Churchill; the film had been made at the request of Churchill, who

Alec Guinness in The Bridge on the River Kwai. *Because of the Hollywood blacklist, Foreman and his collaborator Michael Wilson received no screenplay credit for this film.*

greatly admired *The Guns of Navarone*. During this period, Foreman produced all his own scripts and helped produce, but did not write, *The Mouse that Roared* (1959), *Born Free* (1966), *Otley* (1969), and *The Virgin Soldiers* (1970).

During nearly twenty-five years abroad, Foreman retained his American citizenship, and in 1975 he returned to the United States and took up his career in Hollywood again. Since then, he has served on the Advisory Board of the American Film Institute, the Executive Board of the Writers Guild of America, the Public Media Panel of the National Endowment for the Arts, and the Board of Directors of Los Angeles's Center Theatre Group. He lectures frequently at colleges and universities. He has been the executive producer of several movies for television, and one of these, *The Golden Gate Murders* (1979), received some theatrical release after its television airing.

Foreman has done little screenwriting since his return to the United States. He wrote the screen story for the sequel to *The Guns of Navarone*, *Force 10*

from Navarone (1978), for American International Productions. A three-year contract with MCA-Universal resulted in only a few unproduced screenplays. In February 1980, he signed a five-year contract to produce and write four films for Warner Bros. The first of these, *When Time Ran Out* (1980), was cowritten with Stirling Silliphant. One of the last "disaster" movies, it depicted a group of people trying to escape an erupting volcano. The movie was a critical and financial failure, and Foreman has not had a screenplay produced since.

Carl Foreman has left an indelible mark on the history of screenwriting with three films which must be considered classics: *High Noon*, *Bridge on the River Kwai*, and *The Guns of Navarone*.

References:

Hollis Alpert, "Someone Worth Fighting For," *Saturday Review* (28 December 1963): 16-18;

Marshall Berges, "Eve and Carl Foreman," *Los Angeles Times*, Home Section, 15 January 1978, pp. 29-32;

Mary Blume, "Blacklist," *Los Angeles Times*, Calendar Section, 16 June 1960, p. 16;

Gordon Gow, "Interrogation," *Films and Filming* (August 1972): 14-17;

Penelope Houston and Kenneth Cavender, "Interview with Carl Foreman," *Sight and Sound* (Summer 1958): 220;

Paul Jacobs, "Good Guys, Bad Guys and Congressman Walter," *Reporter* (15 May 1958): 29-31;

Arthur Knight, "Carl Foreman, the Lesson of History," *Hollywood Reporter* (10 February 1978): 10;

Knight, "Carl Foreman, Professional as Teacher," *Hollywood Reporter* (14 April 1978): 10;

John Francis Lane, "Big Guns," *Films and Filming* (August 1960): 28;

Joe Medjuck, "Carl Foreman," *Take One*, 3 (9 November 1973): 21;

M. Yacower, "Cyrano de H.U.A.C.," *Journal of Popular Film*, 1 (January 1976): 68-75.

Daniel Fuchs
(25 June 1909-   )

Gabriel Miller
Rutgers University

See also the Fuchs entry in *DLB 9, American Novelists, 1910-1945*.

MOTION PICTURES: *The Day the Bookies Wept* (RKO, 1939), story;

The Big Shot (Warner Bros., 1942), story; screenplay by Fuchs, Bertram Millhauser, and Abem Finkel;

The Hard Way (Warner Bros., 1942), screenplay by Fuchs and Peter Viertel;

Between Two Worlds (Warner Bros., 1944), screenplay;

The Gangster (Allied Artists, 1947), screenplay adapted by Fuchs from his novel *Low Company*;

Hollow Triumph (Eagle Lion, 1948), screenplay;

Criss Cross (Universal, 1949), screenplay;

Panic in the Streets (20th Century-Fox, 1950), adaptation;

Storm Warning (Warner Bros., 1951), screenplay by Fuchs and Richard Brooks;

Taxi (20th Century-Fox, 1952), screenplay by Fuchs and D. M. Marshman, Jr.;

The Human Jungle (Allied Artists, 1954), screenplay by Fuchs and William Sackheim;

Love Me or Leave Me (M-G-M, 1955), screen story; screenplay by Fuchs and Isobel Lennart;

Interlude (Universal, 1957), screenplay by Fuchs and Franklin Coen;

Jeanne Eagels (Columbia, 1957), screenplay by Fuchs, Sonya Levien, and John Fante.

Daniel Fuchs (Culver Pictures)

BOOKS: *Summer in Williamsburg* (New York: Vanguard, 1934; London: Constable, 1935);

Homage to Blenholt (New York: Vanguard, 1936; London: Constable, 1936);

Low Company (New York: Vanguard, 1937; London: Constable, 1937);

Stories, by Fuchs and others (New York: Farrar, Straus & Cudahy, 1956; London: Gollancz, 1957);

West of the Rockies (New York: Knopf, 1971; London: Secker & Warburg, 1971);

The Apathetic Bookie Joint (New York: Methuen, 1979; London: Secker & Warburg, 1980).

SELECTED PERIODICAL PUBLICATIONS: "Dream City or the Drugged Lake," *Cinema Arts* (Summer 1937);

"A Hollywood Diary," *New Yorker*, 14 (6 August 1938): 22-27;

"Writing for the Movies," *Commentary*, 33 (February 1962): 104-116;

"Days in the Gardens of Hollywood," *New York Times Book Review*, 18 July 1971.

Daniel Fuchs was born in New York City and grew up in the poor section of Brooklyn that became the setting for his early novels. His parents were Jacob Fuchs, a newsstand owner, and Sara (Cohen) Fuchs. Fuchs's writing talent developed early; after serving as editor of his high-school paper, he went on to City College of New York, where he majored in philosophy and graduated in 1930. Soon after that, he sent a long account of growing up in Williamsburg to the *New Republic*, where editor Malcolm Cowley encouraged Fuchs to turn it into a novel and also published part of it in the magazine as "Where Al Capone Grew Up" (1931). During this time Fuchs was working as a permanent substitute teacher in the Brooklyn public school system. He wrote his first two novels during summer vacations. In 1932 he married Susan Chessen; they have two sons. Fuchs's first novel, *Summer in Williamsburg* (1934), was the story of a young writer's struggle in the ghetto. His second, *Homage to Blenholt* (1936), was lighter in tone, the story of a young man's plans to attend the funeral of Blenholt, the sewer commissioner. Fuchs's third novel, his last before going to Hollywood, was *Low Company* (1937), set in Neptune Beach (a fictional representative of Brighton Beach).

In 1937 Fuchs received his first Hollywood offer, a thirteen-week contract with RKO. Disgusted by the poor sales of his books, he accepted the offer and left for California. Like most Eastern novelists, Fuchs was horrified by the studio system, feeling that quality work was rejected and mediocrity encouraged. He wrote several satiric essays about his experiences, notably "A Hollywood Diary" and "Dream City or the Drugged Lake." When his contract expired without his accomplishing much, he went back East, vowing never to return. But he changed his mind in 1940, and with the exception of a few years in the military and two stints in Europe working for Sam Spiegel, he has been in California ever since.

Despite the fact that Fuchs has worked at several different studios, his work contains a thematic unity; his most successful scripts, like his novels, are concerned with the underside of life. The characters he fashioned for the screen are not the debonair, elegant individuals that his fictional characters dream about, but troubled people who have their own frustrations, fears, and disappointments. His heroes rarely win out; his endings are not happy, the plots never escapist.

Fuchs's name appears on fourteen films, although he worked on many others. He received his first film credit for the story to *The Day the Bookies Wept* (1939)—an adaptation of his short story "Crazy over Pigeons"—but he did not work on the script. His first screenplay credit was for *The Big Shot* (1942), a Warner Bros. film starring Humphrey Bogart as a man who is convicted of robbery and escapes from prison. Fuchs's characteristic sense of inescapable fate is enforced by the flashback device of the hero narrating the events of the story from his deathbed.

The Hard Way (1942) was the first of Fuchs's show-business films. These films have more in common with his work in the crime genre than with the usual Hollywood success story, for even the characters who manage to succeed in Fuchs's world do so at a price that nullifies their achievements. *The Hard Way*, like *The Big Shot*, is narrated from a deathbed, and its protagonist, like the characters in many of Fuchs's gangster films, will die as punishment for a misspent life. The story centers on two sisters (Ida Lupino and Joan Leslie) who escape from a dreary mining-town existence by joining a pair of itinerant dancers, whom they later abandon when offered a chance at "the big time." One of the sisters claws her way up to the top, ruining the lives of everyone around her until at last, having failed in an attempt at suicide, she tells her story from her deathbed.

After adapting Sutton Vane's fantasy play *Outward Bound* into *Between Two Worlds* (1944), Fuchs wrote three more crime films. *The Gangster*

Jack Palance and Zero Mostel in Panic in the Streets

(1947) was taken from his novel *Low Company* and presents the most tormented of Fuchs's criminal protagonists. He is not obsessed with success but content with his small prostitution business. Unlike the typical motion-picture gangster, he does not drive a car or carry a gun. At the end, he is killed not because of overreaching ambition but because he himself wishes to be killed; his sense of despair has convinced him that death is the only exit from an empty existence.

Another Fuchs film interesting for the complex characterization of its protagonist is *Hollow Triumph* (1948). A former medical student (Paul Henreid) has turned to crime and almost gets away with impersonating a psychiatrist who strongly resembles him. The personalities of the criminal and psychiatrist are well developed and the criminal's efforts in plotting his hoax are ingeniously worked out. Fuchs's characters, however, never escape the forces of fate, and the student, too, is trapped and destroyed by forces beyond his control.

The air of impending doom is most effectively handled in *Criss Cross* (1949). The film presents two rival gangsters, Steve Thompson (Burt Lancaster) and Slim Dundee (Dan Duryea), involved in a rob-

bery scheme. Thompson is in love with Dundee's wife, Anna (Yvonne De Carlo), and this relationship provides the essence of the film's fatalistic mood. Thompson changes his mind about the robbery and turns Dundee in. Then he tries to run away with Anna, but they are both killed by Dundee. *Criss Cross* is a very skillfully written film noir, well directed by Robert Siodmak.

In *Panic in the Streets* (1950) Fuchs deals with a claustrophobic, closed situation; the working title of his version, "Quarantine," emphasizes this no-exit theme. (Despite the fact that most of Fuchs's ideas are retained in the final version, Fuchs only received credit for adapting the story by Edward and Edna Anhalt; Richard Murphy is credited with the screenplay.) The film centers on the efforts of a public-health official (Richard Widmark) and a police captain (Paul Douglas) to find two murderers who unknowingly came into contact with pneumonic plague. Naturally the criminals (Zero Mostel and Jack Palance) evade the authorities who cannot announce the presence of plague lest they create widespread panic. Fuchs was nominated for a Writers Guild award for his work on this film.

Fuchs followed *Panic in the Streets* with *Storm*

6-18-54   P.17

As Johnny, disgusted, exits with Georgie,   33
who's grinning -   CONT'D
                                                   (2)

                    Stage Manager (calling over)
Mr. Frobisher, they can't rehearse without music!

              Frobisher (disinterestedly)
So hum to them.

                              DISSOLVE TO:

                                                   34 OUT

     INT. LAUNDRY - JOHNNY AND GEORGIE   35

as they go past big vats, piles of wetwash,
etc., towards an office made of glass parti-
tions. Near it the Gimp stands with Ruth,
proudly showing off his joint.

                    Marty (to Ruth)
You notice how the help wears gloves? Once the
wash is washed, it ain't touched by a human hand.
Maybe I'm crazy, but I like things clean!

                    Ruth (admiringly)
That's wonderful, Mr. Snyder --

                    Georgie (interrupting, proudly)
I got him, boss - the piano player.

     Marty turns, as does Ruth - who looks at
     Johnny quickly once and then away. Marty
     nods at him, gestures towards the office.
     As they all follow him into it -

     INT. OFFICE   36

     Marty sits down behind the desk - gestures
     Ruth to a chair near it, but doesn't ask
     Johnny to sit. Getting right to business -

                    Marty (to Johnny)
How much you get an hour to coach?

                    Johnny (puzzled)
Coach -- ?

                    Marty (indicating Ruth)
Miss -- uhhh - Miss Etling. She wants to sing.
          (he shrugs, indicating how silly this is)
She's got some idea it's important right at the
beginning she shouldn't make bad habits, she should
have arrangements and -- and all like that.

     Hiding a smile, Johnny looks over at Ruth,
     who meets his eyes calmly.

Page from the screenplay by Fuchs and Isobel Lennart for Love Me or Leave Me

Robert Keith, James Cagney, and Doris Day in Love Me or Leave Me. *Fuchs's story for this motion picture won an Academy Award in 1955.*

Warning (1951), a violent film about rape and a small town terrorized by the Ku Klux Klan. Next came *Taxi* (1952), an entertaining but slight comedy about a New York cab driver (Dan Dailey) trying to help an Irish girl find her husband; the film is enlivened by the effective dialogue characteristic of Fuchs's best screen work. *The Human Jungle* (1954), with its documentarylike treatment of a typical day at a precinct station, is in keeping with Fuchs's interest in the underside of life.

    Love Me or Leave Me (1955) won Fuchs an Academy Award for best original story (he also co-wrote the screenplay with Isobel Lennart) and is probably his best-known film. It is a study of 1930s singer Ruth Etting (Doris Day) and her relationship with Martin Snyder (James Cagney), the small-time racketeer who takes charge of her career and eventually marries her. The film succeeds mainly because of the realistic portrayal of its two main characters, whose relationship is examined unsparingly, and for the crisp, tense dialogue that is Fuchs's hallmark as a writer. The picture won the Writers Guild award for best written American musical and received an Academy Award nomina-

tion for best screenplay. Cagney was also nominated as best actor.

    The success of *Love Me or Leave Me* was followed by *Interlude* (1957), about a married composer in love with another woman, and *Jeanne Eagels* (1957), another, less effective film about show business. As in *Love Me or Leave Me*, the heroine in *Jeanne Eagels* (Kim Novak) is given a break by a tough male (Jeff Chandler). She rises to the top, has an unhappy marriage, becomes dependent on alcohol and drugs, and finally dies. The film suffers from poor characterizations and an episodic, loosely organized script. Although Fuchs received screen credit, most of his original script was discarded.

    Fuchs's last film was *Oceans Eleven* (1960), a caper film on which he worked with Harry Brown and Charles Lederer. At his own request, he received no credit. Since then he has continued to write fiction and has published two essays about his Hollywood experiences: "Writing for the Movies" and "Days in the Gardens of Hollywood." His Hollywood novel, *West of the Rockies*, was published in 1971, and a collection of short stories, *The Apathetic Bookie Joint*, was published in 1979.

References:

Irving Howe, "Daniel Fuchs: Escape from Williamsburg," *Commentary* (6 July 1948): 29-34;

Gabriel Miller, *Daniel Fuchs* (Boston: Twayne, 1979).

Samuel Fuller

(12 August 1912-   )

Lee Tsiantis

MOTION PICTURES: *Hats Off* (Grand National, 1937), screen story and screenplay by Fuller and Edmund Joseph;

It Happened in Hollywood (Columbia, 1937), screenplay by Fuller, Ethel Hill, and Harvey Ferguson;

Adventure in Sahara (Columbia, 1938), screen story;

Federal Man-Hunt (Republic, 1938), story by Fuller and William Lively;

Gangs of New York (Republic, 1938), screen story; screenplay by Fuller, Wellyn Totman, and Charles Francis Royal;

Bowery Boy (Republic, 1941), screen story by Fuller and Sidney Sutherland;

Confirm or Deny (20th Century-Fox, 1941), story by Fuller and Henry Wales;

Power of the Press (Columbia, 1942), screen story;

Gangs of the Waterfront (Republic, 1945), screen story;

I Shot Jesse James (Lippert, 1949), screenplay;

The Baron of Arizona (Lippert, 1950), screen story and screenplay;

The Steel Helmet (Lippert, 1951), screen story and screenplay;

Fixed Bayonets (20th Century-Fox, 1951), screen story and screenplay;

Park Row (United Artists, 1952), screen story and screenplay;

Pickup on South Street (20th Century-Fox, 1953), screenplay;

Hell and High Water (20th Century-Fox, 1954), screenplay by Fuller and Jesse Lasky, Jr.;

House of Bamboo (20th Century-Fox, 1955), additional dialogue;

Run of the Arrow (Universal, 1957), screen story and screenplay;

Forty Guns (20th Century-Fox, 1957), screen story and screenplay;

China Gate (20th Century-Fox, 1957), screen story and screenplay;

Verboten! (Columbia, 1959), screen story and screenplay;

The Crimson Kimono (Columbia, 1959), screen story and screenplay;

Underworld, USA (RKO/Columbia, 1961), screen story and screenplay;

Merrill's Marauders (Warner Bros.,1962), screenplay by Fuller and Milton Sperling;

Shock Corridor (Allied Artists, 1963), screen story and screenplay;

The Naked Kiss (Allied Artists, 1964), screen story and screenplay;

Shark! (Heritage Calderon, 1969), screenplay by Fuller and John Kingbridge;

Dead Pigeon on Beethoven Street (Bavaria/Atelier/Gesellschaft Productions, 1972), screenplay;

The Deadly Tracker (Warner Bros., 1973), screen story;

The Klansman (Paramount, 1974), screenplay by Fuller and Millard Kaufman;

The Big Red One (Lorimar Productions/United Artists, 1980), screenplay;

White Dog (Paramount, 1982), screenplay by Fuller and Curtis Hanson.

TELEVISION: "It Tolls For Thee," *The Virginian* (NBC, 1962), script;

"High Devil," *The Iron Horse* (ABC, 1966), script;

"Hellcat," *The Iron Horse* (ABC, 1966), script by Fuller and Oliver Crawford.

BOOKS: *Burn, Baby, Burn!* (New York: Phoenix Press, 1935);

Test Tube Baby (New York: William Godwin, 1936);

Make Up and Kiss (New York: William Godwin, 1938);

The Dark Page (New York: Duell, Sloan & Pearce, 1944);

144 Piccadilly (New York: R.W. Baron, 1971; London: New English Library, 1972);

Samuel Fuller (photo by Maureen Lambray)

Dead Pigeon on Beethoven Street (New York: Pyramid, 1974);

The Big Red One (New York: Bantam, 1980; London: Corgi, 1980).

PERIODICAL PUBLICATIONS: "What is a Film?," *Cinema*, 2 (July 1964): 22-24; republished in *Hollywood Directors 1941-76*, edited by Richard Kozarski (New York: Oxford, 1977), pp. 339-347;

"News That's Fit to Film," *American Film*, 1 (October 1975): 20-24;

"War That's Fit to Shoot," *American Film*, 2 (November 1976): 58-62.

Samuel Fuller is the writer-director (and often producer) of all of the films he has made since 1949—a creative accomplishment approached in the American cinema only by Orson Welles, Joseph L. Mankiewicz, and Preston Sturges. Fuller has produced an intensely personal body of work within the confines of Hollywood's established "B" feature genres: war movies, Westerns, gangster films. Violence, irony, and paradox are at the heart of Fuller's cinema; his scripts are simple, direct, and crude; his protagonists emotional, obsessed outsiders often living on the fringes of society.

Samuel Michael Fuller was born in Worcester, Massachusetts. His father died when he was ten, and his family moved to New York City, where he found a job as a newspaper hawker. Quitting high school, Fuller became a copyboy for Hearst editor Arthur Brisbane. At seventeen he became the youngest crime and police reporter in the country, working for the *New York Evening Graphic*, the most sensational of the city's tabloids. He later moved to the West Coast as a waterfront reporter for the *San Diego Sun*. Fuller wrote three pulp novels between 1935 and 1938, drawing on his experiences as a newspaperman. It was also during this time that he started working in the movies, ghostwriting stories for established screenwriters. His first screen credit was for *Hats Off* (1937). Between 1937 and 1945, he was credited with the screenplay or screen story for eight more films, including *It Happened in Hollywood* (1937), *Adventure in Sahara* (1938), *Federal Man-hunt* (1938), *Gangs of New York* (1938), *Bowery Boy* (1941), *Confirm or Deny* (1941), *Power of the Press*

(1942), and *Gangs of the Waterfront* (1945).

Fuller served as a corporal in the First Infantry Division (known as The Big Red One) in World War II and fought in North Africa and Europe. Returning to Hollywood after the war, Fuller became a screenwriter in the studio stable at Warner Bros. None of his work at the time made it to the screen, but his reputation began to spread, and in 1948 he was approached by Robert Lippert, a producer who specialized in low-budget Westerns, and asked to write a script. Fuller insisted that he be paid minimum scale to write and direct. The result was *I Shot Jesse James* (1949), filmed in ten days for $110,000.

Fuller's experience as an infantryman and journalist influenced his next two films, both Korean war dramas, as incidents and situations remembered from fighting in The Big Red One were filtered through his tabloid newsman's sensibility. *The Steel Helmet* and *Fixed Bayonets* (both 1951) formulated Fuller's ground rules for war movies: "Leave the soldiers dirty, tired, and unshaven. Never put girls into war films." *The Steel Helmet* depicts the circumstances of one American sergeant (Gene Evans) during the early days of the Korean War; it has become one of Fuller's most highly regarded films. In *Fixed Bayonets*, a rear-guard platoon in Korea is left behind by an American force to give the impression of remaining strength. The platoon corporal (Richard Basehart), psychologically unable to kill, assumes command as the officers are picked off; gradually he acquires the ability to kill. The film displays much of the bitter humor that was to become a Fuller trademark.

The Steel Helmet cost $103,000 to make and grossed a phenomenal $2,000,000. Fuller used his share of the profits to finance *Park Row* (1952), one of his finest films, and one that combines his love for movies with his love for journalism. In *Park Row*, heroes of New York's rambunctious early newspaper days—James Gordon Bennett, Horace Greeley, Charles E. Dana, and Joseph Pulitzer—are combined in one character, editor Phineas Mitchell. Mitchell gets fired from the reigning daily, the *Star*, and resolves to found the *Globe*. Almost every legend of journalism's early days finds its way into Fuller's script, which dramatizes the genesis of the phrase "off the cuff," the birth of the newsstand, and the waging of the first circulation war.

Park Row's relative failure disappointed Fuller, but he rebounded with *Pickup on South Street* (1953), which won a Bronze Lion Award at the

Thelma Ritter and Richard Kiley in Pickup on South Street, *winner of the Bronze Lion Award at the Venice Film Festival*

Venice Film Festival and garnered an Academy Award nomination for supporting actress Thelma Ritter. The first of Fuller's crime films in a modern setting, *Pickup on South Street* has as its protagonists pickpocket Skip McCoy (Richard Widmark), police informer Moe (Ritter), and prostitute Candy (Jean Peters). The pickpocket takes the contents of the prostitute's purse including, unknowingly, a piece of top-secret microfilm she was carrying for one of her customers, a Communist agent (Richard Kiley). The police and the F.B.I. appeal to McCoy for help; he refuses, but is forced to battle the Communist agent himself. *Pickup on South Street* has been discussed largely for its seeming paradox: it is an anti-Communist film, but its protagonists are not patriots but criminals.

Hell and High Water (1954) is noteworthy less for Fuller's screenplay than for its technical accomplishments. This Cold War melodrama was thrust on Fuller to see if conventional camera movements could be made in a confined space (a submarine) with the new Cinemascope ratio. Fuller's script credit for his next film, *House of Bamboo* (1955), was for additional dialogue only. The film was a remake of *The Street with No Name* (1948) and depicted the efforts of an American police officer (Robert Stack) to infiltrate a crime ring run in Tokyo by American expatriates.

In 1957 Fuller wrote and directed two Westerns, *Run of the Arrow* and *Forty Guns*, both depictions of conflicting ideologies. *Run of the Arrow* is about a Southerner (Rod Steiger) who joins the Sioux nation because he is embittered by the outcome of the Civil War. He quarrels with a Union lieutenant (Ralph Meeker) he shot and wounded during the war and is eventually forced to kill the lieutenant to save him from torture by the Sioux.

Forty Guns tells of the love of gunman Griff Bonnell (Barry Sullivan) for powerful landowner Jessica Drummond (Barbara Stanwyck). Jessica's brother Brockie (John Ericson) kills Griff's brother Wes (Gene Barry) and forces Griff, who has not killed a man in ten years, to kill him. Most important for Fuller is the attraction-repulsion in the relationship between Griff and Jessica—the former representing government, law and order, the latter capitalist free enterprise.

Fuller's next films, *China Gate* (1957), *Verboten!* (1959), and *The Crimson Kimono* (1959), all deal with the question of national identity. The hero of *China Gate* cannot accept his child by an Occidental-looking Eurasian because the child has Oriental features. An American soldier in love with a German woman in *Verboten!* is plagued with doubt over

whether or not she is a Nazi. A nisei policeman in *The Crimson Kimono* is in love with an American woman and she with him, but he resents his feelings toward her.

It was in the late 1950s that Fuller's international reputation began to grow, with the support of a group of young European cineastes. In 1957 Jean-Luc Godard wrote an admiring review of *Forty Guns* in the French magazine *Cahiers du Cinéma*, extolling the virtues of a film "so rich in invention—despite an incomprehensible plot—and so bursting with daring conceptions that it reminds one of the extravagances of Abel Gance and Stroheim, or purely and simply of Murnau." The rebellious *Cahiers du Cinéma* critics were reassessing Hollywood cinema at the time, in the process coining a new word, *auteur*, for the critical vocabulary. They wanted to wrest films from the purely literary conventions by which cinema was then being judged by most reviewers, and it was in this spirit that they took Fuller's iconoclasm to heart. Both *Breathless* (1960), Godard's first feature film, and François Truffaut's *The Bride Wore Black* (1968) pay homage to Fuller by reprising scenes from *Forty Guns*.

Fuller's first marriage ended in divorce in 1959. He married German-born actress Christa Lang in 1965, and they have a daughter, Samantha, born in 1975.

In 1961 Fuller made *Underworld, USA*, about a man (Cliff Robertson) trying to avenge the death of his father, who was murdered by organized crime. As in *House of Bamboo*, the protagonist infiltrates the gang and strikes from within. He destroys the villains but is killed in the process, a victim of his own passion for revenge. This was followed by *Merrill's Marauders* (1962), a financially successful war film.

Fuller's next two films, *Shock Corridor* (1963) and *The Naked Kiss* (1964), were extremely personal projects, expressing general disenchantment and pessimism. In *Shock Corridor*, a journalist poses as an inmate of an asylum to solve a murder committed there; he wins a Pulitzer Prize for the resulting story. Fuller makes it clear from the start that the journalist is already a borderline psychotic, and at the film's end he has lost his sanity. Fuller uses the other inmates to address problems of the early 1960s: a deserter from the Korean War believes he is Jeb Stuart; the only Negro at a Southern university believes he is a Klansman; a nuclear scientist believes he is a child. *Shock Corridor* was hailed as a masterpiece in Europe, but it was totally ignored in America.

The Naked Kiss is about a prostitute who attempts to reform, almost achieving respectability by becoming engaged to a small town's most prominent citizen, but on the night before their marriage she discovers he is a child molester and bludgeons him to death. She is exonerated when a child confirms her story, but she leaves town anyway. Fuller's ultimate irony is that the world of "legitimacy" and "respectability" in all its hypocrisy has proved more disillusioning than a life of prostitution; the woman returns to her former life.

The Naked Kiss was a critical and commercial failure; it was also the last film Fuller was to complete with American financing for more than a decade. Frustrated with his inability to raise money for projects, he went to France, making appearances as himself in Godard's *Pierrot le Fou* (1965) and Luc Moullet's *Brigitte et Brigitte* (1966). (Fuller has continued to make appearances in films of other directors who wish to pay tribute to him in this way: Dennis Hopper's *The Last Movie* [1971]; Wim Wenders's *The American Friend* [1977], *Hammett* [1982], and *The State of Things* [1982]; and Steven Spielberg's *1941* [1979].) "Caine," an adventure story starring Burt Reynolds and filmed in Mexico in 1967, was recut against Fuller's wishes, retitled *Shark!*, and released in 1969. Although Fuller demanded that his name be taken off the final product, he did receive credit on the film. Deal after deal fell through, and *Dead Pigeon on Beethoven Street* (1972), a gangster melodrama shot in Germany, did nothing to enhance his reputation. He provided the story for *The Deadly Tracker* (1973) and was set to direct the film but was fired; in 1974 he coauthored the screenplay for *The Klansman*, about racial problems in the South.

Finally, through Peter Bogdanovich's intercession, Lorimar productions came through with financing for Fuller's most cherished project, *The Big Red One*. Fuller's most autobiographical film, it is based on his World War II experiences and depicts the war as seen by an experienced sergeant (Lee Marvin) and four young recruits (Mark Hamill, Robert Carradine, Bobby DiCicco, Kelly Ward). Shooting began in 1978, but a long postproduction period was spent getting the film down to a manageable length, and it was not released until 1980. The film was given uniformly positive reviews, many commenting that it was good to see Fuller back at work again. The film was an American entry in the 1980 Cannes Film Festival. Fuller wrote a novel from his film script; it was published at the time of the film's release.

Fuller considered several projects following the success of *The Big Red One* —he has always written six full screenplays a year—and finally cowrote

and directed *White Dog*, based on an episode from Romain Gary's book. The film, about a dog trained to attack blacks, was considered too controversial to be released. It was given very limited test engagements in 1982 but taken out of distribution, recut, and relegated to cable television. Always appreciated most in France, Fuller went there for his next project, "Thieves After Dark," which he directed and coauthored. It has not been released.

Fuller's career as a filmmaker may be best defined by his appearance in Godard's *Pierrot le Fou*. In that movie, he gave his personal definition of cinema: "Film is a battleground: love, hate, action, violence, death, . . . in a word, emotion." Fuller's achievement has been to take that emotion and leaven it with irony and humor, producing a body of work unique for its narrative drive and stylistic flourish, at once straightforward, uncompromising, and unsentimental.

Interviews:
Stig Bjorkman and Mark Shivas, "Samuel Fuller: Two Interviews," *Movie*, 17 (Winter 1969-70): 25-31;
Eric Sherman and Martin Rubin, *The Director's Event* (New York: Atheneum, 1970), pp. 123-191;
Richard Thompson, "Hey, Mom, Where's My Suicide Note Collection?," *Movietone News*, 50 (June 1976): 1-8;
Thompson, "The Flavor of Ketchup," *Film Comment*, 13 (January-February 1977): 25-31;
Russell Merritt and Peter Lehman, "Being Wrong is the Right Way of Living," *Wide Angle*, 3, No. 3: 66-75.

References:
Manny Farber, "Samuel Fuller," in *Negative Space* (New York: Praeger, 1971), pp. 129-133;
Nicholas Garnham, *Samuel Fuller* (New York: Viking, 1971);
Jean-Luc Godard, "Forty Guns," in *Godard on Godard*, edited by Jean Narboni and Tom Milne (New York: Viking, 1972), pp. 61-62;
Phil Hardy, *Samuel Fuller* (New York: Praeger, 1970);
Richard T. Jameson, "Creative Contact," *Movietone News*, 50 (June 1976): 19-26;
Daniel Melnick, "An Old Pro On the Go Again," *New York Times Magazine*, 4 May 1980, pp. 48, 58-78;
Andrew Sarris, "Samuel Fuller," in his *The American Cinema: Directors and Directions 1929-1968* (New York: Dutton, 1968), pp. 93-94.

Jules Furthman
(5 March 1888-22 September 1966)

Renée D. Pennington

MOTION PICTURES: *Steady Company* (Rex/Universal, 1915), story;

Bound on the Wheel (Rex/Universal, 1915), story;

Mountain Justice (Rex/Universal, 1915), story;

Chasing the Limited (Bison/Universal, 1915), story;

Quits (Rex/Universal, 1915), story;

Souls in Pawn (American/Mutual, 1917), story and scenario;

The Frame Up (American/Mutual, 1917), story and adaptation; released again as *High Gear Jeffrey* (American, 1921);

The Camouflage Kiss (Fox, 1918), story; screenplay by Furthman, as Stephen Fox, and Ralph H. Spence;

More Trouble (Anderson-Bruton/Pathé, 1918), scenario, as Stephen Fox;

A Japanese Nightingale (Astra Film/Pathé, 1918), scenario, as Stephen Fox;

Hobbs in a Hurry (American/Pathé, 1918), scenario, as Stephen Fox;

Mantle of Charity (American/Pathé, 1918), scenario, as Stephen Fox;

All the World to Nothing (American/Pathé, 1918), scenario, as Stephen Fox;

Wives and Other Wives (American/Pathé, 1918), story and scenario, as Stephen Fox;

When a Man Rides Alone (American/Pathé, 1918), story and scenario, as Stephen Fox;

Where the West Begins (American/Pathé, 1919), story and scenario, as Stephen Fox;

Brass Buttons (American/Pathé, 1919), story and scenario, as Stephen Fox;

Some Liar (American/Pathé, 1919), scenario, as Stephen Fox;

A Sporting Chance (American/Pathé, 1919), story and scenario, as Stephen Fox;

This Hero Stuff (American/Pathé, 1919), story and scenario, as Stephen Fox;

Six Feet Four (American/Pathé, 1919), scenario, as Stephen Fox;

Victory (Famous Players-Lasky/Paramount, 1919), scenario, as Stephen Fox;

The Valley of Tomorrow (American/Pathé, 1920), story and scenario, as Stephen Fox;

Treasure Island (Famous Players-Lasky/Paramount, 1920), scenario, as Stephen Fox;

Jules Furthman

Would You Forgive? (Fox, 1920), story and scenario;

Leave It to Me (Fox, 1920), scenario;

The Twins of Suffering Creek (Fox, 1920), scenario;

The White Circle (Famous Players-Lasky/Paramount, 1920), scenario by Furthman and Jack Gilbert;

The Man Who Dared (Fox, 1920), story and scenario;

The Skywayman (Fox, 1920), story and scenario;

The Great Redeemer (Metro, 1920), adaptation by Furthman and Gilbert;

The Texan (Fox, 1920), scenario by Furthman and Lynn Reynolds;

The Iron Rider (Fox, 1920), scenario;

The Land of Jazz (Fox, 1920), story with Barbara La Marr Deely;

The Cheater Reformed (Fox, 1921), story; scenario by Furthman and Scott Dunlap;

The Big Punch (Fox, 1921), story and scenario;

The Blushing Bride (Fox, 1921), story and scenario;

Colorado Pluck (Fox, 1921), scenario;

Singing River (Fox, 1921), scenario;

119

The Last Trail (Fox, 1921), scenario by Furthman and Paul Schofield;

The Roof Tree (Fox, 1921), scenario;

Gleam O'Dawn (Fox, 1922), scenario;

The Ragged Heiress (Fox, 1922), story and scenario;

Arabian Love (Fox, 1922), story and scenario;

The Yellow Stain (Fox, 1922), story and scenario;

Strange Idols (Fox, 1922), scenario;

Calvert's Valley (Fox, 1922), scenario;

The Love Gambler (Fox, 1922), scenario;

A California Romance (Fox, 1922), story;

Pawn Ticket 210 (Fox, 1922), scenario;

Lovebound (Fox, 1923), scenario by Furthman and Josephine Quirk;

St. Elmo (Fox, 1923), scenario;

North of Hudson Bay (Fox, 1923), story and scenario;

The Acquittal (Universal-Jewel, 1923), scenario;

Condemned (Ben Wilson Productions/Grand-Asher Distributing Corp., 1923), story and scenario;

Try and Get It (Samuel V. Grand/Producers Distributing Corp., 1924), scenario;

Call of the Mate (Phil Goldstone Productions/Renown Pictures, 1924), story and scenario;

Sackcloth and Scarlet (Kagor Productions/Paramount, 1925), scenario by Furthman, Tom Geraghty, and Julie Herne;

Any Woman (Famous Players-Lasky/Paramount, 1925), scenario by Furthman and Beatrice Van;

Before Midnight (Banner Productions/Henry Ginsberg Distributing Corp., 1925), story and scenario;

Big Pal (Royal Pictures/Henry Ginsberg Distributing Corp., 1925), story and scenario;

The Wise Guy (Frank Lloyd Productions/First National, 1926), story;

You'd Be Surprised (Famous Players-Lasky/Paramount, 1926), story and screenplay;

Hotel Imperial (Famous Players-Lasky/Paramount, 1927), screenplay;

Casey at the Bat (Famous Players-Lasky/Paramount, 1927), screenplay;

Fashions for Women (Famous Players-Lasky/Paramount, 1927), adaptation by Furthman and Herman J. Mankiewicz;

Barbed Wire (Paramount Famous Lasky, 1927), screenplay by Furthman and Rowland V. Lee;

The Way of All Flesh (Paramount Famous Lasky, 1927), screenplay;

The City Gone Wild (Paramount Famous Lasky, 1927), screenplay; story by Furthman and Charles Furthman;

The Dragnet (Paramount Famous Lasky, 1928), adaptation; scenario by Furthman and Charles Furthman;

The Docks of New York (Paramount Famous Lasky, 1928), scenario;

Abie's Irish Rose (Paramount Famous Lasky, 1929), adaptation;

The Case of Lena Smith (Paramount Famous Lasky, 1929), screenplay;

Thunderbolt (Paramount Famous Lasky, 1929), screenplay; story by Furthman and Charles Furthman;

New York Nights (United Artists, 1929), adaptation;

Common Clay (Fox, 1930), dialogue and screenplay;

Renegades (Fox, 1930), adaptation, continuity, and dialogue;

Morocco (Paramount-Publix, 1930), screenplay and dialogue;

Body and Soul (Fox, 1931), screenplay;

Merely Mary Ann (Fox, 1931), screenplay;

The Yellow Ticket (Fox, 1931), screenplay;

Over the Hill (Fox, 1931), screenplay and dialogue by Furthman and Tom Barry;

Shanghai Express (Paramount-Publix, 1932), screenplay;

Blonde Venus (Paramount-Publix, 1932), story and screenplay by Furthman and S. K. Lauren;

The Girl in 419 (Paramount, 1933), story;

Bombshell (M-G-M, 1933), screenplay by Furthman and Johnny Lee Mahin;

China Seas (M-G-M, 1935), screenplay by Furthman and James Kevin McGuinness;

Mutiny on the Bounty (M-G-M, 1935), screenplay by Furthman, Talbot Jennings, and Carey Wilson;

Come and Get It! (United Artists, 1936), screenplay by Furthman and Jane Murfin;

Spawn of the North (Paramount, 1938), screenplay by Furthman and Jennings;

Only Angels Have Wings (Columbia, 1939), screenplay;

The Shanghai Gesture (United Artists, 1941), screenplay by Furthman, Josef von Sternberg, Geza Herczeg, and Karl Vollmoeller;

The Outlaw (United Artists, 1943), screen story and screenplay;

To Have and Have Not (Warner Bros., 1945), screenplay by Furthman and William Faulkner;

The Big Sleep (Warner Bros., 1946), screenplay by Furthman, Faulkner, and Leigh Brackett;

Moss Rose (20th Century-Fox, 1947), screenplay by Furthman and Tom Reed;

Nightmare Alley (20th Century-Fox, 1947), screenplay;

Pretty Baby (Warner Bros., 1950), screen story by Furthman and John Klorer;

Peking Express (Paramount, 1951), adaptation;

Jet Pilot (Universal, 1957), screen story and screen-
    play;
Rio Bravo (Warner Bros., 1959), screenplay by
    Furthman and Brackett.

BOOK: *Morocco, and Shanghai Express: Two Films by
    Joseph von Sternberg* (New York: Simon &
    Schuster, 1973; London: Lorrimer, 1973).

SELECTED PERIODICAL PUBLICATIONS:
"The Whip Hand: A Hard Rock Story," *Saturday
    Evening Post,* 185 (22 February 1913): 24-29;
"The Inn of Youth," *Smart Set,* 40 (August 1913):
    1-7.

During a career that began in the recesses of
silent film history, bridged the transition to sound,
and concluded with the script for *Rio Bravo* in 1959,
Jules Furthman epitomized the Hollywood screenwriter whose reputation as a collaborative writer
obscured his distinctive talents. His current reputation began to develop amid the analytic interest in
screenwriters that supplemented auteurism in the
early 1970s. Critics have isolated Furthman's patterns of authorship across various acting and directing styles, distinct correspondences of characterization, incident, and dialogue connecting his
scripts for such radically different filmmakers as
Josef von Sternberg and Howard Hawks. Furthman, as Hawks said, "did things differently," but
did them recognizably.

Throughout his career he wrote fictional
screen narrative, either based upon original story
treatments or adapted from other sources. His earliest scripts for silent films were comedies or melodramas, often blended with other genres such as the
Western. Most of these early efforts no longer exist,
and the film plots synopsized in the *American Film
Institute Catalogue* of features from 1921 through
1930 barely indicate the thematic explorations of
personal relationships and commitment that
characterize some of Furthman's extant silents and
much of his postsilent work. With the addition of
sound, Furthman's male characters embark on a
verbal collision course with his women, whom
Pauline Kael characterized by their "good-bad-girl
glamour." These women, however, are notable for
their differences as well as their similarities; the
degrees of eroticism, self-awareness, and humor are
variables, while the qualities of resilience and independence are constants. With a few exceptions, the
male-female relationship is a theme central to
Furthman's development of the narrative as a complex interrelationship of characters, situations, and
events. Equally important is Furthman's examina-

tion of the society of males; frequently his films
depict the loyalty that exists between men working
together under difficult, even dangerous, conditions.

Born in Chicago, Julius Grinnell Furthmann
(he later dropped one *n* from his name) spent his
childhood in the Rogers Park section of Chicago's
North Side. His father, Edmund Furthmann, was a
German immigrant who achieved prominence in
Chicago as an attorney. In 1886, Edmund Furthmann served on the prosecuting staff of the
Haymark Riot trial, and he and Sara Ford Furthmann subsequently named their youngest son after
his mentor on the case, State's Attorney Julius S.
Grinnell.

As a boy, Furthman was frequently ill, and
during convalescences he read a great deal—a habit
that led to his writing and remained with him
throughout his life. Illness, and possibly indiffer-
ence, affected his schoolwork as well, since his
grades and attendance record at the Northwestern
University Preparatory school for his only two
semesters—1904-1905—were mediocre. After he
left school, his father's death and strained relations
with his brothers at home prompted a move to Denver, where he lived with an uncle before traveling
throughout the Southwest and Mexico. He began
writing for magazines in his twenties and had at
least two short stories published in 1913. The first of
these was "The Whip Hand: A Hard Rock Story," a
melodramatic tale of rival cowhands in Montana
which appeared in the *Saturday Evening Post.* Written at a time when Western themes pervaded
popular culture (including the nascent cinema),
"The Whip Hand" is a conventional literary attempt
and foreshadows the Western motifs of Furthman's
silent film work. Six months later, the *Smart Set*
published "The Inn of Youth," a quasiauto-
biographical story about a family's domestic crisis
that reflects Furthman's own family in character
names but suggests dramatic manipulation of personal experience in the incidents it depicts.

By 1915 Furthman was selling stories to film
companies, and within two years he was writing
scripts for the American Film Company in Santa
Barbara, California. His earliest filmmaking association began there in 1917 with director Henry King,
who remembers that Furthman "wrote a story and
screenplay, *Souls in Pawn* (1917), which was originally called 'A Woman in Black.' Furthman did a
most excellent job on the screenplay."

On temporary assignment at Fox studios in
early 1918, Furthman began using the pseudonym
Stephen Fox and continued its use at American and
Paramount until March 1920, presumably because

postwar antipathy toward Germany made film companies hesitant about giving screen credit to a writer surnamed Furthman. During this period he wrote nine films directed by King and starring William Russell. *Six Feet Four* (1919), a Western drama based on a novel by Jackson Gregory, was the last of these five-to-six-reel features and the only one still known to exist.

Toward the end of 1919 Furthman left America to adapt Joseph Conrad's 1915 novel *Victory* for Maurice Tourneur. Novel and film center on the isolation of Axel Heyst on an island in the East Indies. Heyst rescues a young woman, Alma, from a neighboring island, and they become the target of three criminals. The film develops the relationship between Heyst and Alma amid a series of melodramatic events that conclude in Heyst's declaration of love for her. His commitment to action on her behalf ensures not only her emotional regeneration but also his own; it is this depth of motivation, response, and growth in the relationship that confirms *Victory* as a thematic prelude to Furthman's work with Sternberg and Hawks.

During most of 1920 Furthman was a contract writer at Fox, where his screenplays were no longer credited to Stephen Fox but to Jules Furthman. About this time, he met a young actress named Sybil Travilla, a former Mack Sennett Bathing Beauty, and in 1921 they married and she retired from films. Furthman continued his prolific output of scripts at Fox until he left the studio in 1923 and free-lanced for a few years. By 1926 Furthman was establishing himself at Paramount, where he wrote *You'd Be Surprised* (1926), a satire of drawing-room mysteries starring Raymond Griffith. It was a commercial success, and Furthman's next assignments included screenplays for two major Pola Negri vehicles, *Hotel Imperial* (1927) and *Barbed Wire* (1927), as well as *The Way of All Flesh* (1927), for which Emil Jannings won the Academy Award for Best Actor.

Furthman was the foremost screenwriter at Paramount when he began collaborating with his brother Charles, who was also a writer there but considerably less eminent. Their intermittent partnership spanned two years — 1927-1929 — and is crucial to the argument that Jules Furthman, without receiving screen credit, assisted or influenced Charles Furthman's adaptation of the Ben Hecht story for *Underworld* (1927). An early gangster film thematically concerned with the moral forces exerted by love and friendship, *Underworld* was Jules Furthman's first association with Josef von Sternberg. After its immense popularity, Jules and Charles Furthman cowrote the screenplay of

another gangster film directed by Sternberg, *The Dragnet* (1928). Contemporary reviewers dismissed it as an inferior follow-up to *Underworld*; there are no known prints in existence.

Working with Sternberg again, Furthman adapted John Monk Saunders's story "The Dockwalloper" for the script of *The Docks of New York* (1928). In the film Sadie (Betty Compson) an embittered prostitute, throws herself into the ocean but is rescued by Bill Roberts (George Bancroft), a stoker on a tramp steamer who "never missed a ship" in his life. In a drunken revelry, Bill marries Sadie and then abandons her, but jumps ship to return to her. In a situation reminiscent of *Victory*, Bill revives Sadie's trust, and her strength of character regenerates his faith in humanity. A silent film released amid the novelty of talking pictures, *The Docks of New York* was ignored by both contemporary critics and the public. Today it is a highly regarded film.

Following *The Docks of New York*, Furthman wrote the screenplay for *The Case of Lena Smith* (1929), which was the last — and reputedly the finest — of the Sternberg silents, but like *The Dragnet*, it is a lost work.

The Furthmans' next collaboration, *Thunderbolt* (1929), was for the screen story only; Furthman wrote the screenplay alone. *Thunderbolt* was conceived as a silent film but was generally released in its sound version. In the silent film, Furthman's dialogue subtitles frequently treat a balance between metaphor and colloquialism; the spoken dialogue retains this balance but with the dimension of sound seems unduly artificial. The film tells the story of the gangster Thunderbolt (George Bancroft) and his moll Ritzy (Fay Wray), who wants to go straight and marry her honest former love Bob Moran (Richard Arlen). Ritzy betrays Thunderbolt to the police so that he cannot hurt Bob. In retaliation, Thunderbolt frames Bob for murder, but finally admits Bob is innocent.

After *Thunderbolt*, Sternberg filmed *The Blue Angel* (1930) in Germany and returned to Hollywood with the film's star, Marlene Dietrich. Furthman scripted three of the six films made by Sternberg and Dietrich at Paramount. The first, *Morocco* (1930), preceded the release of *The Blue Angel* in the United States and so introduced Dietrich to the American audience, which responded by elevating it among the top moneymaking films of the year. Dietrich played a singer with a dubious past torn between two men: wealthy and stoical La Bessiere (Adolph Menjou) and Foreign Legionnaire Tom Brown (Gary Cooper).

Betty Compson and George Bancroft in a scene from The Docks of New York

Adapting Harry Hervey's original story, Furthman constructed a romantic imbroglio for Sternberg's fourth film with Dietrich. *Shanghai Express* (1932) begins at a railway station in Peking and presents a group of passengers whose facades are revealed and exploited during the journey by Henry Chang (Warner Oland), who ostensibly is a Eurasian merchant but actually is the leader of rebel troops that will hijack the train at Te Shan. The core of the narrative which connects with increasing complexity to the evolving plot intrigue and to the interactions of other characters concerns the rekindled affair between Shanghai Lily (Dietrich) and Captain Donald Harvey (Clive Brook), who had left her five years before. Since then, she has "lived by her wits along the China Coast" and has "wrecked a dozen men." *Shanghai Express* was the most financially successful of the Dietrich films directed by Sternberg.

After the narrative precision of *Morocco* and

Shanghai Express, the elliptical structure of *Blonde Venus* (1932) marks a departure in Furthman's work for the Dietrich series. With writer S. K. Lauren (and, uncredited, Sternberg), Furthman developed a story about maternal self-sacrifice. Helen Faraday (Dietrich) is the wife of chemist Edward Faraday, a man facing imminent death from radiation poisoning unless enough money can be raised to save him. She resumes her stage career and becomes involved in an affair that provides money for her husband's medical treatment but also causes him to forbid her to see their son (Dickie Moore). She flees with the child and supports him by becoming a prostitute but eventually surrenders him to her husband and becomes a very successful singer in Paris. Helen chooses the steps toward her degradation and her regeneration, operating with shrewd awareness in situations controlled by men. She makes no atonement for her actions, and eventually the smugly hypocritical Faraday accepts her return to her family. Dismissed by critics at its release, *Blonde Venus* is still criticized for its narrative wanderings, although its many episodes successively reaffirm the emphasis in *Morocco* and in *Shanghai Express* on the Dietrich character as a projection of—and challenge to—male attitudes.

By December 1932 Furthman had joined M-G-M and begun work on "Soviet," a script for Irving Thalberg based on a story by Frances Marion. But Thalberg finally shelved the project, after at least twenty-four other writers had also tackled the screenplay. In 1933 Furthman and Harry Behn cowrote a screenplay based on William Faulkner's short story "Honor," but M-G-M decided against producing that project as well. After uncredited contributions to the scripts of two 1933 releases, *The White Sister* and *The Prizefighter and the Lady*, Furthman received his first screen credit at M-G-M for *Bombshell* (1933). Although he occasionally worked at other studios, Furthman remained under contract to M-G-M until the end of 1939, writing some forty story treatments or scripts there. Most of his assignments eventually became films, yet he received screen credit on only three. Despite the labyrinth of credited and uncredited collaborators on scripts at M-G-M, Furthman's contributions can be discerned in two screenplays written for Jean Harlow that reflect his stylistic idiosyncrasies as well as represent an abrupt departure from his films for Dietrich. The subtly cadenced dialogue that he structured for her was not transferable to Harlow's stridency; characterization necessarily changed as well: Dietrich radiated sensuality, while Harlow advertized it.

For *Bombshell*, Furthman and cowriter John Lee Mahin transformed an unproduced play by Caroline Francke and Mack Crane into a satirical view of Hollywood. Jean Harlow, reigning female sex symbol at Metro, portrayed Lola Burns, reigning female sex symbol at Monarch Pictures. She is surrounded by her parasitic family, innumerable retainers, and a conniving publicity agent (Lee Tracy). The frivolous star wants successively to rendezvous with an alleged marquis (Ivan Lebedeff); renew her romance with a director (Pat O'Brien); adopt a baby; and marry a man she believes to be a Boston socialite (Franchot Tone). The film cleverly manipulates the interweaving of acting and life by blending in allusions to contemporary Hollywood personalities and creating in Lola a hectic amalgam of screen, public, and private persona. The essence of characterization in *Bombshell* is the wisecracking dialogue, and though it limits character depth, it is hilariously appropriate to the script's farcical content and its rapid-fire pacing.

Bombshell was popular with critics and filmgoers, and in 1934 Furthman became part of Irving Thalberg's writers unit at M-G-M. Occasionally, Thalberg assigned special projects such as the story treatment entitled "Buck Rogers, 2432 A.D." that Furthman wrote in 1935 but never developed further. In any case, two of Furthman's scripts did become films that year, and they were resounding box-office hits.

Two years after *Bombshell* Furthman began work on *China Seas* (1935), based on Crosbie Garstin's 1930 novel. Directed by Tay Garnett, the film depicts an act of piracy organized by ship passenger McArdle (Wallace Beery). McArdle's villainy is cushioned by his affection for China Doll (Jean Harlow), who in turn actively pursues the ship's captain, Alan Gaskell (Clark Gable). Gaskell overcomes the pirates and resumes a relationship with Sybil Barclay (Rosalind Russell), rejecting China Doll and his life at sea. Although cowritten with James Kevin McGuinness, *China Seas* remains Furthman's most personal screenplay at M-G-M, particularly because of its dialogue and plot construction. Indeed, more than one reviewer commented on the narrative similarities between this romantic adventure and *Shanghai Express*.

Furthman received his only Academy Award nomination, which he shared with cowriters Talbot Jennings and Carey Wilson, for M-G-M's adventure epic *Mutiny on the Bounty* (1935). Their adaptation of Charles Nordhoff and James Norman Hall's *Bounty* trilogy centers on the conflict between the brutal command of Captain Bligh (Charles Laughton) and the humanistic attitude of Fletcher Christian (Clark Gable), a ship's officer and subsequent leader of the mutineers. The pivotal character, though, is midshipman Roger Byam (Franchot Tone). Personally sympathetic to Christian but professionally bound to his oath of duty, Byam exemplifies the film's theme: duty must be based on mutual respect between officers and men. The screenplay did not win the Oscar, but the film won the Academy Award for Best Picture and thus became Furthman's most prestigious credit.

By special arrangement with Thalberg, producer Samuel Goldwyn secured Furthman's services for the screenplay of *Come and Get It!* (1936). Furthman and Jane Murfin coauthored this adaptation of Edna Ferber's 1935 novel, which was ultimately directed by Howard Hawks and William Wyler. Furthman's first work with Hawks, *Come and Get It!* concerns the rise of a man (Edward Arnold) from chore boy in a timber camp to Wisconsin

Charles Laughton as Captain Bligh and Clark Gable as Fletcher Christian in Mutiny on the Bounty, *winner of the 1935 Academy Award for Best Picture*

lumber magnate during the late nineteenth century. He falls in love with a saloon singer (Frances Farmer) but rejects her for a lucrative marriage to his employer's daughter, and the singer marries his best friend (Walter Brennan, who won an Oscar for the role). Years later, the lumber magnate tries to gain the love of his former girlfriend's daughter (also played by Farmer) but fails. The daughter is barely described in the book, so this film character is largely Furthman's creation. She possesses qualities he developed for women in the Sternberg films: innate decency, cynical wariness of men, and candor.

Within three years of the critical and commercial success of *Come and Get It!*, Furthman wrote *Only Angels Have Wings* (1939) for Howard Hawks, using the director's recollections of his flying experiences as a basis for the screenplay. The film is set mostly at a saloon in a South American seaport. There, entertainer Bonnie Lee (Jean Arthur) is gradually initiated into the group of mail pilots who frequent the saloon. The leader of the group (Cary Grant) handles the business side of the missions as well as

the flights that are too hazardous for anyone else because of the region's adverse weather conditions. More than any other screenplay by Furthman, *Only Angels Have Wings* achieves its impact through dialogue; the pilots use callous jokes to buffer themselves against the emotional consequences of their dangerous work. Less concerned with the plausibility of events than with the consequences of action and its meaning to character relationships, *Only Angels Have Wings* brilliantly redefines the adventure genre.

Furthman's penultimate collaboration with Sternberg, *The Shanghai Gesture* (1941), was adapted from John Colton's Broadway melodrama set in a brothel. The objections of censors had defeated previous attempts at filming the play, but in the spring of 1941 the Hays Office approved a preliminary script by Geza Herczeg. Sternberg and Furthman then contributed additional elements that disassociate the film from its theatrical past. The film explores the corrupt city of Shanghai, where Sir Guy Charteris (Walter Huston) heads a redevelopment combine that is divesting certain businesses of their tenancy, his principal target being "Mother" Gin Sling (Ona Munson), who owns the largest gambling casino. She retaliates by arranging for his daughter (Gene Tierney) to incur heavy gambling debts and in the process discovers that Charteris is her former husband. Still believing he stole her inheritance and abandoned her to slavery years earlier, she intensifies her attempts at revenge. In *The Shanghai Gesture* verbal nuances create a fatalistic current characteristic of Furthman's work. But the abstract exploration of decadence in the film confused reviewers searching for social realism, although it allowed the film to elude the rigid screen censorship of the era that Furthman's next film, *The Outlaw* (1943), confronted directly.

In December 1940, Howard Hughes hired Furthman to rewrite the Ben Hecht script for *The Outlaw* after director Howard Hawks and Hecht had left the project after a few days into the filming. *The Outlaw* was subject to censorship troubles from the beginning; it was exhibited by a single theater in 1945 and widely released in 1946, but did not receive complete freedom of circulation until 1949. The film depicts the friendship between gunslingers Doc Holliday (Walter Huston) and Billy the Kid (Jack Buetel), a friendship that is threatened by sheriff Pat Garrett (Thomas Mitchell) and Rio McDonald (Jane Russell). Controversy centered on director Hughes's preoccupation with Jane Russell's breasts and the story's sexual overtones. Whether Hecht's original story treatment or

12.

4 (Cont.4)

                        MORGAN:
                    (returning to wheel)
                Slack it to him --

                        JOHNSON:
                He hasn't got it --

                        MORGAN:
                Yes, he has. And he's a big one.
                I'll bet he'll go a thousand pounds --

                        JOHNSON:
                I tell you he hasn't got it --

In reply, the marlin jumps straight up beside the boat,
and Johnson rises up in his chair as though he was
being derricked, and he stands there clinging to the
rod for a second and the rod bending like a bow, and
then the butt catches him in the belly and the whole
works goes overboard, rod, reel, tackle, and all.

                        MORGAN:
                    (shutting off engine)
                Well, I guess that's enough for
                one day --

Johnson sits down, holding onto his belly where the rod
butt had hit him.

                        JOHNSON:
                    (dazedly)
                What happened?

                        MORGAN:
                Nothing. You just had the drag screwed
                down tight again, that's all, and when
                the fish struck, it just naturally lifted
                you right out of your chair and you
                couldn't hold it.

                        HORATIO:
                    (chuckling)
                You had the harness on, that fish'd've
                taken you along with him.

                        EDDY:
                    (slapping Johnson
                    on the back)
                Mr. Johnson, you're just unlucky.
                Now, maybe you're lucky with women.
                Mr. Johnson, what d'you say we go out
                tonight?

                        JOHNSON:
                    (rising enragedly and
                     hitting Eddy in the face)
                I'll lucky you, you dirty rummy --

                                            (CONTINUED)

Page from the screenplay by Furthman and William Faulkner for To Have and Have Not *(University of Virginia Library)*

Hughes's predilections influenced Furthman, the film incorporates Furthman's characteristic stylization of dialogue. *The Outlaw* received negative reviews in the 1940s, but its atypical treatment of relationships also invoked many interpretations and analyses.

To Have and Have Not (1945) was adapted from Ernest Hemingway's novel by Furthman and William Faulkner, with uncredited contributions by Howard Hawks. The screenplay presented a narrative that incorporates political involvement into a framework of individual commitment and personal responsibility. The film takes place in Fort-de-France, the capital of French Martinique, in the summer of 1940. Harry Morgan (Humphrey Bogart), who runs a charter boat for fishing trips with his alcoholic friend Eddy (Walter Brennan), is asked to aid Free French efforts by transporting a resistance leader—a request he refuses. He meets Marie Browning (Lauren Bacall), and they begin a relationship that progresses from defensive bantering to mutual acceptance. Morgan is eventually spurred to political action, largely because of the casual brutality of Gestapo agents in the city, who abuse Marie and Eddy. Personal and political commitments, inextricably linked, end his detachment, and he complements his independence, self-respect, and ethical code through involvement with a woman who shares these qualities.

Adapting Raymond Chandler's novel *The Big Sleep* for the 1946 film was a challenge to Hawks and three screenwriters. In 1944 William Faulkner and Leigh Brackett worked on the script but left for other projects; in 1945 and 1946 Furthman made some revisions and additions, basically condensing the second half of the complex script and rewriting the ending that Brackett had devised but censors had rejected. The film opens with General Sternwood hiring detective Philip Marlowe (Humphrey Bogart) to discover who is responsible for blackmail attempts on his nymphomaniacal daughter Carmen (Martha Vickers). This situation is further complicated by the general's report that his companion, Shawn Regan, has disappeared and by the interest Sternwood's elder daughter, Vivian Rutledge (Lauren Bacall), shows in Marlowe. She thinks Marlowe has been hired to find Regan, and Marlowe becomes intrigued with her concern, its relevance to gambler Eddie Mars, and the connection of Mars to the blackmailing angle and to Regan's disappearance. The script is faithful to the novel's plot structure, caustic wit, and moral ambience. The role of Vivian Rutledge, however, was expanded in order to repeat the romantic team-

work of Bogart and Bacall in *To Have and Have Not*.

In 1945 Howard Hughes hired Furthman to write and produce a jet-age film that would emphasize aerial footage. *Jet Pilot* (1957) sets Soviet-American relations within the boundaries of sexual politics as American colonel Jim Shannon (John Wayne) and a Russian pilot (Janet Leigh) who is posing as a defector enter a relationship that fluctuates between love and hate. The film was delayed before its release because of Hughes's attention to the flying sequences; both he and Furthman were responsible for redirecting and updating segments of the film. When it finally opened, critical reaction ranged from hostile to indifferent.

In 1948 Furthman wrote an outline titled "Bread Upon the Waters," based on the story of Lew Resse, a businessman who revived a dying town by building a pottery business during the depths of the Depression. The outline was optioned by M-G-M, revised by Furthman, and turned into a completed script but never filmed.

Shortly after the completion of *Jet Pilot*, Furthman began to work on one of his most successful efforts. Although Leigh Brackett had written a couple of preliminary versions, the final script for *Rio Bravo* (1959) was a collaborative venture. "We worked together," she recalled in January 1976. "Primarily it was a business of story conferences, where Hawks, Furthman, and I would talk. . . . In strict truth, Furthman contributed much more to the final version than I did. He was in a position to argue with Hawks over story points."

Rio Bravo, an acknowledged Western classic, relegates plot line to the background, with character development and relationships in the foreground. John T. Chance (John Wayne), a sheriff in a Southwestern town, arrests a man for killing an unarmed man. The killer's brother and his hired guns plan to free him from jail, and Chance must stand against them with only a little help from his drunken deputy, Dude (Dean Martin), the gunslinger Colorado (Rick Nelson), a crippled old man called Stumpy (Walter Brennan), and a woman named Feathers (Angie Dickinson). Furthman and Hawks paid conscious attention to *Underworld* in constructing *Rio Bravo*: Feathers takes her name from a character in the earlier film, and the opening scene, when Dude starts to grovel for a coin in a spittoon but is stopped by Chance, was inspired by a scene from *Underworld*. The film also recasts themes, relationships, and even specific situations and lines of dialogue from *Only Angels Have Wings* and *To Have and Have Not*. *Rio Bravo* fully defines Furthman's craftsmanship: the importance of dialogue; the arrangement of

Lauren Bacall, Humphrey Bogart, Walter Brennan, and Hoagy Carmichael (at the piano) in a scene from To Have and Have Not

scenes within the overall context of the narrative; and the structural interlocking of character and incident intrinsic to such films as *Morocco* and *Shanghai Express*. *Rio Bravo* was the eighth highest grosser of 1959, and although its success tempted Furthman and Hawks to work together again, it stands as their final collaboration and as Furthman's last screen credit. Furthman retired from films the following year and only occasionally dictated a story treatment in subsequent years.

After leaving films, Furthman devoted his time to two of his avocations that dated from the early 1930s. He owned an orchid farm that was legendary throughout Hollywood for its size and its capacity to fill orders across the country and around the world. Furthman was also a collector of first editions. In 1966 he traveled to Oxford in search of a rare book. He suffered a stroke there and died on 22 September. His wife, Sybil Furthman, accompanied his body on the return to Los Angeles, and on 29 September, funeral services were held at Forest Lawn.

References:

John Baxter, *The Cinema of Josef von Sternberg* (New York: A. S. Barnes, 1971), pp. 52-62, 75-80, 90-109, 154-157, 162-166;

André Bazin, *"The Outlaw,"* in *What Is Cinema?*, volume 2, selected and translated by Hugh Gray (Berkeley, Los Angeles & London: University of California Press, 1971), pp. 163-168;

John Belton, *The Hollywood Professionals*, volume 3: *Howard Hawks, Frank Borzage, Edgar G. Ulmer* (New York: A. S. Barnes, 1974), pp. 31-36, 44-49;

Richard Corliss, *Talking Pictures: Screenwriters in the*

American Cinema 1927-1973 (Woodstock, N.Y.: Overlook Press, 1974), pp. 265-274;

Richard T. Jameson, "Talking and Doing in *Rio Bravo*," *Velvet Light Trap*, 12 (Spring 1974): 26-30;

Richard Koszarski, "The Golden Years: Jules Furthman," in *The Hollywood Screenwriters*, edited by Richard Corliss (New York: Avon, 1972), pp. 51-63;

Douglas McVay, "From the Lily to the Poppy: Von Sternberg's *The Shanghai Gesture*," *Bright Lights*, 2 (1977): 17-22;

James Monaco, "Notes on *The Big Sleep*, Thirty Years After," *Sight and Sound*, 44 (Winter 1974-1975): 34-38;

Thomas H. Pauly, "Howard Hughes and his Western: The Maverick and *The Outlaw*," *Journal of Popular Film*, 6, 4 (1978): 350-368;

Andrew Sarris, *The Films of Josef von Sternberg* (Garden City: Doubleday, 1966), pp. 13-24, 28-30, 34-37, 47-52;

Robin Wood, "The Have (Directed) and Have Not (Written): Reflections on Authorship," *Film Comment*, 9 (May-June 1973): 30-35;

Wood, *Howard Hawks* (Garden City: Doubleday, 1968), pp. 17-57;

Wood, "Venus de Marlene," *Film Comment*, 14 (March-April 1978): 58-63.

Frances Goodrich
(1891-)

Albert Hackett
(16 February 1900-)

Evelyn Ehrlich

SELECTED MOTION PICTURES: *The Secret of Madame Blanche* (M-G-M, 1933), screenplay;

Penthouse (M-G-M, 1933), screenplay; filmed again as *Society Lawyer* (M-G-M, 1939), screenplay by Goodrich, Hackett, Leon Gordon, and Hugo Butler;

Fugitive Lovers (M-G-M, 1934), screenplay by Goodrich, Hackett, and George B. Seitz;

The Thin Man (M-G-M, 1934), screenplay;

Hide-Out (M-G-M, 1934), screenplay;

Naughty Marietta (M-G-M, 1935), screenplay by Goodrich, Hackett, and John Lee Mahin;

Ah, Wilderness! (M-G-M, 1935), screenplay;

Rose Marie (M-G-M, 1936), screenplay by Goodrich, Hackett, and Alice Duer Miller;

Small Town Girl (M-G-M, 1936), screenplay by Goodrich, Hackett, Mahin, and Edith Fitzgerald;

After the Thin Man (M-G-M, 1936), screenplay;

The Firefly (M-G-M, 1937), screenplay;

Another Thin Man (M-G-M, 1939), screenplay;

Lady in the Dark (Paramount, 1944), screenplay;

The Hitler Gang (Paramount, 1944), screen story and screenplay;

The Virginian (Paramount, 1946), screenplay;

It's a Wonderful Life (RKO, 1946), screenplay by Goodrich, Hackett, and Frank Capra;

The Pirate (M-G-M, 1948), screenplay;

Summer Holiday (M-G-M, 1948), screenplay;

Easter Parade (M-G-M, 1948), screen story; screenplay by Goodrich, Hackett, and Sidney Sheldon;

In the Good Old Summertime (M-G-M, 1949), screenplay by Goodrich, Hackett, and Ivan Tors;

Father of the Bride (M-G-M, 1950), screenplay;

Father's Little Dividend (M-G-M, 1951), screen story and screenplay;

Too Young to Kiss (M-G-M, 1951), screenplay;

Give a Girl a Break (M-G-M, 1954), screenplay;

Seven Brides for Seven Brothers (M-G-M, 1954), screenplay by Goodrich, Hackett, and Dorothy Kingsley;

The Long, Long Trailer (M-G-M, 1954), screenplay;

Gaby (M-G-M, 1956), screenplay by Goodrich, Hackett, and Charles Lederer;

A Certain Smile (20th Century-Fox, 1958), screenplay;

The Diary of Anne Frank (20th Century-Fox, 1959), screenplay;

Five Finger Exercise (Columbia, 1962), screenplay.

Albert Hackett and Frances Goodrich

PLAYS: *Up Pops the Devil* (New York, Masque Theatre, 1 September 1930);
Bridal Wise (New York, Cort Theatre, 30 May 1932);
The Great Big Doorstep (New York, Morosco Theatre, 26 November 1942);
The Diary of Anne Frank (New York, Cort Theatre, 5 October 1955).

SELECTED BOOKS: *Up Pops the Devil* (New York & London: French, 1933);
The Great Big Doorstep (Chicago: Dramatic Publishing, 1943);
The Diary of Anne Frank, Dramatized by Frances Goodrich and Albert Hackett (New York: Dramatists Play Service, 1958; London: French, 1958).

Frances Goodrich and Albert Hackett are among Hollywood's lesser-known writing teams, yet their careers span the years when American film production reached its peak. From *The Secret of Madame Blanche* (1933) to *Five Finger Exercise* (1962), Goodrich and Hackett's films exemplify the professionalism and popular appeal that were the hallmarks of Hollywood screenwriting at its best. Their working union was so organic, in fact, that Goodrich once said, "Each of us writes the same scene. Then each looks at what the other has done, and we try to decide which of us has done the better. We advise each other and then go back at it again. We argue but we don't quarrel. When a scenario or play is finished, neither of us can recognize his own work."

Both Goodrich and Hackett began their careers as actors. Born in New York City to an acting couple, Albert Maurice Hackett made his New York stage debut at the age of six and performed in silent films and on stage. Frances Goodrich was born in Belleville, New Jersey, and graduated from Vassar

College in 1912. After performing with a Massachusetts stock company, she made her Broadway debut in *Come Out of the Kitchen* (1916). While pursuing her acting career, she was married first to screen actor Robert Ames in 1917, then in 1927 to writer Hendrik Willem Van Loon. Both marriages ended in divorce.

Goodrich and Hackett began their writing collaboration in 1927 when they were both acting in a stock company in Denver. Their earliest efforts were unsuccessful, but in 1930 their play *Up Pops the Devil* opened in New York. A comedy set in a writer's milieu in Greenwich Village, it dealt with the marital complications arising from a two-career family. Goodrich and Hackett were married on 7 February 1931.

When *Up Pops the Devil* was filmed in 1931, Albert Hackett was brought out to Hollywood as dialogue director. Because the contract called for Albert Hackett's services only, the couple returned to New York, where they wrote *Bridal Wise* (1932). This play, although not filmed, again led to a Hollywood contract, this time for both. Their contract with M-G-M stipulated that if the couple had no writing assignment, Hackett could be called on for acting duties, but the studio never had to exercise that clause—between 1933 and 1939 Goodrich and Hackett were credited with writing thirteen films, many of them box-office successes.

These early films reveal the literate and sophisticated dialogue that became Goodrich and Hackett's trademark. Their first assignment was to adapt Martin Brown's 1923 Broadway melodrama, *The Lady*; the film was released in 1933 as *The Secret of Madame Blanche*. It was followed by two story adaptations, *Penthouse* (1933), a gangster tale set in high society, and *Fugitive Lovers* (1934), a gangster melodrama. Although these films are nearly forgotten today, when first released they were praised by critics for their amusing dialogue and excellent performances.

Actors appearing in films written by Goodrich and Hackett have often received critical acclaim for their performances. In part, this was because Goodrich and Hackett films starred many first-rate actors, but much of the credit must be attributed to the scripts. Having been actors, Goodrich and Hackett were especially concerned with providing witty lines and appropriate mannerisms for the actors in their films. An example of this matching of script to actor was their first major popular and critical success, *The Thin Man* (1934).

Based on the novel by Dashiell Hammett and directed by W. S. Van Dyke, *The Thin Man* typifies the best of Hollywood in the 1930s. Nick and Nora Charles (William Powell and Myrna Loy) are wealthy, happy-go-lucky dipsomaniacs who stumble into a murder mystery that keeps them pleasantly engaged while offering little real danger. Goodrich and Hackett developed Nick and Nora Charles beyond the characterizations given in the novel, and although the Charleses were conceived by Hammett, the details—the camaraderie and equality within the marriage, the playful gestures that give the marriage its sense of fun—were fleshed out by Goodrich and Hackett. Credit, of course, cannot be given to the screenwriters alone. The film's success resulted from a happy combination of talents, including those of the director, screenwriters, actors, and technicians. By working together, they succeeded in capturing a vision of America as it would have liked to be in 1934.

The Thin Man was an immediate success and won Goodrich and Hackett an Academy Award nomination. M-G-M, foreseeing the box-office potential of a Thin Man series, engaged all the principals for two sequels. Both *After the Thin Man* (1936) and *Another Thin Man* (1939) combined the ingenuity of Hammett's mysteries (Hammett wrote the screen stories for both films) with the witty sophistication of Goodrich and Hackett's dialogue.

Between the Thin Man films, M-G-M assigned Goodrich and Hackett to a variety of projects ranging from the melodramatic *Chained* (1934), for which they received no credit, to the lavish spectacles of the Jeanette MacDonald-Nelson Eddy operettas. Goodrich and Hackett's first musical assignment was the first pairing of MacDonald and Eddy in the highly successful *Naughty Marietta* (1935). The film was based on the well-known operetta by Victor Herbert and Rita Johnson Young. Goodrich, Hackett, and John Lee Mahin rewrote dialogue from the operetta and revised the story line in order to create a film that would appeal to contemporary audiences. More musical assignments followed, limited to standard operettas such as *Rose Marie* (1936) and *The Firefly* (1937). Goodrich and Hackett's job was to take well-known but exceedingly old-fashioned stories and rewrite them in a modern idiom. In at least one case, their updating may have given them the opportunity to editorialize: some critics suggested that the new plot and dialogue for *The Firefly*, with its story of a Spanish dancer during the Napoleonic wars, provided a parallel to the Spanish Civil War. As a rule, however, these assignments rarely gave the screenwriters an opportunity to do more than a perfunctory linking of songs.

William Powell and Myrna Loy in a publicity shot for The Thin Man

Similarly, their nonmusical assignments in the later 1930s (aside from the Thin Man series) left little room for creative intervention. Although they received an Academy Award nomination for their screenplay adaptation of Eugene O'Neill's *Ah, Wilderness!* (1935), the film was essentially a routine M-G-M vision of Americana which provided appropriate parts for the studio's family of actors: Mickey Rooney, Wallace Beery, and Lionel Barrymore. Goodrich and Hackett's other M-G-M projects during this period included an ordinary comedy, *Small Town Girl* (1936), and a remake of their own screenplay for *Penthouse*, retitled *Society Lawyer* (1939). With an increasing lack of enthusiasm for Hollywood, Goodrich and Hackett returned to Broadway, where Hackett resumed his acting career in the long-running play *Mr. and Mrs. North* (1941). In 1942 their own play *The Great Big Doorstep* opened on Broadway but closed after twenty-eight performances.

Goodrich and Hackett returned to Hollywood, this time to work for Paramount, and were assigned to one of that studio's biggest and most prestigious projects. They began work on adapting *Lady in the Dark*, the 1941 Broadway musical hit written by Moss Hart with music by Kurt Weill and lyrics by Ira Gershwin. Paramount, feeling that the play's subject matter—psychoanalysis—might not be popular with audiences, decided to stress the film's production; the lavishly costumed and decorated dream sequences became the film's focal point, eclipsing the complicated story and replacing eight of the play's original songs. The complex subject of psychoanalysis was simplified to the level of emphasizing the fantastic, but the producers, and not Goodrich and Hackett, should be blamed for the superficiality of the treatment of the subject. Their screenplay was inoffensively amusing, and the interplay between Ginger Rogers as the magazine editor and Ray Milland as the art editor benefited from Goodrich and Hackett's dialogue, with its usual good-natured banter.

It became painfully obvious in the years following *Lady in the Dark* that Paramount did not know what to do with Goodrich and Hackett. Despite that studio's reputation for sophisticated comedy, the team was next assigned to two projects for which they were little suited. *The Hitler Gang* (1944) was a semidocumentary on Hitler's rise to power, incorporating German footage. An even more inappropriate assignment for the pair was a remake of *The Virginian* (1946), this version with Joel McCrea.

Goodrich and Hackett left Paramount in 1946 for more rewarding assignments; one of these was *It's a Wonderful Life* (1946), about a man (James Stewart) who considers his life a failure. He contemplates suicide, but his guardian angel appears and shows him he is wrong. As Frank Capra, who collaborated on the screenplay, details the origins of the film in his memoirs, the idea originated with a story written by Philip Van Dorn Stern as a Christmas card for his friends. RKO bought the rights and assigned several writers, including Dalton Trumbo, Mark Connelly, and Clifford Odets, to work on the treatment. Capra's usual collaborators were unavailable, and he hired Goodrich and Hackett because, he said, they were "perceptive, human writers." As Capra describes the scriptwriting process: "The story came back to me, more beautiful than ever. The Hacketts were writing some bright, sensitive scenes, but why didn't the scenes move me? I sat down and wrote some key scenes. The Hacketts melded them with their own. I had the script I wanted. Take it or leave it—things had to be done my way."

The resulting film does seem to be more Capra's work than Goodrich and Hackett's. The New York sophistication of Goodrich and Hackett's writing is almost totally missing in the script that celebrates those small-town values that the screenwriters were wont to satirize in films such as their later *Father of the Bride* (1950). The characterization of George Bailey (Stewart), however, is more rounded than the one-dimensional characters found in other Capra films. Although it was well received critically, *It's a Wonderful Life* was not an immediate box-office success; yet it seems to have touched a sentimental streak among movie audiences, leading to its sustained popularity over the decades.

With the completion of their assignment for Capra, Goodrich and Hackett returned to M-G-M, where they reestablished their reputation as writers of trenchant comedy dialogue. Their first assignment was on a project that several writers, including Anita Loos and Joseph Than, had already attempted: *The Pirate* (1948), an adaptation of S. N. Behrman's 1942 play. Since *The Pirate* had not been a musical play, Goodrich and Hackett had the responsibility of integrating the new Cole Porter score with the film's dialogue.

The story of *The Pirate* allowed far more character delineation than plot development. On a Caribbean island in the nineteenth century, Manuela (Judy Garland) dreams of the dashing pirate Macoco, who in reality is her unattractive fiancé (Walter Slezak). The actor Serafin (Gene Kelly) impersonates the pirate in order to win Manuela's affections. *The Pirate* was another case of matching actor to script: Goodrich and Hackett's dialogue for the fiery Manuela and the wily Serafin perfectly suited the temperamental Garland and the flippant Kelly. Despite the commercial and critical failure of the film, producer Arthur Freed immediately assigned Goodrich and Hackett to another musical project to star Kelly and Garland. For this one, the writers started with little more than the song title "Easter Parade"; working closely with Freed and Irving Berlin, Goodrich and Hackett formulated a script for *Easter Parade* (1948). The script was partially rewritten when Kelly was replaced by Fred Astaire, and there is some dispute as to the responsibility for the final script; Sidney Sheldon shares credit with Goodrich and Hackett. The film was enormously successful at the box office, and the screenplay won Goodrich and Hackett a Writers Guild award.

The Hacketts followed *Easter Parade* with another hit musical, *In the Good Old Summertime* (1949), and two more films which perfectly suited their talents and are among their finest work: *Father of the Bride* (1950) and *Father's Little Dividend* (1951). *Father of the Bride*, based on the novel by Edward Streeter and directed by Vincente Minnelli, presents an American middle-class wedding as seen from the point of view of the seemingly extraneous father (Spencer Tracy). As in *The Thin Man*, character development was primary, and comedy derived more from the characters' interaction than from the plot. The film was greeted with delight by both public and critics. It was nominated for Academy Awards for best picture, best screenplay, and best actor (Tracy), and was seventh on *Variety*'s list of top-grossing films of 1950. *Father's Little Dividend* nearly equaled the popularity of its predecessor. Goodrich and Hackett wrote both the original story and the screenplay for this film, and they sustained the satiric intent of the earlier film by

From The Diary of Anne Frank, *left to right: Diane Baker, Ed Wynn, Joseph Schildkraut, Gusti Huber, Richard Beymer, and Millie Perkins*

examining the rituals surrounding the birth of the first grandchild.

These two films presented Goodrich and Hackett with their last opportunity to write sophisticated domestic comedy for the screen. Routine assignments followed these successes and included such projects as *Too Young to Kiss* (1951), a farce with June Allyson and Van Johnson, and *Give a Girl a Break* (1954), a musical comedy with Marge and Gower Champion. Goodrich and Hackett worked on the big-budget musical *Seven Brides for Seven Brothers* in 1954; it was a box-office success and earned the screenwriters another Academy Award nomination. But neither it nor *The Long, Long Trailer* (1954), an extended situation comedy designed to exploit the television popularity of Lucille Ball and Desi Arnaz, provided characters or situations that allowed for the witty dialogue exchanges or the acting tours de force that had been the basis of Goodrich and Hackett's best comedies. Their last film for M-G-M was *Gaby* (1956), a remake of *Waterloo Bridge* (1940), with Leslie Caron. This wartime melodrama was followed by a drama about marriage for 20th Century-Fox, *A Certain Smile*

(1958), a toned-down version of the then-shocking novel by Françoise Sagan. Neither film was well received by audiences or critics.

If Goodrich and Hackett's screen work in the mid-1950s lacked the wit of their previous efforts, it is possible that their interests were engaged elsewhere. After a long and respected career in Hollywood and on Broadway, the writing team finally received public recognition for a project that was one of their last efforts. *The Diary of Anne Frank*, which opened on Broadway in 1955, was the high point of their careers, bringing them critical acclaim, international popular success, and recognition from their peers. The play received the New York Drama Critics Circle Award, the Tony Award, and the Pulitzer Prize in 1956. Adapted from the diary that Anne Frank kept while she and her family hid from the Nazis, the play occupied most of Goodrich and Hackett's time and attention from 1953 to 1955. The subject was a departure for them, and they researched the material scrupulously, producing a play the critics praised for its fidelity to the spirit of the girl's diary. For the 1959 film version Goodrich and Hackett added a few incidents to the script but maintained the claustrophobic atmosphere and conveyed the tension of the Franks' life in hiding. The film received critical acclaim but was not popular with the public.

The Diary of Anne Frank had been a labor of love for Goodrich and Hackett. "No one working on *Diary* thought about money," Hackett commented in 1956. "We all felt we were working for a cause, not just a play." Nevertheless, the commercial failure of the film, combined with the disappointing reception of their last film, *Five Finger Exercise* (1962), persuaded Goodrich and Hackett to leave Hollywood and return to New York. Although they have discussed screenwriting projects since, they have not written a film since 1962.

Frances Goodrich and Albert Hackett exemplify Hollywood screenwriters during the studio era. Although they were nominated for six Academy Awards, they received little recognition from the press and continue to be little known today. Yet during their Hollywood careers they wrote screenplays that appealed to the audiences of the time and that have, in some cases, endured to become classics.

James Edward Grant

(2 July 1905-19 February 1966)

Blake Lucas

MOTION PICTURES: *Grand Jury* (RKO, 1936), screen story by Grant and Thomas Lennon;

Big Brown Eyes (Paramount, 1936), story;

The Ex-Mrs. Bradford (RKO, 1936), screen story;

The Women Men Marry (M-G-M, 1937), screenplay by Grant, Harry Ruskin, and Donald Henderson Clark;

Danger–Love at Work (20th Century-Fox, 1937), screen story; screenplay by Grant and Ben Markson;

She's No Lady (Paramount, 1937), screen story;

She Had To Eat (20th Century-Fox, 1937), screen story by Grant and M. M. Musselman;

There's That Woman Again (Columbia, 1938), screenplay by Grant, Philip G. Epstein, and Ken Englund;

We're Going To Be Rich (20th Century-Fox, 1938), story;

Josette (20th Century-Fox, 1938), screenplay;

Music In My Heart (Columbia, 1939), screen story and screenplay;

Miracles For Sale (Columbia, 1939), screenplay by Grant, Ruskin, and Marion Parsonnet;

I Can't Give You Anything But Love, Baby (Universal, 1940), screen story;

They Dare Not Love (Columbia, 1941), screen story;

The Lady Is Willing (Columbia, 1941), screen story; screenplay by Grant and Albert McCleery;

Johnny Eager (M-G-M, 1942), screen story; screenplay by Grant and John Lee Mahin;

Belle of the Yukon (RKO, 1945), screenplay;

The Great John L (United Artists, 1945), screen story and screenplay;

Angel and the Badman (Republic, 1947), screen story and screenplay;

The Plunderers (Republic, 1948), story;

Johnny Allegro (Columbia, 1949), screen story;

Sands of Iwo Jima (Republic, 1949), screenplay by Grant and Harry Brown;

Rock Island Trail (Republic, 1950), screenplay;

Father Is a Bachelor (Columbia, 1950), story; screenplay by Grant and Aleen Leslie;

Surrender (Republic, 1950), screen story; screenplay by Grant and Sloan Nibley;

Bullfighter and the Lady (Republic, 1951), screenplay;

California Passage (Republic, 1951), screen story and screenplay;

Flying Leathernecks (RKO, 1951), screenplay;

Big Jim McLain (Warner Bros., 1952), screenplay by Grant, Richard English, and Eric Taylor;

Hondo (Warner Bros., 1953), screenplay;

Ring of Fear (Warner Bros., 1954), screen story and screenplay by Grant, Paul Fix, and Philip MacDonald;

The Last Wagon (20th Century-Fox, 1956), screenplay by Grant, Delmer Daves, and Gwen Bagni Gielgud;

Three Violent People (Paramount, 1957), screenplay;

The Sheepman (M-G-M, 1958), screen story; screenplay by Grant and William Bowers;

The Alamo (United Artists, 1960), screen story and screenplay;

The Comancheros (20th Century-Fox, 1961), screenplay by Grant and Clair Huffaker;

Donovan's Reef (Paramount, 1963), screenplay by Grant and Frank Nugent;

McLintock! (United Artists, 1963), screen story and screenplay;

Circus World (Paramount, 1964), screenplay by Grant, Ben Hecht, and Julian Halevy;

Hostile Guns (Paramount, 1968), screen story by Grant and Nibley;

Support Your Local Gunfighter (United Artists, 1971), screenplay.

A successful Hollywood writer for thirty years, James Edward Grant is best represented by three works: *Angel and the Badman* (1947), *Hondo* (1953), and *The Alamo* (1960). All three films are in the Western genre and were produced by John Wayne. Although Grant demonstrated great versatility, particularly in his early career, the Western stimulated his finest creative work. He was also Wayne's favorite writer.

Grant was born in Chicago and worked as a journalist and magazine writer before coming to Hollywood. With the *Chicago Herald*, he was responsible for a syndicated column titled "It's a Racket." He received his first screen credit for the screen story to *Grand Jury* in 1936 and until 1940 worked mostly on undistinguished comedies, musicals, and melodramas. The most appealing of these is *Big Brown Eyes* (1936), for which Grant contributed the original story. The film is a comedy about newspaper publishing and reflects the writer's background better than many of his other efforts. Raoul Walsh directed and Cary Grant starred.

Grant became established in Hollywood when he wrote "A Lady Comes to Burkburnett," the story that served as the basis of *Boom Town* (1940), a film about two wildcat oil drillers (Clark Gable and Spencer Tracy) who come into conflict over women and moral principles as wealth tarnishes one but not the other. In 1942 Grant wrote the story for *Johnny Eager* and collaborated on the screenplay with John Lee Mahin, who had written the script for *Boom Town*. This early film noir was about a gangster (Robert Taylor) in love with the district attorney's daughter (Lana Turner); Van Heflin won an Oscar as best supporting actor for his role as the gangster's alcoholic friend. The theme of an outlaw reformed by a good woman is repeated in *Angel and the Badman*, Grant's next important film and possibly the one which reveals his gifts most eloquently.

Grant's other work in the early 1940s included the screen story for a comedy, *The Lady Is Willing* (1941), and the screenplay for *Belle of the Yukon* (1945), another story of an outlaw reformed by his girl. He also wrote and produced *The Great John L* (1945), a biography of John L. Sullivan. Then he went to work on *Angel and the Badman*, his first

Western script as well as his first film with John Wayne; it is also the first film Grant directed. The film draws on the tradition of the "good badman" that dates back to the silent Westerns in its story of an outlaw whose noble impulses are revealed when he falls in love with a Quaker woman. What sets the script apart from predecessors in the tradition is the degree of sexual explicitness in the relationship between the two; by later standards the romance is discreet, but the sexual attraction which gives it credibility is treated in an adult manner. The most interesting scenes are the intimate ones, rather than those involving conventional Western action. A sensibility rarely revealed in Grant's other work is shown in this film. *Angel and the Badman* had a lasting effect on Grant's career. He returned to Western films with increasing frequency, and the impression he made on Wayne is evident.

After working on another Western, *The Plunderers* (1948), and a gangster film, *Johnny Allegro* (1949), Grant collaborated with Harry Brown on the screenplay for the celebrated war film *Sands of Iwo Jima* (1949), based on Brown's story and directed by Allan Dwan. Grant's ability to write effectively for Wayne is evident in the incisive characterization of Sergeant Stryker, an extremely tough but ultimately fair-minded professional marine. The

Robert Stack and Gilbert Roland in Bullfighter and the Lady

John Wayne, Geraldine Page, Tom Irish, and Ward Bond in Hondo

sudden and unexpected death of Stryker is especially well realized and reflects Grant's disregard for elaborate sentiment. Wayne was nominated for an Academy Award for his performance.

Grant followed *Sands of Iwo Jima* with three "B" movies for Republic studios—*Rock Island Trail* (1950), *Surrender* (1950), and *California Passage* (1951)—and a comedy, *Father Is a Bachelor* (1950) for Columbia. He then wrote five films which were produced by and/or starred John Wayne. The first, *Bullfighter and the Lady* (1951), is a character study of an American (Robert Stack) who is taught to be a matador by an experienced Mexican (Gilbert Roland). Grant wrote his script from an autobiographical story by the film's director, Budd Boetticher.

John Wayne starred in *Flying Leathernecks* (1951), a war film in which the character he portrays is very similar to Stryker from *Sands of Iwo Jima*. Nicholas Ray directed this story of pilots in World War II. In 1952 Grant was one of three writers on *Big Jim McLain*, a film designed to show producer-star Wayne's anti-Communist beliefs. The film was about a U.S. operative tracking down Communist subversives in Hawaii; Grant's major contribution was creating a proper characterization for Wayne.

Grant was sole adaptor of Louis L'Amour's novel *The Gift of Cochise*. His screenplay *Hondo* reveals again the artist behind the craftsman who had been responsible for *Angel and the Badman*. *Hondo* is a sensitive screenplay in which the hero, played by Wayne, kills the husband of the woman with whom he has fallen in love. Again, Grant provided adult scenes between hero and heroine, played in this instance by Geraldine Page, who was nominated for an Oscar. Additionally, relations between whites and Indians are portrayed with a mature attitude. Grant's understanding of the subject cannot be faulted, and his ability to create the archetypal Wayne character was never more evident.

Grant directed, as well as cowrote, *Ring of Fear* (1954), a circus melodrama that Wayne produced. Grant then returned to the Western, although he did not work for Wayne again until *The Alamo* six years later. In these intervening years, Grant wrote two films which deserve special recognition. *The Last Wagon* (1956) was a collaboration with writer-director Delmer Daves and Gwen Bagni Gielgud, based on the latter's story. The film, about a condemned killer (Richard Widmark) who saves the survivors of a wagon train raided by Indians, is a serious moral study of the ambiguity of good and evil, a subject which had previously interested

A scene from The Alamo

Grant. *The Sheepman* (1958) is in a very different mood, playing for comedy the battle between a sheep raiser (Glenn Ford) and cattlemen. The film succeeds because comedy is presented as part of a solid dramatic structure. Grant received his only Academy Award nomination for this film.

As with *Hondo* and *Angel and the Badman*, Grant was the sole screenwriter of *The Alamo,* an ambitious project which John Wayne had long wanted to make. Grant had done initial work on it ten years earlier, and when Wayne was finally able to set up the production, Grant returned to write the final script and act as associate producer. On the whole, Grant's screenplay is dramatic, intelligent, and moving. There are weak moments, particularly the Republic speech delivered by Wayne as Davy Crockett and expressing Wayne's personal sentiments. The three major characters—Crockett, William Travis (Laurence Harvey), and Jim Bowie (Richard Widmark)—are all richly detailed in Grant's script. As a result, when the three men die, the effect is emotionally powerful, even though their deaths were preordained by the subject and thus expected by the audience.

After *The Alamo*, Grant worked on four more films for Wayne. The only one of the four on which Grant was the sole writer is *McLintock!* (1963), a broad Western farce about a cattle baron feuding with his rebellious wife (Maureen O'Hara). He collaborated on *The Comancheros* (1961) with Western novelist Clair Huffaker, and that film blends some fresh characterization with a traditional adventure narrative about two men (Wayne, Stuart Whitman) fighting white renegades selling guns to the Comanches.

Donovan's Reef (1963) allowed Grant to work with John Ford, a director he had long admired. The story's primary interest is Boston heiress Amelia Dedham's (Elizabeth Allen) reconciliation with her estranged father (Jack Warden) on a Pacific island. John Wayne's role as Donovan is not central but does serve two functions: he is romantic interest for Amelia and provides comic relief in his antagonism to "Boats" Gilhooley (Lee Marvin).

Circus World (1964) has a curious history. The original story for the Samuel Bronston production was written by Philip Yordan and Nicholas Ray, but no film resulted, and the project was taken on by Frank Capra. When Wayne insisted on bringing in Grant, Capra quit, but the new director of the film, Henry Hathaway, had little use for Grant and employed Ben Hecht to write the final version of the script. Although the work of many hands, the film is an appealing one, and the characterization of Wayne as the circus owner does reflect Grant's work.

Grant died on 19 February 1966. After his death, the Western *Hostile Guns* (1968) was filmed from his screen story. His script for *Support Your Local Gunfighter* was filmed in 1971.

James Edward Grant was a fine professional screenwriter, though rarely intent on asserting his own personality. Consequently, although his association with John Wayne and his contributions to *The Last Wagon* and *The Sheepman* assure him a place in the history of the Western, he has never been as central to the development of the genre as have other screenwriters such as Borden Chase and Dudley Nichols. The key films in Grant's career, *Angel and the Badman, Hondo,* and *The Alamo*, demonstrate both passion and purpose. It is in these films that his love of complex characterization and mature view of history are best revealed.

References:
Allen Eyles, *John Wayne and The Movies* (New York:

Grosset & Dunlap, 1976);
T. F. James, "The Man Who Talks Back to John Wayne," *Cosmopolitan* (August 1960): 60-65.

John Michael Hayes
(11 May 1919-   )

Willard Carroll

MOTION PICTURES: *Red Ball Express* (Universal, 1952), screenplay;
Thunder Bay (Universal, 1953), screen story; screenplay by Hayes and Gil Doud;
Torch Song (M-G-M, 1953), screenplay by Hayes and Jan Lustig;
War Arrow (Universal, 1954), screen story and screenplay;
Rear Window (Paramount, 1954), screenplay;
To Catch a Thief (Paramount, 1955), screenplay;
It's a Dog's Life (M-G-M, 1955), screenplay;
The Trouble with Harry (Paramount, 1956), screenplay;
The Man Who Knew Too Much (Paramount, 1956), screenplay by Hayes and Angus McPhail;
Peyton Place (20th Century-Fox, 1957), screenplay;
The Matchmaker (Paramount, 1958), screenplay;
But Not for Me (Paramount, 1959), screenplay;
Butterfield 8 (M-G-M, 1960), screenplay by Hayes and Charles Schnee;
The Children's Hour (United Artists, 1961), screenplay;
The Chalk Garden (Universal, 1964), screenplay;
The Carpetbaggers (Paramount, 1964), screenplay;
Where Love Has Gone (Paramount, 1964), screenplay;
Harlow (Paramount, 1965), screenplay;
Judith (Paramount, 1966), screenplay;
Nevada Smith (Paramount, 1966), screen story and screenplay.

In the classification of American screenwriters working within the studio system, the term *Hollywood professionals* most accurately describes those writers who, through a great amount of talent and a lesser amount of compromise, have achieved a staying power in commercial filmmaking. The amalgam of personal expression and craftsmanship coupled—of necessity—with productivity and an awareness of controlling externals can be well observed in the work of screenwriter John Michael Hayes. Under contract at different times to several major studios, Hayes, known primarily as an adaptor, did not simply fulfill the basic requirements deemed necessary for the commercial success of a particular property. The surface fundamentals are adhered to, of course, and the majority of films produced from his screenplays have been successful at the box office. A Hayes screenplay, however, also brings with it a concern for style and form, an investigation of forces (such as the stifling social environment of *Peyton Place*) that motivate his characters, and an uncanny sensitivity for milieu.

Born in Worcester, Massachusetts, Hayes was sickly as a child, a situation that contributed to an early development of eclectic reading habits ranging from the works of Hemingway and Dos Passos to *Tom Swift*. Following a family relocation in Michigan, Hayes's desire to write manifested itself in short articles printed in a Detroit newspaper. As Hayes continued contributing to newspapers from a Boy Scout weekly to, ultimately, the *Boston Globe*, he developed a talent for feature articles and fiction, at the same time becoming fascinated with radio dramas. On leaving high school—he never graduated, owing to illness—Hayes entered Massachusetts State College, financing his education by writing weekly radio shows. When he moved to Hollywood in the early 1940s, he was assigned to the Lucille Ball radio comedy *My Favorite Husband*. Hayes followed this show with radio plays for such programs as *Suspense* and *The Adventures of Sam Spade*, as well as the less successful comedy *Sweeney and March*. Hayes's talents brought him to the attention of Universal Pictures, and in 1952 he embarked on his screenwriting career, accompanied by the precise knowledge of the cogent force of carefully scripted dialogue that he had acquired through his radio experience.

Hayes is a dialogue specialist. His carefully structured, finely polished screenplays are distinguished by well-defined characters who are provided with witty, pungent dialogue. As a writer of radio plays, Hayes formed his personal style of dialogue composition: he did not employ mundane talk; rather, his characters indulge in colloquies which play on film as well as they read on paper.

Hayes's first works as a screenwriter, at Universal in the early 1950s, demonstrate his early grasp of the film medium—the function of dialogue in a visual art form, punctuated by a keen sense of film language manifested in the overall structure of the screenplays. *Thunder Bay* (1953), one of the early Universal screenplays, demonstrates Hayes's abilities.

A contemporary action drama with strong ecological overtones, *Thunder Bay* details the effects of an offshore drilling operation on a Louisiana fishing village. The film, which emphasizes atmosphere over plot mechanics, evinces Hayes's concern with character and environment, specifically the role which the latter plays in regard to the individual. The inhabitants of Thunder Bay, fearful that both their environment and their morals will be corrupted by big business, resent the intrusion of the oil drillers. Hayes did not deal with this conflict in simple terms of man and his general environment; he concentrated on the extrinsic elements, specifically an unarticulated code of behavior fostering xenophobic suspicion, exclusion of outsiders, and an inbred resistance to progress. This basic theme of unspoken laws and taboos would later blend perfectly with Alfred Hitchcock's concepts in *The Trouble with Harry* (1956) and achieve its ultimate expression in *Peyton Place* (1957).

In 1954, after writing star vehicles for Joan Crawford at M-G-M (*Torch Song*, 1953) and Jeff Chandler at Universal (*War Arrow*, 1954), Hayes moved to Paramount. There he entered into partnership with Alfred Hitchcock, an association which was to produce four films in two years. Hayes was Hitchcock's most frequent collaborator during the director's American period, furnishing screenplays for *Rear Window* (1954), *To Catch a Thief* (1955), *The Trouble with Harry*, and *The Man Who Knew Too Much* (1956). Hayes's usually refined, sophisticated character creations are the perfect inhabitants of Hitchcock's world, regardless of the

tone imposed upon the material in the directorial synthesis.

The graceful byplay between Jeffries and Lisa in *Rear Window*, for example, forms a point-counterpoint relationship to the silent murder happening across the courtyard. In *To Catch a Thief*, the elegant byplay is the very core of the film, one of Hitchcock's few whodunits that emphasizes romantic elements over suspense. With *The Man Who Knew Too Much*, Hayes contrasts the emotional strengths of man and wife, which, as executed by Hitchcock, result in shifting tone as the film's progression mirrors the heroine's increasing anxiety. In *The Trouble with Harry* the inhabitants of a New England village discuss coolly and matter-of-factly the recurring inconvenience of disposing of a corpse.

Rear Window is considered by many critics the quintessential screenplay for a Hitchcock film. As with most of his screenplays, Hayes worked as an adaptor, taking his script from a short story by Cornell Woolrich. The action occurs over a period of several days and, save a brief sequence, is confined to a single Greenwich Village apartment overlooking a courtyard bordered on all sides by other apartments. L. B. Jeffries (James Stewart) is a news photographer injured on assignment and recovering from a broken leg. Jeffries's idle gazings lead him to suspect that a murder has been committed in the apartment facing his. This discovery, his difficulty in convincing the police of his assumptions, his enlisting the aid of his girl friend Lisa Fremont (Grace Kelly) in securing evidence, and his eventual peril at the hands of the killer form the surface elements of *Rear Window*. Interwoven into this framework is the film's second layer—an examination of the noncommittal relationship between Jeffries and Lisa. Jeffries's inability to deal effectively with his own relationships is tied directly to his ability in analyzing and documenting the lives of others.

Hayes's complex, multilayered screenplay matched in both style and tone the director's cynical nature, and *Rear Window* is regarded as one of Hitchcock's masterpieces. In 1954, owing to its deceptively slick dialogue and characterization, the film was regarded by many critics as little more than a romantic comedy. Critical reaction centered on an assessment of *Rear Window*'s surface gloss and commercial potential while disregarding its more subtle pleasures, only later to be appreciated fully. Hayes earned an Academy Award nomination for his screenplay.

If *Rear Window* was misjudged, romantic comedy was exactly what the next Hayes-Hitchcock project, *To Catch a Thief*, intended. The screenplay

Thelma Ritter, Grace Kelly, and James Stewart in Rear Window, *Hayes's first film for Alfred Hitchcock*

concentrates on the romance between a retired cat burglar (Cary Grant) and a vacationing beauty (Grace Kelly) who suspects that he is responsible for the wave of jewel thefts on the French Riviera. Hayes and Hitchcock examine in this relationship the interplay of an aura of danger and sexual attraction, and the scenes are fraught with innuendo and sexual energy. The screenplay in its initial stages had undergone heavy rewriting with elimination of several subplots as the film was steered from the traditional whodunit to other directions. Certainly no one was better suited than Hayes to write the sharp dialogue for the now expanded love scenes, and enjoyment of *To Catch a Thief* depends on its being accepted as a romance and as a change of pace from the customary Hitchcock offerings.

Hayes and Hitchcock followed *To Catch a Thief* with an artistically successful change of pace. *The Trouble with Harry*, one of Hitchcock's favorite films, is a black comedy set in Vermont. The trouble with Harry is that he is dead. Further complicating matters and providing the dark humor of the film is

Harry's stubbornness in not staying buried, for Hayes's characters scurry about digging up and replanting the body to cover up for a loved one they suspect did Harry in. Hayes and Hitchcock were concerned with placing their clever story in the proper setting and constructing the proper atmosphere. The pastoral New England countryside forms the immediate reality of the characters—a reality thrown off balance by the intrusion of the dead Harry, an improper and undesirable element which must be dealt with in order to maintain a false sense of security and to restore harmony.

Hayes brought to *The Trouble with Harry* a perceptive view of Puritanism running rampant, commenting on the connections between sex and death, neither of which is ever talked about openly. The derisive wit that marks *The Trouble with Harry* did not make for financial success; Hayes and Hitchcock returned to a more straightforward, conventional work with *The Man Who Knew Too Much*, their final team effort.

A remake of Hitchcock's own 1934 British

original, *The Man Who Knew Too Much* is remembered chiefly for its carefully constructed set pieces, principally a ten-minute nondialogue sequence which climaxes with the heroine's foiling an assassination attempt with a well-timed shriek during a concert in Albert Hall. The globetrotting events detailing the efforts of a couple (James Stewart and Doris Day) to retrieve their kidnapped child seem to call for a realistic approach. Hitchcock emphasized the visceral aspects of the screenplay; Hayes's inherent sense of pacing, scene construction, and character development were relegated to a secondary position.

In 1957 both Hayes and Hitchcock left Paramount, and Hayes went to 20th Century-Fox. That year he embarked on his most detailed screenplay, the adaptation of Grace Metalious's best-selling novel *Peyton Place*. The novel was considered unfilmable because of its explicit dialogue and its abundance of sex. Hayes's adaptation omitted the more graphic sequences of the novel, turning it into a perceptive analysis of small-town life,

concentrating on the inherent hypocrisy of Puritanism and the effects of its stifling atmosphere on the inhabitants of Peyton Place, Maine.

The film, like the novel, is narrated by Allison MacKenzie (Diane Varsi), an impressionable, articulate, would-be writer, desperately struggling to establish an identity. The relationship between Allison and her mother-dominated friend, Norman Page (Russ Tamblyn), forms the crux of the film. Their two extended scenes together—as teenagers on a hill overlooking the town, and at a chance meeting aboard a homebound train several years later—serve as barometers in gauging the effects of the values imposed on them by the town's societal rules.

Hayes's pacing and structure of the elements in *Peyton Place* allows, especially in the first third of the film, for a detailed portrayal of location and atmosphere. The quiet streets, the Harrington Mills (economic backbone of the town), and the Fourth of July parade contrast sharply with the tar-paper shacks looked upon as an embarrassment by the

Russ Tamblyn and Diane Varsi in a publicity shot for Peyton Place

prominent members of the community. Hayes weighs the components exactly, and the use of incidents associated with small-town life contributes to the overall reality in which Hayes places his characters. The everyday incidents and the talks between Allison and Norman are somehow more effective than the melodramatics which take precedence in the last section of the film.

On its release, *Peyton Place* was praised for its tasteful reworking of what in print was for many a literary mess, for its sensitivity in regard to character and situation, and for its sense of Americana. Hayes received his second Academy Award nomination for his screenplay, and his reworking and tempering of the characters in *Peyton Place* are the bases for all characterizations in subsequent versions. The film was followed by the sequel *Return to Peyton Place* (1961), a long-running television series, a daytime serial, and the television movie *Murder in Peyton Place* (1977), all owing more to Hayes's screenplay than to the original source material.

Hayes's output in the next few years after *Peyton Place* consisted of a series of film adaptations of successful plays and an adaptation of John O'Hara's novel *Butterfield 8* (1960), for which Elizabeth Taylor won an Academy Award. *The Matchmaker* (1958) is a faithful adaptation of Thornton Wilder's play scripted with an excellent period flavor. *But Not for Me* (1959), the third film version of Samson Raphaelson's play *Accent on Youth*, is marked by acute observations of the New York theater world, recounting a down-and-out producer's attempt to regain his popularity while making his secretary a Broadway star.

Hayes's reputation for dealing effectively with sensitive subject matter, garnered mainly because of his tasteful handling of *Peyton Place*, made him an ideal choice as adaptor of Lillian Hellman's play *The Children's Hour* in 1961 and Enid Bagnold's drama *The Chalk Garden* in 1964. A recurring theme in Hayes's work and one that he deals with particularly well is concern for truth in a struggle to survive in a hostile environment. Hayes does not always present this theme in terms of a problem common to an entire community as he did in *Peyton Place* and *Thunder Bay*; frequently the theme is examined on an intimate level—in the case of both *The Children's Hour* and *The Chalk Garden*—by studying the specific effect of innuendo upon a person's life. In both plays the catalyst for tragedy is a child; in *The Children's Hour* a spoiled, dangerous schoolgirl accuses her two female instructors (Shirley MacLaine and Audrey Hepburn) of being lovers; in *The Chalk Garden* a disturbed, neglected child's (Hayley Mills) desire to disgrace her governess (Deborah Kerr) leads to the discovery of a hidden incident in the governess's past.

Hayes expanded on several basic themes in the plays, concentrating mainly on the varying degrees of corruptibility—both inherent and learned—and on the motivating factors which influence the children's actions. At the same time, Hayes softened, particularly in *The Chalk Garden*, some of the characters' hard edges, making them more accessible to a general audience. Mainly, however, Hayes was called on to bring to the original works his knowledge of film structure in order to open up the plays, thereby rendering them more cinematic.

In 1964 Hayes made two alliances: he accepted an executive position at Avco Embassy Pictures and undertook to adapt several works of novelist Harold Robbins for the screen: *The Carpetbaggers* (1964) and *Where Love Has Gone* (1964) were completed within the year; *The Adventurers* was planned but produced in 1970 by another studio with Hayes's screenplay unused; and *Nevada Smith* (1966) used Hayes's virtually original screenplay based on characters in *The Carpetbaggers*.

Inspired by the exploits of Howard Hughes, *The Carpetbaggers* is most effective in its handling of time period (the saga spans two decades) and the changing mores of the 1920s and the 1930s. The film was a success primarily by virtue of its exploitative qualities, but Hayes's screenplay does contain some sharply written dialogue, and the story is well fashioned.

Where Love Has Gone followed almost immediately, directed by Edward Dmytryk, who also did *The Carpetbaggers*. This film, however, did not enjoy the success of its predecessor. Again based loosely on fact—the stabbing death of Lana Turner's lover, Johnny Stompanato, by her daughter—the film suffers from unsympathetic characters and a tendency on Hayes's part to overwrite the dialogue.

Next Hayes adapted Irving Shulman's biography of Jean Harlow in *Harlow* (1965) and adapted a Lawrence Durrell short story, filmed as *Judith* (1966), before returning to Harold Robbins for inspiration in *Nevada Smith*.

In the course of *The Carpetbaggers*, Jonas Cord, Jr., reveals his knowledge of the past of lifelong friend Nevada Smith—Smith's wild West days when he was known as Max Sand, a half-breed avenging his parents' brutal slaying. Hayes's final feature screenplay uses the Max Sand character as a starting point, detailing the past only hinted at in *The Carpetbaggers*. *Nevada Smith* recounts the quest of Max

George Peppard and Elizabeth Ashley in The Carpetbaggers

Sand (Steve McQueen) for the killers of his parents, a search which ironically results in his attainment of knowledge and a moral education. *Nevada Smith* is Hayes's second excursion into the Western genre, the other being an early work, *War Arrow*. The success of *Nevada Smith* is not due to a reworking of clichés, as in the case of *War Arrow*, but to examination of a virtual innocent and the demands which a hostile environment places on him. *Nevada Smith* is one of Hayes's few original screenplays and a fitting close to a productive feature-film writing career. It embodies the best aspects of Hayes's screenplays: it has well-developed characters, a strong central theme, and complex interplay between man and his environment.

It is regrettable that a proposed collection of Hayes's screenplays in book form did not come to fruition. His screenplays have not only served as the blueprints for many celebrated films but are also immensely readable in themselves. The construction of dialogue and the detailed descriptions of

time and place form a coherent whole rarely found in the screenwriting medium. In his screenplays Hayes deals with universal concerns in a poetic, accessible manner. In films such as *Rear Window*, *Thunder Bay*, *The Chalk Garden*, and *Nevada Smith*, the facades which characters construct to block out affection and human interaction are ultimately subverted through an increased awareness. The "plain wrappers" of *Peyton Place* are stripped away, the characters laid bare, the truth exposed and examined.

The stylish craftsmanship which was the earmark of Hayes's screen work was out of fashion by the late 1960s, with the trend toward realism taking precedence over the traditional Hollywood film. Carefully constructed scenes gave way to improvisations as the fiction film experimented with new directions. After *Nevada Smith*, Hayes continued in his executive capacity at Avco through the 1970s, writing frequently for television projects. Undaunted by the film-going public's change of tastes,

Hayes also continued with his feature output, although he has not had a theatrical film property produced since *Nevada Smith*. In an interview in the early 1970s Hayes analyzed his quandary: "Since '66, if I was keeping track of the unproduced scripts which I have written, and which haven't been made, the number would be something like eight. The producers were caught in an economic bind. There was a sudden change in movies.... the subject matter didn't have broad enough appeal. Suddenly with expensive pictures, studios were losing money—expensive pictures got dangerous and they stopped making them." Hollywood has again come full circle, but the present trend toward inflated big-budget productions has not brought with it a return to structural basics. Title cards bearing the credit line "Screenplay by John Michael Hayes" are missing not only in regard to this specific screenwriter's contributions but also in terms of all it implies: a mastering of craft and an overriding professionalism.

References:

J. D. Marshall, ed., *Blueprint on Babylon* (New York: Phoenix House, 1978), pp. 213-233, 325;

"Screenwriters Symposium," *Film Comment*, 6 (Winter 1970-1971): 86, 91-92, 101;

François Truffaut, *Hitchcock* (New York: Simon & Schuster, 1967).

Ben Hecht

(28 February 1894-18 April 1964)

Randall Clark

See also the Hecht entries in *DLB 7, Twentieth-Century American Dramatists; DLB 9, American Novelists, 1910-1945;* and *DLB 25, American Newspaper Journalists, 1901-1925.*

SELECTED MOTION PICTURES: *Underworld* (Paramount, 1927), story;
The Big Noise (First National, 1928), screenplay by Hecht and Tom Geraghty;
Unholy Night (M-G-M, 1929), story;
The Green Ghost (M-G-M, 1929), story;
Roadhouse Nights (Paramount, 1930), story;
The Great Gabbo (Sono Art World Wide, 1930), story;
Unholy Garden (United Artists, 1931), screenplay by Hecht and Charles MacArthur;
Scarface (United Artists, 1932), adaptation;
Hallelujah, I'm a Bum (United Artists, 1933), story;
Turn Back the Clock (M-G-M, 1933), screenplay by Hecht and Edgar Selwyn;
Design for Living (Paramount, 1933), screenplay;
Upper World (Warner Bros., 1934), story;
Twentieth Century (Columbia, 1934), screenplay adapted by Hecht and MacArthur from their play;
Crime Without Passion (Paramount, 1934), screenplay adapted by Hecht and MacArthur from Hecht's short story;
Viva Villa! (M-G-M, 1934), screenplay;

Once in a Blue Moon (Paramount, 1935), screenplay by Hecht and MacArthur;
The Scoundrel (Paramount, 1935), screenplay by Hecht and MacArthur;
Barbary Coast (United Artists, 1935), screenplay by Hecht and MacArthur;
Soak the Rich (Paramount, 1936), screenplay by Hecht and MacArthur;
Nothing Sacred (United Artists, 1938), screenplay;
Goldwyn Follies (United Artists, 1938), screenplay;
Let Freedom Ring (M-G-M, 1939), screen story and screenplay;
It's a Wonderful World (M-G-M, 1939), screen story by Hecht and Herman Mankiewicz; screenplay;
Lady of the Tropics (M-G-M, 1939), screen story and screenplay;
Gunga Din (RKO, 1939), screen story by Hecht and MacArthur;
Wuthering Heights (United Artists, 1939), screenplay by Hecht and MacArthur;
Angels Over Broadway (Columbia, 1940), screen story and screenplay;
Comrade X (M-G-M, 1940), screenplay by Hecht and Charles Lederer;
Lydia (United Artists, 1941), screenplay by Hecht and Samuel Hoffenstein;
Tales of Manhattan (20th Century-Fox, 1942), screen

story and screenplay by Hecht and others;

China Girl (20th Century-Fox, 1942), screenplay;

The Black Swan (20th Century-Fox, 1942), screenplay by Hecht and Seton I. Miller;

Spellbound (United Artists, 1945), screenplay;

Specter of the Rose (Republic, 1946), story and screenplay;

Notorious (RKO, 1946), screen story and screenplay;

Her Husband's Affairs (Columbia, 1947), screen story and screenplay by Hecht and Lederer;

Kiss of Death (20th Century-Fox, 1947), screenplay by Hecht and Lederer;

Ride the Pink Horse (Universal, 1947), screenplay by Hecht and Lederer;

The Miracle of the Bells (RKO, 1948), screenplay by Hecht and Quentin Reynolds;

Whirlpool (20th Century-Fox, 1950), screenplay by Hecht (as Lester Bartow) and Andrew Solt;

Where the Sidewalk Ends (20th Century-Fox, 1950), screenplay;

Actors and Sin (United Artists, 1952), story and screenplay;

Monkey Business (20th Century-Fox, 1952), screenplay by Hecht, Lederer, and I. A. L. Diamond;

Ulisse (Ulysses) (Lux Films/Paramount, 1955), screenplay by Hecht and others;

The Indian Fighter (United Artists, 1955), screenplay by Hecht and Frank Davis;

Miracle in the Rain (Warner Bros., 1956), screenplay adapted by Hecht from his novel;

The Iron Petticoat (M-G-M, 1956), screen story and screenplay;

Legend of the Lost (United Artists, 1957), screen story and screenplay by Hecht and Robert Presnell, Jr.;

A Farewell to Arms (20th Century-Fox, 1957), screenplay;

Circus World (Paramount, 1964), screenplay by Hecht, Julien Halevy, and James Edward Grant.

SELECTED PLAYS: *The Wonder Hat* (Detroit, Arts and Crafts Theatre, 1916), by Hecht and Kenneth S. Goodman;

The Hero of Santa Maria (New York, Comedy Theatre, 12 February 1917), by Hecht and Goodman;

The Egotist (New York, Thirty-ninth Street Theatre, 25 December 1922);

The Front Page (New York, Times Square Theatre, 14 August 1928), by Hecht and Charles MacArthur;

The Great Magoo (New York, Selwyn Theatre, 2 December 1932), by Hecht and Gene Fowler;

Ben Hecht (Culver Pictures)

Twentieth Century (New York, Broadhurst Theatre, 29 December 1932), by Hecht and MacArthur;

Jumbo (New York, Hippodrome, 16 November 1935), by Hecht and MacArthur;

To Quito and Back (New York, Guild Theatre, 6 October 1937);

Ladies and Gentlemen (New York, Martin Beck Theatre, 17 October 1939), by Hecht and MacArthur;

Christmas Eve (New York, Henry Miller's Theatre, 27 December 1939);

Fun to Be Free, Patriotic Pageant (New York, Madison Square Garden, 1941), by Hecht and MacArthur;

Lily of the Valley (New York, Windsor Theatre, 26 February 1942);

We Will Never Die (New York, Madison Square Garden, 9 March 1943);

Swan Song (New York, Booth Theatre, 15 May 1946), by Hecht and MacArthur;

A Flag Is Born (New York, Alvin Theatre, 5 September 1946);

Hazel Flagg (New York, Mark Hellinger Theatre, 11 February 1953);

Winkelberg (New York, Renata Theatre, 14 January 1958).

SELECTED BOOKS: *The Wonder Hat*, by Hecht and Kenneth S. Goodman (New York: Shay, 1920);

The Hero of Santa Maria, by Hecht and Goodman (New York: Shay, 1920);

Erik Dorn (New York & London: Putnam's, 1921);

1001 Afternoons in Chicago (Chicago: Covici McGee, 1922);

Gargoyles (New York: Boni & Liveright, 1922);

Fantazius Mallare: A Mysterious Oath (Chicago: Covici McGee, 1922);

The Florentine Dagger: A Novel for Amateur Detectives (New York: Boni & Liveright, 1923; London: Heinemann, 1924);

Cutie, A Warm Mamma, by Hecht and Maxwell Bodenheim (Chicago: Hechtshaw, 1924);

Humpty Dumpty (New York: Boni & Liveright, 1924);

Broken Necks and Other Stories (Girard, Kans.: Haldeman-Julius, 1924);

Tales of Chicago Streets (Girard, Kans.: Haldeman-Julius, 1924);

The Kingdom of Evil: A Continuation of the Journal of Fantazius Mallare (Chicago: Covici, 1924);

The Wonder Hat and Other One-Act Plays, by Hecht and Goodman (New York & London: Appleton, 1925);

Broken Necks (Chicago: Covici, 1926);

Count Bruga (New York: Boni & Liveright, 1926);

Infatuation, and Other Stories of Love's Misfits (Girard, Kans.: Haldeman-Julius, 1927);

Jazz, and Other Stories of Young Love (Girard, Kans.: Haldeman-Julius, 1927);

The Policewoman's Love-Hungry Daughter and Other Stories of Chicago Life (Girard, Kans.: Haldeman-Julius, 1927);

The Sinister Sex and Other Stories (Girard, Kans.: Haldeman-Julius, 1927);

The Unlovely Sin and Other Stories (Girard, Kans.: Haldeman-Julius, 1927);

Christmas Eve (New York: Covici Friede, 1928);

The Front Page, by Hecht and Charles MacArthur (New York: Covici Friede, 1928; London: Richards & Toulmin, 1929);

The Champion from Far Away (New York: Covici Friede, 1931);

A Jew in Love (New York: Covici Friede, 1931);

The Great Magoo, by Hecht and Gene Fowler (New York: Covici Friede, 1933);

Actor's Blood (New York: Covici Friede, 1936);

To Quito and Back (New York: Covici Friede, 1937);

A Book of Miracles (New York: Viking, 1939; London: Nicholson & Watson, 1940);

Ladies and Gentlemen, by Hecht and MacArthur (New York, Los Angeles & London: French, 1941);

Fun to Be Free, Patriotic Pageant, by Hecht and MacArthur (New York: Dramatists Play Service, 1941);

1001 Afternoons in New York (New York: Viking, 1941);

Miracle in the Rain (New York: Knopf, 1943);

A Guide for the Bedevilled (New York: Scribners, 1944);

I Hate Actors! (New York: Crown, 1944);

The Collected Stories of Ben Hecht (New York: Crown, 1945);

A Flag Is Born (New York: American League for a Free Palestine, 1946);

A Child of the Century (New York: Simon & Schuster, 1954);

Charlie: The Improbable Life and Times of Charles MacArthur (New York: Harper, 1957);

The Sensualists (New York: Messner, 1959);

Perfidy (New York: Messner, 1961);

Gaily, Gaily (Garden City: Doubleday, 1963);

Letters from Bohemia (Garden City: Doubleday, 1964);

In the Midst of Death (London: Mayflower, 1964).

OTHER: *Wuthering Heights*, in *Twenty Best Film Plays*, edited by John Gassner and Dudley Nichols (New York: Crown, 1943);

Spellbound, in *Best Film Plays, 1945*, edited by Gassner and Nichols (New York: Crown, 1946).

Ben Hecht was one of the most successful screenwriters in the history of motion pictures. In a career that spanned forty years, Hecht was credited with writing the screen stories or screenplays for more than fifty films and worked without credit on many others. He could produce a screenplay in two weeks and, according to his autobiography, never spent more than eight weeks on a script. He never liked writing for the movies and looked on it as just a means of obtaining ready cash, but he continued to write screenplays until his death.

Hecht was born in New York City, the son of Russian-Jewish immigrants. The family later moved to Racine, Wisconsin, and when Hecht was in his early teens he would spend his summers with an uncle who owned a circus in Chicago. At sixteen he ran away to Chicago and found work as a reporter, first for the *Chicago Journal*, then for the *Chicago Daily News*. Hecht married Marie Armstrong in

1915; they had a daughter, Edwina.

From 1918 to 1919 Hecht served as foreign correspondent in Berlin for the *Daily News*. There he discovered the works of Dadaists and German Expressionists—influences later evident in his own writing, especially his novel *Fantazius Mallare* (1922) and his films *Crime Without Passion* (1934) and *Angels Over Broadway* (1940).

Hecht began his career as playwright in 1914, when he collaborated with Kenneth Sawyer Goodman on a series of one-act plays. His first full-length play, *The Egotist*, was produced in New York in 1922. Hecht met fellow reporter Charles MacArthur in Chicago; they decided to move to New York and collaborate on a play. The resulting work, *The Front Page*, began a successful Broadway run of 281 performances in August 1928. Hecht was divorced in 1925 and married that same year to Rose Caylor; they had a daughter, Jenny.

Although Anita Loos says that Hecht supplied the idea for the film *Double Trouble* in 1915, his screenwriting career did not really begin until the late 1920s. Former newspaperman and drama critic Herman Mankiewicz sent him a telegram urging him to come to Hollywood. Hecht soon became the highest paid screenwriter in Hollywood, receiving from $50,000 to $125,000 per script. He divided his life, spending half the year in New York and the other half in Hollywood.

Hecht frequently argued with his producers and directors, sometimes walking out on a film before it was completed. For his first movie, *Underworld* (1927), Hecht prepared an eighteen-page treatment, then demanded his name be removed from the film when director Josef von Sternberg changed one scene. He finally agreed to take credit for the film, and went on to win the Academy Award for Best Original Story the first year the awards were presented. *Underworld* was the story of a petty hoodlum with political pull; it was based on a real Chicago gangster Hecht knew, Dion O'Bannon, a beer baron. The film began the gangster film genre that was popular in the early 1930s.

Following *Underworld* Hecht contributed the original stories for several films and worked without credit on the first film version of his play *The Front Page* in 1931. His first full screenplay was *Unholy Garden* (1931), which he cowrote with Charles MacArthur. The film starred Ronald Colman, who played the sort of gentleman adventurer he had made popular with *Bulldog Drummond* (1929) and *Raffles* (1930).

Hecht had helped to start the gangster film with *Underworld*; his next film, *Scarface* (1932), be-

Paul Muni in a scene from Scarface

came one of the best films in that genre. Hecht wrote the screen story from a novel by Armitage Trail. The film was directed by Howard Hawks, who became one of the few directors with whom Hecht enjoyed working. *Scarface* was the story of an Al Capone-like gangster, played by Paul Muni. At the time of its release, the film encountered some censorship troubles not just because of its violence but also because of its suggestions of incest.

Hawks also directed *Twentieth Century* (1934), which Hecht and Charles MacArthur adapted from their play of the same title. John Barrymore stars as a Broadway producer who is about to lose his leading lady (Carole Lombard) to Hollywood. When she travels west by train, he sneaks aboard, willing to do anything to convince her to return. *Twentieth Century* is a fast-paced, witty film that contains the rapid-fire dialogue for which Hecht became famous. It is one of the first, and finest, of the screwball comedies of the 1930s.

Hecht's third film for Hawks was *Viva Villa!* (1934), about the Mexican rebel. Some critics complained that the film took liberties with the facts, but the movie was still a great success. Hecht received an Academy award for his screenplay.

In 1934 Hecht and Charles MacArthur formed their own film company and began work on four films which they wrote, produced, and directed at the Paramount Astoria Studios: *Crime Without Passion* (1934), *Once in a Blue Moon* (1935), *The Scoundrel* (1935), and *Soak the Rich* (1936). *Crime Without Passion* is the story of a crooked attorney (Claude Rains) who almost gets away with murder. *Once in a Blue Moon* is about a ballet troupe fleeing revolutionary Russia. *The Scoundrel* was based on a play which Hecht wrote with his wife Rose Caylor. An immoral rake (Noel Coward) dies and cannot be completely put to rest until someone cries for him. Hecht and MacArthur won Oscars for their screenplay. *Soak the Rich* concerns an heiress who participates in a student revolt to promote a tax plan that will penalize the rich.

Hecht and MacArthur again worked with Howard Hawks on *Barbary Coast* (1935), set in San Francisco in the late nineteenth century and pitting a dance-hall girl (Miriam Hopkins) against the man (Edward G. Robinson) who runs the town. During

that same year *Man-Eating Tiger*, another play Hecht had written with his wife, was made into the film *Spring Tonic* (1935).

Hecht's first assignment after his film company failed was *Nothing Sacred* (1938), which he adapted from his play *Hazel Flagg*. Carole Lombard stars as a small-town girl who is diagnosed as having radium poisoning. A reporter makes her case a cause célèbre of the newspapers. Although she realizes she will live, she goes along with him for awhile. *Nothing Sacred* allowed Hecht to work with one of his favorite themes, hypocrisy (especially among journalists); he took the themes of lying, decadence, and immorality and made them into a sophisticated screwball comedy.

After becoming one of the many writers to work without credit on *Gone with the Wind* (1939) and cowriting with MacArthur what was to become one of Hollywood's greatest action-adventure films, *Gunga Din* (1939), Hecht was hired by Samuel Goldwyn to adapt Emily Brontë's *Wuthering Heights*. MacArthur worked with him. The completed

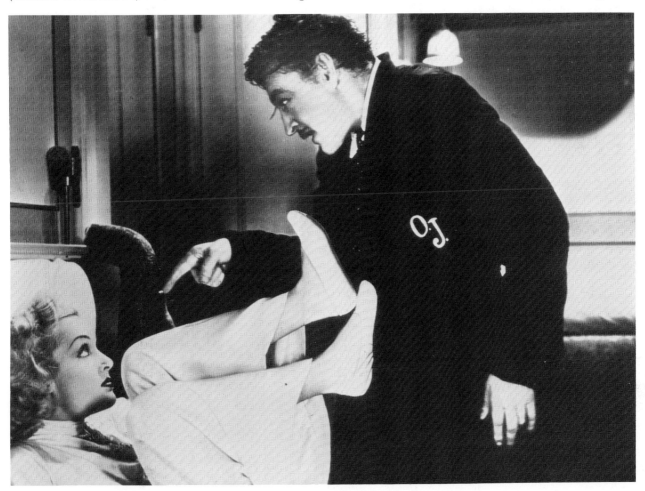

Carole Lombard and John Barrymore in Twentieth Century

screenplay was deemed too long to film by Goldwyn, who cut it off at the halfway point. Obviously the film was not entirely faithful to the novel; besides ending at the seventeenth chapter, it also omitted certain scenes and expanded others. The film was a critical and financial success in spite of these liberties, and Hecht and MacArthur were nominated for Academy awards. This was the last screenplay they wrote together.

In between writing screenplays for Hollywood, Hecht returned to directing with *Angels Over Broadway* (1940), the only movie he directed, produced, and wrote originally for film. In the film a group of people are stranded during a ten-hour rainstorm; one (Douglas Fairbanks, Jr.) tries to convince another (Rita Hayworth) to join him in an embezzling plot. Hecht received another Academy award nomination for this film.

In 1940 Hecht worked without credit on *The Shop Around the Corner*, *Foreign Correspondent*, and *His Girl Friday*, which was the second film version of *The Front Page*, directed by Howard Hawks. Screenplay credit on *His Girl Friday* went to Charles Lederer, and this was the beginning of a film collaboration between the two men that would last until

the early 1960s. That same year, 1940, they wrote the comedy *Comrade X*, about an American man (Clark Gable) in love with a Russian woman (Hedy Lamarr).

In 1945 and 1946, Hecht wrote two films for Alfred Hitchcock, for whom he had worked without credit on *Foreign Correspondent*. *Spellbound* (1945) is the story of an amnesiac (Gregory Peck) who is aided by a psychiatrist (Ingrid Bergman) in unraveling a murder he thinks he has committed. *Notorious* (1946) deals with a woman (Ingrid Bergman) who marries a Nazi spy (Claude Rains) and tries to help an American agent (Cary Grant). Hecht received his final Academy award nomination for this film. He is also said to have worked without credit on two other Hitchcock films, *The Paradine Case* (1947) and *Rope* (1948), but there is some question as to whether his contributions were used. Arthur Laurents, the credited screenwriter of *Rope*, has said that Hecht "wasn't responsible for one word of the screenplay used."

Hecht wrote and directed *Specter of the Rose* (1946) from his own short story about a ballet dancer accused of murder. He then teamed with Charles Lederer for three films in 1947. The first,

Cary Grant and Ingrid Bergman in Notorious, *Hecht's second film for Alfred Hitchcock (Museum of Modern Art Film Stills Archive)*

Her Husband's Affairs, was an unsuccessful comedy about a jealous wife (Lucille Ball). *Kiss of Death*, directed by Henry Hathaway, was among the best American films noirs, a violent movie about a criminal (Victor Mature) turned informer. The film contains the now-famous scene in which a psychopath (Richard Widmark, who received an Oscar nomination for the role) pushes a woman in a wheelchair down a flight of stairs. Also a film noir, but considerably less violent, was *Ride the Pink Horse*, which Hecht and Lederer adapted from Dorothy B. Hughes's novel about an ex-GI (Robert Montgomery) who comes to a Mexican village during its annual fiesta looking for an old enemy, a gangster he intends to blackmail.

From 1948 to 1951, Hecht was blacklisted in England because of his criticism of British policies in Palestine. Hecht's films were banned in England, and those which were released in that country were shown with his name removed from the credits.

In the early 1950s Hecht wrote his final two films for Howard Hawks. He and Charles Lederer wrote *The Thing* (Hecht worked without credit), a science-fiction film that Hawks produced and is said to have directed, at least in part. Hecht, Lederer, and I. A. L. Diamond wrote *Monkey Business* (1952). In this film a scientist played by Cary Grant attempts to find a rejuvenation formula; what he discovers is a serum that causes adults to act like children. He, his wife (Ginger Rogers), his boss (Charles Coburn), and his boss's secretary (Marilyn Monroe) are all affected. *Monkey Business* was a screwball comedy in the old tradition, and it was Hecht's last true success as a screenwriter.

Actors and Sin (1952) was Hecht's final film as a director. The film consists of two stories, both adaptations of his own short stories. "Actor's Blood" is about a former actor concerned with his daughter's career; in "Woman of Sin" a literary agent represents a nine-year-old child. For the remainder of the 1950s, Hecht worked either as an uncredited contributor to successful films —*The Greatest Show on Earth* (1952), *Roman Holiday* (1953)—or as cred-

ited screenwriter of failures. *Miracle in the Rain* (1956) is a surprisingly sentimental story of a woman (Jane Wyman) whose husband is killed in the war, while *The Iron Petticoat* (1956) is an unsuccessful attempt to make a comedy team of Katharine Hepburn and Bob Hope. *A Farewell to Arms* (1957) reduces Ernest Hemingway's novel to a simplistic romance.

In the 1960s, Hecht worked without credit on *Mutiny on the Bounty* (1962), his final film with Lederer; he then was brought in by director Henry Hathaway to work on the John Wayne film *Circus World* (1964). Hecht was one of several writers asked to contribute additional material for the big-budget James Bond spoof *Casino Royale* (1967). Shortly after completing his work on that film, Hecht died of a heart attack at age seventy.

References:

George Bluestone, *From Novels Into Film* (Berkeley: University of California Press, 1968), pp. 91-114;

Geoff Brown, "Better Than Metro Isn't Good Enough; Hecht and MacArthur's Own Movies," *Sight and Sound*, 44 (Summer 1975): 153-155ff;

Richard Corliss, *Talking Pictures* (New York: Penguin, 1974);

Doug Fetherling, *The Five Lives of Ben Hecht* (Toronto: Lester & Orpen, 1977);

Stephen Fuller, "Ben Hecht: A Sampler," *Film Comment*, 6 (Winter 1970/1971): 33-39;

Penelope Houston, "Scripting; The Return of Hecht," *Sight and Sound*, 21 (August/September 1951): 30ff;

Peter Wollen, *Signs and Meaning in the Cinema* (Bloomington: Indiana University Press, 1969), pp. 80-94.

Papers:

The Newberry Library, Chicago, holds the largest collection of Ben Hecht's papers.

Buck Henry

(9 December 1930-)

Nan Morrison
College of Charleston

MOTION PICTURES: *The Troublemaker* (Janus, 1964), screen story and screenplay by Henry and Theodore Flicker;

The Graduate (Embassy Pictures, 1967), screenplay by Henry and Calder Willingham;

Candy (Cinerama, 1968), screenplay;

Catch-22 (Paramount, 1970), screenplay;

The Owl and the Pussycat (Columbia, 1970), screenplay;

What's Up, Doc? (Warner Bros., 1972), screenplay by Henry, Robert Benton, and David Newman;

The Day of the Dolphin (Avco Embassy, 1973), screenplay;

First Family (Warner Bros., 1980), screenplay.

TELEVISION: *The Steve Allen Show* (ABC, September-December 1961), writer;

That Was the Week That Was (NBC, January 1964-May 1965), writer;

Get Smart (NBC, September 1965-September 1969; CBS, September 1969-September 1970), creator and story editor with Mel Brooks;

Captain Nice (NBC, January 1967-August 1967), producer, creator, writer;

Quark (NBC, February 1978-April 1978), creator.

PERIODICAL PUBLICATION: "Diary of Planes, Pilots, and Pratfalls," *Life* (12 June 1970): 46.

Buck Henry

Buck Henry was born Buck Henry Zuckerman, the son of Paul Zuckerman, a U.S. Army Air Forces general who became a stockbroker, and Ruth Taylor Zuckerman, an actress. He grew up in New York City, beginning an acting career as a teenager by appearing in a production of *Life with Father*. Henry graduated from Dartmouth College in 1952 with a B.A. in English, and from 1952 to 1954 he served in the U.S. Army as a helicopter mechanic and as a member of the Seventh Army Repertory Company, which toured Germany with a musical comedy which he wrote and directed. After leaving the service, he continued his acting career, appearing in productions of *No Time for Sergeants*, *Fortress of Glass*, and *Bernardine*. In 1960 he joined the off-Broadway improvisational group called The Premise. His work with them gave him invaluable training as a comic writer and actor and led to his employment as a writer for the *Steve Allen Show*, an experience which he says was not a happy one but taught him a lot about jokes. He later wrote for other television shows, including the satiric *That Was the Week That Was*, and for many television comedians.

Henry's first film work was on *The Troublemaker* (1964), for which he wrote the screen story and screenplay in collaboration with Theodore Flicker, who also directed the film. The film, which stars actors from The Premise, reflects the group's approach to comedy. The script goes in several directions, allowing the actors to improvise their own jokes, which are sometimes exaggerated and obscene. *The Troublemaker* centers on an honest young man who comes to New York to open a coffeehouse, where "people may do as they please," but who first has to grease the palms of policemen and public officials who control licenses. Henry also acted in the film. Although the satire is effective, the slapstick is overdone, the humor is broad, and the improvisations lead to a lack of unity. *The Troublemaker* was neither a financial nor a critical success.

Henry spent the years following *The Troublemaker* working mostly for television. In 1965 he and Mel Brooks created the highly successful comedy series *Get Smart*, for which he also served as story editor and for which he won an Emmy Award in 1966. He also created, produced, and wrote *Captain Nice*, a super-hero spoof, which ran on NBC from January to August 1967.

Henry's next film, *The Graduate* (1967), the first of three movies he wrote for director Mike Nichols, was a huge success at the box office and garnered for Henry and his collaborator Calder Willingham an Academy Award nomination, the New York Film Critics Award, the British Film Academy Award, and the Writers Guild of America Award for best comedy. Henry and Willingham adapted Charles Webb's novel *The Graduate* to the screen, adhering to its story but adding brilliant dialogue and sharp satire of the materialistic, per-

missive society of the 1960s. In the film young, naive, college graduate Benjamin Braddock (Dustin Hoffman) returns home to his rich, vulgar parents in California before facing the realities of the world and is shortly introduced to sexual realities by his parents' friend Mrs. Robinson (Anne Bancroft). Their affair produces a humorous contrast between his innocence and ineptitude and her experience, and the relationship is complicated by Benjamin's falling in love with her daughter Elaine (Katharine Ross). After Elaine discovers his affair with her mother and therefore consents to marry a young man who is a friend of her family's, Benjamin interrupts the marriage and flees with Elaine. *The Graduate* became one of the key films of the 1960s, and its success made Henry one of the most in-demand screenwriters in Hollywood.

Henry's next film, *Candy* (1968), was almost as big a failure as *The Graduate* was a success. Again he was adapting a novel to the screen, this time Terry Southern and Mason Hoffenberger's 1959 parody of pornographic novels. While the novel *Candy* enjoyed a mild critical success, much of its humor

Katharine Ross and Dustin Hoffman in The Graduate

derives from novelistic conventions that did not translate well to the screen. The heroine of the film is a young, innocent, nubile teenager who wanders about the world encountering various strange characters, most of whom are parodies of stock types—doctor, poet, general, guru. The humor in the film was criticized as crude and smutty.

Henry's next movie, *Catch-22* (1970), an adaptation for Mike Nichols of Joseph Heller's novel, represents his best work as a screenwriter. The narrative line of the film was unclear to some because it consisted of flashbacks within a flashback, a structure suggested by the novel. Henry did a good job of compressing the story line while preserving as many of the elements of the novel as possible—truncating events, eliminating some characters, and reordering events so that he could juxtapose scenes from the novel to create the effect of cinematic montage. According to Henry, this screenplay is the only one of his works for film for which he made up the structure completely and "wrote it down on a half million index cards" before he began the actual composition. The other excellent feature of the film for which Henry is responsible is the dialogue. In its illogic, fragmentation, and manic repetition, it reflects the absurdity of the lives of the air force officers on the island of Pianoso during World War II—the madness of the bombardier Yossarian (Alan Arkin), the panic, isolation, and desperate humor of the other characters.

Although Henry's next screenplay, *The Owl and the Pussycat* (1970), was well received by the public, it was criticized by reviewers. Adapted from a play by Bill Manhoff, the film depicts the relationship of a mismatched couple: Doris (Barbra Streisand), an uneducated prostitute, and Felix, an intellectual aspiring writer (George Segal). Henry's script is not up to his usual standards for comedy, perhaps because Manhoff's play is too contrived and strains too hard for humor. The comedy is sarcastic and often based on insults. Although the movie is inoffensive, the plot is predictable, and Henry's usual intelligent, crisp dialogue is missing.

Henry next did the final rewrite on Robert Benton and David Newman's screenplay for *What's Up, Doc?* (1972), developed from a story by Peter Bogdanovich, who also directed the film. Intended as a tribute to the screwball comedies of the 1930s, the movie, Bogdanovich says, was inspired by *Bringing Up Baby* (1938). Like *The Owl and the Pussycat*, *What's Up, Doc?* presents a mismatched couple: Jody Maxwell (Barbra Streisand), a carrot-chomping free spirit, and Howard Bannister (Ryan O'Neal), a serious musicologist. The complications

Barbra Streisand and George Segal in The Owl and the Pussycat

in the plot stem from the existence in one hotel of four identical bags, each carrying a different load—igneous rocks, jewels, stolen Pentagon papers, and Jody's clothes. The critics differed on the merits of the script. Some thought the humor was too derivative, while others thought it witty and inventive. The Screen Writers Guild gave it an award for best comedy of the year, and it was immensely popular with the public.

In 1973 Henry adapted Robert Merle's novel for the Mike Nichols movie *The Day of the Dolphin*, inspired by the research of American scientists who had spent years trying to teach dolphins to speak English. In the film, two scientists (George C. Scott and Trish Van Devere) find a way to communicate with dolphins, only to have the dolphins taken away from them by a mysterious government agency that plans to use them in an assassination attempt. The plot and the dialogue are dull.

For the next several years, Henry devoted his efforts to activities other than script writing. He appeared as an actor in the film *The Man Who Fell to Earth* (1976) and made frequent appearances as a television performer. In 1978, he created the television series *Quark*, a spoof of science-fiction programs; it ran on NBC for about three months. The same year Henry made his directorial debut when he and Warren Beatty directed *Heaven Can Wait* (1978), a remake of *Here Comes Mr. Jordan*, about an athlete who is taken to heaven prematurely and then placed in another body and returned to earth. (Henry may also have rewritten the script without credit; he is listed as coauthor on a working draft, but Beatty and Elaine May received screenplay credit on the film.) The film was nominated for an Academy Award for Best Picture, and Henry and Beatty were nominated for the Oscar for best director.

Henry also directed his next screenplay, a political satire titled *First Family* (1980), which centers on the attempts of an incompetent president (Bob Newhart) to establish diplomatic relations with an emerging African nation. At the same time, he must deal with problems caused by his alcoholic wife (Madeline Kahn), his nymphomaniac daughter (Gilda Radner), and his eccentric staff and advisers. Unfortunately, Henry's screenplay left the pos-

sibilities for political humor unrealized; *First Family* was a critical and popular failure.

Henry works most effectively with satire. His satirical scripts are sharp, brisk, and provocative. He accurately portrays the insanities of the modern age, yet allows even the most ridiculous of his characters to remain human and sympathetic. Because he has a fine sense of structure, his scripts are skillfully and economically crafted, with little superfluous action or dialogue. As a comedy writer, he has a perfect sense of timing; he builds up to a joke gradually and lets it explode, or he lets one-liners flow freely and quickly. Henry has said, "The good screenwriter should be able to see a movie in his head, or at the very least, hear it. But it's not enough to have a good ear for dialogue. You have to know where the beats and pauses are." The dialogue in his best scripts—*The Graduate* and *Catch-22*—reflects this sensitivity to the nuances of language as well as to character and theme.

References:

William Froug, *The Screenwriter Looks at the Screenwriter* (New York: Macmillan, 1972);

M. Seligson, "Hollywood's Hottest Writer," *New York Times Magazine*, 19 June 1970, pp. 11-12;

C. Thegze, "I See Everything Twice," *Film Quarterly*, 24 (Fall 1970): 7-17;

P. D. Zimmerman, "Bucking the System," *Newsweek* (9 October 1970): 11-12.

Colin Higgins

(28 July 1941-   )

William Frankfather

MOTION PICTURES: *Harold and Maude* (Paramount, 1971), screenplay;

Silver Streak (20th Century-Fox, 1976), screenplay;

Foul Play (Paramount, 1978), screenplay;

9 to 5 (IPC Productions, 1980), screenplay by Higgins and Patricia Resnick;

The Best Little Whorehouse in Texas (Universal, 1982), screenplay by Higgins, Larry L. King, and Peter Masterson.

PLAYS: *Harold and Maude*, translated by Jean-

Claude Carrière (Paris, 1972);

The Ik, by Higgins and Dennis Cannon, translated by Carrière and produced as *Les Iks* (Paris, Theatre des Bouffes du Nord, 12 January 1975); produced in English (London, Round House, 15 January 1976).

TELEVISION: *The Devil's Daughter* (ABC, January 1973).

BOOK: *Harold and Maude* (Philadelphia: Lippin-

Colin Higgins (photo by Bonnie Colodzin)

cott, 1971; London: Heinemann, 1971).

OTHER: *Opus One* in *Films on the Campus*, by
   Thomas Fensch (South Brunswick: A. S.
   Barnes, 1970);
Silver Streak in *Screenplay: The Basics of Screenwriting*,
   by Syd Field (New York: Dell, 1979).

Colin Higgins was born in Noumea, New
Caledonia, a French island in the Pacific, to Joy
Kelly Higgins, an Australian, and John Edward
Higgins, an American. He attended school in Oakland, California, and later in Sydney, after his family moved to Australia in 1950. He graduated with
honors in 1958 from his high school, St. Anthony's
College in Robertson, New South Wales, and the
following year he enrolled in Stanford University,
where he became interested in theater and wrote
and acted in several student productions. In 1960,
after his freshman year, he hitchhiked to New York,
where he worked as a page at ABC television and
studied acting at the Actors Studio. In 1962, after a
second year at Stanford, he enlisted in the army,
and upon graduating from the Armed Forces
Communications School at Fort Slocum, New York,
he was assigned to work as assistant editor on the

2nd Division *Bayonet* at Fort Benning, Georgia. He
was assigned overseas in 1963 and traveled
throughout Europe as a journalist with the 8th Division *Arrow* and *Stars and Stripes*. Following his discharge in 1965, he studied for six months at the
Sorbonne in Paris and made his film acting debut in
Louis de Funes's *Le Gendarme à New York* (1965).
Returning to Stanford in 1966 to study creative
writing under Wallace Stegner, Higgins worked
nights as a professional actor with the Stanford
Repertory Theatre at the Comedia Repertory Company in Palo Alto. He also appeared in his first
American film, as an extra in *Petulia* (1968). After
graduating from Stanford in 1967 with a B.A. degree, he signed on as an ordinary seaman on a
merchant ship bound for the Orient, and for six
months he toured Japan, Hong Kong, and the
South Pacific. Later in 1967 he entered graduate
school at UCLA to study film and continue his acting career. In 1969 the Student Theatrical Society
voted him Best Actor of the Year at UCLA for his
performance in the title role of *The Importance of
Being Earnest*. Also at UCLA he made two student
films: *Opus One*, a satire on student films, and *Re-
treat*, which won grand prize at the Long Beach film
festival. As a graduate assistant in his last year at
UCLA, he taught courses in beginning film and
studio production, and the University of Minnesota
invited him to judge their Of Media Festival. His
master's thesis, a screenplay entitled *Harold and
Maude*, won second prize in the annual Samuel
Goldwyn Awards. After receiving his M.F.A. degree in 1970, Higgins formed his own production
company and made a deal with Paramount Pictures
to produce the film with Hal Ashby directing.

Harold and Maude, the bizarre story of a love
affair between a young man, Harold (Bud Cort),
and an elderly woman, Maude (Ruth Gordon), who
are brought together by their mutual fascination for
death, funerals, and suicide, was not an immediate
success in the United States, probably because of its
offbeat humor. Although it was not received well
critically or at the box office, it did attract a strong
following on college campuses, and critics soon
labeled it a cult film. Its appeal to students and
young people seems to lie in its rejection of the
establishment values represented by Harold's
wealthy and domineering mother—who tries to get
him to drive a sports car instead of a hearse, to go
with the "right" girls she has selected for him, and to
try to make something of himself—and by the
military, represented by Harold's uncle, a hawkish,
one-armed general. Finding conventional values
absurd, Harold repeatedly stages mock suicide at-

Bud Cort and Ruth Gordon in a scene from Harold and Maude

tempts. Harold finds Maude, who is seventy-nine years old and plans to commit suicide on her eightieth birthday, invigorating and falls in love with her. Though heartbroken by her suicide, he is converted to her love of life and learns to accept it—but on his own terms.

Despite its relative failure in the United States, *Harold and Maude* was instantly successful in France, running in one movie house for more than two years. At the urging of Jean-Louis Barrault, Higgins adapted his screenplay for the stage. Translated by the French playwright-screenwriter Jean-Claude Carrière, the play opened successfully in Paris in 1972 and ran for more than four years. It has since been produced in the United States, Germany, Japan, Spain, Argentina, Czechoslovakia, England, and Canada. Higgins also expanded the screenplay into a novel, which was published in 1971 and has been translated into a half-dozen foreign languages.

While in Paris, Higgins joined Peter Brook's international theater group as playwright-in-residence, and with English playwright Dennis

Cannon he collaborated on a stage adaptation of Colin Turnbull's book *The Mountain People*. The play, *The Ik,* was translated by Jean-Claude Carrière and on 12 January 1975 opened successfully as *Les Iks* in Brook's theater in Paris. In 1976 it was produced in London, and also in 1976 the French government, as a bicentennial gift, sponsored a tour of *The Ik* throughout the United States.

Higgins's next two films, *Silver Streak* (1976) and *Foul Play* (1978), are marked by their similarity to earlier Hollywood movies. Both are derivative celebrations of the old-fashioned suspense thrillers that audiences have enjoyed for years. Films of form rather than content, they are slick, fast-paced adventure-comedies meant to thrill and entertain. Both were big box-office hits.

Originally entitled "Super Chief," *Silver Streak* is about a man (Gene Wilder) who falls in love with another passenger (Jill Clayburgh) on a cross-country trip and is innocently caught up in mystery and intrigue. A sudden murder, strange disappearances, and steely-eyed villains lurking inside Pullman cars combine to recreate past moments of

Goldie Hawn in Foul Play, *the film that marked Higgins's debut as a director*

Hollywood films. Although criticized for being too derivative of older films, particularly *North by Northwest*, *Silver Streak* was one of the surprise successes of its year.

Higgins made his directorial debut with his next film, *Foul Play*. Most critics have pointed out Higgins's tribute to Alfred Hitchcock in this picture, particularly in the romance between the heroine (Goldie Hawn) and the police detective (Chevy Chase) assigned to protect her. Murders abound, bodies seem to disappear, and the heroine is chased, chloroformed, and kidnapped before she can convince the police that someone is out to get her. The climactic scene in which the hero and heroine, trying to prevent the assassination of the Pope, chase through an opera house during a performance of *The Mikado* harkens back to Hitchcock's *The Man Who Knew Too Much*. There is even a humorous nod to *Psycho* with a spoof of its famous shower scene. Like *Silver Streak*, *Foul Play* received mixed reviews, but it was a financial success, so much so that it inspired a television series which ran briefly in 1980.

Higgins's next film, for which he rewrote a

screenplay by Patricia Resnick, *9 to 5* (1980), became his biggest commercial success. The film, about three secretaries (Jane Fonda, Lily Tomlin, Dolly Parton) who conspire to get rid of their domineering, sexist boss (Dabney Coleman), was written by Resnick as a black comedy; the humor was to come from the secretaries' unsuccessful attempts to murder their boss. Higgins was asked to lighten the tone, and he changed the story so that the secretaries only fantasize about killing the boss. When one of the fantasies is nearly realized by accident, the secretaries kidnap the boss and then blackmail him. *9 to 5* was transformed into a television series in 1981.

The Best Little Whorehouse in Texas (1982), which Higgins adapted from the Broadway musical with the play's authors, Larry L. King and Peter Masterson, was Higgins's first nonoriginal screenplay and his first written in collaboration. The film and play are based on a well-known brothel in Texas, the Chicken Ranch, which operated for decades with the consent of the populace, becoming a virtual institution in the state. It was finally shut down when a television personality alleged that the Chicken Ranch had ties with organized crime. The film centers mostly on the romance (which was not in the play) between the sheriff (Burt Reynolds) and madam Mona Strangely (Dolly Parton). The sheriff does his best to save the Chicken Ranch, but it is finally closed when the governor discovers that a majority of voters want such an action. After the ranch is abandoned, the sheriff marries Miss Mona. Like earlier Higgins films, *The Best Little Whorehouse in Texas* received mixed, mostly poor, reviews but

was a huge financial success.

With the possible exception of *Harold and Maude*, Colin Higgins's films are to a large extent about moviemaking, but they are more than remakes, serving commentary on the best techniques of American film. Higgins is one of a new generation of student filmmakers come of age—writers and directors who went to school to study the history of American cinema and filmmaking techniques. If his small body of work is a fair test, Colin Higgins learned his lessons well.

Sidney Howard

(26 June 1891-23 August 1939)

Joanne Yeck

See also the Howard entry in *DLB 7, Twentieth-Century American Dramatists*.

MOTION PICTURES: *Bulldog Drummond* (United Artists, 1929), screenplay by Howard and Wallace Smith;

Condemned (United Artists, 1929), screenplay;

Raffles (United Artists, 1930), screenplay; filmed again (United Artists, 1939), screenplay by Howard and John Van Druten;

One Heavenly Night (United Artists, 1930), screenplay;

A Lady to Love (M-G-M, 1930), screenplay adapted by Howard from his play *They Knew What They Wanted*;

Arrowsmith (United Artists, 1931), adaptation;

The Greeks Had a Word for Them (United Artists, 1932), adaptation;

Dodsworth (United Artists, 1936), screenplay;

Gone With The Wind (M-G-M, 1939), screenplay.

SELECTED PLAYS: *Swords* (New York, National Theatre, 1 September 1921);

S.S. Tenacity (Belmont Theatre, 2 January 1922);

Bewitched (New York, National Theatre, 1 October 1924), by Howard and Edward Sheldon;

They Knew What They Wanted (New York, Garrick Theater, 24 November 1924);

Lucky Sam McCarver (New York, Playhouse, 21 October 1925);

Ned McCobb's Daughter (New York, John Golden Theatre, 29 November 1926);

The Silver Cord (New York, John Golden Theatre, 20 December 1926);

Half Gods (New York, Plymouth Theatre, 21 December 1929);

The Late Christopher Bean (New York, Henry Miller's Theatre, 31 October 1932);

Alien Corn (New York, Belasco Theatre, 20 February 1933);

Dodsworth (New York, Shubert Theatre, 24 February 1934);

Yellow Jack (New York, Martin Beck Theatre, 6 March 1934);

Paths of Glory (New York, Plymouth Theatre, 26 September 1935);

The Ghost of Yankee Doodle (New York, Guild Theatre, 22 November 1937);

Lute Song (New York, Plymouth Theatre, 6 February 1946), by Howard and Will Irwin;

Madame, Will You Walk? (New York, Phoenix Theatre, 1 December 1953).

SELECTED BOOKS: *Swords* (New York: Doran, 1921);

Three Flights Up (New York: Scribners, 1924);

Casanova (New York: Brentano's, 1924);

Lexington (Lexington, Mass.: Lexington Historical Society, 1925);

They Knew What They Wanted (Garden City: Doubleday, Page, 1925);

Lucky Sam McCarver (New York: Scribners, 1926);

Sidney Howard (photo by Vandamm)

Howard was the son of John Lawrence Howard, a steamship company executive, and Helen Coe Howard, a pianist and organist. Ill with tuberculosis at nineteen, Howard spent a year at a Swiss sanatorium. This isolation and introspection resulted in his first serious writings of journals and letters. He was educated at the University of California, Berkeley, and then at Harvard, where he received an M.A. in literature. During World War I he was an ambulance driver and later a flyer, receiving the Silver Star.

Howard began his first professional writing as a journalist. He joined the editorial staff of *Life* after the war, becoming literary editor by 1922. Between 1920 and 1924 he wrote articles revealing his concern for social problems for *Collier's*, *New Republic*, and *Hearst's International*. The year 1921 saw the first professional production of a Howard play, *Swords*. Howard married a member of the cast, Clare Jenness Eames, on 1 June 1922. He won a Pulitzer Prize in 1925 for *They Knew What They Wanted*. The play was filmed three times and inspired the Broadway musical *The Most Happy Fella* in 1956. Several of Howard's other plays were filmed, although from screenplays usually by others.

When sound revolutionized the movies in 1927, it was natural for the producers to comb Broadway for new voices and writers. Howard's prestige as a playwright put him at the forefront of the talent exodus which brought Ben Hecht, Charles MacArthur, and later Maxwell Anderson, Lillian Hellman, and others to California. Samuel Goldwyn courted Howard with a promise to make him a millionaire. More enticing than riches was the challenge represented by the new film form. Howard observed that while the playwright "sees through many eyes," the scenarist writes for "a single lens." He was sensitive to the specific needs of the dialogue screenplay, and his ten produced screenplays advanced talking pictures both structurally and thematically.

Ned McCobb's Daughter (New York: Scribners, 1926);
The Silver Cord (New York: Scribners, 1927);
Olympia (New York: Brentano's, 1928);
Half Gods (New York & London: Scribners, 1930);
Alien Corn (New York & London: Scribners, 1933; London: Gollancz, 1933);
The Late Christopher Bean (New York: French, 1933);
Dodsworth: Play in Three Acts (New York: Dramatists Play Service, 1934);
Yellow Jack (New York: Harcourt, Brace, 1934);
Paths of Glory (New York & London: French, 1935);
The Ghost of Yankee Doodle (New York & London: Scribners, 1938);
One, Two, Three (New York: French, 1952);
Lute Song (Chicago: Dramatic Publishing, 1955);
Madame, Will You Walk? (New York: Dramatists Play Service, 1955);
"Gone With The Wind": The Screenplay, edited by Richard Harwell (New York: Collier, 1980).

Sidney Coe Howard was born in Oakland, California, but found his spiritual home on the East Coast. After he began screenwriting, Howard was torn between the unique qualities of the West Coast and his base in the East. However, his insistence on spending most of his time in the East only slightly hampered his career.

Howard did not believe, as did many literary types, that the screenplay was sacrosanct. He felt it should provide the director with "rhythms and ideas." Howard knew the screenplay would be passed from structure specialist to dialogue doctors and through a censor's scrutiny. He was concerned not about the integrity of his work but about the drama his rhythms and ideas could inspire.

When Howard went to work for Goldwyn, the chief star at the studio was Ronald Colman, and Goldwyn, eager to have Colman make a successful transition to sound films, assigned Howard to write his first three screenplays. Writing dialogue for the continuity by Wallace Smith, Howard first adapted the popular Bulldog Drummond stories by Sapper (H. C. McNeile), changing Drummond from a sadistic right-winger to a suave, witty, highly articulate gentleman adventurer. In the film *Bulldog Drummond* (1929), a bored Drummond places a newspaper ad seeking adventure and receives a response from a young woman trying to free her uncle from the clutches of a band of sinister extortionists who have imprisoned him in a fake hospital. With this film Howard was one of the first screenwriters to rediscover the powers of silence. A serious problem of the early sound film was talk—too much of it. Howard broke away from the stagey screenplay, writing the fast-paced action and witty dialogue that films were then lacking. *Bulldog Drummond* was a great financial success; Ronald Colman was nominated for an Academy Award, and 20th Century-Fox produced a sequel in 1934.

Howard's second film for Goldwyn and Colman was *Condemned* (1929), suggested by Blair Nile's book *Condemned to Devil's Island*. The book is largely documentary, and Howard's screenplay is mostly his own invention. This time Colman plays a debonair convict who falls in love with the wife of the penal colony's brutal governor. He escapes, is recaptured and made to serve out his term, but is reunited with his lover by the film's end. Critics praised Howard for the economy of his dialogue but faulted *Condemned* for being static in parts. Howard felt that the still crude state of sound equipment dulled the dialogue. The boothbound camera and immobile microphones contributed to the film's stagelike quality. He further observed that it was difficult to "spark up" a film without the interplay of dialogue and action.

Howard's next project, *Raffles*, was filmed twice, first in 1930 with Ronald Colman and again in 1939 with David Niven. Howard's skill gave both versions a verbal sophistication, whether lines were read smoothly by Colman or by Niven with his snappy sarcasm. An aristocrat who at night turns gentleman thief and safecracker, the character Raffles was created at the beginning of the century by Ernest William Hornung and became a popular figure on stage and in silent films. Howard's screenplay borrowed material from two plays, *Raffles, the Amateur Cracksman* (1903) by Hornung and Eugene Wiley Presbrey; and *A Visit from Raffles* (1909) by Hornung and Charles Samsam. In the film, audiences are kept sympathetic with Raffles, who wins them with his romantic bravado and

Ronald Colman and Lilyan Tashman in Bulldog Drummond

Ronald Colman, John Qualen, and Adele Watson in Arrowsmith

amuses them with his cleverness in outwitting the police. But though audiences were pleased with *Raffles*, the critics found it too talky and static.

Howard's fourth film for Goldwyn was a 1930 adaptation of Louis Bromfield's *One Heavenly Night*. Burdened with musical numbers, the film was not a success. His next film was one of two not produced by Goldwyn and was the first Howard adapted from one of his own plays. *A Lady to Love* (1930), based on *They Knew What They Wanted*, did not recreate the play's stage success. That year Howard divorced Clare Eames and in 1931 married Leopoldine Blaine Damrosch, daughter of conductor Walter Damrosch.

Howard's screenwriting career reached a new high in 1931 with his adaptation of Sinclair Lewis's Pulitzer Prize-winning novel *Arrowsmith*, the story of an idealistic doctor dedicated to medical research. Howard's screenplay necessarily condensed and oversimplified Lewis's novel and left out much of the satire against the medical establishment, but Howard also omitted some of Lewis's heavy-handedness and created a script that is more consistent in tone than the original. Ronald Colman played the lead, and his performance and Howard's script kept the role from being preachy. Sinclair

Lewis announced himself entirely satisfied with the production. As one of the decade's first "message pictures," *Arrowsmith* was a hit with the critics as well as the public. The *New York Times* named it one of the Ten Best of 1931, and it was nominated for four Academy awards, including best picture and best screenplay.

Howard's first screen comedy, an adaptation of Zoë Akins's play *The Greeks Had a Word for It*, did not at first meet with Hays Office approval. The film censors were particularly concerned with the title; Clara Bow had given the word "it" an unmistakable sexual connotation. The film was called *The Greeks Had a Word for Them* (1932), with *Them* referring to the play's three unscrupulous golddiggers. Despite the interference, Howard was successful at keeping the play's original sophistication, if not all of its racy repartee.

Pleased with the way Goldwyn had produced *Arrowsmith*, Sinclair Lewis offered him the film rights to *Dodsworth* for $20,000. When Goldwyn turned Lewis down, Howard bought the dramatic rights to the novel and turned it into a successful play. After its impressive run in New York in 1934, Goldwyn bought the rights to Howard's play for $165,000 and brought him back to Hollywood after a four-year absence to adapt the play to the screen.

The title character in *Dodsworth* is a middle-aged manufacturer who retires and travels to Europe, where he and his wife experience a testing of their Midwestern values. Howard's screenplay minimized Lewis's elaborate and sometimes didactic comparison of American and European values and concentrated on Dodsworth's marital situation. Goldwyn recreated the Broadway version as much as possible, even bringing the New York leads, Walter Huston and Ruth Chatterton, to star. The movie was an enormous critical and popular success. It received eight Academy Award nominations, including one for best screenplay.

Howard wrote three screenplays for Goldwyn that were never produced: "The Brothers Karamazov," "It Can't Happen Here," and "The Light that Failed." Howard and Goldwyn had seven successful years together, from 1929 to 1936. Goldwyn kept his word on making Howard wealthy, paying him as much as $15,000 for treatments and $25,000 for screenplays. Most of all, he was understanding about Howard's insistence on living in the East and allowed him to do a great deal of writing in New York.

In October of 1936, Howard signed with producer David O. Selznick to adapt Margaret Mitch-

ell's Pulitzer Prize-winning novel *Gone With The Wind*. The massive saga of the old South centers on Southern belle Scarlett O'Hara, her survival of the hardships of the Civil War and Reconstruction in Georgia, her prolonged infatuation for the aristocratic Ashley Wilkes, and her stormy marriage to Rhett Butler. Reducing the intricacies of *Gone With The Wind*'s epic dimensions was a herculean task. Despite his efforts, Howard's first submission was far too long; it would have required at least six hours to film. Howard cut what he could and turned the script over to Selznick. Selznick wanted Howard to remain on the set to make revisions as the film was shooting, but Howard refused to leave New England. As a result, revisions were handled by a host of local writers, including Ben Hecht, Charles MacArthur, F. Scott Fitzgerald, and John Van Druten. By the time of the film's release in 1939, there was some question as to who should receive screen credit. But despite the number of writers and changes, the final script was remarkably close to Howard's version. The fact that Howard's name alone appears on the credits may have been as much a gesture to his memory as to his writing, for in 1939 Sidney Howard died tragically at age forty-eight, crushed by a tractor on his farm in Tyringham, Massachusetts. His death came before the premiere of *Gone With The Wind* and that season's Academy Awards ceremony. Howard's only Oscar was awarded posthumously in the spring of 1940.

Howard once wrote, "The novelist prefers writing to anything; the dramatist prefers acting to anything. The drama does not spring from a literary impulse but from a love of the brave, ephemeral, beautiful art of acting. When such a love becomes the obsession of genius, the great plays are written and great dramatists appear, as Ibsen, Shakespeare and Chekhov appeared." Howard's modesty would have prevented him from admitting genius, but his obsessive love of drama added much to the success of the films he wrote and to the state of the art of filmmaking in the 1930s.

Clark Gable and Vivien Leigh in Gone With The Wind. *Howard died shortly before the premiere of this film, for which he won his only Academy Award.*

References:

Alvin H. Marill, *Samuel Goldwyn Presents* (New York: A. S. Barnes, 1976), pp. 21ff;

Sidney Howard White, *Sidney Coe Howard: Criticism and Interpretation* (Boston: Twayne, 1977).

Papers:

The Sidney Howard Collection is housed at the University of California, Berkeley.

John Huston
(5 August 1906-   )

James Goodwin
University of California, Los Angeles

MOTION PICTURES: *Jezebel* (Warner Bros., 1938), screenplay by Huston, Clements Ripley, and Abem Finkel;

The Amazing Dr. Clitterhouse (Warner Bros., 1938), screenplay by Huston and John Wexley;

Juarez (Warner Bros., 1939), screenplay by Huston, Wolfgang Reinhardt, and Aeneas Mackenzie;

Dr. Ehrlich's Magic Bullet (Warner Bros., 1940), screen story and screenplay by Huston, Heinz Herald, and Norman Burnside;

High Sierra (Warner Bros., 1941), screenplay by Huston and W. R. Burnett;

Sergeant York (Warner Bros., 1941), screen story and screenplay by Huston, Finkel, Harry Chandlee, and Howard Koch;

The Maltese Falcon (Warner Bros., 1941), screenplay;

Report from the Aleutians (U.S. Army documentary, 1943), script;

The Battle of San Pietro (U.S. Army documentary, 1945), script;

Let There Be Light (U.S. Army documentary, 1946), script by Huston and Charles Kaufman;

Three Strangers (Warner Bros., 1946), screen story and screenplay by Huston and Koch;

The Treasure of the Sierra Madre (Warner Bros., 1948), screenplay;

Key Largo (Warner Bros., 1948), screenplay by Huston and Richard Brooks;

We Were Strangers (Columbia, 1949), screenplay by Huston and Peter Viertel;

The Asphalt Jungle (M-G-M, 1950), screenplay by Huston and Ben Maddow;

The Red Badge of Courage (M-G-M, 1951), screenplay;

The African Queen (United Artists, 1951), screenplay by Huston and James Agee;

Moulin Rouge (United Artists, 1952), screenplay by Huston and Anthony Veiller;

Beat the Devil (United Artists, 1954), screenplay by Huston and Truman Capote;

Moby Dick (Warner Bros., 1956), screenplay by Huston and Ray Bradbury;

Heaven Knows, Mr. Allison (20th Century-Fox, 1957), screenplay by Huston and John Lee Mahin;

John Huston

The Night of the Iguana (M-G-M, 1964), screenplay by Huston and Veiller;

The Kremlin Letter (20th Century-Fox, 1970), screenplay by Huston and Gladys Hill;

The Man Who Would Be King (Associated Artists, 1975), screenplay by Huston and Hill.

PLAYS: *Frankie and Johnny* (New York, Republic Theatre, 25 September 1930);

In Time to Come (New York, Mansfield Theatre, 28 December 1941), by Huston and Howard Koch.

BOOKS: *Frankie and Johnny* (New York: Boni, 1930);

The Maltese Falcon [pictures and dialogue from the feature motion picture], edited by Richard Anobile (London: Macmillan, 1974);

The Asphalt Jungle: A Screenplay, by Huston and Ben Maddow (Carbondale & Edwardsville: Southern Illinois University Press, 1980);

An Open Book (New York: Knopf, 1980; London: Macmillan, 1981).

OTHER: *In Time to Come,* by Huston and Howard Koch, in *Best Plays of 1941-1942,* edited by Burns Mantle (New York: Dodd, Mead, 1942);

Juarez, by Huston, Wolfgang Reinhardt, and Aeneas Mackenzie, in *Twenty Best Film Plays,* edited by John Gassner and Dudley Nichols (New York: Crown, 1943);

The African Queen, by Huston and James Agee, in *Agee on Film,* volume 2 (New York: McDowell, Obolensky, 1960).

PERIODICAL PUBLICATIONS: "Fool," *American Mercury,* 16 (March 1929): 347-351;

"Figures of Fighting Men," *American Mercury,* 23 (May 1931): 113-115;

"The African Queen," *Theatre Arts* (February 1952): 42-49, 92;

"Home Is Where the Heart Is—and So Are Films," *Screen Producers Guild Journal* (March 1963): 3.

Best known as a film director and, in recent years, as a screen actor, John Huston has had a no less productive and distinctive career as a screenwriter. He was born to Rhea and Walter Huston in 1906 in a Missouri town named Nevada. At the time his father had given up ambitions as a stage actor to raise a family on his earnings as a civil engineer. But Walter Huston returned to vaudeville and the stage in 1909; he went on to become a highly successful actor on Broadway and in motion pictures. John Huston's parents divorced in 1913, and shortly thereafter his mother resumed her career in journalism, which she had abandoned in favor of marriage. Huston's boyhood and adolescence were spent in a series of boarding schools; his vacations brought him in contact alternately with the world of theater and that of the popular press. Huston ended his formal education at age fifteen, after two years of high school, in order to become a boxer. According to his own account, he was a smart but not overpowering fighter, winning twenty-three of twenty-five semiprofessional bouts. A broken nose prompted him to reconsider boxing as a career, and he left Los Angeles to join his father in New York.

With his father playing a lead role in Eugene O'Neill's *Desire Under the Elms,* Huston tried his acting talents in two off-Broadway productions and had some small roles in films. He saw no future for himself in the acting profession and became a cavalry officer in the Mexican army. For two years he served in Mexico as a member of the army's ceremonial horse guard. After returning to the United States and appearing in the guard's public performance at Madison Square Gardens, young Huston resigned his commission as a lieutenant.

While in Mexico, Huston wrote a play entitled *Frankie and Johnny,* based on the familiar ballads known by that title. The relatively easy sale of the manuscript convinced Huston that writing was a viable career. H. L. Mencken, then editor of *American Mercury,* bought two Huston stories, "Fool" and "Figures of Fighting Men," which appeared in 1929 and 1931. Later, Huston's stories and features would be published in *Esquire, Theater Arts,* and the *New York Times.* During his early years, Huston worked for a while on the *New York Graphic,* but his job as a city reporter then ended abruptly when he confused the names of victim and criminal in a murder story. In 1931 he left New York for California and the prospect of writing for the screen.

For the first six months of Huston's stay in Hollywood he was a contract writer for Goldwyn Studios. Having received not one assignment in that period, he quit to work for Universal Studios, where his father was by then a star. His first efforts in Universal's script department were writing dialogue for such 1932 films as *Murders in the Rue Morgue, A House Divided,* and *Law and Order* (the last two starred his father). *A House Divided* was directed by William Wyler, who gave Huston an inside view of the filmmaking process during its production.

Between 1932 and 1938 Huston traveled to Europe, settled for a while in New York City, then Chicago, and tried his luck and talent at play writing, painting, editing, and stage acting. During this time he was married twice, to Dorothy Harvey and to Leslie Black.

Huston returned to Hollywood for a writer's contract with Warner Bros., where he received his first credit as screenwriter in collaboration with Clements Ripley and Abem Finkel for *Jezebel* (1938), for which Bette Davis won the Academy Award as best actress. He collaborated on the scripts for *The Amazing Dr. Clitterhouse* (1938), *Juarez* (1939), *Dr. Ehrlich's Magic Bullet* (1940), *High Sierra* (1941), and *Sergeant York* (1941). Given the practices in Hollywood of the studio system of the 1930s and 1940s, it is difficult to identify Huston's specific contributions to these scripts.

Huston's opportunity to direct a film came in

Bette Davis and Henry Fonda in Jezebel, *the film for which Huston received his first screen credit*

1941, when Jack Warner approved for production Huston's treatment of Dashiell Hammett's 1930 novel *The Maltese Falcon*. Huston's treatment was intended to preserve and intensify much of the novel's plot, characterization, and hard-boiled manner of expression; a great deal of the dialogue was simply transposed from Hammett. In preparation for his first directing job, Huston sketched each shot and made notations on camera position, lighting, and compositional scale. While Huston did not always adhere to these drawings, the preparations indicate that he conceived of the adaptation process essentially in visual terms. He received an Academy Award nomination for his screenplay. Since *The Maltese Falcon*, Huston has directed all his own screenplays except *Three Strangers* (1946).

Huston and Howard Koch, who had collaborated on the script for *Sergeant York*, wrote a play about Woodrow Wilson's life titled *In Time to Come*, which ran on Broadway for forty performances beginning in December 1941. Koch is credited with the screenplay for Huston's next film, *In This Our Life* (1942), although it is generally acknowledged that Huston assisted Koch in adapting Ellen Glasgow's Pulitzer Prize-winning novel, a commentary on the decay of Southern aristocracy. Huston began directing *Across the Pacific* (1942), but the film was completed by Vincent Sherman after Huston was activated by the United States Army to serve as a filmmaker.

Huston's first six-month tour of duty was on the island of Adak, at the tip of the Aleutians in the north Pacific. An American air base was being constructed for bomber attacks against the Japanese, which began in full force toward the end of 1942. With a six-man camera crew, Huston documented this series of events, from construction of the landing strips to the actual missions, which Huston accompanied on fifteen occasions, often under heavy enemy fire. In July 1943 the War Department released *Report from the Aleutians*, which runs forty-seven minutes and is narrated by Walter Huston reading commentary prepared by John Huston.

The documentary Huston produced next for the U.S. Army, *The Battle of San Pietro* (1945), stirred controversy among the military. Assigned in the winter of 1943 to cover the American campaign in Italy, Huston and his crew joined an infantry regiment during the assault on San Pietro, a hillside village held by the Germans. Nightly, after each day's action in the field, Huston worked on the film's narration in order to account for the conflict's sudden turns. Huston submitted a final print running about fifty minutes to the Pentagon, but army authorities refused to permit its release, saying the film would demoralize new troops who viewed it before departing for overseas duty. General George C. Marshall interceded, and the film was circulated after being cut to thirty-two minutes.

Huston's last film as a commissioned officer in the armed services, *Let There Be Light* (1946), was shot at the Mason General Hospital on Long Island, New York, and depicts the treatment and rehabili-

tation of soldiers suffering neuropsychiatric disorders. The prologue, written by Huston and read by his father, states that nearly twenty percent of the war's casualties were of this nature. Using hidden cameras, the film details the often anguishing process of medical and psychological treatment. The footage also documents the remarkable recovery of many veterans. *Let There Be Light* was so controversial that it was banned by the War Department and not shown publicly until 1981.

In 1946 Jean Negulesco directed *Three Strangers* from a screenplay Huston had written before joining the army. Under studio direction, Howard Koch revised the script during production to stress the story's romantic angles. Conceived by Huston as a tale of intrigue and murder in the mold of *The Maltese Falcon*, the film brings together an unlikely trio—Crystal (Geraldine Fitzgerald), Arbutny (Sidney Greenstreet), and Johnny West (Peter Lorre)—whose only shared goal is wealth, which each is finally unwilling to share. In an ironic

Humphrey Bogart, Peter Lorre, Mary Astor, and Sidney Greenstreet in The Maltese Falcon–*Huston's first film as screenwriter and director*

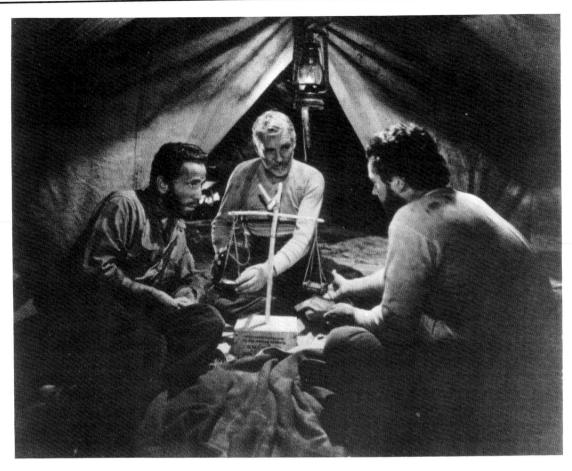

Humphrey Bogart, Walter Huston, and Tim Holt in The Treasure of the Sierra Madre. *Huston's screenplay for this film won an Academy Award, and his father, Walter Huston, received an Oscar for his portrayal of prospector Howard.*

conclusion typical of other Huston screen stories, Johnny holds a winning sweepstakes ticket but cannot claim the prize of £30,000 because to do so would implicate him in the death of Crystal, who was bludgeoned by Arbutny. During the same year, Huston worked uncredited on two other productions. According to Robert Siodmak, *The Killers* (1946) relied extensively on a scenario by Huston, which was subsequently reworked by Anthony Veiller. Orson Welles and Huston collaborated with Veiller (who received sole writing credit) on Welles's *The Stranger* (1946), the story of a Nazi criminal (Welles) who has settled in a New England town under an assumed name. Huston was married this year for the third time, to actress Evelyn Keyes.

Huston's next work as a writer-director, *The Treasure of the Sierra Madre* (1948), is one of the three or four films that established his reputation as a filmmaker. He had read B. Traven's novel soon after its American publication in 1935 but did not have an opportunity to adapt it until after the war.

The screenplay Huston prepared contains the character types, idiosyncrasies in dialogue, and central plot Traven presents, but it does not retain the novelist's overt concern with social issues and political factions. Three men—Dobbs (Humphrey Bogart), Howard (Walter Huston, who won an Oscar for the role), and Curtin (Tim Holt)—mine a gold claim in the Sierra Madre mountains. Once they have struck it rich, Dobbs becomes obsessed with the idea of guarding his share of the gold, while Howard warns that gold can disease a man's mind. Dobbs dies as a result of his own greed, and Howard and Curtin survive, only to see the gold dust blown away. High praise was given *The Treasure of the Sierra Madre* upon its release, and the praise has continued unabated. Huston won the Writers Guild Award and the Academy Award for best screenplay, the New York Film Critics Award, and the One World Award for best direction. The film was nominated for the Academy Award for best picture.

Key Largo (1948) was adapted by Huston in

collaboration with Richard Brooks from Maxwell Anderson's play, which Brooks and Huston changed considerably. The central character was changed from a Spanish Civil War volunteer with feelings of cowardice to a bitter World War II veteran (Humphrey Bogart) who travels to the Florida Keys to visit the father (Lionel Barrymore) and widow (Lauren Bacall) of a soldier killed while under his command. He finds them in the hotel they run, held captive by a gangster (Edward G. Robinson) and his men. With the drama confined mainly inside the hotel, the film is primarily an exercise in tension. The screenplay was nominated for a Writers Guild Award, and Claire Trevor won an Oscar for her performance as the gangster's alcoholic mistress.

In 1947 Huston formed a group with William Wyler and screenwriter Philip Dunne to protest the House Un-American Activities Committee investigations in Hollywood. He was married again in 1949 to Enrica Soma, who died in 1969. Their daughter, Anjelica, is an actress. Also in 1949, Huston wrote one of his least successful films, *We Were Strangers*, about a daring and ill-fated attempt to assassinate a Cuban dictator during the political unrest of the early 1930s.

In *The Asphalt Jungle* (1950), Huston again explores the drama of a conspiratorial quest for wealth. He collaborated with Ben Maddow on the script, which is based on a novel by W. R. Burnett. Like *We Were Strangers*, *The Asphalt Jungle* displays deep attention to the ingenuity of a daring plot and to the difficulties of carrying it out. The masterful criminal Doc (Sam Jaffe) has devised a jewel heist and enlists a driver (James Whitmore), a gunman (Sterling Hayden), and a safecracker (Anthony Caruso). The scenes detailing every step in the robbery have the attentiveness and thoroughness of a documentary—an approach which allows Huston to establish the professionalism of these criminals and, with intended irony, to make their scheme seem respectably enterprising. The gang ultimately acquires the jewels, but, as one would expect in a Huston film, all the members are either killed or captured before any use can be made of the riches. Huston and Maddow were nominated for the Writers Guild Award and the Academy Award for their screenplay.

Huston's experiences during World War II had caused him to become deeply interested in Stephen Crane's novel *The Red Badge of Courage*, and in 1951 he was able to film the novel. M-G-M drastically altered the film before its release, cutting the running time from eighty-eight to sixty-nine min-

utes, adding a narrator who reads sections from Crane's book, and deleting the death of "the tattered soldier," a scene Huston considered crucial. While the studio version was not faithful to Crane or Huston, it remains a powerful film.

For his next film, Huston acquired the rights to C. S. Forester's 1935 novel *The African Queen* and cowrote the adaptation with James Agee, who had long admired Huston's work. Both novel and film tell of an imagined incident in German East Africa shortly after World War I has started in Europe. Rose Sayer (Katharine Hepburn), a strong-willed English spinster who aids her brother at his religious mission, and Charlie Allnut (Humphrey Bogart, who won an Oscar), a gin-guzzling riverboat operator, find that with the change in political circumstances they are considered enemy aliens. Inclined to sit out the war, Charlie is cajoled into collaborating with Rose in her fantastic scheme to maneuver his dilapidated boat downstream, through natural dangers and past a German fortress to a lake patrolled by an enemy gunboat, which she intends to sink with a homemade torpedo. Consistent with patterns set in his earlier stories about improbable quests, Huston planned to have the couple die before their scheme could succeed. Upon the urging of the film's producer, Sam Spiegel, the ending was rewritten to allow them to survive. *The African Queen* (1951) is Huston's most successful film financially, and it remains one of his finest works. He and Agee both received Academy Award nominations for their screenplay.

For *Moulin Rouge* (1952) Huston worked with Anthony Veiller in adapting the 1950 Pierre La Mure novel on Toulouse-Lautrec's life, which proposes that artistic genius is the product of personal agony. The artist, played by José Ferrer, is depicted as a man morbidly obsessed with his own deformity and self-destructively devoted to a prostitute (Colette Marchand). Huston received another Writers Guild nomination for the screenplay.

Humphrey Bogart persuaded Huston to film a novel by James Helvick entitled *Beat the Devil*, feeling it offered an opportunity to recreate the success of *The Maltese Falcon*. Huston worked with Anthony Veiller and Peter Viertel on several early versions, but by the time he had arrived in Italy to begin production he had hired Truman Capote to collaborate on a new script. The two decided to parody the formulas of crime and adventure genres and conceived a story of two married couples and assorted criminals trying to claim land in Africa where uranium deposits are supposedly located. *Beat the Devil* (1954) succeeds as a parody of Hus-

Colette Marchand and José Ferrer in a scene from Moulin Rouge

ton's customary preoccupation with conspiratorial quests.

For his next film, Huston turned to another classic in American literature: Herman Melville's *Moby-Dick*. Ray Bradbury collaborated with Huston on the script, which concentrates on the novel's whaling action. The film places strong dramatic emphasis on the sermon about Jonah and God's will delivered before the *Pequod* sails; but once under-way the film's voyage remains more a sea venture than a spiritual quest. The screenplay necessarily deletes practically all of Melville's cetology, but along with it goes most of the symbolism.

Under contract with 20th Century-Fox, Huston was assigned to adapt a novel by Charles Shaw entitled *Heaven Knows, Mr. Allison*. Like *The African Queen*, the Huston-John Lee Mahin script, which Huston also directed, pairs a pious woman with an impious man. The scene is a South Pacific island in 1944; the pair are a novice nun (Deborah Kerr) and marine corporal Allison (Robert Mitchum). The two manage to fend off natural threats and a Japanese attack. The screenplay was nominated for a Writers Guild Award and an Academy Award.

Huston then went to work on a film version of Hemingway's *A Farewell to Arms* (1957). Huston re-worked a script by Ben Hecht to restore material from the novel and received Hemingway's personal approval for the film. But producer David Selznick was not pleased with the script, and Huston left the project. Hecht received sole screen credit.

Since 1957, Huston has worked primarily as a director and actor; only four films have been pro-duced from his screenplays. The films for which he is credited as director only include *The Barbarian and the Geisha* (1958), *The Roots of Heaven* (1959), *The Unforgiven* (1960), *The Misfits* (1961), *Freud* (1962), *The List of Adrian Messenger* (1963), *The Bible* (1966), *Reflections in a Golden Eye* (1967), *Sinful Davey* (1969), *A Walk with Love and Death* (1969), *Fat City* (1972),

The Life and Times of Judge Roy Bean (1972), *The Mackintosh Man* (1973), *Independence* (1976), *Wise Blood* (1979), *Phobia* (1980), *Victory* (1981), and *Annie* (1982). By this stage in Huston's career, directing a film meant authoring it; the *auteur* Huston is evident in the mise-en-scènes of these films.

In 1964 Huston wrote with Anthony Veiller an adaptation of Tennessee Williams's play *The Night of the Iguana*, about a defrocked minister given to womanizing and drink. The script altered the play, making the minister (Richard Burton) as much a figure of comedy as a tragic figure and updating the setting from the 1940s. A prologue was added, showing the minister before his congregation as he berates them for their prudery and provincialism and confesses his own excesses. This same year Huston was given the Laurel Award by the Writers Guild for the body of his work.

Huston began an acting career in 1963 with his performance in *The Cardinal*, for which he was nominated for an Oscar. He has continued to work as an actor, occasionally appearing in his own movies. In 1967 Huston was one of five directors who worked on the James Bond spoof *Casino Royale*, for which he worked without credit on the screenplay.

With his screenplay for *The Kremlin Letter* (1970), based on a best-selling novel by Noel Behn, Huston collaborated with Gladys Hill, a writer and story editor who had worked with him since the 1950s. The story presents a tale of international intrigue involving American spies on a dangerous mission to Moscow which proves to be a cover for a more sinister plot.

For over twenty years, Huston had wanted to film a Rudyard Kipling story, and with *The Man Who Would Be King* (1975) he fulfilled that wish. Working again with Gladys Hill, Huston adapted the Kipling short story, which tells the fantastic adventures of two rogues (Sean Connery, Michael Caine) who travel to an unmapped region beyond Britain's empire in the East in search of legendary riches.

Since *The Man Who Would Be King*, Huston has worked only as a director and actor. In 1982 he received the American Film Institute's Life Achievement Award.

Some critics are negative in their assessments of John Huston's film career, but few would deny that *The Maltese Falcon*, *The Treasure of the Sierra Madre*, and *The African Queen* are, on the basis of script and direction, enduring achievements in American cinema. By comparison, the adventures in later films like *The Kremlin Letter* are ultimately chaotic. But in virtually all of Huston's film work as writer-director, a heroic quest—even if it involves questionable motives or destructive alliances—is preferable to the spiritless, amoral routines of life.

References:

Gideon Bachman, "How I Make Films" [interview with Huston], *Film Quarterly* (Fall 1965): 3-13;

Robert Hughes, ed., *Film Book 2: Films of Peace and War* (New York: Grove, 1962);

Stuart Kaminsky, *John Huston: Maker of Magic* (Boston: Houghton Mifflin, 1978);

Axel Madsen, *John Huston* (Garden City: Doubleday, 1978);

William Nolan, *John Huston: King Rebel* (Los Angeles: Sherbourne, 1965);

Gerald Pratley, *The Cinema of John Huston* (New York: Barnes, 1977);

Lillian Ross, *Picture* (New York: Rinehart, 1952).

Nunnally Johnson

(5 December 1897-25 March 1977)

Thomas Bohn
University of Tulsa

SELECTED MOTION PICTURES: *A Bedtime Story* (Paramount, 1933), screenplay by Johnson and Waldemar Young; adaptation by Johnson, Young, and Benjamin Glazer;

Mama Loves Papa (Paramount, 1933), screenplay by Johnson and Arthur Kober;

Moulin Rouge (20th Century/United Artists, 1934), screenplay by Johnson and Henry Lehrman;

The House of Rothschild (20th Century/United Artists, 1934), screenplay;

Bulldog Drummond Strikes Back (20th Century/United Artists, 1934), screenplay;

Kid Millions (United Artists, 1934), screenplay by Johnson, Arthur Sheekman, and Nat Perrin;

Baby Face Harrington (M-G-M, 1935), adaptation;

Thanks a Million (20th Century-Fox, 1935), screenplay;

The Man Who Broke the Bank at Monte Carlo (20th Century-Fox, 1935), screenplay by Johnson and Howard Ellis Smith;

The Prisoner of Shark Island (20th Century-Fox, 1936), screenplay;

Banjo on My Knee (20th Century-Fox, 1936), screenplay;

Jesse James (20th Century-Fox, 1939), screenplay;

Wife, Husband and Friend (20th Century-Fox, 1939), screenplay; filmed again as *Everybody Does It* (20th Century-Fox, 1949);

Rose of Washington Square (20th Century-Fox, 1939), screenplay;

The Grapes of Wrath (20th Century-Fox, 1940), screenplay;

Chad Hanna (20th Century-Fox, 1940), screenplay;

Tobacco Road (20th Century-Fox, 1941), screenplay;

Roxie Hart (20th Century-Fox, 1942), screenplay;

The Pied Piper (20th Century-Fox, 1942), screenplay;

Life Begins at Eight-Thirty (20th Century-Fox, 1942), screenplay;

The Moon Is Down (20th Century-Fox, 1943), screenplay;

Holy Matrimony (20th Century-Fox, 1943), screenplay;

Casanova Brown (RKO-Radio, 1944), screenplay;

Woman in the Window (RKO-Radio, 1944), screenplay;

The Keys of the Kingdom (20th Century-Fox, 1945), screenplay by Johnson and Joseph L. Mankiewicz;

Along Came Jones (RKO-Radio, 1945), screenplay;

The Dark Mirror (Universal-International, 1946), screenplay;

Mr. Peabody and the Mermaid (Universal-International, 1948), screenplay;

Three Came Home (20th Century-Fox, 1950), screenplay;

The Mudlark (20th Century-Fox, 1950), screenplay;

The Long Dark Hall (Eagle Lion-United Artists, 1951), screenplay;

The Desert Fox (20th Century-Fox, 1951), screenplay;

Phone Call From a Stranger (20th Century-Fox, 1952), screenplay;

We're Not Married (20th Century-Fox, 1952), screenplay;

My Cousin Rachel (20th Century-Fox, 1952), screenplay;

How to Marry a Millionaire (20th Century-Fox, 1953), screenplay;

Night People (20th Century-Fox, 1954), screenplay;

Black Widow (20th Century-Fox, 1954), screenplay;

How To Be Very, Very Popular (20th Century-Fox, 1955), screenplay;

The Man in the Gray Flannel Suit (20th Century-Fox, 1956), screenplay;

The Three Faces of Eve (20th Century-Fox, 1957), screenplay;

The Man Who Understood Women (20th Century-Fox, 1959), screenplay;

The Angel Wore Red (M-G-M, 1960), screenplay;

Flaming Star (20th Century-Fox, 1960), screenplay by Johnson and Clair Huffaker;

Mr. Hobbs Takes a Vacation (20th Century-Fox, 1962), screenplay;

Take Her, She's Mine (20th Century-Fox, 1963), screenplay;

The World of Henry Orient (United Artists, 1964), screenplay by Johnson and Nora Johnson;

Nunnally Johnson

The Dirty Dozen (M-G-M, 1967), screenplay by Johnson and Lukas Heller.

PLAYS: *The World's Full of Girls* (New York, Royal Theatre, 6 December 1943);
Park Avenue (New York, Shubert Theater, 4 November 1946), book by Johnson and George S. Kaufman;
Henry Sweet Henry (New York, Palace Theatre, 23 October 1967), book.

BOOK: *There Ought to Be a Law* (Garden City: Doubleday, Doran, 1931).

OTHER: *The Grapes of Wrath*, in *Twenty Best Film Plays*, edited by John Gassner and Dudley Nichols (New York: Crown, 1943).

Once described as the world's highest-paid writer and one of its greatest humorists, Nunnally Johnson was the perfect example of a talented Hollywood contract writer able to put his pen to almost any subject. In addition, he was an astute studio executive who produced many of his screenplays, and toward the end of his active career he turned his talents to directing. Primarily remembered for his screenplay for *The Grapes of Wrath* (1940), Johnson authored some fifty screenplays over a thirty-year career that began with early sound films and ended in the 1960s. As a result of his acclaimed work on *The Grapes of Wrath*, Johnson gained a certain critical respect that he was unable to sustain with later efforts. However, his great commercial success as a writer, producer, and occasional director was due primarily to his working on a variety of films, most of which were geared toward popular acceptance, rather than to his development of a consistent filmic profile or theme. He had the ability to work in a wide variety of styles and genres with many directors, using material from many sources. His role as producer in the majority of his films obviously played a large part in what he chose to write about. Johnson the producer preferred to hire Johnson the writer. As he told one interviewer in the early 1940s: "The nice thing about it is that since I'm hired as a producer, I can go out on a lot where a director is kicking my script around and say, 'Listen, what we want you to do is make this picture the way it's written here on the paper.' "

Born in Columbus, Georgia, to Pearl Patrick and James Nunnally Johnson, in 1915 Johnson began his professional writing career as a newspaper reporter for the *Columbus Enquirer-Sun*. He served in the U.S. Army from 1916 to 1918 and after his discharge resumed his newspaper career, this time in Savannah, Georgia. He moved to larger papers and during the 1920s enjoyed great success on such newspapers as the *Brooklyn Daily Eagle* and *New York Herald Tribune*. He was also a columnist for the *Eagle* and the *New York Evening Post*. In addition, he wrote numerous articles and fiction for many magazines, including the *Saturday Evening Post*. In 1931 his volume of short stories, *There Ought to Be a Law*, was published.

Johnson came to Hollywood in 1932 with a host of writers, singers, actors, and actresses as the movie studios, in the wake of the sound revolution, imported anyone qualified who had any experience with the spoken word. Talking pictures had taken the studios by surprise, and they quickly discovered that they did not have under contract the right type of writers, directors, and screen personalities. Johnson had already established a reputation as journalist and writer of short stories, and he was brought to Hollywood, ultimately to team up with Darryl F. Zanuck at 20th Century-Fox.

One of Johnson's first films, *Bulldog Drummond Strikes Back* (1934), was his own favorite among his screenplays. A sequel to the immensely popular *Bulldog Drummond* (1929), which was Ronald Colman's first talking film, *Bulldog Drummond Strikes Back* was the first of three films that Colman made at 20th Century-Fox after breaking his contract with Goldwyn. The studio was eager to do a superior job, and Johnson's witty blend of comedy and suspense is an improvement over the original film. The next year he wrote another light comedy for Colman entitled *The Man Who Broke the Bank at Monte Carlo*.

Also written in 1934 was *The House of Rothschild*, a historical drama starring the grand old man of the genre, George Arliss. Johnson was used primarily as a dialogue writer to add a modern style and faster pace to the somewhat stolid and ponderous film. Apparently he succeeded, because the film achieved popular box-office success and received favorable reviews. In 1935 Johnson worked on *Cardinal Richelieu*, another historical drama starring Arliss, but requested that his name be removed from the credits when Arliss made changes in the script.

Historical dramas soon ran through their cycle of popularity, and Johnson was quickly assigned to the newest popular film genre, the musical comedy. He wrote the screenplays for four musicals, including *Kid Millions* (1934) starring Eddie Cantor, *Thanks a Million* (1935) with Dick Powell and Fred Allen, and *Banjo on My Knee* (1936) with Barbara Stanwyck. Here his primary function was to write the humorous dialogue that served as the bridges between songs, although he was credited with writing the complete screenplays for all the films. His dialogue for Cantor was somewhat lost amidst the seemingly endless songs and vaudeville routines in *Kid Millions*, but with *Thanks a Million* Johnson received special praise for his writing for Fred Allen, who was making his screen debut.

Up to this point in his career there is little suggestion of Johnson's later work with powerful social dramas. However, in 1936 he wrote the first of only two original screenplays, *The Prisoner of Shark Island* (1936), a historical drama based on the life of Dr. Samuel Mudd, the physician who innocently set John Wilkes Booth's broken leg and eventually became a national scapegoat. Directed by John Ford, the film had a strong feel for the historical period and the emotions surrounding Lincoln's assassination. Although criticized by some for overplaying certain dramatic episodes—such as the yellow fever epidemic in which Mudd heroically works to save the people on Shark Island, ultimately winning a presidential pardon—Johnson's script was given praise for its clarity and forcefulness. His only other original screenplay was *Jesse James* (1939). Johnson worked directly from material supplied by relatives of James and was able to reach a balance between romantic respectability and realism. Jesse James (Tyrone Power) is driven into crime by the land-grabbing schemes of the railroad. At first he is another Robin Hood, but his life as an outlaw brutalizes him until his brother Frank (Henry Fonda) denounces him as having turned vicious. At the end, Jesse James is redeemed by his wife and son but too late to escape his fate. Johnson was the associate producer on this film and was quickly establishing himself as a powerful force at 20th Century-Fox. Some indication of his rise is evident in his rapidly escalating salary, from $300 a week to $2,000 a week by 1938.

Following his success with *Jesse James*, in 1939 Johnson wrote screenplays for *Wife, Husband and Friend*, from James M. Cain's novel *Career in C Major*, and *Rose of Washington Square*. He was then assigned to work on *The Grapes of Wrath* (1940). Johnson was chosen to write the screenplay because among the many writers in Zanuck's studio, he had one of the most successful track records, had worked with the film's director, John Ford, on a film with strong realistic overtones (*The Prisoner of Shark Island*), and was a trusted member of Zanuck's inner family circle. Johnson began work on the screenplay in an atmosphere of secrecy, as Zanuck attempted to walk the line between people who said he would never make the movie for fear of offending vested political interests and the people he was actually afraid of offending, local and state officials in Oklahoma and California. As a result of the potentially explosive effect of the film, Johnson made several changes in the screenplay that drastically altered the original tone and theme of John Steinbeck's novel. Specifically, Johnson greatly reduced Steinbeck's treatment of political manipulation and instead focused primarily on the themes of love of the land, the family, and the nobility of the human spirit. In this way, Johnson was clearly appealing to the movie audience's tastes. This is nowhere more dramatically illustrated than in the ending of the movie, where Johnson uses a speech that occurs about two-thirds of the way through the book, with Ma Joad saying, "We'll go on forever, Pa. We're the people." Thus the film ends on a note of affirmation, while the novel ends less hopefully. Beyond these major thematic changes, Johnson deleted, added, and reorganized some of the novel's elements simply because of the requirements of

The Joad family in The Grapes of Wrath. *In front, left to right: Charley Grapewin, Dorris Bowdon, Jane Darwell, Russell Simpson, Darryl Hickman, Shirley Mills, Frank Darien, Eddie Quillan, and John Carradine. In back: Henry Fonda, Frank Sully, and O. Z. Whitehead.*

motion-picture time and plot. Critical and popular reaction to Johnson's work and to the film as a whole was overwhelmingly favorable. Johnson was nominated for an Academy Award, and the film was nominated for Oscars for best picture and best actor (Henry Fonda). John Ford won the Academy Award for Best Director, and Jane Darwell was voted best supporting actress for her performance as Ma Joad.

Teaming up once more, and for the last time, with John Ford, Johnson followed *The Grapes of Wrath* with a highly sterilized and undistinguished screenplay for *Tobacco Road* (1941). Johnson's process of alteration and change, so successful in *The Grapes of Wrath*, met with faint praise. Perhaps taking his cue from this less than successful effort, Johnson abandoned serious social drama and wrote as well as produced *Roxie Hart*, *The Pied Piper*, and *Life Begins at Eight-Thirty*, all in 1942. It was with

these films that Nunnally Johnson the producer and studio executive took over from Nunnally Johnson the writer. Although he continued to write screenplays for almost all the films he produced, it was perhaps more from a desire to control his films as much as possible than from any dedication to the art of screenwriting.

One of his most notable films of the war years was his version of Steinbeck's *The Moon Is Down* (1943). Johnson toned down the controversy involving charges that Steinbeck's novel was defeatist and too sympathetic to the Germans and gave definition to the theme that the will of a free and noble people cannot be suppressed by violence. Johnson muted much of the emotional impact of the novel, replacing it with a cool, almost dispassionate indictment of the German New Order. Johnson was at his best here as he once again used Steinbeck's dialogue and violent physical action to paint a vivid picture of Nazi brutality.

Alternating between comedy and drama, Johnson next wrote and produced *Holy Matrimony* (1943), in which a harassed artist assumes the identity of his late butler to avoid publicity. The film brought Johnson his second Academy Award nomination. This was followed in 1945 by *The Keys of the Kingdom*, from A. J. Cronin's novel about a Catholic missionary (Gregory Peck) in China. It was at this time that Johnson decided to leave 20th Century-Fox and become an independent producer. His first effort was a mild farce, *Casanova Brown* (1944), about a husband (Gary Cooper) who is separated from his wife and kidnaps their baby. An improvement was *Along Came Jones* (1945), a satiric Western that Johnson wrote for Cooper, in which a mild-mannered cowboy is mistaken for a murderous outlaw.

Throughout the decade of the 1940s Johnson persistently developed this pattern of alternating mild comedies and satires with relatively strong and usually effective dramas. In 1944, for instance, he teamed with director Fritz Lang to produce a taut suspense story, *Woman in the Window*, in which a professor (Edward G. Robinson) kills an assailant in self-defense and then attempts to cover up his crime. Two years later, he wrote and produced *The Dark Mirror* (1946), about a murder that is committed by one of identical twin sisters (Olivia de Havilland) and solved when a psychologist (Lew Ayres) notes the mental differences in the two women.

Johnson returned to Zanuck and 20th Century-Fox in 1948 and continued his pattern of selecting stories that were commercial successes with *Everybody Does It* (1949), a remake of his earlier hit *Wife, Husband and Friend*. This was followed by *Three Came Home* (1950), a realistic account of the true story of a woman's imprisonment by the Japanese in World War II; *The Mudlark* (1950), from Theodore Bennett's sentimental story of a London street urchin who falls in love with a picture of Queen Victoria (Irene Dunne); and *The Long Dark Hall* (1951), which explored the problems of a married man who plays around with a chorus girl and is accused of her murder. In *The Long Dark Hall* Johnson developed a strong courtroom atmosphere that was both suspenseful and realistic.

Perhaps Johnson's best work of the early 1950s was *Phone Call From a Stranger* (1952), for which he received the prize for best screenplay at the Venice Film Festival. The story revolves around David Trask (Gary Merrill) who, while running away from his family, meets three strangers on a plane. They are killed in a crash, but Trask survives, and to redeem himself and bring meaning back into his life he first phones, then visits the families of the three dead travelers. Although perhaps a little too commercially slick in places, the film is an excellent example of Johnson's ability to interweave several lines of action smoothly and efficiently.

In 1952 Johnson wrote one of his more successful comedies, *We're Not Married*. The movie consists of several episodes, as several couples discover that their marriages are technically invalid. This was followed by another well-received comedy, *How to Marry a Millionaire* (1953), in which three single women (Lauren Bacall, Betty Grable, and Marilyn Monroe) work together to snare wealthy husbands. Johnson drew his screenplay from two stage plays, *The Greeks Had a Word for It* by Zoë Akins (filmed in 1932 as *The Greeks Had a Word for Them*) and *Loco* by Dale Eunson and Katherine Albert. Johnson was nominated by the Writers Guild for his screenplay; the film inspired a television series in the late 1950s.

By 1954 the studio system was in a state of mild chaos due to competition from television, blacklisting, and the Supreme Court ruling that the studios could no longer control all three activities of production, distribution, and exhibition. The studios were forced to sell their vast theater holdings, thus

Marilyn Monroe, Lauren Bacall, and Betty Grable in
How to Marry a Millionaire

Joanne Woodward won an Academy Award for her performance in The Three Faces of Eve.

creating an open market for film exhibition. Johnson capitalized on the situation and his significant power as writer and producer to direct his first film, *Night People*, in 1954. His directorial debut met with critical and commercial success as he utilized Cold War espionage in Berlin to create a first-rate commercial melodrama.

Johnson continued his triple role as producer, writer, and director throughout the remainder of the 1950s, making six films with varying degrees of success. His most popular and creative films were *The Man in the Gray Flannel Suit* (1956), the story of an executive and the problems that surround his attempts to be successful; *The Three Faces of Eve* (1957), the story of a young woman's (Joanne Woodward, who won an Oscar) battle with acute schizophrenia; and *The Man Who Understood Women* (1959), in which a fading Hollywood director (Henry Fonda) marries a young woman (Leslie

Caron) and then drives her into the arms of another man. All three films dealt with complex patterns of emotional pressures, crises, and events that make up the fabric of modern life. Johnson presented his characters and their problems in clean, forceful, almost documentary style and was able to effectively translate complex issues and themes into memorable screen images. In 1959 Johnson was honored by the Screenwriters Branch of the Writers Guild of America-West, given its annual Laurel Award for writing that "had contributed most to the literature of the screen."

The films from the 1950s represented the last of what can be called vintage Johnson efforts. In 1960 he wrote and directed *The Angel Wore Red*, a story about the Spanish Civil War that centers around the love affair between a prostitute in Loyalist Spain (Ava Gardner) and a priest (Dirk Bogarde). This was followed by *Flaming Star* (1960), an unpretentious Western that served as a vehicle for Elvis Presley. Johnson next wrote two family comedies, *Mr. Hobbs Takes a Vacation* (1962) and *Take Her, She's Mine* (1963); in both James Stewart plays a slightly harassed and befuddled father trying to understand the problems of the younger generation. *Mr. Hobbs Takes a Vacation* was nominated for a Writers Guild award, as was Johnson's 1964 film, *The World of Henry Orient*, about two teenage girls who admire an eccentric pianist (Peter Sellers). On this movie he shared screenplay credit with his daughter Nora Johnson, who also wrote the novel on which the film was based.

Johnson was clearly approaching the end of his long career. He was sixty-seven years old in 1964 and had become part of a passing era in film. The studio system had all but crumbled, foreign films were making definite inroads on the domestic market, and Johnson's slick type of domestic comedy and drama was out of touch with the new waves breaking on American screens. In 1967 he coauthored with Lukas Heller his final film, *The Dirty Dozen*, the story of a dozen military prisoners freed from prison and secretly trained for a commando raid behind German lines prior to D-Day. Johnson spent the last ten years of his life in retirement, occasionally taking on writing projects but never again assuming an active production role. He died on 25 March 1977, survived by his wife, Dorris Bowdon Johnson, and five children, two of whom were from an earlier marriage.

Nunnally Johnson's strengths as a screenwriter were his abilities to streamline, clarify, and engineer a story to fit the time and structure requirements of the motion-picture medium. He also had a finely tuned sense of audience expectations and matched those expectations with films consciously designed to appeal to a broad spectrum of thoughts and emotions. Johnson's strongest stylistic characteristic was his ear for dialogue and speech that was clean, honest, and true to his characters and situations. Johnson was a consummate craftsman who created over a thirty-five-year career pleasant, occasionally absorbing, and, in several masterful moments, classic films that entertained in the best and broadest sense of the word.

Letters:

The Letters of Nunnally Johnson, selected and edited by Dorris Johnson and Ellen Leventhal (New York: Knopf, 1981).

Reference:

Tom Stempel, *Screenwriter: The Life and Times of Nunnally Johnson* (San Diego & New York: A. S. Barnes, 1980).

Howard Koch

(12 December 1902-   )

William Hughes
Essex Community College

SELECTED MOTION PICTURES: *The Sea Hawk* (Warner Bros., 1940), screen story and screenplay by Koch and Seton I. Miller;

The Letter (Warner Bros., 1940), screenplay;

Shining Victory (Warner Bros., 1941), screenplay by Koch and Anne Froelich;

Sergeant York (Warner Bros., 1941), screen story and screenplay by Koch, Abem Finkel, Harry Chandlee, and John Huston;

In This Our Life (Warner Bros., 1942), screenplay;

Casablanca (Warner Bros., 1943), screenplay by Koch and Julius and Philip Epstein;

Mission to Moscow (Warner Bros., 1943), screenplay;

In Our Time (Warner Bros., 1944), screen story and screenplay by Koch and Ellis St. Joseph;

Rhapsody in Blue: The Story of George Gershwin (Warner Bros., 1945), screenplay by Koch and Elliot Paul;

Three Strangers (Warner Bros., 1946), screen story and screenplay by Koch and Huston;

Letter from an Unknown Woman (Universal, 1948), screenplay;

No Sad Songs for Me (Columbia, 1950), screenplay;

The 13th Letter (20th Century-Fox, 1951), screenplay;

The Intimate Stranger (Great Britain) / *Finger of Guilt* (United States), (Angla-Amalgamated/RKO-Radio, 1956), screenplay, as Peter Howard;

Howard Koch

Loss of Innocence (Columbia, 1961), screenplay;

The War Lover (Columbia, 1962), screenplay;

633 Squadron (United Artists, 1964), screenplay by Koch and James Clavell;

The Fox (Claridge Pictures, 1968), screenplay by Koch and Lewis John Carlino.

SELECTED PLAYS: *Great Scott!* (New York, 49th St. Theatre, 2 September 1929);

Give Us This Day (New York, Booth Theatre, 27 October 1933);

The Lonely Man (Chicago, Blackstone Theatre, 1935);

In Time to Come (New York, Mansfield Theatre, 28 December 1941), by Koch and John Huston;

Dead Letter (New York, 1971).

RADIO: "Invasion from Mars," *Mercury Theatre On the Air* (CBS, 30 October 1938), script.

BOOKS: *The Panic Broadcast* (Boston: Little, Brown, 1970);

As Time Goes By: Memoirs of a Writer (New York: Harcourt Brace Jovanovich, 1979);

Mission to Moscow, edited with an introduction by David Culbert (Madison: University of Wisconsin Press, 1980).

OTHER: *In Time to Come*, by Koch and John Huston, in *Best Plays of 1941-1942*, edited by Burns Mantle (New York: Dodd, Mead, 1942);

"Introduction" and "The Chairman's Report," in *Thought Control in the U.S.A. The Collected Pro-*

ceedings of the Conference on the Subject of Thought Control in the U.S., called by the Hollywood Arts, Sciences & Professions Council, PCA, July 9-13, 1947, edited by Harold J. Salemson (Hollywood: Hollywood A.S.P. Council, Progressive Citizens of America, Southern California Chapter, 1947);

Casablanca: Script and Legend, compiled by Koch (Woodstock, N.Y.: Overlook Press, 1973)—includes the screenplay for *Casablanca* by Koch and Julius and Philip Epstein.

Howard Koch is best known for his work on *Casablanca* (1943), which earned him and his collaborators, Julius and Philip Epstein, an Academy Award in 1944. That film bears the imprint of his style: skillful narrative construction and intelligent dialogue written from a liberal point of view. And though Koch brought these qualities to other films, *Casablanca* remains the high point of a career generally limited to respectable adaptations of minor works by prominent authors and topical melodramas in the characteristic Warner Bros. manner—efficiently produced, fast-paced, hard-hitting stories full of incident. Blacklisted during the 1950s for his leftist politics, Koch has written only sporadically since 1961.

Koch was born in New York City but grew up in Kingston, New York, where his father, Frederick Koch, worked for the New York Board of Water Supply. Of French-German ancestry, the Kochs were outsiders in this provincial Hudson River Valley community dominated by old-line Dutch families. Koch recalls, "we hung precariously to our bourgeois status by the grace of my father's white collar." At age sixteen Koch became the youngest student ever to attend St. Stephen's College (now Bard College) at Avondale-on-the-Hudson and graduated with his B.A. in 1922. He went on to Columbia Law School, earning his LL.B. in 1925. Dissatisfied with his life as a small-town lawyer in Hartsdale, New York, and inspired by the plays he saw on Broadway, Koch decided to become a dramatist. He spent idle hours at his law office analyzing a copy of *The Butter and Egg Man* by George S. Kaufman, who was then considered one of Broadway's finest craftsmen. Before long Koch was drafting his own scenes. He made his way from Hartsdale to Hollywood by way of an uneven apprenticeship in the theater and a meteoric stint in radio.

Koch's early plays reflected the influence of such contemporary playwrights as Eugene O'Neill, Sidney Howard, and Robert E. Sherwood. He wanted to write well-constructed, satirical plays about current social issues. A campus radical of the 1920s, he intended to expose "the lies and hypocrisies that had been fed me . . . seeking out the most uncomfortable truths and wearing them like a hair shirt." From these beginnings Koch went on to enlist in many liberal causes, both political and cultural, from the New Deal and the Federal Theatre in the 1930s to the Hollywood Writers Mobilization and the Arts, Sciences, and Professions Council of the Progressive Citizens of America in the 1940s. Koch saw drama as a weapon against social injustice; his early works display talent without craft, passion without understanding. His first play, "He Went to College" (produced on Broadway in 1929 as *Great Scott!*), was about a student, much like himself, who attempts to impose his newly acquired radical ideas on family, friends, and fellow workers. *Give Us This Day* (1933) exposed the corrosive effects of inherited wealth.

The Lonely Man (1935) marked the end of Koch's apprenticeship as a playwright; this time he placed his theme in broader political and social context, and his craft and understanding were equal to his ambitions. In *The Lonely Man*, Koch has Abraham Lincoln return to Depression-era America to confront slavery in its contemporary forms, such as racial discrimination and exploitation of industrial workers. Staged in Chicago by the WPA's Federal Theatre Project, one of many repertory companies committed to social theater during the 1930s, *The Lonely Man* ran for a full season. It was a turning point in the playwright's career, for it eventually led him to Orson Welles's radio program, and Koch's association with the play's star, John Huston, later smoothed the way to Hollywood.

In the summer of 1938 John Houseman, who had read and liked *The Lonely Man*, hired Koch to script a new radio series, *Mercury Theatre on the Air*. The job gave the dramatist a regular salary and the opportunity to work with Orson Welles, who had only recently established himself as the newest genius of the American theater. For his Halloween program Welles asked Koch to update H. G. Wells's *The War of the Worlds* in the form of news bulletins and first-person narratives. Koch's script, "Invasion from Mars," became the basis for perhaps the most famous broadcast in radio history, for this realistic treatment of a Martian invasion set off a minor, though well-publicized, panic. In the aftermath of the controversial episode, Welles gained commercial sponsorship for his program, and Koch got a raise and an offer from Hollywood.

Warner Bros. hired Koch in 1939 on the strength of his radio work and some urging by John

Huston. Eager to show what he could do in motion pictures, Koch agreed to help revise the script for *Virginia City* (1940), but to the surprise of studio executives, their new writer declined a credit for his work because he did not believe his slight contribution merited recognition. He further shocked his supervisors by rejecting an assignment to script *The Sea Hawk* (1940). These were bold decisions for a young writer with no screen credits, but Koch had his reasons, which he later explained in *As Time Goes By: Memoirs of a Writer* (1979): "From the start I had made a practice of turning down assignments whose subject matter was alien or of no interest to me. Since the accumulation of credits is the screenwriter's stock-in-trade, this involved a certain risk, including at times the displeasure of the front office, since contract writers were expected to accept whatever was assigned to them. In the long run it worked to my advantage. I escaped the trap of being typed for one or another kind of movie whose repetition invited formula treatment." Koch did not entirely avoid being typed, but more than most contract writers he attempted to turn his scripts into personal statements. That is why the themes, if not the subjects, of his early screenplays were so often consistent with his work for the theater.

The Sea Hawk is a case in point. Although Koch initially rejected the assignment, he eventually agreed to develop a script (with Seton I. Miller), but only after the studio accepted his contention that the film should not be just another formula swashbuckler. *The Sea Hawk* takes its title from the novel by Rafael Sabatini about an Elizabethan sea captain who becomes a Barbary corsair; the novel had been filmed once before in 1924. For the remake, Koch and Miller retained only the title and the historical period, creating an entirely new story about Geoffrey Thorpe (Errol Flynn), an English privateer whose career resembles that of Sir Francis Drake. Characteristically, Koch infused the film with topical concerns, even attempting to insert a patriotic speech that used the film's historical conflict—the threat of an invasion by the Spanish Armada—to stir support for an England threatened by Nazi Germany.

Koch's next job was to adapt Somerset Maugham's play *The Letter* as a vehicle for Bette Davis, Warner Bros.'s leading actress. This time there were no objections from the screenwriter. The property had impressive literary origins, and the assignment gave Koch a chance to work with William Wyler, one of Hollywood's most respected directors.

The Letter (1940) opens with Leslie Crosby (Davis), the wayward wife of an English planter in Malaysia, killing her lover—in defense of her honor, she says. The plot hinges on an incriminating letter held by the victim's native lover (Gale Sondegaard), and the efforts of Leslie and her lawyer (James Stephenson) to keep the evidence from surfacing during the inquest. Protected by respectability—and a web of lies—Leslie is acquitted. Here, Koch creates a new ending in which the murdered man's mistress kills Leslie. Many reviewers attributed this to the Hays office's insistence that a murderer must be punished, but Koch claims full credit for the finish: "The film needed something less prosaic and more dramatic."

Koch followed *The Letter* with two more melodramas. *Shining Victory* (1941), written with Anne Froelich from a play by A. J. Cronin, was a formula picture about a brilliant young doctor (James Stephenson) and his research assistant (Geraldine Fitzgerald) who fall in love, only to have her die heroically, sacrificing herself to save the doctor's data from a fire. Critics generally dismissed the movie as inconsequential, but praised its literate script. *In This Our Life* (1942), based on a novel by Ellen Glasgow, was about two sisters (Bette Davis and Olivia de Havilland), one good, one bad. It is noteworthy mainly for its references to racial discrimination and sympathetic portrayal of a sensitive young Negro, reflecting, perhaps, the liberal views of Koch and director (and uncredited collaborator) John Huston.

Earlier Huston and Koch had collaborated on two historical projects with topical implications. Both the film *Sergeant York* (1941) and *In Time to Come* (1941), a play about Woodrow Wilson's campaign for world peace after World War I, disavowed isolationism, which had dominated American diplomacy since the Versailles treaty.

Howard Hawks directed *Sergeant York*, the movie biography of Alvin York (Gary Cooper), a poor Appalachian farmer who had in World War I single-handedly captured an entire company of German soldiers. Apart from the military heroics, the film is about the conflict between York's fundamentalist-inspired pacifism and his military obligations. For the writers, the main challenge was to find a convincing way for the hero to reconcile these contradictory impulses without sacrificing his essential idealism. The assignment created a personal dilemma for Koch, an avowed pacifist. Under the prodding of Huston, Koch eventually acceded to the collective judgment that the message of *Sergeant York* was the right one for that moment in the nation's history. The writer's pacifism gave way

Dooley Wilson, Humphrey Bogart, and Ingrid Bergman in Casablanca, *winner of the 1943 Academy Awards for best screenplay, best direction, and best picture*

to his realization that "the defaults and misjudgments of various European governments had allowed a situation to develop in Germany which seemingly left no alternative to war."

Though American participation in yet another European war was a very real possibility in 1941, not all those who saw *Sergeant York* shared the filmmakers' views on the matter. Critics, even those who otherwise liked the picture, criticized its propagandistic elements. On the balance, reviewers praised the film's depiction of York. Gary Cooper won an Academy Award for his performance as York, and Koch and Huston were nominated for their screenplay.

Koch was on the verge of his greatest success: *Casablanca*. Experience had sharpened his skills without diminishing the earnestness, romanticism, and idealism of his early period. And he retained his knack for infusing his material with topical concerns. Koch was brought in to work on the script after Julius and Philip Epstein had left for another project, and though he does not remember which of

Casablanca's famous lines are his and which are the Epsteins', he does remember that he shaped the film's politics. Aside from the characterizations, he was most interested in "the political intrigues with their relevance to the struggle against fascism." The issue of isolationism is at the heart of the picture, despite its romantic overtones. The main concern, after all, is whether Rick (Humphrey Bogart), the expatriate, will sustain his isolation in the face of various pressures: money, love, self-preservation, ideology. Of course, there is more to *Casablanca* than its political message; otherwise it would not have retained its appeal. In 1943 critics praised the film more for its entertainment value than its message; it won the Academy Award for Best Picture, and the script won the Oscar for best screenplay.

Doubtless it was on the strength of Koch's handling of the political elements in *Casablanca* that Jack Warner asked him to script *Mission to Moscow* (1943), begun by Erskine Caldwell from a bestselling book by Ambassador Joseph Davies. Koch's script concentrated on Ambassador Davies's favorable impressions of Joseph Stalin and the Soviet Union. It touted Soviet industrial progress, pointed out similarities between Russian communism and American capitalism, found a way to justify the infamous purge trials, and depicted Stalin as a good friend of the United States. *Mission to Moscow* was blatantly propagandistic. It repeatedly tampered with history, sometimes for purely dramatic reasons, other times for political purposes. Unfortunately for Koch, the political message of the film, which was so acceptable, even patriotic, during wartime, became subversive by Cold War standards and led to his being subpoenaed during the House Un-American Activities Committee's hearings on Communists in the film industry.

While working on *Mission to Moscow*, Koch met and married writer Anne Green; it was his second marriage. He is the father of three children.

During the early 1940s Koch tried to obtain his release from Warner Bros. when it appeared that the studio had become cautious about making topical films of social significance. Before leaving the studio, he scripted three more films. *In Our Time*

(1944), written with Ellis St. Joseph, was a tale of lovers who are separated by class and national barriers in prewar Poland; Koch called it an anti-Fascist film. *Rhapsody in Blue* (1945) was notable for its musical score; as a biography of George Gershwin it lacked clarity, continuity, and insight. Koch shared the writing credit with Elliot Paul, though director Irving Rapper recalls that Clifford Odets was the main writer on the project. *Three Strangers* (1946), by Koch and Huston, was a taut mystery drama about three people (Geraldine Fitzgerald, Sidney Greenstreet, and Peter Lorre) who become partners in a sweepstakes ticket. The story, with its theme that fate rules lives, shows the hand of John Huston, while the fluent dialogue is very much in the Koch manner.

In 1947 the House Un-American Activities Committee questioned studio chief Jack Warner about *Mission to Moscow*. Warner denied that there had been any Communist propaganda in his films and said that he had refused to renew the contracts of writers who had tried to advance the Communist line in their scripts. Among those writers he men-

Dudley Field Malone as Winston Churchill and Walter Huston as Ambassador Joseph Davies in Mission to Moscow

tioned was Howard Koch. Koch, who had openly opposed the Committee and its goals, was subpoenaed to appear before the House panel. The Committee cancelled his subpoena at the last minute, perhaps because Jack Warner's testimony would not survive close scrutiny. Koch could prove that he was not fired by Warner Bros. in a purge of "Communists" but had, in fact, sought his release from his contract, which the studio granted him only after he agreed to pay them $10,000. That revelation and the cancellation of his subpoena did not end the matter, for during the controversy, and after, Koch persistently defended the political record of the progressive Left in Hollywood, whether liberal or Communist. Still, he found it necessary to buy space in the trade papers to announce that he had never been a Communist, but added that he reserved the right to refuse to repeat the statement before HUAC.

Following Jack Warner's HUAC appearance, Howard Koch became "graylisted"—producers continued to offer him writing assignments, but with diminishing frequency, even though no official agency had cited the writer as a Communist. Koch next scripted an independent production, *Letter from an Unknown Woman* (1948), about the bittersweet romance between a young woman (Joan Fontaine) and a Viennese concert pianist (Louis Jourdan). She is left pregnant and marries a man she does not love, but on her deathbed forgives the pianist, telling him in a letter that she had always loved him. Her letter makes him realize the emptiness of his life, and he dies in a duel with her husband. When it was first released, *Letter from an Unknown Woman* was slighted by critics and ignored by audiences, but it has since become a cult film because of its poignantly romantic script and director Max Ophuls's stylized evocation of late nineteenth-century Vienna.

Koch's next script, *No Sad Songs for Me* (1950), was good enough to lure Margaret Sullavan back to the screen after a seven-year absence. She played a dying mother who must prepare her family to go on without her. The story has all the ingredients of a formula tearjerker, but Koch's script turned them into a fine drama.

In 1951 Koch wrote the screenplay for *The 13th Letter*. The story by Louis Chavance had been the basis for a French film by H. G. Clouzot. Otto Preminger asked Koch to write an English version set in Canada. The story explored a community's reaction to a series of poison-pen letters directed against a new doctor in town. In the original, Clouzot showed how the corrosive effects of suspicion and false accusations spread throughout the community. In 1951 it was unlikely that Koch, given his HUAC experiences, and Preminger, given his liberal views, would not see parallels between McCarthyism and the situation depicted in *The 13th Letter*. Yet they uncharacteristically chose to deemphasize the social and political implications of their story, turning the film into a rather straightforward mystery.

Koch was blacklisted following *The 13th Letter*. United Artists turned down a Joseph Mankiewicz project because the producer wanted Koch; the sponsors of the *U.S. Steel Hour* vetoed a production of Koch and Huston's Woodrow Wilson play; and CBS overruled John Houseman's offer to hire Koch to write for his proposed *Seven Lively Arts* television program. Eventually Koch left Hollywood for Woodstock, New York, then exile in Europe, where he supported his family by working under an assumed name. As Peter Howard, he wrote the screenplay for *The Intimate Stranger* (1956), a British film released in the United States as *Finger of Guilt*. He returned to the United States in 1956, but soon found he could not get a writing contract, despite interest from the studios, as long as his name appeared on any list of "unemployables."

Finally in 1961, Koch's attorney Edward Bennett Williams was able to have the writer's name removed from the last list of so-called subversives. Columbia Pictures hired Koch to script *Loss of Innocence* (1961). Based on Rumer Godden's novel *The Greengage Summer*, the film dealt with a young English girl's (Susannah York) romantic awakening.

Two undistinguished war movies followed. *The War Lover* (1962) was based on John Hersey's 1959 novel about a bomber pilot who enjoys the danger and excitement of war as well as the anonymous killing that modern war sanctions. Koch's screenplay stripped away the crude, and basically uncinematic, psychologizing of the original, but that left only a commonplace story about two American pilots (Steve McQueen and Robert Wagner) competing for the same Englishwoman (Shirley Ann Field). *633 Squadron* (1964), written primarily by James Clavell, was about a British squadron assigned to bomb a German rocket factory in Norway. The script was turgid and pretentious; the film was negligible. Koch came to the project late, as a script-doctor, when the producers realized their film had serious deficiencies.

Koch's skills were better suited to his next project, *The Fox* (1968), an adaptation of D. H. Lawrence's novella. Lawrence's original told the story of two women whose close relationship, based on years of living together, is suddenly disrupted by a young man who comes to their isolated farm in the English midlands. Koch's treatment was faithful to Lawrence, but the producer, Raymond Stross, and director, Mark Rydell, wanted to make the sexual implications of the story less symbolic and more explicit. Koch objected to the addition of a scene that would establish a lesbian relationship between the two women and took his case unsuccessfully to the Writers Guild. Another writer, Lewis John Carlino, was hired to prepare a shooting script which owes little to Lawrence.

Howard Koch resides in Woodstock, New York. He turns down offers to write screenplays, preferring to write for the theater because it offers "the chance to write what you want." He has written an anti-nuclear war play, as yet unproduced, and is nearing the completion of a pair of novels about the last years of this century. Tentatively titled "The Coldest War" and "Game's End," the novels are not science fiction but political fiction, based on Koch's projections of forces currently at work in the world.

References:

Richard J. Anobile, ed., *Michael Curtiz's Casablanca* (New York: Universe Books, 1974);

Gregory D. Black and Clayton R. Koppes, "OWI Goes to the Movies: The Bureau of Intelligence's Criticism of Hollywood, 1942-43," *Prologue: The Journal of the National Archives*, 6 (Spring 1974): 44-59;

Larry Ceplair and Steven Englund, *The Inquisition in Hollywood: Politics in the Film Community, 1930-1960* (Garden City: Doubleday / Anchor Press, 1980);

John Cogley, *Report on Blacklisting, Volume 1, Movies* (N.p.: The Fund for the Republic, 1956);

Richard Corliss, ed., *The Hollywood Screenwriters* (New York: Avon, 1972);

Corliss, *Talking Pictures* (Woodstock, N.Y.: Overlook Press, 1974);

David Culbert, "Our Awkward Ally: *Mission to Moscow*," *American History / American Film: Interpreting the Hollywood Image*, edited by John E. O'Connor and Martin A. Jackson (New York: Ungar, 1979), pp. 121-145;

John Davis, "Notes on Warner Brothers Foreign Policy, 1918-1948," *The Velvet Light Trap*, 17 (Winter 1977): 19-31;

John Higham, *Warner Brothers* (New York: Scribners, 1975);

John Houseman, *Front and Center* (New York: Simon & Schuster, 1979);

Houseman, *Run-Through: A Memoir* (New York: Simon & Schuster, 1972);

John Huston, *An Open Book* (New York: Knopf, 1980);

Pare Lorentz, *Lorentz on Film: Movies 1927 to 1941* (New York: Hopkinson & Blake, 1975);

Axel Madsen, *William Wyler: The Authorized Biography* (New York: Crowell, 1973);

Victor S. Navasky, *Naming Names* (New York: Viking, 1980);

Richard Schickel, "Some Nights in Casablanca," *Favorite Movies: Critics' Choice*, edited by Philip Nobile (New York: Macmillan, 1973), pp. 114-125;

Ted Sennett, *Warner Brothers Presents* (New Rochelle, N.Y.: Arlington House, 1972);

David Thomson, *America in the Dark: Hollywood and the Gift of Unreality* (New York: Morrow, 1977);

Michael Wood, *America in the Movies* (New York: Basic Books, 1975).

Papers:

Manuscripts by Koch are housed in the Film and Manuscript Archive, Wisconsin Center for Film and Theater Research, State Historical Society of Wisconsin, Madison.

Norman Krasna

(7 November 1909-   )

Irene Atkins

MOTION PICTURES: *Hollywood Speaks* (Columbia, 1932), screen story; dialogue by Krasna and Jo Swerling;

That's My Boy (Columbia, 1932), screenplay;

So This is Africa (Columbia, 1933), story and screenplay;

Meet the Baron (M-G-M, 1933), story by Krasna and Herman J. Mankiewicz;

Love, Honor and Obey (Universal, 1933), screenplay by Krasna and Eddie Buzzell;

Parole Girl (Columbia, 1933), story and screenplay;

The Richest Girl in the World (RKO, 1934), story and screenplay;

Romance in Manhattan (RKO, 1934), story with Don Hartman;

Four Hours to Kill (Paramount, 1935), screenplay adapted by Krasna from his play *Small Miracle*;

Hands Across the Table (Paramount, 1935), screenplay by Krasna, Herbert Fields, and Vincent Lawrence;

Wife Versus Secretary (M-G-M, 1936), screenplay by Krasna, John Lee Mahin, and Alice Duer Miller;

Fury (M-G-M, 1936), screen story;

As Good as Married (Universal, 1937), screen story;

The King and the Chorus Girl (Warner Bros., 1937), screen story and screenplay by Krasna and Groucho Marx;

Big City (M-G-M, 1937), screen story;

The First Hundred Years (M-G-M, 1938), screen story;

You and Me (Paramount, 1938), screen story;

Bachelor Mother (RKO, 1939), screenplay;

It's a Date (Universal, 1940), screenplay;

Mr. and Mrs. Smith (RKO, 1941), screen story and screenplay;

The Flame of New Orleans (Universal, 1941), screen story and screenplay;

The Devil and Miss Jones (RKO, 1941), screen story and screenplay;

It Started with Eve (Universal, 1941), screenplay by Krasna and Leo Townsend; filmed again as *I'd Rather Be Rich* (Universal, 1946), screenplay by Krasna, Townsend, and Oscar Brodney;

Princess O'Rourke (Warner Bros., 1943), screen story and screenplay;

Bride By Mistake (RKO, 1945), screen story;

Norman Krasna

Practically Yours (Paramount, 1945), screen story and screenplay;

The Big Hangover (M-G-M, 1950), screen story and screenplay;

White Christmas (Paramount, 1954), screen story and screenplay by Krasna, Melvin Frank, and Norman Panama;

The Ambassador's Daughter (United Artists, 1956), screen story and screenplay;

Bundle of Joy (RKO, 1956), screenplay by Krasna, Robert Carson, and Arthur Sheekman;

Indiscreet (Warner Bros., 1958), screenplay adapted by Krasna from his play *Kind Sir*;

Who Was That Lady? (Columbia, 1960), screenplay adapted by Krasna from his play *Who Was That Lady I Saw You With?*;

Let's Make Love (20th Century-Fox, 1960), screen

186

story and screenplay;

My Geisha (Paramount, 1962), screen story and screenplay;

Sunday in New York (M-G-M, 1964), screenplay adapted by Krasna from his play.

SELECTED PLAYS: *Louder, Please* (New York, Masque Theatre, 12 November 1931);

Small Miracle (New York, John Golden Theatre, 26 September 1934);

Man With Blonde Hair (New York, Belasco Theatre, 4 November 1941);

Dear Ruth (New York, Henry Miller's Theatre, 13 December 1944);

John Loves Mary (New York, Booth Theatre, 4 February 1947);

Time for Elizabeth (New York, Fulton Theatre, 27 September 1948), by Krasna and Groucho Marx;

Kind Sir (New York, Alvin Theatre, 4 November 1953);

Who Was That Lady I Saw You With? (New York, Martin Beck Theatre, 3 March 1958);

Sunday in New York (New York, Cort Theatre, 29 November 1961);

Watch the Birdie! (Miami, Florida, Coconut Grove Playhouse, Summer 1964);

Love in E-Flat (New York, Brooks Atkinson Theatre, 13 February 1967);

We Interrupt This Program (New York, Ambassador Theatre, 1 April 1975).

BOOKS: *Louder, Please* (New York: French, 1932);

Small Miracle (New York: French, 1935);

Dear Ruth (New York: Random House, 1945);

John Loves Mary (New York: Dramatists Play Service, 1947);

Time for Elizabeth, by Krasna and Groucho Marx (New York: Dramatists Play Service, 1948);

Kind Sir (New York: Dramatists Play Service, 1954);

Who Was That Lady I Saw You With? (New York: Random House, 1958);

Sunday in New York (New York: Random House, 1962);

Love in E-Flat (New York: Dramatists Play Service, 1967);

Watch the Birdie! (New York: Dramatists Play Service, 1969);

Bunny (New York: French, 1970).

OTHER: *Fury*, in *Twenty Best Film Plays*, edited by John Gassner and Dudley Nichols (New York: Crown, 1943).

PERIODICAL PUBLICATIONS: "The Return of the Native or Man Overboard," *Hollywood Reporter*, 23 (21 September 1934);

"My Father and the Picture Business," *Daily Variety*, 97, no. 35 (1957).

In 1935 Norman Krasna was hailed by his colleagues as the Boy Wonder of Hollywood. By age twenty-five, he had written stories and screenplays for several film comedies, and his original story for *The Richest Girl in the World* (1934) had received an Academy award nomination. His second play, *Small Miracle*, was running on Broadway and had been bought by a film company. Indeed, during the 1930s and through the 1940s and 1950s, Krasna wrote film scripts that lifted the genre of screwball comedy to a level of sophisticated entertainment. Mistaken identity, the Cinderella story, and the humanizing of cynics and curmudgeons are the chief elements of Krasna's plots. His characters and their surroundings are often drawn from his own experiences and include newspapermen, press agents, employees of department stores, and servicemen back from the war. By the 1960s, however, his plots had worn thin and were less engaging.

Norman Krasna was born to Benjamin and Beatrice Mannison Krasna in the Corona section of Queens, New York. After graduation from public high school, he attended New York University in 1927, Columbia University in 1928, and the night law school of Saint John's University in Brooklyn in 1928. His interests turned to journalism, and in 1928 he took a job as copyboy and then assistant to Louis Weitzenkorn, drama editor of the *New York World*. When Weitzenkorn left the *World* late that year for the *New York Evening Graphic*, Krasna accompanied him, and in 1929 became the *Graphic*'s drama editor and critic. Krasna has said that while working as a drama critic, he typed the complete manuscript of Ben Hecht and Charles MacArthur's *The Front Page* ten times to learn the rhythms of playwriting.

In 1930 Krasna left the *Graphic* to join the staff of the *Exhibitors Herald-World*, a film trade paper for which he wrote a column. This position, in turn, led to a fifty-dollar-a-week job in Hollywood in the publicity department at Warner Bros. His experiences there provided him with material for his first play, *Louder, Please* (1931), in which the protagonist, a Hollywood press agent, stages the phony disappearance of the star he is publicizing.

Soon after, Krasna was hired by Columbia Pictures as a screenwriter. His first film, *Hollywood Speaks* (1932), written in collaboration with Jo

Crowd scene from Fury

Swerling, is a comedy-melodrama about the tribulations of an aspiring screen actress who is befriended by a sympathetic newspaperman. After working on "B" pictures at various studios, Krasna won his first widespread recognition for his story and screenplay for *The Richest Girl in the World*, starring Miriam Hopkins, Joel McCrea, and Fay Wray. Mistaken identity—a plot device that recurs throughout Krasna's work—provides the basis for this comedy. An heiress changes places with her secretary hoping that a young man will fall in love with her for herself, not her millions.

In 1935 Krasna adapted his play *Small Miracle* for the screen under the title *Four Hours to Kill*. The story takes place in the lounge of a theater during a stage performance, with a *Grand Hotel* kind of plot about intertwining lives. The film was well received by critics but was not a financial success.

Later in 1935 Krasna collaborated with Herbert Fields and Vincent Lawrence on the screenplay for *Hands Across the Table* (1935). Based on the story by Vina Delmar, the film is another tale of mistaken identity. Manicurist Regi Allen (Carole Lombard) is

determined to marry for money but instead falls in love with Theodore Drew (Fred MacMurray), an impoverished young man whom she believes to be wealthy. *Hands Across the Table* was the first starring role tailored expressly for Lombard, and her manicurist is a complex, moody character. The flippant comedy in the film is tempered with serious introspective moments that give the characters dimension unusual in screwball comedies. Excellent fast-paced dialogue also distinguishes the film, which was a box-office hit and became a classic of 1930s comedy.

Next Krasna worked with Alice Duer Miller and John Lee Mahin in adapting Faith Baldwin's *Wife Versus Secretary* (1936). Although the film is a stereotyped tale of a wife's suspicions about her husband's involvement with his beautiful secretary, the popularity of its stars—Clark Gable, Myrna Loy, and Jean Harlow—ensured its commercial success. Krasna then ventured away from comedy and wrote the original story for *Fury* (1936), a denunciation of mob violence. Fritz Lang wrote the screenplay with Bartlett Cormack and also directed the film. *Fury* is an account of a man (Spencer Tracy) wrongfully identified and arrested for kidnapping; when a lynch mob sets fire to the jail where he is imprisoned, he escapes and seeks revenge. Krasna's original story was nominated for an Academy award.

In spite of his proven ability with dramatic material, Krasna returned to writing light comedies in 1937 and collaborated with Groucho Marx on the original screenplay for *The King and the Chorus Girl*, with Cary Grant as a bored monarch. The film capitalized on the headlines created by the abdication of King Edward VIII. Krasna and Marx remained close friends for many years, collaborating again on *Time for Elizabeth* (1948), a play that had a short Broadway run.

In 1937 Louis B. Mayer was seeking producers to help fill the void left at M-G-M by the death of Irving Thalberg. Krasna was hired as producer and between 1937 and 1938 made three films for M-G-M: *Big City* (1937) and *The First Hundred Years* (1938), based on his original stories, and *Three Loves Has Nancy* (1938).

Krasna's screenplay for *Bachelor Mother* (1939) combined farce based on mistaken identity with warm, believable characters. Critics were almost unanimous in their praise for this story of a young woman (Ginger Rogers) thought to be the mother of a baby she found outside a foundling home, and the film played to a large audience throughout its run. Garson Kanin directed.

In 1941 Krasna sold the script of *Mr. and Mrs. Smith* to RKO as a vehicle for Carole Lombard with the proviso that he would direct the film. Lombard declined to appear in a director's debut, and the film about a couple (Lombard and Robert Montgomery) who find their marriage is not technically legal was instead directed by Alfred Hitchcock. Also in 1941, Krasna wrote his favorite script, *The Devil and Miss Jones*, about a department store owner (Charles Coburn) posing as a worker in his own store to spy on his employees. The film was an immediate box-office success, and Krasna's original screenplay was nominated for an Academy award.

In 1942 Krasna signed a contract with Warner Bros. to write and direct several films but completed only *Princess O'Rourke* (1943) before entering the U.S. Army Air Force. In this film that won the Academy Award for Best Original Screenplay, a young American flyer (Robert Cummings) falls in love with a woman who he thinks is a penniless refugee (Olivia de Havilland), only to find she is an exiled, wealthy princess. He loves the princess, but not enough to give up his American citizenship or

defer his war service. Krasna was praised by the critics for both his writing and directing.

Krasna joined the U.S. Army Air Force's first motion-picture unit in 1943 and served there until 1945. He flew as an observer on several missions over Europe, while writing and directing training films. Part of his service years were spent at "Fort Roach," the former Hal Roach Studios in Culver City, California, where he wrote and directed propaganda films, including several that starred air force officer Clark Gable. Krasna was awarded the Bronze Star for his efforts.

After the war, Krasna divided his time between screenwriting, film directing, and playwriting. His play *Dear Ruth*, about a woman whose sister had used her name while corresponding with a soldier overseas, had a successful Broadway run in 1944-1945 and was filmed from a screenplay by Arthur Sheekman in 1947. In 1947 Krasna wrote another Broadway hit, *John Loves Mary*, about a man who marries his best friend's girl to get her into the United States. It was filmed in 1949 from a screenplay by Phoebe and Henry Ephron.

In the 1950s, Krasna wrote, directed, and produced *The Big Hangover* (1950) and *The Ambassador's Daughter* (1956). Both films did well at the box office, but the criticism of each was kinder to Krasna as director than as writer of what were now beginning to be regarded as rather overworked situations and gags. *The Big Hangover* is about a man (Van Johnson) who is so allergic to brandy that even a whiff of it gives him hallucinations; *The Ambassador's Daughter* is the story of a young woman (Olivia de Havilland) who wants to convince her father, a U.S. senator, that GIs are well-mannered enough to use Paris as a recreation city.

In 1950 Krasna and Jerry Wald formed Wald-Krasna Productions, an independent company that distributed films through RKO. Wald and Krasna were both known for their energy and aggressiveness, and each had been mentioned as the prototype for Sammy Glick, the protagonist for Budd Schulberg's 1941 Hollywood novel *What Makes Sammy Run?* Krasna and Wald produced three films together: *The Blue Veil* (1951), a melodrama of self-sacrifice; *Behave Yourself* (1951), a comedy murder mystery, and *Clash by Night* (1952), an adaptation of a stark drama by Clifford Odets coproduced with Harriet Parsons. None of the films was a critical or box-office success, and Krasna sold his interest in the company to Wald in 1952.

Krasna's 1953 Broadway play *Kind Sir* was not a success but his film adaptation, entitled *Indiscreet* (1958), was a critical and financial hit. Krasna

Cary Grant and Ingrid Bergman in Indiscreet

changed the setting from New York to London, but the premise remained the same—a bachelor pretends to be married to protect himself from ardent women. Stanley Donen directed the film, which starred Cary Grant and Ingrid Bergman.

In 1959, Krasna's fellow screenwriters presented him with the Writers Guild of America's Laurel Award, an honor bestowed for the body of a writer's work rather than for any individual script. That same year, Krasna left Hollywood for Switzerland. It was a move that had been made by many others in the film industry, mostly for tax purposes. Feeling that "writers can write anywhere," Krasna continued writing for stage and screen and commuted from Switzerland to New York and Hollywood. His marriage to Ruth Frazee had dissolved in 1950, and in 1951 he had married Erle Galbraith Jolson, the widow of Al Jolson.

Krasna adapted his successful play *Who Was That Lady I Saw You With?* (1958), a spy comedy-drama,to the screen as *Who Was That Lady?* in 1960. That same year, he sold his original screenplay *Let's Make Love*, about a billionaire (Yves Montand) pretending to be an actor and falling in love with a

showgirl (Marilyn Monroe), to 20th Century-Fox. Krasna and Hal Kantor (Kantor wrote additional dialogue for the film) were nominated for a Writers Guild award.

Krasna returned to Broadway in 1961 with *Sunday in New York*, a romantic comedy about a virginal young woman visiting New York City. He adapted the play for the screen in 1964; this was followed by *I'd Rather Be Rich*, a remake of his earlier film *It Started with Eve*. Since 1964, Krasna has written no screenplays. He has had three plays produced: *Watch the Birdie!* (1964), *Love in E-Flat* (1967), and *We Interrupt This Program* (1975).

Although the best of Krasna's films, notably *Bachelor Mother, The Devil and Miss Jones*, and *Fury*, are often enjoyed at retrospective screenings, his name has been overlooked by many film scholars. The reasons for this lack of recognition could be that the Krasna themes are a little less profound, or the characters not as deep as those in the films of his peers. Yet as examples of inventiveness, a remarkable ability to juggle complicated plots, and skillful dialogue writing, Krasna's films have aged gracefully and deserve a close look by those who are interested in the craft of screenwriting.

References:

Hector Arce, *Groucho* (New York: Putnam's, 1979);

David Chierichetti, *Hollywood Director* (New York: Curtis Books, 1973);

Richard Corliss, *Talking Pictures* (Woodstock, N.Y.: Overlook Press, 1974), pp. 62-72;

Henry Ephron, *We Thought We Could Do Anything* (New York: Norton, 1977);

Paul M. Jensen, *The Cinema of Fritz Lang* (New York: Barnes, 1969);

"Screenwriters Symposium," *Film Comment*, 6 (Winter 1970-1971): 86-100;

Donald Spoto, *The Art of Alfred Hitchcock* (New York: Hopkinson & Blake, 1976).

Stanley Kubrick

(26 July 1928-   )

Joseph Adamson III

MOTION PICTURES: *Killer's Kiss* (United Artists, 1955), screen story and screenplay;

The Killing (United Artists, 1956), screenplay;

Paths of Glory (United Artists, 1957), screenplay by Kubrick, Calder Willingham, and Jim Thompson;

Dr. Strangelove, or: How I Learned to Stop Worrying and Love the Bomb (Columbia, 1964), screenplay by Kubrick, Peter George, and Terry Southern;

2001: A Space Odyssey (M-G-M, 1968), screen story and screenplay by Kubrick and Arthur C. Clarke;

A Clockwork Orange (Warner Bros., 1971), screenplay;

Barry Lyndon (Warner Bros., 1975), screenplay;

The Shining (Warner Bros., 1980), screenplay by Kubrick and Diane Johnson.

BOOK: *Stanley Kubrick's A Clockwork Orange. Based on the Novel by Anthony Burgess* (New York: Ballantine, 1972; London: Lorrimer, 1972).

PERIODICAL PUBLICATIONS: "Stanley Kubrick—Movie Maker," *London Observer Weekend Review*, 4 December 1960;

"Words and Movies," *Sight and Sound*, 30 (Winter 1961);

"Lolita and the Press," *London Observer*, 24 June 1962;

"How I Learned to Stop Worrying and Love the Cinema," *Films and Filming* (June 1963);

"Quotesmanship," *Action* (May-June 1968);

"Critics and Film," *Action* (January-February 1969);

"What Directors are Saying," *Action* (January-February 1971);

"Now Kubrick Fights Back," *New York Times*, 27 February 1972.

Stanley Kubrick is an exceptional filmmaker whose control over his films is so complete that it

Stanley Kubrick in the 1950s

extends from the supervision of every production detail to the planning of elaborate advertising and distribution campaigns; from the film editing to the inspection of the projector for opening night; from the selection of the subject matter to the writing of his own screenplays.

The precocious son of a middle-class doctor, Kubrick was born in the Bronx, New York. He watched many films with his mother, learned chess at age ten from his father, was playing the game for money at twelve, and exhibited a mania for photography at thirteen. Though active as a drummer and the class photographer, he was bored at William Howard Taft High School and reportedly graduated with a sixty-seven average. In 1945 he began a four-year stint as a photographer for *Look* magazine. A photographic innovator, Kubrick was a pioneer in the use of infrared light.

But chess and the movies still fascinated him. When he was not taking pictures, Kubrick was hustling the players at Washington Square and frequenting every movie house in town. He made his first motion picture at age twenty-two, basing it on "Day of the Fight," a *Look* photo study he had done on middleweight boxer Walter Cartier. He wrote, produced, directed, and edited the one-reel short and sold it at a small profit to RKO Radio Pictures, which released it in 1952 as part of their *This Is America* series. That year Kubrick's first marriage, to Toba Metz, ended in divorce.

Kubrick next wrote and directed *The Flying Padre* (1952) for RKO-Pathé's Screenliner series and directed and photographed other informational films for various sponsors, including *The Seafarers* for Seafarers International Union in 1953. During this period he was able to independently produce and direct his first feature, *Fear and Desire* (1955), from a Howard O. Sackler screenplay about a unit of soldiers on patrol. The film was distributed to a limited art-house circuit by Joseph Burstyn.

Collaborating with Sackler, Kubrick quickly wrote the script for his second feature, a series of inexpensive action scenes linked by a narrative thread just strong enough to tie them together. He raised the production money from friends and relatives, deferred salaries and lab costs during the shooting of the film, worked nearly twenty-four hours a day, and lived on unemployment checks. The resulting film was *Killer's Kiss* (1955), a bleak film noir about a boxer's attempts to save a young dancer from a gangster boss. United Artists bought the film and gave it worldwide distribution as a second feature on double bills. It proved so profitable that United Artists offered Kubrick a contract

to deliver low-budget programmers on a regular basis. He refused, preferring to maintain his independence.

The next project he undertook was cast in the mold of *Killer's Kiss*. Designed as an inexpensive film to be shot on available locations, "Lunatic at Large" was written at Kubrick's behest by novelist Jim Thompson. But by the time Thompson had finished it, Kubrick had read Lionel White's novel *Clean Break* (1955) and had been fascinated by its "perfect crime" framework, wherein a team of cheap hoods engineer a heist of two million dollars from a racetrack. Kubrick and Thompson abandoned "Lunatic at Large" and set about purchasing the rights to *Clean Break*. The result, *The Killing* (1956), another B movie in the film noir vein, was hailed as the sleeper of the year and given international recognition. Kubrick considers *The Killing* his first finished work. He takes no pride in his earlier films.

Kubrick continued his involvement with Jim Thompson and attempted unsuccessfully to interest United Artists in filming Thompson's novel *The Killer Inside Me*. When this failed, he began searching for another project. Kubrick and James B. Harris, Kubrick's partner in his production company, were signed to develop stories for Dore Schary, head of production at M-G-M. The studio owned so many properties that it took two weeks just to read the synopses; they finally selected Stefan Zweig's "The Burning Secret," from which Kubrick prepared a screenplay with novelist Calder Willingham. By the time this was completed, Schary was no longer in power at M-G-M, and the contract was not binding. Kubrick therefore abandoned that project and reached back to his childhood memories of Humphrey Cobb's novel *Paths of Glory*; he subsequently bought the rights with Harris and wrote the script with Thompson and Willingham.

Based on a true story from World War I, *Paths of Glory* is about three privates in the French army who were executed by a firing squad to serve "as an example." The downbeat subject matter and ending kept studio heads from agreeing to go ahead, but because of Kirk Douglas's interest and willingness to play the lead, Kubrick was able to secure a United Artists contract. Somewhere in the process of raising financing, however, the uncompromising ending had been changed to what James Harris called "a very corny last minute reprieve." Douglas did not see the new script until he arrived on location in Germany, and the change so enraged him that he threatened to abandon the production immediately. Kubrick, Harris, and Willingham supported his position, and the original ending was restored. The terrible inevitability of the final execution is now one of *Paths of Glory*'s most powerful moments, as well as a necessary realization of the tragic vision of Cobb's novel. Released in 1957, *Paths of Glory* was a great critical success, and its reputation has continued to grow.

Kubrick's second marriage, to dancer Ruth Sobotka, had ended, and in 1958 he married Suzanne Christiane Harlan, an actress who had appeared in *Paths of Glory*. They have two daughters, Anya and Vivian.

From *Killer's Kiss* to *Paths of Glory*, Kubrick progressively developed fatalistic themes. The happy ending of *Killer's Kiss* (much debated at the time; Kubrick shot several alternative endings) never rings true, but the slaughter of the criminals in *The Killing* is grimly appropriate to everything that has gone before, and the execution at the end of *Paths of Glory* is the final episode in a series of grim but unavoidable incidents. For each of these films, the setting is violent and hostile to romantic or optimistic visions, and the stories all concern plans that go wrong.

Kubrick professed at this time a fascination for the soldier and the criminal: losers, he said, before they even started. Though he was yet to have a true box-office success, he was increasingly aware of the

difficulty in uniting the issues that obsessed him with the demands of the marketplace. Within a narrow scope, Kubrick had perfected a type of story that was consistent with his view of life; rather than settle comfortably into a career of producing such films indefinitely, he set about to broaden his range.

But after *Paths of Glory* Kubrick encountered frustration. Jim Thompson began work on an original story called "I Stole a Million Dollars" but was unable to complete it due to illness. Kubrick wrote "two scripts no one wanted." For six months he worked with Marlon Brando and Calder Willingham on the preparation of *One-Eyed Jacks* (1961) until Brando dispensed with him at the last minute and directed the film himself. Kubrick's hand is evident in the structure and tone of the finished film; only his visual style and control over actors are missing. Subsequently, Kubrick replaced Anthony Mann as director of Kirk Douglas's production of *Spartacus* (1960) from Dalton Trumbo's screenplay based on Howard Fast's novel. The project has always caused Kubrick much pain, bearing as it does his name but not his full control.

Before Vladimir Nabokov's novel *Lolita* (1955) reached the top of the best-seller lists, Kubrick and Harris read it and wanted to make it into a film. The story of a cultured European who falls in love with a pubescent American teenager, the novel has a com-

Sue Lyon and James Mason in Lolita

pelling combination of poetry and sensationalism that appealed to them both. They bought the rights, knowing that the major studios had already declined the novel fearing that the Motion Picture Production Code would not approve of such a delicate subject.

Kubrick and Harris turned down a deal with Warner Bros. guaranteeing one million dollars and percentages for the two of them but leaving final control in the hands of the studio; they produced the film independently and secured M-G-M release upon completion. Nabokov was hired to write the screenplay, and after many conferences, six months of work, and two drafts, Nabokov prepared—on the basis of Kubrick's suggestions—a workable script. The producers then spent thirty days rewriting it, retaining only a few of Nabokov's scenes and fragments of his dialogue. Kubrick and Harris allowed the script to be revised further by the improvisations of the actors, particularly Peter Sellers, who interpolated wildly in the role of Claire Quilty. In the end, by Nabokov's own admission, "only ragged odds and ends of my script had been used." He

was given sole credit to protect the filmmakers from outraged film critics who might complain about liberties taken with the book.

Despite this precaution, *Lolita* (1962) was not a success with the critics, who gave Kubrick and Harris bad notices. In later years, Kubrick noted that, hedged in by the Hays Office and pressure from the Roman Catholic Legion of Decency, he had had to tone down the erotic content of the novel to the point that true love between Humbert and Lolita was unintentionally implied from the beginning. Kubrick agrees that this cripples the film's final scene, when Humbert should realize for the first time that he is in love with Lolita. Following the release of *Lolita*, Kubrick left the United States and went to live in England.

Concerned about the nuclear arms race, Kubrick researched the subject extensively before turning up Peter George's novel *Red Alert* (1958), about a nuclear showdown. Kubrick used it as the basis for his nightmare comedy about the end of the world: *Dr. Strangelove, or: How I Learned to Stop Worrying and Love the Bomb* (1964). He settled on a farci-

Slim Pickens (right) as Major T. J. King Kong in Dr. Strangelove, or: How I Learned to Stop Worrying and Love the Bomb

cal approach to the film only after repeated efforts to deal seriously with such a grotesque situation. Soon after starting work on the project, Kubrick parted amicably with Harris, who wanted to do his own directing, leaving Kubrick to do his own producing.

After months of working on the screenplay with Peter George, Kubrick met Terry Southern, a writer whom *Esquire* had assigned to write an article on the upcoming film. Impressed by Southern's comic flair, Kubrick hired him to contribute additional material. (Southern later had only one comment to make about the Kubrick-George script: "It wasn't funny.") Whatever the contributions of the collaborators and actors (Peter Sellers and George C. Scott improvised much of their material), Kubrick is undeniably responsible for holding the wackiness of the dialogue to the overall satirical tone of the film. The viewer is shocked into laughing *at* the horror of the threat of nuclear destruction rather than in spite of it. "The only way to tell the story," Kubrick claimed, "was as a black comedy, or better, a nightmare comedy, where the things you laugh at most are really the heart of the paradoxical postures that make a nuclear war possible."

Some doubted the legitimacy of this approach, claiming that premonitions of a nuclear Armageddon were just not funny. But in its attitudes, its hyperbole of factual conditions, its nomenclature (President Merkin Muffley, Colonel Bat Guano), its facetious opening, and its nihilistic ending, the film conforms to the patterns of classical satire. Kubrick considered it very much in the tradition of American comedy: "The best comedy," he said, "certainly the best American comedy, has always been based on a nightmare combination of danger, imbecility, physical pain, rudeness, deflation of authority, destruction, and viciousness. Just two examples: Donald Duck, Tom and Jerry." In pointing out man's all-too-human inability to be the perfect master of the massive destruction apparatus he had constructed, the film was conforming to the basic pattern of all comedy.

With *Dr. Strangelove* Kubrick's daring venture had become that rarity of film history, the critical success that is also a box-office winner. Though condemned by the United States State Department as "irresponsible filmmaking at its worst," the film won more than seventy-five awards internationally. *Dr. Strangelove*'s reputation has solidified over the years, as time has revealed it to be a landmark film, one of the most important of its decade.

By the time *Dr. Strangelove* was released, Kubrick was immersed in the research for what would prove to be another of the key films of the 1960s, what he envisioned from the beginning as a "good" science-fiction film. Plowing through existing science-fiction novels and finding none worthy of his purpose, he proceeded to have a story written. Contacting Arthur C. Clarke, Kubrick initiated a series of meetings that stretched from April 1964 to June 1966. They decided to base the new project on Clarke's short story "The Sentinel," about a lunar alarm clock presumably planted millions of years ago by extraterrestrials.

As production progressed, Kubrick dispensed with more and more of the science in his science fiction and cut reams of written dialogue, including an informative omniscient narration similar to that which he had used in *The Killing* and *Dr. Strangelove*. Kubrick's decision to transform *2001: A Space Odyssey* (1968) into a nonverbal experience (in which much of the dialogue is intentionally inane) caused a great deal of confusion among those accustomed to more verbally and theatrically oriented films. The film received a hostile reaction from New York critics, who called it boring, bothersome, and bewildering, and reviews elsewhere in the country were mixed, with even the positive ones cautious.

Actually, *2001*, far from being nonlinear, is carefully structured, divided into four acts that serve as the exposition, development, conflict, and resolution of the basic narrative; each of the four acts incorporates an exposition, development, conflict, and resolution of its own. The story concerns a bizarre monolith that appears first to the Pliocene apes, then to the Americans exploring the moon, then to astronaut David Bowman who is in orbit around Jupiter. This object represents a catalytic device, prompting the species into evolutionary leaps.

Although the completed film dismayed M-G-M executives as surely as it baffled New York critics, it turned out to be one of M-G-M's most profitable pictures of the period, saving the studio from bankruptcy. And in spite of the predictions of the critics, the "boring" film immediately made an impact, attracting a large coterie of followers who came back for repeated viewings.

Kubrick immediately announced that his next project would be "Napoleon" and set about reading extensively about the French emperor. As the decade neared its end, it became clear that multimillion-dollar projects of the kind Kubrick envisioned could not be financed, and once again he found a project involving months of work indefinitely postponed.

Almost as a reflex, he turned to a novel given

A scene from 2001: A Space Odyssey

to him by Terry Southern, spent three days immersed in the challenges posed by Anthony Burgess's *A Clockwork Orange* (1962), and began planning a small, flexible production more suited to the temper of the times. Convinced as he is that "the screenplay is the most incommunicative form of writing ever devised," he chose the response that seemed most appropriate to a man of his resources and devised a new form. The screenplay for *A Clockwork Orange* was written in the reverse of the conventional form, so that dialogue ran all the way across the page and action passages became concentrated in the center.

The precise nature and intent of Kubrick's film version of *A Clockwork Orange* (1971) have been the subjects of a heated controversy. Made in the emotionally high-strung period of the early 1970s, the film intentionally raises many issues viewers could conceivably feel disturbed about and then flashes vivid pictures of the issues' furthest extremes on the screen in nightmare images. Not only the usual sources of controversy—sex and violence—but also political domination, technological manipulation, religious sanctimony, and ideological hysteria are hyperbolized and thrust in front of viewers. Much of the negative reaction to the film stemmed from the mistaken notion that the audience was meant to like and identify with its savage main character, Alex (Malcolm McDowell), whose raping and murdering end after he is subjected to a process meant to condition him out of his antisocial behavior. In truth, the film, like the book, goes to great pains to discourage full identification with the character and strives to portray Alex as a beast to be feared as well as a prodigy to be ambivalently admired.

Along with intense negative reactions, the film garnered some excellent reviews and inspired many interesting critical analyses. It also won new respect for a filmmaker capable of producing such a variety of provocative, unusual, and important films and box-office grosses far beyond the expectations generated by the modest two-million-dollar budget of *A Clockwork Orange*.

Still unsuccessful in raising the capital for "Napoleon," Kubrick next chose to adapt the first novel of William Makepeace Thackeray, *The Luck of Barry Lyndon* (published serially in 1844). After three films speculating on possible futures of the human race, Kubrick decided to venture into the past for the first time since *Spartacus* and for the first time as a writer since *Paths of Glory*. The resulting film implies Kubrick's view that man was just as deluded and corrupted a creature in the romantic past as he is in the degenerate present and will be in the apocalyptic future. Redmond Barry (Ryan O'Neal), a commoner who becomes a man of means by marrying the widow Lyndon (Marisa Berenson), is a rogue who begins as an innocent and is corrupted gradually by a society that seems to favor chicanery over integrity.

Barry Lyndon (1975) received some rave reviews and became the fourth consecutive Kubrick film to receive Academy Award nominations for best picture, best director, and best screenplay. Despite these successes, it was Kubrick's least profitable venture since *Paths of Glory*—perhaps inevitably, since the enormous production cost would have required an enormous return. Barry, another

Malcolm McDowell as Alex in A Clockwork Orange *(Museum of Modern Art Film Stills Archive)*

character impossible to identify with fully, proves not so worthy an object of contemplation as Alex. Also, Kubrick's narrative drive, at its peak in the tight structures of *Paths of Glory* and *Dr. Strangelove*, fails in *Barry Lyndon* to achieve any but the most cerebral cohesion. Intellectually brilliant but emotionally alienating (a study, in fact, of eighteenth-century alienation), the film lacks the surface sensationalism that had made Kubrick's past intellectual constructs more palatable to the mass audience.

In a move seemingly calculated to regain his preeminent position in the film industry, Kubrick once again turned to a best-selling novel containing themes that both appealed to him and had the potential to attract a large audience, Stephen King's Gothic novel *The Shining* (1977). The story is about a struggling writer (Jack Nicholson) who is forced into the thankless role of winter caretaker at a summer resort and is too desperately in need of the work to deal rationally with the warnings of his precognitive son that bloody atrocities await the whole family. As the family stays in the hotel, the father is gradually possessed by the evil spirits that

exist there. Cut off from society by a snowstorm, the mother (Shelley Duvall) and son (Danny Lloyd) must find a way to survive as the father becomes increasingly irrational. The plot shows Kubrick's concern with the man-made horrors to which the human race is heir. The element of precognition offers the right touch of determinism, and the presence of gore affords the opportunity to create the ultimate horror film by invoking the audience's repressed fears.

The Shining (1980) was a financial success, though not as great a one as had been hoped, but, like other Kubrick films, it puzzled and irritated the critics. While they recognized Kubrick's stunning visual style and mastery of the techniques of camera movement, they nevertheless found fault in the narrative dislocation and the ambiguous ending.

Because he has rejected elements of filmmaking he deems not relevant to his purposes and generally avoids techniques aimed at gaining audience acceptance, Stanley Kubrick has moved farther away from the conventional film narrative and character identification than any other screenwriter in the commercial mainstream. This is in part responsible for the controversy that surrounds his films; he makes idea films that are structured on narrative frameworks, while most critics and audiences are geared for story films that might tangentially contain ideas. The triumph of Kubrick's ironic, sardonic sensibility has been to reconcile seemingly irreconcilable conflicts and embody in a single concept elements that have always been considered diametrically opposed. At his best, he arrives at the radical through the traditional and at emotional involvement through a sense of impersonal detachment.

Interviews:

William Kloman, "In 2001, Will Love Be a Seven-Letter Word?," *New York Times*, 14 April 1968;

Charles Kohler, "Stanley Kubrick Raps," *Eye*, 1 (August 1968);

Eric Norden, "Playboy Interview: Stanley Kubrick," *Playboy* (September 1968);

Maurice Rapf, "A Talk with Stanley Kubrick," *Action*, 6 (January-February 1969);

Joseph Gelmis, *The Film Director as Superstar* (Garden City: Doubleday, 1970);

Penelope Houston, "Kubrick Country," *Saturday Review* (25 December 1971);

Andrew Bailey, "A Clockwork Utopia," *Rolling Stone* (20 February 1972);

Bernard Weintraub, "Kubrick Tells What Makes 'Clockwork Orange' Tick," *New York Times*, 31 December 1972.

References:

Jerome Agel, *The Making of Kubrick's 2001* (New York: New American Library, 1970);

John Allen, "High Voltage on Four Circuits," *Christian Science Monitor*, 10 May 1968;

Hollis Alpert, "Offbeat Director in Outer Space," *New York Times Magazine*, 6 January 1966;

Alpert, "Tell Me, Who is Kubrick?," *Esquire* (July 1958);

Jeremy Bernstein, "How About a Little Game?," *New Yorker* (12 November 1966);

Robert Brustein, "Out of This World," *New York Review of Books*, 6 February 1964;

Arthur C. Clarke, *The Lost Worlds of 2001* (New York: New American Library, 1972);

Carolyn Geduld, *Filmguide to 2001: A Space Odyssey* (Bloomington: Indiana University Press, 1973);

Tim Hunter, Stephen Kaplan, and Peter Jaszi, "2001: A Space Odyssey," *Film Heritage* (Summer 1968);

Norman Kagan, *The Cinema of Stanley Kubrick* (New York: Holt, Rinehart & Winston, 1972);

Max Kosloff, "2001," *Film Culture* (Spring 1970);

Peter Lyon, "The Astonishing Stanley Kubrick," *Holiday* (February 1964);

F. Anthony Macklin, "The Comic Sense of 2001," *Film Comment* (Winter 1969);

Macklin, "Sex and Dr. Strangelove," *Film Comment*, III (Summer 1965);

Stephen Mamber, "A Clockwork Orange," *Cinema*, VII (Winter 1972-1973);

Annette Michelson, "Bodies in Space," *Artforum* (February 1969);

Tom Milne, "How I Learned to Stop Worrying and Love Stanley Kubrick," *Sight and Sound* (Spring 1964);

Gene D. Philips, *Stanley Kubrick: A Film Odyssey* (New York: Popular Library, 1975);

Joanne Stang, "Film Fan to Film Maker," *New York Times Magazine*, 12 October 1958;

Loudon Wainwright, "The Strange Case of Strangelove," *Life* (13 March 1964);

Alexander Walker, *Stanley Kubrick Directs* (New York: Harcourt Brace Jovanovich, 1971).

Ring Lardner, Jr.

(19 August 1915-   )

Joyce Olin

SELECTED MOTION PICTURES: *Meet Dr. Christian* (RKO-Radio, 1939), screenplay by Lardner, Ian McLellan Hunter, and Harvey Gates;

The Courageous Dr. Christian (RKO-Radio, 1940), screen story and screenplay by Lardner and Hunter;

Woman of the Year (M-G-M, 1942), screen story and screenplay by Lardner and Michael Kanin;

The Cross of Lorraine (M-G-M, 1944), screenplay by Lardner, Kanin, Alexander Esway, and Robert Andrews;

Tomorrow the World (United Artists, 1944), screenplay by Lardner and Leopold Atlas;

Cloak and Dagger (Warner Bros., 1946), screenplay by Lardner and Albert Maltz;

Forever Amber (20th Century-Fox, 1947), screenplay by Lardner and Philip Dunne;

The Forbidden Street (20th Century-Fox, 1949), screenplay;

Four Days Leave (Film Classics, 1950), additional dialogue;

Virgin Island (Films-Around-the-World, 1959), screenplay by Lardner and Hunter as Philip Rush and by Pat Jackson;

The Cincinnati Kid (M-G-M, 1965), screenplay by Lardner and Terry Southern;

M*A*S*H (20th Century-Fox, 1970), screenplay;

The Greatest (Columbia, 1977), screenplay.

BOOKS: *The Ecstasy of Owen Muir* (London: Cape, 1954; New York: Cameron & Kahn, 1954);

The Lardners: My Family Remembered (New York: Harper & Row, 1976).

Ring Lardner, Jr., 1937

The screenwriting career of Ring Lardner, Jr., began in 1937 at Selznick International Pictures, was disrupted from 1947 to 1963 when he was blacklisted in the film and television industries, and resumed in 1965 with his screen credit for *The Cincinnati Kid*. The son of Ellis Abbot and sportswriter and humorist Ring Lardner, Lardner grew up in a journalistic household. After a two-year stint at Princeton, he worked briefly for the *New York Daily Mirror* in 1935. Hoping to learn the movie business, Lardner traveled to Hollywood and was signed to a contract by David O. Selznick which specified that

Selznick could assign Lardner to any sort of work he wanted him to do. After giving Lardner a screen test, Selznick decided he should become a writer and assigned him to the studio publicity department, where Lardner worked from 1936 to 1937. He married Silvia Schulman, Selznick's secretary, in 1937; they had two children. Lardner met Budd Schulberg, who was working in the story department, and they collaborated on two screenplays that they hoped would impress Selznick. Selznick apparently read neither, but Lardner and Schulberg did get to rewrite (without credit) the final scene of *A Star Is Born* (1937), providing the scene in which Vicki Lester identifies herself as Mrs. Norman Maine.

Lardner was next assigned to rewrite the ending of Ben Hecht's screenplay for *Nothing Sacred* (1938). In 1937 he began attending Marxist study

Spencer Tracy and Katharine Hepburn in Woman of the Year, *for which screenwriters Lardner and Michael Kanin won an Academy Award*

groups along with Budd and Virginia Schulberg. In 1938, frustrated by the lack of opportunities with Selznick, he moved over to the B-picture unit at Warner Bros., hoping to get some practical experience as a writer. He found that instead of writing new screenplays, he was only supposed to rewrite scripts from Warner's huge backlog of properties. He prepared two such scripts, but neither was produced.

At the recommendation of writer Jerry Wald, Lardner was promoted to the Warner's A unit and was assigned to work on an adaptation of a screen story by Dalton Trumbo, which was used as the basis of *The Kid from Kokomo* (1939). Lardner found that his script was to be used only as a guideline for two other writers. In the fall of 1938 he left Warner Bros. to work with Ian McLellan Hunter on a project for RKO. It was never filmed, but Lardner and Hunter did write two films based on Jean Hersholt's

"Dr. Christian" radio series: *Meet Dr. Christian* (1939) and *The Courageous Dr. Christian* (1940). Both pictures were criticized for their formulaic presentation of the infallible, kindly, country doctor who invariably heals all physical, emotional, and social ills.

After working on an unproduced screenplay with Austrian writer Fritz Potter, Lardner cowrote *Woman of the Year* with Michael Kanin in 1942. They sent a ninety-page version of the story to Katharine Hepburn, who liked it and sent it directly to Louis B. Mayer, suggesting it as her next project for M-G-M. She negotiated the deal for Lardner and Kanin herself, thinking correctly that she would have more bargaining power than two unknown writers. Lardner and Kanin received $100,000 each for their script.

Woman of the Year is the story of an intense, sophisticated newspaper woman (Hepburn), respected in the world of international reporting, who falls in love with and marries an easygoing sportswriter (Spencer Tracy). The conflict centers on the questions of men's and women's roles and where to draw the line between professional and personal lives. *Woman of the Year* won Lardner and Kanin an Academy Award and upped their salaries from $250 to $1000 a week. It was the first of nine movies starring Hepburn and Spencer Tracy.

Lardner and Kanin next collaborated on *Marriage Is a Private Affair* (1944) for M-G-M, but the script was rewritten in order to build up the Lana Turner character and according to Lardner had no resemblance to their original script. They received no screen credit. Their final joint effort for M-G-M was *The Cross of Lorraine* (1944), a propaganda film about a French prisoner of war. It is a grim depiction of the capitulation of the French army, told through a group of men who surrender and are taken to a Nazi prison camp but regain the energy and commitment to fight for a free France.

In 1944 Lardner also cowrote an adaptation of the Broadway play *Tomorrow the World*, about a Nazi teenager (Skip Homeier) who is brought to the United States by an uncle (Fredric March) after the deaths of his parents in a concentration camp. Believing Nazi dogma, the boy hates the memory of his father, who was an anti-Nazi intellectual; he tries to inculcate racial intolerance and anti-Semitism in the small Midwestern town and to steal war department documents from his uncle. Following this, Lardner worked without credit on *Laura* (1944).

During the next two years Lardner worked on several unproduced scripts, including "Up Front" (based on Bill Mauldin cartoons) on which he collaborated with his brother John, who was writing for *Newsweek* and the *New Yorker*. Lardner's next film was *Cloak and Dagger* (1946), a melodramatic spy film about the OSS directed by Fritz Lang.

Lardner's first marriage had ended in divorce in 1945, and he married actress Frances Chaney in 1946. They have a son, James.

Roger Bowen, Donald Sutherland, Tom Skerritt, John Schuck, Fred Williamson, and Elliott Gould in a scene from M*A*S*H. *Lardner's screenplay won an Oscar and a Writers Guild Award.*

Lardner went to work at 20th Century-Fox. Under Otto Preminger he was asked to collaborate with Philip Dunne on a rewrite of Dunne's script for *Forever Amber* (1947), about a lower-class beauty who, through a series of marriages and lovers, makes her way up the ladder of Restoration society to the court of Charles II. The screenplay encountered many censorship problems, and the final film was considerably tamer than the novel on which it was based.

The Forbidden Street (1949), based on the novel *Britannia Mews* by Margery Sharp, was Lardner's last script before his testimony before the House Un-American Activities Committee and subsequent blacklisting at the studios. When he was questioned in 1947 by Congressman J. Parnell Thomas about his political activities, Lardner's response was "I could answer the way you want, Mr. Chairman, but I'd hate myself in the morning." His silent resistance resulted in an indictment for contempt of Congress, and he served nine months of a one-year sentence (in 1950-1951) at the Federal Correctional Institution in Danbury, Connecticut. It was at Danbury that Lardner began work on his novel, *The Ecstasy of Owen Muir* (1954), first published in England by Jonathan Cape. Lardner had difficulty finding an American publisher because of the blacklisting.

In 1950 Lardner was able to find work contributing additional dialogue to the film *Four Days Leave*, about an American soldier in Switzerland. The next year, he wrote for Joseph Losey (also a victim of the blacklist) *The Big Night* (1951), a melodrama about a rebellious teenager; he received no credit. After that, he was forced to work anonymously. Most of his work was for television; with Ian McLellan Hunter, also blacklisted, he wrote for the British television programs *Sir Lancelot* and *The Adventures of Robin Hood*. He and Hunter also wrote the film *Virgin Island* (1959) under the joint pseudonym Philip Rush.

In the early 1960s, Ingo Preminger, brother of Otto, became Lardner's agent and got him a job rewriting the film *A Breath of Scandal* (1960). While working on the film, Lardner employed the name Rick Spencer, but received no screen credit, pseudonymously or otherwise. At his brother's suggestion, Otto Preminger hired Lardner to adapt Patrick Dennis's novel *Genius*, but the project was abandoned.

Sam Peckinpah hired Lardner to adapt Richard Jessup's novel *The Cincinnati Kid*, about backroom gambling in New Orleans. Peckinpah was fired and replaced by Norman Jewison, who had Lardner's script rewritten by Terry Southern, but

Lardner still received credit when the film was released in 1965, his first under his own name since the blacklist began.

When Ingo Preminger became a motion-picture producer, he hired Lardner to write his first film. *M*A*S*H* (1970), based on a novel about the Korean War written by a former army surgeon under the pseudonym Richard Hooker, established Lardner again as a major studio writer for 20th Century-Fox, the same studio that had helped consign him to the blacklist twenty-two years earlier. The film follows surgeons Hawkeye (Donald Sutherland), Trapper John (Elliot Gould), and Duke (Tom Skerritt) while they, as Lardner put it, "maintain sanity in the rampant insanity of war" by being alternately nasty and compassionate, indulging in pranks, morbid operating room humor, and demonstrating general belligerence toward military order. In commenting on the screenplay, Lardner has said that "a lot of words had been wasted . . . discussing whether or not it was an 'antiwar film.' . . . This one does have an incidental comment to make about a special kind of war, an American one on the Asian mainland, and our habit of taking our culture along with us and ignoring the local variety. . . ." *M*A*S*H* won Lardner the Academy Award for Best Screenplay of 1970 and the Writers Guild Award. The film won the Cannes Film Festi-

Lardner, 1977

val Grand Prix and was nominated for Oscars for best picture and best director (Robert Altman).

Following *M*A*S*H*, Lardner devoted less of his time to screenwriting and more to writing fiction and nonfiction. He explained that this was the result of his having been blacklisted. "In a way it was good for me. I had been quite successful as a screenwriter quite young, and it would have been hard to resist the temptation to continue in that field. As a result

of the blacklist, I wrote a novel and got away from southern California." Lardner worked without credit on the thriller *The Deadly Trap* (1972) and wrote scripts for television and articles for magazines. His family history, *The Lardners*, was published in 1976. In 1977, he wrote the screenplay for *The Greatest*, a film adaptation of Muhammad Ali's autobiography.

Arthur Laurents
(14 July 1918-   )

Dale Winogura

MOTION PICTURES: *Rope* (Warner Bros., 1948), screenplay;
Caught (M-G-M, 1949), screenplay;
Anna Lucasta (Columbia, 1949), screenplay by Laurents and Philip Yordan;
Anastasia (20th Century-Fox, 1956), screenplay;
Bonjour Tristesse (Columbia, 1958), screenplay;
The Way We Were (Columbia, 1973), screenplay adapted by Laurents from his novel;
The Turning Point (20th Century-Fox, 1977), screenplay.

PLAYS: *Home of the Brave* (New York, Belasco Theatre, 27 December 1945);
Heartsong (New Haven, Shubert Theatre, 27 February 1947);
The Bird Cage (New York, Coronet Theatre, 22 February 1950);
The Time of the Cuckoo (New York, Empire Theatre, 15 October 1952);
A Clearing in the Woods (New York, Belasco Theatre, 10 January 1957);
West Side Story (New York, Winter Garden Theatre, 26 September 1957), book;
Gypsy (New York, Broadway Theatre, 21 May 1959);
Invitation to a March (New York, Music Box Theatre, 29 October 1960);
Anyone Can Whistle (New York, Majestic Theatre, 4 April 1964), book;
Do I Hear a Waltz? (New York, Forty-sixth Street Theatre, 15 March 1965), book;
Hallelujah, Baby! (New York, Martin Beck Theatre, 27 April 1967), book;

Arthur Laurents

The Enclave (New York, Theatre Four, 15 November 1973);
Scream (Houston, Alley Theatre, 1978);
The Madwoman of Central Park West (New York, 22 Steps, 13 June 1979), by Laurents and Phyllis Newman.

James Stewart, Douglas Dick, Joan Chandler, Sir Cedric Hardwicke, Constance Collier, John Dall,
and Farley Granger in a scene from Rope

BOOKS: *Home of the Brave* (New York: Random House, 1946);

The Bird Cage (New York: Dramatists Play Service, 1950);

The Time of the Cuckoo (New York: Random House, 1953);

A Clearing in the Woods (New York: Random House, 1957; revised edition, New York: Dramatists Play Service, 1960);

West Side Story (New York: Random House, 1958; London: Heinemann, 1959);

Gypsy (New York: Random House, 1960);

Invitation to a March (New York: Random House, 1961);

Anyone Can Whistle (New York: Random House, 1965);

Do I Hear a Waltz? (New York: Random House, 1966);

The Way We Were (New York: Harper & Row, 1972; London: Allen, 1973);

The Enclave (New York: Dramatists Play Service, 1974);

The Turning Point (New York: NAL, 1977; London: Corgi, 1978).

Arthur Laurents is a successful playwright who writes only occasionally for the screen. Most of his screenplays are romantic melodramas, ranging from the Gothic and bleak (*Caught*, 1949) to the elegant (*Anastasia*, 1956), to the socially relevant (*The Way We Were*, 1973).

Born in New York City, the son of Irving and Ada Robbins Laurents, he graduated from Cornell University in 1937. He started writing for radio and, after serving in the army during World War II, received a Variety radio award in 1945 for his *Assignment: Home* series. Also in 1945 he wrote his first play, *Home of the Brave*. Based on his experiences during the war, this play deals sentimentally, but honestly, with prejudice against a Jewish soldier.

His success as a playwright brought Laurents to Hollywood in 1948. The first screenplay he worked on was *The Snake Pit* (1948), but he had little to do with the final film and received no screen credit. That same year he worked with Alfred Hitchcock to adapt Patrick Hamilton's one-set play, *Rope*, a fictionalization of the Leopold-Loeb case. For his work Laurents received his first screen credit. The challenge of *Rope* was to make a simple, theatrical play cinematic. In the film two young men (John Dall and Farley Granger) murder a friend for thrills and then hide the body in a chest, on which they serve dinner to guests. They drop clues to the crime throughout the dinner party, and one of the guests (James Stewart), a professor who taught them Nietzsche's "Superman" philosophy, gradually realizes what they have done. From the film's opening moments, when the body is first hidden in the chest, suspense and terror build. Hitchcock's daring use of smooth ten-minute takes—although it dominates the film—never detracts from Lau-

rents's script. The adaptation also remains close to the original play, restricting Laurents's own writing personality to a degree. (There have been reports that Ben Hecht wrote much of the screenplay, but Laurents says none of Hecht's work was used.)

Laurents's screenwriting style comes through more clearly in *Caught*, directed by Max Ophuls. Believing she must find a rich husband to be truly happy, department-store model Lenora Ames (Barbara Bel Geddes) marries neurotic millionaire Smith Ohlig (Robert Ryan), who alternately mistreats and neglects her after their marriage. She leaves Ohlig, goes to work for Dr. Quinada (James Mason), who runs a ghetto clinic, and falls in love with him. Quinada, who knows nothing about her past, wishes to marry her, but Ohlig promises her he will change and convinces her to return. After Lenora spends one night with her husband, she realizes he will never change and returns to Quinada, only to discover she is pregnant. Ohlig promises her a divorce if she will give him custody of

Ingrid Bergman and Yul Brynner in Anastasia

Shirley MacLaine, Anne Bancroft, Tom Skerritt, and Phillip Saunders in The Turning Point

the child; she refuses but subsequently has a miscarriage and is granted her divorce. *Caught* might have become ludicrous melodrama in the wrong hands, but Laurents carefully avoids clichés and deals with his material sensitively.

That same year he adapted *Anna Lucasta* (1949), Philip Yordan's play about a promiscuous woman (Paulette Goddard) whose boyfriend leaves her when he finds out her true nature. The film failed critically and commercially. Laurents next wrote another play, *The Time of the Cuckoo* (1952), which later became one of David Lean's finest films, *Summertime* (1955), about a spinster traveling in Europe who falls in love with a married man. The screenplay maintains the play's delicate wit and romanticism, much to the film's advantage.

A good, but stagy, adaptation of Marcelle Maurette's play *Anastasia* was Laurents's next film, directed by Anatole Litvak and released in 1956. Based on the case of Anna Anderson, who claimed to be the only survivor of the assassinated family of Czar Nicholas II, the film depicts a man (Yul Brynner) trying to train a seeming impostor (Ingrid Bergman, who won an Oscar) to be exactly like

Anastasia. The man soon falls in love with his creation, who may or may not be the real missing daughter of the czar. Laurents wisely kept the romantic element inconspicuous and subtle, never interfering with the dramatic progression.

Following *Anastasia*, Laurents worked on an adaptation of Françoise Sagan's novel *Bonjour Tristesse*, about a teenaged girl (Jean Seberg) who tries to end the romance between her widowed father (David Niven) and his mistress (Deborah Kerr). Directed by Otto Preminger, the 1958 film is expressively austere, but many critics found it a heavy-handed interpretation of Sagan's existential ideals.

Laurents did not write another screenplay for fifteen years. He spent that time working on a series of musical plays, most notably *West Side Story* (1957) and *Gypsy* (1959). He also completed a novel, *The Way We Were* (1972), which became the basis for his 1973 film of the same name, a love story with political undertones, directed by Sydney Pollack. The first half of the film details the offbeat romance of two opposites, liberal Jewish Katie (Barbra Streisand) and conservative waspish Hubbell (Robert Redford), while the remainder shows the romance's dissolution by the McCarthy hearings of the early 1950s. Though it is Katie's activist character that provides the major cause for their separation, Hubbell's apparently innocent association with party members is the catalyst. In the long run both of them prove to be equally responsible for the breakup of their marriage, but Laurents never judges them bluntly or insensitively. *The Way We Were* was harmed by prerelease cutting that removed much of the political subplot, but it remains a successful film.

Laurents's next film, *The Turning Point* (1977), was undeniably personal to him and the film's director, Herbert Ross, as it examines the close relationship between life and art. A former ballerina turned dance instructor, Deedee (Shirley MacLaine) finds herself at odds with an old friend, Emma (Anne Bancroft), now a successful ballerina.

Deedee also sees her daughter (Leslie Browne) making some of her own past mistakes in life and love. Ross's direction resulted in a film with broad and sentimental characterizations, but *The Turning Point* received eleven Academy Award nominations, including those for best picture, best screenplay, best director, best actress (Bancroft and MacLaine), best supporting actress (Browne) and best supporting actor (Mikhail Baryshnikov). Despite this recognition, Laurents has written no more screenplays, but has instead occupied himself with his work in the theater.

Arthur Laurents has intelligently adapted works by others into some of the best romantic films ever made. Despite the sparsity of his work, he remains an important screenwriter, creating scripts in a genre that has otherwise been almost completely abandoned.

Charles Lederer
(31 December 1910-5 March 1976)

Scott Levine

MOTION PICTURES: *The Front Page* (United Artists, 1931), dialogue by Lederer and Bartlett Cormack; filmed again as *His Girl Friday* (Columbia, 1940), screenplay;
Cock of the Air (United Artists, 1932), story and screenplay by Lederer and Robert E. Sherwood;
Double or Nothing (Paramount, 1937), screenplay by Lederer, Erwin Gelsey, John C. Moffitt, and Duke Atteberry;
Mountain Music (Paramount, 1937), screenplay by Lederer, Moffitt, Atteberry, and Russel Crouse;
Broadway Serenade (M-G-M, 1939), screenplay;
Within the Law (M-G-M, 1939), screenplay by Lederer and Edith Fitzgerald;
Comrade X (M-G-M, 1940), screenplay by Lederer and Ben Hecht;
I Love You Again (M-G-M, 1940), screenplay by Lederer and George Oppenheimer;
Love Crazy (M-G-M, 1941), screenplay by Lederer, William Ludwig, and David Hertz;
The Youngest Profession (M-G-M, 1943), screenplay by Lederer, Oppenheimer, and Leonard Spigelgass;

Slightly Dangerous (M-G-M, 1943), screenplay by Lederer and Oppenheimer;
Her Husband's Affairs (Columbia, 1947), screen story and screenplay by Lederer and Hecht;
Kiss of Death (20th Century-Fox, 1947), screenplay by Lederer and Hecht;
Ride the Pink Horse (Universal, 1947), screenplay by Lederer and Hecht;
I Was a Male War Bride (20th Century-Fox, 1949), screenplay by Lederer, Spigelgass, and Hagar Wilde;
Red, Hot and Blue (Paramount, 1949), story;
Wabash Avenue (20th Century-Fox, 1950), screen story and screenplay by Lederer and Harry Turgend;
The Thing (RKO, 1951), screenplay;
Fearless Fagan (M-G-M, 1952), screenplay;
Monkey Business (20th Century-Fox, 1952), screenplay by Lederer, Hecht, and I. A. L. Diamond;
Gentlemen Prefer Blondes (20th Century-Fox, 1953), screenplay;
Kismet (M-G-M, 1955), screenplay by Lederer and Luther Davis;
Gaby (M-G-M, 1956), screenplay by Lederer, Frances Goodrich, and Albert Hackett;

Adolphe Menjou and Pat O'Brien in The Front Page

The Spirit of St. Louis (Warner Bros., 1957), adaptation;

Tip on a Dead Jockey (M-G-M, 1957), screenplay;

Never Steal Anything Small (Universal, 1959), screen story and screenplay;

It Started with a Kiss (M-G-M, 1959), screenplay;

Can-Can (20th Century-Fox, 1960), screenplay by Lederer and Dorothy Kingsley;

Ocean's Eleven (Warner Bros., 1960), screenplay by Lederer and Harry Brown;

Follow That Dream (United Artists, 1962), screenplay;

Mutiny on the Bounty (M-G-M, 1962), screenplay;

A Global Affair (M-G-M, 1964), screenplay by Lederer, Arthur Marx, and Robert Fisher.

PLAY: *Kismet*, by Lederer and Luther Davis (New York, Ziegfeld Theatre, 3 December 1953).

Charles Lederer was born in New York City, the son of two then-prominent figures in the American theater—producer George Lederer and singer Reine Davies. After his parents were separated in 1912, Lederer and his sister, Pepi, were raised by his mother's sister, actress Marion Davies, the protégée of William Randolph Hearst. Lederer detested his dependence on Hearst's support of the family and separated himself from Hearst's patronage as he grew older. His relationship with Hearst affected his later work: his screenplays frequently delve into the corrosive influences of wealth and power.

After graduating from the University of California, Lederer began a career in journalism. When he was nineteen, he became friends with Ben Hecht, who introduced him to the New York literati, especially the members of the Round Table group that met at the Algonquin Hotel. The friendship with Hecht led to Lederer's being hired in 1931 to write additional dialogue for the film version of Hecht and Charles MacArthur's 1928 play *The Front Page*. The next year, he collaborated with Robert E. Sherwood on *Cock of the Air* (1932), a comedy about an army air force lieutenant (Chester Morris) who flies his fiancée from Italy to Paris so she can drink champagne at the Ritz bar. In 1933, he made contributions to Hecht's screenplay for *Topaze*, but neither of them received screen credit.

Following *Topaze*, Lederer was largely inactive in film work, not receiving another screen credit until 1937, when he collaborated on two musicals, *Double or Nothing* and *Mountain Music*. His first solo screenplay, *Broadway Serenade* (1939), was a thinly plotted vehicle for Jeanette MacDonald, who played a singer whose career ruins her marriage to her songwriter husband (Lew Ayres).

Lederer married Virginia Welles, former wife of Orson Welles, in 1940. That same year he wrote what has remained his most popular and critically acclaimed screenplay, *His Girl Friday*, a remake of *The Front Page*. At the suggestion of the film's director, Howard Hawks, Lederer changed the sex of the lead character, Hildy Johnson, from male to female (played by Rosalind Russell) and then complicated the situation by making her the former wife of Walter Burns (Cary Grant), the tyrannical editor. The basic plot of the story is retained, as is much of the original dialogue. In fact, Lederer's greatest achievement in restructuring the original was his ability to change the context of the biting repartee from that of an entirely male world to one of a once-married couple.

From 1940 to 1943 Lederer worked at M-G-M, where he wrote a series of light comedies, usually centering on mismatched couples. *Comrade X* (1940), written in collaboration with Ben Hecht and directed by King Vidor, is the story of an American in Russia (Clark Gable) who falls in love with a streetcar conductor (Hedy Lamarr). More successful was his collaboration with George Oppenheimer on *I Love You Again* (1940), about a respected small-town citizen (William Powell) who becomes an amnesiac and reverts to his earlier way of life as a con man. Matters are complicated by the attempts of his confused wife (Myrna Loy) to divorce him. Powell and Loy also starred in *Love Crazy* (1941), a screwball comedy about a married couple who separate due to a misunderstanding. Lederer then worked with Leonard Spigelgass and Oppenheimer on *The Youngest Profession* (1943), about young autograph hunters stalking M-G-M stars, and then reteamed with Oppenheimer on *Slightly Dangerous* (1943). Designed as Lana Turner's first comedy, the film is about a waitress (Turner) who loses her job, feigns amnesia, is adopted by a millionaire (Walter Brennan) who has mistaken her for

Cary Grant and Rosalind Russell in His Girl Friday, *the 1940 remake of* The Front Page

his long-lost daughter, and then marries the man who fired her (Robert Young).

After leaving M-G-M, Lederer went through another unproductive period before teaming with Hecht to write two highly successful films noirs: *Kiss of Death* and *Ride the Pink Horse* (both 1947). Directed by Henry Hathaway, *Kiss of Death* centers on small-time criminal Nick Bianco (Victor Mature) who is pressured by the police, first to become an informer and then to testify against killer Tommy Udo (Richard Widmark). Lederer's attitudes toward the misuse of power are revealed when Bianco is caught between cruel forces: criminal elements (calculating and homicidal) and the law (dangerous because of its arrogance). *Kiss of Death* was praised for its carefully balanced mixture of realism and melodrama; particularly effective is the well-known scene in which Udo pushes an old woman in a wheelchair down a flight of stairs.

Based on the novel by Dorothy B. Hughes, *Ride the Pink Horse* is about a mysterious former GI, Gagin (Robert Montgomery), who appears at a fiesta in a small New Mexico town. Gagin, who has come to blackmail gangster Frank Hugo (Fred Clark), is being followed in turn by F.B.I. agent Bill Retz (Art Smith), who wants the incriminating material Gagin has on Hugo. The aloof and friendless Gagin gradually changes his outlook after meeting an Indian girl (Wanda Hendrix), and Retz kills Hugo.

After collaborating again with Hecht on a slight comedy, *Her Husband's Affairs* (1947), Lederer was hired by Howard Hawks to work on *I Was a Male War Bride* (1949), about a French army officer (Cary Grant) who marries a WAC. He then finds that he must be classified as a war bride and even has to disguise himself as a woman to get past some overzealous military police onto the boat that will bring him to America.

Between 1949—the year of his second marriage, to actress Anne Shirley—and 1953, Lederer wrote six pictures. Three of them were inconsequential: he wrote the story for *Red, Hot and Blue* (1949), a Betty Hutton vehicle; collaborated on the screen story and screenplay for *Wabash Avenue* (1950), a Betty Grable musical and a remake of her earlier *Coney Island* (1943); and wrote the screenplay for *Fearless Fagan* (1952), about a young man who enters the army with his pet lion. His other films from this period were written for Howard Hawks and became his most highly regarded screenplays: *The Thing* (1951), *Monkey Business* (1952), and *Gentlemen Prefer Blondes* (1953).

The Thing is based on a short story by noted science-fiction writer John W. Campbell, Jr., in which an Antarctic military base is invaded by an alien creature that can take human guise. Hawks read the story while shooting *I Was a Male War Bride*, was impressed with it, and had Lederer prepare the screenplay in less than a week. (Ben Hecht is also believed to have worked on the script, but he received no screen credit, and, while Hawks received only producer credit, some believe that he, not his former film editor Christian Nyby, directed the film as well.) Lederer's screenplay deviates greatly from Campbell's story, making the monster a vegetablelike creature rather than one that changes shape. The script maintains suspense as scientists protect the alien for the glory of knowledge, even after it begins to pose a great threat to the community's safety and eventually causes violent death. The head scientist, who continues to sabotage efforts to destroy the intruder, is repaid for his efforts by being killed by the monster, which is then destroyed by the men. Lederer's dialogue is particularly adept at portraying the easy camaraderie in such relationships as that between Captain Patrick Henry (Ken Tobey) and a scientist's secretary, Nikki Nicholson (Margaret Sheridan). Their banter is similar to but more tender than the repartee in *His Girl Friday*. *The Thing* received mixed reviews but was one of the top-grossing movies of 1951.

The following year, Lederer and Hecht joined forces with I. A. L. Diamond for *Monkey Business*, in which an absentminded scientist, Barnaby Fulton (Cary Grant), who is working on a youth elixir, inadvertently swallows a potion concocted by a lab chimpanzee. Suddenly shedding his inhibitions, he acts like a happy child, and, because the potion has been dumped into a water cooler, other characters, including Fulton's wife, Edwina (Ginger Rogers), drink it also and begin to behave with infantile abandon. Lederer had dealt with the sudden release of repressed personalities in earlier films, particularly *I Love You Again* and *Mountain Music*, but this film was his most successful exploration of the theme.

Gentlemen Prefer Blondes, one of Lederer's solo efforts, was adapted from Anita Loos's 1925 novel, the subsequent 1926 stage hit and 1928 film by Loos and her husband, John Emerson, and the successful 1949 musical play. Lederer's film version depicts two golddiggers, blonde Lorelei Lee (Marilyn Monroe) and brunette Dorothy Shaw (Jane Russell), who sail to Europe on a trip sponsored by Lorelei's rich and naive fiancé, Gus Esmond (Tommy Noonan). After several musical numbers and a

Marilyn Monroe and Jane Russell in the 1953 version of Gentlemen Prefer Blondes

series of minor crises, the two women become brides together in a double ceremony. *Gentlemen Prefer Blondes* was a great commercial and critical success. One of its most enthusiastic critics was Loos, who said that Lederer "had made the perfect transition of my book of which every novelist dreams. Hardly an incident of the story survived but Charlie's replacements were so much in character; his motivations so utterly correct, that the flavor of the novel remained intact."

Lederer next took a year off from screenwriting to work with Luther Davis on a musical version of Edward Knoblock's 1911 play, *Kismet*, set in the time of the Arabian Nights and centering on an itinerant poet who clashes with an evil wazir. Lederer also produced the play, which opened on 3 December 1953 and ran for 583 performances. It won a Tony Award in 1954, and the next year Lederer and Davis collaborated on a film adaptation, which was unable to duplicate the play's success.

Lederer next collaborated with Frances Goodrich and Albert Hackett on *Gaby* (1956), a remake of the film *Waterloo Bridge* (1940), itself based on a play by Robert E. Sherwood. In *Gaby* Leslie Caron plays a ballerina who falls in love with a soldier during World War II. Lederer then began work with Billy Wilder on *The Spirit of St. Louis* (1957), based on Charles Lindbergh's autobiographical account of his flight over the Atlantic, but he quarreled with Wilder and left the project. Wilder finished the film with Wendell Mayes, and Lederer was credited as adaptor.

The Spirit of St. Louis was Lederer's last significant film work. Of the eight films that followed, most were vehicles for established stars—Frank Sinatra (*Can-Can* and *Ocean's Eleven*, both 1960), Elvis Presley (*Follow That Dream*, 1962), Bob Hope (*A Global Affair*, 1964)—made by minor directors. Lederer's only attempt at directing one of his own screenplays was *Never Steal Anything Small* (1959). (He had earlier directed, but not written, *Fingers at the Window*, 1942, and *On the Loose*, 1951.) Based on a play by Maxwell Anderson and Rouben Mamoulian, *Never Steal Anything Small* is a musical comedy-drama about a labor leader desperate to win a union election. Lederer's penultimate film, a remake of *Mutiny on the Bounty* (1962), was also his final collaboration with Ben Hecht (who again worked without credit). While critics differed in their opinions of the merits of this film, nearly all agreed it was inferior to the original 1935 version.

Charles Lederer often produced lively adaptations and worked well in collaboration with others, but when an original play or story was frail or when the other members of his writing team did not possess the genius of a Ben Hecht, Lederer's writing lost the sparkle and wit present in his best screenplays. He deserves recognition for his acerbic adaptations and collaborative screenplays of the 1940s and early 1950s.

Anita Loos
(26 April 1893-18 August 1981)

Joanne Yeck

See also the Loos entries in *DLB 11, American Humorists, 1800-1950,* and *DLB Yearbook 81*.

SELECTED MOTION PICTURES: *The New York Hat* (Biograph, 1912), scenario;
The Power of the Camera (Biograph, 1913), scenario;
A Horse on Bill (Biograph, 1913), scenario;
A Hicksville Epicure (Biograph, 1913), scenario;
Highbrow Love (Biograph, 1913), scenario;
Pa Says (Biograph, 1913), scenario;
The Widow's Kids (Biograph, 1913), scenario;
The Lady in Black (Biograph, 1913), scenario;
His Hoodoo (Biograph, 1913), scenario;
A Fallen Hero (Biograph, 1913), scenario
A Cure for Suffragettes (Biograph, 1913), scenario;
The Suicide Pact (Biograph, 1913), scenario;
Bink's Vacation (Biograph, 1913), scenario;
How the Day Was Saved (Biograph, 1913), scenario;
The Wedding Gown (Biograph, 1913), scenario;
A Bunch of Flowers (Biograph, 1914), scenario;
When a Woman Guides (Biograph, 1914), scenario;
The Road to Plaindale (Biograph, 1914), scenario;
The Saving Presence (Biograph, 1914), scenario;
The Meal Ticket (Biograph, 1914), scenario;
Where the Roads Part (American Film Manufacturing, 1914), scenario;
The Suffering of Susan (Biograph, 1914), scenario;
The Tear on the Page (Biograph, 1915), scenario;
Pennington's Choice (Metro Pictures, 1915), scenario;
A Corner in Cotton (Quality Pictures, 1916), scenario;
His Picture in the Papers (Triangle Film, 1916), scenario;
Macbeth (Lucky Film Producers, 1916), titles;
Intolerance (D. W. Griffith, 1916), titles;
In Again, Out Again (Artcraft Pictures, 1917), scenario;
Wild and Woolly (Artcraft Pictures, 1917), scenario;
Down to Earth (Artcraft Pictures, 1917), scenario;
Reaching for the Moon (Artcraft Pictures, 1917), scenario by Loos and John Emerson;
Let's Get a Divorce (Famous Players Lasky, 1918), scenario;
Hit-the-Trail Holiday (Famous Players Lasky, 1918), scenario by Loos and Emerson;
Come On In (Famous Players Lasky, 1918), scenario by Loos and Emerson;
Good-Bye Bill (Famous Players Lasky, 1918), scenario by Loos and Emerson;
Oh, You Women! (Famous Players Lasky, 1919), scenario by Loos and Emerson;
Getting Mary Married (Marion Davis Film Co., 1919), scenario by Loos and Emerson;
A Temperamental Wife (Constance Talmadge Film Co., 1919), scenario by Loos and Emerson;
A Virtuous Vamp (Joseph M. Schenck, 1919), scenario by Loos and Emerson;
The Isle of Conquest (Select Pictures, 1919), scenario by Loos and Emerson;
In Search of a Sinner (Joseph M. Schenck, 1920), scenario by Loos and Emerson;
The Perfect Woman (First National, 1920), scenario by Loos and Emerson;
The Love Expert (Joseph M. Schenck, 1920), scenario by Loos and Emerson;
Two Weeks (First National, 1920), scenario by Loos and Emerson;
The Branded Woman (Joseph M. Schenck, 1920), scenario by Loos and Albert Parker;
Dangerous Business (First National, 1921), scenario by Loos and Emerson;
Mama's Affair (First National, 1921), scenario by Loos and Emerson;
A Woman's Place (Joseph M. Schenck, 1921), scenario by Loos and Emerson;
Polly of the Follies (First National, 1922), scenario by Loos and Emerson;
Red Hot Romance (Joseph M. Schenck, 1922), scenario by Loos and Emerson;
The Americano (Tri-Stone Pictures, 1923), scenario by Loos and Emerson;
Dulcy (Joseph M. Schenck, 1923), scenario by Loos and Emerson;
Three Miles Out (Kenma, 1924), scenario by Loos and Emerson;
The Social Secretary (Tri-Stone Pictures, 1924), scenario by Loos and Emerson;
Learning to Love (First National, 1925), scenario by Loos and Emerson;
Stranded (Sterling Pictures, 1927), scenario;
Publicity Madness (Fox Film, 1927), scenario;
Gentlemen Prefer Blondes (Paramount Famous Lasky, 1928), screenplay adapted by Loos and Emer-

Hollywood's shortest writer, Anita Loos, teamed with the tallest director, Malcolm St. Clair, to make the 1928 screen version of Gentlemen Prefer Blondes.

son from their play;

The Struggle (D. W. Griffith, 1931), screenplay by Loos and Emerson;

Red-Headed Woman (M-G-M, 1932), screenplay;

Blondie of the Follies (M-G-M, 1932), dialogue;

The Barbarian (M-G-M, 1933), screenplay by Loos and Elmer Harris;

Hold Your Man (M-G-M, 1933), story; screenplay by Loos and Howard Emmett;

Midnight Mary (M-G-M, 1933), original story;

The Girl from Missouri (M-G-M, 1934), screenplay by Loos and Emerson;

Biography of a Bachelor Girl (M-G-M, 1934), screenplay;

Riffraff (M-G-M, 1936), screenplay by Loos, Frances Marion, and H. W. Hanemann;

San Francisco (M-G-M, 1936), screenplay;

Mama Steps Out (M-G-M, 1937), screenplay;

Saratoga (M-G-M, 1937), screenplay by Loos and Robert Hopkins;

The Women (M-G-M, 1939), screenplay by Loos and Jane Murfin;

Susan and God (M-G-M, 1940), screenplay;

They Met in Bombay (M-G-M, 1941), screenplay by

Loos, Edwin Justin Mayer, and Leon Gordon;

Blossoms in the Dust (M-G-M, 1941), screenplay;

When Ladies Meet (M-G-M, 1941), screenplay by Loos and S. K. Lauren;

I Married an Angel (M-G-M, 1942), screenplay.

Between 1912 and 1928 Loos wrote over 100 films. According to her book *Cast of Thousands*, the following is a list of films Loos claims to have written but which cannot be located in the United States Catalog of Copyright Entries:

He Was a College Boy (1912);

The Earl and the Tomboy (1912);

A Hicksville Romance (1913);

A Fireman's Love (1913);

Fall of Hicksville's Finest (1913);

Yiddish Love (1913);

Gentlemen and Thieves (1913);

The Deacon's Whiskers (1913);

His Awful Vengeance (1913);

All for Mabel (1913);

The Fatal Deception (1913);

For Her Father's Sins (1913);

Unlucky Jim (1913);

All on Account of a Cold (1913);

The Saving Grace (1913);

A Narrow Escape (1913);

Two Women (1913);

The Wall Flower (1913);

Queen of the Carnival (1913);

The Mayor Elect (1913);

The Making of a Masher (1913);

Path of True Love (1913);

A Girl Like Mother (1913);

The Mother (1913);

The Great Motor Race (1913);

The Chieftain's Daughter (Some Bull's Daughter, 1914);

The Fatal Dress Suit (1914);

The Girl in the Shack (1914);

His Hated Rival (1914);

A Corner in Hats (1914);

Nearly a Burglar's Bride (1914);

The Fatal Curve (1914);

The Million-Dollar Bride (1914);

A Flurry in Art (1914);

Nellie, the Female Villain (1914);

His Rival (1914);

A No Bull Spy (1914);

A Balked Heredity (1914);

A Blasted Romance (1914);

Mortimer's Millions (1914);

A Life and Death Affair (1914);

The Sensible Girl (1914);

At the Tunnel's End (1914);
The Deadly Glass of Beer (1914);
The Last Drink of Whiskey (1914);
Nell's Eugenic Wedding (1914);
The School of Acting (1914);
A Hicksville Reformer (1914);
The White Slave Catchers (1914);
The Style Accustomed (1914);
The Deceiver (1914);
How They Met (1914);
The Cost of a Bargain (1915);
Sympathy Sal (1915);
Nelly, the Female Victim (1915);
Mixed Values (1915);
How to Keep a Husband (1915);
The Burlesquers (1915);
The Fatal Fourth (1915);
The Fatal Fingerprints (1915);
Wards of Fate (1915);
Heart that Truly Loved (1915);
The Little Liar (1915);
Mountain Bred (1915);
Wild Girl of the Sierras (1916), with F. M. Pierson;
Calico Vampire (1916);
Laundry Liz (1916);
French Milliner (1916);
The Wharf Rat (1916);
The Half-Breed (1916);
The Great Canadian (1938).

SELECTED PLAYS: *The Whole Town's Talking* (New York, Bijou Theatre, 29 August 1923), by Loos and John Emerson;
The Fall of Eve (New York, Booth Theatre, 31 August 1925), by Loos and Emerson;
Gentlemen Prefer Blondes (New York, Times Square Theatre, 28 September 1926), by Loos and Emerson;
The Social Register (New York, Fulton Theatre, 9 November 1931), by Loos and Emerson;
Happy Birthday (New York, Broadhurst Theatre, 31 October 1946);
Gentlemen Prefer Blondes [musical] (New York, Ziegfeld Theatre, 8 Deeember 1949), book by Loos and Joseph Fields;
Gigi (New York, Fulton Theatre, 24 November 1951);
The Amazing Adele (Philadelphia, Shubert Theatre, 26 December 1955), book;
Chéri (New York, Morosco Theatre, 12 October 1959);
Gogo Loves You (New York, Theatre de Lys, 9 October 1964), book;
Lorelei; or Gentlemen Still Prefer Blondes (New York,

Palace Theatre, 27 January 1974).

BOOKS: *How to Write Photoplays*, by Loos and John Emerson (New York: McCann, 1920);
Breaking into the Movies, by Loos and Emerson (New York: McCann, 1921);
"Gentlemen Prefer Blondes": The Illuminating Diary of a Professional Lady (New York: Boni & Liveright, 1925; London: Brentano's, 1926);
"But Gentlemen Marry Brunettes" (New York: Boni & Liveright, 1928; London: Brentano's, 1928);
"The Struggle," by Loos and Emerson (New York: Griffith, 1931);
Happy Birthday: A Play in Two Acts (New York, Los Angeles & Toronto: French, 1947);
A Mouse Is Born (Garden City: Doubleday, 1951; London: Cape, 1951);
No Mother to Guide Her (New York, Toronto & London: McGraw-Hill, 1961; London: Barker, 1961);
A Girl Like I (New York: Viking, 1966; London: Hamilton, 1967);
Twice Over Lightly: New York Then and Now, by Loos and Helen Hayes (New York: Harcourt Brace Jovanovich, 1972);
Kiss Hollywood Good-by (New York: Viking, 1974; London: Allen, 1974);
Cast of Thousands (New York: Grosset & Dunlap, 1977);
The Talmadge Girls: A Memoir (New York: Viking, 1978);
San Francisco: A Screenplay (Carbondale & Edwardsville: Southern Illinois University Press, 1979).

OTHER: *The Women*, by Loos and Jane Murfin, in *Twenty Best Film Plays*, edited by John Gassner & Dudley Nichols (New York: Crown, 1943).

Anita Loos, one of the century's most gifted humorists, was the author of over 150 screenplays. Spanning three decades, her screenwriting career accompanied her success as a novelist and playwright. Loos helped to create what has come to be known as the "Golden Era" of Hollywood.

Born in Sisson (now Mount Shasta), California, to R. Beers and Minnie Ellen Smith Loos, Loos was one of three children. Her father introduced her to theater life at a young age. Loos became a star at age five.

At nineteen, Loos submitted an unsolicited "photoplay" to the Biograph Company. *The New York Hat* (1912) earned her twenty-five dollars and starred the not-yet-famous cast of Lillian and

Dorothy Gish, Mary Pickford, and Lionel Barrymore. By Loos's account, between 1912 and 1915 she wrote 105 scenarios, only 4 of which were rejected by Biograph. Even these were sold to lesser studios. A majority of the photoplays were slapstick comedies in the Keystone Cop tradition. She wrote and submitted one or two a month while acting in her father's San Diego stock company.

In early 1914, A. Loos (as she signed her early scripts, afraid the studio would reject plots from a woman) was invited to interview at Biograph. A discontented bride, she left her young husband after one night of marriage and headed for Hollywood. She was accompanied by her mother, who was mistaken for the "little lady" who had been sending her screenplays. Looking even younger than she was, with braids down her back and dressed in a sailor suit, Loos went to work for the silent era's greatest director, D. W. Griffith.

Against Griffith's strong admonition that "people don't go to the movies to read!," Loos introduced satire to the silent film. Her dialogue cards were bright with sharp wit, exposing her real talent for verbal comedy. Her first satirical success starred a robust young actor, Douglas Fairbanks. *His Picture in the Papers* (1916), produced by Triangle Company, was directed by John Emerson, who would become Loos's second husband. The comedy earned Loos $500, and she continued as the sole writer for the Fairbanks unit. The three worked together molding Fairbanks's comic persona. Loos admitted she spent most of her time dreaming up situations that could facilitate the famous Fairbanks leap.

As a result of the success of *His Picture in the Papers*, Griffith realized his mistake in mistrusting the written word on the screen. He ordered Loos to write the titles for his epic *Intolerance* (1916). Loos would later poke fun at the film and at Griffith in her novel *"Gentlemen Prefer Blondes"* (1925).

After ten films for the Triangle Company and Fairbanks's own production company, the Emerson-Loos-Fairbanks group broke up. Emerson and Loos worked at various studios: Paramount, First National, and Cosmopolitan Pictures. At First National, Loos scripted eleven films

Lobby poster and scene from the 1936 film starring Clark Gable as Blackie Norton

for Constance Talmadge and two for Norma Talmadge. Loos's biography *The Talmadge Girls* (1978) traces their careers and contributions to silent film.

In the 1920s Emerson and Loos moved East. Emerson's heart was in the New York theater society, and Loos found herself at home with the East Coast elite. Emerson had amassed a fortune in Hollywood and was now playing the stock market. The couple enjoyed Palm Beach in the winter and the continental hospitality of expatriates such as Gertrude Stein and the Fitzgeralds.

The marriage to Emerson was ill-fated almost from the start. He had an eye for the ladies and an ego that had to be constantly indulged. As a result, they settled on a father-daughter relationship (Emerson being twenty years Loos's senior), and after the stock-market crash she supported him the rest of his life. Although his name appears on most of her screen work after their meeting, Loos confided in her autobiography that after their marriage Emerson's contribution was minimal.

In 1925 Loos started the diary of Lorelei Lee, professional golddigger. The idea started as a little piece to make fun of H. L. Mencken's flirtation with a "stupid little blonde." The sketch turned into a serial for *Harper's Bazaar* and finally into the book *"Gentlemen Prefer Blondes."* The novel has been translated into fourteen languages and has been transformed into plays, films, and musicals. In 1928 Loos adapted the story for its first screen success.

Loos returned to Los Angeles in December 1931, this time to work with the reigning genius of the talkies, Irving Thalberg. Although she disliked life in Hollywood, the obligations she felt to Emerson kept her working for M-G-M at the impressive salary of $3,500 a week. Under Thalberg's guidance, Loos learned the basics of talking pictures. Thalberg believed that a film's narration emerged from the characters rather than from contrived situations, so typical of the films of the 1930s. Loos learned well; her dialogue in classic films like *San Francisco* and *The Women* (1939) earned her a reputation that overshadowed her contribution to silent comedy.

Her first assignment for M-G-M was *Red-Headed Woman* (1932), starring Jean Harlow. Loos brought out Harlow's natural sense of humor and capitalized on the actress's flippant attitude toward sex and men. The screenplay for the film, with its lighthearted view of sex, started the national protest of women's clubs and church groups that eventually culminated in the formation of the Breen Office in 1934. Loos even directed a sequence of *Red-Headed Woman* at the Santa Monica Pier. She became so

discouraged with the problems of even one day's shooting that it was her first and last effort at directing.

In 1927 Loos had met Wilson Mizner, a rogue of the Barbary Coast who later came to Hollywood, where he became famous for his wisecracks. After Mizner's death, Loos collaborated with his friend and coworker Robert Hopkins to write a tribute to his memory. The result was *San Francisco*, M-G-M's fictionalization of the 1906 Great San Francisco earthquake and fire. An original script idea was hard to sell during a period when most dramatic stories were adaptations from plays and novels. But gagman Hopkins sold Thalberg on the possibilities.

Loos tailored the script for M-G-M stars Clark Gable, Spencer Tracy, and Jeanette MacDonald. Gable played Mizner's film counterpart Blackie Norton. W. S. Van Dyke was assigned to direct, but his misdirection of Gable threatened to ruin the film. Loos came on the set, writing revisions daily and working with Hopkins and Van Dyke to keep true the interpretations of the characters. Such input and control were seldom achieved by a screenwriter. Thalberg's pictures were usually more prestigious than they were financially successful; however, *San Francisco* profited $2,237,000 and was by far the most commercially successful film Thalberg ever produced.

Loos reteamed with Hopkins for *Saratoga* (1937), a Gable vehicle costarring Jean Harlow. Another original screenplay, *Saratoga* lacked the passion and purpose of *San Francisco*. An uneven comedy set at the famous New York spa and racetrack, it probably would have remained another standard Gable movie, but Jean Harlow's tragic death during the filming created a great deal of publicity. The shooting was completed with a double, and the film was released. It became, essentially, an obituary.

In 1939 Loos, with Jane Murfin, adapted Clare Booth's successful Broadway play *The Women*. Since it was too racy for the strict Breen standards, Loos was assigned to "clean up" the dialogue, retaining the venom of the play without the sexiness. An expert at writing backbiting, hard-as-nails dialogue, Loos was the perfect doctor for the script. The cast was led by Norma Shearer, Joan Crawford, Rosalind Russell, Mary Boland, Paulette Goddard, and Joan Fontaine—in all 135 women worked on the film and not a single man, except for director George Cukor. Although the film is now berated by feminist critics as sexist, it remains a delight substantially because of an inspired script. Certainly it is the epitome of the "woman's film"—by women, for

*Norma Shearer, Joan Crawford, and Rosalind Russell
in* The Women

women, about women, its portrayal of women notwithstanding.

Loos's next adaptation, in 1940, was from the Rachel Crothers play *Susan and God*. Again directed by George Cukor, the film starred Joan Crawford and Fredric March. Although Crawford recreated with some success Gertrude Lawrence's stage performance of a society woman who puts her religious obsession ahead of her family, the story was dramatic, and the film does not represent the Loos élan for which she was so famous.

Her remaining pictures at M-G-M, though always first-class productions, were never essentially comedies and never gave her the opportunity to use her comic talents fully. *They Met in Bombay* (1941) is a love story starring Clark Gable and Rosalind Russell. Gable plays a jewel thief, and Russell is his sticky-fingered partner and antagonist.

When Ladies Meet (1941), another script based on a Rachel Crothers play, cast Joan Crawford as the heroine, an author who thinks she is in love with her friend's husband. The best scenes are between

Greer Garson and Robert Taylor as the friend and her husband. These characters develop a rapport, a sense of playfulness and sarcasm that is unmistakably Loos. Unfortunately, like *Susan and God, When Ladies Meet* is weighted down by its lead character, and Loos's clever dialogue never has a chance to overcome the plot.

Blossoms in the Dust (1941), another script for Greer Garson, was the fictionalization of the story of Edna Gladney, the Texan woman who founded an orphanage and fought for modern laws to protect illegitimate children. Today the film is remembered mainly as the first teaming of Garson with her frequent costar Walter Pidgeon, but it has been championed as one of the few films of the period that portray a woman in a positive light.

Like *Blossoms in the Dust, I Married an Angel* (1942) is remembered mostly for its stars: Jeanette MacDonald and Nelson Eddy. But it is distinctly different from their long run of operettas. A dream-fantasy, the film tells the story of playboy Count Willie Palaffi's transformation when he meets and marries an angel, Brigitta, and falls sincerely in love for the first time. It is a satirical musi-

Nelson Eddy as the count in I Married an Angel

cal comedy, underrated and misunderstood.

I Married an Angel was Anita Loos's last screenplay; she had been unhappy working in Hollywood since the death of Irving Thalberg in 1936. After leaving motion pictures, Loos continued writing plays, novels, and nonfiction, including three autobiographies, *A Girl Like I* (1966), *Kiss Hollywood Good-by* (1974), and *Cast of Thousands* (1977). Loos died on 18 August 1981.

Herman Mankiewicz

(7 November 1897-5 March 1953)

Don Kilbourne

SELECTED MOTION PICTURES: *The Road to Mandalay* (M-G-M, 1926), story by Mankiewicz and Tod Browning;

The Dummy (Paramount Famous Lasky, 1929), adaptation and dialogue,

The Man I Love (Paramount Famous Lasky, 1929), story, screenplay, and dialogue;

Thunderbolt (Paramount Famous Lasky, 1929), dialogue;

Men Are Like That (Paramount Famous Lasky, 1930), adaptation and dialogue;

Honey (Paramount Famous Lasky, 1930), adaptation;

Ladies Love Brutes (Paramount Famous Lasky, 1930), adaptation and dialogue by Mankiewicz and Waldemar Young;

Love Among the Millionaires (Paramount-Publix, 1930), dialogue;

The Vagabond King (Paramount-Publix, 1930), additional dialogue;

True to the Navy (Paramount-Publix, 1930), dialogue;

The Royal Family of Broadway (Paramount-Publix, 1931); script by Mankiewicz and Gertrude Purcell;

Man of the World (Paramount-Publix, 1931), original story and script;

Ladies' Man (Paramount-Publix, 1931), script and dialogue;

The Lost Squadron (RKO-Radio, 1932), additional dialogue by Mankiewicz and Robert S. Presnell;

Dancers in the Dark (Paramount-Publix, 1932), screenplay;

Girl Crazy (RKO-Radio, 1932), adaptation by Mankiewicz and Tim Whelan;

Another Language (M-G-M, 1933), script by Mankiewicz and Donald Ogden Stewart;

Dinner at Eight (M-G-M, 1933), screenplay by Mankiewicz and Frances Marion;

Meet the Baron (M-G-M, 1933), original story by Mankiewicz and Norman Krasna;

The Show-off (M-G-M, 1934), script;

Stamboul Quest (M-G-M, 1934), script;

After Office Hours (M-G-M, 1935), script;

Escapade (M-G-M, 1935), script;

John Meade's Woman (Paramount, 1937), screenplay by Mankiewicz and Vincent Lawrence;

My Dear Miss Aldrich (M-G-M, 1937), screen story and screenplay;

It's a Wonderful World (M-G-M, 1939), screen story by Mankiewicz and Ben Hecht;

Keeping Company (M-G-M, 1941), screen story;

Citizen Kane (RKO, 1941), screen story and screenplay by Mankiewicz and Orson Welles;

Rise and Shine (20th Century-Fox, 1941), screenplay;

Pride of the Yankees (RKO, 1942), screenplay by Mankiewicz and Jo Swerling,

Stand by for Action (M-G-M, 1943), screenplay by Mankiewicz, George Bruce, and John L. Balderston;

Christmas Holiday (Universal, 1944), screenplay;

The Enchanted Cottage (RKO, 1945), screenplay by Mankiewicz and DeWitt Bodeen;

The Spanish Main (RKO, 1945), screenplay by Mankiewicz and George Worthing Yates;

A Woman's Secret (RKO, 1949), screenplay;

The Pride of St. Louis (20th Century-Fox, 1952), screenplay.

Herman J. Mankiewicz was widely regarded as one of the most brilliant wits ever to work in Hollywood. During his early years there, his presence

Herman Mankiewicz in the early 1940s
(International News Photo)

entered Columbia University, where he began life as a writer by creating plays for the local college audiences. As Mankiewicz matured, the rivalry between him and his father grew. Franz Mankiewicz always seemed determined to top his son's achievements and went back to school at the same time Herman was attending Columbia, eventually receiving his doctorate.

While working as a cub reporter, Herman Mankiewicz met his future wife, Shulamith Sara Aaronson, through whom he gained some of the approval and acceptance he never received from his father. After brief service in the U.S. Marines, which included a trip to Germany just after the World War I Armistice was signed, Mankiewicz landed a job with the Red Cross press service. He married Sara Aaronson in 1920 and took her to Berlin for their honeymoon. Mankiewicz had lost his job by that time and spent several difficult months in Germany trying to earn money on which to live. Eventually he joined some of the American newspaper crowd in Berlin. He did some reporting, but even at this time his drinking and general unreliability were a bane to his employers.

After his son Don, a future screenwriter, was born in 1922, Mankiewicz managed to obtain a job as publicity man for dancer Isadora Duncan, then on tour throughout Europe. Duncan, like Mankiewicz, was an impulsive person who spent whatever money she had and borrowed when she had none. Mankiewicz's paychecks from her were quite irregular, and their association ended after a few months.

When the Mankiewiczes finally arrived back in America in 1922, the newspaper contacts Herman had made overseas proved to be valuable, and he became George S. Kaufman's assistant on theater coverage for the *New York Times*. His association with Kaufman led to his coming into contact with the Algonquin Round Table, a group of literary lights that included Kaufman, Robert Benchley, Dorothy Parker, Robert Sherwood, and Ben Hecht. As a group, they sometimes helped Mankiewicz financially and often assisted with contacts, but their influence on him as a writer was not entirely benign. Mankiewicz often felt out of place—the only one in the group with strong opinions on serious subjects. The group did serve to fire his ambition to be a playwright. Unfortunately, his few attempts in the mid-1920s were flops, and as a result he set off for Hollywood.

With the exception of *The Road to Mandalay* (1926), which was based on an original story by Mankiewicz and Tod Browning, his first few Hol-

was in demand at the homes of some of America's most famous and powerful people. In addition, he was regarded as a master of dialogue and was often called upon to fix other writers' screenplays. Despite all this, his own luster from his masterpiece *Citizen Kane* (1941) was tarnished by a continuing battle over how much of the screenplay he actually wrote.

Herman Jacob Mankiewicz was born in New York City. He was a bookish, introspective child who, despite his intelligence, was never able to win approval from his demanding father. Franz Mankiewicz, for many years an editor of a German-language newspaper, was constantly belittling his son's achievements. Although Herman was supposed to have gained his wit from his mother, she never had as strong an influence on his life as his father did.

After spending part of his childhood in Wilkes Barre, Pennsylvania, Mankiewicz moved back to New York with his family in 1913. (His brother Joseph, also a screenwriter, was born in 1901.) He

lywood jobs were as title writer for silent films. For Mankiewicz, writing titles came naturally, and he gained a reputation as the master of the witty title, which through his influence was to come into vogue as a replacement for the overly sentimental ones associated with earlier silent films. He contributed titles for over two dozen films between 1926 and 1930.

Starting in 1929, Mankiewicz began writing stories, dialogue, and screenplays for what would turn out to be dozens of films in the next few years. From the beginning, he held a cynical attitude toward his work in Hollywood, perhaps best summed up in his famous telegram to Ben Hecht urging Hecht to come to Hollywood: "Millions are to be made out here and your only competition is idiots. Don't let this get around." Despite his negative attitude, Mankiewicz was responsible for persuading many New York writers to come to Hollywood, and they did strongly influence movies with their tough, sardonic writing.

A look at Mankiewicz's own screenplays shows very little in the way of brilliance or originality. Even the films based on his original screen stories were generally clichéd and uninteresting. What did distinguish them were occasional flashes of the Mankiewicz humor and satire that proved to be a foreshadowing of a new type of slick, satirical, typically American film that depended almost totally on dialogue for its success.

Mankiewicz is credited with working on at least twenty films between 1929 and 1935. The ones he doctored while others got credit are not all known. One of his earliest screenplays, *The Dummy* (1929), was based on the O. Henry story "The Ransom of Red Chief." Reviewers, at the time perhaps still accustomed to the silent cinema, complained of too much talk and of a script that did not make sense. They also felt that the kidnapped boy was too precocious.

Mankiewicz followed *The Dummy* with a boxing story, *The Man I Love* (1929); several comedies; a combination musical/gangster film, *Dancers in the Dark* (1932); and a crime melodrama, *Man of the World* (1931). Between 1930 and 1932 Mankiewicz served as producer or associate producer on four comedies and worked without credit on all four screenplays: *Laughter* (1930), *Monkey Business* (1931), *Horse Feathers* (1932), and *Million Dollar Legs* (1932). Joseph Mankiewicz received the screenwriting credit for *Million Dollar Legs*, but Herman was later to claim that he, and not his brother, actually wrote the script. *Million Dollar Legs* starred W. C. Fields in the story of a fictional country whose

people take part in the Olympics to raise money for their empty treasury. Many critics considered it to be one of the funniest comedies of the early 1930s. It also marked the start of the rivalry between Herman and Joseph Mankiewicz, for as Joseph became more famous, Herman became increasingly bitter, often referring to his brother publicly in disparaging terms.

Dinner at Eight (1933), based on the George S. Kaufman / Edna Ferber play, was one of Herman Mankiewicz's best efforts, even if it was not original. In the 1932 stage version, the story of a dinner party given by a snobbish woman merely served as an excuse for some clever repartee. In transferring the play to the screen, Mankiewicz and his collaborator Frances Marion changed little, but they did condense some of the material. There is much bitterness and cynicism beneath the comic lines, and the characters are hardly admirable. In any event, the film was one of the most popular comedies of the time, and it has remained a favorite of critics.

A string of generally mediocre films followed *Dinner at Eight*. Mankiewicz, besides patching up other writers' dialogue, was taken off assignments for excessive drinking or erratic work habits. The result was that he lost credit on several films on which he had spent a great deal of time. By 1936 Mankiewicz's drinking habits and general insensitivity to the egos of his bosses had put his screenwriting career in jeopardy, so he returned to New York and started working on a play called "The Tree Will Grow," an examination of the life of John Dillinger from the viewpoints of several who knew him. Although this play was not produced, Mankiewicz was to incorporate this method of looking at a character into his screenplay for *Citizen Kane* several years later.

Mankiewicz's excesses were also causing him to lose the once-plentiful invitations to the homes of the rich and famous. One of his admirers in the early 1930s was William Randolph Hearst, who for a time regularly invited him to San Simeon for weekends. Mankiewicz absorbed much information from his visits with Hearst and was to put this to good use in his work on *Citizen Kane*. A one-time admirer of the publisher, Mankiewicz had grown disgusted with Hearst's positions in his later years. Although Hearst enjoyed Mankiewicz's wit, he soon found his carryings-on too much. When his onetime guest satirized him brutally on film, Hearst was to pursue a longtime vendetta.

Between 1936 and 1940 Mankiewicz wrote only three credited screenplays (although the Screenwriters Guild also credits him with *The Em-*

Mankiewicz with Diane Ellis, Nancy Carroll, and Fredric March (at the piano) on the set of Laughter. *Mankiewicz worked without credit on the screenplay for this 1930 film, which he also produced.*

peror's Candlesticks in 1937): *John Meade's Woman* (1937), *My Dear Miss Aldrich* (1937), and *It's a Wonderful World* (1939). M-G-M did not renew Mankiewicz's contract at the end of 1939, although he was kept on payroll until Louis B. Mayer fired him for gambling. After being let go, Mankiewicz decided to go back to New York again and set out by car. An accident resulted in a severely broken leg for Mankiewicz and, ironically, a chance to work on his masterpiece.

One of Mankiewicz's visitors in the hospital was Orson Welles, who had met him earlier and was a great admirer of his wit. He first offered Mankiewicz uncredited writing jobs for his Mercury Theatre radio program. After these were completed, the two men gradually set about thrashing out the ideas that led to *Citizen Kane*. With Mankiewicz's idea of a portrait of a famous figure through the eyes of several associates and Welles's

"March of Time" gimmick serving as an introduction and overview, the next thing they needed to decide upon was the subject for their story. They eventually decided to pattern their hero on Hearst, a person known to Welles as well as to Mankiewicz. Once that was decided, Mankiewicz, Welles, and John Houseman, a cofounder of the Mercury Theatre, took a place in the desert, and the task of creating *Citizen Kane* began.

The question of who actually did what in the creation of *Citizen Kane* is one of the most controversial in the history of American film and one that can probably never be answered completely. Both Mankiewicz and Welles received Academy Awards for their screenplay—the only award *Citizen Kane* received—but over the years, as Mankiewicz's career waned, Welles took increasing credit for the screenplay. Mankiewicz was once quoted as saying, "There is hardly a comma that I did not write."

Orson Welles in a scene from Citizen Kane. *Welles and collaborator Mankiewicz won an Oscar for their screenplay.*

Whatever the controversy over credits, there is little over the merits of the film. *Citizen Kane* is regarded by many as the greatest achievement in the history of film.

Certain elements in the film were taken from Mankiewicz's own experience: the sled Rosebud was based—according to some sources— on a very important bicycle that was stolen from him. The scene in which Kane finishes a review for his drunken critic friend, Jed Leland, was modeled on an incident involving Mankiewicz during one of his bouts.

Much of the information for *Citizen Kane* came from already-published material about Hearst; in fact, there was a lawsuit several years later by the author of a book on Hearst. Some of Kane's speeches are almost verbatim copies of Hearst's. When Welles denied that the film was about the still-influential publisher, he did not convince many people. Hearst at first threatened a libel suit but after dropping that, put pressures on several studio heads not to exhibit the film in their theaters. Hearst's gossip columnist, Louella Parsons, threatened smears against virtually everyone connected with the film. The negative publicity kept the film from being a financial success and probably did

a lot to deny Welles such tight control over his other films. From a personal standpoint, though, Mankiewicz suffered most from the controversy over *Citizen Kane*. Perhaps because he was once a guest at Hearst's house, the magnate felt an increased sense of betrayal over Mankiewicz's involvement in the project. Mankiewicz was to bear the brunt of Hearst's attacks over the next several years, and when he got involved in a drunk-driving accident, coverage in the Hearst papers was so brutal that Mankiewicz turned to the American Civil Liberties Union for help.

Despite all the problems, *Citizen Kane* restored Mankiewicz's career—for a while. At least it made him in demand again. For a time, he stopped drinking and began to work in a reasonably disciplined manner. *Rise and Shine* (1941) followed *Citizen Kane*, and it was successful, a wacky satire on college football. Mankiewicz's next film, *Pride of the Yankees* (1942), written with Jo Swerling, won an Academy Award nomination. The film, the life story of Lou Gehrig (Gary Cooper), seemed to be what America needed in the early days of the war, and it was well received by most. The screenplay consisted of a series of homilies about a shy young man, his immigrant parents, and the girl he loved (Teresa Wright).

Pride of the Yankees was not a happy experience for Mankiewicz, who encountered problems with Samuel Goldwyn. Unsure of Mankiewicz's ability, the producer hired another screenwriter to produce a parallel script, and Mankiewicz found out about it. Around this time his father, the strongest although most negative influence in his life, died. It was not long before Mankiewicz started drinking again.

Adding to his problems was the fact that his next screenwriting efforts were not particularly successful. *Stand by for Action* (1943), written with two others, was the old story about the cocky young military recruit who must learn the service code. The screenplay went from drama to broad comedy when the recruit found himself taking care of a boatload of young babies. *Christmas Holiday* (1944) was based on the Somerset Maugham story of a young woman (Deanna Durbin) who gets into serious trouble standing by her murderer husband (Gene Kelly). Robert Siodmak directed the picture.

Mankiewicz was drinking heavily at this time and was being fired and rehired on an almost regular basis. He managed to obtain two screenwriting jobs in 1945, *The Enchanted Cottage* and *The Spanish Main*. The first, based on Arthur Wing Pinero's 1922 play, told of a homely woman (Dorothy

In Pride of the Yankees *Gary Cooper (right) starred as Lou Gehrig.*

McGuire) and a maimed veteran (Robert Young) who find beauty in a small New England cottage, which metaphorically represents the love they have for each other. *The Spanish Main* was a pirate film. Mankiewicz's screenplay was light in tone and fast-moving enough to keep the clichés from becoming unbearable.

In the next few years, Mankiewicz planned several screenplays. One of the most intriguing projects was "Woman on the Rock," a *Citizen Kane*-like look at evangelist Aimee Semple McPherson. The proposed film ran into trouble not only with the Production Code but also with McPherson's children, who threatened a libel suit when Mankiewicz showed them the screenplay.

Mankiewicz both produced and wrote *A Woman's Secret* (1949), which incorporated flashback sequences to show the reasons a woman (Maureen O'Hara) killed the singer (Gloria Grahame) she had built up to success. Nicholas Ray directed, and the film, if not profound, was well done and intriguing.

Mankiewicz's last film was *The Pride of St. Louis*

(1952), in which baseball played second to character as it had in *The Pride of the Yankees*. The film portrayed pitcher Dizzy Dean (Dan Dailey) as a warm, colorful guy whose biggest victory was not on the ballfield but in court in a battle with a group of English teachers who objected to his misuse of language on baseball broadcasts.

By this time Mankiewicz's drinking had led to severely declining health and greater and greater depression. He was hospitalized for treatment for edema in early 1953; his condition steadily worsened, and he died a few days later. His obituaries in the *Hollywood Reporter* and *Los Angeles Examiner* made no mention of *Citizen Kane*; the *Los Angeles Times* made greater note of his Oscar-winning brother Joseph.

References:

Pauline Kael, *The Citizen Kane Book* (New York: Bantam Books, 1971);

Gavin Lambert, *On Cukor* (New York: Putnam's, 1972);

Frances Marion, *Off With Their Heads* (New York: Macmillan, 1972);

Richard Meryman, *Mank: The Wit, World, and Life of*

Herman Mankiewicz (New York: Morrow, 1978);

James Naremore, *The Magic World of Orson Welles* (New York: Oxford University Press, 1978).

Wendell Mayes
(1919-   )

Tanita C. Kelly

MOTION PICTURES: *The Spirit of St. Louis* (Warner Bros., 1957), screenplay by Mayes and Billy Wilder;

The Way to the Gold (20th Century-Fox, 1957), screenplay;

The Enemy Below (20th Century-Fox, 1957), screenplay;

From Hell to Texas (20th Century-Fox, 1958), screenplay by Mayes and Robert Buckner;

The Hunters (20th Century-Fox, 1958), screenplay;

The Hanging Tree (Warner Bros., 1959), screenplay by Mayes and Halsted Welles;

Anatomy of a Murder (Columbia, 1959), screenplay;

Advise and Consent (Columbia, 1962), screenplay;

Von Ryan's Express (20th Century-Fox, 1965), screenplay by Mayes and Joseph Landon;

In Harm's Way (Paramount, 1965), screenplay;

Hotel (Warner Bros., 1967), screenplay;

The Stalking Moon (National General, 1968), screenplay;

The Poseidon Adventure (20th Century-Fox, 1972), screenplay by Mayes and Stirling Silliphant;

The Revengers (National General, 1972), screenplay;

Death Wish (Paramount, 1974), screenplay;

Bank Shot (United Artists, 1974), screenplay;

Go Tell the Spartans (Avco Embassy, 1978), screenplay;

Love and Bullets (Associated Film, 1979), original story; screenplay by Mayes and John Melson;

Monsignor (20th Century-Fox, 1982), screenplay by Mayes and Abraham Polonsky.

SELECTED TELEVISION: *The Most Blessed Woman, Kraft Theatre* (NBC, 1957), script.

Wendell Mayes has had a successful screenwriting career since the late 1950s. Most of his work has called on his skills as an adaptor; sixteen of his nineteen screenplays have been based on novels. He has also worked repeatedly within the same genres and with the same directors and actors.

Mayes was born in Hayti, Missouri. He attended Johns Hopkins and Columbia universities but graduated from neither. He left school to join the U.S. Navy and served in the Pacific in World War II. After leaving the navy, Mayes went to New York City to pursue a career as an actor. He also began writing plays.

In 1957 one of his plays, *The Most Blessed Woman*, was produced on television and received good reviews. This led Billy Wilder to ask Mayes to work on *The Spirit of St. Louis* (1957), an adaptation of Charles Lindbergh's autobiography for the screen.

In 1957 and 1958, four of Mayes's scripts were produced by 20th Century-Fox. The first was *The Way to the Gold*, about efforts to find a hoard of stolen gold hidden in a contemporary Western town. This was followed by *The Enemy Below* (1957), which Mayes adapted from the novel by Commander D. A. Rayner. Although the screenplay for this war story which pitted an American ship against a German submarine adheres closely to Rayner's story line, some of the original's sense of a cat-and-mouse naval battle leading inevitably to mutual destruction is lost in the film. In 1958 Mayes and Robert Buckner wrote *From Hell to Texas*, adapting Charles O. Locke's Western novel *The Hell-Bent Kid*. This story of a young man (Don Murray) on the run after accidentally killing a man emphasized character more than action. That same year, Mayes wrote another war film, *The Hunters*, which had the same director, Dick Powell, and star, Robert Mitchum, as *The Enemy Below*.

In 1959 Mayes collaborated on another psychologically oriented Western, *The Hanging*

Wendell Mayes confers with Rod Taylor during production of the 1967 film Hotel

Tree, based on Dorothy M. Johnson's novelette of the same title. It is about a frontier doctor (Gary Cooper) treating a young woman (Maria Schell) who was blinded after a stagecoach robbery. He finds that she is not suffering from overexposure to the sun but from the shock of having seen her father killed by the robbers. *The Hanging Tree* was not well received upon its release, but its critical reputation has grown since.

At Billy Wilder's suggestion, Otto Preminger hired Mayes to adapt Robert Travers's novel *Anatomy of a Murder* for the screen. The novel was controversial, and Mayes turned it into an equally controversial film, dealing frankly with rape and using language that had never before been heard in films. Mayes was nominated for an Academy Award and the Writers Guild Award for his screenplay.

Mayes and Preminger worked together on two

more films, *Advise and Consent* (1962), a study of Washington politics, and *In Harm's Way* (1965), a big-budget war film about the events immediately before and after Pearl Harbor. In between these films, Mayes wrote *Von Ryan's Express* (1965), about American and British prisoners of war escaping from an Italian prison camp.

By the late 1960s Mayes was enjoying great success as a screenwriter, making five thousand dollars a week for his work. He acted as producer as well as writer on his next project, *Hotel* (1967), based on Arthur Hailey's novel. Like *In Harm's Way* and *Advise and Consent*, it was a multicharacted story, interweaving the problems of the hotel's guests, its owner, and its manager.

In 1968 Mayes worked on the Western film *The Stalking Moon*, which, like his earlier Westerns, emphasized character more than action. For this

Lee Remick, James Stewart, and Ben Gazzara in Anatomy of a Murder

film starring Gregory Peck and Eva Marie Saint, Mayes worked not only from the novel by Theodore V. Olsen but also from an earlier script by Alvin Sargent; he received sole screenplay credit.

In 1972, with Stirling Silliphant, Mayes co-wrote *The Poseidon Adventure*, the first of the series of disaster movies made in the 1970s. That same year he wrote another Western, *The Revengers*. This was Mayes's first produced screenplay that was not an adaptation of a book; for this film, however, he worked from someone else's screen treatment.

Mayes next wrote the screenplay for *Death Wish* (1974), based on Brian Garfield's novel. When the film—about a man (Charles Bronson) who turns vigilante after criminals attack his wife and daughter—was released in 1974 it became the center of controversy. Although some accused it of being exploitative and encouraging violence, other critics found it well-made and credible. Vincent Canby called *Death Wish* "despicable," "a bird-brained movie to cheer the hearts of the far-right wing," but Judith Christ lauded it as a "first-rate suspenser . . . that provides . . . more empathy and

Aristotelian purgation for the beleaguered city dweller than a monthful of Lone Rangers or a legion of Shanes in our innocent Western-oriented past." Mayes's other 1974 project, *Bank Shot*, was also a crime story but was completely different from *Death Wish*. It was a comedy taken from Donald E. Westlake's novel about a group of inept thieves. Mayes called it "the most fun-writing job I've ever had."

For years Mayes had been trying to find a producer for a film about the Viet Nam War, and in 1978 that film, *Go Tell the Spartans*, was made. Mayes's screenplay was nominated for the Writers Guild Award.

In 1979 for the first time a film based on an original screenplay by Mayes was produced. Capitalizing on the success of *Death Wish*, Mayes wrote an action/suspense script for the earlier film's star, Charles Bronson. The film, *Love and Bullets*, was dismissed as another Bronson vehicle and was neither a critical nor a financial success.

Since 1979 Mayes has written for television and completed the film *Monsignor* (1982), which he wrote in collaboration with Abraham Polonsky. Based on Jack Alain Leger's novel about a young priest (Christopher Reeve) involved in the European black market during World War II, *Monsignor* suffered from prerelease cutting that removed much of its intricate plot. It was a critical and financial failure.

Despite his many successes and his setbacks, Mayes has retained a sense of humor. In a recent letter he remarked, "I always find it astounding that anyone can find so much to write about movies. Me, I think screenwriting and making movies are pretty much on the same level as making mud pies and just about as interesting."

Dudley Nichols

(6 April 1895-4 January 1960)

Stephen O. Lesser

MOTION PICTURES: *Men Without Women* (Fox, 1930), screenplay and dialogue;
On the Level (Fox, 1930), adaptation;
Born Reckless (Fox, 1930), screenplay and dialogue;
One Mad Kiss (Fox, 1930), adaptation and dialogue;
A Devil With Women (Fox, 1930), screenplay and dialogue;
Seas Beneath (Fox, 1931), screenplay and dialogue;
Not Exactly Gentlemen (Fox, 1931), screenplay by Nichols and William Conselman;
Hush Money (Fox, 1931), dialogue;
Skyline (Fox, 1931), screenplay and dialogue by Nichols and Kenyon Nicholson;
This Sporting Age (Columbia, 1932), screenplay, adaptation, and dialogue;
Robber's Roost (Fox, 1932), screenplay;
Pilgrimage (Fox, 1933), dialogue;
The Man Who Dared (Fox, 1933), original screenplay by Nichols and Lamar Trotti;
Hot Pepper (Fox, 1933), story;
You Can't Buy Everything (M-G-M, 1934), original screenplay by Nichols and Trotti;
Hold That Girl (Fox, 1934), screenplay and dialogue by Nichols and Trotti;
The Lost Patrol (RKO, 1934), screenplay;
Wild Gold (Fox, 1934), story by Nichols and Trotti;
Call It Luck (Fox, 1934), story by Nichols and George Marshall; screenplay by Nichols and Trotti;
Judge Priest (Fox, 1934), screenplay by Nichols and Trotti;
The Mystery Woman (Fox, 1935), story by Nichols and E. E. Paramore, Jr.;
The Informer (RKO, 1935), screenplay;
The Arizonian (RKO, 1935), story and screenplay;
The Crusades (Paramount, 1935), screenplay by

Dudley Nichols

Nichols, Harold Lamb, and Waldemar Young;
Steamboat Round the Bend (20th Century-Fox, 1935), screenplay by Nichols and Trotti;
The Three Musketeers (RKO, 1935), screenplay by Nichols and Rowland V. Lee;
Mary of Scotland (RKO, 1936), screenplay;

The Plough and the Stars (RKO, 1936), screenplay;

The Toast of New York (RKO, 1937), screenplay by Nichols, John Twist, and Joel Sayre;

The Hurricane (United Artists, 1937), screenplay;

Bringing Up Baby (RKO, 1938), screenplay by Nichols and Hager Wilde;

Carefree (RKO, 1938), story and adaptation by Nichols and Wilde;

Stagecoach (United Artists, 1939), screenplay;

The 400 Million (Garrison Films, 1939), narration;

The Long Voyage Home (United Artists, 1940), screenplay;

Man Hunt (20th Century-Fox, 1941), screenplay;

Swamp Water (20th Century-Fox, 1941), screenplay;

This Land Is Mine (RKO, 1943), screen story and screenplay;

Air Force (Warner Bros., 1943), screen story and screenplay;

For Whom the Bell Tolls (Paramount, 1943), screenplay;

Government Girl (RKO, 1943), screenplay;

It Happened Tomorrow (United Artists, 1944), screenplay by Nichols and René Clair;

The Sign of the Cross (Paramount, 1944), prologue;

And Then There Were None (Fox, 1945), screenplay;

The Bells of St. Mary's (RKO, 1945), screenplay;

Scarlet Street (Universal, 1946), screenplay;

Sister Kenny (RKO, 1946), screenplay by Nichols, Alexander Knox, and Mary McCarthy;

Mourning Becomes Electra (RKO, 1947), adaptation;

The Fugitive (RKO, 1948), screenplay;

Pinky (20th Century-Fox, 1949), screenplay by Nichols and Philip Dunne;

Rawhide (20th Century-Fox, 1951), screen story and screenplay;

Return of the Texan (20th Century-Fox, 1952), screenplay;

The Big Sky (RKO, 1952), screenplay;

Prince Valiant (20th Century-Fox, 1954), screenplay;

Run for the Sun (United Artists, 1956), screenplay by Nichols and Roy Boulting;

The Tin Star (Paramount, 1957), screenplay;

The Hangman (Paramount, 1959), screenplay;

Heller in Pink Tights (Paramount, 1960), screenplay by Nichols and Walter Bernstein.

PLAY: *Come Angel Band* (New York, 46th Street Theatre, 18 February 1936), by Nichols and Stuart Anthony.

OTHER: *The Informer*, in *Modern British Dramas*, edited by Harlan Hatcher (New York: Harcourt, Brace, 1941);

Twenty Best Film Plays, edited by Nichols and John Gassner (New York: Crown, 1943)—includes *Stagecoach* and *This Land Is Mine* by Nichols;

Best Film Plays, 1943-1944, edited by Nichols and Gassner (New York: Crown, 1945).

PERIODICAL PUBLICATIONS: "The World and William Ink," *Stage* (February 1941);

"Film Writing," *Theatre Arts*, 26 (December 1942);

"The Writer and the Film," *Theatre Arts*, 28 (October 1943);

"Death of a Critic," *Theatre Arts*, 31 (April 1947).

Few Hollywood screenwriters have enjoyed the professional respect, the salary, and the national recognition given to Dudley Nichols during the 1930s and 1940s. Known as "one of filmdom's most literate personalities," Nichols wrote fourteen scripts for director John Ford; he also wrote for Howard Hawks, Fritz Lang, Jean Renoir, George Cukor, René Clair, Cecil B. De Mille, and Elia Kazan. He adapted for the screen works by Ernest Hemingway, Eugene O'Neill, Liam O'Flaherty, and Graham Greene. His screenplays for *The Informer* (1935) and *Stagecoach* (1939) have been termed masterpieces. Hollywood professionals still speak of Nichols with a respect bordering on awe, but his posthumous reputation has suffered from critical reevaluation. Even his best screenplays have been termed heavy-handed, schematic, and simplistic.

Nichols was born in Wapakoneta, Ohio, the son of Dr. Grant Byron and Mary (Means) Nichols. In his youth he displayed a quick and agile mind, open to the new technological forces that were changing the country. One part-time job demanded that Nichols repair tension wires while the lines were still hot, which meant that he had to replace the poles and insulators without shutting off the 33,000 volt current. That job turned his interests toward radio, and at age eighteen he worked as a radio operator on ships that crossed the Great Lakes. In the fall of 1915 he enrolled in the University of Michigan, supporting himself as a student assistant in the radio laboratory. Nichols invented a new type of electronic discharger that was later adopted by commercial radio companies. His flair for technical invention continued to show itself when he devised a method for electrical protection of minesweepers. Put into operation at the end of World War I, Nichols's method enabled the U.S. Navy to sweep up 50,000 mines in the North Sea without the loss of a man or a ship.

Nichols himself served in the navy, stationed first in London and then on a mine-laying detail in the North Sea. In 1920 he was awarded the Distinguished Service Medal. He was married to Esta Vacez Gooch-Collins in 1924.

Like many in his generation, Nichols used his wartime experience to enter the field of journalism. In September 1919 he had a piece published in the Sunday magazine of the *New York Times* entitled "The Art of Sweeping Up Mines." The *Times* offered him a job, but he turned it down because the managing editor was a family friend. Nichols wanted to make it on his own. He started at the *New York Evening Post* and then switched to the *New York World*. For ten years Nichols worked as a journalist in New York City.

The *World* published stories, reviews, and columns by some of the best-known writers of the 1920s. The executive editor, Herbert Baynard Swope, assembled a group of journalists noted for their wit, ambition, and sheer talent—a group that included Heywood Broun, Dorothy Parker, Alexander Woollcott, and Frank Sullivan. Nichols joined this incandescent company, learning how to use words quickly, accurately, and graphically.

The years as a journalist in New York gave Nichols the experiences that influenced his later work as a screenwriter. As a reporter, Nichols covered major court trials in the city. At the end of the 1920s he contributed free-lance articles to the *Nation* about a rural murder in the Susquehanna Valley in Pennsylvania and the New York City trial of Mary Dare Dennette for "sexual heresy." Several of Nichols's films end with dramatic courtroom confrontations, such as *This Land Is Mine* (1943), which concludes with a ringing defense of democracy.

Nichols also acquired a taste for the theater. He covered the opening of Eugene O'Neill's *Strange Interlude* in 1926 and wrote a discriminating review for the *World*. Throughout his life, Nichols remained attached to the theater, bringing such works as Maxwell Anderson's *Mary of Scotland*, Sean O'Casey's *The Plough and the Stars*, and O'Neill's *Mourning Becomes Electra* to the screen. The film versions showed a great respect for the original productions. After he moved west, Nichols kept a residence in Connecticut, and even in Hollywood he often chose friends from theater circles, such as Walter Wicclair, a fine, classically trained actor from the German stage who was driven into exile by the Nazis. In 1936 Nichols coauthored the play *Come Angel Band* that opened on Broadway in February. It closed within the month, having received devastating reviews. Having experimented once with Broadway, Nichols did not try again.

After working for ten years as a daily journalist, Nichols was ready for a change. He wanted to free himself from the tight restrictions of writing urgent copy and had planned a long trip to Spain to work on a book. He even secured an advance from a publisher and then turned to Winifred Sheehan, a former *World* reporter, for letters of introduction to Sheehan's friends in Spain. At that time, Sheehan was working at the Fox Studios in Hollywood. Sheehan offered to double Nichols's old salary at the *World* if he would give up the idea of Spain and come to Hollywood and work on scripts. Years later, Nichols told the story in a letter to Lindsay Anderson: "I knew nothing about films and told him so. I had seen one film I remembered and liked, Ford's *The Iron Horse*. So I arrived rather tentatively and experimentally, intending to leave if I found it dissatisfying. Sheehan assigned me to John Ford. . . . Working with Ford closely, I fell in love with the cinema."

Men Without Women (1930) was Nichols's first screenplay and also the first of fourteen films on which he and John Ford collaborated. The Ford-Nichols relationship was critical in the developing careers of both men, although Nichols's contribution to Ford's style has become a matter of dispute. In recent times, the weight of opinion has swung against Nichols, claiming that Ford only revealed himself as a poet of the cinema once free from the schematic bonds of Nichols's screenplays. On the other hand, it was only after Ford had discovered Nichols that Ford achieved the critical success needed to fuel his career and establish his reputation.

It is safe to say that the two men shared similar outlooks and worked well together, each bringing out tendencies in the other that resulted in a symbolic, atmospheric style of filmmaking. As Ford explained in an interview with Peter Bogdanovich about *Men Without Women*: "These guys are trapped in a submarine and eventually rescued but one man has to stay behind. He [Nichols] had never written a script before, but he was very good, and he had the same ideas [as I] about the paucity of dialogue."

Two points emerge from Ford's statement: first, the screenplay by Nichols showed a fondness for a particular kind of situation—a group of men trapped by their physical environment, who are forced to examine the bases of their lives. This device was repeated in several of Nichols's later pictures: *The Lost Patrol* (1934), *The Long Voyage Home* (1940), and *Stagecoach* (1939). Nichols viewed the sealed dramatic enclosure with no exits as—in his words—"the search for truth through the artistic lie," in which a character has no choice but to un-

Victor McLaglen in The Informer. *McLaglen won an Academy Award for his portrayal of Gypo Nolan in this 1935 film.*

ravel, shedding his defenses until he has reached his core as a man. Second, Nichols saw the role of dialogue as subordinate to that of the image. In a published essay, Nichols wrote: "One is not a screenwriter until one writes as a camera. You key your visualizing faculties to all the possibilities—and limitations of the camera. The eye of the mind must be dominant, for only when you have exhausted the possibilities of projecting an idea, a character or a conflict visually, does the competent screenwriter turn to the more complicated dimension of the word."

After the success of *Men Without Women* Nichols and John Ford collaborated on *Born Reckless* (1930) and *Seas Beneath* (1931), but neither was as successful as *Men Without Women*. As a result, Nichols did not work again for Ford until 1934. He continued writing screenplays, many of them for Fox, throughout the 1930s. His major collaborator was Lamar Trotti, with whom he worked on seven

films: *The Man Who Dared* (1933), *You Can't Buy Everything* (1934), *Hold That Girl* (1934), *Wild Gold* (1934), *Call It Luck* (1934), *Judge Priest* (1934), and *Steamboat Round the Bend* (1935).

In their fourth collaboration, *The Lost Patrol* (1934), Nichols and Ford created a film of uncanny brilliance. *The Lost Patrol* is the story of British soldiers lost in the Mesopotamian desert, prey to an unseen Arab foe that kills the patrol one by one. The anguished men try to catch a glimpse of their enemy but fail. Each succumbs to a treacherous attack until only the sergeant is left alive. As the Arabs come over the hill to finish him off, he rocks with insane laughter, wildly firing his machine gun at the hordes. Weird streaks of light flash across the desert, lending an almost mystical quality to the film to emphasize the emptiness and futility of the patrol's efforts to make sense of its predicament.

In 1935 RKO released one of the two masterpieces of the Ford-Nichols canon, *The Informer*, starring Victor McLaglen as the man who betrays his friend. The story comes from the novel by Liam O'Flaherty. Nichols devoted only five weeks to the script, and the film was shot in just three weeks at a budget of $218,000. It was nominated for the Academy Award for Best Picture of 1935, and McLaglen won the Oscar for best actor.

The Informer, while lacking social complexity and subtlety, does create a convincing amalgam of mood, atmosphere, image, and dialogue. The screenplay demonstrates Nichols's intention to visualize, to create a scene through the eye of the camera. Roaming through the city, the camera picks up symbolic details that recur throughout the film. Objects become indicators of the protagonist Gypo Nolan's mental state, as he passes from temptation through betrayal to redemption.

Nichols rearranged some of the scenes from the novel and added episodes that were not in the book. He provided a convincing rationale for Gypo's conduct: immediately after seeing the poster offering twenty pounds reward for information about Frankie McPhillip, Gypo meets Katie, who needs twenty pounds to buy a ticket to America. Nichols also fleshed out the betrayal scene itself, with Gypo's giving the information about Frankie to the British soldiers. Gypo is kept waiting in the office until Frankie has been killed. When the news is communicated by telephone, as the screenplay has it, "a riding crop pushed the money across the table" to Gypo. The ending of the film, which has been criticized for its sentimentality, comes directly from the novel. Gypo dies, crying in a loud voice, "Frankie, yer mother has forgiven me." Nichols adds, "we follow him until he comes to the foot of a great carved Christ, where, with a gurgling sound, he falls at the foot of the statue, dead."

The Motion Picture Academy honored Nichols with the Oscar for Best Screenplay Adaptation, but he refused the award. In a polite but firmly worded letter to the Academy, Nichols stated: "To accept it would be to turn my back on nearly a thousand members of the Writers Guild, to desert those fellow members who ventured everything in the long drawn out fight for a genuine writers' organization, to go back on convictions honestly arrived at, and to invalidate years of work in the Guild. . . ."

The rejection stems directly from Nichols's work to upgrade the standing of screenwriters in Hollywood. From his first days as a screenwriter, he had been engaged in improving the status of the writer from that of a free-lance independent who sells his talent at the going rate to that of a profes-

sional protected by union minimums and regulations that guaranteed him credit for work done. Nichols was involved with Guild activities throughout the 1930s and early 1940s, trying to strengthen its bargaining position. In 1938-1939 he was president of the Screen Writers Guild. It was the dispute over his screenplay for Hemingway's *For Whom the Bell Tolls* (1943) that gave the Guild the right to assign the final screen credit to its members. Up to then the producers would participate in awarding the all-important screen credit to film writers.

It appears that Nichols passed through a period of genuine political radicalism; his work on the pictures he wrote before the war, however, does not reveal a radical slant. Indeed, the records on Nichols's career show that he was used as a talented craftsman, ready to be assigned to projects. From 13 July to 3 October 1936, Nichols worked on such scripts as *The Plough and the Stars* (1936), *The Toast of New York* (1937), and *Gunga Din* (1939, for which he received no credit) at the rate of $1,500 a week. The following year his salary went up to $1,750, and he turned his talents to *Bringing Up Baby* (1938), *Carefree* (1938), and "Memory of Love."

Bringing Up Baby shows a different side of Nichols's talents. Directed by Howard Hawks, the film is one of the craziest of the screwball comedies, starring Cary Grant as a mild-mannered paleontologist who gets involved with a zany woman— Katharine Hepburn—and her pet, Baby—a leopard. The comedy is farcical, the acting inspired. Nichols worked with Hager Wilde, Robert McGowan, and Gertrude Purcell on the screenplay, which was adapted from the story by Wilde (McGowan and Purcell received no credit). The film proves Nichols's adaptability as a writer, his capacity to work successfully in different genres. *Bringing Up Baby* is free from the morose sentimentality which critics have termed the Nichols style.

In 1939 the Ford-Nichols film *Stagecoach* was released. From the moment it appeared before the public, the film was described as a classic, the archetypical Western that has inspired a thousand imitations. It reversed a momentary decline in Ford's career and allowed Nichols to write the significant dramas in the 1940s.

Stagecoach is based on a short story by Ernest Haycox entitled "Stage to Lordsburg." The script is terse and economical. The characters move in predictable patterns, lacking resonance, inner complexity, or ambiguity, with the possible exception of the gambler, Hatfield, whose past is never really explained. We are never convinced that we are dealing with real people, and there is almost a

Cary Grant and Katharine Hepburn in Bringing Up Baby

blatant simplemindedness to the dialogue. Dallas (Claire Trevor), the prostitute, after explaining herself, says, "You have to live, no matter what happens," to which Ringo (John Wayne) replies, "Yeah, that's it."

John Ford's direction compensates for what the script lacks. The panoramic camera shots of Arizona's Monument Valley reveal the massive and empty desert, the towering monuments of buttes and mesas that heighten the isolation as the stagecoach proceeds toward its destination. The grouping of characters—where they sit on the stagecoach—shows the sure feeling for visual organization. The use of light, how day and then night fuse with the plot, how the camera moves from the general to the particular, from the group to the individual—these are indications of Ford's strength as a director.

In the early 1940s Ford became interested in remaking his 1928 antiwar film *Four Sons*. When Darryl F. Zanuck refused the project Nichols

suggested that four one-act plays by Eugene O'Neill—*In the Zone, The Moon of the Carribees, Bound West for Cardiff,* and *The Long Voyage Home*, all set aboard an English freighter during World War I—be used as the basis of one film. Under the title *The Long Voyage Home*, this Nichols-Ford collaboration was released in 1940. Although reviewers were enthusiastic, the film, one of Nichols's personal favorites among his scripts, lost money at the box office because of its grim subject matter.

In 1941 Nichols also teamed with French director Jean Renoir to make *Swamp Water*, about a fugitive from the law (Walter Brennan) who decides to hide out in the Georgia swamps. Nichols and Renoir then decided to make an anti-Fascist film, and, according to Nichols, they were given by RKO "complete freedom to make a film, without any other impediment than our own shortcomings." In *This Land Is Mine* Charles Laughton plays a French schoolteacher who is moved to action by the Nazi occupation of France. He becomes a national hero, and the film concludes with a trial scene that becomes a defense of freedom.

In 1943 *For Whom the Bell Tolls*, adapted by Nichols from Hemingway's novel, was released with great fanfare as a three-hour epic starring Ingrid Bergman as Maria and Gary Cooper as the American Robert Jordan. As a vehicle to show the couple's doomed love affair in the Spanish mountains, the picture accomplished its purpose, but in the process the Hemingway novel was lost. Whereas Hemingway dealt with the complexities and ambiguities of political alliances in Spain, the picture is basically void of politics. Nichols's original script was altered by Paramount so that the word *fascist* never appeared; instead, the word became *nationalist*. No background or explanation is given for the Spanish Civil War. Romance lures the viewer away from history and politics.

It has been alleged that Paramount showed Nichols's script to representatives of the Spanish government before the shooting began and acted on their suggestions. The studio claims that it was advised by the U.S. State Department to submit the film to Spanish diplomats based in San Francisco but that this in no way constituted censorship. In any event, what emerged was a film denuded of political content, keeping the action and romance of Hemingway's plot but stripping it of any greater significance.

By 1944 Nichols was at the apogee of his career. He enjoyed the respect of the industry, and the increase of salary testified to his standing as a professional. Nichols moved from writing into directing. In a letter written in 1941 to J. R. McDonough, then vice-president of RKO, Nichols said: "The business hasn't developed enough directors. Consequently, it has to build the few fine talents up too big and they get out of hand."

As a director, Nichols did not add to his reputation. His first directorial effort was for *Government Girl* (1943), a romantic comedy set in wartime Washington. *Sister Kenny* (written and directed by

George Bancroft, John Wayne, and Louise Platt in Stagecoach

Nichols in 1946) is the true story of an Australian nurse who pioneered a new treatment for infantile paralysis. Star Rosalind Russell took an interest in Sister Kenny and sponsored a short-subject about her, then interested RKO and Nichols in the idea of a full-length drama.

In 1947 Nichols produced and directed the film version of the Eugene O'Neill play *Mourning Becomes Electra*. There was no screenplay credit, but Nichols adapted the play, retaining O'Neill's dialogue and adding offstage scenes. The film was severely cut for commercial distribution and was a box-office failure.

Nichols's last film with John Ford was *The Fugitive* (1948), based upon Graham Greene's novel *The Power and the Glory*. John Ford observed that in 1947 it was impossible to film the story of a whiskey priest with an illegitimate child, so *The Fugitive* makes Greene's incorruptible police officer the father of the child and turns the priest (Henry Fonda) into a simple and sober peasant, thus destroying the point of the novel and leaving only the story of a martyrdom in anticlerical Mexico.

The 1949 film *Pinky* was more daring, treating the question of racial discrimination in a strong and courageous manner. Pinky (Jeanne Crain), a light-skinned Negro, returns home to the South after having passed for white in the North. She is a nurse and has fallen in love with a white doctor. Her black grandmother convinces her that her place is at home, as a black woman, to fight to better her people. Characteristic of Nichols, the film ends with a courtroom drama in which Pinky vindicates her claim to the estate of the old woman whom she nursed.

Between 1951 and 1959 Nichols wrote eight films, all of them action stories and most of them Westerns. *Rawhide* (1951) was a tense psychological Western in which a group of captives at a stagecoach station defeat the outlaws holding them prisoner. *Return of the Texan* (1952) was an unsuccessful Western about a man's efforts to save his ranch; Delmer Daves directed. Nichols adapted the first half of

A. B. Guthrie's novel *The Big Sky* for Howard Hawks in 1952. *Prince Valiant* (1954) was based upon Harold Foster's comic strip. *Run for the Sun* (1956) was an updating of the 1932 film *The Most Dangerous Game*.

In 1957 Nichols wrote the best of his later scripts, *The Tin Star*. Anthony Mann directed this film about a former sheriff (Henry Fonda) turned bounty hunter who agrees to help the inexperienced young sheriff (Anthony Perkins) of another town. Nichols received an Academy award nomination for his screenplay. The film was later turned into the television series *The Deputy*. Nichols followed *The Tin Star* with another, less successful Western, *The Hangman* (1959).

Dudley Nichols died in 1960. His last film, *Heller in Pink Tights* (1960), about the problems of a traveling show in the old West, was released after his death.

References:

Lindsay Anderson, "On the Films of John Ford," *Cinema*, 3 (Spring 1971);

Peter Bogdanovich, *John Ford* (Berkeley: University of California Press, 1968);

Roger Boussinot, *L'Encyclopedie du cinéma* (Paris: Bordas, 1969);

Richard Corliss, *Talking Pictures: Screenwriters in American Cinema* (Woodstock, N.Y.: Overlook Press, 1974);

Paul Jensen, "The Career of Dudley Nichols," *Film Comment* (Winter 1970-1971);

Nancy Warfield, *The Structure of John Ford's Stagecoach* (New York: Warfield, 1974).

Papers:

The UCLA Library Department of Special Collections houses a Dudley Nichols collection. The UCLA Theatre Arts Library and the Library of the Motion Picture Academy of Arts and Sciences hold most of his screenplays. The RKO Library, Los Angeles, has correspondence and the worksheets detailing salary and time spent on RKO projects.

Clifford Odets

(18 July 1906-14 August 1963)

James Goodwin
University of California, Los Angeles

See also the Odets entry in *DLB 7, Twentieth-Century American Dramatists.*

MOTION PICTURES: *The General Died at Dawn* (Paramount, 1936), screenplay;
None But the Lonely Heart (RKO, 1944), screenplay;
Deadline at Dawn (RKO, 1946), screenplay;
Humoresque (Warner Bros., 1946), screenplay by Odets and Zachary Gold;
Sweet Smell of Success (United Artists, 1957), screenplay by Odets and Ernest Lehman;
The Story on Page One (20th Century-Fox, 1960), screen story and screenplay;
Wild in the Country (20th Century-Fox, 1961), screenplay.

PLAYS: *Waiting for Lefty* (New York, Civic Repertory Theatre, 5 January 1935);
Awake and Sing! (New York, Belasco Theatre, 19 February 1935);
Till the Day I Die (New York, Longacre Theatre, 26 March 1935);
Paradise Lost (New York, Longacre Theatre, 9 December 1935);
Golden Boy (New York, Belasco Theatre, 4 November 1937);
Rocket to the Moon (New York, Belasco Theatre, 24 November 1938);
Night Music (New York, Broadhurst Theatre, 22 February 1940);
Clash by Night (New York, Belasco Theatre, 27 December 1941);
The Russian People (New York, Belasco Theatre, 29 December 1942);
The Big Knife (New York, National Theatre, 24 February 1949);
The Country Girl (New York, Lyceum Theatre, 10 November 1950);
The Flowering Peach (New York, Belasco Theatre, 28 December 1954);
The Silent Partner (New York, Actor's Studio, 11 May 1972).

SELECTED BOOKS: *Three Plays by Clifford Odets* (New York: Covici-Friede, 1935)—includes

Clifford Odets, 1936

Awake and Sing!, Waiting for Lefty, Till the Day I Die;
Rifle Rule in Cuba, by Odets and Carleton Beals (New York: Provisional Committee for Cuba, 1935);
Paradise Lost (New York: Random House, 1936);
Waiting for Lefty (London: Gollancz, 1937);
Golden Boy (New York: Random House, 1937; London: Gollancz, 1938);
Rocket to the Moon (New York: Random House, 1939);
Six Plays of Clifford Odets (New York: Random House, 1939)—includes *Waiting for Lefty, Awake and Sing!, Till the Day I Die, Paradise Lost, Golden Boy, Rocket to the Moon;*

Night Music (New York: Random House, 1940);

Clash by Night (New York: Random House, 1942);

The Big Knife (New York: Random House, 1949);

The Country Girl (New York: Viking, 1951); republished as *Winter Journey* (London: French, 1955);

The Flowering Peach (New York: Dramatists Play Service, 1954).

OTHER: *None But the Lonely Heart*, in *Best Film Plays, 1945*, edited by John Gassner and Dudley Nichols (New York: Crown, 1946).

PERIODICAL PUBLICATIONS: "I Can't Sleep: A Monologue," *New Theatre and Film*, 3 (February 1936): 8-9;

"Silent Partner," *New Theatre and Film*, 4 (March 1937): 5-9.

Born in Philadelphia to Louis J. and Pearl Geisinger Odets, Clifford Odets grew up in a Jewish section of the Bronx. Though Odets at times suggested that he was raised under the shadows of poverty, his father became a prosperous businessman in the 1920s, and the family continued to enjoy financial security in the Depression years. Late in life, Odets said of his boyhood that it was middle-class and "very ordinary." A negligent student, he quit high school after two years, vaguely in pursuit of a future as a poet. His father's disapproval of this career culminated one night in his smashing the son's typewriter.

Odets's next pursuit was stage acting, which met with his parents' halfhearted support. He joined an amateur company named the Drawing Room Players, which produced one-acts, and soon moved to the Poet's Theatre. With associates from these two groups, Odets formed a small acting troupe, and they performed in radio plays, vaudeville, and summer stock during the years 1925-1927, with Odets taking turns as actor and director. He began to compose original material for radio drama and acted professionally with the Mae Desmond Stock Company, the Theatre Guild, and, in 1930, the Group Theatre. Odets could not make a living from the theater, and he returned home for a period, then moved to Manhattan and stayed in a series of cheap furnished rooms. That milieu exposed Odets to the language, personalities, and experiences of people struggling to survive and salvage some dignity during the Depression's first years, all of which he used in his early plays.

Odets began to write more ambitious dramatic pieces. In 1933, under the working title "I Got the Blues," he completed a full-length play about an embattled Jewish family; in 1934 *Waiting for Lefty* won the New Theatre League-*New Masses* playwriting contest. That same year Odets joined the Communist party, which he abandoned after eight months. In 1935, when "I Got the Blues" was retitled *Awake and Sing!* and produced on Broadway, Odets became an overnight sensation, but that same year his *Paradise Lost* was a failure. Odets regained his reputation in 1937 with the production of *Golden Boy*, the most successful play in the Group Theatre's history. His last two plays with the Group Theatre —*Rocket to the Moon* (1938) and *Night Music* (1940)—received unfavorable reviews and little public support. In the remaining twenty-three years of his life, Odets completed only four original plays: *Clash by Night* (1941), *The Big Knife* (1949), *The Country Girl* (1950), and *The Flowering Peach* (1954). His 1942 production, *The Russian People*, was an adaptation of Konstantin Simonov's *The Russians*.

Offers from Hollywood came soon after the successful Broadway openings of *Waiting for Lefty* and *Awake and Sing!* Odets resisted the promise of lucrative contracts, at terms as high as $4,000 a week, until the production of his *Paradise Lost* ran into trouble at the box office. Upon accepting a contract with Paramount, he wired money to the Group Theatre, but the play failed anyway. During his first stay in Hollywood, Odets completed three screenplays—"Gettysburg," "The River Is Blue," and *The General Died at Dawn* —but only the last one was produced. Set in contemporary China, *The General Died at Dawn* (1936) involves the efforts of an idealistic American named O'Hara (Gary Cooper) to assist the common people in their fight against the oppressive rule of a local warlord (Akim Tamiroff). Comparing the film story with Odets's plays, many critics found *The General Died at Dawn* inconsequential. Odets insisted that the screenwriter did not have to sacrifice art and ideas in his works: "People can be given a sense of problems, a heightened perception of life, and at the same time be entertained and even gripped."

Odets wrote and directed his next film, *None But the Lonely Heart* (1944), which is based on a novel by Richard Llewellyn. The original story concerns the coming of age of a young tough, Ernie Mott, in the slums of prewar London. Preproduction decisions by the studio forced Odets to alter the story considerably: "I asked who they had in mind for the lead and they said Cary Grant. There was silence for a moment and I asked if anyone *read* this book. It seemed no one had. Well, it's about a nineteen-year-old boy with pimples whose two desires in life

Madeleine Carroll (in front at right) in The General Died at Dawn. *Seated behind her is novelist John O'Hara, who played a bit part in this 1936 film.*

are to have a girl and get a new suit of clothes." At Grant's request, the studio assigned Odets to direct the film, and Odets's sympathies for common people and his faith in them are evident in the film's writing and direction. The role of the Cockney wanderer Ernie was rewritten for an older man who walks the precarious path between impoverished gentility and profitable crime. By the end he proves himself a loyal British subject and a loyal son to Ma Mott (Ethel Barrymore, who won an Oscar for the role), who is dying of cancer.

None But the Lonely Heart was well received by the critics, and on the strength of such a reception, M-G-M signed Odets to a generous contract to write and direct several films. After spending a full year under contract without one of his projects being accepted for production, Odets cancelled the deal and returned East to resume playwriting. According to director Irving Rapper, Odets was largely responsible for the screenplay for the film *Rhapsody*

in Blue (1945), the fictionalized film biography of George Gershwin, although he received no screen credit. His next screen work was *Deadline at Dawn* (1946), based on a novel by William Irish (Cornell Hopley-Woolrich). The film's central character is a young sailor (Bill Williams) on leave in New York City; in the span of six hours, he must prove himself innocent of murder. In the quest to clear himself, the sailor is aided by a dance-hall girl (Susan Hayward) and a philosophical cab driver (Paul Lukas). The plot serves Odets as an occasion for speeches, mostly delivered by the cabbie, on the meaning of urban existence. That same year, Odets collaborated with Zachary Gold on an adaptation of the Fannie Hurst novel *Humoresque*, about the love affair between a struggling violinist (John Garfield) and his unstable patroness (Joan Crawford). Jean Negulesco directed the movie with distinct touches of film noir.

Odets did not have another screenplay pro-

Cary Grant and Ethel Barrymore in None But the Lonely Heart, *written and directed by Odets. Barrymore won an Academy Award for her portrayal of Ma Mott.*

duced until 1957. In the interim, three of his plays were made into films. Screenwriter Alfred Hayes and director Fritz Lang adapted *Clash by Night* in 1952. In 1954 *The Country Girl* was released as a motion picture, adapted and directed by George Seaton. Although Odets completed a screen treatment of his play *The Big Knife*, the Robert Aldrich film adaptation released in 1955 is based on a later treatment prepared by James Poe. Earlier, in 1939, Rouben Mamoulian directed an adaptation of *Golden Boy*, a play with a Hollywood plot about a youth who abandons classical music and the dream of becoming a concert violinist for a career as a prizefighter.

Sweet Smell of Success (1957) was Odets's next writing assignment for Hollywood. Ernest Lehman wrote the first draft of the screenplay from his own short story; when rewrites were needed after Lehman became ill, Odets was brought in to work on the project. Odets's influence shows on the film, which is set in New York and tells of the corruption of the Broadway and nightlife scene. The

screenplay details the dealings of the syndicated columnist J. J. Hunsecker (Burt Lancaster), who boasts a readership of sixty million people, and his protégé, Sidney Falco (Tony Curtis), a publicity agent by day and hatchet man by night. The plot and characters are gross exaggerations, but their total effect strikes a suitable image for a world kept in motion by puffery and gossip.

Jerry Wald, the producer who had brought earlier Odets projects to the screen, encouraged the playwright to direct his original screenplay *The Story on Page One* (1960). The story follows the trial of Jo Morris (Rita Hayworth) and her lover, Larry Ellis (Gig Young), for the murder of her husband. Larry is a lonesome widower who, at age thirty-five, is still ruled by his mother. Jo's husband finds the lovers one night, draws his service revolver, and accidentally kills himself. The legal proceedings occupy fully one hour of screen time; flashbacks present scenes of the love affair and the husband's death. Predictably, Larry leaves the court with Jo, finally breaking free of his mother's domination.

Wild in the Country (1961), Odets's last screenplay, was an Elvis Presley vehicle about a moody and rebellious farmboy with a talent for writing. After a series of misdirections and mishaps, including a trial for manslaughter, he escapes his past and heads for college on a scholarship. That Odets was credited as screenwriter astounded film reviewers. But the storyline and dialogue exhibit, in an extreme form, characteristics to be found even in the best of Odets's work. The premise that a backwoods juvenile delinquent is destined to become a world-famous novelist is not, finally, any more exaggerated than the connections between the fight arena and the concert stage in *Golden Boy*.

By the time of Clifford Odets's death in 1963, the consensus among American theater critics was that the playwright had sold his creative soul to Hollywood. At times Odets feared as much himself. Many consider his finest film work the collaboration with Ernest Lehman on *Sweet Smell of Success*, and, in retrospect, motion pictures seem to have well served Odets's reputation as a dramatic writer. Those films adapted by other scenarists and directors from Odets's plays—particularly *Golden Boy*, *Clash by Night*, and *The Big Knife*—remain engaging works of American cinema and interesting signs of their cultural times.

References:

Margaret Brenman-Gibson, *Clifford Odets, American Playwright: The Years from 1906 to 1940* (New York: Atheneum, 1981);

Harold Cantor, *Clifford Odets, Playwright-Poet* (Metuchen, N.J.: Scarecrow Press, 1978);

John McCarten, "Revolution's Number One Boy," *New Yorker*, 13 (22 January 1938);

Michael J. Mendelsohn, *Clifford Odets: Humane Dramatist* (Deland, Fla.: Everett/Edwards, 1969);

Edward Murray, *Clifford Odets: The Thirties and After* (New York: Ungar, 1968);

Robert Baird Shuman, *Clifford Odets* (New York: Twayne, 1962);

Robert S. Warshow, "Poet of the Jewish Middle Class," *Commentary*, 1 (May 1946): 17-22.

Papers:
The Library of Congress and the Performing Arts Research Center of the New York Public Library at Lincoln Center hold collections of Odets's papers.

Norman Panama
(21 April 1914-)

Melvin Frank
(13 August 1913-)

Jonathan Kuntz
Los Angeles Southwest College

MOTION PICTURES: *My Favorite Blonde* (Paramount, 1942), story;

Star Spangled Rhythm (Paramount, 1942), sketches by Frank, Panama, George Kaufman, Arthur Ross, and Fred Saidy;

Happy Go Lucky (Paramount, 1942), screenplay by Frank, Panama, and Walter DeLeon;

Thank Your Lucky Stars (Warner Bros., 1943), screenplay by Frank, Panama, and James V. Kern;

And the Angels Sing (Paramount, 1944), screenplay;

Duffy's Tavern (Paramount, 1945), screen story and screenplay;

Our Hearts Were Growing Up (Paramount, 1946), screenplay;

Monsieur Beaucaire (Paramount, 1946), screenplay;

Road to Utopia (Paramount, 1946), screen story and screenplay;

It Had to Be You (Columbia, 1947), screenplay;

Mr. Blandings Builds His Dream House (RKO, 1948), screenplay;

A Southern Yankee (M-G-M, 1948), screen story;

Norman Panama

Melvin Frank

The Return of October (Columbia, 1949), screenplay;

The Reformer and the Redhead (M-G-M, 1950), screenplay;

Strictly Dishonorable (M-G-M, 1951), screenplay;

Callaway Went Thataway (M-G-M, 1952), screen story and screenplay;

Above and Beyond (M-G-M, 1953), screenplay by Frank, Panama, and Beirne Lay, Jr.;

Knock on Wood (Paramount, 1954), screen story and screenplay;

White Christmas (Paramount, 1954), screen story and screenplay by Frank, Panama, and Norman Krasna;

The Court Jester (Paramount, 1956), screen story and screenplay;

That Certain Feeling (Paramount, 1956), screenplay by Frank, Panama, I. A. L. Diamond, and William Altman;

The Trap (Paramount, 1959), screen story and screenplay by Panama and Richard Alan Simmons;

Li'l Abner (Paramount, 1959), screenplay;

The Jayhawkers (Paramount, 1959), screen story and screenplay by Frank, Joseph Petracca, Frank Fenton, and A. I. Bezzerides;

The Facts of Life (United Artists, 1960), screen story and screenplay;

The Road to Hong Kong (United Artists, 1962), screen story and screenplay;

Strange Bedfellows (Universal, 1965), screen story and screenplay by Frank and Michael Pertwee;

Not With My Wife You Don't! (Warner Bros., 1966), screen story; screenplay by Panama, Larry Gelbart, and Peter Barnes;

A Funny Thing Happened on the Way to the Forum (United Artists, 1966), screenplay by Frank and Pertwee;

Buona Sera, Mrs. Campbell (United Artists, 1968), screen story and screenplay by Frank, Sheldon Keller, and Denis Norden;

A Touch of Class (Avco Embassy, 1973), story and

screenplay by Frank and Jack Rose;

The Duchess and the Dirtwater Fox (20th Century-Fox, 1976), screenplay by Frank and Barry Sandler;

I Will, I Will . . . For Now (20th Century-Fox, 1976), screenplay by Panama and Albert E. Lewin;

Lost and Found (Columbia, 1979), story and screenplay by Frank and Jack Rose.

PLAY: *Li'l Abner* (New York, St. James Theatre, 15 November 1956), book.

BOOK: *The Glass Bed*, by Panama and Albert Lewin (New York: Morrow, 1980).

Melvin Frank and Norman Panama, authors of more than thirty films, have achieved a unique position among successful Hollywood writing teams. By becoming not only the coauthors but also the coproducers and codirectors of their films, Frank and Panama have gained a large measure of control over their screenplays. Since their earliest collaborations writing for radio, Frank and Panama have been closely associated with major comic performers. They have carefully tailored films to the particular talents of Bob Hope (seven films), Danny Kaye (three films), and Bing Crosby (five films), and have provided material for such performers as Lucille Ball, Red Skelton, Zero Mostel, and Goldie Hawn. Their films—notably *Knock on Wood* (1954), *The Court Jester* (1956), and *The Road to Hong Kong* (1962)—often center on characters who are performers or entertainers. Frank and Panama's comedy films are often fantasies in which the comic figure is forced to perform heroic deeds, and the contrast between the everyday, self-deprecating personality of the comedian and the death-defying personality of his fantasy hero side provides the source of humor.

Melvin Frank and Norman Panama were both raised in Chicago. They both attended the University of Chicago and began writing plays together. An unproduced comedy led to a series of radio gag-writing stints, first for Milton Berle. During World War II they wrote material for comedians and others to be broadcast on Armed Forces Radio. Paramount bought their original story *My Favorite*

Basil Rathbone and Danny Kaye in The Court Jester

Blonde (1942) for Bob Hope and put them under contract. In 1946 they coauthored two more films for Hope: *Monsieur Beaucaire* and *Road to Utopia*. Both were successful, and *Road to Utopia* earned them an Academy Award nomination. Reaching the end of their Paramount contract, Frank and Panama established themselves as independent coproducers, giving them the opportunity to supervise directly the development of their work.

Their first product as a producer-screenwriter team was *Mr. Blandings Builds His Dream House* (1948), about a city dweller (Cary Grant) who longs to get away from it all and decides to build a house in the country. The film's humor benefits from Frank and Panama's sharp eye for the details of family life in the late 1940s and the comic reversal of the plot—here, the city residents are conned by the hicks.

After the success of *Mr. Blandings Builds His Dream House*, Frank and Panama signed a contract with M-G-M to codirect, coauthor, and coproduce their films. Of the five films that resulted, two are particularly noteworthy: *Callaway Went Thataway* (1952), a spoof of the then-popular Hopalong Cassidy films, and *Above and Beyond* (1953), their first successful drama, which starred Robert Taylor as the pilot of the plane that bombed Hiroshima and depicts the effect the mission has on his marriage.

Leaving M-G-M, Panama and Frank next wrote three films for Danny Kaye: *White Christmas* (1954), *Knock on Wood*, and *The Court Jester*. *Knock on Wood* and *The Court Jester* are among Kaye's finest films, both tailored to his unique talents. In *Knock on Wood* he is a ventriloquist whose dummy has been uncontrollably ruining his love life. Seeking help from a psychiatrist (Mai Zetterling), he is unwittingly involved in an international spy plot. Sought as a murderer, he must wear a series of disguises to escape his pursuers. In *The Court Jester*, Kaye is a member of a band of outlaws, caring for an infant king who has been deposed by a usurper. Kaye disguises himself as the court jester, enters the castle, and is hypnotized and given a dashing, heroic personality which he shifts in and out of. The Kaye films were successful, and *Knock on Wood* earned Frank and Panama their second Academy Award nomination and their third nomination for a Writers Guild Award (the first two had been for *Mr. Blandings Builds His Dream House* and *Above and Beyond*).

In 1956 Frank and Panama wrote a Broadway musical based on the comic strip "Li'l Abner." This play no doubt influenced their next film, *That Certain Feeling* (1956)—in which Al Capp had a cameo—about an egotistical cartoonist (George Sanders). The cartoonist's ghostwriter (Bob Hope) is also the ex-husband of the cartoonist's fiancée (Eva Marie Saint). Frank and Panama collaborated on the screenplay with I. A. L. Diamond and William Altman. This film was followed by the screen version of *Li'l Abner* (1959), which was nominated for another Writers Guild Award.

Frank and Panama received their third Oscar nomination and fifth nomination by the Writers Guild for *The Facts of Life* (1960), about two middle-class, middle-aged suburban neighbors (Bob Hope and Lucille Ball) who break out of the repetitions of their married lives and have a brief affair. After many comic mishaps that sabotage their affair at every turn, the two give up and return to their respective families and their old roles as just friends.

The Road to Hong Kong (1962) was the seventh and last of the Bob Hope-Bing Crosby Road pictures. Crosby and Hope play con men who become involved in a scheme that gets them caught up in the race for mastery of outer space. They end up as passengers in a space capsule, replacing the apes that had originally been selected. The plot generates a series of gags, but critics found the film strained and tired.

Bob Hope in Panama and Frank's last collaboration,
The Road to Hong Kong

Jack Gilford, Michael Hordern, Zero Mostel, and Phil Silvers in A Funny Thing Happened on the Way to the Forum.
Frank was producer and coauthor of this film, one of his first after he parted with Panama.

The Road to Hong Kong was Frank and Panama's last full screenplay as a team. In the mid-1960s Frank collaborated with Michael Pertwee on the screen story and screenplay for the comedy *Strange Bedfellows* (1965), and Panama did the screenplay for *Not With My Wife You Don't!* (1966) with Larry Gelbart and Peter Barnes.

Panama and Frank established offices in London during the early 1960s. Projects and duties had become progressively individualized, and they ceased working together after 1966. They parted amicably, and each has since continued to work with collaborators, including Jack Rose and Sheldon Keller. Frank produced and coauthored *A Funny Thing Happened on the Way to the Forum* (1966), directed by Richard Lester. Panama directed *How to Commit Marriage* (1969), another Bob Hope film, and several made-for-television films.

Frank's *Buona Sera, Mrs. Campbell* (1968) is an interesting combination of motifs from the earlier comedies. In World War II Italy, a young woman slept with three American soldiers and had a child;

she convinced each soldier the child was his. When the men (Phil Silvers, Telly Savalas, and Peter Lawford) return to Italy with their families for a twenty-year reunion, Mrs. Campbell (Gina Lollobrigida) is forced to admit the truth to them and her daughter (Janet Margolin), who thought her father had been killed in the war.

Like *The Facts of Life*, Frank's *A Touch of Class* (1973) traces the love affair between two independent individuals. Vicki Allesio (Glenda Jackson) is a divorced woman with a successful career; she is pitted against Steve Blackburn (George Segal), a thoroughly married businessman. *A Touch of Class* was Frank's most successful film since the split from Panama; it was nominated for Academy Awards for best picture and best screenplay, and Glenda Jackson won the Oscar for best actress.

Independent of each other, Frank and Panama have continued making films. In 1976 Panama wrote and directed *I Will, I Will . . . For Now*, about a straying couple (Elliott Gould and Diane Keaton) who rediscover each other. That same year, Frank cowrote and directed *The Duchess and the Dirtwater Fox*, an unsuccessful Western comedy about a gambler (George Segal) and a dance-hall girl (Goldie Hawn). In *Lost and Found* (1979), Frank reteamed George Segal and Glenda Jackson for a romantic comedy that placed a newly married couple in an academic setting but failed to recapture the success of *A Touch of Class*.

The comedy films of Frank and Panama, starring such performers as Hope, Kaye, and Ball, have often been consigned to the category of light amusement. Yet their years together resulted in a body of social comedy/dramas representative of major trends in American film since World War II. Extending from the comic fantasies of Bob Hope and Danny Kaye to the family comedies of the 1950s and finally to the man/woman confrontations of the 1970s, Frank and Panama's films trace the evolution of the American comedy film.

Abraham Polonsky
(5 December 1910-   )

Keith Kelly
Institute of Fine Art, New York University

MOTION PICTURES: *Golden Earrings* (Paramount, 1946), screenplay by Polonsky, Frank Butler, and Helen Deutsch;

Body and Soul (United Artists, 1947), screen story and screenplay;

Force of Evil (M-G-M, 1949), screenplay by Polonsky and Ira Wolfert;

I Can Get It for You Wholesale (20th Century-Fox, 1951), screenplay;

Madigan (Universal, 1968), screen story and screenplay by Polonsky and Harry Kleiner;

Tell Them Willie Boy Is Here (Universal, 1969), screenplay;

Avalanche Express (20th Century-Fox, 1979), screenplay;

Monsignor (20th Century-Fox, 1982), screenplay by Polonsky and Wendell Mayes.

BOOKS: *The Goose is Cooked*, by Polonsky and Mitchell Wilson (New York: Simon & Schuster, 1940);

The Enemy Sea (Boston: Little, Brown, 1943);

The World Above (Boston: Little, Brown, 1951);

A Season of Fear (New York: Cameron Associates, 1956);

Zenia's Way (New York: Harper & Row, 1980).

PERIODICAL PUBLICATIONS: "The Case of David Smith," *Hollywood Quarterly*, 1 (January 1946): 185-198;

"Hemingway and Chaplin," *Contemporary Reader*, 1 (March 1953): 21-31;

"The Troubled Mandarins," *Masses and Mainstream*, 9 (August 1956): 35-47;

"Une Expérience Utopique," *Présence du Cinéma*, 14 (June 1962): 5-7;

"Making Movies," *Sight and Sound*, 40 (Spring 1971): 101;

"Nuits Blanches Pendant la Liste Noire, Extrait de Journal," *Positif* (December-January 1977-1978).

Abraham Polonsky's importance as a screenwriter rests both on his body of work—one of the strongest, continuously radical political statements in commercial American film—and on his role as symbol of the oppressed Hollywood writer, driven underground by Cold War hysteria, only to reemerge undaunted, still creative, and still radical. Polonsky was a successful screenwriter and had just begun a career as director when he was blacklisted in 1951. One of the last in Hollywood to break the blacklist, he did not receive a screen credit for another seventeen years. His early films, particularly *Force of Evil* (1949), have gained in reputation over the years; his output since 1968 has been limited but distinctive.

Abraham Lincoln Polonsky was born in the East Side of New York City, the son of a Russian émigré pharmacist, Henry Polonsky, and Rebecca Rosoff Polonsky. He has described his youth as "the usual restless street life," and he was a member of a gang as a teenager. Polonsky was reared in a socialist Jewish environment, and the reminiscences of his parents, and particularly his atheist socialist grandmother, were to influence his screenplays and

Abraham Polonsky (photo by Maureen Lambray)

fiction. While attending City College of New York, he wrote for its literary magazine, *Lavender*. After receiving his B.A. in 1932, he taught at City College to support his studies at Columbia Law School, which granted him an LL.B. in 1935. During these years, Polonsky joined the American Communist party.

In 1937, Polonsky married Sylvia Marrow, with whom he subsequently had three children, and, as a young attorney, he was sent to Hollywood to work with the production staff for a radio serial, "The Goldbergs." Eventually he wrote some scripts for the series, and, after he returned to New York, he abandoned law to continue writing radio scripts and returned to teaching at City College. His first novel, "The Discoverers," was accepted for publication then withdrawn as "unreadable." His novel *The Enemy Sea* (1943) was published and led Paramount Pictures to hire Polonsky as a screenwriter. Immediately after signing with Paramount, Polonsky left for Europe to serve as a civilian volunteer in

World War II, so his first screenplay was not produced until 1947.

Polonsky spent 1943-1945 working for the Office of Strategic Services as a European operative involved in projects aimed at undermining enemy morale. When he returned to the United States in 1945, he became involved with the Hollywood Writer's Mobilization, and in 1946 he served on the editorial board of the *Hollywood Quarterly*.

Polonsky worked on several unproduced scripts for Paramount before being assigned to "an incredible, romantic melodramatic stew," *Golden Earrings* (1946). While he intended the film to become a study of Gypsies suffering from persecution by the Nazis, it emerged as a story of a Gypsy woman spying against the Germans. Polonsky later said, "I know there isn't a single word or scene of mine in it," but he received screen credit along with Helen Deutsch and Frank Butler.

After a year at Paramount, Polonsky left to work at the newly formed independent Enterprise

Clockwise from left: John Garfield, Anne Revere, Lilli Palmer, and Joseph Pevney in Body and Soul

Productions, where he was asked to write a boxing drama in the vein of Clifford Odets's *Golden Boy*. The resulting film, *Body and Soul*, released by United Artists in 1947, became one of the most successful films of the year and earned Polonsky an Oscar nomination.

In Polonsky's film Charlie Davis (John Garfield) becomes a fighter hoping to break out of working-class poverty and allies himself with Roberts, a gangster-promoter who runs boxing. As Charlie becomes a successful fighter, he alienates those close to him and remains indifferent to the corruption around him, even refusing to act when Roberts causes the death of his best friend Shorty. Charlie agrees to throw a fight for Roberts, but when his trainer Ben dies, he changes his mind and wins the match.

Polonsky's social ethics are clear in *Body and Soul*. Money is presented as a source of evil; all of Charlie's problems are caused by his greed ("I want money, money, money!," he shouts at one point). Charlie knows he is choosing to be a prizefighter not

for love of the sport but because it offers him his only escape from poverty, and he also knows the price he will have to pay in loss of identity and integrity, as he sells himself to the gangster who runs the fight racket. The film's ending, with Charlie's rejecting the criminals with whom he has been associated, is the result of the idealism of Polonsky and his coworkers on the film: director Robert Rossen, producer Bob Roberts, and John Garfield, who had founded Enterprise Productions with the intention of making films that were socially relevant.

Polonsky was on the set constantly during the shooting of *Body and Soul*, and Roberts and Garfield suggested he direct, as well as write, their next project, *Force of Evil*, based on Ira Wolfert's novel *Tucker's People*. In *Force of Evil* Joe Morse (Garfield), a young lawyer who has become crooked, is now in the service of Ben Tucker, a numbers-racket boss who has exploited Joe's talents to become a legitimate businessman while still retaining underworld power. In helping Tucker to gain a monopoly on the numbers racket, Joe destroys a small-time num-

246

bers business run by his older brother, Leo, and because Leo resists incorporation into the mob, he is killed. Joe realizes his own responsibility for the murder and vows to aid the police in destroying Tucker and his crime empire.

A major premise of *Force of Evil* is one Polonsky shares with other Marxist filmmakers: the criminal underworld is a mirror image of corporate capitalism. The film repeatedly equates the goals and methods of gangsters with those of legitimate businessmen. Joe's rise from honest lawyer to powerful and wealthy criminal thereby becomes a perverted success story. In this scathing critique of the American dream, the "force of evil" is the profit motive.

For Polonsky, in a corrupt system all people are corrupted to some degree. Leo, whose resistance to the lure of big-time crime makes him seem somehow respectable, is himself a crook, albeit on a smaller scale than Joe and Tucker. Doris, Leo's secretary, who represents the strongest force for morality in the film, is corrupted both through her service to Leo and her attraction to Joe when he is at the height of his criminal involvement. The characters are all infected by capitalist greed, jealousy, and fear. True to a Marxist perspective, relationships are dominated by economic considerations, people become objectified into commodities, and there is total alienation of the individual from nature, work, fellow man, and self.

Force of Evil was ignored by American critics when first released, but it was praised overseas, particularly by the British magazine *Sight and Sound*. In the 1960s, it found new admirers in the French new-wave critics. Today, though seldom seen, it has a growing reputation in the United States. Andrew Sarris has called it "one of the great films of the modern American cinema."

In 1950, Polonsky suggested to Alvah Bessie the idea for Bessie's screen story *Cross of Gold* (1951), about a group of escaped convicts in nineteenth-century California, who are reformed by a group of immigrants fleeing religious persecution.

Polonsky's next screen credit was for *I Can Get It for You Wholesale* (1951), another tale of greed, depicting a designer in the garment business who will do anything to succeed. It is based on a novel by Jerome Weidman, and Weidman wrote a treatment for the film from which Polonsky worked to create a finished script.

After completing this assignment, he traveled to Europe with the intention of writing a novel (he eventually completed it years later) and of obtaining the film rights to Thomas Mann's *Mario and the Magician*. He returned to America and signed to write and direct a film for 20th Century-Fox, but before he could begin work on that film, Polonsky was blacklisted.

In 1950, Richard Collins, Meta Rosenberg, and Sterling Hayden identified Polonsky to the House Committee on Un-American Activities as a Communist. Polonsky was subpoenaed and appeared before the committee on 25 April 1951, at which time he invoked the Fifth Amendment. Labeled by Congressman Harold H. Velde as "the most dangerous man in America," Polonsky was blacklisted from commercial filmmaking until 1968.

After being blacklisted, Polonsky returned to writing fiction and magazine articles. A novel, *The World Above*, published in 1951, was followed by another, *A Season of Fear* (1956), which carried a blurb stating that Polonsky had left filmmaking "to go abroad and devote himself to serious fiction." He also wrote on the black market, producing scripts for the television series *You Are There* and *Danger* and doctoring screenplays from time to time. Director Robert Wise has revealed that Polonsky wrote *Odds Against Tomorrow* (1959) without credit. He also worked on a pet project, "The Sweet Land," a screenplay about the migration of blacks from the South after the Civil War, but it was never produced. Unlike some writers, Polonsky did not suffer financially during blacklisting; in fact, he made more money than he had before. He later said of this period, "The guerilla life I pretended to practise in the war I played with some amusement and frequent disgust in the jungle of TV as a blacklisted writer. Likewise in films."

In 1965 Polonsky wrote under his own name "The Last Clear Chance" for NBC's *Kraft Suspense Theatre*, and in 1968 he was brought in to replace Howard Rodman on *Madigan*, a film about a policeman's efforts to track a sadistic killer. Producer Frank Rosenberg gave Polonsky screen credit, and his blacklisting was ended.

The success of *Madigan* brought Polonsky an offer to write and direct a film for television, *Tell Them Willie Boy Is Here* (1969). After Polonsky had begun work on the teleplay, however, he was able to convince Universal to produce it as a film. Polonsky said of the film—which was based on a true story of a young Indian who kills the father of his intended wife and is pursued by the police—"What particularly interested me is the fact that the Indian is a kind of exile in his own country, and so am I—or was—for a brief period: twenty years. I thought my reaction to his problem might be interesting in

Robert Redford as the deputy sheriff in Tell Them Willie Boy Is Here

terms of my reaction to my own." Although some critics complained that the film was sometimes heavy-handed in its portrayal of conflicts between Indians and whites, nearly all agreed that it was well made, and several found Willie, as portrayed by Robert Blake, to be similar to the John Garfield characters in *Body and Soul* and *Force of Evil.*

In 1971 Polonsky directed but did not write *Romance of a Horse Thief*, about a group of Polish Jews plotting against a Cossack captain and his men at the beginning of the twentieth century. For this film, Polonsky drew heavily on the stories told him as a child by his grandmother, saying, "It is her voice I hear all through the movie, and it was her voice and her face which toured the locations."

Although he worked on several unproduced scripts, including an adaptation of Arthur C. Clarke's *Childhood's End*, Polonsky did not receive another screen credit until *Avalanche Express* (1979).

A standard espionage film about a Soviet official defecting to the United States, it was a box-office failure.

In 1981, Polonsky worked without credit on *Mommie Dearest*, based on the memoir by Joan Crawford's daughter Christina. For the same director and producer, Frank Perry and Frank Yablans, Polonsky wrote with Wendell Mayes *Monsignor* (1982), about a priest who is attached to the Vatican during World War II and finds himself dealing with the European black market. The original screenplay was reportedly impressive, but the final version of the film was severely edited, omitting transitional scenes and major characters. The film was a financial failure and poorly received by critics, though, as with *Tell Them Willie Boy Is Here*, some critics remarked favorably on the similarities between this film's protagonist and the protagonist in *Force of Evil.*

Interviews:

William Pechter, interview (1961 or 1962), in *Interviews with Film Directors*, edited by Andrew Sarris (New York: Avon, 1967), pp. 384-397;

Eric Sherman and Martin Rubin, *The Director's Event: Interviews with Five American Filmmakers* (New York: Atheneum, 1969), pp. 3-37;

James Pasternak and William Howton, interview (1970), in *The Image Maker*, edited by Ron Henderson (Richmond: John Knox Press, 1971), pp. 16-27;

Sherman, interview (1974), in *The American Film* Institute, Louis B. Mayer Oral History Collection, part I, no. 16 (Glenn Rock, N.J.: Microfilming Corporation of America, 1977).

References:

Jack Shadoian, *Dreams and Dead Ends: The American Gangsters/Crime Film* (Cambridge: MIT Press, 1977), pp. 134-148;

Barbara Zheutlin and David Talbot, *Creative Differences: Profiles of Hollywood Dissidents* (Boston: South End Press, 1978), pp. 55-99.

Robert Riskin

(30 March 1897-20 September 1955)

Sam Frank

MOTION PICTURES: *Men in Her Life* (Columbia, 1931), adaptation and dialogue;

Platinum Blonde (Columbia, 1931), dialogue;

Three Wise Girls (Columbia, 1931), dialogue;

The Big Timer (Columbia, 1932), story, adaptation, and dialogue;

American Madness (Columbia, 1932), story, screenplay, and dialogue;

Night Club Lady (Columbia, 1932), screenplay;

Virtue (Columbia, 1932), screenplay;

Shopworn (Columbia, 1932), dialogue by Riskin and Jo Swerling;

Ann Carver's Profession (Columbia, 1933), screenplay and dialogue;

Lady for a Day (Columbia, 1933), screenplay;

It Happened One Night (Columbia, 1934), screenplay;

Broadway Bill (Columbia, 1934), screenplay;

Carnival (Columbia, 1935), story and screenplay;

The Whole Town's Talking (Columbia, 1935), screenplay by Riskin and Jo Swerling;

Mr. Deeds Goes to Town (Columbia, 1936), screenplay;

When You're In Love (Columbia, 1937), screenplay;

Lost Horizon (Columbia, 1937), screenplay;

You Can't Take It With You (Columbia, 1938), screenplay;

Meet John Doe (Warner Bros., 1941), screenplay;

The Thin Man Goes Home (M-G-M, 1944), screen story by Riskin and Harry Kurnitz; screenplay by Riskin and Dwight Taylor;

Magic Town (RKO, 1947), screen story by Riskin and Joseph Krumgold;

Mister 880 (20th Century-Fox, 1950), screenplay;

Half Angel (20th Century-Fox, 1951), screenplay;

Here Comes the Groom (Paramount, 1951), story by Riskin and Liam O'Brien.

SELECTED PLAYS: *She Couldn't Say No* (New York, Booth Theatre, 31 August 1926);

A Lady in Love (New York, Lyceum Theatre, 21 February 1927);

Bless You, Sister (New York, Forrest Theatre, 26 December 1927), by Riskin and John Meehan;

The Lady Lies (New York, Little Theatre, 26 November 1928);

Many a Slip (New York, Little Theatre, 3 February 1930).

Though his credits for stage and screen were numerous, Robert Riskin is most often remembered for the films he wrote for director Frank Capra. These nine motion pictures contain Riskin's finest work and demonstrate his ability to create populist heroes. His hallmarks were an ear for down-to-earth, sometimes poetic dialogue and an aptitude for stories that dealt with earthy themes or "bread-and-butter" issues.

Robert Riskin was born in New York City, one of five children of Russian immigrants. His father and grandfather spent much time discussing

Robert Riskin

philosophy; his mother treated life with a touch of humor. These influences enriched the lives of the young Riskins and compensated for the very modest financial circumstances of their early years. Riskin was educated in New York and Baltimore. At thirteen, he left school and went to work as an office boy in a textile mill.

During the years at the mill, Riskin tried his hand at writing short stories. They were rejected by magazine editors but impressed Riskin's employer so much that he asked the young man to write a love letter for him. Pleased with the letter, the employer asked Riskin's opinion of some short films he and other textile men had produced for Famous Players-Lasky. It was Riskin's opinion that the films "stank" and that Lasky wouldn't touch them. When a Lasky executive confirmed this opinion, the textile men turned to Riskin for advice. Riskin suggested they would be better off making one-reelers with a famous stage star. Before long Riskin had the title "studio manager." This meant he wrote, coproduced, and directed ten-minute comedies in Florida with actor Victor Moore for Famous Players-Lasky; he earned five thousand dollars for each. By the time he turned eighteen and volunteered for navy duty during World War I, Riskin had made many one-reel quickies.

When Riskin returned from war duty in 1918,

movie jobs were at a premium, so he tried writing plays. He wrote and, with his brother Everett, produced several, including *She Couldn't Say No* (1926), *A Lady in Love* (1927), and *The Lady Lies* (1928). Riskin met and became friends with playwright Edith Fitzgerald, with whom he later collaborated. He was making a name for himself when the stock-market crash of 1929 reduced his holdings to a handful of dollars. He tried to get a screenwriting job at Paramount but was turned down by B. P. Schulberg; this rejection filled him with defiance, and he proceeded to write and sell three more plays, all in collaboration with Edith Fitzgerald.

In February 1930, Columbia Pictures bought the rights to *Bless You, Sister*, a play by Riskin and John Meehan that was loosely based on the evangelism of Aimee Semple McPherson. The play was filmed as *The Miracle Woman* (1931) and directed by Frank Capra, and although Riskin did not write the screenplay, it was this project that introduced him to Capra.

By this time, Riskin was well on his way to making a name for himself in Hollywood. His previous experience with short films had proved invaluable when it came to switching from stage to screen. Riskin was commissioned by Columbia's president, Harry Cohn, to cowrite a low-budget feature. He turned in a draft of two hundred pages, not knowing that Cohn had a rule forbidding scripts to run over ninety pages.

Cohn kept Riskin on and, at Frank Capra's request, assigned him to write the dialogue for *Platinum Blonde* (1931). In this film a high-society woman (Jean Harlow) marries a newspaper reporter (Robert Williams) with social aspirations. He discovers he is out of place in the upper class and that his heart really belongs to the earthy, workaday world of his newspaper chums. Riskin was clearly in his element here, writing snappy, street-smart dialogue for the characters in the script.

Capra was as impressed with Riskin as a person as he was with his facility as a writer. They became friends as well as collaborators. Writing of this partnership, Capra said, "Bob was a fine writer, a simpatico man. Natty, witty as they come, he loved life, sports and women, and vice-versa. We had many things in common, but two stood out: 1) our skulls vibrated to the same lady's hair massager and 2) our funnybones vibrated to the same tuning fork in humor. . . . And never was there a better 'ear' for the spoken word than Riskin's."

Riskin's work for Capra following *Platinum Blonde* has several basic characteristics: the hero is always a blue-collar type, either by profession or by temperament; the heroine is almost always a brassy, self-sufficient, wisecracking woman with undertones of sexual aggression who becomes the hero's helper—a role most often played by Jean Arthur; the hero is forced by circumstance to call upon inner reserves of courage, integrity, and idealism in dealing with a social dilemma; the brassy, cynical heroine is converted to this idealism by the hero's innate but never saccharine sincerity and goodness; the hero and heroine are always victorious in their social cause, though the happy endings are sometimes achieved through deus ex machina.

There are exceptions to this formula, notably the wisecracking, aggressive reporter in *It Happened One Night* (1934), (the one time the brassy role was played by a man), the diplomat's lover in *Lost Horizon* (1937), and the moon-eyed daughter in *You Can't Take It With You* (1938). Basically, though, the world of Riskin and Capra is one in which populist heroes right social wrongs, demonstrating that folksy common sense and immediate action are the only possible cures for an American society groping its way out of Depression.

After *Platinum Blonde* came the first of the eight films for which Riskin is most noted, *American Madness* (1932), about a banker (Walter Huston) who insists on lending money to people of good character with no regard for collateral. Riskin's screenplay was just the sort of populist movie Depression audiences needed. Critics pounced on the film for its idealism, but the public loved its bold, commonsense approach to problems.

Lady for a Day (1933), Riskin's next screenplay for Capra, was an adaptation of Damon Runyon's short story "Madame La Gimp." In the film an aging flower-seller (May Robson) enlists the help of some gangster friends with hearts of gold in convincing her long-absent daughter and future son-in-law she is well-heeled. The ruse is eventually uncovered, but all ends well, the point being that even the worst of us can be decent if given the chance. *Lady for a Day* was one of the greatest box-office successes of 1933 (Capra remade it in 1961 as *Pocketful of Miracles*).

By now Riskin was working exclusively for Capra. He had written seven screenplays for other directors, but none had enjoyed the public favor of the Capra films. It was clear that Columbia had a winning partnership. *Lady for a Day*—the first Columbia picture ever nominated for an Oscar—had been nominated for Academy awards for best screenplay, best director, and best actress.

The 1934 Riskin-Capra film *It Happened One Night* was based on a short story by Samuel Hopkins Adams called "Night Bus." It went through several revisions and rejections by major stars before it ended up as a comedy classic with Clark Gable and Claudette Colbert. In the film a spoiled, runaway heiress tangles with a reporter; he sees her as a headline to boost his sagging reputation; she sees him as a means of getting back to her playboy fiancé. By the end of 1934, *It Happened One Night* had broken box-office records throughout the country. The film won Academy awards for best picture, best director, best screenplay, best actor, and best actress—the first time one film had won all the major awards.

Before the release of *It Happened One Night*, Riskin and Capra began work on their next project, *Broadway Bill* (1934), an important film in the Riskin-Capra canon because it marks the transition between their escapist comedies and their populist ones. Dan Brooks (Warner Baxter) is a misfit businessman who forsakes his unsympathetic wife (Helen Vinson) and the factory run by his tycoon father-in-law (Walter Connolly) to enter his beloved

Clark Gable and Claudette Colbert in It Happened One Night, *the first film to win the five major Academy awards—for best screenplay, best director, best actor, best actress, and best picture.*

Gary Cooper (with tuba) in Mr. Deeds Goes to Town

but broken-down horse, Broadway Bill, in an important meet. In the end Broadway Bill does win the race, only to drop dead instantly from a burst heart. The father-in-law is so moved that he divests himself of his wealth and joins Brooks on the road.

Riskin's next two screenplays were for directors other than Capra. *Carnival* (1935) was directed by Walter Lang. John Ford directed *The Whole Town's Talking* (1935), about a timid man who looks like a famous gangster (Edward G. Robinson played both parts). The film has most of the characteristics that mark the Riskin-Capra works. Riskin collaborated on the screenplay with Jo Swerling.

Mr. Deeds Goes to Town (1936) was the first Riskin-Capra film to use a protagonist who becomes a social savior despite himself. Small-town boy Longfellow Deeds (Gary Cooper) inherits a fortune from a distant uncle. Eventually Deeds is persuaded to utilize his fortune as a means of putting thousands of unemployed men to work as farmers. Some greedy would-be heirs are enraged by Deeds's act and have him put on trial for insanity, but he is found "the sanest man who ever walked into this courtroom." *Mr. Deeds Goes to Town* was one of the most commercially successful Riskin-Capra films, and it was also the prototype for many of the populist motifs outlined earlier. The film was nominated for the Academy Award for Best Picture and won awards from the New York Film Critics and the National Board of Review. Riskin's screenplay was also nominated for an Academy Award.

The sneak-preview success of *Mr. Deeds Goes to Town* enabled Capra to talk Harry Cohn into buying James Hilton's best-selling fantasy *Lost Horizon*. The film version of Hilton's novel is certainly the supreme example of Riskin's talent for shaping basically uncinematic material into an escapist epic with popular appeal, improving on the original in the process. In *Lost Horizon* an idealistic diplomat named Robert Conway (Ronald Colman) is hijacked, along with four others, to a mystical Tibetan utopia called Shangri-La. The High Lama (Sam Jaffe) is about to die and feels Conway is the man to carry on his work maintaining Shangri-La as a cultural treasure-house for mankind. What Riskin did was to transform Hilton's utopia from a passionless, loveless, sexless paradise into just the opposite: a happy, loving, sensual community whose reason for being offers a vision of what man can be in his best moments. The novel is singularly lacking in humor, but Riskin injects a good deal of it, not only into the portrayal of Conway's fellow travelers, but into Conway as well. Riskin was able to imbue the novel's intellectual idealism with a warm sense of humanity, thereby making Shangri-La a paradise worthy of its goals. The film was a success, though not phenomenally so until its subsequent rereleases.

After the success of *Mr. Deeds Goes to Town* and *Lost Horizon*, Riskin used his now-considerable clout to persuade Cohn to let him direct a film in addition to writing it. The result was *When You're In Love* (1937), about a woman (Grace Moore) who pays a man to pretend to be her husband and then really falls in love with him. The film, which was not a financial success, disappointed Riskin; he never directed another film.

In 1936 Capra, who had been away from Columbia for a year because of litigation, asked Riskin

to adapt George S. Kaufman and Moss Hart's 1936 Broadway hit *You Can't Take It With You*. This comedy about an amiable family who live as they please was a huge popular success, earning Riskin another Oscar nomination and winning the Academy Award for Best Picture.

After completing *You Can't Take It With You*, Riskin left Columbia and became an associate producer for Samuel Goldwyn. He worked on two films: *They Shall Have Music* (1939) and *The Real Glory* (1939).

In 1940 Capra also left Columbia and formed a new kind of partnership with Riskin. They would jointly produce independent features for which Riskin would write the scripts and distribute them through a major studio which would provide financial backing. (Common today, the procedure was a precedent then.) Warner Bros. was the studio, and the one film made was *Meet John Doe* (1941), for which Riskin and Capra each received $500,000 in salary.

Meet John Doe is about a newspaper columnist (Barbara Stanwyck) who has created a fictional

A scene from Lost Horizon

character to represent the problems of the little man and named him John Doe. A bum (Gary Cooper) is found to impersonate John Doe, and he becomes involved with the plan of a ruthless tycoon (Edward Arnold) to run for president. This was the first Riskin-Capra film to have serious narrative problems. They started filming without an ending in mind and wound up shooting five different endings. Despite this, the film was a success, but Riskin never worked with Capra again, except for writing the screen story for *Here Comes the Groom* (1951).

In August 1941, at the invitation of the British government, Riskin went to London to act in an advisory capacity in the use of film for propaganda purposes. He returned to the United States in 1942, joining the Office of War Information, where he created its Overseas Motion Picture Bureau and functioned as its chief until May 1945. Riskin produced twenty-six features and shorts on various aspects of American life, including the acclaimed documentary *Toscanini* (1944), about the great conductor.

On 23 August 1942, Riskin married actress Fay Wray; they had three children, Susan, Robert Jr., and Victoria. During this time, he also wrote and produced *The Thin Man Goes Home* (1944), the penultimate film in the Thin Man series.

In 1945, Riskin formed Robert Riskin Productions and signed to produce and cowrite a series of independent features for RKO. Only one film resulted from this deal—*Magic Town* (1947), about a pollster (James Stewart) who finds what he thinks is the perfect middle-American town for a survey of American opinion on basic issues. *Magic Town* was the last populist film of its type, partly because Riskin's attempt to duplicate his earlier successes with Capra was out of step with postwar America.

Liam O'Brien, a young writer for whom Riskin had great hopes, joined Riskin's company, and they collaborated on the screen story for *Here Comes the Groom*, about a man (Bing Crosby) bent on keeping his former fiancée (Jane Wyman) from marrying a millionaire. Following the financial failure of *Magic Town*, Riskin sold the story to Paramount in 1949 and dissolved his company. *Here Comes the Groom* was filmed by Capra in 1951; Riskin and O'Brien were nominated for the Academy Award for Best Original Story.

Riskin next went to work at 20th Century-Fox, where he wrote his last two screenplays. The first, *Mister 880* (1950), was based on *New Yorker* articles about a counterfeiter; the film presented a charming old man (Edmund Gwenn) who had spent ten years making and circulating counterfeit dollar bills. *Half Angel* (1951), also based on fact, was a romantic comedy about a woman (Loretta Young) who takes on a new personality when she sleepwalks.

Shortly after completing his work on *Half Angel*, Riskin suffered a stroke. He underwent surgery during Christmas week 1950, but the operation failed, leaving him permanently paralyzed on his left side. On 28 February 1955, the Writers Guild of America presented Riskin with a Laurel Award for his "distinguished contributions to the film medium"; Fay Wray accepted on his behalf. On 20 September that same year, Riskin died, having been bedridden for nearly five years.

References:

Frank Capra, *The Name Above the Title* (New York: Macmillan, 1971);

Richard Corliss, "Capra and Riskin," *Film Comment*, 8 (November 1972): 18-21;

William T. Levy and Victor Scherle, *The Films of Frank Capra* (Secaucus, N.J.: Citadel Press, 1977);

Bob Thomas, *King Cohn* (New York: Putnam's, 1967).

Papers:
The major collection of Riskin's papers is part of the Fay Wray Collection at the University of Southern California. There is a smaller collection of Riskin materials at the Margaret Herrick Library of the American Academy of Motion Picture Arts and Sciences, Beverly Hills, California.

Allen Rivkin

(20 November 1903-   )

Stephen O. Lesser

SELECTED MOTION PICTURES: *Is My Face Red* (RKO, 1932), story by Rivkin and Ben Markson;

The Devil Is Driving (Paramount, 1932), adaptation by Rivkin and P. J. Wolfson;

Madison Square Garden (Paramount, 1932), screenplay by Rivkin and Wolfson;

Night World (Universal, 1932), story by Rivkin and Wolfson;

70,000 Witnesses (Paramount, 1932), dialogue by Rivkin and Wolfson;

Dancing Lady (M-G-M, 1933), screenplay by Rivkin and Wolfson;

Cheating Cheaters (Universal, 1934), screenplay by Rivkin and Gladys Unger;

Black Sheep (Fox, 1935), screenplay;

Our Little Girl (Fox, 1935), screenplay by Rivkin and Stephen Avery;

Bad Boy (20th Century-Fox, 1935), screenplay;

Champagne Charley (20th Century-Fox, 1936), screenplay;

Half Angel (20th Century-Fox, 1936), screenplay by Rivkin, Bess Meredyth, and Gene Fowler;

Love Under Fire (20th Century-Fox, 1937), screenplay by Rivkin, Fowler, and Ernest Pascal;

This Is My Affair (20th Century-Fox, 1937), screen story and screenplay by Rivkin and Lamar Trotti;

Straight, Place and Show (20th Century-Fox, 1938), screenplay by Rivkin and M. M. Musselman;

It Could Happen to You (20th Century-Fox, 1939), screenplay by Rivkin and Nathanael West;

Let Us Live (Columbia, 1939), screenplay by Rivkin and Anthony Veiller;

Typhoon (Paramount, 1940), screenplay;

Dancing on A Dime (Paramount, 1940), screenplay by Rivkin, Anne Morrison Chapin, and Maurice Rapf;

Behind the News (Republic, 1941), screen story by Rivkin and Dore Schary;

Singapore Woman (Warner Bros., 1941), screenplay by Rivkin and M. Coates Webster;

Highway West (Warner Bros., 1941), screenplay by Rivkin, Charles Kenyon, and Kenneth Gamet;

Kid Glove Killer (M-G-M, 1942), screenplay by Rivkin and John C. Higgins;

Allen Rivkin (photo © Norman B. Samuels)

Joe Smith, American (M-G-M, 1942), screenplay;

Sunday Punch (M-G-M, 1942), screenplay by Rivkin, Fay Kanin, and Michael Kanin;

Till the End of Time (RKO, 1946), screenplay;

The Thrill of Brazil (Columbia, 1946), screen story and screenplay by Rivkin, Harry Clark, and Devery Freeman;

Dead Reckoning (Columbia, 1946), adaptation;

The Guilt of Janet Ames (Columbia, 1946), screenplay by Rivkin, Louella MacFarlane, and Freeman;

The Farmer's Daughter (RKO-Radio, 1947), screenplay by Rivkin and Laura Kerr;

My Dream Is Yours (Warner Bros., 1949), adaptation by Rivkin and Kerr;

Tension (M-G-M, 1950), screenplay;

Gambling House (RKO, 1951), screenplay by Rivkin and Marvin Borowsky;

Grounds for Marriage (M-G-M, 1951), screenplay by Rivkin and Kerr;

The Strip (M-G-M, 1951), screen story and screenplay;

It's a Big Country (M-G-M, 1952), screenplay by Rivkin and others;

Battle Circus (M-G-M, 1953), story by Rivkin and Kerr;

Prisoner of War (M-G-M, 1954), screen story and screenplay;

Timberjack (Republic, 1955), screenplay;

The Road to Denver (Republic, 1955), screenplay by Rivkin and Horace McCoy;

The Eternal Sea (Republic, 1955), screenplay;

Girls on the Loose (Universal, 1958), screenplay by Rivkin, Dorothy Raison, and Alan Friedman;

Live Fast, Die Young (Universal, 1958), screenplay by Rivkin and Ib Melchoir;

The Big Operator (M-G-M, 1959), screenplay by Rivkin and Robert Smith.

PLAY: *Knock on Wood* (New York, Cort Theatre, 28 May 1935).

BOOKS: *I Wasn't Born Yesterday: An Anonymous Autobiography,* by Rivkin and Leonard Spigelgass (New York: Macauley, 1935);

Hello, Hollywood!: A Book About the Movies by the People Who Make Them, by Rivkin, Laura Kerr, and others (Garden City: Doubleday, 1962).

The film career of Allen Rivkin follows two paths. As a screenwriter Rivkin worked on over sixty scripts and collaborated with most of Hollywood's leading producers, directors, and stars. But equally important, he has been closely associated for over forty years with the Screen Writers Guild, where he helped formulate the policies that govern the working world of the screenwriter. Rivkin's involvement with the Guild has given him a unique vantage point, as participant and as observer, on the changing status of the Hollywood screenwriter. To celebrate Rivkin's seventy-fifth birthday in 1978, the Guild's board of directors gave him a large party; it was the first time an individual has been so honored. As a former president of the Guild and winner of its Valentine Davies Award in 1963, he has been serving as its director of public relations and special projects since 1963.

Allen Rivkin was born in Hayward, Wisconsin, the son of Samuel Richard and Rose (Rosenberg) Rivkin. His father worked for the Weyerhauser Corporation and moved to Cloquet, Minnesota, where Rivkin attended public school. At the Uni-

versity of Minnesota Rivkin was drawn to college dramatics and journalism, editing the school's yearbook. Following graduation he worked on a series of daily newspapers including the *Minneapolis Journal* and the *Chicago Tribune*, eventually going to New York to enter the field of public relations.

Rivkin came to Hollywood in 1931 at the invitation of Hy Daab, then director of RKO publicity and advertising, and joined the publicity unit for the feature film *Cimarron*. A colleague, Howard Estabrook, advised him, "Write about what you know," which led to Rivkin's first screen credit for *Is My Face Red* (1932), a film about a Broadway gossip columnist.

Rivkin's active screenwriting career continued for twenty-seven years, during which he wrote scripts and worked, in his own words, as "clean-up man" on numerous other projects. He also wrote over sixty television shows and served as a producer and head writer for the late 1950s series *Troubleshooter*. As a screenwriter, Rivkin's output is marked by versatility. His work ranges from Westerns (*The Road to Denver*, 1955) to South Seas epics (*Typhoon*, 1940) to crime drama (*Dead Reckoning*, 1946) to historical romance (*This Is My Affair*, 1937), war stories (*Prisoner of War*, 1954), and musical comedy (*Dancing Lady*, 1933).

A political liberal, Rivkin tried to point out, often in a painless and humorous manner, imperfections in American society. His light touch and his flair for a strong narrative story sprang from his commitment to expressing his views. In a recent interview Rivkin said that there had to be a political content to the story; "otherwise I couldn't get fascinated." In his personal life Rivkin has been active in social and political causes. Along with Dore Schary and Leonard Spigelgass, he joined a group called Fight for Freedom that tried to alert the country to the menace of fascism before the United States entered the war. Later, he served as director and entertainment producer of the Democratic National Convention in Los Angeles in 1960. Beginning in 1948 he was national director of the Committee for the Arts for the Democratic National Committee; in this position he helped win the support of Hollywood celebrities for the Democratic party.

Rivkin's best films reflect an awareness of social issues. *Is My Face Red*, one of the first films for which Rivkin wrote, is about a newspaper columnist (Ricardo Cortez) who abuses his powerful position. *Love Under Fire* (1937) uses the Spanish Civil War as the background for a routine love story. In *This Is My Affair*, which Rivkin wrote with Lamar Trotti, a military officer (Robert Taylor) works under orders from President McKinley to expose a criminal gang. Rivkin collaborated with Anthony Veiller on *Let Us Live* (1939), about an innocent man (Henry Fonda) convicted of murder. Rivkin and John C. Higgins wrote the screenplay for one of director Fred Zinnemann's first feature films, *Kid Glove Killer* (1942), about a police chemist trying to thwart an assassination plot. *Joe Smith, American* (1942) was an anti-Nazi thriller about a munitions worker kidnapped by the Germans.

One of Rivkin's strongest presentations of a social problem was *Till the End of Time* (1946), based on the novel *They Dream of Home* by Niven Busch. The film concerns the difficulties faced by the World War II veterans returning to civilian life. Rivkin remembers this film with particular pleasure because he received a telephone call from a legless veteran who had been planning suicide on the very night that he saw *Till the End of Time*. Inspired by one character, a marine prizefighter who lost both legs at Guadalcanal, the veteran had changed his mind.

The next year, 1947, Rivkin treated another social problem in *The Farmer's Daughter*, one of his most successful films. It is a political comedy, the story of the Scandinavian maid Katie (Loretta Young won an Oscar for her performance) who finds herself first working in the home of a con-

Joseph Cotton and Loretta Young in The Farmer's Daughter. *Young's portrayal of the Scandinavian maid Katie won her the 1947 Academy Award for Best Actress.*

gressman and is later nominated and elected to Congress herself. The approach is humorous, the underlying message more serious. The film satirizes the carnivallike atmosphere of American politics, pointing to the weaknesses in how Americans choose and elect candidates to national office. (The movie inspired a considerably less satirical television series in the 1960s.)

During the 1940s Rivkin also worked on three highly successful mystery films. John Cromwell directed *Dead Reckoning*, about an ex-GI (Humphrey Bogart) who thinks his army buddy was murdered by gangsters. *The Guilt of Janet Ames* (1946) has a similar plot that details a woman's investigation of her husband's mysterious death. One of Rivkin's few solo screenplays was *Tension* (1950), about a man (Richard Basehart) who seeks revenge on his wife.

In the 1950s Rivkin collaborated on three films set during the Korean War: *It's a Big Country* (1952), for which he wrote segment 5, *Letter From Korea*; *Battle Circus* (1953); and *Prisoner of War*. He also worked on four movies concerned with the growing problem of urban crime: *Gambling House* (1951), *Timberjack* (1955), *Girls on the Loose* (1958), and *Live Fast, Die Young* (1958).

On 10 November 1952, Rivkin married writer Laura Hirnickel who, as Laura Kerr, collaborated with him on *The Farmer's Daughter* and four other screenplays. Rivkin completed his last script in 1959, working as "clean-up operator" for the Albert Zugsmith production of *The Big Operator*. Subsequently, he devoted his energies, at first on a part-time and later on a full-time basis, to the Writers Guild. He spent his time working on public relations for the Guild without fee until 1963, when he was asked to join the staff. He is responsible for the Guild's awards presentation, for special projects, and the theatre and film society. He also edits the Guild's newsletter.

From his earliest days in Hollywood, Rivkin has been associated with the Writers Guild. As he remembers it, he attended a meeting, asked a question, and found himself serving on a committee. In the early 1930s, he served on the Guild's board of directors. The initial struggle of the Guild was to establish itself as a recognized union, separate from the Motion Picture Academy, that protected and served the screenwriter. At first its position was weak, but through the turbulent 1930s, despite severe internal schism, the Guild managed to win many of its positions. A major issue of the 1930s was to prevent studios from imposing mandatory salary cuts on writers as a means of saving money during the Depression. The Guild fought the studios' attempt. The Guild's decision in 1936 to amalgamate with the larger Author's League of America caused a split in Guild ranks, and many members resigned and joined a company union sponsored by the studios. When a National Labor Relations Board election between the two organizations resulted in an overwhelming Guild victory, the Guild decided not to join the Author's League. During this period, Rivkin was active as a Guild supporter, urging, cajoling, and persuading members not to leave the Guild.

Rivkin served on numerous negotiation and arbitration committees, but most of his activities centered on preparing Guild publications, such as the *Screen Writer*. He worked with Donald Ogden Stewart and Ralph Block in these areas.

The period following World War II was also a time of trouble for the Guild. Public reaction and governmental pressure as a result of the Red scare forced the Guild into a defensive position, unable to protect its members against the anti-Communist hysteria. Rivkin, a liberal, wanted to protect the Guild from organized pressure, either by the government or a left-wing block. He successfully defeated the practice of "all-time" proxy voting by which a few activists were able to corral proxies from less involved members and use them for an

indefinite period. Rivkin, along with Abel Buffington, Paul Gangelin, and Art Arthur, spent a busy weekend, gathering eight hundred seventy proxies to defeat the block voting and the granting of all-time proxies in the future.

Rivkin points to three issues that concern the Guild in Hollywood. The first is the problem of "possessory credit" when a director's name appears above the film title (in 1966 the writers were able to have possessory credit dismissed, but the Screen Directors Guild won it back three years later). Another problem is the desire for a clause giving writers cost-of-living increases in forthcoming contracts. A final question involves the new technologies, particularly cable television, and the writer's share of proceeds.

Both paths of Rivkin's Hollywood career, as a screenwriter and as an organizational man on behalf of other screenwriters, have led to accomplishment and success. His recognition is deserved, for few have helped the community of screenwriters in Hollywood as much as Allen Rivkin.

Papers:

Screenplays and other materials related to Rivkin's films can be found at the Library of the Academy of Motion Picture Arts and Sciences, Beverly Hills, California.

Reginald Rose
(10 December 1920-   )

Carola Kaplan
California State Polytechnic University, Pomona

MOTION PICTURES: *Crime in the Streets* (Allied Artists, 1956), screen story and screenplay;
Dino (Allied Artists, 1957), story and screenplay;
12 Angry Men (United Artists, 1957), screenplay;
Man of the West (United Artists, 1958), screenplay;
Man in the Net (United Artists, 1959), screen story and screenplay;
Baxter! (National General, 1973), screenplay;
Somebody Killed Her Husband (Columbia, 1978), screenplay;
The Wild Geese (Allied Artists, 1978), screenplay;
The Sea Wolves (Lorimar, 1980), screenplay;
Whose Life Is It Anyway? (M-G-M, 1981), screenplay

by Rose and Brian Clark;
The Final Option (M-G-M/United Artists, 1983), screenplay.

SELECTED TELEVISION: *The Bus to Nowhere* (1951), script;
12 Angry Men, *Studio One* (CBS, 1954), script;
The Expendable House, *Philco-Goodyear Television Playhouse* (NBC, 1955), script;
The Sacco and Vanzetti Case, *Armstrong Circle Theatre* (NBC, 1960), script;
The Defenders [series] (CBS, 1961-1965), creator and scriptwriter;

Reginald Rose

Dear Friends (CBS, 1967), script;
The Zoo Gang [series] (NBC, 1975), creator and
　scriptwriter.

BOOKS: *Six Television Plays* (New York: Simon &
　Schuster, 1956);
The Thomas Book (New York: Harcourt Brace
　Jovanovich, 1972).

Reginald Rose was born in New York City and
attended City College. After graduation, he worked
at a series of odd jobs: receiving clerk, window
cleaner, and camp counselor. He then served in the
United States Army in World War II, completing
his service as a first lieutenant.

After the war, Rose returned to New York
City, where he worked first for the publicity department of Warner Bros. studio and then as a
copywriter for a small advertising agency. In 1951
he sold his first teleplay, *The Bus to Nowhere*, then
went on to write numerous television scripts in the
1950s and 1960s, including *12 Angry Men*, for which
he won an Emmy award. He created, supervised,
and wrote many episodes of the successful television
series *The Defenders* (1961-1965), for which he received Emmy awards in 1962 and 1963.

Rose's early years as a television writer shaped
and colored his entire career. During his emergence
in the 1950s, a golden age for original television
drama which nurtured many fine writers, including
Paddy Chayefsky, Robert Alan Aurthur, and Rod
Serling, Rose tailored his craft to the particular
strengths of the medium. His scripts were topical
and controversial; he used narrow, often indoor
settings, and he centered conflicts on small but crucial individual moral choices. As a writer of motion
pictures, Rose has continued to produce the kind of
social, timely, personal dramas he created for television. Rose's main subjects are crime; juvenile delinquency; the problems of children and adolescents;
and contemporary social issues, including bigotry,
poverty, and urban blight. He has treated these
problems in a variety of forms—Westerns, war
movies, urban and courtroom dramas—but however exotic or prosaic the setting and whatever the
form, at its best Rose's work is powerful, committed,
intense; at its worst it is didactic or descends from
drama into sociology.

Rose's first screenplay was for *Crime in the
Streets* (1956), about teenage gang members who
plan but do not carry out the murder of an old man
who has slapped their psychotic leader, Frankie
(John Cassavetes). The film ends in a confrontation
between Frankie and the younger brother (Sal
Mineo) of another gang member who talks Frankie
out of the crime by professing love and concern for
his brother. Compared by many critics with *The
Blackboard Jungle* (1955) and *Rebel Without a Cause*
(1955), the film shows Rose's weaknesses as a writer
in the script's didactic emphasis on the social causes
of juvenile delinquency and the saving power of
love.

Rose's second film, *Dino* (1957), is a variation
on the same theme. Dino (Sal Mineo) is a young man
who returns from reform school and is entreated by
his younger brother to lead the neighborhood gang
in holding up a gas station. Dino agrees; he is angry
and bitter, the victim of a brutal father and a slum
childhood. But with the love of a neighborhood girl
(Susan Kohner) and the understanding of a settlement worker (Brian Keith), Dino begins to change.
Finally, determined to save his brother from making the same mistakes he has made, Dino refuses to
go through with the holdup and asks the settlement
worker to help himself and his brother in building a
better life. Critical response to the film was mixed.
Some critics, while acknowledging that the material
was somewhat threadbare, applauded Rose's treatment of juvenile delinquency and of the regeneration of a young criminal. Other critics accused the

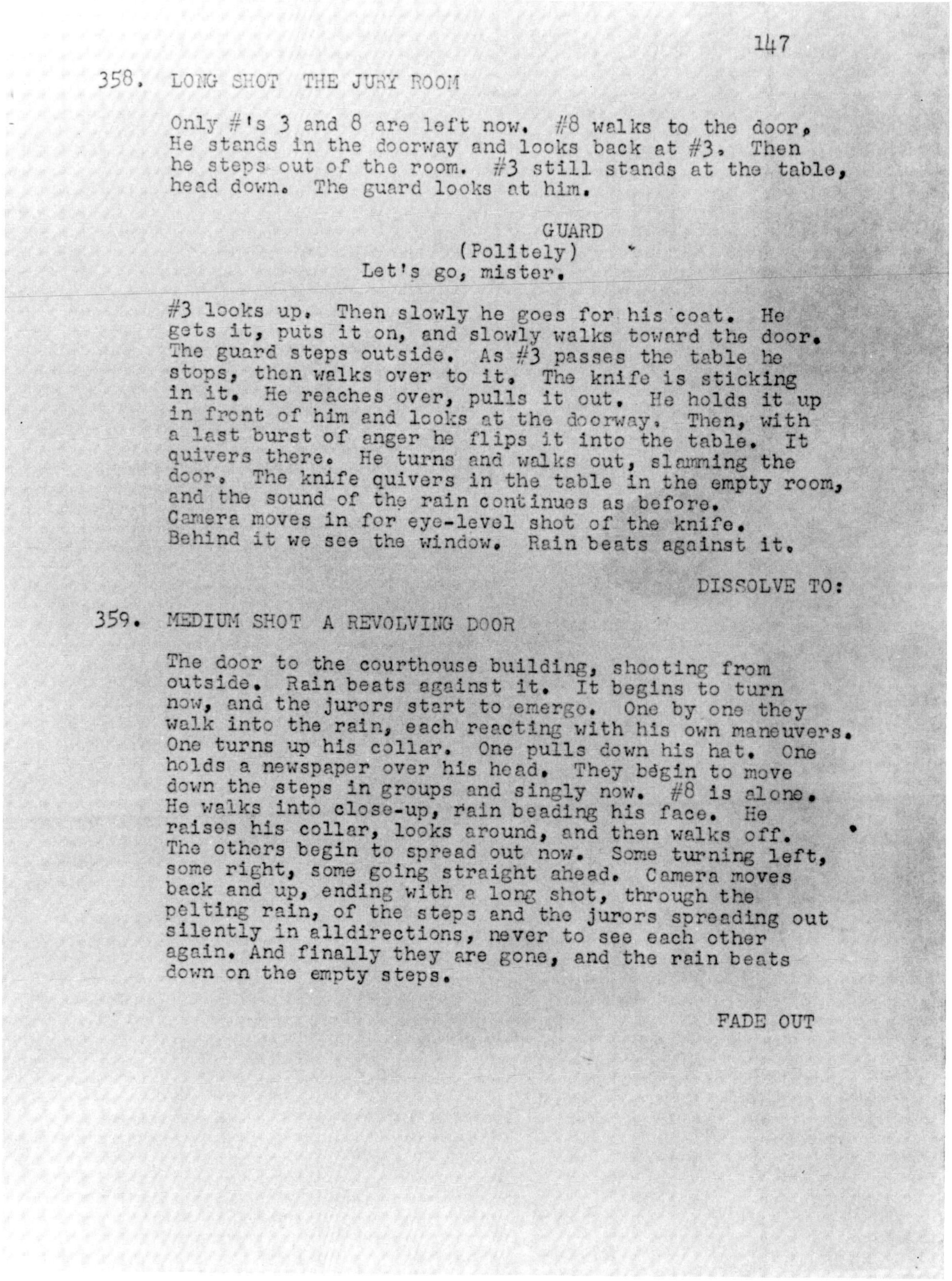

147

358. LONG SHOT THE JURY ROOM

Only #'s 3 and 8 are left now. #8 walks to the door.
He stands in the doorway and looks back at #3. Then
he steps out of the room. #3 still stands at the table,
head down. The guard looks at him.

> GUARD
> (Politely)
> Let's go, mister.

#3 looks up. Then slowly he goes for his coat. He
gets it, puts it on, and slowly walks toward the door.
The guard steps outside. As #3 passes the table he
stops, then walks over to it. The knife is sticking
in it. He reaches over, pulls it out. He holds it up
in front of him and looks at the doorway. Then, with
a last burst of anger he flips it into the table. It
quivers there. He turns and walks out, slamming the
door. The knife quivers in the table in the empty room,
and the sound of the rain continues as before.
Camera moves in for eye-level shot of the knife.
Behind it we see the window. Rain beats against it.

> DISSOLVE TO:

359. MEDIUM SHOT A REVOLVING DOOR

The door to the courthouse building, shooting from
outside. Rain beats against it. It begins to turn
now, and the jurors start to emerge. One by one they
walk into the rain, each reacting with his own maneuvers.
One turns up his collar. One pulls down his hat. One
holds a newspaper over his head. They begin to move
down the steps in groups and singly now. #8 is alone.
He walks into close-up, rain beading his face. He
raises his collar, looks around, and then walks off.
The others begin to spread out now. Some turning left,
some right, some going straight ahead. Camera moves
back and up, ending with a long shot, through the
pelting rain, of the steps and the jurors spreading out
silently in alldirections, never to see each other
again. And finally they are gone, and the rain beats
down on the empty steps.

> FADE OUT

Last page of the screenplay for 12 Angry Men

From left, the jurors in 12 Angry Men: *Jack Warden, Edward Binns (behind Warden), E. G. Marshall, John Fieldor (behind Marshall), Henry Fonda, Ed Begley, Robert Webber, Jack Klugman (in front), George Voskovec, Martin Balsam, and John Sweeney. Absent from the photo is the twelfth juror, played by Lee J. Cobb.*

film of being slick and formulaic.

In marked contrast, the screenplay for Rose's next film, *12 Angry Men* (1957), shows to greatest advantage his strengths as a writer and presents in a persuasive way some of the concerns unconvincingly dealt with in *Crime in the Streets* and *Dino*. Sidney Lumet directed the film, which has become Rose's most acclaimed and best-known work. Adapted from Rose's earlier teleplay, the movie is about a jury that must reach a verdict in the trial of a teenager accused of murdering his father. The jury becomes deadlocked because one juror (Henry Fonda) refuses to vote guilty with the others. He insists that the other jury members reconsider the evidence, articulate the reasons for their opinions, and examine their own consciences. In a methodical way, he analyzes the prosecution's arguments so that the evidence of the boy's guilt, all circumstantial, falls away piece by piece. As he does so, the other members of the jury are forced to confront their hasty judgments and prejudices.

12 Angry Men focuses on important social issues with clarity and restraint, makes these issues personal ones through complex characterization, and brilliantly matches the technical aspects of the film to its subject matter and themes. As in Rose's previous work, the film deals with social injustices—the boy on trial is the victim of a brutal father and sordid environment. The film also deals with the conflict between young and old; the boy is accused of murdering his father and is tried by a jury of men who are old enough to be his father. One of the virtues of the film is that it does not present the problem as an abstract issue but through dramatic confrontations between the jurors, one of whom (Lee J. Cobb) hates all young people because of his anger at his own son. Another juror (Ed Begley) hates the Puerto Rican boy because of his own prejudice. Perhaps the best feature of the movie is its matching of technique to theme. With virtually all the action confined to the jury room, the film has an unnerving claustrophobic quality. The ninety-five minutes that the film runs is the length of time it takes the jurors to reach a verdict. *12 Angry Men* was a great critical success, earning Academy Award nominations for best picture and best screenplay.

Rose's next film script, *Man of the West* (1958), is a complex, psychological Western. Based on the novel *The Border Jumpers* by Will C. Brown and directed by Anthony Mann, the film is about Link, a bandit (Gary Cooper) who, having reformed and become a respectable family man, is entrusted by his community with a large sum of money to use in hiring a schoolteacher. On the train to Fort Worth to find the teacher he meets a dance-hall singer, Billie Ellis (Julie London), and an old gambler, Sam Beasley, for whom he takes responsibility when the train is robbed and they are left stranded. A nearby cabin in which they seek shelter proves to be a hideout for Link's old gang, headed by his crazed uncle, Dock Tobin (Lee J. Cobb). In order to protect himself, Billie, and Sam, Link pretends to rejoin the gang and volunteers to take charge of a bank robbery in a nearby town. As he is forced to spend time with his old cronies, Link is disturbed to find himself becoming more and more like them, reverting to his old, violent ways. He is finally driven to action when a gang member named Coaley (Jack Lord) forces Billie to strip and later shoots at Link but kills Sam instead. Link kills most of the gang members before having a final gunfight with Tobin, whom he also kills. In the end Link plans to leave Billie, who has fallen in love with him, and return to his family and community.

Man of the West returns to several of Rose's previous themes—the relationship between generations in a family (Tobin and Link) and the need for the individual to make his own moral decisions. As Link confesses to Billie that he has been just as evil and vicious as the other members of Tobin's gang, he affirms, "One day I grew up. There comes a point where you either grow up or you rot like that bunch." This statement points to another of Rose's themes—that the criminal can reform if given the opportunity to assume responsibility and to earn people's trust.

Rose's next film, *Man in the Net* (1959), is a steamy melodrama, a murder mystery in which an executive-turned-painter (Alan Ladd) takes his alcoholic, promiscuous wife (Carolyn Jones) to a small town in Connecticut. When she is murdered shortly

Jack Lord as Coaley, Gary Cooper as Link, and Julie London as Billie in Man of the West

after their arrival, he is accused of the crime. The whole town believes him guilty except a group of children who hide him in a cave and help him solve the case and exonerate himself. Not surprisingly, critics found the script lacking in credibility, and the film was neither a critical nor a financial success. The film does demonstrate again Rose's thesis that an innocent man may be trapped in a net of circumstantial evidence and that people should suspend their judgments until offered clear proof of guilt. Its strongest features are Rose's charming and natural characterizations of the children who come to the aid of the accused man.

Television scripts and other projects kept Rose away from motion pictures following *Man in the Net*; it was fourteen years before another film was made from a screenplay by Rose. His sympathetic treatment of children—his understanding of their needs and motivations—is the focus of the 1973 film, *Baxter!*, based on Kin Platt's novel *The Boy Who Could Make Himself Disappear*. The story of an adolescent boy (Scott Jacoby) rejected by his divorced parents, the film follows the boy on a traumatic move from Los Angeles to London, where he establishes relationships with three different people who help him. The strength of the film is characterization, particularly of the boy Roger Baxter, whose sharp wit and self-mockery reveal his hurt and his need for love and understanding. He finds his needs temporarily fulfilled by his caring speech therapist (Patricia Neal) and by a pair of lovers, Chris Bentley and Roger Tunnell (Britt Ekland and Jean-Pierre Cassel), who reach out to this lonely boy. When Chris dies of pneumonia, the boy Roger withdraws into catatonia but begins to emerge as the grieving Roger Tunnell turns to him to share his grief and his essential faith in life. The film is one of Rose's better efforts; it could have become maudlin, but it remains moving and absorbing.

Rose's next film, *Somebody Killed Her Husband* (1978), is a slight, screwball comedy created as a vehicle for Farrah Fawcett. An unhappy housewife (Fawcett) meets an unpublished children's book writer (Jeff Bridges) who is employed as a toy salesman in a department store. They fall in love, but no sooner does their affair begin than they find her husband murdered. Knowing they will be suspects, they conceal the murder and set out to find the killer. Critics found the film implausible and contrived, and it was a failure with audiences as well.

Having failed with this rare attempt at comedy, Rose returned to drama with *The Wild Geese* (1978), based on a novel by Daniel Carney. Four soldiers of fortune (Richard Burton, Richard Harris, Hardy Kruger, Roger Moore) are hired to lead a force into Africa and rescue a recently overthrown president. After they reach the president, the men are betrayed and abandoned by their employer. *The Wild Geese* is a lengthy and detailed film, an attempt to create an epic adventure movie. It was not a financial success in the United States but did very well in Europe, and a follow-up film was planned that would reunite the creative team of *The Wild Geese*: Rose, director Andrew V. McLaglen, and producer Euan Lloyd. *The Sea Wolves* (1980), based on the novel *The Boarding Party* by James Leasor, is about a British cavalry unit brought out of retirement during World War II and sent to destroy a German radio base in India. The film was unable to repeat the success of *The Wild Geese*; a financial failure overseas, it was held out of American release for over a year and then received very limited distribution.

In 1981 Rose worked with playwright Brian Clark in adapting Clark's *Whose Life Is It Anyway?* for the screen. In this film, sculptor Ken Harrison (Richard Dreyfuss) is paralyzed from the neck down as a result of an auto accident. After learning of his condition, Harrison asks to be discharged from the hospital and sent home, where he is certain to die. When his doctor (John Cassavetes) refuses, Harrison takes the case to court and is finally granted the right to leave the hospital. Though highly praised by critics, *Whose Life Is It Anyway?* was not a financial success; perhaps audiences were kept away by the unpleasant subject matter.

Rose next wrote another action film for Euan Lloyd, but he made certain the film had an underlying political message. *The Final Option* (1983) suggests that the nuclear disarmament movements in Europe have been infiltrated and manipulated by terrorists who are in turn manipulated by foreign governments. A special British task force sends an agent (Lewis Collins) to act as an undercover operative in one antiwar group. At a political gathering in London, the group takes hostages, including the American secretary of state (Richard Widmark), and then demands that an atomic bomb be detonated in Scotland to demonstrate the horrors of nuclear war. The agent must find a way to communicate with his superiors and free the hostages before the terrorists' thirty-six-hour deadline elapses. *The Final Option* was criticized both for implausibilities in the script and for Rose's heavy-handedness in moralizing; like *The Sea Wolves* it was distributed in the United States a year after its European release and was a financial success on neither continent.

Rose's work is noteworthy for his willingness to take on difficult social issues and to deal with the darker aspects of human psychology, for his deep commitment to social justice, for his in-depth characterizations and sharp, compact scenes. Yet his writing shows an unwillingness to probe beyond a certain point: his desire to see justice done sometimes creates happy endings that are unconvincing, and his general optimism seems unjustified. In an overall view of Rose's screenplays, one must ask whether he tries to appease his audience in limiting the complexity of the issues he asks them to consider. As Rose himself describes it, "In all my work, . . . my main purpose has always been to project my own view of good and evil—and this is the essence of controversy."

Robert Rossen

(16 March 1908-18 February 1966)

Tom Wiener

MOTION PICTURES: *They Won't Forget* (Warner Bros., 1937), screenplay by Rossen and Aben Kandel;

Marked Woman (Warner Bros., 1937), story and screenplay by Rossen and Abem Finkel;

Racket Busters (Warner Bros., 1938), screen story and screenplay by Rossen and Leonardo Bercovici;

Dust Be My Destiny (Warner Bros., 1939), screenplay;

The Roaring Twenties (Warner Bros., 1939), screenplay by Rossen, Jerry Wald, and Richard Macaulay;

A Child Is Born (Warner Bros., 1939), screenplay;

Blues in the Night (Warner Bros., 1941), screenplay;

The Sea Wolf (Warner Bros., 1941), screenplay;

Out of the Fog (Warner Bros., 1941), screenplay by Rossen, Wald, and Macaulay;

Edge of Darkness (Warner Bros., 1942), screenplay;

A Walk in the Sun (20th Century-Fox, 1946), screenplay;

The Strange Love of Martha Ivers (Hal Wallis Productions/Paramount, 1946), screenplay;

Johnny O'Clock (Columbia, 1947), screenplay;

Desert Fury (Paramount, 1947), screenplay;

All the King's Men (Columbia, 1949), screenplay;

Mambo (Produzione Ponti De Laurentiis/Paramount, 1955), story and screenplay by Rossen, Guido Piovene, Ivo Perilli, and Ennio de Concini;

Alexander the Great (United Artists, 1956), screen story and screenplay;

They Came to Cordura (Columbia, 1959), screenplay by Rossen and Ivan Moffat;

The Hustler (20th Century-Fox, 1961), screenplay by Rossen and Sidney Carroll;

Lilith (Columbia, 1964), screenplay.

PLAYS: *The Body Beautiful* (New York, Plymouth Theatre, 31 October 1935);

The Cool World (New York, Eugene O'Neill Theatre, 22 February 1960).

BOOK: *Three Screenplays*, edited by Steven Rossen (Garden City: Doubleday/Anchor, 1972)—includes *All the King's Men*, *The Hustler* by Rossen and Sidney Carroll, and *Lilith*.

Robert Rossen

PERIODICAL PUBLICATION: "The Face of Independence," *Films & Filming*, 8 (August 1962): 7.

Robert Rossen began his screenwriting career as a contract writer in Hollywood during the 1930s and in the late 1940s became a successful producer and director. Rossen's career was interrupted by the blacklisting of the McCarthy era, but it resumed in the mid-1950s with a series of forceful and original films. As a screenwriter and later a producer and director, Rossen preferred to work with contemporary American stories and themes, but his range extended to historical epics and dramas with foreign locales. Although the quality of his work varies, it displays a remarkable continuity in theme, often focusing on the effects of power and ambition on the individual. Several of his films, most notably *Body and Soul* (1947), *All the King's Men* (1949), and *The Hustler* (1961), hold respected places in the history of postwar American cinema.

Robert Rossen was born in the Rivington Street section of New York's East Side. After attending New York University, Rossen boxed professionally for a short time before becoming involved with theater groups both as a director and playwright. He directed Richard Maibaum's *The Tree* (1932) and the anti-Nazi drama *Birthright* (1932), both of which received kind critical notices during their short runs. Among the plays Rossen wrote were "Corner Pocket," an unproduced work set in a pool hall, and *The Body Beautiful*, which ran for four performances on Broadway in 1935. The latter play led to a contract with Warner Bros., and in 1936 Rossen moved to Hollywood.

Shortly after arriving in California, Rossen joined the Communist party. The association was born out of an idealism not unusual for many intellectuals during the Depression. For a time, Rossen was intensively involved in party work, but he eventually withdrew from any political activity.

As a young contract writer for Warner Bros., Rossen was in the perfect place to put his social beliefs to work. Warner Bros. films in the 1930s often dealt with social problems such as injustice, discrimination, urban crime, and poverty. Rossen's first film, *They Won't Forget* (1937), was written with Aben Kandel and directed by Mervyn LeRoy. Based on a fictionalized account of the Leo Frank case, in which a Jewish factory owner was lynched in 1913 in Georgia for the alleged murder of a thirteen-year-old girl, the film received glowing reviews from critics of the time and is still regarded as one of the most realistic studies of mob violence on film. The script was Rossen's favorite of those he wrote at Warner Bros.

With varying degrees of authenticity and success, Rossen's next three screenplays also dealt with social problems. *Marked Woman* (1937) concentrates on the attempts of a district attorney (Humphrey Bogart) to expose a gang controlling the city's prostitutes. *Racket Busters* (1938), as the title implies, follows much the same plot, with Bogart playing a character on the other side of the law and George Brent as the district attorney. *Dust Be My Destiny* (1939) was an early vehicle for John Garfield, who plays a young misfit trying to break out of the slums.

Rossen's first big break came with his screenplay for *The Roaring Twenties* (1939). Directed by Raoul Walsh and starring Humphrey Bogart and James Cagney as rival mobsters during Prohibition,

the film prefigured the concerns of many later Rossen films. Working with Jerry Wald and Richard Macaulay on the script, Rossen created in the character of Eddie Bartlett (James Cagney) a man whose drive for power and success eventually leads to his ruin. A veteran of World War I, Eddie becomes involved in the bootlegging rackets that flourished with the enactment of Prohibition. The film was enormously popular at the box office and also managed to portray honestly the economic realities that figured in Eddie's corruption.

Rossen wrote five more screenplays for Warner Bros. after *The Roaring Twenties*. His concerns became less focused, and each film seemed more like an assignment than a project of genuine interest to him. *A Child Is Born* (1939) is about the maternity ward of a city hospital; *Blues in the Night* (1941) chronicles the breakup of a jazz band. With his adaptation of Jack London's 1904 novel *The Sea Wolf* (1941), Rossen returned to the theme of the man whose lust for power corrupts him. Larsen (Edward G. Robinson) is portrayed with such brutality, however, that he is hardly a sympathetic figure. *Out of the Fog* (1941) stars John Garfield as a gangster who attempts to dominate a Brooklyn family; it was based on Irwin Shaw's play *The Gentle People*.

Edge of Darkness (1942), a drama of the Norwegian resistance to the Nazi occupation, was Rossen's last screenplay for Warner Bros. It was also the first of three collaborations with director Lewis Milestone. First, however, came Rossen's break with Hollywood and the Communist party. In 1944 he moved to New York to spend a year there with his wife and three children. He returned to Hollywood, but only for short intervals and not at all after 1953. The demands upon his time by the party and his increasing disillusionment with shifts in the party line ate away all Rossen's devotion to the cause. By 1947 he had severed all formal ties with the party.

Rossen's two postwar collaborations with Milestone, *A Walk in the Sun* (1946) and *The Strange Love of Martha Ivers* (1946), are now regarded as among the best films in the careers of both men. Taken from Harry Brown's novel, *A Walk in the Sun* is a probing study of men attempting to deal with the pressures of combat. Rossen and Milestone eliminated lengthy action scenes in order to concentrate on full and believable characterizations. In *The Strange Love of Martha Ivers*, Rossen and Milestone dramatized the effects of ill-gotten inherited wealth on a young woman (Barbara Stanwyck).

Before beginning to direct his own screenplays, Rossen wrote one last script, *Desert Fury*

(1947), for another director, Lewis Allen. The film is a melodrama about gamblers, a subject subsequently explored in Rossen's first film as writer and director, *Johnny O'Clock* (1947). In *Johnny O'Clock* Dick Powell stars as a gambling-hall proprietor who is framed for murder.

Rossen's next directorial effort, *Body and Soul*, was highly praised upon its release and still has not diminished in reputation. The screenplay was credited to Abraham Polonsky, although Rossen worked closely with him. The story concerns the rise to fame and the eventual corruption and redemption of a prizefighter named Charlie Davis (John Garfield). As played by Garfield (whose company produced the film), Charlie is the prototypical Rossen protagonist—a loner involved in a quest, aggressive and unafraid to bend or break the rules to get what he wants.

After adding director to his credits, Rossen further extended his duties by producing three films for Columbia Pictures. The first, *The Undercover Man* (1949), was a gangster film directed by Joseph H. Lewis and written by Sydney Boehm. With *All the King's Men*, Rossen became a producer-writer-director. This adaptation of Robert Penn Warren's 1946 novel about Willie Stark (Broderick Crawford), a Southern demagogue with more than a passing resemblance to Huey Long, is a stunning achievement. Hailed by critics as one of the best political films ever to come out of Hollywood, the film received a number of awards, including Academy awards for best picture, best actor (Crawford), and best supporting actress (Mercedes McCambridge). Rossen received nominations for best director and best screenplay.

Rossen later admitted that his work on *All the King's Men* was influenced by the Italian postwar neorealistic movement, which emphasized the use of amateur actors, extensive location shooting, and a rough, almost improvised style of dialogue. The

Broderick Crawford and John Ireland in All the King's Men, *which won the Oscar for best picture in 1949. Crawford's portrayal of Willie Stark earned him the award for best actor.*

Paul Newman, Myron McCormick, and Jackie Gleason in The Hustler

film's writing is vivid, and although it necessarily coalesces much of the detail and nuance of Warren's novel, it is remarkably faithful to the spirit of the book. Perhaps this was because Rossen was dealing with a favorite theme—the corrosive effects of power—on a grander scale than in any of his previous films. Rossen followed *All the King's Men* with two more films for Columbia: *The Brave Bulls* (1951), which he produced and directed, and *No Sad Songs for Me* (1950), which he produced as a contract obligation and for which he received no credit.

Events developed in Rossen's personal life that would affect his career for several years to come. Named in 1947 by the House Un-American Activities Committee as one of nineteen unfriendly witnesses, Rossen was spared from appearing when the committee broke off its proceedings after the first ten witnesses had testified. Nevertheless, Rossen was hounded by the specter of his Communist associations, and in 1950 Columbia broke its producing contract with him.

Rossen did testify before the committee in June 1951, and, although he repudiated the party,

he also refused to discuss his past activities. Several years of forced inactivity followed, and in May 1953 Rossen finally agreed to discuss his Communist party association and to confirm published lists of persons he knew to have been party members.

Free to work again, Rossen turned his energies toward a personal project, a film about Alexander the Great. First, however, he agreed to accept an assignment in Europe, a romantic film called *Mambo* (1955), which he wrote and directed for Carlo Ponti and Dino Di Laurentiis. The result pleased neither Rossen nor the critics, and by the time of its release, he was well into shooting *Alexander the Great* (1956).

Alexander the Great received less than enthusiastic reviews. As Rossen's first attempt at an epic, it suffered many of the problems of the genre, in particular the overemphasis of pomp and spectacle in place of characterization. Rossen later admitted that in editing the film from a rough cut of three hours to one hundred forty-one minutes, much of Alexander's motivation was sacrificed. Nevertheless, Rossen added another character to his gallery of men for whom power is an end in itself.

With *They Came to Cordura* (1959), Rossen

worked for producer William Goetz, who had paid a great deal of money for the screen rights to Glendon Swarthout's Western novel of survival in the desert and was eager to protect his investment. Rossen and Ivan Moffat wrote the screenplay, with Goetz insisting on more expository dialogue and an overly long cavalry charge to open the film. The result was not satisfying to audiences or critics, but the film does deal with themes of interest to Rossen: the definitions of honor and courage and the notion of performing well under pressure.

With *The Hustler*, Rossen's career revived significantly. In this film, he returned to a familiar milieu: the world of pool sharks that he knew well from his youth in New York and had explored in his early play "Corner Pocket." The hustler "Fast" Eddie Felsen (Paul Newman) is a man like Willie Stark and Charlie Davis who reaches for something by which he can define himself, unaware of the consequences of his actions.

Working with Sidney Carroll from Walter

Tevis's novel of the same title, Rossen fashioned a screenplay that is both lean and detailed. It captures perfectly the language rhythms of the hoods, gamblers, and defeated men whose lives revolve around the pool halls of urban America. At the same time, Rossen achieved a depth of characterization that reflected his maturity as both a writer and a director. The major characters—Eddie; the alcoholic cripple, Sarah (Piper Laurie); the gambler Bert (George C. Scott); and the ultimate pool shark Minnesota Fats (Jackie Gleason)—are sharply drawn. Rossen achieved in *The Hustler* his one undisputed masterpiece as both screenwriter and director. The film was nominated for Academy awards for best picture, best director, and best screenplay, and the screenplay won the Writers Guild Award.

In the early 1960s, Rossen began to feel the effects of a rare skin disease and the complications that resulted from medicine he took to treat it. Nevertheless, he continued to write, working on a

Jean Seberg in the title role of Lilith

script about life in a Florida town near Cape Canaveral titled "Cocoa Beach." That was put aside for another project, *Lilith* (1964), which proved to be his last film and also his most controversial. It was entered in the 1964 Venice Film Festival, but the festival director severely criticized the film and Rossen angrily withdrew it. When released to the general public, *Lilith* was treated with some scorn from critics and met with bewilderment by audiences.

Lilith is certainly Rossen's most pessimistic film. The film focuses on Vincent (Warren Beatty), a young veteran who goes to work in a mental hospital and becomes involved with Lilith (Jean Seberg), a beautiful patient. Vincent intends to help Lilith, but by the end of the film, he has been brought under her spell and begins questioning his own sanity. The French film journal *Cahiers du Cinéma* listed *Lilith* as one of the ten best films of the year. It has gained a following over the years and has done much to revive interest in Rossen's career.

Following the release of *Lilith*, Rossen's illness worsened, and he was unable to devote much time to "Cocoa Beach." He underwent surgery in November 1965, and on 18 February 1966 he died of complications from that operation.

Rossen's legacy as a screenwriter is significant. His apprenticeship at Warner Bros. taught him his craft as he worked on a variety of projects with the American underworld that provided him with his best material. Rossen's concern for the effects of environment on the individual and the means by which men acquire and use power are recurrent themes in his work. His desire to produce and direct films was born out of the need to express his ideas with as little restriction as possible. His scripts were sometimes criticized for moralizing, especially in their resolutions, and it is true that he was torn between dealing honestly with social issues and the acute realization of the limitations of commercial filmmaking. But he was able on many occasions to resolve this conflict and produce work of lasting merit. Rossen's career was damaged by the blacklist, but in the long run he managed to achieve an important place in contemporary American film history.

References:

Henry Burton, "Notes on Rossen Films," *Films in Review*, 13 (June-July 1962): 335-341;

Alan Casty, "The Films of Robert Rossen," *Film Quarterly*, 20 (Winter 1966-1967): 3-12;

Casty, *The Films of Robert Rossen* (New York: The Museum of Modern Art, 1969);

Casty, "Robert Rossen," *Cinema*, 4 (Fall 1968): 18-22;

Saul R. Cohen, "Robert Rossen and the Filming of *Lilith*," *Film Comment*, 3 (Spring 1965): 3-7;

Henry Hart, "Notes on Robert Rossen," *Films in Review*, 13 (June-July 1962): 333-335;

Jean-Louis Noames, "Lessons Learned in Combat," *Cahiers du Cinéma in English*, 7 (January 1967): 20-29;

John Springer, "A Rossen Index," *Films in Review*, 13 (June-July 1962): 341-342;

Daniel Stein, "An Interview With Robert Rossen," *Arts in Society*, 4 (Winter 1966-1967): 46-58.

Morrie Ryskind

(20 October 1895-   )

Joseph Adamson III

SELECTED MOTION PICTURES: *The Cocoanuts* (Paramount Famous Lasky, 1929), adaptation;

Animal Crackers (Paramount-Publix, 1930), screenplay adapted by Ryskind from his play with George S. Kaufman;

Palmy Days (United Artists, 1931), dialogue and story by Ryskind, Eddie Cantor, Keene Thompson, and David Freedman;

A Night at the Opera (M-G-M, 1935), screenplay by Ryskind and Kaufman;

My Man Godfrey (Universal, 1936), screenplay by Ryskind and Eric Hatch;

Stage Door (RKO, 1937), screenplay by Ryskind and Anthony Veiller;

Room Service (RKO, 1938), screenplay;

Man About Town (Paramount, 1939), screenplay;

Penny Serenade (Columbia, 1941), screenplay;

Claudia (20th Century-Fox, 1943), screenplay;

Where Do We Go From Here? (20th Century-Fox,

George S. Kaufman and Morrie Ryskind (in front) with Ira and George Gershwin, their collaborators on Strike Up the Band, Of Thee I Sing, *and* Let 'Em Eat Cake *(Gershwin Collection)*

1945), story and screenplay;
It's in the Bag (United Artists, 1945), contributor;
Heartbeat (RKO, 1946), adaptation.

PLAYS: *The '49ers* (New York, Punch and Judy Theater, 7 November 1922), sketches and lyrics;
Garrick Gaieties (New York, Garrick Theater, 8 June 1925), sketches and lyrics;
Americana (New York, Belmont Theatre, 26 July 1926), lyrics;
Merry-Go-Round (New York, Klaw Theatre, 31 May 1927), sketches and lyrics by Ryskind and Howard Dietz;
Animal Crackers (New York, 44th Street Theatre, 23 October 1928), book by Ryskind and George S. Kaufman;
Strike Up the Band (New York, Times Square Theatre, 14 January 1930), book by Ryskind and Kaufman;
Of Thee I Sing (New York, Music Box Theatre, 26 December 1931), book by Ryskind and Kaufman;
Let 'Em Eat Cake (New York, Imperial Theatre, 21 October 1933), book by Ryskind and Kaufman;

Bring on the Girls (Washington, D.C., National Theatre, 22 October 1934), script by Ryskind and Kaufman;
Louisiana Purchase (New York, Imperial Theatre, 28 May 1940), book.

BOOKS: *Unaccustomed As I Am* (New York: Knopf, 1921);
The Home Movie Scenario Book, by Ryskind, C. F. Stevens, and James Englander (New York: R. Manson, 1927);
The Diary of an Ex-President, as John P. Wintergreen (New York: Minton Balch, 1932).

OTHER: *My Man Godfrey*, in *Twenty Best Film Plays*, edited by John Gassner and Dudley Nichols (New York: Crown, 1943).

SELECTED PERIODICAL PUBLICATION: "Socratic Dialogue," by Ryskind and George S. Kaufman, *Nation* (12 April 1933).

A man of very definite ideas and convictions, Morrie Ryskind has created a body of work that examines the general folly of the human race. He never worked as sole scenarist, but the scripts he wrote with others brought him into contact with some of Hollywood's most prodigious talents: the Marx Brothers, Carole Lombard, Katharine Hepburn, Jack Benny, and directors Howard Hawks and George Stevens. Ryskind had a major role in creating such classic films as *Animal Crackers* (1930), *Ceiling Zero* (1935), *A Night at the Opera* (1935), *My Man Godfrey* (1936), *Stage Door* (1937), *Penny Serenade* (1941), and *It's in the Bag* (1945).

The son of Abraham Ryskind, a storekeeper, and Ida Eddleston Ryskind, Morris Ryskind began contributing to the New York literary scene while still in high school. By the time he graduated from Townsend Harris High School in 1912, he had frequently contributed to Franklin P. Adams's column, "The Conning Tower," and was so well received that Adams once allowed Ryskind's contributions to fill an entire day's space. At Columbia University, Ryskind became acquainted with Herman Mankiewicz, Richard Rogers, and Lorenz Hart and helped George S. Kaufman with his chores as drama editor of the *New York Times*. During this period Ryskind contributed, as he put it, "a song here, a sketch there" to several Broadway revues and shows; he also had poems published in some of the better magazines of the day.

A major break for Ryskind came in 1925, when George S. Kaufman, who was working on a musical play for the Marx Brothers, hired Ryskind to be his assistant. The resulting work, *The Cocoanuts*, combined the buffoonery of the Marx Brothers with topical satire of the Florida land boom. In 1928 Ryskind became Kaufman's collaborator on *Animal Crackers*, another play for the Marx Brothers. In both plays, the writers' main problem was to structure a definite story line and at the same time allow enough flexibility for the semi-improvisational routines of their star comedians. Their success earned them Groucho Marx's lifelong admiration for being "the best writers we ever had."

Ryskind's first screenwriting opportunity arose when Chico Marx convinced Paramount Pictures to film *The Cocoanuts* at Paramount's Astoria Studios in Long Island. Hollywood, in its transition from silent films, was turning in desperation to Broadway talents for the new talkies, and Paramount commissioned Ryskind to fashion a screenplay from the successful and by then often-performed musical. Ryskind met the challenge by simply adding camera terminology to the existing script. The result was a 140-minute film that was necessarily cut to 96 minutes—cutting that resulted in fragmented continuity and days of wasted shooting. Nevertheless, the picture was a tremendous success, grossing two million dollars in its first few months after release and securing repeat business in many theaters; the Marxes were established as film personalities, and Ryskind was suddenly a screenwriter.

Hired to write the script for *Animal Crackers*, Ryskind did much of the necessary cutting before shooting started; he sat in the audience while the play was touring the United States and eliminated lines and scenes that seemed weak. The plot centered around the efforts of the Marx Brothers to find a stolen painting. Again, the film proved a roaring success, faring well even in a 1974 rerelease and holding up far better than its predecessor.

In 1929 Ryskind married Mary House (they have three children). In 1931 he traveled to Hollywood and there collaborated on *Palmy Days* with Eddie Cantor, Keene Thompson, and David Freedman. The film spoofed phony spiritualists, physical educationalists, and even Florenz Ziegfeld's Paramount musical *Glorifying the American Girl*. *Palmy Days* now seems dated; much of the humor that accounted for its 1931 success (and critical raves by French cineasts) has today evaporated.

Ryskind continued to write for the Broadway stage in the 1930s. His zealous antiwar tirades con-

vinced George S. Kaufman that they should collaborate on a pacifist musical. The resulting work, *Strike Up the Band* (1930), ran for 191 performances. Expanding their horizons, the two concocted a musical burlesque that satirized the United States government. *Of Thee I Sing*, with music and lyrics by George and Ira Gershwin, opened in New York December 1931. The production was so pointed a satire and so effective a musical that it prompted comparisons with Gilbert and Sullivan. Some critics felt its significance surpassed the current Broadway dramas of Maxwell Anderson, S. N. Behrman, Robert E. Sherwood, Elmer Rice, and Eugene O'Neill. *Of Thee I Sing* became the first musical to win the Pulitzer Prize for drama.

But all attempts to follow it failed. The sequels, *Let 'Em Eat Cake* (1933) and the 1934 play *Bring on the Girls*, were disastrous. *Of Thee I Sing* was so topical that even a 1933 revival was in need of updating; the play became an antique almost as soon as Roosevelt entered the White House. Partly for this reason, all attempts to translate this work into film ran aground. There were offers, as Ryskind says, "every election year," but its authors wanted to keep tight control over the project and desired a deal whereby they could prepare the screenplay and Kaufman could direct the film, and the studios never agreed to these demands; even attempts to film the play as a Marx Brothers vehicle were unsuccessful.

When the Marxes' career at Paramount deteriorated with the financial disappointment of *Duck Soup* (1933) and their new project at M-G-M was encountering script difficulties, they prevailed upon their producer Irving Thalberg to bring Kaufman and Ryskind to Hollywood. The project was *A Night at the Opera* (1935), and before the script was completed it had employed the talents of Ryskind, Kaufman, James Kevin McGuiness, Bert Kalmar, Harry Ruby, Al Boasberg, George Seaton, and Robert Pirosh in combination with the substantial improvisatory talents of the Marx Brothers. The script went through several drafts and a western vaudeville tour to test the laugh-provoking potential of the comedy scenes. "Those were not the good old days," Ryskind recalls, "and Salt Lake City in the height of the Depression was not a place where people were just roaring." But after a weak start the Marxes found their footing, and with Ryskind and Boasberg along to provide new lines, the material was metamorphosed. Ryskind and Boasberg were on hand to rewrite during shooting, a practice costly to the studio but greatly beneficial to the end result.

A Night at the Opera retained the satirical bent

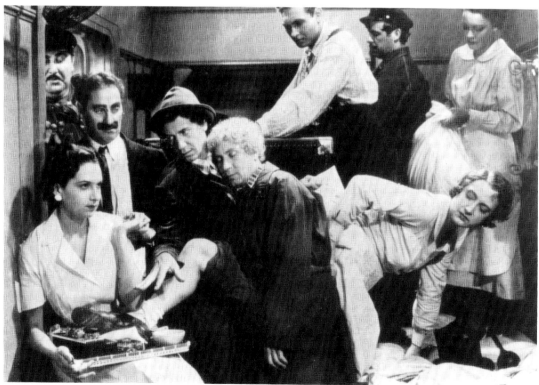

Scenes from two of Ryskind's films for the Marx Brothers: top, The Cocoanuts;
bottom, A Night at the Opera

of *The Cocoanuts* and *Animal Crackers*, combining it with a carefully constructed romantic tale. The film reportedly grossed three million dollars on its initial release and has remained a favorite among Marx Brothers fans ever since. Groucho called it his favorite of the team's films.

Also in 1935, Ryskind was cast in another of the roles to which Hollywood assigned its screenwriters: the script doctor. Ryskind had an astute sense of characterization and story construction stemming from his years as a successful playwright and could apply his skill to much more than the burlesque comedy fare the studios had so far assigned him. "If I was called in to doctor a script, I'd go after the weak spot—and that often means a complete rewrite of several scenes." His first work as script doctor was on *Ceiling Zero* (1935), an aviation story directed by Howard Hawks. In 1936 Ryskind did rewriting without screen credit for the musical comedy *Anything Goes* and for Bing Crosby's musical Western *Rhythm on the Range*. Also in 1936, Ryskind worked as associate producer on *The Luckiest Girl in the World*.

But Ryskind's most important comedy work apart from the Marx Brothers came from his association with Gregory La Cava, the cartoonist-turned-director. Ryskind worked well with La Cava and respected his directorial abilities: "One thing I learned, the director is boss—and rightly so—on the screen, as compared to the stage. I could argue about scenes and their content, but never the best camera angles to put them over. And sometimes a brilliant angle, that only a director could think of, makes even the best written dialogue doubly effective." La Cava suggested that Ryskind write the scenes as if they were for the stage and leave it to the director to break the script up into shots. Ryskind still feels that is the only way for a writer-director team to work.

In the first Ryskind-La Cava collaboration, *My Man Godfrey* (1936)—for which the term "screwball comedy" was coined—believable characters make snappy wisecracks that are even funnier because the remarks are true to each character's personality. Eugene Palette as the master of the house complains to his free-spending family, the Bullocks: "You people have confused me with the treasury department!"; free-loading artist Mischa Auer rejects money as a topic for polite conversation by labeling it "the Frankenstein monster that destroys souls!"; and Irene Bullock (Carole Lombard) responds gleefully to being chastised by Godfrey, played by William Powell: "Godfrey loves me, he put me in the shower." The contrasts between rich and poor and

between responsibility and irresponsibility are dramatically highlighted by the witty dialogue.

When La Cava approached Ryskind in 1937 with the idea of adapting George S. Kaufman and Edna Ferber's play *Stage Door* (1936) to the screen, the writer hedged. He felt that the premise of the play—an aspiring actress loses artistic integrity when she goes to Hollywood—was dishonest. La Cava eventually convinced Ryskind to write an opening scene, and as he delivered the pages he voiced doubt about where he could go from there. "You go home and work on it from there," La Cava replied, "because we're shooting this scene Tuesday." And in this way the shooting continued for weeks. "I'd be literally a day ahead of him, and just hoping and praying," Ryskind recalls. "But that's basically the way we'd done *My Man Godfrey*." The finished film was something of a turnabout on the original Broadway-versus-Hollywood dichotomy and revealed that Broadway involved its own compromises as well. Like *My Man Godfrey*, *Stage Door* is full of wisecracks that serve to reveal character. The girls at a Broadway boardinghouse make cracks about the food, each other's dates, and the shows they appear in to protect themselves from the uncertainties of life as chorus girls.

In 1938 Ryskind adapted the hit play *Room Service* for a Marx Brothers movie. The same year he worked as a script doctor on the Thin Man-style comedy *There's Always a Woman* and on the romantic satire about summer camp *Having Wonderful Time*. *Man About Town*, a Jack Benny comedy for which Ryskind wrote the screenplay, was released in 1939.

In 1940 Ryskind returned to writing for the stage. He adapted *Louisiana Purchase*, another political satire cum music, from a story he and B. G. De Sylva had coauthored. Featuring Irving Berlin's music, the play starred Victor Moore as a prudish senator hoodwinked by a con man. The play's conservative politics were obvious, but the emphasis was clearly on comedy rather than commentary. In 1941 the musical was made into a movie with a screenplay by Jerome Chodorov and Joseph Fields, and Moore costarred with Bob Hope.

Also in 1941 Ryskind initiated the final stage of his screenwriting career, adapting the melodrama *Penny Serenade* from a *McCall's* story by Martha Cheavens. The film's comic touches are adroitly placed by Ryskind and director George Stevens and serve to heighten the tragic elements of this story about a couple (Cary Grant and Irene Dunne) who adopt a child after the wife miscarries. The finished film was uncommonly affecting, and its blatantness in tugging at the heart strings was

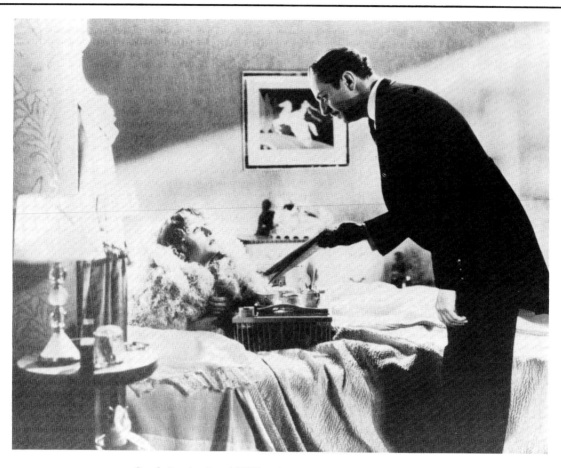

Carole Lombard and William Powell in My Man Godfrey

generally overlooked because of its success in doing so.

Less graceful was *Claudia* (1943), adapted almost verbatim from Rose Franken's play and directed by Edmund Goulding. On doing the adaptation, Ryskind remarked, "I just let it alone, just put it in the movie terms and I didn't have to get in the way of transforming it." It is perhaps this faithfulness to a dated original that makes *Claudia* seem such a labored effort; the dialogue is alternately snappy enough to be scintillating and too glib to be anything but cute, and the film remains a minor story about a silly girl (Dorothy McGuire) who enters womanhood through a series of traumas.

Twentieth Century-Fox produced *Claudia* and Ryskind's next screenplay, *Where Do We Go From Here?* (1945), a historical fantasy-satire made at a time when it was well known in Hollywood that fantasy, satire, and historical subjects spelled disaster at the box office. The satire lacked impact and took as a target an ambitious Hessian general during the Revolutionary War mulling over how to go

about conquering the world: "America, and then Europe, then Africa, and then—I'll be ready for Notre Dame." The extravaganza featured music and lyrics by Ira Gershwin and Kurt Weill and was generally received as a pleasant show, but little more.

It's in the Bag (1945), starring Fred Allen, was Ryskind's next project. The film is based on an old story about a man who inherits a fortune only to find it is hidden inside some old chairs he has already sold. (Mel Brooks based the 1970 film *The Twelve Chairs* on the same story.) Fred Allen and Alma Reville worked on the script, along with Lewis R. Foster and Jay Dratler, but Ryskind's dialogue and gag contributions were substantial enough to be acknowledged by a special credit. Ryskind was present at all stages of filming, supplying last-minute dialogue and situations. The film was a critical and popular success, making a reported profit of $200,000.

Ryskind's last work for the screen was a remake of the French film *Battement de Coeur*; it was filmed in 1946 as *Heartbeat*. The film, about a pickpocket (Ginger Rogers) and a diplomat (Adolphe Menjou) who fall in love, was criticized for lacking the raciness and cynicism of the original.

After finishing work on *Heartbeat*, Ryskind retired from screenwriting to devote his time to political efforts. He was a key figure in many of the organizations that supported Joseph McCarthy, including the Motion Picture Alliance for the Preservation of American Ideals. He was a close friend and scriptwriter for the outspoken anti-Communist Lela Rogers. In 1960 Ryskind found a forum for his political opinions in "The Morrie Ryskind Column," which he wrote for the *Los Angeles Times* and later the *Washington Star* syndicate. By this time Ryskind had lost a great deal of contact with the film and theater worlds. He told an interviewer in 1969, "There are guys today who never heard of me, and frankly, I never heard of them."

For a man capable of astonishing extremes, Ryskind was perhaps at his best when he found the delicate balance between flippant humor and deeply held beliefs. Whether sanity is more to be found in the balance than in the extremes, however, is impossible to say. As Ryskind himself put it,

"Stage, screen or novel, no writer is completely sane."

References:

Joe Adamson, *Groucho, Harpo, Chico and Sometimes Zeppo* (New York: Simon & Schuster, 1973);

Hector Arce, *Groucho* (New York: Putnam's, 1978);

Charlotte Chandler, *Hello, I Must Be Going: Groucho and His Friends* (Garden City: Doubleday, 1978);

Richard Corliss, "Screenwriters Symposium," *Film Comment*, 6 (Winter 1970-1971);

Corliss, *Talking Pictures* (Woodstock, N.Y.: Overlook Press, 1974);

Scott Meredith, *George S. Kaufman and His Friends* (Garden City: Doubleday, 1974);

Frederick C. Othman, "Comedians, but with Sad Faces," *Hollywood Citizen-News*, 2 October 1944;

Howard Teichmann, *George S. Kaufman: An Intimate Portrait* (New York: Atheneum, 1972);

Robert Wilson, *The Film Criticism of Otis Ferguson* (Philadelphia: Temple University Press, 1971).

John Monk Saunders

(22 November 1897-10 March 1940)

Anthony Slide

MOTION PICTURES: *Too Many Kisses* (Famous Players-Lasky/Paramount, 1925), story;

The Shock Punch (Famous Players-Lasky/Paramount, 1925), story;

Wings (Paramount Famous Lasky, 1927), story;

The Legion of the Condemned (Paramount Famous Lasky, 1928), story; scenario by Saunders and Jean de Limur;

The Docks of New York (Paramount Famous Lasky, 1928), story;

She Goes to War (Inspiration/United Artists, 1929), dialogue and titles;

The Dawn Patrol (First National, 1930), story; filmed again (Warner Bros., 1938);

The Finger Points (First National, 1931), story and screenplay by Saunders and W. R. Burnett; dialogue by Saunders;

The Last Flight (First National, 1931), screenplay;

The Eagle and the Hawk (Paramount, 1933), story;

Ace of Aces (RKO, 1933), story; screenplay by Saunders and H. W. Hanemann;

West Point of the Air (M-G-M, 1935), story by Saunders and James K. McGuinness;

Devil Dogs of the Air (Cosmopolitan/Warner Bros., 1935), story;

I Found Stella Parish (First National/Warner Bros., 1935), story;

A Yank at Oxford (M-G-M, 1938), story idea.

PLAY: *Nikki* (New York, Longacre Theatre, 29 September 1931), book.

BOOKS: *Wings* (New York: Grosset & Dunlap, 1927);

Single Lady (New York: Brewer & Warren, 1931).

Saunders with his second wife, Fay Wray (Culver Pictures)

PERIODICAL PUBLICATION: "Looking ahead at Twenty-Seven: The Confessions of a Career-Hound," *Liberty*, 2 (12 September 1925): 5-7.

John Monk Saunders was born in Hinckley, Minnesota. His family was prosperous and his father served as U.S. District Attorney to the city of Seattle. Saunders attended the University of Washington, where he was described as "a brilliant student and a champion swimmer." He was awarded a Rhodes scholarship and received his master's degree from Oxford in 1923. Saunders served in the U.S. Flying Corps during World War I and, because of his flying skills, was made an instructor. Tall, lean, and good-looking, Saunders probably had everything a young man might want: excitement, glamour, wealth, and celebrity status. In 1928, after a divorce from his first wife, he married the young screen star Fay Wray, who received screen immortality with her role in *King Kong* (1933).

After graduation from Oxford, Saunders worked as a reporter for the *Los Angeles Times* and occasionally wrote editorials. With a letter of recommendation from veteran *Times* writer Harry Carr, Saunders went to New York, working first as a reporter on the *New York Tribune* and later as an associate editor of *American Magazine* and a regular contributor to *Cosmopolitan* and *Liberty* magazines.

In September 1924 Famous Players-Lasky purchased the screen rights to one of Saunders's *Cosmopolitan* stories, "The Maker of Gestures," and filmed it as *Too Many Kisses* (1925). Directed by Paul Sloane, the film starred Richard Dix and Frances Howard in the story of a wealthy man's son who is sued for breach of promise. To keep him away from his many female admirers, his father sends him off to the Basque region of Spain, because the women there will not marry outside of their race. A few months later, Famous Players-Lasky filmed *The Shock Punch* (1925), from a *Liberty* story by Saunders. The critics loved this comedy melodrama about a millionaire's son (Richard Dix) who poses as a boxer with a knockout "shock punch," and who, in the course of the story, scales a half-finished skyscraper in the tradition of Harold Lloyd's *Safety Last* (1923).

A year later, 1925, Saunders met with Jesse L. Lasky, head of production at Famous Players-Lasky/Paramount, and discussed a proposed novel about two Americans in the flying corps during World War I who see active duty in France and behind enemy lines. Lasky liked the idea but would only agree to undertake the project if Saunders could obtain the support of the War Department, which Saunders accomplished. In 1926 Paramount purchased the screen rights to an unfinished novel *Wings* (1927) for $39,000—an unprecedented sum of money for that time. The novel was only published as a movie edition by Grosset and Dunlap after the film was released. Like the film, it was dedicated to "Those young warriors of the sky whose wings are folded about them forever."

Charles "Buddy" Rogers and Richard Arlen were featured as the two young flyers in love with the same girl, played by Clara Bow. Gary Cooper appeared in a brief, poignant cameo as a doomed flyer. The production was shot in Hollywood and on location near San Antonio, Texas, with a cast that included 3,500 servicemen and more than 65 pilots. The director, William Wellman, had served in both the American and French Flying Corps during World War I and had been a member of the famed Lafayette Escadrille. The film was a tremendous critical and box-office success and received the first Academy Award (1927-1928) for Best Picture. Al-

Charles "Buddy" Rogers, Clara Bow, and Richard Arlen in Wings, *winner of the first Academy Award for Best Picture*

though *Wings* premiered and received an initial, roadshow release in 1927, it was not generally released until 1929, when a music and sound-effects track was added.

As soon as *Wings* was completed, Saunders began work on a sequel, *The Legion of the Condemned* (1928). Critics agreed that the story of an American newspaperman and the members of an unattached flying unit at the front was no *Wings*, but they were nonetheless lavish in their praise. William Wellman again directed, and Gary Cooper and Fay Wray costarred. The young actress and Saunders met on the set of *The Legion of the Condemned* and were married in Maryland while she was on location for her next film, *The First Kiss* (1928).

Before his marriage to Fay Wray, Saunders wrote an original story, "The Dockwalloper," on which Jules Furthman based the script for *The Docks of New York* (1928). Directed by Josef von Sternberg, the film tells the story of a hard-drinking, hard-fighting stoker on a tramp steamer

(George Bancroft) who goes ashore on leave and marries a waterfront derelict (Betty Compson). Far from successful on its original release, the film is recognized today as one of von Sternberg's finest silent films—a pictorial essay in the use of light and shadow.

Contemporary trade papers announced that Saunders was working on a number of scripts for films to star his wife. Although two of these projects were filmed and did feature Fay Wray—*The Four Feathers* (1929) and *Dirigible* (1931)—Saunders did not receive credit for any contribution to their scripts. He did, however, receive credit for the dialogue and titles in a part-talkies, *She Goes to War* (1929), concerning a wealthy, spoiled girl who serves as a canteen worker in France during World War I and later takes her fiancé's place at the front. The film was directed by Henry King and featured Eleanor Broadman and John Holland.

Closer to the success of *Wings* was *The Dawn Patrol* (1930), for which Saunders wrote the original story about a group of upper-class English gentle-men who experience the grim realities of war in the Royal Flying Corps. Like *Wings*, this film had a basically pacifist attitude towards war. Howard Hawks, who coadapted the story with Dan Totheroh and Seton I. Miller, directed the film which featured Richard Barthelmess, Douglas Fairbanks, Jr., and Neil Hamilton. *The Dawn Patrol* gained Saunders an Academy Award for best original story in 1931; it was remade in 1938 by Warner Bros. and starred Errol Flynn, Basil Rathbone, and David Niven.

Saunders next collaborated with W. R. Burnett, the author of *Little Caesar* and coscreenwriter on *Scarface, Shame of a Nation* (1932). Their film, *The Finger Points* (1931), is the story of the gangland murder of a Chicago reporter. Richard Barthelmess played the newpaper reporter who investigates gangsters in his city and who is killed by machine-gun fire after the gang leader "points the finger" at him. Regis Toomey played the reporter's colleague who avenges his death by writing the story that cleans up the city, and Fay Wray played the girl both reporters loved.

During 1930 John Monk Saunders published a series of short stories in *Liberty* magazine which were collectively titled "Nikki and Her War Birds," about a wealthy American girl living in Paris. Nikki, best described as eccentric, befriended a group of American flyers ("war birds") who had stayed on in Paris after World War I for lack of anything better to do with their lives. In 1931 the series was published in novel form under the title *Single Lady*. It was the writer's first novel, and he described it as "the result of a holiday spent in and about the taverns, cafes, and bullrings of Lisbon." Reviews were generally favorable, with many critics comparing the book to Ernest Hemingway's *The Sun Also*

A scene from The Dawn Patrol, *which won Saunders the 1931 Oscar for Best Original Story*

Rises and Michael Arlen's *The Green Hat*.

As soon as the novel was published, First National and Warner Bros. began production on a script by Saunders, based on *Single Lady*. With the working title "Spent Bullets," the film was released in late summer 1931 as *The Last Flight*. It starred Helen Chandler as Nikki (first appearing on the screen with a champagne glass containing a pair of false teeth) and Richard Barthelmess, Johnny Mack Brown, David Manners, and Elliott Nugent as the four "war birds."

This literate film about a disillusioned group of flyers (two of whom almost gladly accept death) and a girl who is as respectable as she is goofy, has come to be recognized as a minor masterpiece of the cinema. It is the story of the friendship and affection which exists between men who have faced death together, and, for all its witty dialogue, it contains moments of gentle emotion and warmth.

Saunders wrote the script and Philip Charig the music for the musical comedy version, *Nikki*, starring Fay Wray, which opened at the Longacre Theatre, New York, on 29 September 1931. One of the four flyers was played by Archie Leach, who later went to Hollywood and changed his name to Cary Grant.

The Last Flight, the third outstanding film of Saunders's career, marked his last major contribution to the screen. He did, however, coscript one additional film, *Ace of Aces* (1933), a pacifist story about a young sculptor urged by his fiancée to become a fighter pilot. He also wrote the original stories for two other films, *West Point of the Air* (1935) and *Devil Dogs of the Air* (1935), which were World War I flying yarns, and provided the original idea for a third, *A Yank at Oxford* (1938), partially based on his own experiences at that school.

When asked about writing for the screen, John Monk Saunders was quoted as saying, "Action is the thing. Action! Action! Action!" But his films offer far more than just action scenes. His three major works have many tender moments which add depth to their characters and plots. Much of his work for the screen demonstrates a strong pacifist philosophy; he obviously glories in the comradeship that war can offer a man, but does not overlook the harsh realities of war. In *Wings* Buddy Rogers gives a fond farewell kiss to his dying comrade Richard Arlen, illustrating Saunders's sensitivity to emotion and his view that the hidden emotions of men are seldom released except under severe conditions, such as during war.

Saunders and Fay Wray separated in the summer of 1938, and on 18 January 1939, the actress filed suit for divorce, mentioning his drinking and narcotics. On 10 March 1940, Saunders was found hanging in his beach cottage in Fort Myers, Florida. He left no note.

In a 1925 *Liberty* magazine piece, John Monk Saunders mused about his future: "Shall I, at fifty, be a major or a minor figure? Shall I go up like a rocket, blacken against the sky, and come down like a dead stick? Or shall I go up at all?" Saunders need not have worried. His film work in general and *Wings*, *The Dawn Patrol*, and *The Last Flight* in particular have ensured his place in American cinema history.

Reference:

"Sold down the River to the Movies, So They Said," *Washington Post*, 12 February 1928.

Papers:

Two scrapbooks, one covering the period 1925-1928 and the other "Nikki and Her War Birds" and its various reincarnations, are in the Fay Wray Collection at the University of Southern California, Los Angeles.

Budd Schulberg

(27 March 1914-   )

Stephen O. Lesser

See also the Schulberg entries in *DLB 6, American Novelists Since World War II, Second Series*, and *DLB Yearbook: 1981*.

MOTION PICTURES: *Little Orphan Annie* (Paramount, 1938), screenplay by Schulberg and Samuel Ornitz;

Winter Carnival (United Artists, 1939), screen story; screenplay by Schulberg, Maurice Rapf, and Lester Cole;

Weekend for Three (RKO, 1941), story;

City Without Men (Columbia, 1943), screen story by Schulberg and Martin Berkeley;

Government Girl (RKO, 1943), adaptation;

On the Waterfront (Columbia, 1954), screen story and screenplay;

A Face in the Crowd (Warner Bros., 1957), story and screenplay;

Wind Across the Everglades (Warner Bros., 1958), screen story and screenplay.

PLAYS: *The Disenchanted* (New York, Coronet Theatre, 3 December 1958), by Schulberg and Harvey Breit;

What Makes Sammy Run? (New York, Fifty-fourth Street Theatre, 27 February 1964), book by Schulberg and Stuart Schulberg.

Budd Schulberg (The Granger Collection)

BOOKS: *What Makes Sammy Run?* (New York: Random House, 1941; London: Jarrolds, 1941);

The Harder They Fall (New York: Random House, 1947; London: Bodley Head, 1948);

The Disenchanted (New York: Random House, 1950; London: Bodley Head, 1951);

Some Faces in the Crowd (New York: Random House, 1953; London: Bodley Head, 1954);

Waterfront (New York: Random House, 1955; London: Bodley Head, 1956);

A Face in the Crowd: A Play for the Screen (New York: Random House, 1957);

Across the Everglades: A Play for the Screen (New York: Random House, 1958);

The Disenchanted: A Drama in Three Acts, by Schulberg and Harvey Breit (New York: Random House, 1959);

What Makes Sammy Run?: A New Musical, by Schulberg and Stuart Schulberg (New York: Random House, 1964);

Sanctuary V (New York & Cleveland: New American Library / World, 1969; London: Allen, 1971);

Loser and Still Champion: Muhammad Ali (Garden City: Doubleday, 1972; London: New English Library, 1972);

The Four Seasons of Success (Garden City: Doubleday, 1972; London: Robson, 1974);

Swan Watch, by Schulberg and Geraldine Brooks (New York: Delacorte, 1975);

Everything That Moves (Garden City: Doubleday, 1980);

On the Waterfront: A Screenplay (Carbondale & Edwardsville: Southern Illinois University Press, 1980);

Moving Pictures: Memories of a Hollywood Prince (New

York: Stein & Day, 1981).

OTHER: *From the Ashes: Voices of Watts,* edited by
Schulberg (New York: New American Library, 1967);
William Spratling, *File on Spratling,* edited by Schulberg (Boston & Toronto: Little, Brown, 1967).

Budd Wilson Schulberg was born in New York
City, the son of Benjamin P. and Adeline (Jaffe)
Schulberg. In 1919 the family moved to Hollywood,
where B. P. Schulberg became head of production
at Paramount Famous-Lasky. A genuine Hollywood mogul, B. P. Schulberg was one of the dominant personalities in a fiercely competitive business;
he has been credited with developing the careers of
Gary Cooper, Claudette Colbert, Clara Bow, and
Fredric March. He brought Emil Jannings and
Marlene Dietrich from Germany. At the height of
his power, B. P. Schulberg earned $10,000 a week,
but his collapse was as legendary as his ascent. He
divorced his wife, turned to drink, became a compulsive gambler, lost his job, and was finally reduced to begging for employment in an advertisement in *Daily Variety.* He died in 1957.

Budd Schulberg grew to know the successes
and failures of Hollywood. Reminiscing about his
childhood in *Los Angeles* magazine (September
1965), he wrote that Hollywood was "flamboyant,
show off, unabashedly theatrical, a razzle-dazzle
example of the Veblen theory of conspicuous con-
sumption. When Paramount moved to its present
real estate on Marathon Street near Melrose I used
to pedal my bike through the big studio gate nearly
every day and use the back lot as my private playground." He went on to say, "If life is a series of
disenchantments through which we prepare ourselves for mature enchantments, then I was richly
endowed, for our castles were built on glamorous
quicksand."

Following graduation from Dartmouth in
1936, Schulberg returned to Hollywood to work as a
junior writer at various studios. He added dialogue
to the film *A Star Is Born* (1937), writing with Ring
Lardner, Jr., the final scene in which the heroine,
Vicki Lester, presents herself as "Mrs. Norman
Maine" (neither Schulberg nor Lardner received
screen credit). He quit working for David O.
Selznick's story department after Selznick refused
to read two scripts Schulberg and Lardner had cowritten and denied Schulberg a raise from seventy-
five to one hundred dollars a week. Schulberg
began spending more time on his political and literary interests, contributing short stories to *Collier's,*

Esquire, Liberty, and other national magazines. He
joined a study group that later became a Communist Party Youth League Group but quit in 1940
when the group criticized his stories as "too indi-
vidualistic and decadent."

Schulberg's first screen credit came in 1938
with the Paramount release of *Little Orphan Annie,*
which he coauthored with Samuel Ornitz. The film
received poor reviews, but it represents Schulberg's
first story about boxing, with Annie convincing a
tenement neighborhood victimized by a loan shark
to underwrite the training expenses of a boxer.

In 1939 Schulberg received credit for both the
screen story and the joint screenplay for *Winter Carnival,* a Walter Wanger-United Artists film. The
movie is more famous for the production problems
encountered in its making than for the story itself.
Schulberg had been engaged by Wanger, also a
graduate of Dartmouth, to write a screenplay using
the background of the Dartmouth Winter Carnival
and incorporating a love story to be played by stars
Ann Sheridan and Richard Carlson. Wanger assigned F. Scott Fitzgerald to collaborate with Schulberg, and the two authors took notes on each other.
Fitzgerald was fascinated by Schulberg's stories
about growing up in Hollywood and included many
of them in his posthumously published novel *The
Last Tycoon.* Schulberg used the entire collaborative
relationship as the basis for his novel *The Disenchanted* (1950). As for the picture itself, *Winter Carnival* was a failure, and Schulberg moved to Vermont to work on his first novel, *What Makes Sammy
Run?,* which was published in 1941.

What Makes Sammy Run? brought Schulberg
instant fame and established his reputation as a
critic of Hollywood. Published on his twenty-
seventh birthday, the book is still considered a
minor classic, an impressive indictment of a system
of values. The novel follows the career of Sammy
Glick, who begins as a New York copyboy and ends
as a Hollywood writer. Sammy betrays everyone
who did him a good deed, and predictably, he himself is betrayed by the one person he trusted.

The story is told through a first-person narrator who represents an older standard of values
and principles. But even the narrator, Al Mannheim, is pulled to Hollywood in Sammy's wake,
where he too becomes a screenwriter. The novel
covers much of the social history of Hollywood in
the late 1930s from the screenwriter's point of view,
such as the writers' abortive strike and meetings of
the Writers Guild. Above all, *What Makes Sammy
Run?* overflows with telling, discerning remarks, the
observations of Mannheim on Sammy Glick.

Marlon Brando in On the Waterfront. *The film won eight Oscars, including those for best actor (Brando), best supporting actress (Eva Marie Saint), best screenplay, and best picture.*

In the early 1940s Schulberg wrote for three films: *Weekend for Three* (1941), *City Without Men* (1943), and *Government Girl* (1943). *City Without Men* was produced by B. P. Schulberg and Samuel Bronston and was about women waiting for their husbands or boyfriends to be released from prison. *Government Girl* was adapted from a serial by Adela Rogers St. John about a government secretary in wartime Washington, D.C. Dudley Nichols wrote the screenplay and directed the film.

In February 1943, Schulberg married Victoria Anderson. During World War II he served in the U.S. Navy as a lieutenant junior grade assigned to the Office of Strategic Service. He was awarded the Army Commendation Ribbon for gathering photographic evidence of war crimes for the Nuremberg trials.

In the later 1940s, Schulberg had two novels published. *The Harder They Fall* (1947) is a realistic

exposé of the world of boxing. Schulberg is at home in the violent world of the sport. There is a gritty realism to the novel, and Schulberg does not spare the reader the details of racketeering and chicanery. He also indicts the public for its blood lust to witness tragedy in the ring. The novel was filmed in 1956, without Schulberg's participation, and he was not pleased with the results. "I don't think they really smelled or breathed the fight atmosphere of Eighth Avenue. How could they expect to make a picture working out of the St. Regis Hotel?"

For his third novel, *The Disenchanted*, Schulberg returned to Hollywood, where he created the character Manley Halliday, who is partially based on F. Scott Fitzgerald. This is a novel of personal memory and, as Schulberg claims, a composite of the experiences of many screenwriters in Hollywood. Much of the book consists of a running dialogue between the narrator, Shep, who represents a socially committed young writer of the 1930s, and Halliday, the prodigy of the 1920s who could not adjust to the new environment. The novel was adapted for the stage by Schulberg and Harvey Breit in December 1958.

After completing *The Disenchanted*, Schulberg turned his energies to the subject of corruption in labor unions and created his most distinguished and successful screenplay, *On the Waterfront* (1954). Schulberg based the screenplay on the series "Crime on the Waterfront" which ran in twenty-four articles in the *New York Sun* from November through December 1948. In 1949 Malcolm Johnson, the reporter, won a Pulitzer prize. Schulberg saw the personal angle in the story—the awakening of man's conscience and how one man rose up against union corruption and vindicated honesty and integrity.

On the Waterfront almost did not get made. It was turned down by every major studio and finally produced independently by Sam Spiegel. Even after shooting began, the film encountered a series of problems. The director Elia Kazan needed a bodyguard to protect him against intimidation. Joe Ryan, union boss of the New York docks, threatened a labor boycott of the movie production crew. There were several suits against Spiegel and Schulberg, including one by a man named Sam Shaw, who claimed to have assisted in the scripting at "Schulberg's request."

On the Waterfront was one of the most successful films of 1954. It cost $820,000 to produce and grossed over $6,000,000. The film won eight Academy awards, including the awards for best picture, best actor (Marlon Brando), best supporting actress (Eva Marie Saint), best director, and best screenplay. The subject matter gripped Schulberg's interest so intensely that when he finished the screenplay, he wrote a novel on the same subject entitled *Waterfront* (1955).

Following the acclaim of *On the Waterfront*, Schulberg again worked with Kazan to write *A Face in the Crowd* (1957). The film looks forward to *Network* (1976) and other movies that try to point out the dangers of mass manipulation through television. In *A Face in the Crowd* Schulberg examines the role of commercial television in American life, developing a pointed morality story about the rise and fall of an opportunistic but clever lout, Lonesome Rhodes (Andy Griffith), a hobo with a good singing voice who climbs to national prominence through radio. His nature—he is a lecherous cynic—is at complete variance with his public personality. Schulberg has said that he used a composite of

Walter Winchell and Will Rogers as the model for Lonesome Rhodes. Lonesome plays on the public's need for heroes, exploiting its gullibility. He is adopted by right-wing political forces. But the microphone, the very instrument that brought him his initial success, causes his ruin.

Schulberg and his brother Stuart formed their own company to make *Wind Across the Everglades* (1958). The film grew out of the period when Schulberg lived in Florida on the outskirts of the Everglades National Wildlife Refuge and became fascinated by that "unique and unknown corner of America." Nicholas Ray directed this story of a schoolteacher (Christopher Plummer) from the North who, when he is refused the job promised him in Miami, becomes a warden in the Everglades for the Audubon Society. He risks his life to stop the slaughter of the egret, whose feathers were sold to fashionable ladies. Unfortunately, the movie was not able to communicate Schulberg's intense feelings in a convincing manner; the film received poor reviews and was a commercial failure.

Schulberg began the 1960s by returning to an old theme: racketeering in organized labor. He prepared a script entitled "The Enemy Within,"

Patricia Neal, Percy Waram, and Andy Griffith in A Face in the Crowd

George Voskovec, Christopher Plummer, and Gypsy Rose Lee in Wind Across the Everglades

based on the book by Attorney General Robert Kennedy about his campaign against dishonest labor leaders. The screenplay was completed for Jerry Wald productions in August 1962, but Wald's death put an end to the project. The script reveals characteristic Schulberg themes: abuse of public trust, personal corruption, and the dogged persistence of one individual to get to the truth.

Although Schulberg has written several treatments and scripts, he has not had a screenplay produced since *Wind Across the Everglades*. In 1964,

with his brother Stuart Schulberg, he adapted *What Makes Sammy Run?* into a musical; he was divorced from Victoria Anderson and married actress Geraldine Brooks that same year. Although Schulberg has continued to work as a novelist and writer of nonfiction, his most recent book is a volume of memoirs entitled *Moving Pictures: Memories of a Hollywood Prince* (1981). Progress on that book had been interrupted by Brooks's death in 1977. In 1979 he married Betsy Ann Langman. They currently reside on Long Island.

Rod Serling

(25 December 1924-28 June 1975)

F. Jeffrey Armstrong

MOTION PICTURES: *Patterns* (United Artists, 1956), screen story and screenplay;
Saddle the Wind (M-G-M, 1958), screenplay;
Requiem for a Heavyweight (Columbia, 1962), story and screenplay;
The Yellow Canary (20th Century-Fox, 1963), screenplay;
Seven Days in May (Paramount, 1964), screenplay;
Assault on a Queen (Paramount, 1966), screenplay;
Planet of the Apes (20th Century-Fox, 1968), screenplay by Serling and Michael Wilson;
The Man (Paramount, 1972), story and screenplay;
The Salamander (ITC, 1982), adaptation.

SELECTED TELEVISION: *Patterns*, *Kraft Theatre* (NBC, 1955), script;
Requiem for a Heavyweight, *Playhouse 90* (CBS, 1956), script;
The Comedian, *Playhouse 90* (CBS, 1957), script;
The Twilight Zone [series] (CBS, 1959-1964), creator and scriptwriter;
Night Gallery [series] (NBC, 1969-1973), creator and scriptwriter.

SELECTED BOOKS: *Patterns: Four Television Plays with the Author's Personal Commentary* (New York: Simon & Schuster, 1957);
Stories from the Twilight Zone (New York: Bantam, 1960);
More Stories from the Twilight Zone (New York: Bantam, 1961);
Requiem for a Heavyweight (New York: Bantam, 1962);
New Stories from the Twilight Zone (New York: Bantam, 1965);
The Season to Be Wary (Boston: Little, Brown, 1967);
Night Gallery (New York: Bantam, 1971);
Night Gallery 2 (Toronto & New York: Bantam, 1972);
Rod Serling's Other Worlds (New York: Bantam, 1978).

Rod Serling left behind an impressive body of work for television. Hundreds of his teleplays were aired during his twenty-five-year career. By comparison, his writing for the screen seems slight—he

Rod Serling

wrote the screenplays for only nine films, and he never had an original screenplay produced; all of his screenplays were adaptations of his own teleplays or of stories or novels by others.

Edward Rodman Serling was born in Syracuse, New York, the son of a wholesale butcher, Samuel L. Serling, and Esther Cooper Serling. He grew up in Binghamton, New York, and after high school he entered the army, where he served as a paratrooper in the Philippines during World War II and received the Purple Heart. Upon leaving the army, he entered Antioch College under the G.I. bill; there he began writing radio and television scripts, teaching himself as he wrote. He married Carol Kramer on 31 July 1948. Before he graduated in 1950, he had sold his first television script (after forty rejections). Until 1953 he wrote for a Cincinnati television station. Turning to free-lance writing for the new medium of television, he developed his craft and found an individual style along the way.

Sérling's work during this period in many ways typifies the work of the first generation of television writers, a group which includes Paddy Chayefsky and Reginald Rose. His teleplays were serious, often dealing with contemporary issues in an emotional and powerfully direct manner. Serling placed special emphasis on character psychology and motivation, and perhaps his greatest strength as a writer was his handling of dialogue—always forceful and direct, with effective use of pauses and unusual wordplay. Serling's attitude toward his characters was humanistic, and his stories were characterized by moralizing.

In 1955 *Patterns*, a powerful *Kraft Theatre* drama about the pressures of corporate politics and ruthless power games in big business, made Serling an overnight success and brought him the first of six Emmies. He followed this success with a string of fine teleplays, including two more Emmy winners (both written for *Playhouse 90), Requiem for a Heavyweight* (1956), a pathetic story about the loneliness and confusion facing a boxer at the end of his career, and *The Comedian* (1957), which focuses on an obnoxious, self-centered comedian who exploits those around him to further his own goals.

Serling's early days in television were filled with conflicts with networks and sponsors who attempted to censor his work. Eventually these censorship battles led to Serling's abandoning live drama to work on his own television series, *The Twilight Zone*. Because most of the series' episodes were in the science-fiction/fantasy genre, Serling felt that he could say things he could never get away with in more "realistic" screenplays.

The Twilight Zone, which Serling is credited with creating, aired from 1959 to 1964. The weekly stories were memorable tales of imagination and possibility, of modern science and ancient superstition. A central theme of episodes written by Serling was that there were universal mysteries and forces before which man, even modern, scientific man, must inevitably humble himself. The general tone of many was cautionary: man can never be too sure of anything. Again Serling the humanist and moralist emerged. He rewarded the good and punished the evil, often in appropriately ironic ways.

The success of his television work led Serling to write his first screenplays, and like Chayefsky and

Rose, he based his earliest scripts on his television plays. *Patterns*, made into a film in 1956, was brought to the screen virtually unchanged, with most of the same cast members and the same director, Fielder Cook. *Requiem for a Heavyweight* was made into a film in 1962, and although Serling added a new ending and made minor changes, it too was quite faithful to the original. Neither suffered in the transition to the big screen. In between these films, Serling wrote *Saddle the Wind* (1958), one of many adult Westerns to be made in the late 1950s, with a clash between cattlemen and sheepherders serving as backdrop for a conflict of brother versus brother (Robert Taylor and John Cassavetes).

Television kept Serling busy until 1963, when he wrote *The Yellow Canary*, adapted from the novel *Evil Come, Evil Go* by Whit Masterson. Designed as a vehicle for Pat Boone, the film is a drama about a popular singer who changes his self-centered ways when he must turn amateur sleuth to retrieve his kidnapped baby. The movie benefits from Serling's insights into the world of the entertainer. *Assault on a Queen* (1966), based on the novel by Jack Finney, is one of Serling's weakest screenplays, a caper film about an attempt to rob the *Queen Mary* using a submarine.

Serling's two best screenplays were his adaptations of novels whose subject matter intersected with his own interests and specialties: *Seven Days in May* by Fletcher Knebel and Charles W. Bailey and *Planet of the Apes* by Pierre Boulle. *Seven Days in May* (1964) is a drama about an attempted military takeover of the United States government by high-ranking officers who are alarmed by the President's decision to carry out a nuclear disarmament pact with the Soviet Union. The military angle obviously attracted Serling, as did the high-level power games played between the White House and the Pentagon. With Serling's tight pacing, and under John Frankenheimer's skillful direction, *Seven Days in May* moves with a swift, calculated momentum. Serling the humanist again emerges in the screenplay's celebration of peace and democracy and in its condemnation of war, suspicion, and the undemocratic wielding of power. And Serling the critic of technological man emerges in a speech the President (Fredric March) delivers about the nuclear age: "Our enemy is an age. It happens to have killed man's faith in his ability to influence what happens to him. And out of this comes a sickness. A sickness of frustration."

Pierre Boulle's novel *Planet of the Apes*, about a space traveler from earth who, after years in space, lands on a planet ruled by apes, where humans are

Linda Harrison, Charlton Heston, and Maurice Evans in Planet of the Apes

no better than animals, has a premise that would have made a good *Twilight Zone* episode. The surprise ending of *Planet of the Apes* (1968) is also reminiscent of *The Twilight Zone*: the space traveler discovers to his horror that the planet run by apes is his own planet earth, changed during his absence. Boulle's novel, which satirizes human vanity, condemns the entrenchment of blind authority, and mocks social conventions, approaches Swiftian irony. In the film, Boulle's themes are made timely to late-1960s America; the film takes jabs at governmental authority, the military, racial prejudice, and class divisions. Serling wrote the screenplay with Michael Wilson, but his hand is visible throughout, particularly in the soliloquy delivered by one of the space travelers (Charlton Heston) at the beginning of the film, as he looks across space toward an earth that has aged centuries during his

voyage: "Tell me, though. Does man, that marvel of the universe, that glorious paradox who sent me to the stars, still make war against his brother, keep his neighbor's children starving?"

After *Planet of the Apes*, Serling again devoted his efforts to television, particularly his television series *Night Gallery*, an anthology series similar to *The Twilight Zone*. His next screenplay was actually done for television: he adapted Irving Wallace's *The Man* as a telefilm, but Paramount was so impressed with the results that the film was released in theaters in 1972. The film is about an unimportant cabinet member (James Earl Jones) who, through an unexpected chain of events, becomes the first black president of the United States. Not one of Serling's best scripts, *The Man* failed as the timely social commentary it aspired to be.

In 1973, after *Night Gallery* was cancelled,

Serling returned to Upstate New York and taught at Ithaca College. On 28 June 1975 he died of complications stemming from open-heart surgery. His death was mourned as tragically premature. He received a special posthumous Emmy award in the fall of 1975, and his memory has been kept alive since his death mostly by his series *The Twilight Zone*. In 1980 his wife, Carol Serling, announced the publication of *Rod Serling's Twilight Zone* magazine, featuring fiction in the vein of the television show, and in 1982, *Twilight Zone–the Movie*, consisting of three remade episodes of the series, was released.

Some years after his death, Serling's last screenplay was finally filmed. *The Salamander* (1982), based on Morris West's novel about European espionage, was a critical and financial failure.

Rod Serling's relatively small output of screenplays should be weighed against the fact that,

unlike many other early television dramatists, he remained loyal to the medium that gave him his start, even though it did not always treat him well. He will be remembered as one of our best television writers, and beyond that, as a writer whose devotion to his craft was total. To preface its obituary of Rod Serling, *Writer's Digest* chose to borrow these lines from *Requiem for a Heavyweight*: "He had . . . a kind of greatness you don't see very often."

References:

Gary Gerani and Paul H. Shulman, *"The Twilight Zone" and "Night Gallery," Fantastic Television* (New York: Harmony Books, 1977), pp. 35-47, 127-133;

Gilbert Millstein, " 'Patterns' of a Television Playwright," *New York Times Magazine*, 2 December 1956, pp. 24, 57, 59-60.

Robert E. Sherwood
(4 April 1896-14 November 1955)

Ralph Haven Wolfe
Bowling Green State University

See also the Sherwood entry in *DLB 7, Twentieth-Century American Dramatists*.

MOTION PICTURES: *The Lucky Lady* (Famous Players-Lasky/Paramount, 1926), scenario by Sherwood and James T. Donohue;

Oh, What a Nurse (Warner Bros., 1926), screen story by Sherwood and Bertram Bloch;

Age for Love (United Artists, 1931), dialogue;

Around the World in 80 Minutes with Douglas Fairbanks (United Artists, 1931), commentary;

Cock of the Air (United Artists, 1932), screenplay by Sherwood and Charles Lederer;

Roman Scandals (United Artists, 1933), screen story by Sherwood and George S. Kaufman;

The Scarlet Pimpernel (United Artists, 1935), screenplay by Sherwood and Arthur Wimperis;

The Ghost Goes West (United Artists, 1936), screenplay;

Thunder in the City (Columbia, 1937), screenplay by Sherwood, Aben Kandel, and Akos Tolnay;

The Adventures of Marco Polo (United Artists, 1938), screenplay;

The Divorce of Lady X (United Artists, 1938),

screenplay by Sherwood and Lajos Biro;

Idiot's Delight (M-G-M, 1939), screenplay;

Abe Lincoln in Illinois (RKO, 1940), screenplay;

Rebecca (United Artists, 1940), screenplay by Sherwood and Joan Harrison;

The Best Years of Our Lives (RKO, 1946), screenplay;

The Bishop's Wife (RKO, 1947), screenplay by Sherwood and Leonardo Bercovici;

Man on a Tightrope (20th Century-Fox, 1953), screenplay;

Main Street to Broadway (M-G-M, 1953), screen story.

PLAYS: *The Road to Rome* (New York, Playhouse, 31 January 1927);

The Love Nest (New York, Comedy Theatre, 22 December 1927);

The Queen's Husband (New York, Playhouse, 25 January 1928);

Waterloo Bridge (New York, Fulton Theatre, 6 January 1930);

This Is New York (New York, Plymouth Theatre, 28 November 1930);

Reunion in Vienna (New York, Martin Beck Theatre, 16 November 1931);

Robert E. Sherwood (Metropolitan Photo Service)

Acropolis (London, Lyric Theatre, 23 November 1933);

The Petrified Forest (New York, Broadhurst Theatre, 7 January 1935);

Idiot's Delight (New York, Shubert Theatre, 24 March 1936);

Tovarich (New York, Plymouth Theatre, 15 October 1936);

Abe Lincoln in Illinois (New York, Plymouth Theatre, 15 October 1938);

There Shall Be No Night (New York, Alvin Theatre, 29 April 1940);

The Rugged Path (New York, Plymouth Theatre, 10 November 1945);

Miss Liberty (New York, Imperial Theatre, 15 July 1949);

Small War on Murray Hill (New York, Ethel Barrymore Theatre, 3 January 1957).

BOOKS: *The Road to Rome* (New York: Scribners, 1927);

The Queen's Husband (New York & London: Scribners, 1928);

Waterloo Bridge (New York & London: Scribners, 1930);

This Is New York (New York & London: Scribners, 1931);

The Virtuous Knight (New York: Scribners, 1931);

Reunion in Vienna (New York: Scribners, 1932);

The Petrified Forest (New York & London: Scribners, 1935);

Idiot's Delight (New York & London: Scribners, 1936; London: Heinemann, 1938);

Tovarich (New York: Random House, 1937; London: French, 1938);

Abe Lincoln in Illinois (New York & London: Scribners, 1939);

There Shall Be No Night (New York: Scribners, 1940);

Roosevelt and Hopkins (New York: Harper, 1948); republished as *The White House Papers of Harry L. Hopkins,* 2 volumes (London: Eyre & Spottiswoode, 1949);

Small War on Murray Hill (New York: Dramatists Play Service, 1957).

SELECTED PERIODICAL PUBLICATION: "They're Film Writers, Not Juke Boxes," *New York Times Magazine,* 1 December 1946, p. 15ff.

Robert E. Sherwood first distinguished himself as a film critic producing a weekly column for the humor magazine *Life* for almost eight years (1921-1928). He next turned to drama, writing thirteen original plays during his career and winning the Pulitzer Prize for drama three times: for *Idiot's Delight* in 1936, *Abe Lincoln in Illinois* in 1939, and *There Shall Be No Night* in 1941. Intermittently from 1926 to 1953 he wrote for the movies, being involved in twenty-three films and winning an Academy Award for his screenplay for *The Best Years of Our Lives* in 1946. Sherwood also wrote television scripts, short fiction, one novel, and a nonfiction book, *Roosevelt and Hopkins* (1948), for which he won another Pulitzer Prize, in 1949.

Robert Emmet Sherwood was born in New Rochelle, New York, the fourth of five children born to Arthur Murray and Rosina Emmet Sherwood. A brilliant child, Sherwood was educated at Milton Academy in Massachusetts and at Harvard, from which he received a B.A. in 1918. In 1917 during his junior year he enlisted in the Canadian Black Watch and then went to France. He was twice gassed and wounded in both legs at Amiens.

After returning home from World War I, Sherwood went to New York, where he began work in 1919 as a drama and film critic for *Vanity Fair.* Leaving after a dispute the next year, he went on to *Life*, where he wrote movie reviews until 1928 and after 1924 served as editor. He next worked briefly as literary editor for *Scribner's Magazine*, but the success of his first play, *The Road to Rome*, which opened in January 1927 and ran for 392 performances, soon enabled him to devote his full time to writing.

Sherwood's first work for the movies came in 1924 when he was paid $2,500 for rewriting the subtitles for *The Hunchback of Notre Dame*. Next he coscripted *The Lucky Lady* (1926) with James T. Donohue, and with Bertram Bloch wrote the screen story for *Oh, What a Nurse* (1926). *The Lucky Lady*, based on a story by Bloch and directed by Raoul Walsh, is a romantic comedy about a princess who, betrothed to a count by her father, falls in love with an American tourist. *Oh, What a Nurse* is also based on disguise: a man (Sydney Chaplin) dresses up as a widow and then as a nurse to protect his girl friend from villains.

Howard Hughes hired Sherwood for two weeks in 1931 to write the dialogue for his first talkie, *Age for Love*. Adapted from Ernest Pascal's novel about a couple who divorce and then regret it, the film was directed by Frank Lloyd and starred Billie Dove and Edward Everett Horton. Sherwood followed *Age for Love* by furnishing the commentary for *Around the World in 80 Minutes with Douglas Fairbanks* (1931). In 1932 he and Charles Lederer wrote the script for *Cock of the Air*, a comedy about an army pilot who flies from Italy to Paris with his girl friend so that they can have cocktails at the Ritz.

After working without credit on *Rasputin and the Empress* (1932), Sherwood was hired by Samuel Goldwyn in 1933 to work with George S. Kaufman on a script for a musical version of George Bernard Shaw's *Androcles and the Lion* to star Eddie Cantor. The assignment resulted in a lawsuit against Goldwyn, who, according to Sherwood and Kaufman, refused to pay them because he said they had only given him a rough draft and not an acceptable film script. Nevertheless, Kaufman and Sherwood were given credit when the film, retitled *Roman Scandals* (1933), was released.

While in England in 1935 Sherwood was hired by Alexander Korda to write with Arthur Wimperis a script for Baroness Orczy's novel of the French Revolution, *The Scarlet Pimpernel*. The result of this collaboration was Sherwood's first really successful film venture. Directed by Harold Young and starring Leslie Howard, who had recently acted in Sherwood's play *The Petrified Forest* (1935), *The Scarlet Pimpernel* was exceedingly popular. Following this success, Korda asked Sherwood to do extra script work on *Rembrandt*. Next Sherwood took on

full-script responsibility for *The Ghost Goes West* (1936), the first English-language picture to be directed by René Clair. The film script, based on the story "Sir Tristram Goes West" by Eric Keown, is about an American millionaire who buys a haunted Scottish castle and moves it to America. Unbeknownst to the buyer, a ghost goes along with the purchase. The success of this production was the result not only of the first-rate script but also of Clair's skillful direction and the performance of Robert Donat as both the eighteenth-century ghost haunting the castle and the ghost's twentieth-century descendant.

After working without credit on *Conquest* (1937), about a romance between Napoleon (Charles Boyer) and a Polish countess (Greta Garbo), Sherwood next worked with Aben Kandel and Akos Tolnay in scripting *Thunder in the City* (1937), about an American con man who sells a new metal named magnalite in England. This mediocre film was helped by Sherwood's clever dialogue.

Goldwyn hired Sherwood in 1938 to write the script for *The Adventures of Marco Polo*, which was directed by Archie Mayo, with assistance from John Ford and John Cromwell. Sherwood's lighthearted script begins with Marco Polo leaving Venice to go on a business trip for his father to the court of Kubla Khan in Peking. Polo (Gary Cooper) falls in love with the Khan's daughter (Sigrid Gurie), who has been promised to the Persian king and been subjected to the evil designs of Ahmed, the Saracen (Basil Rathbone). Polo ingratiates himself into the good graces of the Khan (George Barbier) and as a result is sent on a mission to the rebel camp of Kaidu (Alan Hale). After Polo saves Kaidu's life, he asks for Kaidu's assistance in saving the Khan's throne from Ahmed. In the final scene, Polo uses the newly discovered gunpowder to rescue the Khan and the princess. *The Adventures of Marco Polo* was a great success. The film's popularity is largely due to its tongue-in-cheek nature, with much of the humor coming from the exchanges between Polo and his servant and traveling companion Binguccio and from his discoveries of Chinese culture.

After completing *The Adventures of Marco Polo*, Sherwood worked with Lajos Biro in scripting Biro's play *Counsel's Opinion*. Retitled *The Divorce of Lady X* (1938), the film was produced by Alexander Korda and directed by Tom Whelan. In this comedy Sherwood again worked with disguise or mistaken identity as a plot device. Leslie (Merle Oberon), fogged in in London at the Park Lane Hotel, appropriates the bedroom of a young lawyer, Logan (Laurence Olivier), while he sleeps outside

Judith Anderson, George Sanders, Joan Fontaine, Laurence Olivier, and C. Aubrey Smith in Rebecca, *winner of the 1940 Academy Award for Best Picture*

on the floor. The next day Lord Mere (Ralph Richardson), on hearing that a lady looking like his wife was seen leaving the Park Lane early in the morning, brings divorce proceedings against her through Logan, who eventually realizes that Leslie has been mistaken for Lady Mere.

Between 1938 and 1940 Sherwood was extremely busy working without credit on *Marie Antoinette* (1938), writing film versions of his plays *Idiot's Delight* and *Abe Lincoln in Illinois*, and coscripting *Rebecca* (1940). He is also said to have worked on *Northwest Passage* (1940), though he received no screen credit.

Idiot's Delight (1939), based on Sherwood's Pulitzer Prize-winning play of 1936, was the first of his plays that he adapted for film. Directed by Clarence Brown, it starred Norma Shearer and Clark Gable in the roles made famous on the stage by Lynn Fontanne and Alfred Lunt. The play, about two former lovers who are reunited in prewar Italy, is a strongly pacifist work. Although Sherwood altered the play's tragic ending and made the film much less specifically antiwar, the film still shows

the essential idiocy and pointlessness of militarism. The characterizations remain virtually the same, although a long sequence was added to establish the fact that Shearer and Gable had once had a love affair during a stay in Omaha while on a vaudeville tour.

Also adapted from one of Sherwood's Pulitzer Prize-winning plays, *Abe Lincoln in Illinois*, released in 1940, was directed by John Cromwell with Raymond Massey repeating his Broadway role. Containing fewer controversial ideas than *Idiot's Delight*, *Abe Lincoln in Illinois* allowed Sherwood to concentrate in his adaptation on ways the shooting could enhance the stage material. With the camera Sherwood could move out of the dimensions of the stage, enabling him to portray Lincoln's life on a larger scale by showing the Illinois landscape and the Mississippi. The intimacy of the camera also allowed Sherwood to convey the feeling and sincerity of Lincoln without dependence upon dialogue. A critical success upon its release, *Abe Lincoln in Illinois* remains a highly regarded film.

In working on *Rebecca*, Sherwood was writing

for Alfred Hitchcock's first film in America. Based on Daphne du Maurier's extremely popular novel, the film, which starred Joan Fontaine and Laurence Olivier, won the Academy Award for Best Picture and has become a classic. Sherwood and Hitchcock's longtime associate Joan Harrison followed the novel closely, tightening it up and adding few new scenes.

Busy as an adviser and speech writer in the Roosevelt administration, Sherwood did not write again for the screen until 1945. It was then that he was summoned to Hollywood by Goldwyn to help director William Wyler adapt MacKinlay Kantor's novel *Glory for Me*, about three servicemen returning to civilian life after World War II. The novel served merely as a basis for *The Best Years of Our Lives* (1946). Wyler and Sherwood made changes, most significantly changing the character Homer Parrish from a spastic to a sailor who had lost both his hands so that Harold Russell, a genuine amputee, could portray him. Some of the film's best-known scenes are likewise not in the novel: Homer trying to get

ready for bed, Fred Derry (Dana Andrews) reliving wartime memories while sitting in the nose of an abandoned B-17, and Al Stephenson's (Fredric March) drunken speech at a banquet. Wyler and Sherwood also changed the outcome of the Derry and Stephenson stories. In the novel, Derry goes into partnership with the owner of a drugstore and Stephenson enters the nursery business after quitting his job at the bank. In the movie, Derry goes into the construction business and Stephenson stays at the bank to help veterans get loans. The film ends with Homer's marriage to his sweetheart, who continues to love him despite his handicap.

While much of the film's dialogue is Sherwood's, the script was worked out in careful consultation with Wyler. At one point, when Sherwood describes Derry's climb into the B-17, he merely writes "and here Mr. Wyler will have to invent something cinematic." *The Best Years of Our Lives* opened on 22 November 1946 in New York, where it became an immediate success. It swept the Academy Awards that year, winning Best Picture,

Harold Russell, Dana Andrews, and Fredric March in The Best Years of Our Lives. *Russell and March won Oscars for their performances in this film, voted best picture in 1946; Sherwood's screenplay also received an Academy Award.*

Best Screenplay, Best Director, Best Actor (March), and Best Supporting Actor (Russell).

Sherwood worked again for Goldwyn on *The Bishop's Wife* (1947). Based on Robert Nathan's novel, the film deals with an angel (Cary Grant) who comes to earth as an answer to the prayer of an Episcopal bishop (David Niven). The angel straightens out the difficulties in the bishop's marriage, transforms a wealthy woman into a generous benefactor so that a new cathedral can be built, brings romance back into the life of the bishop's wife (Loretta Young), and then returns to heaven. Sherwood wrote the screenplay with Leonardo Bercovici.

Sherwood's last screenplay was *Man on a Tightrope* (1953), in which he returned to concerns he had dealt with before: the need for human dignity and freedom. The plot centers on the escape of a Czechoslovakian circus from behind the Iron Curtain: by organizing the circus into a parade, the manager (Fredric March), troupe, and animals race across the guarded border. Sherwood's final film work was the screen story for *Main Street to Broadway* (1953), about an ambitious young playwright (Tom Morton) who tries to make the jump from the lower East Side to Broadway and in the process neglects his small-town girl friend (Mary Murphy), who becomes enamored of a hardware dealer.

In 1952 Sherwood signed a contract with NBC television, a relationship that lasted until February 1955. In the same month he finished what was to be his last play, *Small War on Murray Hill*, and in March was ready to begin on a film script of *War and Peace* for Mike Todd. But soon thereafter he became ill and underwent surgery in mid-August. While recuperating from the operation, he had a heart attack on 12 November and died on 14 November 1955.

References:

Andrew Anderegg, *William Wyler* (Boston: Twayne, 1979);

John Mason Brown, *The Worlds of Robert E. Sherwood Mirror to His Times 1896-1939* (New York: Harper & Row, 1962);

Robert Gessner, *The Moving Image: A Guide to Cinematic Literacy* (New York: Dutton, 1968);

E. R. Hagemann, "An Extraordinary Picture: The Film Criticism of Robert E. Sherwood," *Journal of Popular Film*, 1 (Spring 1972): 81-104;

Karol Kulik, *Alexander Korda: The Man Who Could Work Miracles* (New York: Arlington House, 1975);

Axel Madsen, *William Wyler* (New York: Crowell, 1973);

Seton Margrave, *Successful Film Writing* (New York: Methuen, 1936);

Alvin Marill, *Samuel Goldwyn Presents* (New York: A. S. Barnes, 1976);

Frances Marion, *How to Write and Sell Film Stories* (New York: Garland, 1937);

Walter J. Meserve, *Robert E. Sherwood, Reluctant Moralist* (New York: Pegasus, 1970);

R. Baird Shuman, *Robert E. Sherwood* (New York: Twayne, 1964);

Donald Spoto, *The Art of Alfred Hitchcock: Fifty Years of His Motion Pictures* (New York: Hophanson & Blake, 1976).

Stirling Silliphant

(16 January 1918-)

Randall Clark

MOTION PICTURES: *5 Against the House* (Columbia, 1955), screenplay by Silliphant, William Bowers, and John Barnwell;

Huk! (United Artists, 1956), screenplay;

Nightfall (Columbia, 1957), screenplay;

The Lineup (Columbia, 1958), screenplay;

Damn Citizen (Universal, 1958), screen story and screenplay;

Village of the Damned (M-G-M, 1960), screenplay by Silliphant, Wolf Rilla, and George Barclay;

The Slender Thread (Paramount, 1965), screenplay;

In the Heat of the Night (United Artists, 1967), screenplay;

Charly (Selmur, 1968), screenplay;

Marlowe (M-G-M, 1969), screenplay;

The Liberation of L. B. Jones (Columbia, 1970), screenplay by Silliphant and Jesse Hill Ford;

A Walk in the Spring Rain (Columbia, 1970), screenplay;

Murphy's War (Paramount, 1971), screenplay;

The New Centurions (Columbia, 1972), screenplay;

The Poseidon Adventure (20th Century-Fox, 1972), screenplay by Silliphant and Wendell Mayes;

Shaft in Africa (M-G-M, 1973), screenplay;

The Towering Inferno (20th Century-Fox/Warner Bros., 1974), screenplay;

The Killer Elite (United Artists, 1975), screenplay;

The Enforcer (Warner Bros., 1976), screenplay by Silliphant and Dean Reisner;

Telefon (United Artists/M-G-M, 1977), screenplay by Silliphant and Peter Hyams;

The Swarm (Warner Bros., 1978), screenplay;

Circle of Iron (Avco Embassy, 1979), screenplay by Silliphant and Stanley Mann;

When Time Ran Out (Warner Bros., 1980), screenplay by Silliphant and Carl Foreman.

SELECTED TELEVISION: *The Mickey Mouse Club* (ABC, 1955-1959), writer;

The Naked City (ABC, 1958-1963), creator and contributor of scripts;

Route 66 (CBS, 1960-1964), creator and contributor of scripts;

Longstreet (ABC, 1971-1972), creator and contributor of scripts;

Pearl [mini-series] (ABC, 1978), script;

Golden Gate [pilot] (1981), script;

Fly Away Home [pilot] (1981), script;

Travis McGee [pilot] (1983), script.

SELECTED BOOKS: *Maracaibo* (New York: Farrar, Straus, 1955);

Steel Tiger (New York: Ballantine, 1983).

OTHER: Neil D. Isaacs, *Fiction into Film* (Knoxville: University of Tennessee Press, 1970)— includes Silliphant's screenplay for *A Walk in the Spring Rain*.

Stirling Silliphant is representative of the large group of Hollywood screenwriters respected more for their ability to produce marketable scripts than for artistic achievement. He has had steady and lucrative employment in films and television since the 1950s. Most of his work has been on action or suspense films more intended to please audiences than critics, but he has also received acclaim and awards for his scripts for *In the Heat of the Night* (1967) and *Charly* (1968). Silliphant has been called "the ultimate screenwriting professional."

Stirling Dale Silliphant was born in Detroit, Michigan, to Leigh Lemuel and Ethel May Noaker Silliphant. He has been married three times and has two children. Silliphant attended the University of Southern California, graduating magna cum laude in 1938. At school he became interested in writing and began entering his short stories and essays in college competitions. Upon graduating, he worked briefly as a reporter for the *Glendale News-Press* before taking a job as publicist with Walt Disney Studios. In 1942 he left Disney for a position in the 20th Century-Fox East Coast publicity department but left the same year to enter the navy. He returned to the studio as publicity director in 1946 and remained until 1953.

In 1953 Silliphant produced a low-budget film, *The Joe Louis Story*. Although he received no credit as screenwriter, Silliphant says he did "considerable rewriting" on the script. Two years later he broke into television writing, working on Walt Disney's *The Mickey Mouse Club*. He also published a novel, *Maracaibo* (1955); the novel was filmed in

Silliphant (right) and director Norman Jewison review Silliphant's script for In the Heat of the Night *(photo by Marv Newton).*

1958, but Silliphant did not write the screenplay.

Between 1955 and 1958 five films were produced from Silliphant's scripts. All the films were in the crime-suspense genre, and although he was working on B movies, Silliphant was teamed with now highly regarded directors Don Siegel, Jacques Tourneur, and Phil Karlson. Silliphant also co-produced the first of these films, *5 Against the House* (1955), about an attempt to rob a casino. Little more than a standard "caper" movie, it marked the first time Silliphant used a situation he was to return to often (and in films as different as *The Slender Thread*, 1965, and *The Poseidon Adventure*, 1972): a mixed group of people working toward a goal.

Silliphant's next film, *Huk!* (1956), is a simple story of a young man (George Montgomery) out to avenge his father's murder. *Nightfall* (1957) is more intriguing. Based on David Goodis's novel *The Dark Chase*, the film is about a man (Aldo Ray) who is wanted by the police for a crime he did not commit and is pursued by the real criminals, who think he has their loot. On the run, he meets and falls in love with a model (Anne Bancroft) who agrees to help him, and they team with an insurance investigator who is also looking for the money. In *Nightfall*, Silliphant combined standard B-movie scenes with

his own unusual touches, such as a scene in which the villain is killed by falling under a snowplow. The film is considered one of the last genuine films noirs.

Silliphant's next film, *The Lineup* (1958), taken from a television series and directed by Siegel, pits two policemen against a pair of heroin smugglers. Silliphant's script largely ignores the police (the main characters from the series) and instead focuses on the criminals, Dancer and Julian, who are clearly psychopaths. *The Lineup* has received attention for its depiction of the villain as outcast and its use of symbolism and pop psychology. It developed a sizable cult following. Silliphant followed *The Lineup* with *Damn Citizen* (1958), about one man (Keith Andes) who attempts to clean up a corrupt police force.

In the late 1950s, television was a writer's market. There was a great demand for scripts, but more important to many writers was the artistic freedom they were allowed. Silliphant had been working in television since 1955 but now put most of his efforts into his television work, creating two series, *The Naked City* (1958-1963) and *Route 66* (1960-1964). The series were noted for their location shooting (something fairly new to television), their realism, and their well-developed characters. Silliphant received praise for creating programs that were entertaining but not mindless, and most episodes offered the viewers a distinct moral. Silliphant learned to write quickly for television. In four years he wrote seventy-one scripts for *Route 66* while still working on other projects.

During this period, Silliphant did almost no writing for motion pictures, and over seven years only one film was produced from one of his scripts. *Village of the Damned* (1960), based on John Wyndham's novel *The Midwich Cuckoos*, is a science-fiction thriller about children with strange powers. Silliphant shared screenplay credit with the film's director, Wolf Rilla, and producer, Ronald Kinnoch (who used the pseudonym George Barclay), because Rilla and Kinnoch felt that Silliphant's screenplay showed a lack of knowledge of the film's English setting and rewrote the script. The film was intelligently made and successful enough to inspire a sequel (which Silliphant did not work on). It is considered a classic science-fiction movie.

In 1965, with both his series off the air, Silliphant returned to film and wrote the screenplay for *The Slender Thread*, about a woman (Anne Bancroft) who takes an overdose of sleeping pills and then telephones a suicide-prevention clinic, where a volunteer (Sidney Poitier) tries to locate and help her. The movie is a work of suspense—all the action is supposed to occur in under one hour—but because the woman is white and the volunteer is black it is also a subtle statement about race relations.

Silliphant's next film also dealt with racial matters, and it also used a suspense framework. This time the social commentary was less subtle. *In the Heat of the Night* (1967), based upon John Ball's novel, deals with a stranger, black and from the North, who is picked up as a suspicious person after a murder has occurred in a small Southern town. The black man, Virgil Tibbs (Sidney Poitier), turns out to be a police detective, better trained and more intelligent than the town's sheriff (Rod Steiger). The sheriff forces Tibbs to stay in town and help with the investigation. Tibbs insists on being treated

Sidney Poitier and Lee Grant in In the Heat of the Night. *Silliphant won an Academy Award, a Golden Globe Award, and the Mystery Writers of America Edgar Award for his screenplay.*

as an equal by the sheriff, and he is intelligent, aggressive, and offensive to the townspeople. The two men begin to understand each other and to cooperate. *In the Heat of the Night* was a huge success: it won Academy Awards for Best Picture, Best Actor (Steiger), and Best Screenplay, and it inspired two more Virgil Tibbs films. In addition to his Oscar, Silliphant won a Golden Globe Award and the Mystery Writers of America's Edgar for his screenplay.

Following *In the Heat of the Night*, Silliphant went to work on an adaptation of Daniel Keyes's short story "Flowers for Algernon." (Silliphant had adapted the story for television in the early 1960s.) Released as *Charly* in 1968, the film tells the story of a retarded man (Cliff Robertson) who undergoes a series of experimental operations on his brain. As a result, his intelligence begins to grow, and he becomes a genius. Still emotionally immature, he cannot accept the changes in his life. He begins an unhappy relationship with one of his therapists (Claire Bloom), but the romance ends when he begins reverting to his earlier mental state. *Charly* was a commercial success, winning Robertson an Oscar and Silliphant another Golden Globe Award. Silliphant's standing in Hollywood was improved accordingly; the next year three films were produced from his screenplays.

The first of these was *Marlowe*, taken from Raymond Chandler's novel *The Little Sister*. A Chandler fan, Silliphant worked hard to ensure that the film would remain true to Chandler's novel. He was working on the first film adapted from a Chandler novel since the 1940s and was faced with the potential problem of making Chandler's work seem contemporary. Yet Silliphant thought "Marlowe seemed . . . to work even better today—his shabby knight with all kinds of chinks in his worn armor—seemed even more vulnerable—more noble, somehow, in today's society than in the forties." In spite of his efforts, Silliphant was not pleased with the film that resulted. He felt it was too light in tone, that director Paul Bogart had removed the irony and violence from his screenplay to the point that "we could have held the premiere on NBC Sunday night at 7 O'clock and never have to cut a frame or bloop a sound." Silliphant also wrote an adaptation of Chandler's novel *The Long Goodbye*, but it was not used when the novel was filmed.

The Liberation of L. B. Jones (1970), Silliphant's third film dealing with racial matters, is his favorite of the three. (He has said he despises *In the Heat of the Night*.) Based on a novel by Jesse Hill Ford, who cowrote the screenplay, the film, like earlier Sil-

Cliff Robertson earned the 1968 Oscar as best actor for his portrayal of the title character in Charly.

liphant efforts, is a suspense story with a moral. A black ex-convict (Yaphet Kotto) returns to his hometown seeking revenge on the white cop (Arch Johnson) who sent him to prison. The film has many subplots—a newlywed couple (Lee Majors and Barbara Hershey) returning to the husband's hometown and clashing with his racist mentor (Lee J. Cobb), and a bigoted white cop (Anthony Zerbe) and his black lover (Lola Falana)—and a good deal of violence (the cop castrates and murders his lover's husband, then dies himself in a baling machine). The film was criticized for being melodramatic and needlessly violent, but Silliphant defends it: "*Liberation* continues to be—to me—and possibly in the whole cinematic world alone to me—one of the best films ever made about race relations in this country. It was the film which made everybody feel uncomfortable. It let nobody off the hook. And to this minute, I stand on what the film says. You do not solve racial tension in any other way, in my mind, than by mutual absorption of the hostile races, each of the other, one of each other, and in time, the truth will prevail—and what is the truth? Whatever happens. But in the process of absorption, of conquest, of crushing and being crushed, there are hideous moments and there are moments of humanity. Races do not settle their differences by smiling at each other. *Liberation* said this. It said this harshly and dramatically and nobody wanted to hear *that* kind of message." Whatever the reason, *The Liberation of L. B. Jones* was not a financial success.

When he began work on *A Walk in the Spring Rain* (1970), Silliphant decided to act as producer as well as writer, something he had not done since *5 Against the House* in 1955. Adapted from Rachel Maddux's novel, the film is a love story about a college professor's wife (Ingrid Bergman) and a Tennessee mountain man (Anthony Quinn). It was not a success, nor was *Murphy's War* (1971), about a British soldier (Peter O'Toole) in World War II.

As the 1970s began, Silliphant was enjoying great success. He owned his own production company and made $500,000 a year (claiming his salary was kept this low for tax purposes). He created another television series, *Longstreet*, which ran for two years, and produced a successful film, *Shaft* (1971), which earned him the NAACP "Image" Award.

Adapting Joseph Wambaugh's *The New Centurions* gave Silliphant the chance to write an action film that was really about people and how they get along in difficult situations. *The New Centurions* deals with how very different people function under pressure as policemen and how their personal lives are affected by their jobs. Silliphant replaced Robert Towne as screenwriter, and, after Towne removed his name from the film, Silliphant received sole credit.

In 1972 Silliphant and Wendell Mayes wrote *The Poseidon Adventure*, the first of a series of disaster films that were popular in the 1970s. The film was a huge money-maker, and two years later Silliphant wrote *The Towering Inferno* for the same producer, Irwin Allen. (In between, he had produced the second Shaft film, *Shaft's Big Score*, in 1972 and written the third, *Shaft in Africa*, in 1973.) Two studios had optioned separate books, *The Tower* and *The Glass Inferno*, with almost identical plots. When the studios decided to coproduce one film, Silliphant was asked to combine the two novels into a single screenplay. *The Towering Inferno* was another success and was nominated for an Academy Award for Best Picture. That year Silliphant received the Box Office Writer of the Year Award from the National Association of Theatre Owners.

Following *The Towering Inferno*, Silliphant worked on three action films, each a major Christmas release of its year. *The Killer Elite* (1975), di-

rected by Sam Peckinpah, is about a mercenary (James Caan) pursuing his double-crossing partner (Robert Duvall). *The Enforcer* (1976) was the third Clint Eastwood Dirty Harry movie. Silliphant reteamed with director Don Siegel for *Telefon* (1977), a film about Soviet saboteurs in the United States.

In 1978 Silliphant went back to work for Irwin Allen, writing *The Swarm*, about a Texas town attacked by killer bees. This disaster film was a failure. Allen and Silliphant worked on one more project, *When Time Ran Out* (1980), about a group of people fleeing a volcano. It was also a failure and was the last of the big "disaster" movies.

His work on such big-budget commercial films hurt Silliphant's critical reputation. As he told *Emmy* magazine, "Whenever I speak before college communication groups students ask 'Whatever happened to the Stirling Silliphant who was? How come you took that movie, that pilot?' I try to explain the business of movies and television. In any year, you have a standard of living planned for your family . . . you need to feed your family and keep your name before the industry. Suddenly someone calls: 'Hey, we've got a project.' It turns out to be a film with a box office star, but not much else. You write it: the grosses are good. Now they start coming to you for more of the same. Somewhere along the line you just have to be a canny businessman until you're financially secure enough to break away and do better work."

In 1979 Silliphant was able to "break away" and work on what is his most personal project to date, *Circle of Iron*, a film about a young man's rites of trial as he searches for a secret book of knowledge. This project gave Silliphant the opportunity to use his longtime interest in martial arts and Eastern philosophy. Silliphant had developed the idea with martial arts expert Bruce Lee and actor James Coburn as a project for the three of them. Lee's death in 1973 suspended work on the film. It was finally produced in 1979 as a low-budget effort, the first Silliphant film since *Charly* that was not produced by a major studio.

After the failure of *When Time Ran Out*, Silliphant went back to television. He wrote a miniseries about Pearl Harbor, *Pearl* (1978), and created pilots for two television series: *Golden Gate* (1981), about a newspaper publishing dynasty, and *Fly Away Home* (1981), an elaborate war drama. Neither series sold. His pilot for a *Travis McGee* series was aired in 1983, and that year he signed to adapt James Michener's best-seller *Space* into a miniseries.

Reference:
Kenneth von Gunden and Stuart H. Stock, *Twenty*

All-Time Great Science Fiction Films (New York: Arlington House, 1982), pp. 150-158.

Stewart Stern
(22 March 1922-   )

Edwin T. Kephart
New York University

MOTION PICTURES: *Teresa* (M-G-M, 1951), screen story and screenplay by Stern and Alfred Hayes;
Benjy (Paramount, 1951), screenplay;
Rebel Without a Cause (Warner Bros., 1955), screenplay;
The Rack (M-G-M, 1956), screenplay;
The James Dean Story (Warner Bros., 1957), screen story and screenplay;

Thunder in the Sun (Paramount, 1959), adaptation;
The Outsider (Universal, 1961), screenplay;
The Ugly American (Universal, 1963), screenplay;
Rachel, Rachel (Warner Bros.-Seven Arts, 1968), screenplay;
The Last Movie (Alta-Light Productions/Universal, 1971), story by Stern and Dennis Hopper; screenplay;
Summer Wishes, Winter Dreams (Rastar Pictures/

Stewart Stern (photo © V. Tony Hauser)

Columbia, 1973), story and screenplay.

SELECTED TELEVISION:
Thunder Silence, *Philco-Goodyear Television Playhouse*
    (NBC, 1954), script;
Sybil (NBC, 1976), script;
A Christmas to Remember (CBS, 1978), script.

Stewart Stern's screen adaptations and original screenplays focus on ordinary people whose actions and decisions have an emotional price. Stern deals most profoundly with shy, sensitive, tormented characters who are either deprived of love or unable to love. Self-expression for these protagonists is difficult, but it is necessary for their psychic survival, confronted as they often are by guilt or death.

The nephew of Adolph Zukor and a cousin to the Loew family, Stewart Stern seemed destined to play a part in the film world. His father was a doctor and artist in New York, where Stern was born. Stern grew up in New York and was enrolled in the Ethical Cultural schools until 1940. After attending the University of Iowa, Stern entered the military; his World War II experiences form the background for several of his film scripts, from his earliest, *Teresa* (1951), to *Summer Wishes, Winter Dreams* (1973). Stern briefly worked as an actor in New York and then as assistant stage manager for the Broadway production of *The French Touch* (1945-1946). In California with Arthur Loew, Jr., Stern became involved in the motion-picture business and worked for two years (1946-1948) as a dialogue director for Eagle Lion Studios.

Stern's early associations as a screenwriter were with such directors as Nicholas Ray and Fred Zinnemann, whose films examined the establishment of individual moral codes, often in opposition to the dictates of society or of family. These directors were perhaps partially responsible for the moral tone, the compassion, and the poignancy that are characteristic of Stern's work.

In 1948 Stern visited Fred Zinnemann to compliment him on his film *The Search*. At the time, Zinnemann was looking for a screenwriter for his next project. Arthur Loew, Jr., had just shown

James Dean in a scene from Rebel Without a Cause

Zinnemann three of Stern's unpublished short stories, and Zinnemann hired Stern to work on "Sabra," a film project for Montgomery Clift. Stern went to Israel to research the project.

"Sabra" never went beyond a treatment, but Zinnemann did film *Teresa* from a script Stern had written in 1949 about a confused American soldier (John Ericson) who falls in love with a young Italian woman (Pier Angeli) during World War II, marries her, and returns home by himself. Teresa follows later, confronting prejudice in New York while living in an East Side tenement with her husband's mother. Stern's interest in psychiatry and psychoanalysis, incorporated in many of his screenplays, is first evident in *Teresa*. The story is narrated by the husband to the psychiatrist (Rod Steiger) who eventually manages to help the young husband gain control over his life. Although at times sentimental, the film is also uncompromisingly realistic, and Stern and collaborator Alfred Hayes were nominated for Academy awards for their screen story. In 1951 *Benjy*, a thirty-minute documentary based on an original screenplay by Stern, won an Oscar for producer-director Fred Zinnemann.

In the 1950s Stern wrote four plays for television, a medium to which he would not return until 1976, when he wrote the four-hour television movie *Sybil*. His earlier teleplays included *Crip*, *And Crown Thy Good*, *Heart of Darkness*, and *Thunder Silence*. Stern wrote *Thunder Silence* in 1954 for his friend from New York, fledgling actor Paul Newman.

Stern's friendship with James Dean and composer Leonard Rosenman gave him the opportunity to succeed Leon Uris and Irving Shulman as screenwriter on *Rebel Without a Cause* (1955). The film was directed by Nicholas Ray, who also wrote the screen story from Robert M. Lindner's book about a young delinquent under hypnotherapy. The film covers a day and two nights in the lives of three troubled teenagers (James Dean, Natalie Wood, Sal Mineo) who, confronted by their need for love and companionship, experience conflict with their parents. They set out to prove themselves in tests of courage and endurance, get into trouble with the police, and witness the deaths of their friends in gang fights. Psychiatry becomes an important revelatory device when the chief psychiatrist at juvenile hall listens to Judy (Wood) tell what it is like to be a teenager. At the end of the film the young people and their parents begin to reach a new understanding. *Rebel Without a Cause* has often been cited as the quintessential film about the 1950s.

Stern's next film was *The Rack* (1956), for producer Arthur Loew, Jr. Adapted from a Rod Serling teleplay, the film is about Capt. Ed Hall (Paul Newman), a Korean War veteran who is indicted for collaborating with the enemy. As the film progresses, it is disclosed that Captain Hall is a victim of psychological torture by the North Koreans. Probing reveals that Hall, like the veteran in *Teresa* and the teenagers in *Rebel Without a Cause*, has experienced a loveless childhood and now carries a sense of guilt because of his recent behavior.

After James Dean's death in 1955, Stern wrote the script for the documentary *The James Dean Story* (1957), Robert Altman's first film, which he codirected with George W. George. Stern's next credits were for the adaptation for *Thunder in the Sun* (1959), about a group of French Basque immigrants heading west by wagon train, and the screenplay for *The Outsider* (1961), about American Indian Ira Hayes (Tony Curtis) who was one of the marines who raised the flag at Iwo Jima. In the early 1960s Stern went to Southeast Asia to work for producer-director George Englund on the script of *The Ugly American* (1963), based on the Eugene Burdick-William J. Lederer novel about an American ambassador (played by Marlon Brando in the film) who becomes embroiled in political and personal disaster in an Asian country.

Stern and Joanne Woodward read Margaret Laurence's novel *A Jest of God* (1966) while it was still in galleys. They agreed to produce it as a film with Paul Newman as director, Joanne Woodward in the lead, and Stern a full partner in the venture, writing the script and participating in all phases of production. The resulting film, *Rachel, Rachel* (1968), is the story of a thirty-five-year-old spinster schoolteacher who finally accepts her sexuality and achieves a measure of independence. Inspired in conception and sensitive in execution, *Rachel, Rachel* was a commercial success that earned Academy award nominations for best actress, best director, and best screenplay.

Rachel, Rachel examines an opposition that occurs in many Stern scripts—the confrontation between a naive, small-town mentality and a slick, urban one that subscribes to a more cynical (and often more corrupt) philosophy. In Stern's work this type of opposition is often transposed onto geopolitical conflicts (*The Ugly American* and later *The Last Movie*), generational conflicts, as in *Rebel Without a Cause*, or questions of sexual identity and attitudes, as in *Rachel, Rachel* and the later *Summer Wishes, Winter Dreams*. *Rachel, Rachel* was also the first of several films Stern wrote that use such narrative devices as flashbacks, flashforwards, fan-

James Olson and Joanne Woodward in Rachel, Rachel

tasies, memories, and dreams to convey psychological profiles of characters and events.

After the success of his film *Easy Rider* (1969), Dennis Hopper approached Stern with an idea for a film. He wanted to examine what might happen to a remote South American village after an American movie company, involved in making a gory Western, moved out. Stern shaped the material into a screenplay, and the crew set off for Peru to make *The Last Movie* (1971). Unfortunately, director Hopper failed in his attempt to recapture the alienation of *Easy Rider*, and the film became the greatest disappointment in Stern's career. Elements in *The Last Movie* convey some familiar Stern themes. For example, the film's focus on the effects of an urbanized culture on a remote insular one is a varia-

tion on the opposition that informs *Rachel, Rachel* and other Stern scripts.

Stern and Joanne Woodward again worked together on Stern's original screenplay "Death of a Snow Queen," which was filmed as *Summer Wishes, Winter Dreams* (1973). In this story, middle-aged, frigid, and peevish Rita has all the comforts she could want but is unable to give or receive love. Her mother's death and her daughter's rejection force Rita to come to terms with adulthood and to deal with the failure of her marriage. On a second honeymoon in Europe, her husband (Martin Balsam) relives his war experiences (based on Stern's own), and the couple grow closer, beginning to understand one another for the first time in twenty-five years. Although *Summer Wishes, Winter Dreams* failed

Joanne Woodward and Martin Balsam in Summer
Wishes, Winter Dreams

at the box office, it received acclaim from the critics.
Stern has received no screen credit since 1973.

In 1976 he adapted Flora Rheta Schreiber's book *Sybil* for television. The film depicts a young woman (Sally Field) who seeks psychiatric help to overcome a multipersonality disorder; Joanne Woodward plays Dr. Cornelia Wilbur, whose experiences formed the basis of the book. Stern's teleplay is constructed around conversations with a psychiatrist in which Sybil confronts the actions and memories of her several personalities in order to restructure an integrated life. *Sybil* won an Emmy for Best Dramatic Special, and Stern won an Emmy for Best Dramatic Writing. Field won for Best Actress, and Woodward was nominated in the same category. In 1978 Stern adapted for television Glendon Swarthout's novel *The Melodeon*, about a farm couple whose grandson comes to spend his Christmas holidays with them.

Evident in much of Stern's work is the struggle to communicate, the struggle to know oneself and to know others. Perhaps the words of the evangelist in *Rachel, Rachel* best sum up Stern's view of the nature of human relationships and communication: "Walls and words . . . walls and words! The animals are less alone in their roaring than we are with all our words. . . . We're cut off from each other and from God. . . . Isn't . . . our final obligation to be ourselves?"

Reference:
"Dialogue on Film: Stewart Stern," *American Film* (October 1983): 20-22.

Papers:
Stewart Stern's papers and research materials are at the University of Southern California, Los Angeles.

Donald Ogden Stewart

(30 November 1894-2 August 1980)

Duane Byrge

See also the Stewart entries in *DLB 4, American Writers in Paris, 1920-1929*, and *DLB 11, American Humorists, 1800-1950*.

SELECTED MOTION PICTURES: *Brown of Harvard* (M-G-M, 1926), adaptation;
Laughter (Paramount, 1930), dialogue;
Tarnished Lady (Paramount, 1931), screenplay and screen adaptation by Stewart from his story "New York Lady";
Smilin' Through (M-G-M, 1932), dialogue by Stewart and James Bernard Fagan; filmed again (M-G-M, 1941), screenplay by Stewart and John Balderston;
The White Sister (M-G-M, 1933), screenplay;
Another Language (M-G-M, 1933), screenplay by Stewart and Herman J. Mankiewicz;
Going Hollywood (M-G-M, 1933), screenplay;
Dinner at Eight (M-G-M, 1933), additional dialogue;
The Barretts of Wimpole Street (M-G-M, 1934), screenplay by Stewart, Ernest Vajda, and Claudine West;
No More Ladies (M-G-M, 1935), screenplay by Stewart and Horace Jackson;
The Prisoner of Zenda (United Artists, 1937), screenplay by Stewart, Balderston, and Wallis Root;
Holiday (Columbia, 1938), screenplay by Stewart and Sidney Buchman;
Marie Antoinette (M-G-M, 1938), screenplay by Stewart, Vajda, and West;
Love Affair (RKO-Radio, 1939), screenplay by Stewart and Delmer Daves;
Night of Nights (Paramount, 1939), screen story and screenplay;
The Philadelphia Story (M-G-M, 1940), screenplay;
Kitty Foyle (RKO-Radio, 1940), adaptation;
That Uncertain Feeling (United Artists, 1941), screen story and screenplay;
A Woman's Face (M-G-M, 1941), screenplay by Stewart and Elliott Paul;
Tales of Manhattan (20th Century-Fox, 1942), screenplay by Stewart and others;
Keeper of the Flame (M-G-M, 1942), screenplay;
Forever and a Day (RKO, 1944), screenplay by Stewart and others;

Donald Ogden Stewart (Culver Pictures)

Without Love (M-G-M, 1945), screenplay;
Life with Father (Warner Bros., 1947), screenplay;
Cass Timberlane (M-G-M, 1947), screenplay; adaptation by Stewart and Sonya Levien;
Edward My Son (M-G-M, 1949), screenplay;
Europa 51, released in the United States as *The Greatest Love* (I. F. E., 1954), English dialogue;
Escapade (Eros, 1955), screenplay as Gilbert Holland.

PLAYS: *Los Angeles* (New York, Hudson Theatre, 19 February 1927);
Rebound (New York, Plymouth Theatre, 3 March 1930);
Fine and Dandy (New York, Erlanger Theatre, 23 September 1930);
How I Wonder (New York, Hudson Theatre, 30 September 1947);

The Kidders (London, Arts Theatre, 12 November 1957);

Honour Bright (Hammersmith, U.K., Lyric Theatre, 17 June 1958).

BOOKS: *A Parody Outline of History* (New York: Doran, 1921);

Perfect Behavior (New York: Doran, 1922);

Aunt Polly's Story of Mankind (New York: Doran, 1923; London: Brentano, 1927);

Mr. and Mrs. Haddock Abroad (New York: Doran, 1924);

The Crazy Fool (New York: Boni, 1925);

Mr. and Mrs. Haddock in Paris, France (New York & London: Harper, 1926);

Father William: A Comedy of Father and Son (New York & London: Harper, 1929);

Rebound (New York, Los Angeles & London: French, 1931);

By a Stroke of Luck! An Autobiography (London: Paddington Press; New York: Paddington Press/ Two Continents, 1975).

Donald Ogden Stewart was born in Columbus, Ohio. The son of Gilbert Holland Stewart, a judge, and Clara Ogden Stewart, he attended Phillips Exeter Academy and Yale University. While at Yale, he served as assignment editor on the *News* and was elected to the Skull and Bones secret society. Stewart graduated from Yale in 1916, assuming that he would be a banker or businessman like most of his classmates. After graduation, he served in the U.S. Navy and then began a short career with AT&T.

Stewart's work with AT&T, in the capacity of clerk, moved him to Minneapolis in 1919. Living in Saint Paul, Stewart became friends with an as-yet-unpublished writer, F. Scott Fitzgerald. Disillusioned with his "safe" job, Stewart quit AT&T in 1920 and moved to New York City, where Fitzgerald was able to recommend him to Edmund Wilson, who worked for *Vanity Fair*. Seeking a job in the advertising department, Stewart wrote a short parody as a sample of his creative ability. Wilson saw it and asked him to write a parody of James Branch Cabell's *Jurgen*, with the promise of publication if it were good enough. It was, and Stewart became a regular contributor to *Vanity Fair*.

During the 1920s Stewart wrote a series of satiric books: *A Parody Outline of History* (1921), *Perfect Behavior* (1922), *Aunt Polly's Story of Mankind* (1923), *Mr. and Mrs. Haddock Abroad* (1924), *The Crazy Fool* (1925), *Mr. and Mrs. Haddock in Paris, France* (1926), and *Father William: A Comedy of Father*

and Son (1929). Stewart divided his time between New York and Europe. He became friends with Ernest Hemingway in Paris and traveled with him to Pamplona in 1924.

Returning to New York in 1924, Stewart began a lecture tour with a series of lectures titled "Life, Liberty, and the Pursuit of Happiness." This tour eventually brought him to Hollywood in 1925, where he spoke to various women's clubs in and around Los Angeles. Stewart became friends with Jack Pickford, Lew Cody, John Gilbert, whom he met through his lectures, as well as Charlie Chaplin and King Vidor. While in Los Angeles, Stewart worked on the novel *The Crazy Fool*, the story of a young man who inherits a mental institution, which Stewart admittedly wrote with one eye toward a sale to the movies. *The Crazy Fool* achieved best-seller status, and while in Paris Stewart received word that M-G-M had purchased the novel and asked him to come to Hollywood to write the screenplay. Upon arrival in Hollywood, he found that his friend King Vidor had mistakenly sold M-G-M a different book, *Perfect Behavior*. Vidor had told Irving Thalberg the story of *Perfect Behavior*, and Thalberg bought the novel, thinking it was *The Crazy Fool*. Stewart was to find such a mistake typical of the workings of Hollywood and accepted with amusement their first offer to work on a screenplay. It was decided he would be a natural for the project *Brown of Harvard* (1926); Stewart regarded this curiously since he was a Yale graduate. He completed the project, his first and only silent film, and then asked for and was granted a leave of absence by M-G-M.

Stewart returned to Paris, where he finished *Mr. and Mrs. Haddock in Paris, France*. Upon its completion, Stewart signed to write a weekly humor series for the *Chicago Tribune* syndicate. He married Beatrice Ames in 1926; in 1927 they moved to New York where Stewart wrote short pieces for the *New Yorker* and worked on *Father William*. In addition to his literary endeavors, Stewart became an actor. His friend Philip Barry had written the play *Holiday* and had fashioned the role of Nick Potter after Stewart. Deferential about his acting talents, Stewart nonetheless confessed to learning a great deal about dialogue by his participation in *Holiday*, distinguishing between dialogue that works when spoken and dialogue that merely impresses on the written page.

In addition to appearing in *Holiday*, Stewart began writing his own play *Rebound*, which opened in 1930 with Stewart acting in the production. At this time, he was approached by Walter Wanger of Paramount (whose Eastern studios were then on

Stewart with Marion Davies on the set of Not So Dumb. *Stewart made his only screen appearance in this 1930 film.*

Long Island). Wanger wanted him to work with his company on *Laughter*, a romantic comedy in which a former Follies beauty marries an elderly banker. *Laughter* was released in 1930 and is regarded as one of the most sophisticated sound comedies of the time; it was one of the very first sound comedies written specifically for the screen and not the stage. Stewart's facility for writing dialogue for *Laughter* was a talent he had nurtured with his acting in *Holiday* and *Rebound*. He had a ready feel for dialogue, and *Laughter* was a foreshadowing of the screwball comedies that flourished in the latter half of the 1930s.

Stewart's third film, *Tarnished Lady* (1931), was the first of his only two original screenplays. (The other was *Night of Nights*, written in 1939.) Written for Tallulah Bankhead, the film is significant only for the fact that it was George Cukor's first solo effort as a director. The combination of Stewart and Cukor was a happy professional relationship. Cukor was later to direct other Stewart scripts, and Stewart always enjoyed working with Cukor, appreciating the fact that Cukor allowed him on the set to work with the actors.

At this juncture in his career, Stewart obtained an agent, Leland Hayward, who promptly got Stewart a writing assignment for Irving Thalberg at M-G-M. M-G-M was having difficulty with the script for *Smilin' Through* (1932); it needed lively, literate dialogue. This Stewart supplied, later noting that he felt his contribution was a significant one. Thalberg was so pleased with Stewart's dialogue that he gave him a screen credit.

Stewart continued to work for M-G-M, developing a harmonious relationship with Irving Thalberg. Stewart admits to learning a great deal from Thalberg not only about screenwriting but about playwriting as well. He had great admiration for Thalberg's sense of story structure and later likened him to a computer in his rapid sense of structure. Stewart came to take great pride in screenwriting, considering it a craft worthy of respect.

His next job was for Hunt Stromberg, who brought him in to adapt *The White Sister* from the novel by Francis Marion Crawford. *The White Sister*

(1933) is the story of a girl who mistakenly believes her lover is killed in war; she enters a nunnery only to have him return. This production starred Helen Hayes and Clark Gable, and the script was met with trepidation by Gable, who was uneasy about some of the humor Stewart had injected. In addition, Stewart experienced disagreement with Stromberg, who wanted Stewart to write down to his audience. Accordingly, Charles MacArthur was brought in on the project under the auspices of his wife, Helen Hayes, to tone down Stewart's script.

As Stewart continued writing screenplays, he learned that "you should never be the man to write the first draft." Writers were not above changing perfectly good scripts to earn screen credit. Stewart credits Leland Hayward with being sagacious enough to get him involved as the last writer on several scripts, so that there would not be time to bring in another writer. One project for which Stewart was brought in near the end of the writing was *Red Dust* (1932). Hunt Stromberg needed help with the ending, and Stewart supplied the conclusion to this picture. Although he did not receive screen credit, Stewart said, "the general feeling was that I saved the picture." The following year Stewart received screen credit for *Another Language* (1933)—a drama of confrontation between a wife and her domineering mother-in-law—and worked on a musical for Walter Wanger entitled *Going Hollywood* (1933).

A project which greatly satisfied Stewart was *Dinner at Eight* (1933) for David O. Selznick. Selznick needed an ending for the Herman Mankiewicz-Frances Marion screenplay, and he called Stewart in to supply one. Stewart's ending delighted Selznick, and Stewart remarked that a nice epitaph for himself might read "He gave them a laugh at the end."

Not all of Stewart's contributions at M-G-M were as successful or as appreciated. A three-year collaboration with Ernest Vajda and Claudine West on *Marie Antoinette* (1938) resulted in a picture which contained only one line of Stewart dialogue. He had a far happier collaboration with these two writers on *The Barretts of Wimpole Street* (1934), the story of love's triumph over the intransigence of a Victorian father. Stewart's talents as an adaptor were further utilized by M-G-M the following year as he and Horace Jackson adapted *No More Ladies* (1935) from the marital comedy by A. E. Thomas, in which a wife cures her husband's preoccupation with other women by playing up to another man.

During the mid-1930s, Stewart became socially conscious. He joined the Hollywood Anti-Nazi

League and organized a meeting of the Hollywood Women's Club at which an actor read Irwin Shaw's antiwar play *Bury the Dead*. Stewart also found a forum in the *Screen Writer*, the magazine of the Writers Guild; he was featured in the premiere issue with a piece on the fear of censorship. Stewart also became the president of the League of American Writers; with his direction, the League sponsored the Second American Writers Conference in 1937.

While he was involved with these projects, Stewart's marriage of over a decade was coming to an end. Stewart met and fell in love with Ella Winter, the widow of Lincoln Steffens. Stewart's wife left him for another man, and the two were divorced. Stewart and Ella Winter were married in 1938; he brought his two sons to the marriage, and she brought one son.

David O. Selznick asked Stewart to supply additional dialogue to John Balderston's screenplay for *The Prisoner of Zenda*, and Stewart and Balderston received joint screen credit for the 1937 film. Stewart then went to work on the script for *Holiday*, the Philip Barry play in which he had once acted. *Holiday* had fallen out of favor in the early 1930s because audiences were not sympathetic to a man who made money in the stock market and then wanted to take it easy. Stewart is credited with infusing a liberal, down-to-earth tone into the play that made it consistent with the mood of the country. He changed the characters of the Potters from the wealthy sophisticates that they had been in the play to the amusing, genuine couple in the movie. Since Stewart had played the role of Nick Potter in the play, it was a part he was very close to, a part he could skillfully reshape.

Holiday won acclaim for all concerned, particularly its impressive cast (Katharine Hepburn, Cary Grant, Lew Ayres, Edward Everett Horton); it was truly an ensemble accomplishment. Stewart had always admired director George Cukor and got along well with coscreenwriter Sidney Buchman, who was also politically active and a strong anti-Nazi. Although they were given cocredit, Cukor maintains that Buchman received credit only because of studio politics. Stewart realized that a good adaptor was someone who knew what to leave in; it was not always necessary to change things, especially if they were good.

Stewart's next adaptation was for RKO-Radio. He and Delmer Daves were assigned to write the screenplay for *Love Affair* (1939), a shipboard romance based on a story by Mildred Kram and Leo McCarey, who directed the film. *Love Affair* ran into

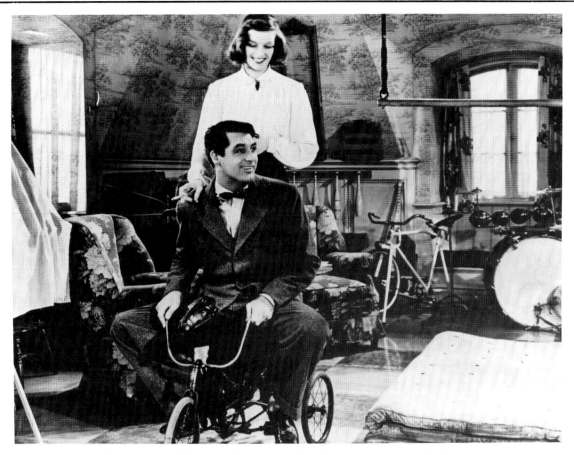

Cary Grant and Katharine Hepburn in the 1938 screen version of Holiday

censorship trouble when the Hays Office decided that the woman's (Irene Dunne) earlier love affair, though only alluded to in the dialogue, was immoral and she must be punished for it. Stewart used a suggestion from the Hays Office for her punishment that was so ludicrous he was amused rather than outraged: on her way to meet her lover, she was run over by a truck.

In 1939 Stewart completed the second work for which he wrote both story and screenplay, *Night of Nights*, about a down-and-out playwright who, upon finding his long-lost daughter, stages a career comeback. Lewis Milestone directed the picture. *Kitty Foyle* (1940), the next film Stewart worked on, was certainly more memorable. Dalton Trumbo reworked Stewart's initial script taken from a Christopher Morley novel about a salesgirl (Ginger Rogers, who won an Oscar) who becomes involved with a socialite. Trumbo received sole screenplay credit.

Stewart won an Academy award for *The Philadelphia Story* (1940), saying it was "the easiest award anybody got, because it was a hell of a play. I just got out of the way." Again, Stewart's sense of

dramaturgy and his respectful approach were the very ingredients the adaptation of Philip Barry's play required. In fact, a recording had been made of the original play in the theater with all the audience responses. Stewart followed this recording, making sure, as the studio insisted, that all the laughs stayed in. As he said, "I was really writing against a tape recorder."

Stewart's next project was *That Uncertain Feeling* (1941). The film, a light comedy set in high society in New York, is the story of a husband's (Melvyn Douglas) fight for his wife's (Merle Oberon) attention by trying to dissipate her infatuation for an eccentric concert pianist (Burgess Meredith). *That Uncertain Feeling* was directed by Ernst Lubitsch, who also directed the 1925 film *Kiss Me Again* on which Stewart based the script. Stewart added topical, light touches of satire, such as the undermining of pop psychology clichés. His next film was *A Woman's Face* (1941), about a woman whose life changes when she undergoes plastic surgery. The film starred Joan Crawford and was directed by George Cukor.

During the next two years, Stewart was twice employed as one of many collaborators on a film, a situation he always found frustrating. He was one of ten writers on *Tales of Manhattan* (1942), in which a dress coat passes through five different owners. Twenty-one writers, seven directors, and eighty star performers were required for *Forever and a Day* (1944), which depicted the inhabitants of a house over a period of years.

Despite his success in Hollywood, Stewart decided to return to playwriting. He purchased a farm in the East and settled there with his wife. Stewart began work on the book for a musical based on Ludwig Bemelmans's Hotel Splendide short stories. However, this project was quickly interrupted when he received an offer to return to Hollywood to adapt the I. A. R. Wylie novel *Keeper of the Flame* (1942). He readily accepted this assignment; he admired the strong anti-Fascist stance of the book and believed it was a project of strong social consequence. Yet Stewart experienced problems in writing the film. The two stars, Spencer Tracy and Katharine Hepburn, believed he was interjecting

needless political sentiments into the script and complained to M-G-M. M-G-M intervened, and Stewart was forced to temper his writing. In spite of this, Stewart has said, "The one film I am the proudest of is *Keeper of the Flame*."

Stewart returned to his farm and began work on the play "Emily Brady" which was optioned by Billy Rose but never produced. Stewart then returned to screenwriting, adapting Philip Barry's play *Without Love* (1945) for Tracy and Hepburn. Then, at the suggestion of his friend Clarence Day, he was chosen to adapt for the screen the Howard Lindsay-Russell Crouse play *Life with Father* (1947).

Stewart's next job was to adapt *Cass Timberlane* (1947) from Sinclair Lewis's novel. The script was a classic melodrama—the story of a marriage between people of two different classes: a Brahmin judge (Spencer Tracy) and a young woman (Lana Turner) of unsuitable social standing. It was with the role of the young woman that Stewart ran into his greatest difficulty. Lana Turner constantly objected to the writing, and Stewart was forced to make many changes for her benefit. In retrospect,

John Howard, Cary Grant, Katharine Hepburn, and James Stewart in The Philadelphia Story. *Donald Ogden Stewart's screenplay for this 1940 film won an Academy Award.*

however, he considered it to be one of his finest pictures.

Stewart continued to work on plays, his outlet for serious writing. He penned a comic fantasy, *How I Wonder*, the story of the dilemma of the scientist in the Atomic Age, that was sponsored by Ruth Gordon and Garson Kanin. It opened on Broadway in 1947 but closed after sixty-three performances.

When the play had run its short course, Stewart left for London to begin another project for M-G-M, the adaptation of the Robert Morley-Lowell Langley play *Edward My Son* (1949). Stewart completed the script in London and then returned to New York to see *Edward My Son* as it was being performed there. While in New York, he was summoned to the Metro offices. It was suggested that he "clear himself" by giving names to the House Un-American Activities Committee. Stewart refused, and as he says, "That was the end of a beautiful contract."

Stewart was now on the blacklist, a position he had been fortunate enough to avoid throughout his last fourteen years of screenwriting, a period when he was very politically involved. Stewart did not attribute his refusal to participate in the activities of the House Un-American Activities Committee to personal bravery: "It was not bravery or anything at all. I felt and still feel so very proud of those years with the anti-Nazi league and to say that I'd been duped into that was just not true."

While in New York, resigned to the fact that his screenwriting career had ended, Stewart began work on a new play, *The Kidders*. *The Kidders* was given a run in Cambridge, Massachusetts, but no producer was interested in supporting it. Feeling that both the motion picture industry as well as the

theater were now closed to him in the United States, Stewart returned to London with his wife in 1951, intent on making England his new home. *The Kidders* was produced there in 1957.

Settling in the London home of former Prime Minister Ramsay MacDonald, Stewart continued to write. Various assignments came his way. He supplied English dialogue for the dubbed version of Roberto Rossellini's *Europa 51* (1952), which was released in the United States as *The Greatest Love* (1954).

Stewart was able to do some work for Hollywood as well. Sam Spiegel, who made use of blacklisted writers, hired him to provide polish to the Harry Kurnitz script *Melba* (1953), the story of an opera singer. Using his father's Christian name, Stewart wrote the screenplay for *Escapade* (1955) as Gilbert Holland. The film was an adaptation of the Roger MacDougall play in which a young child takes off from his boarding school to travel to Vienna to try to bring about world peace. Stewart's final project for the screen was *Moment of Danger* (1960), the story of a robber's flight from London to Spain. The picture was released in the United States with, as conditioned, Stewart's name deleted from the credits.

Stewart and his wife remained in England the rest of their lives. Stewart died on 2 August 1980, following a heart attack, and Ella Stewart died two days later.

Reference:

Gary Carey, "The Many Voices of Donald Ogden Stewart," *Film Comment*, 6 (Winter 1970-1971): 74-78.

Preston Sturges

(29 August 1898-6 August 1959)

James Ursini

SELECTED MOTION PICTURES: *The Big Pond* (Paramount-Publix, 1930), dialogue;
Fast and Loose (Paramount-Publix, 1930), dialogue;
The Power and the Glory (Fox, 1933), story and screenplay;
Thirty Day Princess (Paramount, 1934), screenplay by Sturges and Frank Partos;
We Live Again (Samuel Goldwyn/United Artists, 1934), screenplay by Sturges, Leonard Praskins, and Maxwell Anderson;
The Good Fairy (Universal, 1935), screenplay;
Diamond Jim (Universal, 1935), screenplay;
Hotel Haywire (Paramount, 1937), screen story and screenplay;
Easy Living (Paramount, 1937), screenplay;
Port of Seven Seas (M-G-M, 1938), screenplay;
If I Were King (Paramount, 1938), screenplay;
Never Say Die (Paramount, 1939), screenplay by Sturges, Don Hartman, and Frank Butler;
Remember the Night (Paramount, 1940), screen story and screenplay;
The Great McGinty (Paramount, 1940), screen story and screenplay;
Christmas in July (Paramount, 1940), screen story and screenplay;
The Lady Eve (Paramount, 1941), screenplay;
Sullivan's Travels (Paramount, 1941), screen story and screenplay;
The Palm Beach Story (Paramount, 1942), screen story and screenplay;
The Great Moment (Paramount, 1944), screenplay;
The Miracle of Morgan's Creek (Paramount, 1944), screen story and screenplay;
Hail the Conquering Hero (Paramount, 1944), screen story and screenplay;
The Sin of Harold Diddlebock (United Artists, 1947; rereleased as *Mad Wednesday*, United Artists, 1950), screen story and screenplay;
Unfaithfully Yours (20th Century-Fox, 1948), screen story and screenplay;
The Beautiful Blonde From Bashful Bend (20th Century-Fox, 1949), screenplay;
The Birds and the Bees (Paramount, 1956), by Sturges and Sidney Sheldon;
Les Carnets du Major Thompson (The French They Are a Funny Race) (S.N.E. Gaumont-Paul Wagner, 1957), screenplay.

Preston Sturges

PLAYS: *The Guinea Pig* (New York, President Theatre, 7 January 1929);
Strictly Dishonorable (New York, Avon Theatre, 18 September 1929);
Recapture (New York, Eltinge Theatre, 29 January 1930);
The Well of Romance (New York, Craig Theatre, 7 November 1930);
Child of Manhattan (New York, Fulton Theatre, 1 March 1932);
Make a Wish (New York, Winter Garden Theatre, 18 April 1951).

OTHER: *Miracle of Morgan's Creek*, in *Twenty Best Film Plays*, edited by John Gassner and Dudley Nichols (New York: Crown, 1943);
Hail the Conquering Hero, in *Best Film Plays, 1943-44*, edited by Gassner and Nichols (New York: Crown, 1945).

Preston Sturges was and remains an enigmatic film director. For a decade—from 1940, when he began directing as well as writing, until 1950—Sturges was one of the most successful men in Hollywood. Between 1940 and 1944 he made nine films, all huge critical and financial successes. During those years, he garnered an Academy Award and two Academy nominations and was one of Paramount's highest paid directors. After leaving that studio in late 1943, he merged his creative and monetary forces with multimillionaire Howard Hughes to produce films. By 1947 Sturges had reached the pinnacle of success that he, as much as the many success-hungry characters he created, so frantically desired. But even during these years of financial and critical success, artistic maturity, and energetic creativity, the enigma of Preston Sturges remained. The often bitter, satirical tone so evident in his screenplays of the 1930s became even more pronounced in the 1940s. There was a desperate quality to his films that reflected the conflict between his desire to believe in the Horatio Alger ideals associated with America and his skepticism about those same ideals. Out of this dialectic grew the phenomenon of Preston Sturges, a man of many sides and many contradictions.

Sturges was born Edmond Preston Biden to Mary and Edmond Biden in the Irish district of Chicago. His father was a traveling salesman and his mother a woman of Irish and Italian descent whose ambitions ranged far beyond her Chicago home. After a year of marriage, she took young Preston to Paris, ostensibly to study music. While in France she met dancer Isadora Duncan; they later became constant companions. Mary Biden returned to Chicago, where she divorced Biden and married a successful broker, Solomon Sturges. Sturges legally adopted her son in 1902, and young Biden became Preston Sturges.

After the marriage, Mary and Solomon Sturges agreed that she would spend six months of each year in Europe and the remaining six in Chicago. In accordance with the agreement, Preston Sturges was dragged back and forth across the Atlantic. When he was eleven, his mother and foster father agreed to separate, and Mrs. Sturges took her son back to Europe. There he was enrolled in progressive schools, moving continually from one to another while his mother and Isadora Duncan toured the Continent. Much of the energy, restlessness, and eccentricity of Sturges's own career can be traced back to his experiences during these bohemian years.

As Sturges approached adolescence, his mother married Vely Bey, the son of a Turkish court physician and the possessor of "secret" beauty cream formulas. With his help, Maison Desti, Mrs. Sturges's cosmetic business, was opened in France and later in New York. In 1914, at sixteen years of age, Sturges was taken out of school and put in charge of the Deauville branch of the cosmetic business. But before he could take control, World War I broke out and he was sent to the United States.

While in New York, Sturges had his first chance to work in the arts, becoming assistant stage manager in Augustin Duncan's production of *Oedipus Rex*. Later, Sturges returned to manage Maison Desti, which had been badly run and abandoned by Vely Bey. Sturges solicited famous customers such as Lillian Russell and Mae Marsh, and in a short time the business was again solvent.

After a brief stint in the American Air Service during World War I, Sturges returned to Maison Desti in New York. There, in an attempt to salvage the again-failing business, Sturges took to invention and began patenting new cosmetic products such as "kissproof lipstick." But the business finally failed. Shortly thereafter he married heiress Estelle de Wolfe Mudge and retired to a country home where he occupied himself with inventing such devices as a bantam automobile and a machine that projected ticker tape. Sturges and Estelle separated in 1927; in 1930 he married Eleanor Post Hutton.

During Christmas of 1927, Sturges suffered an attack of acute appendicitis. It was while recuperating that Sturges first turned to playwriting. His first work, *The Guinea Pig*, dealt with a female playwright who attaches herself to a young man in order to observe his romantic behavior and use the data for a new play. Sturges had had a similar encounter earlier in his life, and after the initial unpleasantness was able to recall the incident with laughter. Although it was difficult to find backers for this first effort, Sturges finally managed to raise enough money to take the play on the road, and in early 1929 it opened in New York. The reception there was cool, but there were some favorable reviews. At the same time, in order to learn more about the theater business and earn money for his play, Sturges worked for the celebrated New York producer Brock Pemberton as stage manager and occasional extra.

In 1929 Sturges wrote his second play, *Strictly Dishonorable*. It was produced on Broadway by Pemberton and directed by Antoinette Perry to marvelous reviews and a long and prosperous run. By the end of 1929 Sturges had completed *Recapture*, a play that dealt with a couple's attempts to relive the idyl-

Colleen Moore and Spencer Tracy in The Power and the Glory

lic days of their honeymoon, only to find disappointment and tragedy. The play was produced on Broadway in 1930 and was a failure. It was quickly followed by Sturges's first attempt at a musical with the operetta *The Well of Romance*. It was also a failure, and Sturges was in financial trouble again.

In order to compensate for the losses sustained in these last two productions, Sturges accepted an offer to work as a screenwriter. His first assignment from Paramount's New York offices was to adapt two plays: *The Big Pond* by George Middleton and A. E. Thomas, and *The Best People* by David Gray and Avery Hopwood. *The Best People* was filmed in 1930 as *Fast and Loose*. After selling the screen rights to *Strictly Dishonorable* and his newest play, *Child of Manhattan*, for over $40,000 each, Sturges decided to move where the money and creative opportunities obviously lay—Hollywood. One of his first projects there was an adaptation of H. G. Wells's *The Invisible Man* for Universal, but his script was rejected.

The turning point in Sturges's screen career came with his first dramatic screenplay, *The Power*

and the Glory (1933). As he would later do for character players such as William Demarest and Jimmy Conlin or stars such as Harold Lloyd and Betty Hutton, Sturges wrote the lead for a specific actor, Spencer Tracy. The story of Tom Garner (Tracy), a railroad magnate whose life was an inspiration to some and a mockery to others, is recounted in flashback by one character after Garner's funeral and employs a device Sturges developed and called "narratage." A montage of the narrator's memories was shown as his voice became synchronized with that of another character speaking in the flashback. The ambiguity of the Garner character is communicated through the polarized positions of the narrator, Henry, and Henry's wife. Although the flashbacks are narrated by one person, their objectivity permits observation of both sides of Garner's character—his callousness toward his family as well as his youthful energy and his genuine concern for those he considers friends. Ultimately, with Garner's suicide, the realization of the American dream has turned out to be the American nightmare. Possibly because of this central ambiguity and undoubtedly because of its intricate flashback structure, *The Power and the Glory* is said to have influenced *Citizen Kane* (1941).

After *The Power and the Glory* Sturges became peripherally involved in several projects. He wrote an adaptation for Samuel Goldwyn of Tolstoy's *Resurrection* titled *We Live Again* (1934), but his work was considerably revised by others. He then wrote a screen treatment for Universal of Fannie Hurst's "weeper" *Imitation of Life* (1934). Again, very little of Sturges's work was used, and he received no screen credit for this film. He also participated in the writing of a Carole Lombard vehicle for Universal, *Love Before Breakfast* (1936), but it is doubtful that any of Sturges's screenplay was used. Finally, he adapted a story by Clarence Budington Kelland that was filmed as *Thirty Day Princess* (1934).

The period 1934-1935 marked Sturges's first attempts to break through the barrier between writer and director. In 1934 he negotiated with Universal to direct his own screenplay "A Cup of Coffee" (based on his play of the same title and later to serve as the basis for the film *Christmas in July*, 1940), but his efforts were unsuccessful and negotiations fell through.

After two more adaptations—"Song of Joy," a musical which was shelved, and *The Good Fairy* (1935), from a play by Ferenc Molnár—Sturges's next project was an original screenplay based on the life of tycoon Diamond Jim Brady. *Diamond Jim* (1935) and *Easy Living*, released in 1937, are among Sturges's most mature and fully realized scripts before his burst of creativity in the 1940s. Diamond Jim (Edward Arnold) is one of Sturges's most human and sympathetic characters, combining innocence, vitality, ingenuity, vulgarity, and warmth. His rise to power, like Garner's in *The Power and the Glory*, is rapid. But as was the case with that other tycoon, it brings him little personal happiness. He ends his lonely life eating himself to death. It is a wry comment on a system that places more value on material possessions than on human relationships.

After working without credit on *Next Time We Love* (1936), another adaptation for Universal, Sturges wrote *Hotel Haywire* (1937) for comedy stars George Burns and Gracie Allen. But before shooting could start, Burns and Allen had to withdraw, and the screenplay was revised.

Easy Living was the first of two films on which Sturges worked with Paramount's fine comedy director Mitchell Leisen. It is the 1930s screenplay closest to the kind of screwball comedy which was to become Sturges's trademark. Edward Arnold again plays a millionaire. In a fit of anger, he throws his

wife's mink coat out a window, and it lands on the head of a passerby portrayed by Jean Arthur. She later meets and falls in love with the millionaire's son (Ray Milland). The movie pits her, with her working-class common sense, against the inane and indulgent rich.

Sturges followed *Easy Living* with two more adaptations for the screen, *Port of Seven Seas* (1938), a translation and fairly faithful rendering of Marcel Pagnol's Marseilles trilogy, and *If I Were King* (1938), from Justin Huntly McCarthy's romantic play dealing with part of the life of the fabled French poet and rogue François Villon. The year *If I Were King* was released, Sturges was married for the third time to Louise Tevis. In 1939 *Never Say Die*, with an original script by Sturges, was rewritten by star Bob Hope's regular writers and molded to fit the comedian's style. Sturges's last screenplay before making the transition from writer to writer-director was *Remember the Night* (1940), for Mitchell Leisen.

Tired of having his screenplays indifferently directed, Sturges conceived a plan to break into directing. He approached Paramount with a screenplay he had been peddling for years—*The Great McGinty* (1940). He offered them the script for a minimal fee on the condition that he be allowed to direct it himself. Paying Sturges far less than his usual $1000 to $2500 weekly fee, production chief William LeBaron accepted his proposal.

The Great McGinty was a political satire about a bum (Brian Donlevy) who, through political manipulation, rises to a position of power. The film was a financial and critical success, and the screenplay won an Academy Award. Reviews hailed Sturges as a new American comic genius, a man who could combine the functions of writer and director with apparent ease. Interestingly, the film which garnered all those accolades was Sturges's most bitter. It attacked the American political system savagely, portrayed those in it as fools, and demonstrated several twisted applications of the American success ethic.

Sturges followed *The Great McGinty* with *Christmas in July* (1940), based on his own play about a man (Dick Powell) who enters a contest and then begins to spend his anticipated winnings. *The Lady Eve* (1941) is about a golddigger (Barbara Stanwyck) who sets her sights on a shy and awkward young man (Henry Fonda). She and her father (Charles Coburn) intend to swindle him, but she reforms at the last minute.

In 1941 Sturges wrote and directed *Sullivan's Travels*, the film which many consider to be his most

Akim Tamiroff (second from left), Brian Donlevy, and William Demarest in The Great McGinty

introspective and significant work. In this film John L. Sullivan (Joel McCrea) is a director who wants to direct more "meaningful" movies than the comedies he has worked on most of his career. For his next film, he wants to learn about poverty and misery firsthand. Against the advice of his friends and associates, Sullivan dresses as a hobo and begins his travels. He meets a would-be starlet (Veronica Lake) who joins him in hopping trains, sleeping in flophouses, attending mission revival meetings, and scraping garbage pails. After they return to Hollywood, Sullivan returns to the flophouses and railroad yards he had visited to hand out five-dollar bills to the unfortunate. He is beaten, robbed, and loses his memory. Sullivan winds up in prison, and it is in prison that he learns something essential about himself and his art. The prisoners see a Mickey Mouse cartoon, and as they laugh at it, all their problems vanish. In this sentimental sequence, Sturges defends moviegoing as not only an escape from the grim realities of life but also as an almost religious experience—the film is viewed in a church—where the idea of brotherhood becomes a reality. Though this statement does appear to dis-

count the cinema as a tool for social change, it holds the basically idealistic view of comedy films as a therapeutic experience.

Most of Sturges's films can be categorized as comedies of error, full of deception, confusion, and mistaken identity. *The Palm Beach Story* (1942) is very much in this tradition. Although Gerry and Tom Jeffers (Claudette Colbert and Joel McCrea) love each other deeply, Gerry's materialism makes her desert her inventor-husband in order to find a wealthier prey. She travels to the haven of the rich, Palm Beach, meeting on the way one of the idle rich, billionaire John D. Hackensacker III (Rudy Vallee). Tom also goes to Palm Beach, where he meets Gerry, Hackensacker, and Hackensacker's sister Princess (Mary Astor), who uses her fortune to buy men. Gerry forces Tom to pose as her brother so that her plans can progress without a hitch. If all goes well, she will marry Hackensacker and her "brother" will have enough money to finance his revolutionary new airport. The plot spins around the complications resulting from this masquerade, with the upright Tom winning back his wife.

The Miracle of Morgan's Creek (1944) and *Hail*

Sturges with the cast of The Palm Beach Story: *to his right, Mary Astor and Joel McCrea;*
to his left, Claudette Colbert and Rudy Vallee

the Conquering Hero (1944) are Sturges's contributions to small-town American lore. Morgan's Creek is affected by some of the changes in the country during World War II when soldiers bring new, more liberated social attitudes. The basic premise of the film is a daring one, even for Sturges, and caused him many problems with the Production Code. The constable's daughter Trudy (Betty Hutton) is impregnated by an unknown soldier and convinces country bumpkin Norval Jones (Eddie Bracken) to marry her. Their scheme is uncovered, and Norval is arrested on a series of charges including impairing the morals of a minor, impersonating a soldier, and giving a false name. Trudy gives birth to sextuplets, and the news spreads throughout the state. In an astute political move, the governor pardons Norval, makes him a colonel

in the State Guard, and marries him and Trudy retroactively.

In *The Miracle of Morgan's Creek*, Sturges presented his most extreme version of the bumbling comic hero. Again using Eddie Bracken, Sturges elaborated on that concept with *Hail the Conquering Hero*. Bracken plays a man who is classified 4-F during World War II yet inadvertently becomes hailed as a hero in his home town. Bracken welcomes the attention, which includes plans to run him for mayor; eventually he has second thoughts and admits to the townspeople that he is a fraud.

At the end of 1943 Sturges had finished shooting *Hail the Conquering Hero* and chose not to renew his contract with Paramount because of the studio's constant interference with his films. At the time, the studio had little reason to regret his departure; his last three films had not yet been released, and Sturges had not made them any money since *The Palm Beach Story*. But in 1944 both *Hail the Conquering Hero* and *The Miracle of Morgan's Creek* were nominated for Academy Awards and grossed enormous profits. Although Sturges was offered enviable contracts by Paramount and M-G-M, he refused them both. Independent production was his goal.

Over the years Sturges had nurtured a friendship with the reclusive multimillionaire Howard Hughes and was one of the few men for whom Hughes had developed a liking. The result of this friendship was their joint decision to form an independent film company called California Pictures Corp., with Hughes owning the controlling shares.

Their first project was a vehicle which they hoped would rejuvenate the career of silent film star Harold Lloyd. Sturges proposed his idea to Lloyd for a sequel to *The Freshman* (1925) titled *The Sin of Harold Diddlebock* (1947), about a second-stringer who becomes a hero of a college football game. The film is faithful to the character Lloyd originated during the silent years: that of the all-American boy whose ingenuity, spirit, and stamina enable him to defeat any villain or overcome any difficulty. Lloyd liked the script and agreed to come out of retirement.

Sturges next decided to adapt Prosper Merimée's grim tale of revenge, "Colomba," retitling it *Vendetta*. After completing the screenplay, he hired the German director Max Ophuls. A few weeks later, Hughes saw the film's rushes and fired Ophuls, and Sturges took over the direction. But he lacked enthusiasm for the project, and Hughes became outraged at the lack of progress and particularly at the poor coverage given his newest star, Faith Domergue. Hughes and Sturges clashed frequently, and the company was dissolved.

Sturges departed with no further involvement in his yet unreleased Lloyd comedy or the unfinished *Vendetta*. After a few script revisions and reshooting by three other directors, *Vendetta* was released in 1951 with little of Sturges's work remaining, and he received no screen credit. The Lloyd film was distributed on a limited basis in 1947, withdrawn and reedited, then rereleased in 1950 as *Mad Wednesday*. Whatever the reason for Hughes's handling of the film, a work of true merit was suppressed, and with it part of Sturges's reputation was blackened.

With the dissolution of the Hughes partnership Sturges was again on his own. Refusing to become discouraged, he retrieved one of his earliest projects, *Unfaithfully Yours*, and took the script to Darryl F. Zanuck who agreed to produce the film for 20th Century-Fox.

Unfaithfully Yours (1948) is Sturges's most sophisticated and complex creation. With this film, he hit upon the perfect balance of music, dialogue, and visuals. Sir Alfred De Carter (Rex Harrison), a noted symphony conductor, believes that his wife (Linda Darnell) has been unfaithful with a young man named Tony (Kurt Kreuger). As he conducts a concert, Sir Alfred is driven to fantasy. First he imagines killing his wife and framing the young man, then forgiving her, then killing himself in a game of Russian roulette. After the concert, he attempts to come to grips with the supposedly innocuous circumstances under which she visited Tony's room. Like other characters in Sturges's films, Sir Alfred accepts reassuring appearances rather than chance a deeper exploration of the truth.

Unfaithfully Yours and Sturges's next film, *The Beautiful Blonde from Bashful Bend* (1949)—about a saloon girl (Betty Grable) who becomes a teacher in the Old West—were financial failures. The word was out with these unsuccessful films that Sturges was now a bad risk. His perfectionism and prima donna antics were no longer seen as eccentricities but rather as liabilities.

Sturges never made another American film, although he did receive credit in 1956 for *The Birds and the Bees*, a film based on his earlier screenplay for *The Lady Eve*. After some ill-fated attempts at producing plays, he married Anne Nagle in 1951 and left the United States for France. There he received many offers from American and European producers and directors, but none of these projects was realized. In 1954 he wrote the English subtitles for a French film, *Letters from the Windmill*. His final film, *The French They Are a Funny Race*, was made in France and released in 1957. It was a failure, and most critics agreed that Sturges had lost his creative touch. Sturges finally returned to the United States in the late 1950s. He died in New York in 1959.

References:

"Conversation with P.S.," *Sight and Sound* (Spring 1956);

Richard Corliss, "Preston Sturges," No. 31, *Cinema* (Spring 1972);

James Curtis, *Between Flops: A Biography of Preston Sturges* (New York & London: Harcourt Brace Jovanovich, 1982);

Raymond Durgnat, *The Crazy Mirror, Hollywood*

Comedy and the American Image (London: Faber & Faber, 1969);

Peter Ericsson, "Preston Sturges," *Sequence* (Summer 1948);

Manny Farber, "Preston Sturges, Satirist," *New Republic* (21 December 1942);

Farber and W. S. Poster, "Preston Sturges, Success in the Movies," *Film Culture* (Winter 1962);

Penelope Houston, "Preston Sturges," *Sight and Sound* (Summer 1965);

Alva Johnston, "How To Become a Playwright," *Saturday Evening Post* (8 March and 15 March 1941);

Eric Jonsson (Andrew Sarris), "Preston Sturges and the Theory of Decline," *Film Culture* (Winter 1962);

Siegfried Kracauer, "Preston Sturges or Laughter Betrayed," *Films in Review* (February 1950);

Andrew Sarris, *The American Cinema, Directors, and Directions, 1929-1968* (New York: Dutton, 1968);

Sarris, "Preston Sturges in the Thirties," *Film Comment* (Winter 1970-1971);

Seymour Stern, "Maestro's Return," *New York Times*, 11 July 1948;

James Ursini, *Preston Sturges, An American Dreamer* (New York: Curtis Books, 1973).

Papers:

The Preston Sturges Collection at UCLA contains letters, films, clippings, scripts, and other memorabilia belonging to Preston Sturges.

C. Gardner Sullivan
(18 September 1886-5 September 1965)

Diane Koszarski

SELECTED MOTION PICTURES: *The Italian* (New York Motion Picture Corp./Mutual, 1915), scenario;

On the Night Stage (New York Motion Picture Corp./Mutual, 1915), scenario by Sullivan and Thomas H. Ince;

The Cup of Life (New York Motion Picture Corp./Mutual, 1915), scenario;

The Darkening Trail (New York Motion Picture Corp./Mutual, 1915), scenario;

The Painted Soul (New York Motion Picture Corp./Mutual, 1915), scenario;

The Iron Strain (Ince-Triangle, 1915), scenario;

The Coward (Ince-Triangle, 1915), scenario by Sullivan and Ince;

Matrimony (Ince-Triangle, 1915), scenario;

The Winged Idol (Ince-Triangle, 1915), scenario;

The Golden Claw (Ince-Triangle, 1915), scenario;

The Edge of the Abyss (Ince-Triangle, 1915), scenario;

The Beckoning Flame (Ince-Triangle,1915), scenario;

The Conquerer (Ince-Triangle, 1916), scenario;

The Green Swamp (Ince-Triangle, 1916), scenario;

Honor's Altar (Ince-Triangle, 1916), scenario by Sullivan and Ince;

Peggy (Ince-Triangle, 1916), scenario;

Hell's Hinges (Ince-Triangle, 1916), scenario;

The Moral Fabric (Ince-Triangle, 1916), scenario;

The Stepping Stone (Ince-Triangle, 1916), scenario by Sullivan and J. G. Hawks;

The Aryan (Ince-Triangle, 1916), scenario by Sullivan and William S. Hart;

Civilization's Child (Ince-Triangle, 1916), scenario;

The No-Good Guy (Ince-Triangle, 1916), scenario;

The Beggar of Cawnpore (Ince-Triangle, 1916), scenario;

Not My Sister (Ince-Triangle, 1916), scenario;

The Market of Vain Desire (Ince-Triangle, 1916), scenario;

The Bugle Call (Ince-Triangle, 1916), scenario;

Stranded (Ince-Triangle, 1916), scenario;

Civilization (Ince-Triangle, 1916), scenario;

The Eye of the Night (Ince-Triangle, 1916), scenario;

The Payment (Ince-Triangle, 1916), scenario;

Shell '43 (Ince-Triangle, 1916), scenario;

Home (Ince-Triangle, 1916), scenario;

The Thoroughbred (Ince-Triangle, 1916), scenario;

The Wolf Woman (Ince-Triangle, 1916), scenario;

A Corner in Colleens (Ince-Triangle, 1916), scenario;

The Dawnmaker (Ince-Triangle, 1916), scenario;

Plain Jane (Ince-Triangle, 1916), scenario;

The Return of Draw Egan (Ince-Triangle, 1916), scenario;

The Criminal (Ince-Triangle, 1916), scenario;

Three of Many (Ince-Triangle, 1916), scenario;

C. Gardner Sullivan (Culver Pictures)

The Iced Bullet (Ince-Triangle, 1917), scenario;

The Pinch-Hitter (Ince-Triangle, 1917), scenario;

Happiness (Ince-Triangle, 1917), scenario;

Those Who Pay (Ince-Triangle, 1918), scenario;

Love Me (Paramount, 1918), scenario;

Naughty! Naughty! (Thomas H. Ince/Paramount, 1918), scenario;

Selfish Yates (William S. Hart Productions/Artcraft, 1918), story;

Shark Monroe (William S. Hart Productions/Artcraft, 1918), story;

The Vamp (Thomas H. Ince/Paramount, 1918), story;

The Border Wireless (William S. Hart Productions/Artcraft, 1918), adaptation;

Branding Broadway (William S. Hart Productions/Artcraft, 1918), story and scenario;

Happy Though Married (Thomas H. Ince/Paramount, 1919), adaptation;

The Poppy Girl's Husband (William S. Hart Productions/Artcraft, 1919), scenario;

The Haunted Bedroom (Thomas H. Ince/Paramount, 1919), story;

Other Men's Wives (Thomas H. Ince/Paramount, 1919), story and continuity;

The Virtuous Thief (Thomas H. Ince/Paramount, 1919), story;

Wagon Tracks (William S. Hart Productions/Paramount, 1919), story;

The Market of Souls (Thomas H. Ince/Paramount, 1919), scenario;

Stepping Out (Thomas H. Ince/Paramount, 1919), story;

John Petticoats (William S. Hart Productions/Paramount, 1919), story;

Sahara (W. W. Hodkinson, 1919), scenario;

Dangerous Hours (Thomas H. Ince/Paramount, 1919), scenario;

Sex (J. Parker Read Jr. Productions/W. W. Hodkinson, 1920), story;

The False Road (Thomas H. Ince/Paramount, 1920), story;

Hairpins (Thomas H. Ince/Paramount, 1920), story;

Love Madness (W. W. Hodkinson, 1920), scenario;

Mother O'Mine (Thomas H. Ince/Associated Producers, 1921), adaptation;

Greater Than Love (J. Parker Read Jr. Productions/Associated Producers, 1921), story and scenario;

Good Women (Robertson-Cole Pictures, 1921), story and scenario;

Hail the Woman (Thomas H. Ince/Associated Producers, 1921), story and scenario;

White Hands (Graf Productions/Wid Gunning, Inc., 1922), story;

Human Wreckage (Thomas H. Ince/Film Booking Offices, 1923), story;

Soul of the Beast (Thomas H. Ince/Metro, 1923), story;

Dulcy (Constance Talmadge Film Company/Associated First National, 1923), continuity;

Strangers of the Night (Louis B. Mayer Productions/Metro, 1923), adaptation;

The Dangerous Maid (Joseph M. Schenck Productions/First National, 1923), scenario;

Long Live the King (Metro, 1923), adaptation by Sullivan and Eve Unsell;

The Goldfish (Constance Talmadge Productions/Associated First National, 1924), adaptation;

The Marriage Cheat (Thomas H. Ince/Associated First National, 1924), adaptation;

Wandering Husbands (Regal Pictures/W. W. Hodkinson, 1924), story and scenario;

Dynamite Smith (Thomas H. Ince/Pathé, 1924), story and scenario;

The House of Youth (Regal Pictures/Producers Distributing Corp., 1924), scenario;

The Only Woman (Norma Talmadge Productions/First National, 1924), story;

Cheap Kisses (C. Gardner Sullivan Productions/Film Booking Offices, 1924), story and scenario;

Idle Tongues (Thomas H. Ince/First National, 1924), adaptation;

The Mirage (Regal Pictures/Producers Distributing Corp., 1924), adaptation;

The Monster (Metro-Goldwyn, 1925), titles;

Playing With Souls (Thomas H. Ince/First National, 1925), adaptation;

Wild Justice (United Picture Artists/United Artists, 1925), story;

If Marriage Fails (C. Gardner Sullivan Productions/ Film Booking Offices, 1925), story and scenario;

The Pinch Hitter (Associated Exhibitors, 1925), story;

Tumbleweeds (William S. Hart Company/United Artists, 1925), adaptation;

Three Faces East (Cinema Corp. of America/ Producers Distributing Corp., 1926), adaptation by Sullivan and Monte Katterjohn;

Bachelor Brides (De Mille Pictures/Producers Distributing Corp., 1926), scenario by Sullivan and Garrett Fort;

Sparrows (Pickford Corp./United Artists, 1926), adaptation;

The Bugle Call (M-G-M, 1927), story;

Sadie Thompson (Gloria Swanson Productions/ United Artists, 1928), titles;

Tempest (Joseph M. Schenck Productions/United Artists, 1928), story and adaptation;

The Woman Disputed (United Artists, 1928), scenario and titles;

Alibi (Feature Productions/United Artists, 1929), scenario, titles, and dialogue by Sullivan and Roland West;

The Locked Door (Feature Productions/United Artists, 1929), scenario;

The Cuban Love Song (M-G-M, 1931), screenplay by Sullivan and Bess Meredyth;

Huddle (M-G-M, 1932), dialogue and continuity by Sullivan and Walton Hall Smith;

Strange Interlude (M-G-M, 1932), dialogue and continuity by Sullivan and Meredyth;

Skyscraper Souls (M-G-M, 1932), adaptation;

Men Must Fight (M-G-M, 1933), screenplay;

Father Brown, Detective (Paramount, 1934), screenplay by Sullivan and Henry Myers;

Car 99 (Paramount, 1935), screenplay by Sullivan and Karl Detzer;

Three Live Ghosts (M-G-M, 1936), screenplay;

The Buccaneer (Paramount, 1938), screenplay by Sullivan, Edwin Justus Mayer, and Harold Lamb;

Union Pacific (Paramount, 1939), screenplay by Sullivan, Walter DeLeon, and Jesse Lasky, Jr.;

North West Mounted Police (Paramount, 1940), screen story and screenplay by Sullivan, Alan LeMay, and Jesse Lasky, Jr.;

Jackass Mail (M-G-M, 1942), story.

Charles Gardner Sullivan, who was raised in Saint Paul, Minnesota, began college studies at the University of Minnesota, but left before graduating and in 1907 took a position on the *Saint Paul Daily News*. He worked as a journalist in many major cities, including Chicago, Cleveland, and Philadelphia before settling in New York City, where he wrote a syndicated column for the *Evening Journal*.

In New York Sullivan sold a few sketches to the vaudeville circuit and began submitting stories to film producers in the metropolitan area. The first of his works to be filmed was *Her Polished Family*, a satire on the sensibilities of a recent college graduate, which the Edison Company bought and filmed in 1911. He continued to sell material for one-reelers to Edison and the Lubin Manufacturing Company, while studying the epic films—vigorous, occasionally morbid sagas of the Civil War hero, the vanishing red man, the intrepid pioneer—produced by the California studio of the New York Motion Picture Corp. By 1913 Sullivan had developed a similar "Indian-military thriller" and sold it to New York Motion Picture production head Thomas W. Ince for fifty dollars. Still employed by the *Evening Journal*, Sullivan began contributing regularly to Ince's company, and by 1914 it had produced more than sixty of his scenarios.

In 1914 Ince hired Sullivan to join his California writing staff. Sullivan and his wife were reluctant to leave the lively world of the big city for the unknown rewards of moviemaking in the hamlet of Santa Monica, California; but a handsome salary offer dissolved their resistance, and they found their new life much to their liking. Continuing to work under Ince's aegis, Sullivan wrote vivid stories that blended the narrative capacities of film with the craft of journalism. Ince insisted that each script include annotations for fully developed characterizations and dialogue, set and location breakdowns, and even advice on camera angles, gestures, and makeup.

At the Ince company, Sullivan soon gained an enviable reputation for his pungent stories. Used to short deadlines from his newspaper days and accustomed to seizing the human-interest angle in current topics, Sullivan supplied Ince with everything from bread-and-butter staples such as *In the Sage Brush Country* (1914) and *The Cup of Life* (1915) to big-budget specials such as *Civilization's Child* (1916) and *Peggy* (1916). His deadpan, sardonic

M. Willis (center) as Bad Ike and William S. Hart (at left) in the title role of The Passing of Two-Gun Hicks

humor illuminated genres as diverse as Westerns and drawing-room comedies. Sullivan's puritanical ethos was tempered by his appreciation of cosmopolitan virtues and his interest in Social Darwinism, and while working for Ince, Sullivan explored controversial topics—prostitution, drug addiction, adultery—confident that the visual element would fully portray what titles could only allude to.

Sullivan often observed filming on the studio lots in order to learn more about the process of filmmaking and the special talents of directors and actors that he might use in future stories. Among the directors working for Ince, Sullivan admired the work of Reginald Barker, Charles Miller, and Raymond West, and he designed many of his scripts for their production units. In addition, he liked writing for the newly popular cowboy star William S. Hart, who had joined the Ince company the same year as he had. After one of his earliest scripts for Hart, *The Passing of Two-Gun Hicks* (1914), impressed critics with its combination of action and complex characterizations, Sullivan wrote many more stories in this vein for Hart, both two-reelers

and features that not only brought windfall profits to Ince but also influenced the development of the American Western film by fixing in the public's imagination the character who could be both good and bad.

In 1915 Sullivan moved, under Ince's urging, to the five-reel feature, a format that was increasingly desirable for commercially released films. He wrote easily for the expanded length, using the additional reels to detail dramatic situations and character development more fully. Sullivan was especially good at concocting action-filled climax endings that did not rely too heavily on titles to explain them. Though much of his work, like that of all scenarists, was uncredited in the beginning, by the end of 1914 his name was being listed in trade advertisements as a gauge of reliable drama.

By mid-1915 Ince had allied the New York Motion Picture Corp. studio with the new Triangle Corporation, which would distribute the studio's feature films. Sullivan was made head of the scenario department and supervised the weekly programs of shorts and features that alternated in the Triangle schedule with material from Mack

Announcement in the 1918 Motion Picture Studio Directory

Sennett's Keystone studio and D. W. Griffith's group at Fine Arts. Sullivan's *The Iron Strain*, a contemporary discussion of marriage for money, starring Dustin Farnum, led the Triangle premiere bill at the Knickerbocker Theatre on 23 September 1915. He continued to write for the Ince coterie of actors at Triangle: juvenile Charles Ray, character actors Frank Keenan and Walter Edwards, leading man H. B. Warner, company vamp Louise Glaum, Ince protégée Dorothy Dalton, and William S. Hart. For actress Bessie Barriscale, the versatile Sullivan provided a wide variety of parts ranging from sprightly girl, society matron, country miss, urban working woman—a range that gave full play to Barriscale's intelligence and feminine vitality. One afternoon, after completing her demanding role as a kept woman in *The Payment* (1916), she asked Sullivan to write her a less taxing part. The next morning the obliging author handed her *Plain Jane* (1916), a script he had written the night before. The tale of a love-struck slavey in a college town, *Plain Jane* was as popular with filmgoers as was *The Payment*. By the second year of his association with Triangle, Sullivan was assisting Ince with administrative duties and in 1917 wrote relatively little. In the summer of 1917 Ince left Triangle and secured a new contract as a producer with Adolph Zukor, taking many of his stars and staff, including Sullivan, with him to Paramount.

At Paramount, Sullivan worked with several well-known star-director teams, including Lambert Hillyer and William S. Hart, Jerome Storm and Enid Bennett, Victor Schertzinger and Charles Ray, William Neill and Dorothy Dalton, Fred Niblo and Louise Glaum. By the end of 1919, Zukor was pressuring Thomas Ince productions to move, and Ince left to form Associated Producers with longtime colleagues J. Parker Read, Jr., Allan Dwan, Mack Sennett, Marshall Neilan, and others. He was unable to persuade Sullivan to join them because Sullivan was more interested in forming an independent company with other scenarists such as Monte Katterjohn. But in the end he became a free-lance writer, finding a ready market for his plays with Ince's group and with old collaborators still at work on the Paramount lot.

In the early 1920s Sullivan worked closely with directors John Griffith Wray and Fred Niblo under Ince's auspices, and in 1923 and 1924 Joseph M. Schenck commissioned him to adapt several popular Broadway plays as vehicles for the Talmadge sisters. During the same period, Ince continued to assign Sullivan projects for his actors, including *Dynamite Smith* (1924), Charles Ray's comeback film;

the narcotics-exploitation drama *Human Wreckage* (1923) with Mrs. Wallace Reid; and *Wandering Husbands* (1924), a light sex comedy for Lila Lee and Margaret Livingston. Sullivan reportedly earned $150,000 in 1924, and this was rumored to be the highest pay for a writer at that time.

Sullivan was in the midst of his first independent production, *Cheap Kisses* (1924), a comedy-melodrama about the nouveau-riche, to be directed by John Ince, when Thomas Ince died suddenly on 19 November 1924. Sullivan's association with that shrewd and dynamic producer had been felicitous for both men, and although he continued in a productive, professional capacity at the top levels of the film business, Sullivan would not establish such a fruitful partnership with his subsequent collaborators. During the next year he worked with old acquaintances Ralph and John Ince (the brothers of Thomas Ince), John W. Considine, Jr., and William S. Hart in preparing adaptations and special projects and wrote one more independent film, *If Marriage Fails* (1925), a sensationalist divorce drama.

With *Three Faces East* (1926) Sullivan began his alliance with Cecil B. De Mille, one of the few remaining independent producers of stature in an increasingly studio-dominated industry. As was the custom with De Mille, Sullivan worked with a round table of writers in adapting magazine stories and popular plays. Sullivan, who in the past had written his scenarios alone, shifted to administrative duties and for the next two years worked primarily as supervisor for directors William K. Howard, Rupert Julian, Paul Sloane, and Donald Crisp on such films as *Her Man O' War* (1926), *The Clinging Vine* (1926), *Gigolo* (1926), *Corporal Kate* (1926), *White Gold* (1927), *Yankee Clipper* (1927), *Vanity* (1927), *The Fighting Eagle* (1927), and *Turkish Delight* (1927). During this period Sullivan worked as a scenarist on *Bachelor Brides* collaborating with Garrett Ford.

The last silent films crafted by the longtime master of the form were released in 1928. He titled Raoul Walsh's scenario for *Sadie Thompson*, starring Gloria Swanson, and composed a romantic fantasy about the Russian revolution, *Tempest*, to feature John Barrymore. For Joseph Schenck he prepared a treatment of Guy de Maupassant's *Boule de Suif*. Entitled *The Woman Disputed* (1928), the film was directed by Henry King and benefited from the music and sound effects added for the new sound-market.

During the early sound period Sullivan wrote two adaptations of Broadway plays: For Schenck he collaborated with author-director Roland West on a grim gangster film, *Alibi* (1929), and for producer Joseph Kennedy he wrote the scenario *The Locked Door* (1929), a remake of a 1921 melodrama about murder and blackmail in high society.

In a filmmaking period constrained by the relative immobility of both the camera and the microphone and by the cautious reliance on proven dialogue from Broadway plays, Sullivan again assumed duties as a script supervisor, this time for Universal in 1930 and 1931. He moved to M-G-M in late 1931 and continued there through 1933, working along with other staff writers to adapt the stream of best-sellers and hit plays sought by the studios as story sources. His most significant project during this period was an adaptation of Eugene O'Neill's *Strange Interlude* (1932), which he wrote with Bess Meredyth. After his contract expired in 1933, Sullivan returned to free-lancing, working with old friends such as John W. Considine, Jr., and Cecil B. De Mille on selected projects.

The "dean of silent screenwriting," as *Variety* called him, retired in 1940 after writing more than

375 produced scenarios to enjoy the company of his wife and four children. He died at home on 5 September 1965.

Interviews:
Triangle, 25 March 1916, p. 3;
Triangle, 2 December 1916, p. 3.

References:
Harry C. Carr, "What next?," *Photoplay* (March 1917): 60-63, 146;
Interview with Bessie Barriscale, *New York Telegraph*, 1 October 1916;
Carolyn Lowrey, *The First 100 Noted Men and Women of the Screen* (New York: Moffat, Yard, 1920), pp. 176-177;
Obituary for C. Gardner Sullivan, *Variety*, 8 September 1965, p. 69;
Scott O'Dell, *Representative Photoplays Analyzed* (Hollywood: Palmer Institute of Authorship, 1924), pp. 91-103, 164-165, 274-280.

Dalton Trumbo
(9 December 1905-10 September 1976)

James Moore
Mount San Antonio College

SELECTED MOTION PICTURES: *Love Begins at Twenty* (Warner Bros., 1936), screenplay by Trumbo and Tom Reed;
Tugboat Princess (Columbia, 1936), screenplay;
Road Gang (Warner Bros., 1936), screen story and screenplay by Trumbo, Abem Finkel, and Harold Buckley;
Devil's Playground (Columbia, 1937), screenplay by Trumbo, Liam O'Flaherty, and Jerome Chodorov;
A Man to Remember (RKO, 1938), screenplay;
Fugitives for a Night (RKO, 1938), screenplay;
Sorority House (RKO, 1939), screenplay;
Career (RKO, 1939), screenplay;
The Flying Irishman (RKO, 1939), screen story and screenplay by Trumbo and Ernest Pagano;
Five Came Back (RKO, 1939), screenplay by

Trumbo, Jerry Cady, and Nathanael West;
The Kid from Kokomo (Warner Bros., 1939), screen story;
Heaven with a Barbed Wire Fence (20th Century-Fox, 1940), screen story; screenplay by Trumbo, Leonard Hoffman, and Ben Grauman Kohn;
A Bill of Divorcement (RKO, 1940), screenplay;
Curtain Call (RKO, 1940), screenplay;
Half a Sinner (Universal, 1940), screen story;
The Lone Wolf Strikes (Columbia, 1940), screen story;
Kitty Foyle (RKO, 1940), screenplay;
Accent on Love (20th Century-Fox, 1941), screen story;
You Belong to Me (Columbia, 1941), story;
The Remarkable Andrew (Paramount, 1942), screenplay adapted by Trumbo from his novel;

Dalton Trumbo, mid-1940s

Tender Comrade (RKO, 1943), screen story and screenplay;

A Guy Named Joe (M-G-M, 1943), screenplay;

Thirty Seconds Over Tokyo (M-G-M, 1944), screenplay;

Our Vines Have Tender Grapes (M-G-M, 1945), screenplay;

Jealousy (Republic, 1946), story;

Gun Crazy (United Artists, 1949; released again as *Deadly Is the Female*, 1950), screenplay by Trumbo credited to Millard Kaufman;

The Beautiful Blonde from Bashful Bend (20th Century-Fox, 1949), screen story by Trumbo credited to Earl Felton;

He Ran All the Way (United Artists, 1951), screenplay by Trumbo (credited to Hugh Butler) and Guy Endore;

The Prowler (Universal, 1951), screenplay by Trumbo credited to Butler;

Roman Holiday (Paramount, 1953), screen story by Trumbo credited to Ian Hunter; screenplay by Trumbo and Hunter credited to Hunter;

Carnival Story (RKO, 1954), screenplay by Trumbo, Hans Jacoby, and Kurt Neumann credited to Jacoby and Neumann;

The Brave One (RKO, 1956), screen story as Robert Rich;

The Boss (United Artists, 1956), screen story and screenplay by Trumbo credited to Ben Perry;

Wild Is the Wind (Paramount, 1957), screen story and screenplay as Arnold Schulman;

Cowboy (Columbia, 1958), screenplay by Trumbo and Edmund North credited to North;

Exodus (United Artists, 1960), screenplay;

Spartacus (Universal, 1960), screenplay;

Town Without Pity (United Artists, 1961), screenplay by Trumbo, Sylvia Rinehart, and Georg Hurdalek credited to Rinehart and Hudralek;

The Last Sunset (Universal, 1961), screenplay;

Lonely Are the Brave (Universal, 1962), screenplay;

The Sandpiper (M-G-M, 1965), screenplay by Trumbo and Michael Wilson;

Hawaii (United Artists, 1966), screenplay by Trumbo and Daniel Taradash;

The Fixer (M-G-M, 1968), screenplay;

Johnny Got His Gun (World Entertainments Ltd., 1971), screenplay adapted by Trumbo from his novel;

F.T.A. (American International Pictures, 1972), screenplay by Trumbo and others;
Papillon (Corona/General, 1973), screenplay;
Executive Action (National General, 1973), screenplay.

TELEVISION: *Ishi: The Last of His Tribe* (CBS, 20 December 1978), script by Trumbo and Christopher Trumbo.

PLAY: *The Biggest Thief in Town* (New York, Mansfield Theatre, 30 March 1949).

SELECTED BOOKS: *Eclipse* (London: Dickson & Thompson, 1935);
Washington Jitters (New York & London: Knopf, 1936);
Johnny Got His Gun (Philadelphia & New York: Lippincott, 1939);
The Remarkable Andrew (Philadelphia: Lippincott, 1941);
The Biggest Thief in Town (New York: Dramatists Play Service, 1949; London: English Theatre Guild, 1952);
The Time of the Toad (Hollywood, Cal., 1950?; New York: Harper & Row, 1972).

OTHER: *Thirty Seconds Over Tokyo*, in *Best Film Plays, 1945*, edited by John Gassner and Dudley Nichols (New York: Crown, 1946).

During his lifetime, Dalton Trumbo achieved almost everything a screenwriter could hope for. Trumbo won an Academy Award and a national book award. Twice he was Hollywood's highest paid screenwriter. Blacklisted in the 1940s and 1950s, he became the first screenwriter to "break the blacklist" in 1960. In 1966, when Pauline Kael polled "ten top screenwriters," eight of them called Trumbo "the greatest living screenwriter." At sixty-five, he made his directorial debut. In the last fifteen years of his life, Trumbo was as much admired for his courage and principles as for his writing, but his best work was behind him.

Born in Montrose, Colorado, Trumbo moved to Grand Junction with his family and remained in Colorado until he was twenty and had completed a year at the University of Colorado. In Grand Junction he earned high-school oratory honors and worked as a reporter for the town newspaper. His father, Orus Trumbo, who had been only marginally successful as a provider, suddenly moved the family to Los Angeles in 1925; Orus Trumbo died within a year after the move.

The young Trumbo went to work in a Los Angeles bakery and supported the family while writing six novels, which were never published. According to his biographer, Bruce Cook, it was while working in the bakery that Trumbo learned about "us and them" in society. The admiration for strong, silent loners that is evident in his work seems to stem from his idealization of his maternal grandfather, Millard Tillery, a county sheriff in Colorado.

In 1930 Trumbo wrote an elegant spoof on bootlegging that was accepted by Frank Crowninshield for *Vanity Fair*. Noting that Trumbo lived in Los Angeles, Crowninshield assumed he knew about movies. Trumbo, who knew movies only as a spectator, decided to learn, and soon he was contributing movie reviews and essays to the magazine. In 1934, having ghostwritten a book for a German aristocrat ("I realized later that his house was a nest of Nazis") and written items for the *Hollywood Spectator* for which he received little pay, he followed a friend's tip and got a job reading for the Warner Bros. story department at thirty-five dollars a week.

The next year, which also saw the publication of his first novel, *Eclipse* (1935), Trumbo moved up to screenwriter at one hundred dollars weekly. In 1936 his satirical novel, *Washington Jitters*, appeared. It was moderately well received and, with the novel *Johnny Got His Gun* (1939), overshadowed the films Trumbo did in his first four years of screenwriting; *Johnny Got His Gun* won the American Booksellers Award in 1940.

In the Warners B Unit, learning his craft, Trumbo wrote *Road Gang* (1936), a reworking of *I Am a Fugitive from a Chain Gang*. Also in 1936 Trumbo was pressured by Warner Bros. to resign from the newly formed Screen Writers Guild. He refused, and Warners fired and blacklisted him. Harry Cohn immediately hired him for Columbia, where he received only one screen credit, for *Devil's Playground* (1937).

Trumbo went through bankruptcy in 1938. He married Cleo Beth Fincher, a photographer, on 13 March 1939; they had three children, Nikola, Christopher, and Melissa. Trumbo and his wife settled on a ranch in Frazier Park. He wrote *Johnny Got His Gun* and most of his screenplays there (until he was blacklisted in 1947). It was as a writer for the RKO B Unit that Trumbo first attracted critical attention.

His first film for RKO, *A Man to Remember* (1938), was certainly a B movie; Trumbo wrote it in fourteen days, and Garson Kanin directed it in fifteen. It told the story of a small-town doctor who had died in debt. The merchant-creditors, pressing their claims against his estate, discovered through a series of flashbacks that his life has really enriched their town, bringing it hope and meaning. A Capraesque work, it was adapted from the short story "Failure" by Katherine Haviland-Taylor and in ways seems the sunnier side of Trumbo's 1935 novel, *Eclipse*, which told the story of a successful businessman who failed, later suffering the blow of having all his supposed friends abandon him.

Eight B movies later, Trumbo made a deal for his freedom: RKO would release him from his contract if he would rework a script by Donald Ogden Stewart based upon Christopher Morley's novel. The result was *Kitty Foyle* (1940), which brought Trumbo his first Academy Award nomination.

Kitty Foyle introduced cinematic devices that Trumbo used throughout his career. The screenplay is a triumph of artfully varied flashbacks. Kitty (Ginger Rogers, who won an Oscar for the role) is the daughter and sole support of her hard-drinking, chronically ill Irish father. At her job, she falls in love with her boss, Wyn Strafford (Dennis Morgan), son of an important Philadelphia family. As time passes, their love grows, but it is complicated by the social gulf between them. Impulsively, they marry, but when they confront Wyn's family and understand the full weight of its power, they know their love is doomed. They divorce; Kitty is pregnant, unbeknownst to Wyn, and her baby is stillborn. Later she meets and falls in love with an idealistic young doctor (James Craig). But on the day of their planned wedding, Wyn reappears, urging Kitty to run away with him. Kitty chooses the doctor.

Trumbo tells the story wholly from the perspective of the day of Kitty's decision. The flashbacks are managed through two devices. Getting dressed, Kitty finds her mirrored image talking to her, reminding her of the past, her ups and downs with Wyn. The mirrored Kitty stands for the past and its knowledge; the impulsive, emotional Kitty must listen to it. Trumbo's other device, anticipating *Citizen Kane* by a year, is a glass globe containing a tiny snowman and "snow" which swirls when the globe is rotated. The snow bridges gaps in the larger flashback. When Kitty's father dies, she finds the globe on the floor by his outstretched arm.

Although it is stamped by its era, *Kitty Foyle* reads and screens well. Its most melodramatic sections—the stillbirth, for instance, when Kitty is talking to her lifeless child as her "sweet, tough little candidate for the year 2000"—are done briskly and unsentimentally.

Trumbo's last novel, *The Remarkable Andrew*

(1941), was the basis for his 1942 film for Paramount. In the film, Andrew Long, a small-town bookkeeper, uncovers evidence of civic graft and corruption, only to wind up being accused of the wrongdoing himself; the town's powers twist facts through their political clout. Long's defender is the ghost of Andrew Jackson, visible only to Long. Although Trumbo worked in the genre of fantasy because it was popular, Trumbo was never particularly successful with it, as is the case of *The Remarkable Andrew*.

Before signing with M-G-M in 1943 and becoming for the first time the top-paid screenwriter in Hollywood, Trumbo wrote one final film for RKO. His *Tender Comrade* (1943) is notable mainly for its mention during the 1947 HUAC hearings. Lela Rogers, mother of the film's star, Ginger Rogers, testified that this movie, about how four women moved into a co-op apartment while waiting for their men to come home from the war, was filled with Communist propaganda: one line advised, "Share and share alike."

Trumbo wrote only three films for M-G-M, but they were all hits. By now well settled into his characteristic method of working on a script—sleeping in the daytime and working, in a filled bathtub at a typewriter perched on a specially made board, throughout the night—Trumbo received the kind of reward for which he had joined M-G-M in the first place: a $3000-per week or $75,000-per picture, no-morals-clause contract.

His films for M-G-M were *A Guy Named Joe* (1943), *Thirty Seconds Over Tokyo* (1944), and *Our Vines Have Tender Grapes* (1945). *A Guy Named Joe* is a wartime fantasy in which the ghost of a combat pilot (Spencer Tracy) returns to watch over another pilot (Van Johnson). *Our Vines Have Tender Grapes* is a sentimental small-town story starring Margaret O'Brien. *Thirty Seconds Over Tokyo* is the best of the three and one of Trumbo's best scripts. A war movie without cliché, it succeeds largely because of what is left out. Working from Ted Lawson's real-life memoir of the Doolittle raid on Tokyo, Trumbo wrote a realistic film about men at war. Again flashbacks are his major tool, used here to call up the brief courtship and marriage of the Lawsons, played by Van Johnson and Phyllis Thaxter. Most of the film focuses on the training for the raid and the raid's accomplishment. The film's ending, with amputee Lawson and his pregnant wife embracing on the floor after he has fallen in his eagerness to hug her, blends reality and romanticism in the best Hollywood manner.

In the same year, 1944, Trumbo joined the

Don Defore (second from left) and Van Johnson in a publicity shot for Thirty Seconds Over Tokyo

American Communist party. His time in 1946 and 1947 was mainly taken up delivering speeches, making friends and alienating people, editing the *Screen Writer*, and otherwise playing a central role in the bitter labor battles characteristic of that period in Hollywood. As the battles intensified, they attracted the attention of HUAC, and in October of 1947, the House Un-American Activities Committee convened in Hollywood. Of the ten witnesses later called the Unfriendly Ten, Trumbo and his friend John Howard Lawson emerged as the unfriendliest. All ten refused to answer the question "Are you now, or have you ever been a member of the Communist party?"

Trumbo's defense was an attempt to have read into the record all the scripts he had written. This request was denied, as was a similar request (Trumbo tried to have his movies screened) at the contempt trial which followed two years later. Trumbo set forth the basic position which he maintained throughout his life, one which became identified with his name and made him, to many, a heroic figure: if one is to be criticized or tried, it must be for one's actions, not for purported

thoughts. Trumbo developed his point that the true issue in the HUAC affair was free speech under the First Amendment in a pamphlet called *The Time of the Toad*, which was published in book form in 1972.

In 1949 Trumbo was convicted of contempt of Congress, and in June of 1950 he began serving a year's sentence at Ashland, Kentucky. Before entering prison (a model prisoner, he was out in ten months), Trumbo had already begun his sub-rosa career, although at sharply reduced fees. Millard Kaufman fronted his screenplay for *Gun Crazy* (1949), a film noir inspired by the exploits of Bonnie and Clyde. The film was directed by Joseph H. Lewis and produced by the King Brothers, who eventually produced *The Brave One* (1956), Trumbo's Academy Award-winner. Trumbo wrote the story for Preston Sturges's *The Beautiful Blonde from Bashful Bend* (1949) and the screenplay for John Garfield's last film, *He Ran All the Way* (1951). After his release from prison he worked on *The Prowler* (1951) for blacklisted director Joseph Losey. During the same period, Trumbo's only play, *The Biggest Thief in Town* (1949), a satirical comedy which takes place in an undertaker's parlor, failed in New York, although it later ran for a year in London.

Trumbo worked on a novel in prison and worried about keeping his ranch (he couldn't) and supporting his family; when he was released from prison he followed the example of many victims of the expanding blacklist, moving to Mexico City. Before returning to Los Angeles for good in 1954, Trumbo developed a wide range of pseudonyms for selling scripts. He even sold a magazine story under his wife's maiden name. Variously, he was John Abbott (the protagonist of *Eclipse*) or Lesley Flint or C. F. Demaine or Robert Presnell, Jr., or Sam Jackson or James Bonham (a family name) or Robert Rich. It was possible to get higher fees, sometimes, if a screenwriter friend would lend his name to Trumbo's script. That was how the 1953 original *Roman Holiday* was sold, under the name of Ian Hunter, also later to be blacklisted.

Other "black-market" originals from this period include *Wild is the Wind* (1957), but it is likely that the full productivity of the 1950-1959 period will never be known. Trumbo not only wrote entire screenplays pseudonymously but doctored others

without credit. Before he "broke the blacklist" in 1960, he had made it to the $75,000 per script category. He had also stopped writing novels and plays.

In 1952 Trumbo outlined to the King Brothers "The Boy and the Bull," an original story inspired, to an extent, by a 1936 newspaper clipping about a bull so brave that, by the spontaneous outburst of a Barcelona bullring audience, he was spared. In 1956 this was produced as *The Brave One*, and the Oscar for best motion picture story went to Robert Rich. In 1959 both Frank King and Trumbo publicly acknowledged Trumbo's authorship, but the Academy kept the Oscar until 1975.

Trumbo worked on at least ten more films before his blacklisting was ended in 1960. In January of that year, Otto Preminger announced that Trumbo was writing *Exodus* (1960) for him, and Universal, prodded by Kirk Douglas, responded with a screen credit for Trumbo on the Roman epic *Spartacus* (1960).

Exodus tells only one of the stories from Leon Uris's novel, the straightforward action story of the birth of Israel. *Spartacus*, from the novel by ex-

Michael Ray in The Brave One. *Because of the Hollywood blacklisting, Trumbo, who wrote the screen story for this 1956 film under the pseudonym Robert Rich, did not receive the Academy Award his work earned until 1975.*

Communist Howard Fast, tells the story of a slave rebellion. It was the more artful, if not the more commercially successful of the two, due to Trumbo's script and Stanley Kubrick's direction. Trumbo avoided action and stuck to the figure of Spartacus (Kirk Douglas) himself. At the end, the rebellion crushed, Spartacus retreats into legend, his body crucified, his spirit still with the freedom fighters.

In 1962 Kirk Douglas produced and starred in *Lonely Are the Brave*, which Trumbo had begun while still blacklisted. Working from Edward Abbey's novel *The Brave Cowboy*, Trumbo told the story of a misfit (Douglas), a cowboy who was unable to adjust to the modern, mechanized world. We first see the cowboy at dawn, silhouetted over his beans-and-coffee breakfast before an open campfire, looking up at the trail of a passing airliner. The cowboy gets himself jailed on purpose to help a friend escape from prison. When the friend will not go along with the escape, the cowboy breaks out by himself. He is chased by an understanding opponent, a county sheriff (Walter Matthau), largely based upon Trumbo's idealization of his grandfather. Civilization itself is the cowboy's final downfall: on the superhighway, he is run down by a truck carrying toilet seats.

The Brave One and *Lonely Are the Brave* are the best films Trumbo wrote under the pressure of the blacklist. They are spare and simple (and to some critics, simplistic). They deal with bravery, and their plots are basic. In contrast to the later epics for which Trumbo became, again, the highest paid screenwriter, one finds a skill in dealing with the few. The crowds, the society are only the background, the necessary stage upon which the intense, small-scale drama is enacted.

Trumbo was never again able to achieve the high quality of *Lonely Are the Brave*. The pressure to break the blacklist was off, and perhaps with it went the drive to do his best work. Now he could set his own prices and deadlines. He was not particularly proud of *The Sandpiper* (1965), *Hawaii* (1966), or *The Fixer* (1968), and some critics attacked the last in particular for being ponderous. The story of early twentieth-century Russian pogroms against the Jews, it was sprawling and relentlessly serious; Trumbo had been unable to cut down Bernard Malamud's novel to a size where he could focus clearly.

Trumbo risked money, more than reputation, on the film version of *Johnny Got His Gun* (1971). There had been a previous attempt to film the novel

in 1963, when Luis Buñuel actually shot part of it in Mexico until funding ran out. Trumbo reworked the script and, directing his own material, created a film that won the Prix Special du Jury at the Cannes Film Festival and the International Critics Award, although it did not receive much attention in the United States.

As a novel, *Johnny Got His Gun* was a tour de force. It arose from Trumbo's having read about an incident in which the Prince of Wales had visited a hospital and seen a World War I casualty who had lost his limbs and his ability to speak, hear, smell, and see. Trumbo wrote about such a case from the point of view of the soldier Joe Bonham. The novel uses flashbacks. Joe's entire past is recalled, quite logically, as his still-living mind tries to understand what has happened to him. Each now-imaginary sense is explored with its appropriate memories until the only one left to him—the tactile sense—is revealed as his pipeline to the outside world. Having determined that he is alive and not dreaming, Joe uses Morse code as a method of communication, and a sympathetic nurse finally understands why he is rhythmically thrashing his torso to and fro. She taps out messages on Joe's chest, and he responds.

Trumbo's screenplay is, surprisingly, less dependent on flashbacks than the novel. Joe's story is developed in straight chronology for about the first twenty minutes of the film, to the time he is hit by an artillery shell. From that point, it follows the novel very faithfully, until the end. The later Trumbo wrote more from pity; whereas the novel had Joe raging against the makers of war, the film presents him drifting off to sleep tapping out "SOS, Help me. . . ."

In 1970 Trumbo was given the Laurel Award by the Writers Guild for continued achievement in screenwriting. That same year, a volume of his letters was published as *Additional Dialogue*.

Trumbo contributed material to Jane Fonda and Donald Sutherland's revue *F.T.A.*, a collection of antiwar songs and skits that was performed for troops in Viet Nam. A film was made of the revue in 1972. Working in Jamaica on *Papillon* early in 1973, Trumbo was diagnosed as a lung-cancer victim. He lost a lung and lymph nodes, and his son, Christopher, replaced him on that film as well as on *Executive Action* (1973), a film about a presidential assassination. Neither film was praised; both were criticized for their ponderousness and heavy-handedness. They were Trumbo's last motion pictures. He began a script for television, *Ishi: The Last of His Tribe*, about the plight of the last Yahi Indian;

Trumbo played the French commandant of the Devil's Island prison in the opening scene of Papillon.

Since Dalton Trumbo's death, some harsh criticism has accumulated, but it has generally been overwhelmed by evidence of his ability as commercial, collaborative screenwriter par excellence. The professional's professional, Trumbo seems destined to live on as the embodiment of the blacklist's turmoil, and his reputation will likely prove permanently inextricable from the circumstances, achievements, and defeats of his personal life. He may have realized this himself in 1970, when, receiving the Writers' Guild of America's Laurel Award, he said: "The blacklist was a time of evil, and no one on either side who survived it came through untouched by evil. . . . When you who are in your forties or younger look back with curiosity on that dark time, as I think occasionally you should, it will do no good to search for villains or heroes or saints or devils because there were none; there were only victims."

this was also completed by Christopher Trumbo.

In 1975, after a minor in-house controversy, the Academy presented Trumbo with Robert Rich's award for *The Brave One*. He died the following year.

Letters:

Additional Dialogue, Letters of Dalton Trumbo, 1949-62, edited by Helen Manfull (New York: Evans, 1970).

Biography:

Bruce Cook, *Dalton Trumbo* (New York: Scribners, 1977).

Papers:

Screenplays by Trumbo are on file at the Los Angeles American Film Institute, California, and the library of the Academy of Motion Picture Arts and Sciences, Beverly Hills.

Billy Wilder
(22 June 1906-)

James Moore
Mount San Antonio College

SELECTED MOTION PICTURES: *Menschen am Sonntag (People on Sunday)* (Filmstudio Germania, 1929), screenplay;

Seitensprünge (Dodging) (Universal—Germany, 1930), story idea;

Der Mann, der seinen Mörder Sucht (The Man Who Looked for His Murderer) (UFA, 1931), screenplay by Wilder, Curt Siodmak, and Ludwig Hirschfield;

Der falsche Ehemann (The Wrong Husband) (UFA, 1931), screenplay by Wilder and Paul Franck;

Emil und die Detektive (Emil and the Detectives) (UFA, 1931), screenplay;

Ihre Hoheit Befiehlt (Her Highness' Command) (UFA, 1931), screenplay by Wilder, Franck, and Robert Liebmann;

Das Blaue vom Himmel (The Blue from the Sky) (Aafa-Film AG, 1932), screenplay by Wilder and Max Kolpe;

Ein blonder Traum (A Fairer Dream) (UFA, 1932), screenplay;

Es War Einmal ein Walzer (Once There Was a Waltz) (Aafa-Film AG, 1932), screenplay;

Scampolo, ein Kind der Strasse (Scampolo, a Girl of the Street) (German-Austrian, 1932), screenplay by Wilder and Kolpe;

Madame wünscht keine Kinder (Madame Wants No Children) (Schaftsproduktion, 1933), screenplay by Wilder and Kolpe;

Was Frauen träumen (A Woman's Dreams) (Atrium and Titania Palast, 1933), screenplay by Wilder and Franz Schultz;

Music in the Air (Fox, 1934), screenplay by Wilder and Howard I. Young;

One Exciting Adventure (Universal, 1934), story by Wilder and Schultz;

The Lottery Lover (Fox, 1935), screenplay by Wilder and Schultz;

Champagne Waltz (Paramount, 1937), story by Wilder and H. S. Kraft;

Bluebeard's Eighth Wife (Paramount, 1938), screenplay by Wilder and Charles Brackett;

Midnight (Paramount, 1939), screenplay by Wilder and Brackett;

What a Life (Paramount, 1939), screenplay by Wilder and Brackett;

Billy Wilder (Movie Star News)

Ninotchka (M-G-M, 1939), screenplay by Wilder, Brackett and Walter Reisch;

Rhythm on the River (Paramount, 1940), story;

Arise, My Love (Paramount, 1940), screenplay by Wilder and Brackett;

Ball of Fire (RKO, 1941), screenplay by Wilder and Brackett;

Hold Back the Dawn (Paramount, 1941), screenplay by Wilder and Brackett;

The Major and the Minor (Paramount, 1942), screenplay by Wilder and Brackett;

Five Graves to Cairo (Paramount, 1943), screenplay

by Wilder and Brackett;

Double Indemnity (Paramount, 1944), screenplay by Wilder and Raymond Chandler;

The Lost Weekend (Paramount, 1945), screenplay by Wilder and Brackett;

The Emperor Waltz (Paramount, 1948), screenplay by Wilder and Brackett;

A Foreign Affair (Paramount, 1948), screenplay by Wilder, Brackett, and Richard Breen;

Sunset Boulevard (Paramount, 1950), screenplay by Wilder, Brackett, and D. M. Marshman, Jr.;

Ace in the Hole (later released as *The Big Carnival*) (Paramount, 1951), screen story and screenplay by Wilder, Lesser Samuels, and Walter Newman;

Stalag 17 (Paramount, 1953), screenplay by Wilder and Edwin Blum;

Sabrina (Paramount, 1954), screenplay by Wilder, Ernest Lehman, and Samuel Taylor;

The Seven Year Itch, (20th Century-Fox, 1955), screenplay by Wilder and George Axelrod;

Love in the Afternoon (Allied Artists, 1957), screenplay by Wilder and I. A. L. Diamond;

The Spirit of St. Louis (Warner Bros., 1957), screenplay by Wilder and Wendell Mayes;

Witness for the Prosecution (United Artists, 1957), screenplay by Wilder and Harry Kurnitz;

Some Like It Hot (United Artists, 1959), screenplay by Wilder and Diamond;

The Apartment (United Artists, 1960), screen story and screenplay by Wilder and Diamond;

One, Two, Three (United Artists, 1961), screenplay by Wilder and Diamond;

Irma La Douce (United Artists, 1963), screenplay by Wilder and Diamond;

Kiss Me, Stupid (United Artists, 1964), screenplay by Wilder and Diamond;

The Fortune Cookie (United Artists, 1966), screen story and screenplay by Wilder and Diamond;

The Private Life of Sherlock Holmes (United Artists, 1970), screenplay by Wilder and Diamond;

Avanti! (United Artists, 1972), screenplay by Wilder and Diamond;

The Front Page (Universal, 1974), screenplay by Wilder and Diamond;

Fedora (United Artists, 1978), screenplay by Wilder and Diamond;

Buddy Buddy (M-G-M/United Artists, 1981), screenplay by Wilder and Diamond.

SELECTED BOOKS: *Some Like It Hot*, by Wilder and I. A. L. Diamond (New York: New American Library, 1959);

Irma La Douce, by Wilder and Diamond (New York:

Midwood-Tower, 1963);

The Apartment and The Fortune Cookie, by Wilder and Diamond (New York: Praeger, 1971);

Ninotchka, by Wilder, Charles Brackett, and Walter Reisch (New York: Viking, 1972).

OTHER: *Double Indemnity*, by Wilder and Raymond Chandler, and *The Lost Weekend*, by Wilder and Charles Brackett, in *Best Film Plays, 1945*, edited by John Gassner and Dudley Nichols (New York: Crown, 1946).

Although Billy Wilder won fame for directing films, especially several brilliant ones between 1944 and 1960, he was always a screenwriter. He never directed a film he did not write; his writing career has spanned more than fifty years. Nurtured in the studio system in both Germany and Hollywood, he provides an instructive test of the auteur theory. Although many of Wilder's visual-literary story-telling devices—mistaken identities, disguises, formal narration—are as old as storytelling itself and derive from his silent film experience, his typical themes are highly personal. Over and over Wilder's characters and plots bespeak a love-hate relationship with American life and values, the duality of cynicism and sentimentality, the attraction and repulsion of moviemaking itself, and a growing preoccupation with his own body of work.

Wilder was born in Sucha, in Polish Galicia (then part of Austria) one hundred miles east of Vienna. Born Samuel Wilder, he was nicknamed Billy by his mother, who found it a particularly American-sounding name. His family moved to Vienna in 1914 at the outbreak of World War I, the first of many disruptions in Wilder's life caused by Europe's political agonies. The last of these, the beginning of the anti-Jewish campaign, sent Wilder to America in 1933. His grandmother, mother, and stepfather died at Auschwitz.

Wilder became a journalist early in his life, reporting on sports for *Die Stunde* in Vienna, where he also specialized in personality interviews (Richard Strauss and Arthur Schnitzler were two of his subjects). Moving to Berlin and the *Nachtausgabe*, he became a crime reporter and frequented the Romanisches Cafe, though not the tables where Grosz, Brecht, and Weill presided. For a while he was a professional tea dancer.

By the middle of the 1920s, he was writing silent scenarios. About this phase of his career, as well as others, he has given interviewers different information at different times: the number of these scripts, typically twenty-five-minute vignettes, is reported as one hundred at one time, seventy-five another time. Scholars have identified only fifteen so far, the earliest in 1929.

People on Sunday (1929) was his first solo screenwriting credit, though Robert Siodmak, the director, Curt Siodmak, and Fred Zinnemann also worked on the film, and the nature of Wilder's contribution has been disputed. The movie deals with four young Germans—chauffeur, film extra, salesgirl, and traveling salesman—who spend a day together without getting to know one another or themselves. Traveling from Berlin to Wannsee Lake and back, they voice their aspirations and hopes. The film evokes an empty world with little possible leavening. At the film's end, the four have forgotten their brief escape from routine as they look forward to the week ahead.

Between 1929 and 1933 Wilder's German films were characteristic of the era's mood: there were lighthearted, humorous rags-to-riches tales, mistaken identities, some touches of Expressionism, light looks at street crime. Before he fled Germany in 1933, Wilder made a directorial debut with *Mauvaise Graine* in France.

Wilder arrived in Hollywood in 1933, penniless and speaking no English. He did have friends in Hollywood, and he soon had a job at Columbia, working six weeks for $125 a week, writing nothing. He later told biographers that he listened to the radio twelve hours daily, especially baseball games, and that he lived in the lavatories at the Chateau Marmont, eating nothing but a can of soup per day, shared with Peter Lorre. He quickly picked up American slang and in 1934 got two screen credits—one for turning one of his German scripts written with Franz Schultz into *One Exciting Adventure* and another for working with Howard I. Young on adapting Jerome Kern and Oscar Hammerstein II's *Music in the Air*.

The quick start was deceptive, however, and Wilder had only four American credits by 1938, when Paramount paired him with Charles Brackett for *Bluebeard's Eighth Wife*. His days of writing first in German and then translating finally over, working with the competent professional Brackett, Wilder was ready to start his screenwriting career in earnest at thirty-two. Wilder collaborated with Brackett in the same manner he was to work with his later writing partner, I. A. L. Diamond. Wilder created ideas and tested them on Brackett; Brackett sifted through Wilder's concepts, deciding which were good and which were not usable.

Comparison of the Wilder-Brackett scripts (1938-1950) and the Wilder-Diamond work (begin-

ning in 1957) illustrates the difference between eras. Brackett-Wilder work is much more expository; Wilder-Diamond scripts are quite elliptical, much more visually skilled. Brackett and Wilder balanced conventional wisdom and witty insight. Wilder and Diamond mocked the conventional; their serious moments seemed to come as afterthoughts. By the late 1950s, there were fewer restrictions placed on films, so that Wilder and Diamond had the luxury of letting the bad guys win, the good guys lose; when the good guys won, it was because the film demanded it, not the prevailing morality.

Until 1942, when Wilder began to direct their scripts, Brackett-Wilder screenplays tended to be sophisticated comedies, such as *Bluebeard's Eighth Wife* and *Ninotchka* (1939)—both of which were directed by Ernst Lubitsch—and *Midnight* (1939), directed by Mitchell Leisen. *Bluebeard's Eighth Wife* dealt with an often married man played by Gary Cooper and the little games by which a woman (Claudette Colbert) ensnares him. In *Midnight*, Georges Flamanon (John Barrymore) sets up a penniless ex-chorine (Colbert) in Paris as a fake baroness so she can win the suave playboy Jacques Picot (Francis Lederer) away from Flamanon's daughter (Mary Astor); in *Ninotchka*—which earned Wilder his first Academy Award nomination—communist ideology is shown to be no match for love, let alone the good life.

Although all these films were typical of their era, their central motifs apparently charmed Wilder, and he tucked them away for future reference—Gary Cooper as the dangerous seducer for *Love in the Afternoon* (1957), the tricky business of mixing emotional attachment and self-advancement for *Kiss Me, Stupid* (1964), and the romantic complications of conflicting ideologies for *A Foreign Affair* (1948) and *One, Two, Three* (1961). Characteristically, the later scripts were more ironic.

In *Hold Back the Dawn* (1941), Wilder experimented for the first time with a technique he would use in later films—extended flashback and voice-over narration. Taken from a novel by Ketti Frings, the film dealt in melodramatic fashion with a contemporary phenomenon: the flight of refugees to the United States via Mexico. In this case, a suave European (Charles Boyer) marries a lonely American woman (Olivia de Havilland) in order to gain entry to America. Wilder's screenplay was nominated for an Academy Award.

In the 1941 film *Ball of Fire*, Wilder's authentic voice was heard. This is the tale of good, honest, and dull scholar Bertram Potts (Gary Cooper) and the

Barbara Stanwyck and Fred MacMurray in Double Indemnity

travails of writing his encyclopedia entry on slang. As critics have noted, Wilder is fascinated by the true innocent, the true naif. Potts is the first in a line of Wilder naifs that reaches its height in the 1960s with characters such as Bud Baxter in *The Apartment*. In *Ball of Fire*, when Potts hears stripper Sugarpuss O'Shea's (Barbara Stanwyck) wonderful slang, he realizes that he must go into the world if he is to learn about his subject. Learning from Sugarpuss and her boyfriend, gangland menace Joe Lilac, Potts somehow retains his purity of heart, and of course he wins the girl, proving his bravery at the same time. Wilder received his third Academy Award nomination for *Ball of Fire*.

Wilder began his directorial career with *The Major and the Minor* (1942), a film which owes a great deal to the screwball comedy, then just passing its peak. Lacking the train fare for adult passage home from New York, a woman (Ginger Rogers) is forced to disguise herself as a twelve-year-old, fooling an army major (Ray Milland) and several other adults for days. The film works, despite the implausibility

of the premise, because of the well-constructed script.

Written in collaboration with Raymond Chandler and taken from the novel by James M. Cain, *Double Indemnity* (1944) was made in the film noir tradition, although Wilder resisted calling it film noir, preferring to think of it as film realism along the lines of Erich von Stroheim's film *Greed* (1924). Still, the bitterness of this tale of a corrupt insurance agent (Fred MacMurray), an ambitious and neglected policyholder's wife (Barbara Stanwyck), the murdered policyholder (Porter Hall), and the ethical agent who solves the murder (Edward G. Robinson) cuts across the wishful fantasy which characterized many wartime films.

This film is the first virtuoso use by Wilder of the extended flashback. MacMurray as the corrupted agent tells virtually the whole story to his dictaphone; the voice-over narration to this flashback leads unerringly to the showdown scene with the ethical agent played by Robinson. Wilder remarked later that the device had been so effective

William Holden and Gloria Swanson in Sunset Boulevard, *for which writers Wilder, Charles Brackett, and D. M. Marshman, Jr., won a 1950 Academy Award*

that it rendered unnecessary the original filmed ending of MacMurray going to his execution. *Double Indemnity* is also Wilder's first extensive story of friendship between men. In this film it is the relationship of straightforward father and wayward son that is interrupted and perverted by the worship of money and ambition, personified by a woman. As it would be later with characters such as Joe Gillis of *Sunset Boulevard*, the mistaken Mac-Murray is redeemed at the film's end through self-recognition. This is not only the era's demand: it became a staple of Wilder films for the next twenty years.

Brackett reteamed with Wilder for *Five Graves to Cairo* (1943), a distinguished espionage story. Their next film, *The Lost Weekend* (1945), won Wilder his first Academy Awards, for direction and screenplay. The picture was also named best of the year, and Ray Milland won the award for best actor. Adapting Charles Jackson's novel about an alcoholic writer (Milland), Brackett and Wilder never lost sight of hope for the hero; in this case an understanding fiancée (Jane Wyman) is the agent of

hope, and the writer's pawned typewriter becomes the vehicle by which he is able to overcome his problem. *The Lost Weekend* has a rather standard happy ending—something the novel did not have—which is one reason that the film does not hold up as well as much of Wilder's subsequent work.

Wilder spent time in the mid-1940s as head of the U.S. Army's film division psychological warfare department. In 1949 he married Audrey Young. The previous year the film that seems to have signaled the beginning of the end of the collaborations with Brackett was released. *The Emperor Waltz*, a tentative exploration of the brash-American-in-Europe theme he would develop later, was a mild vehicle for Bing Crosby, who played a salesman at the court of Franz Joseph. *A Foreign Affair* (1948) was better, even though fans complained when Jean Arthur was cast as a McCarthyesque congresswoman. As in *Ninotchka*, the heroine's political convictions melt in the embrace of a not-very-idealistic man, in this case an American captain (John Lund) who is also a German black-market patron. The script received an Academy Award nomination.

Wilder's fondness for extended flashback and voice-over narration led to the tour-de-force flashback of *Sunset Boulevard* (1950), presented from the point of view of Gillis, who is floating dead in Norma Desmond's swimming pool. Joe Gillis (William Holden) has, after an idealistic start as a novelist and storywriter, turned into a hack screenwriter. Down-and-out, in his car he veers into the driveway of an apparently abandoned mansion one afternoon. In the house live Norma Desmond (Gloria Swanson), a faded silent-screen star living in the past, and her ex-husband and current servant, Max Mayerling (Erich von Stroheim). Joe is gradually swept up in the decadent fantasy, which focuses on Norma's returning to the screen in her own script, *Salome*. Gradually assuming all the perquisites of a kept man, he begins to rewrite her script. Roused to a kind of self-knowledge by the young idealistic woman (Nancy Olson) he loves, Joe attempts to hurt Norma. "You used to be big," he sneers. "I *am* big. It's the movies that got small," she replies. Later, Joe attempts to walk out on Norma and she shoots him. Thoroughly mad but thoroughly fascinating, Norma sweeps down the staircase at the film's end, thinking that the newsreel cameras covering the sensational murder are there because of *Salome*. *Sunset Boulevard* is complex and ambivalent, and it shows the direction for the second half of Billy Wilder's career as author of films. *Sunset Boulevard*, the last Brackett-Wilder film, also carried credit for D. M. Marshman, Jr., as a collaborator on the script. The screenplay won an Academy Award.

Even more indicative of the direction Wilder was to take was *Ace in the Hole*, released in June 1951 and retitled *The Big Carnival* in July of that year by Paramount boss Y. Frank Freeman. A washed-up reporter (Kirk Douglas) finds a man trapped in a cave and delays his rescue, exploiting the public's lust for sensation. As in *Sunset Boulevard*, Wilder's protagonist begins to sicken of his own amorality. *Ace in the Hole* was indicative of both Wilder's darkening vision and the commercial problems it would bring. The film failed financially despite its title change, and the relationship between Paramount and Wilder was never quite the same again. *Ace in the Hole* demonstrated what could happen when Wilder's cynical or pessimistic views were not held in tension with either comedy or glamour. American audiences and producers simply would not buy such views by themselves.

Wilder did do two more commercially successful films for Paramount, *Stalag 17* (1953) and *Sa-brina* (1954), both based on Broadway plays. *Stalag 17*, a collaboration with Edwin Blum, solidified William Holden's status as a corrupt-but-good Wilder hero; he played a self-centered man who could be moved to impersonal, idealistic actions—especially when, as in *Stalag 17*, it was in his own interest to discover who the prison camp stool pigeon was. *Sabrina*, like the later *Love in the Afternoon*, put the quintessential 1950s heroine (Audrey Hepburn) in a love situation where the object of her affection (Humphrey Bogart) was too old for her; William Holden also starred as a playboy.

Sabrina marked the end of Billy Wilder's career at Paramount. A 1955 collaboration with George Axelrod for 20th Century-Fox on an adaptation of Axelrod's play *The Seven Year Itch* resulted in a successful but not remarkable film. *The Spirit of St. Louis* (1957), written with Wendell Mayes for Warner Bros., showed Wilder as totally ineffective with conventional heroic material.

Love in the Afternoon (1957), based on Claude Anet's play *Ariane*, was Wilder's only film at Allied Artists, as well as the beginning of the collaboration between Wilder and I. A. L. Diamond. Only *Witness for the Prosecution* (1957), written with Harry Kurnitz, saw Wilder working with another collaborator. *Love in the Afternoon* is vintage Wilder, a kind of tribute to director Ernst Lubitsch, for whom he had written twenty years earlier. In this film Frank Flannagan (Gary Cooper) is a globe-trotting millionaire seducer. Chavasse (Maurice Chevalier) is a Parisian detective. Chavasse's virginal daughter Ariane (Audrey Hepburn) has fallen in love with the idea of Flannagan by reading her father's files. Nothing will do but she seduce him, despite the clear view of his Americanness, which Ariane expresses in some of the film's most humorous lines: "When they're young they have their teeth straightened and their tonsils taken out and gallons of vitamins pumped into them. Something happens to their insides. Everything is immunized and mechanized and airconditioned and hydromatic."

The conclusion of *Love in the Afternoon* is cynical; there is no reason for the viewer to believe that they will live happily. Each has fallen in love with an illusion. Wilder and Diamond created one of their trademarks in *Love in the Afternoon*: the running gag which cuts across the plot's action. Most notable of several in the film is Flannagan's private orchestra of Gypsies which plays at all his trysts.

Some Like It Hot (1959) is the first of three consecutive brilliant, though not equally well-received, Wilder-Diamond films. Based loosely upon a German film, *Fanfares of Love*, it is a marvel-

Marilyn Monroe and Tom Ewell in The Seven Year Itch

ously economical piece of work which drew uniformly brilliant performances from its cast. Two unemployed musicians, Jerry (Jack Lemmon) and Joe (Tony Curtis), masquerade as members of an all-female band to escape the vengeance of a group of Chicago hoods; Joe falls in love with band member Sugar Kane (Marilyn Monroe), while Jerry is pursued by Osgood Fielding, an elderly millionaire (Joe E. Brown). Contemporary audiences and a few critics worried about the implications of transvestism and homosexuality: at the end of the film, Fielding learns that the object of his affections is a man and remarks, "Well, nobody's perfect." But the truth is that the disguises Joe and Jerry don and the transformations they undergo have helped to change them—and Sugar Kane—for the better. For the first time, Sugar is able to relate to men as friends. *Some Like It Hot* is perhaps the first con-

vincing feminization of men in the movies.

Wilder received Academy Award nominations for *Ace in the Hole*, *Sabrina*, and *Some Like It Hot*, and he won his third Oscar with *The Apartment* (1960). This was the third film in which Jack Lemmon portrayed the 1960s Wilder hero, as Holden had in the 1950s. In *The Apartment* Lemmon plays Bud Baxter, the accountant whose apartment is so conveniently located that his supervisors can use it for their after-work dalliances. Harassed, understanding the way the game is played, he is nevertheless a pure-at-heart naif. His female counterpart is Fran Kubelik (Shirley MacLaine), the elevator operator who is carrying on a hopeless affair with the man who can get Bud promoted.

All of Wilder's favorite devices work superlatively in *The Apartment*, including his ear for current slang and his laconic voice-over narration. There are the running gags, such as a neighbor's marveling at Bud Baxter's sexual endurance (he thinks that all the trysts in the upstairs apartment are actually Bud's). *The Apartment* was one of Wilder's greatest successes, financially and critically. It was a film both dry and warm. Both Bud and Fran win out by giving up the fake for the real. Wilder was never able to recapture *The Apartment*'s innocence-conquers-all theme. In addition to receiving the Oscar for best screenplay, Wilder was voted best director, and the film won the award for best picture of 1960.

Wilder's next film, *One, Two, Three* (1961), was brilliantly styled and paced; like *Ninotchka*, the plot involved converting a Communist to capitalism, but the reasons for the conversion were different. James Cagney plays a Coca-Cola executive in Berlin during the early 1960s. He must convert the young communist (Horst Buchholz) who has married his boss's daughter (Pamela Tiffin). At breakneck pace, and purely for self-advancement, the executive does it, so well that the converted Communist gets the plum job while his mentor gets sent to his "Siberia": Atlanta.

From *Irma La Douce* (1963) on, Wilder had few successes, although some films, particularly *The Fortune Cookie* (1966), have done moderately well at the box office. Possibly the greatest disaster of Wilder's career was *Kiss Me, Stupid* (1964). Designed as a bawdy Restoration-style comedy, the film so offended audiences that it evoked a "Condemned" rating from the Roman Catholic Legion of Decency and shouts of moral outrage from nearly everyone. Set in Climax, Nevada, the film is about an aspiring songwriter (Ray Walston) and his wife (Felicia Farr). When singer Dino (Dean Martin) comes to town, a hooker (Kim Novak) agrees to pass herself off as the songwriter's wife and sleep with the singer to get him to promote the husband's songs, but the husband's jealousy extends even to his fake wife. Finally, the real wife sleeps with the singer, and he promises to use one of her husband's songs. *Kiss Me, Stupid* was one of the chief factors contributing to Wilder's decline in the 1960s; condemned as smut, it was passed on by United Artists, the studio that made it, to a subsidiary distributor, and it became a financial as well as a critical failure.

The Fortune Cookie was less corrosive, more along the moral lines of *The Apartment*, but less appealing. Another tale of insurance fraud, it showed the redemption of TV cameraman Harry Hinkle (Jack Lemmon) from the amoral anything-for-a-buck values of an ambulance chaser (played by Walter Matthau, who won an Oscar for the role). At

the film's end, Hinkle and the football player who caused the original "injury" (Hinkle had been knocked unconscious while filming a game) spiritually have both renewed themselves, doffed their burdens; they toss a football around—alone. Wilder received his final Academy Award nomination for this film.

In 1967, Wilder was one of many writers who worked without credit on *Casino Royale*, the big-budget satire of James Bond films, and in 1970, with *The Private Life of Sherlock Holmes*, he may have had his most wounding experience. Ordered cut from its original three-hour version to one hundred twenty-five minutes, the film was particularly dismaying to audiences and critics who thought they knew what a Billy Wilder film would be like. It is a lushly romantic treatment of the melancholy fate of a man who has become trapped in his own legend. With *Ace in the Hole*, it ranks among the least-seen Wilder films. It was pulled from general release after less than three months, but it has developed something of a cult following since.

Wilder did not write any more films until 1972, when he and Diamond coauthored *Avanti!*, an interesting postscript to the Wilder-Lemmon films of the 1960s. In this one, Lemmon plays a harried, ulcer-ridden American businessman who goes to Italy to reclaim the body of his father, recently killed in a car accident. He discovers, when an Englishwoman (Juliet Mills) arrives to claim her mother's body, that not only did both die in the same accident but also that they had been carrying on a love affair in Northern Italy. A parallel love affair develops between the Mills and Lemmon characters until it becomes obvious to both that they cannot live the lives they really want to; they must settle for meeting each year in their parents' old haunts.

In 1974 Wilder's remake of Ben Hecht and Charles MacArthur's *The Front Page* (1931) added nothing new to the classic newspaper tale. This film was followed by four more years of silence, and then, finally, the release of *Fedora* (1978), based on a story in Thomas Tryon's *Crowned Heads* and financed by a German syndicate as a tax shelter.

Fedora was a deliberate return to part of Wilder's own past, specifically *Sunset Boulevard*. Wilder deliberately cast William Holden as his narrator again, so that this time the narrator is old, with his face lined with the kind of compromises Wilder's people—heroes and villains alike—have made throughout the years. In the film, the aging actress Fedora (Hildegarde Neff) forces her daughter Antonia (Marthe Keller) to impersonate her. Antonia becomes the talk of the world as she poses as Fedora, who in her "ageless beauty" has returned to the screen. Only now Fedora is considered "too too old" for the people she falls in love with, and ultimately, because Antonia has lost her identity, she commits suicide. *Fedora* was possibly too derivative of *Sunset Boulevard*, but it remains a fascinating study of the interpenetration of illusion and reality. And the neat twist: Norma Desmond wanted to be perpetually young but was trapped in her age; Antonia, as Fedora, will never be able to act her true youth.

Wilder and Diamond based their screenplay for *Buddy Buddy* (1981) on the French film *A Pain in the A--* (1974). Jack Lemmon and Walter Matthau again starred. Neurotic Victor Clooney (Jack Lemmon) checks into a hotel intending to commit suicide; in the next room is hit-man Trabucco (Matthau), who plans to assassinate a government witness as he enters the courthouse across the street. Trabucco fears Clooney's suicide will draw attention to the hotel, so he constantly thwarts the suicide attempts, and Clooney interprets this as a sign of friendship. Eventually the two trade places, with Trabucco drugged and helpless, and Clooney trying to assassinate his target. *Buddy Buddy* was a financial failure that received generally negative reviews. Many critics panned the film, but a few saw it as a return to Wilder's earlier form.

Throughout his motion picture career, Billy Wilder has rarely attempted to conform to popular tastes. Beginning especially in the middle 1960s, he consistently portrayed, as Joan Didion remarked, "A world seen at dawn through a hangover, a world of double entendres and stale smoke, and drinks in which the ice had melted, the true country of despair." If his reputation has suffered, it is not so much because of a lack of quality as it is that his films are simply out of touch with contemporary views. He is a wisecracking moralist, and his films can properly be read as high satire.

References:

Jon Bradshaw, "You Used To Be Very Big," *New York* (24 November 1975);

Charles Champlin, "Wilder Still Working Without a Net," *Los Angeles Times*, 14 July 1974;

Bernard F. Dick, *Billy Wilder* (Boston: Twayne, 1980);

Stephen Farber, "Magnificent Obsession," *New West* (7 May 1979);

Axel Madson, *Billy Wilder* (London: Secker & Warburg, 1968);

Joseph McBride, "Billy Wilder and I. A. L. Diamond See Grim Future for Comedy Pix," *Variety*, 13 April 1977;

Steve Seidman, *The Film Career of Billy Wilder* (Boston: G. K. Hall, 1977);

Neil Sinyard and Adrian Turner, *Journey Down Sunset Boulevard: The Films of Billy Wilder* (Isle of Wight: BCW Publishing, 1979);

Wayne Warga, "Hollywood, as Viewed by Billy Wilder," *Los Angeles Times*, 29 March 1981;

Maurice Zolotow, *Billy Wilder in Hollywood* (New York: Putnam's, 1977).

Papers:

Original screenplays by Billy Wilder are on file at the American Film Institute.

Waldemar Young
(1 July 1880-30 August 1938)

Elias Savada

SELECTED MOTION PICTURES: *The Car of Chance* (Bluebird Photoplays / Universal, 1917), story; scenario by Young and Eugene B. Lewis;
The Clean-Up (Bluebird Photoplays/Universal, 1917), story and scenario;
The Show-Down (Bluebird Photoplays/Universal, 1917), scenario by Young and Lynn B. Reynolds;
A Stormy Knight (Bluebird Photoplays/Universal, 1917), scenario;
Flirting with Death (Bluebird Photoplays/Universal, 1917), scenario;
The Man Trap (Bluebird Photoplays/Universal, 1917), scenario;
The High Sign (Universal, 1917), scenario;
The Flash of Fate (Universal, 1918), scenario by Young and W. B. Pearson;
Fast Company (Bluebird Photoplays/Universal, 1918), scenario by Young and Lewis;
The Millionaire Pirate (Bluebird Photoplays/Universal, 1919), scenario;
The Little White Savage (Bluebird Photoplays/Universal, 1919), scenario;
A Taste of Life (Universal, 1919), scenario by Young and Fred Myton;
The Light of Victory (Bluebird Photoplays/Universal, 1919), scenario;
The Fire Flingers (Universal, 1919), scenario;
The Unpainted Woman (Universal, 1919), scenario;
Pretty Smooth (Universal, 1919), scenario;
The Spitfire of Seville (Universal, 1919), scenario;
A Petal on the Current (Universal, 1919), scenario;
The Sundown Trail (Universal, 1919), scenario;
Suds (Mary Pickford Co., 1920), adaptation;
The Girl in the Web (Pathé, 1920), scenario;
The Off-Shore Pirate (Metro, 1921), adaptation;
Experience (Famous Players-Lasky / Paramount, 1921), scenario;
Cappy Ricks (Famous Players-Lasky/Paramount, 1921), scenario by Young and Albert Shelby Le Vino;
A Prince There Was (Famous Players-Lasky/ Paramount, 1921), adaptation;
Our Leading Citizen (Famous Players-Lasky / Paramount, 1922), scenario;

Waldemar Young holding the novel on which his 1931 screenplay for First National was based

If You Believe It, It's So (Famous Players-Lasky/ Paramount, 1922), adaptation;
Burning Sands (Famous Players-Lasky/Paramount, 1922), adaptation by Young and Olga Printzlau;
Ebb Tide (Famous Players-Lasky/Paramount, 1922), adaptation and scenario;
Java Head (Famous Players-Lasky/Paramount, 1923), adaptation and scenario;
You Can't Fool Your Wife (Famous Players-Lasky/ Paramount, 1923), story and scenario;
Salomy Jane (Famous Players-Lasky/Paramount, 1923), scenario;
Poisoned Paradise: The Forbidden Story of Monte Carlo (Preferred Pictures/Al Lichtman Corp., 1924), scenario;
The Hill Billy (Jack Pickford Productions/Allied Producers & Distributors, 1924), titles;
Dorothy Vernon of Haddon Hall (Mary Pickford

341

Productions/United Artists, 1924), scenario;

The Dixie Handicap (Metro-Goldwyn, 1925), adaptation;

The Great Divide (Metro-Goldwyn, 1925), continuity;

The Unholy Three (M-G-M, 1925), scenario;

The Mystic (M-G-M, 1925), scenario;

The Black Bird (M-G-M, 1926), scenario;

The Flaming Forest (Cosmopolitan/M-G-M, 1926), scenario;

The Show (M-G-M, 1927), scenario;

Women Love Diamonds (M-G-M, 1927), scenario by Young and Lorna Moon;

The Unknown (M-G-M, 1927), scenario;

London After Midnight (M-G-M, 1927), scenario;

The Big City (M-G-M, 1928), scenario;

West of Zanzibar (M-G-M, 1928), scenario by Young and Elliot Clawson;

The Trail of '98 (M-G-M, 1929), continuity by Young and Benjamin Glazer;

Tide of Empire (Cosmopolitan/M-G-M, 1929), continuity;

Where East is East (M-G-M, 1929), adaptation;

Sally (First National, 1929), screenplay and dialogue;

Ladies Love Brutes (Paramount Famous Lasky, 1930), adaptation and dialogue by Young and Herman J. Mankiewicz;

The Girl of the Golden West (First National, 1930), screenplay and dialogue;

Chances (First National, 1931), adaptation;

Penrod and Sam (First National, 1931), screenplay and dialogue;

The Miracle Man (Paramount, 1932), adaptation; dialogue by Young and Samuel Hoffenstein;

Sky Bride (Paramount, 1932), story;

Sinners in the Sun (Paramount, 1932), screenplay by Young and Hoffenstein;

Love Me Tonight (Paramount, 1932), screenplay by Young, Hoffenstein, and George Marion, Jr.;

The Sign of the Cross (Paramount, 1932), screenplay and dialogue by Young and Sidney Buchman;

Island of Lost Souls (Paramount, 1932), screenplay by Young and Philip Wylie;

A Bedtime Story (Paramount, 1933), screenplay by Young and Nunnally Johnson; adaptation by Young, Johnson, and Glazer;

Men in White (M-G-M, 1934), screenplay;

Cleopatra (Paramount, 1934), screenplay by Young and Vincent Lawrence;

The Lives of a Bengal Lancer (Paramount, 1935), screenplay by Young, John Balderston, and Achmed Abdullah;

The Crusades (Paramount, 1935), screenplay by Young, Harold Lamb, and Dudley Nichols;

Peter Ibbetson (Paramount, 1935), screenplay by Young and Lawrence;

Desire (Paramount, 1936), screenplay by Young, Edwin Justus Mayer, and Hoffenstein;

Poppy (Paramount, 1936), screenplay by Young and Virginia Van Upp;

The Plainsman (Paramount, 1936), screenplay by Young, Lamb, and Lynn Riggs;

Man-Proof (M-G-M, 1938), screenplay by Young, Lawrence, and George Oppenheimer;

Test Pilot (M-G-M, 1938), screenplay by Young and Lawrence.

BOOK: *The Lace of a Thousand Trees and Other Lyrics* (San Francisco: Printed by J. H. Nash, 1933).

Waldemar Young, one of the most colorful and successful scenarists of his day, was admired in Hollywood for his ability to embellish screenplays with lyrical moods and historical perspectives. Although primarily remembered for his sharp wit and keen sense of screenwriting technique, he was also an accomplished poet, playwright, and journalist.

Young was born in Salt Lake City, Utah, to Mormon parents. He was the brother of Mahonri Young, the sculptor, and a grandson of Brigham Young, the Mormon leader. Immediately upon graduation from high school he began working on the editorial staff of the *Salt Lake Herald*. He matriculated at Stanford University in 1900, where he majored in English and pursued interests in economics and history. Young played on Stanford's varsity football team, sang with the glee club, and edited a volume of *The Sequoia*, a yearly collection of college prose and verse. His collaboration with newspaperman Ralph Renaud on the senior class play began Young's career as a playwright.

Leaving Stanford without a degree, Young obtained a job with the *San Francisco Chronicle*, for which he had written feature stories and sports articles during his days at Stanford. He became the *Chronicle*'s sports editor for a time and then worked as drama editor for the *San Francisco Examiner*.

Young took time off from newspaper work to write two plays, *The Dublin Minstrel* and *The House of Kerrigan*. In 1912, he returned to the *Chronicle*, where his column "Bits of Color Round the Town" was very popular. The same year he married Elizabeth Haigh, a journalist and writer.

For a while Young worked as press agent for Gertrude Hoffman and her Russian dance troupe and did free-lance publicity work for other stage and vaudeville personalities. Then, at his wife's suggestion, Young tried scenario writing. His first

Hollywood credits were on comedy-dramas for the acting team of Franklyn Farnum and Brownie Vernon. Produced by Bluebird Photoplays, the films were released through the Universal Film Exchange.

By 1919, Young's screenwriting reputation had grown, and he completed twelve feature scenarios during the year. His material was used by such directors as Jack Dillon, Rupert Julian, Paul Powell, George Siegmann, Rollin Sturgeon, and William Wolbert. Young's 1919 adaptation of Fannie Hurst's *A Petal on the Current* caught the attention of Mary Pickford, and she asked him to rework the play '*Op O' Me Thumb* for her film company. The film was produced as *Suds* in 1920.

During the next few years, Young commuted between the Hollywood and the Astoria, Long Island, studios of Famous Players-Lasky/Paramount, writing vehicles for silent film performers Viola Dana, Richard Barthelmess, Thomas Meighan, Leatrice Joy, and Jacqueline Logan, among others. Again working at Pickford's request, he adapted Charles Major's historical novel *When Knighthood was in Flower* as a vehicle for her. The film was released in 1924 as *Dorothy Vernon of Haddon Hall*. It

was a failure, more because of the audience's reluctance to accept Pickford as an adult than through any fault of Young's script.

Young signed a contract with Metro-Goldwyn in 1924, and his third film there was a career highlight. Young had been friends with director Tod Browning and actor Lon Chaney since the three had worked on *The Wicked Darling* (1919). Now they reteamed to film C. E. Robbins's book *The Unholy Three* (1925), about three sideshow performers—a midget, a ventriloquist, and a strongman—who turn to crime. Young's scenario added dashes of romance, murder, suspense, and a masterfully written set of titles. Chaney contributed a brilliant performance as the ventriloquist, and Browning provided crisp direction and a murky, shadowy atmosphere. Critical acclaim was nearly unanimous, and the film was exceptionally popular at the box office.

Young's next film was also with Chaney and Browning. *The Mystic* (1925) included some of the same themes as *The Unholy Three*, with the opening scenes showing a gypsy clairvoyant in front of a carnival crowd. Young, Browning, and Chaney made five more films together—*The Black Bird*

Gary Cooper, Richard Cromwell, Franchot Tone, and C. Aubrey Smith in The Lives of a Bengal Lancer

Ann Harding, John Halliday, and Gary Cooper in Peter Ibbetson

(1926), *The Unknown* (1927), *London After Midnight* (1927), *The Big City* (1928), and *West of Zanzibar* (1928)—all designed to display Chaney's ability to play grotesque characters.

Young's first all-talking picture was a song-and-dance film. He adapted Florenz Ziegfeld's stage production *Sally* (1929), a musical comedy produced by Ziegfeld and starring Marilyn Miller, who recreated her stage role. This tale of a waitress turned successful actress is embellished with the lavishness of a Follies production.

In the early 1930s, Young wrote four films for Cecil B. De Mille. The first, *The Sign of the Cross* (1932), is a spectacle depicting the faith and heroism of the infant Christian community in Nero's Rome. Paramount made the film in the depths of the Great Depression; the expensive project was a great risk, but it ultimately proved a box-office winner.

Charles Laughton, who had starred in *The Sign of the Cross*, appeared as Dr. Moreau in Young's adaptation of H. G. Wells's *Island of Lost Souls* (1932). Wells publicly repudiated this picture as a vulgarization of his novel, but critics praised it.

Young's second picture for De Mille was *Cleopatra* (1934), a production in De Mille's own familiar, lavish style—the decorative settings, vast crowds, and epic proportions were all on prominent display. A year later Young wrote the screenplay for *The Crusades* (1935), a battle extravaganza about Richard Lion-Heart's journey to the Holy Land to regain possession of the true cross. In De Mille's opinion, this was one of his best pictures, yet it achieved financial success only through subsequent rereleases.

Young greatly admired Gary Cooper, and he wrote four films for Cooper during a two-year period. The first two, directed by Henry Hathaway, were *The Lives of a Bengal Lancer* and *Peter Ibbetson* (both released in 1935). Based on Francis Yeats-Brown's book, *The Lives of a Bengal Lancer* depicts the members of a division that guards the northern frontier of England's empire in India. Young's favorite theme of the fraternity of men is injected into this lively adventure about men living and dying together under the tough military discipline that defines their existence. The film won six

Academy Award nominations, including that for best screenplay. *Peter Ibbetson* is a sensitive drama about a young man who kills his ex-lover's husband and is condemned to prison for life.

The comedy *Desire* (1936) starred Cooper as a Detroit automobile engineer on a European tour. He encounters an international jewel thief (Marlene Dietrich) who hides a stolen necklace on his person as he crosses the border into Spain. To retrieve the jewels, she is forced to flirt with him. They fall in love, and in the end they return to Michigan together. *Desire* was produced by Ernst Lubitsch, known for his spicy innuendo, and directed by Frank Borzage, who flavored his romantic dramas with a soft, sentimental touch.

The Plainsman (1936), Young's final film with Cooper, was also his last with De Mille. The film is set in the American West after the Civil War and tells about the men who sold arms illegally to the Indians. The well-known figures of Wild Bill Hickock (Cooper), Calamity Jane (Jean Arthur), and Buffalo Bill Cody (James Ellison) are dynamically depicted. Critics complained that the film took liberties with history, but audiences did not seem to mind; the film was a remarkable success.

Test Pilot (1938), Young's last film, is a stirring and poignant drama of the early aviation daredevils. Clark Gable played a skillful but irresponsible test pilot, kept from too many binges by his devoted mechanic (Spencer Tracy). The test pilot, flying a new plane across the continent, is forced to land on a farm where he meets a young woman (Myrna Loy), and they soon marry. She realizes that she is married to a man who faces death every time he flies. Director Victor Fleming skillfully realized Young's blend of flesh-and-blood characterizations, comic relief, and realistic action. The production made many "ten best" lists in 1938, and it was one of

Clark Gable and Spencer Tracy in Test Pilot

the biggest grossers in M-G-M's history.

After a lengthy illness, Waldemar Young died of pneumonia at Hollywood Hospital at age fifty-eight. Although Young is often overlooked in surveys of screenwriters today, he was one of the most successful and highly paid members of the field in his time.

Books for Further Reading

BOOKS ON SCREENWRITERS AND SCREENWRITING

The Academy of Motion Picture Arts and Sciences and The Writers Guild of America, West. *Who Wrote the Movie and What Else Did He Write? An Index of Screen Writers and Their Film Works 1936-1969.* Los Angeles: Academy of Motion Picture Arts and Sciences, 1970.

Coffee, L. *Storyline: Recollections of a Hollywood Screenwriter.* London: Cassell, 1973.

Corliss, R., ed. *The Hollywood Screenwriters.* New York: Piscus Books, 1972.

Corliss. *Talking Pictures: Screenwriters in the American Cinema.* Woodstock, N.Y.: Overlook Press, 1974.

Froug, W. *The Screenwriter Looks at the Screenwriter.* New York: Macmillan, 1972.

Guiles, F. L. *Hanging on in Paradise.* New York: McGraw-Hill, 1975.

McCarty, C. *Published Screenplays.* Kent, Ohio: Kent State University Press, 1971.

Pickard, R. *A Companion to the Movies from 1903 to the Present Day: A Guide to the Leading Players, Directors, Screenwriters, Composers, Cameramen and Other Artists Who Have Worked in the English-Speaking Cinema Over the Last Seventy Years.* New York: Hippocrene Books, 1974.

Schwartz, N. L., and S. Schwartz. *The Hollywood Writers Wars.* New York: Knopf, 1982.

Yoekum, L. G., ed. *Television and Screen Writing.* Berkeley: University of California Press, 1958.

FILM HISTORIES

GENERAL HISTORIES

Anderson, J. *The American Theatre* (and) R. Fülöp-Miller, *The Motion Picture in America.* New York: Dial, 1938.

Armes, R. *Film and Reality: An Historical Survey.* Harmondsworth, U.K.: Penguin, 1974.

Balio, T., ed. *The American Film Industry.* Madison: University of Wisconsin Press, 1976.

Bardèche, M., and R. Brasillach. *The History of Motion Pictures,* ed. and trans. I. Barry. London: Allen & Unwin, 1945.

Baxter, J. *Sixty Years of Hollywood.* South Brunswick, N.J.: Barnes, 1973.

Blum, D. *A Pictorial History of the Talkies.* New York: Putnam's, 1958.

Bohn, T. W., and R. L. Stromgren, with D. H. Johnson. *Light and Shadows: A History of Motion Pictures.* Port Washington, N.Y.: Alfred, 1975.

Brode, D. *Crossroads to the Cinema.* Oxford, Mass.: Holbrook, 1975.

Brown, B. *Talking Pictures.* New York: Gordon Press, 1972.

Casty, A. *Development of the Film: An Interpretive History.* New York: Harcourt Brace Jovanovich, 1973.

Cowie, P. *Eighty Years of Cinema.* New York: Barnes, 1977.

Cowie, P. *Seventy Years of Cinema.* South Brunswick, N.J.: Barnes, 1969.

Cowie, P., ed. *A Concise History of the Cinema (in Two Volumes) Volume I: Before 1940. Volume II: Since 1940.* New York: Barnes, 1971.

Cowie, P., ed. *Hollywood 1920-1970.* New York: Barnes, 1977.

Cook, D. *A History of Narrative Film 1889-1979.* New York: Norton, 1981.

Davies, M., J. Anderson, and P. Arnold. *The Hamlyn History of the Movies.* London: Hamlyn, 1975.

Dickinson, T. *A Discovery of Cinema.* London & New York: Oxford University Press, 1971.

Everson, W. K. *The American Movie.* New York: Atheneum, 1963.

Fielding, R., ed. *A Technological History of Motion Pictures and Television: An Anthology from the Pages of the Journal of the Society of Motion Picture and Television Engineers.* Berkeley: University of California Press, 1967.

Freulich, R., and J. Abramson. *Forty Years in Hollywood: Portraits of a Golden Age.* South Brunswick, N.J.: Barnes, 1971.

Fulton, A. R. *Motion Pictures: The Development of an Art from Silent Films to the Age of Television.* Norman: University of Oklahoma Press, 1960.

Garbicz, A., and J. Klinowski. *Cinema, The Magic Vehicle: A Guide to Its Achievement. Journey One: The Cinema Through 1949.* Metuchen, N.J.: Scarecrow, 1975.

Goodman, E. *The Fifty-Year Decline and Fall of Hollywood.* New York: Simon & Schuster, 1961.

Griffith, R., and A. Mayer. *The Movies: The Sixty-Year Story of the World of Hollywood and Its Effects on America, From Pre-Nickelodeon Days to the Present.* New York: Simon & Schuster, 1957.

Hampton, B. *A History of the Movies.* New York: Covici-Friede, 1931.

Higham, C. *The Art of the American Film, 1900-1971.* Garden City: Doubleday, 1973.

Ifkovic, E. *Dream Street: The American Movies and the Popular Imagination 1889-1939.* 2 vols. Brooklyn: Revisionist Press, 1977.

Jackson, C. *In Old Hollywood: The Movies During Their Golden Years.* Hicksville, N.Y.: Exposition, 1977.

Jacobs, L. *The Rise of the American Film: A Critical History,* revised edition. New York: Teachers College Press, 1968.

Jobes, G. *Motion Picture Empire.* Hamden, Conn.: Archon, 1966.

Kardish, L. *Reel Plastic Magic: A History of Films and Filmmaking in America.* Boston: Little, Brown, 1972.

Kennedy, M. *The Mechanized Muse.* London: Allen & Unwin, 1942.

Knight, A. *The Liveliest Art: A Panoramic History of the Movies.* New York: Macmillan, 1957.

Kuhns, W. *Movies in America.* Dayton, Ohio: Pflaum/Standard, 1972.

Lawton, R. *Grand Illusions.* Text by H. Leckey. New York: McGraw-Hill, 1973.

Lawton, R. *A World of Movies: 70 Years of Film History.* New York: Delacorte, 1974.

Leish, K. W. *Cinema.* New York: Newsweek Press, 1974.

Limbacher, J. L. *Four Aspects of the Film.* New York: Brussel & Brussel, 1969.

Limbacher. *A Historical Study of the Color Motion Picture.* Dearborn, Mich.: 1963.

Limbacher. *A Short History of the Sound Motion Picture.* Dearborn, Mich.: Dearborn Public Library, 1962.

Lindgren, E. *A Picture History of the Cinema.* New York: Macmillan, 1960.

Macgowan, K. *Behind the Screen: The History and Techniques of the Motion Picture.* New York: Delacorte, 1965.

Malone, P. *The Film.* Sydney: Chevalier, 1971.

Manvell, R. *The Film and the Public.* Harmondsworth, U.K.: Penguin, 1955.

Mast, G. *A Short History of the Movies.* New York: Pegasus, 1971.

McLaughlin, R. *Broadway and Hollywood: A History of Economic Interaction.* New York: Arno, 1974.

National Film Archive. *Forty Years of Film History, 1895-1935.* London: British Film Institute, ca. 1952.

Reed, S. *The Cinema.* London: Educational Supply Association, 1952.

Rhode, E. *A History of the Cinema: From Its Origins to 1970.* New York: Hill & Wang, 1976.

Robinson, D. *The History of the World Cinema.* New York: Stein & Day, 1973.

Rotha, P. *The Film Till Now: A Survey of World Cinema.* New York: Funk & Wagnalls, 1949.

Rotha, P., and R. Manvell. *Movie Parade 1888-1949: A Pictorial Survey of World Cinema.* London: Studio, 1950.

Scheure, S. H. *The Movie Book.* Chicago: Playboy Press, 1974.

Schickel, R. *Movies: The History of an Art and an Institution.* New York: Basic, 1964.

Shales, T., K. Brownlow, and others. *American Film Heritage: Impressions From the American Film Institute Archives,* ed. K. Karr. Washington, D.C.: Acropolis, 1972.

Shipman, D. *The Story of the Cinema: From Beginnings to "Gone With the Wind."* Vol. I. New York: Hill & Wang, 1982.

Sklar, R. *Movie-Made America: A Social History of American Movies.* New York: Random House, 1975.

Spears, J. *Hollywood: The Golden Era.* South Brunswick, N.J.: Barnes, 1971.

Speed, F. M. *Movie Cavalcade: The Story of the Cinema–Its Stars, Studios and Producers.* London: Raven, 1944.

Strong, H. H. *Then and Now: The Story of the Motion Picture.* Toledo: Strong Electric Corporation, 1943.

Tarbox, C. H. *The Five Ages of the Cinema.* Smithtown, N.Y.: Exposition, 1980.

Taylor, D., M. Peterson, and B. Hale. *A Pictorial History of the Movies.* New York: Simon & Schuster, 1943.

Torrence, B. *Hollywood: The First Hundred Years.* New York: New York Zoetrope, 1982.

Warren, L. *The Film Game.* New York: Gordon Press, 1976.

Wiseman, T. *Cinema.* New York: Barnes, 1965.

Wright, B. *The Long View.* New York: Knopf, 1974.

Silent Films

Bachmann, G., ed. *Dawn of the American Screen, 1893-1916.* New York: Group for Film Study, 1955.

Blum, D. *A Pictorial History of the Silent Screen.* New York: Putnam's, 1953.

Brownlow, K. *The Parade's Gone By.* New York: Knopf, 1968.

Cassaday, R., Jr. *Monopoly in Motion Picture Production and Distribution: 1908-1915.* Los Angeles: Bureau of Business and Economic Research, University of California, 1959.

Everson, W. K. *American Silent Film.* New York: Oxford University Press, 1978.

Grau, R. *The Theatre of Science: A Volume of Progress and Achievement in the Motion Picture Industry.* New York: Broadway, 1914.

Jenkins, R. V. *Images and Enterprise: Technology and the American Photographic Industry, 1839 to 1925.* Baltimore: Johns Hopkins University Press, 1975.

Lennig, A. *The Silent Voice.* Albany: Faculty-Student Association of the State University of New York, 1966.

Lennig. *The Silent Voice: A Sequel.* Troy, N.Y.: Snyder, 1967.

Lennig. *The Silent Voice: A Text.* Troy, N.Y.: Snyder, 1969.

Manchel, F. *When Pictures Began to Move.* Englewood Cliffs, N.J.: Prentice-Hall, 1969.

Niver, K. R. *The First Twenty Years: A Segment of Film History,* ed. B. Bergsten. Los Angeles: Locare Research Group, 1968.

Newark Museum Association. *The Movies Began Making Movies in New Jersey, 1887-1920.* Newark: Newark Museum Association Press, 1977.

North, J. H. *The Early Development of the Motion Picture, 1887-1909.* New York: Arno, 1973.

O'Leary, L. *The Silent Cinema.* New York: Dutton, 1965.

Pfragner, J. *The Eye of History: The Motion Picture From Magic Lantern to Sound Film.* Chicago: Rand McNally, 1964.

Pratt, G., ed. *Spellbound in Darkness: A History of the Silent Film.* Rochester, N.Y.: University of Rochester, 1966.

Ramsaye, T. *A Million and One Nights: A History of the Motion Picture.* New York: Simon & Schuster, 1926.

Slide, A. *Aspects of American Film History Prior to 1920.* Metuchen, N.J.: Scarecrow, 1978.

Slide, with P. O'Dell. *Early American Cinema.* New York: Barnes, 1970.

Thomas, D. B. *The First Colour Motion Pictures.* London: Her Majesty's Stationery Office, 1969.

Wenden, D. J. *The Birth of the Movies.* New York: Dutton, 1975.

The 1920s and Early Sound Films

Geduld, H. M. *The Birth of the Talkies: From Edison to Jolson.* Bloomington: Indiana University Press, 1975.

Green, F. *The Film Finds Its Tongue.* New York: Putnam's, 1929.

Manchel, F. *When Movies Began to Speak.* Englewood Cliffs, N.J.: Prentice-Hall, 1969.

Robinson, D. *Hollywood in the Twenties.* New York: Barnes, 1968.

Seldes, G. *An Hour with the Movies and the Talkies.* Philadelphia: Lippincott, 1929.

Thrasher, F. M., ed. *Okay for Sound: How the Screen Found Its Voice.* New York: Duell, Sloan & Pearce, 1946.

Walker, A. *The Shattered Silents: How the Talkies Came to Stay.* New York: Morrow, 1979.

The 1930s

Baxter, J. *Hollywood in the Thirties.* New York: Barnes, 1968.

Bergman, A. *We're in the Money: Depression America and Its Films.* New York: New York University Press, 1971.

Trent, P. *Those Fabulous Movie Years: The 30's.* Barre, Mass.: Barre, 1975.

Vermilye, J. *The Films of the Thirties.* Williamsburg: Stuart, 1982.

The 1940s

Barbour, A. G. *A Thousand and One Delights.* New York: Macmillan, 1971.

Editors of *Look. Movie Lot to Beachhead: The Motion Picture Goes to War and Prepares for the Future.* Garden City: Doubleday, Doran, 1945.

Fitzgerald, M. *American Movies: The Forties.* Vol. I. 1940-1944. Arlington, N.Y.: Arlington House, 1979.

Higham, C., and J. Greenberg. *Hollywood in the Forties.* New York: Barnes, 1968.

Jones, K. D., and A. F. McClure. *Hollywood at War: The American Motion Picture and World War II*. South Brunswick, N.J.: Barnes, 1973.

Manvell, R. *Films and the Second World War*. South Brunswick, N.J.: Barnes, 1974.

Thomas, T. *The Films of the Forties*. Secaucus, N.J.: Citadel, 1975.

War Activities Committee, Motion Picture Industry. *Movies at War: Reports of War Activities Committee, Motion Picture Industry, 1942-1945*. New York: War Activities Committee, ca. 1946.

Writers' Congress, University of California at Los Angeles. *Writers' Congress: The Proceedings of the Conference Held in October 1943 Under the Sponsorship of the Hollywood Writers' Mobilization and the University of California*. Berkeley: University of California Press, 1944.

Post-World War II

Guback, T. *The International Film Industry: Western Europe and America since 1945*. Bloomington: Indiana University Press, 1969.

Higham, C. *Hollywood at Sunset*. New York: Saturday Review Press, 1972.

Houston, P. *The Contemporary Cinema*. Baltimore: Penguin, 1963.

MacCann, R. D. *Hollywood in Transition*. Boston: Houghton Mifflin, 1962.

Manvell, R. *New Cinema in the USA: The Feature Film Since 1946*. New York: Dutton, 1968.

Sayre, N. *Running Time: Films of the Cold War*. New York: Dial, 1982.

The 1950s

Brode, D. *The Films of the Fifties*. Secaucus, N.J.: Citadel, 1978.

Dowdy, A. *Movies Are Better Than Ever: Wide Screen-Memories of the Fifties*. New York: Morrow, 1973.

Gow, G. *Hollywood in the Fifties*. New York: Barnes, 1971.

The 1960s and 1970s

Baxter, J. *Hollywood in the Sixties*. New York: Barnes, 1972.

Lewis, L., and W. D. Sherman. *The Landscape of Contemporary Cinema*. Buffalo: Buffalo Spectrum, 1967.

Madsden, A. *The New Hollywood: American Movies in the '70s*. New York: Cromwell, 1975.

Toeplitz, J. *Hollywood and After: The Changing Face of Movies in America*, trans. B. Sulik. Chicago: Regnery, 1975.

Documentaries

Alexander, D. *The Documentary Film*. London: British Film Institute, 1945.

Barnouw, E. *Documentary: A History of the Non-Fiction Film*. New York: Oxford University Press, 1974.

Barsam, R. M. *Nonfiction Film: A Critical History*. New York: Dutton, 1973.

Edmonds, R. *About Documentary: Anthropology on Film, A Philosophy of People and Art*. Dayton, Ohio: Pflaum, 1974.

Fielding, R. *The American Newsreel, 1911-1967*. Norman: University of Oklahoma Press, 1972.

Hockings, P., ed. *Principles of Visual Anthropology*. The Hague: Mouton, 1975.

Issair, M. A. *Cinema Verite*. East Lansing: Michigan State University, 1971.

Jacobs, L., ed. *The Documentary Tradition: From Nanook to Woodstock.* New York: Hopkinson & Blake, 1971.

Knight, D., and V. Porter. *A Long Look at Short Films: An A.C.T.T. Report on the Short Entertainment and Factual Film.* New York: Association of Cinematograph, Television and Allied Technicians in association with Pergamon, 1967.

Leyda, J. *Films Beget Films.* New York: Hill & Wang, 1964.

Losey, M. *A Report on the Outlook for the Profitable Production of Documentary Films for the Non-Theatrical Market, for the Sugar Research Foundation.* New York: Film Program Services, 1948.

MacCann, R. D. *The People's Films: A Political History of U.S. Government Motion Pictures.* New York: Hastings, 1973.

Mamber, S. *Cinema Verite in America: Studies in Uncontrolled Documentary.* Cambridge, Mass.: Massachusetts Institute of Technology Press, 1974.

Snyder, R. L. *Pare Lorentz and the Documentary Film.* Norman: University of Oklahoma Press, 1968.

Waldron, G., with C. Starr. *The Information Film: A Report of the Public Library Inquiry.* New York: Columbia University Press, 1949.

Experimental and Avant-Garde Films

Curtis, D. *Experimental Cinema.* New York: Universe, 1971.

Dwoskin, S. *Film Is: The International Free Cinema.* Woodstock, N.Y.: Overlook Press, 1975.

Lawder, S. D. *The Cubist Cinema.* New York: New York University Press, 1975.

Manvell, R., ed. *Experiment in the Film.* London: Grey Walls, 1949.

Mekas, J. *Movie Journal: The Rise of the New American Cinema, 1959-1971.* New York: Macmillan, 1972.

Renan, S. *An Introduction to the American Underground Film.* New York: Sutton, 1967.

Singer, M. *A History of the American Avant-Garde Cinema.* New York: American Federation of Arts, 1976.

Sitney, P. A. *Visionary Film: The American Avant-Garde.* New York: Oxford University Press, 1974.

Tyler, P. *The Underground Film: A Critical History.* New York: Grove, 1969.

Weightman, J. *The Concept of the Avant-Garde: Exploration in Modernism.* La Salle, Ill.: Library Press, 1973.

Young, C. *The American Experimental Film in the Last Decade.* Paris: UNESCO, 1964.

Animation

Falk, N. *How to Make Animated Cartoons: The History and Technique.* New York: Foundation, 1941.

Heraldson, D. *Creators of Life: A History of Animation.* New York: Drake, 1975.

Holman, L. B. *Puppet Animation in the Cinema: History and Technique.* South Brunswick, N.J.: Barnes, 1975.

Madsen, R. P. *Animated Film: Concepts, Methods, Uses.* New York: Interland, 1969.

Manvell, R. *The Animated Film: With Pictures From the Film "Animal Farm" by Halas and Batchelor.* London: Sylvan, 1954.

Stephenson, R. *Animation in the Cinema.* New York: Barnes, 1967.

GENRES

Comedy

Durgnat, R. *The Crazy Mirror: Hollywood Comedy and the American Image.* New York: Horizon, 1970.

Lahue, K. C. *World of Laughter: The Motion Picture Comedy Short, 1910-1930.* Norman: University of Oklahoma Press, 1966.

McCaffrey, D. W. *The Golden Age of Sound Comedy: Comic Figures and Comedians of the Thirties.* South Brunswick, N.J.: Barnes, 1973.

Manchel, F. *Yesterday's Clowns: The Rise of Film Comedy.* New York: Watts, 1973.

Mast, G. *The Comic Mind: Comedy and the Movies.* Indianapolis: Bobbs-Merrill, 1973.

Robinson, D. *The Great Funnies: A History of Film Comedy.* New York: Dutton, 1969.

Sennett, T. *Lunatics and Lovers: A Tribute to the Giddy and Glittering Era of the Screen's "Screwball" and Romantic Comedies.* New Rochelle, N.Y.: Arlington, 1973.

Crime and Suspense

Baxter, J. *The Gangster Film.* New York: Barnes, 1970.

Cameron, I. *A Pictorial History of Crime Films.* London: Hamlyn, 1975.

Clarens, C. *Crime Movies.* New York: Norton, 1980.

Davis, B. *The Thriller: Suspense Film From 1946.* New York: Dutton, 1973.

Everson, W. K. *The Detective in Film.* Secaucus, N.J.: Citadel, 1972.

Gabree, J. *Gangsters From Little Caesar to the Godfather.* New York: Pyramid, 1973.

Gow, G. *Suspense in the Cinema.* New York: Barnes, 1968.

Hammond, L. *Thriller Movies: Classic Films of Suspense and Mystery.* London: Octopus, 1974.

Hossent, H. *Gangster Movies: Gangsters, Hoodlums, and Tough Guys of the Screen.* London: Octopus, 1974.

Karimi, A. M. *Toward a Definition of the American Film Noir (1941-1949).* Dissertation: University of Southern California, 1970.

Karpf, S. L. *The Gangster Film: Emergence, Variation, and Decay of a Genre, 1930-1940.* New York: Arno, 1973.

Lee, R., and B. C. Van Hecke. *Gangsters and Hoodlums: The Underworld in the Cinema.* South Brunswick, N.J.: Barnes, 1971.

McArthur, C. *Underworld USA.* New York: Viking, 1972.

Roscow, E. *Born to Lose: The Gangster Film in America.* New York: Oxford University Press, 1978.

Tuska, J. *The Detective in Hollywood.* Garden City: Doubleday, 1978.

Epics

Cary, J. *Spectacular! The Story of Epic Films,* ed. J. Kobal. London & New York: Hamlyn, 1974.

Hirsch, F. *The Hollywood Epic.* New York: Barnes, 1978.

Horror

Butler, I. *The Horror Film.* New York: Barnes, 1967.

Clarens, C. *An Illustrated History of the Horror Film.* New York: Putnam's, 1967.

Drake, D. *Horror!* New York: Macmillan, 1966.

Gifford, D. *A Pictorial History of Horror Movies.* New York: Hamlyn, 1973.

Huss, R., and T. J. Ross, eds. *Focus on the Horror Film.* Englewood Cliffs, N.J.: Prentice-Hall, 1972.

Musical

Dyer, R. *The Musical: Notes*. London: British Film Institute, Educational Advisory Service, 1975.

Jenkinson, P., and A. Warner. *Celluloid Rock: Twenty Years of Movie Rock*. London: Lorrimer, 1974.

Kobal, J. *Gotta Sing, Gotta Dance! A Pictorial History of Film Musicals*. London & New York: Hamlyn, 1970.

McVay, D. *The Musical Film*. New York: Barnes, 1967.

Sennett, T. *Hollywood Musicals*. New York: Abrams, 1981.

Springer, J. *All Talking! All Singing! All Dancing! A Pictorial History of the Movie Musical*. New York: Citadel, 1966.

Stern, L. E. *The Movie Musical*. New York: Pyramid, 1974.

Romance

Everson, W. K. *Love in the Film: Seventy Years of Romantic Classics*. Secaucus, N.J.: Citadel, 1979.

Kobal J. *Gods and Goddesses of the Movies*. New York: Crescent, 1973.

Science Fiction

Annan, D. *Movie Fantastic: Beyond the Dream Machine*. New York: Bounty, 1975.

Baxter, J. *Science Fiction in the Cinema*. New York: Barnes, 1970.

Gifford, D. *Science Fiction Film*. New York: Dutton, 1971.

Johnson, W., ed. *Focus on the Science Fiction Film*. Englewood Cliffs, N.J.: Prentice-Hall, 1972.

Menville, D. *A Historical and Critical Survey of the Science Fiction Film*. New York: Arno, 1975.

Rovin, J. *The Fabulous Fantasy Films*. New York: Barnes, 1977.

Rovin. *A Pictorial History of Science Fiction Films*. Secaucus, N.J.: Citadel, 1975.

Sobchack, V. C. *The Limits of Infinity: The American Science Fiction Film*. New York: Barnes, 1979.

Social Problem Films

Roseman, P., and J. Purdy. *The Hollywood Social Problem Film: Madness, Despair, and Politics from the Depression to the Fifties*. Bloomington: Indiana University Press, 1981.

White, D. M., and R. Averson. *The Celluloid Weapon: Social Comment in the American Film*. Boston: Beacon, 1972.

War

Butler, I. *The War Film*. South Brunswick, N.J.: Barnes, 1974.

Epstein, E. Z., and others. *Films of World War Two*. Secaucus, N.J.: Citadel, 1975.

Hughes, R., ed. *Film: Book 2, Films of Peace and War*. New York: Grove, 1962.

Isenberg, M. *War on Films: The American Cinema and World War I, 1914-1941*. Madison, N.J.: Farleigh Dickinson, 1979.

Jeavon, C., with M. Unwin. *A Pictorial History of War Films*. London & New York: Hamlyn, 1974.

Jones, K. D., and A. F. McClure. *Hollywood at War: The American Motion Picture and World War II*. South Brunswick, N.J.: Barnes, 1973.

Kagan, N. *The War Film.* New York: Pyramid, 1974.

Manvell, R. *Films and the Second World War.* South Brunswick, N.J.: Barnes, 1974.

Perlmutter, T. *War Movies.* London & New York: Hamlyn, 1974.

Shindler, C. *Hollywood Goes to War.* Boston: Routledge & Kegan Paul, 1979.

Smith, J. *Looking Away: Hollywood and Viet Nam.* New York: Scribners, 1975.

Westerns

Barbour, A. G. *The Thrill of It All.* New York: Macmillan, 1971.

Barbour, A. G., ed. *The "B" Western.* Kew Gardens, N.Y.: Screen Facts, 1966.

Carter, D. *The Western.* Ottawa: Ottawa Film Society, 1966.

Clapham, W. C. *Western Movies: The Story of the West on Screen.* London: Octopus, 1974.

Everson, W. K. *A Pictorial History of the Western Film.* New York: Citadel, 1969.

Eyles, A. *The Western: An Illustrated Guide.* New York: Barnes, 1967.

Fenin, G. N., and W. K. Everson. *The Western: From Silents to Cinerama.* New York: Crown, 1962.

French, P. *Westerns: Aspects of a Movie Genre.* New York: Viking, 1974.

Manchel, F. *Cameras West.* Englewood Cliffs, N.J.: Prentice-Hall, 1971.

Maynard, R. A., ed. *The American West on Film: Myth and Reality.* Rochelle Park, N.J.: Hayden, 1974.

Meyer, W. R. *The Making of the Great Westerns.* Arlington, N.Y.: Arlington House, 1979.

Nachbar, J., ed. *Focus on the Western.* Englewood Cliffs, N.J.: Prentice-Hall, 1974.

Parkinson, M., and C. Jeavons. *A Pictorial History of Westerns.* London & New York: Hamlyn, 1972.

Other

Behlmer, R. *Jungles Tales of the Cinema.* Hollywood, 1960.

Behlmer, R., and T. Thomas. *Hollywood's Hollywood: The Movies About the Movies.* Secaucus, N.J.: Citadel, 1975.

Cameron, I. *Adventure in the Movies.* New York: Crescent, 1973.

Cross, R. *The Big Book of B Movies or How Low Was My Budget.* New York: St. Martin's Press, 1981.

Kaminsky, S. *American Film Genres: Approaches to a Critical Theory of Popular Film.* Dayton, Ohio: Pflaum, 1974.

Thomas, T. *The Great Adventure Films.* Secaucus, N.J.: Citadel, 1976.

Contributors

Joseph Adamson III ....Santa Monica, California
F. Jeffrey Armstrong ....Norfolk, Virginia
Irene Atkins...Pacific Palisades, California
Thomas Bohn...University of Tulsa
Jay Boyer...Arizona State University
Duane Byrge ....Los Angeles, California
Willard Carroll ....Los Angeles, California
Randall Clark..Decatur, Georgia
John P. Driscoll ....University of Washington
Evelyn Ehrlich ....New York, New York
Sam Frank ....Los Angeles, California
William Frankfather...Los Angeles, California
James Goodwin ....University of California, Los Angeles
William Hughes...Essex Community College
Carola Kaplan...........................California State Polytechnic University, Pomona
Keith Kelly...Institute of Fine Art, New York University
Tanita C. Kelly ....Hollywood, California
Edwin T. Kephart ....New York University
Don Kilbourne ....Covina, California
Diane Koszarski ....Elmhurst, New York
Jonathan Kuntz...Los Angeles Southwest College
Stephen O. Lesser..Los Angeles, California
Scott Levine...Chicago, Illinois
Blake Lucas ....Los Angeles, California
Gabriel Miller ....Rutgers University
Joseph R. Millichap ....University of Tulsa
James Moore..Mount San Antonio College
Nan Morrison ....College of Charleston
Joyce Olin...Arlington Heights, Illinois
Renée D. Pennington..East Elmhurst, New York
Nick Roddick ....California State University, Long Beach
Andrea Rosenwein ....Los Angeles, California
Elias Savada..The American Film Institute
Alain Silver ....Culver City, California
Anthony Slide...Studio City, California
Tom Stempel ....Los Angeles City College
Lee Tsiantis ....Atlanta, Georgia
James Ursini..Woodland Hills, California
Malvin Wald ....University of Southern California
Elizabeth Ward ....Santa Monica, California
Tom Wiener ....Washington, D.C.
Dale Winogura ....Hollywood, California
Ralph Haven Wolfe ....Bowling Green State University
Joanne Yeck ....Los Angeles, California

Cumulative Index

Dictionary of Literary Biography, Volumes 1-26
Dictionary of Literary Biography Yearbook, 1980, 1981, 1982
Dictionary of Literary Biography Documentary Series, Volumes 1-4

Cumulative Index

DLB before number: *Dictionary of Literary Biography*, Volumes 1-26
Y before number: *Dictionary of Literary Biography Yearbook*, 1980, 1981, 1982
DS before number: *Dictionary of Literary Biography Documentary Series*, Volumes 1-4

C

L

M

N

T